RIDGWAY
DUELS
FOR KOREA

TEXAS A&M UNIVERSITY

☆ 18 ☆

MILITARY HISTORY SERIES

RIDGWAY DUELS FOR KOREA

By Lt. Col. Roy E. Appleman, AUS (Ret.)

Texas A&M University Press
College Station

The paper used in this book meets the minimum requirements of the
American National Standard for Permanence of Paper for Printed Library
Materials, Z39.48-1984. Binding materials have been chosen for durability.

LIBRARY OF CONGRESS CATALOGING-IN-PUBLICATION DATA

Appleman, Roy Edgar.
    Ridgway duels for Korea / by Roy E. Appleman.
    — 1st ed.
        p.   cm. — (Texas A&M University military
history series ; no. 18)
    Includes bibliographical references.
    ISBN 0-89096-432-7 (alk. paper)
    1. Korean War, 1950–1953—Campaigns.   2. Ridg-
way, Matthew B. (Matthew Bunker), 1895–   .
I. Title.   II. Series: Texas A&M University military
history series ; 18.
DS918.A8   1990
951.904′2—dc20   89-48499
                                                        CIP

Contents

Illustrations

Tables

Maps

Preface

THIS VOLUME covers battlefield events from Gen. Matthew B. Ridgway's assumption of command in Korea on 26 December 1950 to the beginning of truce talks on 10 July 1951, and the end of the war of maneuver in Korea. It is a sequel to *Disaster in Korea: The Chinese Confront MacArthur* and *Escaping the Trap: The US Army X Corps in Northeast Korea, 1950,* which carried the war from 24 November 1950 to 26 December 1950, and they in turn are sequels to *South to the Naktong, North to the Yalu,* the combat narrative of the first six months of the war, which began with the North Korean invasion of South Korea on 25 June 1950.

This volume, like the other three, is a combat history and records the fighting in Korea with only necessary mention of political and diplomatic events associated with the war. It is based on military unit records, command reports, and after-action reports in Record Group 407 in the National Archives, Federal Records Center, Suitland, Maryland. This record group comprises the Korean War official records. Besides researching records in the National Archives, I spent several weeks examining the General Ridgway Papers, deposited in the US Military History Institute at Carlisle Barracks, Pennsylvania. I also have corresponded with and interviewed a great number of participants in the war. The few published works that relate to actual combat operations in Korea are cited in the notes whenever they are used as sources. Most of these relate to UN allies, notably the British, Canadians, and Australians.

I have twice been in Korea, the first time entering Korea in September 1945 in the occupation of the area south of the 38th Parallel with the US XXIV Army Corps from Okinawa, the second time in 1951 during the Korean War, when I saw many of the combat areas across the breadth of the peninsula. At the time I examined the Korean War records in the years 1974–75, they were still classified Secret, and I spent two years in the vaults where they are stored, working in a small cubbyhole provided for my use.

Throughout, an attempt has been made to portray Matthew Ridgway's characteristics as a commander, to relate his leadership to events as they occurred. He alone made the difference in keeping the American Army in Korea, gradually turning it around to face north once again and to emerge as a strong, motivated fighting force in the Chinese 4th and 5th Phase offensives in the winter and spring of 1951. He won back all of South Korea that had been lost and placed the new border north of the old one at the 38th Parallel in a more defensible position.

The maps used throughout the writing of this book were the same ones used in 1950 and 1951 by the troops involved and show the terrain and place-names consistent with records maintained at the time by the units in action.

In writing the narrative I have used the shorter method of referring to command post as "CP." Also, in the citations in the notes I have dropped the National Archives Record Group 407 (RG 407), which applies to all the official Korean War records used, and give only the box number. It can be assumed that each box cited is in RG 407.

I first met General Ridgway in his headquarters in Tokyo as I interviewed him twice in the autumn of 1951. I was impressed then and later with his unassuming humility, his humane understanding of the ordinary soldier and what motivated him, and his courteous, straightforward personality that inspired confidence in those whom he met. I kept in contact with him throughout the years, with the intention of one day writing the story of the Korean War and of his role in it. When I undertook the preparation of this volume, he graciously consented to read the draft chapters as I finished them. From the beginning to the end, over a period of more than two years, he read the chapters as I completed them and returned them quickly to me with his comments. I was gratified and encouraged at his acceptance of them as a credible account of what happened.

Throughout, I have tried to be objective in the narrative, to reveal the bad as well as the good, and to strive for an accurate account of events. My sympathies have been with the rank-and-file, with those who have had to face the terrors of combat, many of whom made the ultimate sacrifice.

Abbreviations

THE USE of abbreviations is common in discussions of the Korean War and in US military usage generally. The following appear throughout the narrative below:

AAA AW	Antiaircraft Artillery, Automatic Weapons
ASP	Ammunition Supply Point
ATIS	Allied Translation and Interrogation Service
BAR	Browning Automatic Rifle
BCT	Battalion Combat Team
BIB	British Independent Brigade
CCF	Chinese Communist Forces
CG	Commanding General
CO	Commanding Officer
CP	Command Post
CTC	Civilian Transport Corps
DA	Department of the Army
DUKW	Amphibious Truck
EUSAK	Eighth United States Army Korea
FA	Field Artillery
FAC	Forward Air Controller
FEC	Far East Command
GHQ	General Headquarters
HQ	Headquarters
I&R	Intelligence and Reconnaissance
JCS	Joint Chiefs of Staff
KATUSA	Korean Augmentation Troops (Attached to the US Army)
KIA	Killed in Action
KMAG	Korean Military Advisory Group
LST	Landing Ship, Tank
MIA	Missing in Action
MLR	Main Line of Resistance

MSR	Main Supply Road
NK	North Korea
NK(P)A	North Korean (People's) Army
OPLR	Outpost Line of Resistance
P&A	Pioneer and Ammunition
PIR	Periodic Intelligence Report, Daily
PLA	People's Liberation Army, Chinese
POR	Periodic Operations Report, Daily
POW	Prisoner of War
R&R	Rest and Recreation
RCT	Regimental Combat Team
ROK	Republic of Korea (South Korea)
SP	Self-propelled
TAC(P)	Tactical Air Control (Party)
TOT	Time-on-Target
UN	United Nations
VT	Variable Time Fuse
WIA	Wounded in Action

RIDGWAY
DUELS
FOR KOREA

1

General Ridgway in Command of Eighth Army

WHEN WORD FLASHED to General MacArthur in Tokyo on 23 December 1950 that General Walker had just died in a traffic accident, he had Maj. Gen. Doyle O. Hickey, his acting chief of staff, immediately get in touch with the Department of the Army in Washington by telecon and ask for Gen. Matthew Bunker Ridgway, deputy chief of staff for Operations and Administration, as replacement for General Walker. It was learned later that General MacArthur and the top command at the Pentagon had previously agreed that, if anything should happen to Walker, his replacement would be Ridgway. Army Chief of Staff J. Lawton Collins had discussed this matter only two weeks before, when he was in the Far East for meetings with General MacArthur. Thus, it was almost automatic that General Collins obtained immediate clearance for the assignment, and he notified General MacArthur that Ridgway would be on his way to the Far East immediately.

General Ridgway knew nothing of this advance arrangement at the time, and he later said that he learned of it only in 1975 in a seminar at the Truman Library Association in Kansas City, when either Averell Harriman or General Collins told him about it. Upon receipt from General Collins of a message confirming that General Ridgway would be immediately assigned to him for command of Eighth Army, General MacArthur sent a message to General Collins that said, "Thanks and deepest appreciation Joe, to you and the Secretary for letting me have Ridgway." MacArthur followed this with a telecon message to Ridgway, saying, "I look forward with the keenest anticipation to your joining this command. Your welcome by all ranks will be of the heartiest. To me, personally, it will mark the resumption of a comradeship which I have cherished through long years of military service." Both messages left Tokyo 23 December 1950.[1]

To Ridgway the news of his appointment to the command came, as he has said, "with the suddenness of a rifle shot." He learned of it in a telephone call from General Collins the evening of 22 December (Washington time) while he and Mrs. Ridgway were at a friend's home in Washington.[2]

It has been alleged by at least one officer of General MacArthur's staff that MacArthur, on 8 August 1950, when Ridgway was a member of a group accompanying Averell Harriman to Japan and Korea, told Ridgway that, if anything happened to Walker, "you are my No. 1 choice." General Ridgway later said privately that General MacArthur never mentioned the subject to him on that visit to the Far East.[3]

Gen. Lauris Norstad, the only other officer in Averell Harriman's party in this Far East Command visit, told Ridgway that MacArthur had said to him that MacArthur wanted to see Ridgway in command of Eighth Army. Ridgway was taken aback at this news and burst out to Norstad, "Oh, don't you breathe a word of that while I am up here anyway, because it would look as though I was seeking a job there, which I am not at all." Later, Ridgway learned that General MacArthur had indeed recommended him as a replacement if anything happened to Walker. But he had the impression that higher officials in the Pentagon had other plans for him.

In a memorandum for record, 16 August 1950, Ridgway relates a conversation he had that day with General Collins after his return from the Far East. He told Collins that Secretary of the Army Frank Pace had asked him for amplification of the report he had made the previous day on conditions in Korea. Lt. Gen Wade H. Haislip, Army vice chief of staff, Ridgway's immediate superior, was present during this conversation with General Collins. In a subsequent conversation with General Collins, Ridgway discussed the question of command in Korea. Collins made the statement in this conversation that "Van Fleet was the natural selection," adding, "you could do it too." Collins then asked Ridgway what his preference would be. Ridgway replied, "If we are going to war, I would prefer to fight in Europe." To this Collins said, "I am planning to put you in Haislip's place when he retires within a year and if I send you to Korea, you might be so involved I couldn't get you out."[4]

This exchange indicates that, by midsummer of 1950, there was consideration of replacing Walker in command of Eighth Army and that Ridgway was under consideration, but the Army chief of staff seemed to have decided to keep Ridgway in the Pentagon and to send Van Fleet to Korea. Afterward Gen. Collins's view seems to have changed, for reasons that are not clear. At some point Averell Harriman and General Collins, and possibly others, discussed the subject of General Walker's replacement, and they agreed that Ridgway would succeed Walker.[5]

General Ridgway's trip to the Far East Command and Korea with the Harriman group in August 1950 was his first and only visit to Korea until he arrived there in December to assume command of Eighth Army. During this visit, Ridgway, in a letter to his mother on 12 August 1950, wrote that Korea looked just like parts of China he had seen.[6]

General Ridgway's first verbal orders to proceed to the Far East came in General Collins's telephone call late in the evening of 22 December 1950. The next day they were more official but still verbal, relieving him of his duties as assistant chief of staff for Operations and Administration, Office Army Chief of Staff, Department of the Army, and assigning him to the Far East Command, Tokyo. The urgency of his departure precluded issuance of the normal printed Department of the Army orders in advance. These confirmatory orders were issued by the adjutant general on 26 December 1950.[7]

In the evening of 23 December General Ridgway proceeded from his quarters at Fort Myer, Virginia, to National Airport in Alexandria, Virginia. Mrs. Ridgway, General Bradley, and other officers were there to see him off. Night had fallen when his Constellation took off on the first leg of the flight to the Far East. Early the next morning, now 24 December and a Sunday, the Constellation landed at Adak Island, in the Aleutians. After leaving Adak the flight crossed the international date line. There the date changed from 24 to 25 December. Just before midnight, 12 hours later, Ridgway landed at Haneda Airport, Tokyo. Maj. Gen. Doyle O. Hickey, acting chief of staff, Far East Command, was there along with other old friends to meet him. They took him at once to the guest house at the American Embassy, where General MacArthur had arranged for him to stay overnight. It was now early 26 December, Tokyo time.[8] (Hereafter, dates will be Far East and Korean time.)

At 9:30 A.M., Tuesday, 26 December, General Ridgway went to General MacArthur's office on the sixth floor of the Dai-Ichi Building to begin talks with MacArthur. General Hickey was the only other person present. He was an old friend, who had a combat command of the 3rd Armored Division in Ridgway's XVIII Airborne Army Corps in the first part of the Battle of the Bulge in Europe in World War II. Ridgway and MacArthur had been acquainted for many years, and he felt he knew MacArthur rather well. He had served under MacArthur at the US Military Academy at West Point as an instructor in charge of the athletic department when MacArthur was superintendent of the academy. Always he had found MacArthur fascinating and compelling.

Now, in Tokyo, once again he found himself giving his whole attention to MacArthur's words and personality. Ridgway characterized his talks with MacArthur that morning as "detailed, specific, frank, and far-ranging." Ridgway's memorandum of record of the conversations, dated 26 December, reflects the substance of MacArthur's view of the situation in Korea and his instructions to Ridgway only hours before the latter enplaned for Korea.

General MacArthur instructed Ridgway to hold a defense line as far north as possible. He was to hold Seoul if that was feasible, largely for psychological and political reasons. These viewpoints seemed to differ considerably from MacArthur's report to the Pentagon a few weeks earlier, when he planned a withdrawal in successive positions to the Pusan area. MacArthur commented that supply discipline in Eighth Army was not good. Where a month earlier he had been supremely confident that his air power would prevent the Chinese from crossing the Yalu River in force and waging strong battle, he now told Ridgway that tactical air power could not isolate the Korean battlefield and stop the flow of enemy troops and supply southward. He felt the Far East Command was operating in a mission vacuum and that political officials in the United States were groping their way diplomatically. MacArthur said the Chinese were wide open to attack in the south of mainland China and that such an attack could be made by Nationalist forces under Chiang Kai-shek from Formosa—that he had so recommended to the Defense Department but that it had not been approved. MacArthur now had come to realize the Chinese were a dangerous foe, and he warned Ridgway not to underestimate them. He mentioned that correspondents (ENTS) accompanying the recently arrived British 29th Brigade had criticized American operations in Korea, something that had never happened with the British 27th Brigade. MacArthur said that General Walker had reported to him on 22 December, the day before he was killed, that the enemy situation on his front was most dangerous and that he expected an attack.

MacArthur told Ridgway the most he expected from the UN forces in Korea was to defeat the enemy forces sufficiently to make possible the retention of South Korea. Gone now, apparently, was any thought of driving the North Koreans and the Chinese military forces out of Korea. MacArthur concluded by saying to Ridgway, "Form your own opinions and use your own judgment. I will support you. I will assume responsibility. You have my complete confidence."

When MacArthur had finished speaking, Ridgway asked him, "If I find the situation to my liking, would you have any objection to my attacking?" MacArthur answered, "The Eighth Army is yours. Do what you think best."[9]

His conference with General MacArthur finished, Ridgway next went to a meeting General Hickey had arranged with the chiefs of the Far East Command general staff sections, together with Vice Adm. C. Turner Joy, commander of Naval Forces Far East, and Lt. Gen. George E. Stratemeyer, commander of the Far East Air Forces. They quickly gave their views of the Korean situation to Ridgway, as seen from their special fields of responsibility. In the course of these discussions Ridgway was told that his counterpart in command of the enemy forces in Korea was Lin Piao, commander of the CCF Fourth Field Army. This statement, widely held and apparently unquestioned in the Far East, was incorrect. Lin Piao was never in Korea during the Korean War and had no command responsibility there whatever, although the CCF divisions facing Eighth Army were from his Fourth Field Army. General Peng Dehuai, vice commander of the Chinese People's Liberation Army (PLA), commanded the Chinese forces in Korea. This meeting ended just before noon. Ridgway then proceeded directly to Haneda Airport, where he boarded a B-17 plane and took off for Korea.[10]

Before leaving Tokyo, Ridgway issued a terse 66-word message to Eighth Army, by which he assumed command of it. The army in Korea was to issue this communication as an order immediately upon his arrival there. This order, sent from Tokyo and dated 26 December 1950, marked PERSONAL FOR ALLEN (Maj. Gen. Leven C. Allen, chief of staff, US Eighth Army), read as follows:

I should like the following General Order in the hands of troops this date, immediately following my message Commanders concerning General Walker, which was sent you last night over the Commander-in-Chief's signature, to the effect that it will be read as soon as practicable by every officer assigned, attached to, or serving with the Eighth Army; and that as circumstances permit, its text be made known to as many of the men as may be practicable, and made available through prompt translations to members of each of our foreign language United Nations contingents.

[The General Order:] I have with little notice assumed heavy responsibilities before in battle, but never with greater opportunities for service to our loved ones and our Nation in beating back a world menace which free men cannot tolerate.

It is an honored privilege to share this service with you and with our comrades of the Navy and Air Force. You will have my utmost. I shall expect yours.

> M. B. Ridgway,
> Lieutenant General
> United States Army,
> Commanding.

In a private letter General Ridgway commented on this order that, "American soldiers do not like rhetoric. They react with either ridicule or indifference."[11]

At four o'clock in the afternoon of the twenty-sixth, Ridgway stepped on Korean soil at Taegu's K-2 airfield. Maj. Gen. Leven C. Allen, Eighth Army's chief of staff, was awaiting him there. Before leaving Japan, Ridgway had Eighth Army patches sewn on the shoulder of his shirt, so he appeared in Korea as a member of that army. General Allen's jeep and driver took the two men over bumpy roads to Eighth Army headquarters. Less than a week earlier, on 20 December, most of Eighth Army Main Headquarters personnel had moved to Taegu from Seoul. Only a skeleton group now remained behind at Eighth Army Advance CP in Seoul. General Allen reminded Ridgway that Eighth Army still operated under General MacArthur's order of 8 December to withdraw south in phase lines until the military situation stabilized and that, at the time of his death, General Walker was operating under those orders. General Allen later commented that Ridgway at this point said, "Well, we are going the other way."[12]

General Allen also said that, when General Collins visited Walker at Seoul on 4 December, he had wanted Walker to plan a perimeter around the Seoul-Inchon area but that Walker would not agree to it and said he would undertake it only under a direct order. At that time Allen said that Walker even wanted specific places in Japan set aside for the Eighth Army if it evacuated Korea.[13]

Before going to bed that night in Taegu, General Ridgway unpacked and laid out his worn European combat dress of World War II, the harness of an airborne trooper. The next morning, 27 December, Ridgway was airborne for Seoul in the gray twilight before dawn, wearing the combat gear he had laid out the night before. There was the web belt and harness, one grenade fastened to the D ring of the right breast shoulder straps, and a first-aid kit fastened to the left breast shoulder straps. A regulation Army .45-caliber automatic pistol was holstered at his belt on the right side.

There has been so much misstatement by writers, even to this day, about Ridgway's wearing two grenades that it seems advisable to quote General Ridgway's words to the author on this subject: "I wore only 1 grenade on the right D-ring of my harness with a bit of adhesive tape over the safety-pin to prevent an accidental pullout. On the other D-ring was one of the special 1st Aid Packets issued only to our paratroopers, I think, though perhaps the glidermen had them also. Each contained a morphine Syrette which we had been shown how to use if alone and badly wounded."[14]

Col. William A. Collier, deputy chief of staff for Eighth Army, was the senior officer at the Eighth Army Advance CP in Seoul. He, with drivers and a guard in two jeeps from the 502nd Reconnaissance Platoon, waited in a bitterly cold dark morning at Kimpo airfield outside Seoul for Ridgway's plane to arrive. Sgt. Eugene Donlin, who later became Ridgway's personal jeep driver, drove Jeep No. 1. Cpl. Randle M. Hurst was a guard in the second jeep. The waiting group could see General Ridgway and Lt. Col. Paul F. Smith of Eighth Army Headquarters, Taegu, peering out through a plane window as the B-17 taxied in. The "old army colonel," as most of the enlisted men at the Advance Headquarters respectfully thought of Collier, greeted General Ridgway. Collier quickly showed the party to their jeep seats, Ridgway and Smith riding with Donlin in Jeep No. 1. Collier moved to Jeep No. 2, and the party started for Seoul. Hurst tells an interesting story of this trip into Seoul. Corporal Sullivan was in the back seat and behind the .50-caliber machine gun in the second jeep, his hands in his pockets because of the cold. Collier said to him, "Get your hands on those spade grips [machine gun]." Sullivan replied, "But sir, it's cold." Collier responded, "I said get your hands on those spade grips and don't take them off before we get to Seoul." Sullivan obeyed.[15]

Five days later, New Year's Day, Hurst wrote to his parents and gave them an initial impression of the army's new commander. He had been a member of the general's jeep guard party in the preceding days as Ridgway traveled to front-line command posts and units along the army line north of Seoul. He wrote, "Obviously, the General is a great go-getter. He doesn't smoke and can't stand the smell of tobacco. He is extremely courteous to enlisted men. He expects the same courtesy in return."[16]

When General Ridgway arrived at the Eighth Army Advance CP at the Main Hall of the University of Seoul about 9:30 A.M., 27 December, he wasted little time. There was much he wanted to do before the day ended, including a hurried visit to the front line north of Seoul. At the Advance CP General Ridgway found, to his "great disappointment only a handful of officers there. The others were back at Taegu, two hundred miles from the front—a situation I resolved to remedy at once."[17]

By 9:40 A.M. Ridgway was in a conference at the CP with Generals Frank W. Milburn and John B. Coulter, commanding I Corps and IX Corps, respectively. They had driven in from their CPs, both near Seoul, for the meeting. General Ridgway had sent a message to General Edward M. Almond, X Corps commander, to meet him there also, but Almond was off in the southeast corner of Korea, at Kyongju, and could not get there quickly. He was on his way. Ridgway, Milburn, Coulter, and Collier discussed the situation north of Seoul, where two American divisions, the 25th and 24th, together with two ROK divisions, the 1st and the 6th, held the defense positions. In this initial conference with his corps commanders, Ridgway stressed his desire to maintain a two-division bridgehead north of the Han River and to improve communications with the ROK III Corps on the right of Coulter's IX Corps. He said he expected close cooperation between Milburn and Coulter and their staffs in planning the defense. He wanted, he said, all front-line units to make reconnaissance to their fronts. He said he intended to make an immediate tour of the battlefront to meet and talk with unit commanders in their Forward CPs, and with his own eyes and ears to form his opinion of Eighth Army's spirit and morale. But first he must call on President Syngman Rhee of South Korea and John J. Muccio, American ambassador to Rhee's government.[18]

Leaving this conference, Ridgway went next to see Ambassador Muccio, who told him that the South Koreans were afraid United States forces were going to leave Korea. President Rhee and others in his government and the ROK Army command, Muccio said, interpreted the recent month-long withdrawal of the UN command from the north of Korea as a prelude to its continued withdrawal, and possibly its departure from Korea.

In this meeting, Muccio spoke most urgently of the danger in central Korea down the Hongchon-Wonju-Chechon corridor, saying that it was wide open to a rapid flanking move of enemy around the UN east, or right, flank. Ridgway saw the force of his comments and had it on his mind the next two days as he made the rounds of the UN line across the peninsula. His conversations with Muccio also convinced him that he must spend most of the days immediately ahead in the Seoul area for psychological reasons, to influence both ROK and American troops. Muccio made clear there might be danger of wholesale defection of the ROK Army if the situation was not handled correctly. Their hurried, wide-ranging conversation ended for the present, Ridgway and Muccio proceeded to a meeting with President Rhee.

Ridgway, Muccio, and Collier met with President Rhee and his minister of defense, General Sihn, at Rhee's residence at 11:40 A.M. President Rhee greeted General Ridgway rather impassively. Ridgway lost no time in civilities. Extending his hand, he said to Rhee that he had not come to Korea to lead Eighth Army out of the country. He said he meant to stay. Ridgway knew it was of the utmost importance to impress the South Koreans at once that this was the American intent. This statement from Ridgway was what the old Korean leader wanted to hear. His face lighted up with a smile, and he grasped Ridgway's extended hand in both his own.

Ridgway and Muccio spent about an hour and fifteen minutes with President Rhee in this meeting, in the course of which they had tea with him and Mrs. Rhee. General Ridgway repeatedly assured President Rhee that he meant to go on the offensive as soon as possible. He also asked the president for as many Korean laborers as could be made available to work on the defenses of Seoul, 30,000 of them if possible. Rhee said he would provide this help, and indeed thousands of Koreans reported for work the next day. Ridgway later told Lt. Gen. Chung Il Kwan, the ROK Army chief of staff, of the American intent to stay in Korea.[19]

A few minutes before noon the conference with President Rhee ended. At 12:30, Ridgway was at General Milburn's I Corps Headquarters. Using a light plane, a helicopter, and a jeep, Ridgway traveled during the afternoon to the British 29th Brigade command post, the US 25th Infantry Division and 27th Infantry Regiment CPs, and the ROK 1st Division and General Coulter's IX Corps CPs. Lt. Col. Paul Smith, who traveled throughout the day with Ridgway, said that, as Ridgway's jeep approached each CP they visited, Ridgway would jump from the jeep before it came to a full stop, give a high salute, and say, "I am not here to get real estate – don't give a damn for that. I am here to defeat the enemy," and pointing his finger at the group in front of him, he added, "and you are going to do it, now!"[20] This performance did not impress most of the viewers.

Meanwhile Maj. Gen. Edward M. Almond was on his way to meet Ridgway. Almond and his X Corps staff, sailing from Hungnam on the USS *Mt. McKinley*, reached their debarkation area near Ulsan on the east coast of Korea above Pusan on the afternoon of 25 December and went at once to Kyongju, where a X Corps Advance CP had been established. There, General Almond received a telephone call from General Allen, Army chief of staff at Taegu, at 10:30 A.M. on 27 December. Allen said that General

Lt. Gen. Matthew Ridgway talks with Maj. Gen. Frank W. Milburn, commanding general of I Corps, on 27 December 1950, Ridgway's second day in command of Eighth Army. *US Army photograph, SC 355279*

Ridgway wanted Almond to attend a corps commanders meeting at Seoul that day. Almond departed Kyongju at noon by jeep, accompanied by his junior aide, Capt. Alexander M. Haig. High winds prevented him from taking off in a light plane. An hour and a half later, Almond reached Taegu, from which he was able to continue by air in a C-47 plane to Seoul. He arrived at Seoul Municipal Airport a few minutes after 3 P.M. Major Woods met him there and drove him to Eighth Army Advance CP. From there he went by jeep to pay his respects to Ambassador Muccio. While he was there, Colonel Collier arrived to tell him that General Ridgway wanted him to come to the IX Corps CP for a conference with him and General Coulter. Almond arrived at IX Corps and had a ten-minute conference with Generals Ridgway and Coulter. Ridgway outlined briefly his intention to have all elements of Eighth Army fight cohesively and take as great a toll in lives as possible, using superior firepower and maneuverability. When Ridgway asked Almond what his attitude was, Almond answered, "Attack on your orders." Ridgway replied, "That's what I want to hear." This was not the typical response Ridgway had received.[21]

On 27 December, when General Ridgway was making his first round of Eighth Army positions above Seoul and conferring with his three corps commanders, it must be realized that X Corps had not yet completed its assembly in South Korea, following its evacuation from northeast Korea, although it was on the point of doing so. All of X Corps was far to the south of the battlefront of Eighth Army at this time and could not be counted on for any help in the immediate future. So, at the time of Ridgway's arrival in Korea, there were only two American divisions, the 24th and 25th, on the line north of Seoul, with the 1st Cavalry Division, at reduced strength, in reserve behind them. The 2nd Infantry Division, following its disaster at Kunu-ri in the last days of November, was still taking in replacements of men and equipment to become combat effective again. But before completing this task, the division had been ordered to the Chungju area in east-central Korea to provide a backstop to the ROK divisions that were being hard hit by North Korean units northward in the Hongchon area.

Three American infantry divisions of X Corps—the 1st Marine Division and the Army 3rd and 7th infantry divisions—were to be moved north and made available to Eighth Army as soon as they had completed their landings in South Korea and had rested, taken in replacements, and re-equipped. The 1st Marine Division had been the first to land at Pusan and had moved to its old assembly area at the northern edge of Masan, where the division established its CP on 16 December. Two days later it passed from X Corps to Eighth Army control. The 7th Infantry Division landed next, and the 3rd Infantry Division, after covering the evacuation of Hungnam, was the last of the major combat elements of X Corps to reach South Korea, its lead units landing over the beaches at Ulsan, north of Pusan, on 18 December. General Almond had sent a small party ahead from Hungnam to establish a X Corps Advance CP at Kyongju. He had barely arrived there when General Ridgway's message reached him on the twenty-seventh to come to the Seoul corps commanders meeting.

After his meeting with Ridgway in the afternoon of 27 December, Almond returned to the Seoul airport and flew to Taegu in the B-17, arriving at Eighth Army's Main Headquarters at 6:15 P.M. There General Almond held a conference with General Allen and then joined him and the senior staff officers at the commanding general's mess for dinner. The main topic of conversation there was the quality of the ROK troops and the general military situation in Korea. After dinner, Almond returned to headquarters with General Allen and Colonel Landrum, a deputy chief of staff, for further conversation. About the conversation at the general's mess, Almond recorded in his diary that, with the exception of General Allen, who was noncommittal, "the entire Eighth Army Staff was extremely low spirited and believed that our forces must retire to the Pusan perimeter in a short time (3–5 days)."[22]

Almond spent the night in Colonel Landrum's quarters and the next day returned to X Corps Headquarters at Kyongju. The same day that Almond met Ridgway at Seoul, 27 December, the X Corps came officially under Eighth Army control. For the first time in Korea all UN forces were under Eighth Army command in unified control. What General Ridgway did not know on 27 December as he flew north to Seoul was that Eighth Army Engineers were preparing demolitions for all bridges along the army's expected line of further withdrawal in anticipation of Walker's Operational Plan 19 and that extra police guards were being placed at the bridges as part of this demolition plan.[23]

General Ridgway did not like what he saw and sensed about Eighth Army and its front-line units on 27 December, and he confirmed his first unfavorable and discouraging feeling about the situation in the next several days, which he spent in going to other command posts and units that he had been unable to see on the afternoon of the twenty-seventh. He traveled along the front in an open jeep, nearly freezing, he said. (Ridgway would not allow a closed vehicle to travel in a combat zone.) He did not even have a pile-lined cap until an unidentified major gave him one with earflaps and fur lining and a good pair of warm gloves to go with it. He wrote that it was clear to him that the troops had lost confidence. He said,

I could sense it the moment I came into a command post. I could read it in their eyes, in their walk. I could read it in the faces of their leaders, from sergeants right on up to the top. They were unresponsive, reluctant to talk. I had to drag information out of them. There was a complete absence of that alertness, that aggressiveness, that you find in troops whose spirit is high. . . . They were not patrolling as they should. Their knowledge of the enemy's location and his strength was pitifully inadequate. There are two kinds of information no commander can do without – information pertaining to the enemy, which we call combat intelligence, and information on the terrain. Both are vital. . . . All intelligence could show me was a big red goose egg out in front of us, with 174,000 scrawled in the middle of it.[24]

"What I told the field commanders in essence was that their infantry ancestors would roll over in their graves could they see how roadbound this army was, how often it forgot to seize the high ground along its route, how it failed to seek and maintain contact in its front, how little it knew of the terrain and how seldom took advantage of it . . . to use runners if the radio and phones were out." He said he found leadership in many instances sadly lacking.[25]

Who was Matthew Bunker Ridgway, the lieutenant general who had suddenly appeared on the Korean scene to direct the American army and its UN allies in the nadir of their military fortunes? Most of the senior officers of the Far East Command in Tokyo and of Eighth Army knew something about his military career in Europe in World War II as an outstanding airborne troop leader. Some of them had been associated with him there. But the rank-and-file knew little or nothing, although favorable rumor began to spread rapidly.

When he arrived in Korea on 26 December 1950, Ridgway was 55 years old, a professional soldier. He stood just under 6 feet tall, weighed 175–80 pounds, and had the rugged, muscular appearance of an athlete. His large brown eyes and high cheekbones in a dark brown-reddish complexion dominated a lean, alert face. At one time, age 33, he had been in training for the 1928 Olympic US Army pentathlon squad. But Gen. Frank R. McCoy asked Ridgway to accompany him to Nicaragua, where McCoy was to supervise a free election in that chaotic country. Ridgway joined General McCoy and never regretted it. He considered McCoy one of the greatest military statesmen he ever knew.

Matthew Ridgway was born 3 March 1895 at Fort Monroe, Virginia, son of Col. Thomas Ridgway and Mrs. Ruth Ridgway. Thomas Ridgway was a graduate of the US Military Academy, West Point, class of 1883, a regular army officer in the Coast Artillery Corps. Matthew's mother played the piano almost at the level of a concert pianist. He had one older sister and no brothers. An uncle, Robert Ridgway, was the chief engineer in the building of the New York subway and consultant for engineering projects in Chicago and Tokyo.

Matthew Ridgway followed in his father's steps, entering West Point as an Army cadet and graduating in the class of 1917, the same class that included Joseph Lawton Collins, Ernest N. Harmon, Mark W. Clark, and Laurence B. Keiser. On 20 April 1917, Matthew Ridgway received appointment as second lieutenant in the regular army.[26]

Ridgway's first assignment was to the 3rd Infantry at Eagle Pass, Texas, on the Mexican border, where he served as a company commander. From there he went in September 1918 to the US Military Academy as an instructor, remaining there until June 1924. From September 1921 he was associated with the athletic department, and from August 1922 as graduate manager of athletics. In June 1924, he entered the company officers course at the Infantry School, Fort Benning, Georgia, and graduated the following May. That summer of 1925 he commanded a company of the 15th Infantry at Tientsin, China. The next year he commanded E Company, 9th Infantry, at Fort Sam Houston, Texas, and later became regimental adjutant. It may be noted that both the 9th Infantry and the 15th Infantry were regiments in Eighth Army when Ridgway assumed command of it in December 1950.

From 1927 to mid-1935, Ridgway spent most of his time working with Gen. Frank McCoy and the American Electoral Commission in Nicaragua, the Commission of Inquiry and Conciliation, relating to the Bolivia-Paraguay boundary dispute, and a tour of duty with the 33rd Infantry at Fort Clayton, Panama Canal Zone. His several years of duty in Central and South America had made him fluent in Spanish, and he already had a passing knowledge of French. In June 1930, he completed the advance course for infantry officers at Fort Benning. He spent 1932–33 as a technical advisor with Gov. Gen. Theodore Roosevelt, Jr., in the Philippine Islands Insular Government. In June 1935, he graduated from the Command and General Staff School at Fort Leavenworth, Kansas. He was then detailed to the General Staff Corps and assigned as assistant chief of staff, G-3, Sixth Corps Area and of Second Army, Chicago, Illinois. Subsequently he attended the Army War College in Washington, D.C., graduating in June 1937. Thereupon he was ordered to the Presidio, San Francisco, California, as assistant chief of staff, G-3, Fourth Army.

In May 1939, Brig. Gen. George C. Marshall, chief of staff designate, asked Ridgway to accompany him on a special mission to Brazil, at least partly because Ridgway was by now considered fluent in Spanish and something of an expert on Latin American affairs. Upon returning from the mission with General Marshall, Ridgway was assigned to the War Department General Staff for duties with the War Plans Division. He remained in that post until January 1942.[27] Things changed rapidly for Ridgway after the Japanese attacked Pearl Harbor on 7 December 1941, as they did for nearly all regular army officers.

Late in January 1942, Gen. George C. Marshall called Ridgway to his office and told him the famous 82nd Division of World War I was being reactivated. He was giving command of it to Gen. Omar Bradley, and Ridgway was to be second in command. A few hours later Ridgway was on his way to Camp Claiborne, Louisiana, where the division cadre was assembling. In March Ridgway officially received his designation as assistant division commander. Some months later, the War Department shifted

Bradley to train the 28th Division, and Ridgway then, on 26 June 1942, became the commander of the 82nd Infantry Division. Two months later the division was redesignated the 82nd Airborne Division, the first such division in the United States Army. The spectacular German parachute and glider drop on the island of Crete had persuaded the American command that it must have similar troops. The 82nd Infantry Division was considered the best then in training, and it was chosen to be the first of the new kind.

Ridgway, now a temporary major general, knew nothing about parachute airborne troop drops. But he wanted to drop with his troops on any practice exercises. He and his artillery commander, Joe Swing, found excuses to get away to Fort Benning, where parachute troops had begun training. He arranged with those in charge of parachute jumping to set him up for a jump the next morning. After breakfast he went to the gymnasium, where a sergeant gave him about ten minutes of instruction. Trussed up in a parachute harness, Ridgway made a jump from the door of a mock-up plane to the floor ten feet below, after being shown how to roll to absorb the shock. He was also shown how to slip out of the harness on landing so that he would not be dragged if a wind were blowing. Then he boarded a plane and went up. Three of them jumped—his old friend Bud Miley, a parachute jump instructor; then Ridgway; and then Swing. Ridgway forgot what the sergeant had told him about guiding his body straight down and "hit going backward and went over on my head with a tooth-rattling crash." But he was not injured. In this way he became an airborne soldier.[28]

General Ridgway took the 82nd Airborne Division to North Africa in April 1943, where it prepared for the first US Army large airborne assault, the attack on Sicily. He led the airborne assault on Sicily in July 1943. Capt. Don C. Faith, Jr., later killed at the Chosin Reservoir in Korea, and posthumously awarded the Congressional Medal of Honor, was Ridgway's aide in the Sicily operation. Ridgway's 82nd Airborne Division was then scheduled to make a drop at Rome to hasten the collapse of the Italian-German resistance and to pave the way for an early capture of the Eternal City, an operation later canceled.

From Sicily, Ridgway had to send the 82nd Airborne on a quick rescue mission to save Gen. Mark Clark's landing at Salerno. From Salerno, the 82nd Airborne Division fought as infantry in the drive to seize Naples.

The next year, on 6 June 1944, General Ridgway parachuted with the leading assault elements of the division into Normandy in the invasion of France. He dropped at the edge of the town of Sainte-Mère-Église. The airborne troops played a critical role on D day of the invasion.

In August 1944, Ridgway was promoted to command the XVIII Airborne Corps. This is not the place to list details of his battle participation in Europe with the XVIII Airborne Corps. But with his aide, Capt. Don

Faith, at his side, he flew in a C-47 to Antwerp, Belgium, and then went forward by jeep to the command post of the 101st Airborne and subsequently to that of the 82nd Airborne Division, both of which had dropped at Eindhoven, Holland, where the British 1st Airborne was virtually destroyed; he and his troops were in the Ardennes battles in Belgium, the crossing of the Rhine River near Wesel, the battle of the Ruhr pocket, the crossing of the Elbe, and finally the advance to junction with Soviet forces on the Baltic on 2 May 1945.

Ridgway returned with the XVIII Airborne Corps to the United States in August 1945 for redeployment to the Pacific Theater for planned operations there against Japan. At that time he flew to the Philippines with some of his staff to meet with General MacArthur, under whom he and his corps were expected to take part in the invasion of the Japanese Home Islands. But the dropping of the atomic bombs on Japan ended the war.

Ridgway was then assigned command in Europe of the Mediterranean Theater. In January 1946, he was named to represent General of the Army Dwight D. Eisenhower on the Military Staff Committee, United Nations— first in London, and then in New York City. In addition to these duties, two months later he became senior US delegate to the Inter-American Defense Board, and chairman of the board.

All of Ridgway's combat experience had been in the European Theater in World War II. He was known for his leadership qualities, and as an officer greatly concerned for the welfare of his men. In his command leadership during combat, Ridgway insisted on being up near his front lines; he felt a commander must see with his own eyes what was happening in a critical area and be there to assume personal command of a critical situation if it developed. On one occasion in March 1945, he went through an area not yet cleared of enemy troops to establish communications between his two separated airborne divisions. He performed the same dangerous mission of passing through enemy to establish contact with the 6th British Airborne Division. On this latter mission his party of two jeeps was ambushed by a German patrol. Ridgway was wounded in this encounter by a German hand grenade.[29]

Something must be said about the inner spirit, the mental coloring, and the truly democratic sympathy of Ridgway for the human individual. There was a certain, hard to define, religious feeling in the man, not associated with any dogma.

A few of Ridgway's principles of action in handling an army in combat may be mentioned as a guide to the type of commander he was. He said, "One must see with his own eyes evidence to support relieving a battlefield commander, and then relieve him only if a better substitute is available; otherwise the situation is made worse." He acted in Korea on the principle that all major units of the army must maintain contact with each other—they must be mutually supporting. No unit, not even a battalion, should be separated from contact with adjacent units; to do so would be to run the risk of sacrificing them, and he would not tolerate such use and management of troop units. He believed that the fundamental requirement of battle leadership in a commander was "to anticipate where a crisis would occur — that it is hardly ever in more than one place at a time — and be there in person to take personal charge if necessary, and if he has not anticipated it to go there in person as quickly as he can get there after it develops."[30]

Ridgway believed that, in war, the foot soldier is the ultimate weapon. He is the only instrument capable of taking and holding ground. Ridgway held that a private's life was just as valuable as a general's, and he tried to avoid undue risk of their lives. He did not lightly venture into any attack or action that might result in a frivolous loss of life. He has expressed his view on this subject.

A commander must have far more concern for the welfare of his men than he has for his own safety. After all, the same dignity attaches to the mission given a single soldier as to the duties of the commanding general. The execution of the soldier's mission is just as vitally important, because it is the sum total of all these small individual missions, properly executed, which produces the results of the big unit. All lives are equal on the battlefield, and a dead rifleman is as great a loss, in the sight of God, as a dead general. The dignity which attaches to the individual is the basis of western civilization, and that fact should be remembered by every commander, platoon or army.[31]

In discussing the failure of soldiers to do their duty on occasion, Ridgway said to the author, "Every man has his breaking point. If treated sympathetically and humanely, a soldier suffering from 'battle fatigue' will return to the line, a brave soldier."[32]

On a visit to Edinburgh, Scotland, Ridgway saw a monument of a soldier sitting head up, rifle across his knees, as if there were a moment's lull in a battle. Carved beneath in the stone was the inscription, "If it be Life that waits, I shall live forever unconquered; if Death, I shall die at last, strong in my pride and free." Ridgway carried a faded picture of that monument and its inscription in his wallet during World War II. Its theme must have become a part of his soldier's creed.

Ridgway had a tremendous sympathy for the ordeals and dangers of the ordinary soldier. The author felt this spirit keenly in his first conversation with Ridgway in Tokyo in October 1951. At one point Ridgway's voice dropped almost to being inaudible and he lowered his eyes as he spoke of the men who had lost their lives in the Korean War. At the door as I left, I spoke of the marvel he had accomplished in turning a field army around, which then drove a previously victorious enemy in front of it. Visibly touched, and with head bent, he said, "Many people had a part in what has been accomplished. One's appeal must be to the spiritual, and if it reaches the mass of soldiers, wonders can be accomplished."

General Ridgway had the reputation in Korea of being a rather grim commander, one who remained somewhat aloof from staff familiarity, but one who would help a soldier who had dropped part of his pack, a man of great personal courage, confidence in his decisions, and one who would relieve a subordinate who did not measure up. When he was asked, "As a Chief of Staff, what qualifications would you look for in key staff officers?" Ridgway replied, "Character first, and professional competence and his professional career."[33]

Soon after Ridgway took command of Eighth Army, he gained the nickname "Wrong-way Ridgway," because he wanted to turn the army around and head it north toward the enemy.[34] But by February 1951, this sobriquet had been forgotten, for all the army by then knew that Ridgway was indeed turning the army around, and it was facing north to drive the enemy toward the 38th Parallel. By February the common soldier in the ranks had complimentary remarks about their new commanding general.

Ridgway carried a Springfield rifle, which had long been his favorite weapon, just as it was with many older officers who had started their careers with it. We know that Ridgway was an unusually good shot. It is said that the Springfield that Ridgway carried in Korea was given to him by the ROK Army.

An opinion that characterized the view of Ridgway commonly held by all ranks in Eighth Army after he had served as the army's commander for a few months was that expressed by Brig. Gen. James F. Brittingham, I Corps Artillery commander: "Finest soldier I ever served with. Had ability to inspire confidence."[35] A comment by an Australian officer, who served with the Australian Battalion in Korea from the summer of 1950, may indicate how a NATO ally remembers his first impression of Ridgway.

I was first introduced to General Ridgway in the winter of 1951, it must have been in January or February, when my General called on him at his tactical headquarters. It has left me with a lasting impression of him. He was quite simply dressed in one of those thick winter shirts with no embellishments save for his stars. His face was strong even in repose and I can recall thinking that he reminded me of a Red Indian. As a young man I was most impressed by his simplicity and strength. . . . I have spoken to both the Commanding Officer at the time and the Intelligence Officer and they have a similar memory of the occasion he arrived.[36]

This was the recollection of Col. David M. Butler, DSO, Australian Military Forces, who later in the Korean War became the personal assistant to Maj. Gen. A. J. H. Cassells, commander of the British Commonwealth Division.

Lt. Gen. William J. McCaffrey has a vivid recollection of General Ridgway's influence on Eighth Army. McCaffrey, then a colonel, was commander of the 31st Infantry Regiment, 7th Division, in central Korea. As a regimental commander he was fully familiar with Ridgway's insistence that all commanders keep their units in positions where they could be supported by others and not cut off and cut up by the enemy. Speaking of one occasion that almost cost him his command, McCaffrey wrote:

[Ridgway] was not sympathetic to corps, division, or regimental commanders who had their units cut off and chewed up by the Chinese. He threatened to relieve me one day while he was at the Division [7th] Headquarters because 7th Division had posted on their situation map a location for one of my battalions that indicated the Bn was beyond the support of the rest of the regiment. Before this [relief from command] occurred, somebody checked and found they had a wrong coordinate. However, when I got the word that afternoon, it was well understood by all of us commanding regiments up and down the line that we jolly well better button up and not get careless.[37]

In a 1969 interview Ridgway spoke of his concept of command leadership in a vein that revealed the man. He said,

Can't say Napoleon's Old Guard was better or worse than Scipio Africanus's Numidian cavalry. . . . It's the same human being each commander deals with; if you have leadership they will rise to any height. If you don't have it, they won't, and that's the key to the whole thing—leadership. How do you produce it? That's an eternally fascinating question. It's not a science; it's an art. . . . It's a question of numerous interrelated factors that affect the nature of man . . . the best of troops will fail if the strain is big enough. It just gets to the point where a man can't take it anymore—that's all. Always be easy on a man like that. Help him get back to the rear. Nine times out of ten he will come out of it all right.[38]

No George Patton speaking there!

To young officers Ridgway in his later years recommended that they read, read, read, and learn from the successes and failures of past great captains. The memoirs and the records of the campaigns of nearly all the great military leaders of the past had been written and published, he said, and they were there for guidance.

It is interesting to compare Ridgway in 1950 with certain aspects of other great soldiers of history. Theodore A. Dodge in his *Great Captains* gives the ages of several at the height of their ability: Alexander the Great was 25; Gustavus Adolphus, 37; Hannibal, 34; Napoleon, 39; Frederick the Great, 45; and Caesar, 52. Ridgway was 55 when he entered on command of Eighth Army in Korea. In size of the armies they commanded, Alexander's largest army in the field was 135,000, Hannibal's less than 60,000, Caesar's about 80,000, Gustavus Adolphus, less than 80,000, Frederick the Great, about 50,000, and Napoleon, 360,000 in the Russian campaign. Ridgway's combined UN command in Korea numbered about 365,000 in December 1950.[39]

From his studies Theodore Dodge believed that great captains have won success "by personal activity and by relying only on themselves in critical matters. In estimating a great soldier, one must remember all his errors of omission and commission. No general may shelter himself behind the lapse of a subordinate. He must stand or fall by what he himself does or fails to do."[40]

Ridgway's philosophy of military leadership was very similar to that of Dodge, which involved

Consideration for the living conditions – food, clothing, and medical care – and above all, consistent with the full accomplishment of my assigned missions, the lives of the men entrusted to me;

Sharing, so far as practicable, their hardships and hazards;

Not asking them to do anything I had not already done myself and stood ready to do again when necessary;

And being at the point of an anticipated crisis before it erupted, if possible, or if not then as soon thereafter as possible.

To my mind these are the basics.[41]

General Ridgway's training in the precepts of military tactics and strategy, as well as that of nearly all officers who came out of West Point until the early twentieth century, may be said to have been based on the principles of Jomini, which the latter summarized in his much-studied work, *Précis de l'art de la guerre*, published in 1838. Baron Antoine Henri Jomini, a Swiss, entered French service in 1806 during the Napoleonic Wars as one of Napoleon's staff officers. Later, Napoleon appointed him chief of staff to Marshal Ney. Jomini was supply conscious and taught that the logistics of any battle or campaign must be well considered. He felt that the basic principles of war were unchanging, objective, and independent of either weapons or time. "Military history," he wrote, "accompanied by sound criticism, is indeed the true school of war." He believed that human nature was and always would be the common denominator of all armed conflict, that control of the human factor in war depended directly upon the qualities of leadership possessed by a commander. He also believed in "moderation in victory to know how to stop in time."[42]

How subservient should a commander be to superior authority when he believes orders received are wrong and, if followed, will result in the destruction of his command? This is far from an academic question, as it was relevant several times in the Korean War. Knowledge of Ridgway's view on this subject adds to an understanding of him. The question the author had in mind was, Is a soldier, no matter how high his rank, ever free not to follow an order? I asked this question of Ridgway, having in mind specific orders that General MacArthur gave to Generals Walker and Almond in the Korean War, and that General Almond in turn gave to Gen. Oliver Smith, commander of the 1st Marine Division in the deployment in northeast Korea that resulted in the Chosin Reservoir campaign.

General Ridgway answered by citing several times in his own career when he believed orders he received were wrong and, if followed, would result in the destruction of his troops, and then by stating the course he followed. Only one of these incidents will be mentioned here. It shows, better than anything one could say, Ridgway's attitude toward command responsibility, devotion to troops commanded, and the necessity in military operations for all levels to follow orders from superior authority. The incident that follows involved the Mediterranean Command's decision in World War II to drop Ridgway's 82nd Airborne Division near Rome after the conclusion of the Sicily campaign, to speed up the conquest of the Italian peninsula and drive Italy out of the war.

General Ridgway utterly opposed the plan. He thought it unsound from many vantage points. Rome was out of range of American fighter-plane support, and his men would be at the mercy of enemy air, since there would be no supporting artillery fire for them once they had landed; it was also well known that there were six good German infantry divisions in the Rome area. The Mediterranean Command promised that Allied infantry would fight their way to the Rome area from the south within five days. Ridgway did not believe that possible and could only foresee that, under all these conditions, his 82nd Airborne Division would be destroyed. They would be all alone if dropped at the edge of Rome, with no chance of success in their mission. Ridgway expressed his views to Gen. Bedell Smith, who advised him to try to see the Mediterranean theater commander, British general Sir Harold R. L. G. Alexander, who had ordered the airborne drop on Rome. Bedell Smith said he could arrange the interview. He did. Ridgway met with Alexander and made his case, asking for a reversal of the order. Alexander brushed him off and dismissed him with the words, "Don't give this another thought, Ridgway. Contact will be made with your division in three days—five at most."

Ridgway, despondent, went back to his division. He talked about the situation with Brig. Gen. Maxwell Taylor, his artillery commander. They agreed that an agent should go to Rome, contact clandestinely the Italian authorities to make a firsthand determination whether the Italians could be counted on to support with strength an airborne drop near Rome. This plan was proposed to General Alexander. He rejected it as too risky. Ridgway had to prepare to carry out the order for the airdrop.

Another twenty-four hours of seething upset about the prospect of sacrificing his beloved airborne division caused Ridgway to ask Bedell Smith to try once more to dissuade General Alexander from the venture. This time Alexander agreed to let General Taylor and Air Force Colonel Gardner make the trip to Rome. They arrived there disguised as captured airmen and met at a secret rendezvous with Italian marshal Badaglio. After their discussions it was clear to General Taylor that the 82nd Airborne drop would be doomed to failure. He sent a coded radio message to General Alexander to that effect.

Meanwhile Alexander's order to make the drop stood, and Ridgway prepared to carry it out. The day arrived. The loaded planes were on their airfields ready for takeoff, and one serial was already airborne. In the following quoted passage General Ridgway answered the author's question.

It never entered my mind for one second to decline to carry out an order from duly constituted superior authority. I laid before my superiors my conscientious convictions as to what the results would be, if the mission as ordered were carried out. When, after my second effort to avert the anticipated tragic sacrifice of as gallant and loyal a unit as ever existed, was disapproved, I proceeded with the completion of our plans to execute the order.

I had inwardly made my peace with my Maker, but on that afternoon just prior to take-off, I sought out the Division Chaplain, Major George Riddle, and asked him to take a walk with me away from all others at my Command Post. What was in my mind was the account of Jesus in the Garden of Gethsemane, and the anguish he knew awaited him, but which he calmly composed and readied himself for the coming ordeal. I do not recall my conversation with Major Riddle, but I remember as vividly as though it were yesterday, that I drew comfort from that walk with him, and that all my anxieties vanished.

I returned to my tent in an almond orchard and asked Doc Eaton, my Chief of Staff, to join me in a game of cribbage. It was then less than one hour before my scheduled take-off. Most of the paratroop units were on their departure fields. Some were already aboard their planes. Eaton and I had that complete mutual understanding and spiritual rapport which should be the ideal relationship between a Commander and his Chief of Staff.

We were at our cribbage game, then probably 20 minutes before leaving for the airfield when General Lemnitzer, an emissary from General Alexander's headquarters, came to me and announced cancellation of the mission. Fearing a message to that effect might arrive too late, he had, on his own initiative, come by plane and jeep to personally deliver the message. Had he not done so, it is possible the 82nd, or some of its units, would already have been airborne.[43]

It is interesting to note that the ground-troops support that General Alexander had assured Ridgway would arrive on the scene near Rome to help in three days, or at the most in five days, did not in fact get there until nearly seven months later. General Ridgway wrote of this episode, "When the time comes that I must meet my Maker, the source of most humble pride to me will not be accomplishments in battle, but the fact that I was guided to make the decision to oppose this thing, at the risk of my career, right up to the top. . . . I deeply and sincerely believe that by taking the stand I took we saved the lives of thousands of brave men." He added a statement that must stand as his view on a commander's duty to his troops:

It seems to me . . . that the hard decisions are not the ones you make in the heat of battle. Far harder to make are those involved in speaking your mind about some hare-brained scheme which proposes to commit troops to action under conditions where failure is almost certain, and the only results will be the needless sacrifice of priceless lives. When all is said and done, the most precious asset any nation has is its youth, and for a battle commander ever to condone the needless sacrifice of his men is absolutely inexcusable. In any action, you must balance the inevitable cost in lives against the objectives you seek to attain. Unless, beyond any reasonable doubt, the results reasonably to be expected can justify the estimated loss of life the action involves, then for my part I want none of it.[44]

This was the man who now faced his supreme test in Korea.

2

The Sword of Damocles over Eighth Army

DEEPENING WINTER, intelligence of enemy probing, and the condition of UN troops hung over General Ridgway's Eighth Army like the mythological sword of Damocles, swinging overhead by a single hair. At the end of his first day at Seoul and his hasty trip to part of the front line north of it, General Ridgway was disturbed.

He spent all the next day, 28 December, continuing his travels over the rest of the line. He visited every corps and division CP that he had not visited on the twenty-seventh, except for the ROK Capital Division at the far eastern end of the line on the Sea of Japan, which at the time was a quiet part of the front.

At the US 24th Infantry Division, Ridgway found that one-third of the men in the division did not have their winter clothing. On the spot, he ordered that this clothing be issued to the troops before midnight. As it chanced, a representative of the division was then in Pusan with requisitions covering the shortages. The items were calculated to weigh 102,000 pounds and to occupy 8,451 cubic feet of space. This information was telephoned from Pusan to the G-4 section of Eighth Army at Taegu. It arranged an airlift from K-9 airfield at Pusan to the 24th Division area northeast of Seoul. The first trucks for transporting this clothing to the Pusan airstrip for the airlift reported to the Pusan Quartermaster Depot at 2:15 P.M. on 28 December. They left the depot three hours later. Three C-54 planes loaded in the afternoon and took off. Four more lifted off the Pusan runway three hours after midnight. The remainder of the winter clothing went forward by air on 30 December.[1]

As General Ridgway traveled from command post to command post and to battalions on the line, he kept in mind Ambassador Muccio's admonition on 27 December that a critical situation was rapidly developing on the central front in the Hongchon and Wonju area, held by the ROK III Corps, because these troops were untrained and unreliable. He found almost universal corroboration from the American officers with whom he discussed the subject on the afternoon of 27 December and during the morning of the twenty-eighth. There was agreement that the central area was vulnerable and that a quick, strong enemy thrust there might place formidable enemy (North Korean) units behind the entire UN command combat forces and between them and Pusan.

Ridgway was convinced and acted immediately. That very day he ordered the US 2nd Infantry Division to send its three regiments to the Wonju-Hongchon area. One regiment was to block at Hongchon against approaches from the north and northeast. The 23rd Regiment was to move to Wonju. The remainder of the division moved up toward these places, but one battalion of the 38th Infantry was to go to Chechon. The next day the 38th Regiment was ordered to Wonju. And Ridgway ordered the 7th Infantry Division to send a regiment north to support the 2nd Division.[2] These orders, on the second and third days after he arrived at Seoul, were among the most important and most far-reaching of any he issued during the Korean War. The 2nd Division and the leading elements of the 7th Division arrived in the Wonju area just in time.

After finishing his hasty tour of Eighth Army's line and major CPs on 28 December, Ridgway returned to Taegu. His next big task was to visit the newly arrived X Corps CP at Kyongju in southeast Korea and to arrange for the X Corps to move quickly north into the central battle line. He left Taegu at 10 A.M., 30 December, by plane for a conference at General Almond's CP in the southeast corner of Korea, far from the Wonju area. At Kyongju, Ridgway conferred with General Almond; Maj. Gen. Clark Ruffner, X Corps chief of staff; Maj. Gen. David Barr, 7th Division commander; Maj. Gen. Oliver Smith, 1st Marine Division commander; and other X Corps officers. The discussion centered on General Ridgway's plans for the immediate movement of the X Corps northward into the mountainous central corridor to reinforce Eighth Army's line with American troops in that vital area.[3]

One must turn now from General Ridgway and his attempt to assess the condition of Eighth Army and its ROK allies in the first few days after his arrival in Korea to note just what was happening at the front during this time, from 27 to 31 December. In the western part of the line, above Seoul, patrols of the 25th Division on 27 December estimated an enemy battalion was opposite its line, the first large group reported to be there. A Chinese prisoner said that the CCF 40th Army was moving to the Imjin River, south of the Munsan-ni–Kaesong road, and that the CCF 50th Army was moving into assembly areas near Kaesong. Meanwhile, Korean laborers continued digging positions and laying tactical wire in front of the division's 24th Regiment. About 400 Korean laborers worked at this regiment's position alone on 27 December. Reports of continued enemy buildup in the west were the rule of the day.[4]

On the eastern and central fronts, in the high mountains back from the east coast, a heavy North Korean attack hit along the boundary of the 28th and 30th regiments of the ROK 9th Division, split them apart, and drove through and past these regiments to a depth of eight miles. This enemy force was now between the ROK 9th and ROK Capital divisions near Yangyang on the coast and south of both divisions. It threatened the entire eastern front, because the North Koreans now sent thousands of their troops through this gap into rear areas of the UN positions to operate in guerrilla fashion to disrupt the ROK II and III Corps front. This was not a probing attack but had to be considered the start of an offensive in the east-central part of the UN line. During the day, 27 December, Eighth Army attached the 1st Marine Division to X Corps, which signaled that it probably would be rushed to the east-central front.[5]

Also during 27 December, the 2nd Infantry Division started moving into position behind the ROK troops in the Hongchon-Chunchon area, but still many miles south of them in the central corridor. The division CP and most of the 9th Infantry were at Chungju, the 23rd Infantry was en route to Wonju, and one battalion of the 38th Infantry was at Yongju and another at Punggi. The attached French Battalion was just north of Chungju along the Han River where it made its big turn from running west to a northwest direction, and the 72nd Tank Battalion was patrolling the Sangu-Mungyong road of the corridor farther south. The Netherlands Battalion, now attached to the 9th Infantry, was at Mungyong. Lt. Col. M. P. A. den Ouden commanded this 600-man battalion. He and most of his staff spoke English. The 2nd Infantry Division G-2 staff section estimated the North Koreans could attack Wonju with at least 7,000 men, and within ten hours after any penetration they could send 22,000 men through the gap.[6]

On 28 December General Ridgway ordered the 2nd Infantry Division to move its troops still farther north and to take defensive positions in the Wonju area. The 37th Field Artillery Battalion was attached to the 23rd Infantry and moved with it to Wonju. The 1st Battalion of the 23rd Infantry dug in on high ground just north of Wonju and prepared to block movements into the town from that direction and to fight delaying actions south along the road to Chungju, and also on the Chupo-ri axis southeast from Wonju to Chungju. The regiment's 2nd and 3rd battalions were to take defensive positions covering all roads into Wonju from the southeast and southwest. The 9th Infantry Regiment and the French and Netherlands battalions were held in division reserve.

The 38th Infantry Regiment, with the 1st Ranger Company attached, had a somewhat different mission to the southeast of Wonju. It was to block any enemy penetration along the Chechon-Tanyang-Yangju-Andong axis. This roadnet, southeast of the Wonju-Chungju road, provided a good avenue for enemy troops to pass the east flank of the 23rd Regiment at Wonju by penetrating the ROK forces eastward in the area where large North Korean units had already pushed past the ROK 9th Division in the mountains. There the 38th Regiment was positioned to stop any further deep penetration of North Korean forces that, on the twenty-seventh, had all but eliminated effective opposition by the ROK 9th Division. The 38th Regiment was to have one battalion at Chechon before dark and block all approaches to the town. The regiment's responsibility extended as far west as Chupori, seven miles west of Chechon. The 2nd Division Operations Order 14 on 28 December covered all its units' movements in some detail. During the day the Eighth Army G-3 submitted a plan to General Ridgway to use the X Corps in the Wonju area and for it to assume control of the 2nd Infantry Division already there. The corps's mission would be to strengthen the Eighth Army's right flank and the ROK divisions in the mountains east of Wonju.[7]

In the west, north of Seoul on 28 December, aerial strikes destroyed several camouflaged tanks and reported many enemy groups moving south out of Kaesong, some following stream beds. The movements in the same area were reported continuing the next day. East of the 25th Division front, a ROK 1st Division patrol engaged an estimated enemy battalion southwest of Korangpo and captured an officer and four enlisted men, all from the North Korean I Corps Engineer Battalion. This group apparently was making a reconnaissance of the Imjin River crossings and ROK defense positions for the Chinese. I Corps intelligence said an attack was imminent.[8]

Somewhat strangely, I Corps ordered the 25th Division to make plans for the evacuation of Seoul on corps orders. It was to block against an enemy advance to allow the ROK 1st Division to withdraw, then the 25th Division would withdraw through the British 29th Brigade to a designated line. The 25th Division would protect the evacuation of Kimpo airfield and of Inchon. It would act as I Corps's rear guard and, once south of the Han River, would reassemble in the vicinity of Chonan as corps reserve. Chonan was a long way south of Seoul and the Han River—about 55 air miles![9]

On 29 December Eighth Army felt the situation near the east coast in the ROK I Corps area was deteriorating, although it had inadequate reports because of poor communication. North Korean troops in unknown numbers were spreading out and moving south in the rear areas of the ROK II and III Corps areas after breaking through the ROK 9th Division. Probably it was some of these enemy troops that the US 9th Infantry, 2nd Division, had met when it reported guerrilla infiltration in its defense sector near Chungju. The ROK 9th Division had to be resupplied by airdrop near Hajinbu, inland from Kangnung, on the twenty-ninth.

Looking to the prospect of extended combat in the central corridor in the future, Eighth Army on 29 December directed the 2nd Division to survey a site at Wonju for the construction of an airstrip large enough to take C-47 planes. When completed, the survey was to be radioed to Eighth

Army with an estimate of the amount of engineer equipment and personnel needed to get the airstrip in operation quickly. The same order gave the 38th Infantry Regiment authority to choose its route and time of withdrawal if it were attacked in overwhelming numbers in its exposed extreme right flank position in the Chechon-Tanyang area. The army gave as its reason for this unusual authority the poor communications between the regiment and division, and between both of them with Eighth Army headquarters. Just before midnight 29 December, the 2nd Division received from Eighth Army a change in its responsibilities; it was now to defend the Hongchon-Wonju area, a zone more limited but farther north than formerly. One regiment was to move to Hongchon to defend it.[10] Meanwhile, the 23rd Infantry, already at Wonju, reported to the 2nd Division that the town would be difficult to defend because of the flat ground around it. A bright note for Eighth Army on the twenty-ninth was word that the 3rd Infantry Division, the last major combat unit of X Corps to arrive in South Korea in the X Corps evacuation from Hungnam, had off-loaded at Pusan and cleared the docks at 4 P.M. that afternoon.[11]

In the west, the continued evidence of a Chinese buildup there led to new orders to the 19th Infantry of the 24th Division to select a new position on the Seoul-Uijongbu road only eight miles from Seoul. This order is hard to understand because, for the past ten days, the regiment and division had apparently been expecting to fight where it was if an enemy attack developed. During the day the 25th Division also reconnoitered a new line only five miles north of Seoul, and large numbers of Korean laborers set to work to dig in and wire this position. ROK 6th Division patrols reported sighting a CCF regiment moving west from Yonchon toward Kaesong. The ROK 1st Division Reconnaissance Company engaged about 100 CCF north of the Imjin River. Aerial reports on 29–30 December reported a total of 160 dead horses, killed by aerial strikes on enemy groups, northwest of Yonchon on the Uijongbu road. The Fifth Air Force continued day-long sorties against all enemy sightings north of the Imjin River.[12]

On 29 December Eighth Army intelligence predicted an enemy attack on Seoul in the west and a secondary attack on Wonju in the central corridor. The Far East Command at the same time speculated the reason the enemy attack had not already started was that they probably were waiting on the arrival of the CCF IX Army Group from the Hungnam-Wonsan area of northeast Korea to reinforce the North Koreans in the east-central part of the front and help to exploit any breakthrough there. It thought these troops might be in place by 3 January. This is only one of numerous American intelligence projections about the commitment of these troops to the enemy line – all wrong. This constant preoccupation with the CCF IX Army Group now assembled in the Wonsan-Hungnam area shows how little reliable intelligence the Far East Command and Eighth Army had about these forces.

During 30 December it became evident that an enemy attack across the front was imminent. On the east-central front the preliminaries were under way. In the west, north of Seoul, signs became more obvious, and CCF prisoner interrogations confirmed that a CCF attack on that section of the front was not far off.

On the east-central front guerrilla action in rear areas increased. Eighth Army decided that, for all practical purposes, the ROK 9th Division there was combat ineffective. North Korean strength continued to build up, especially north of Hongchon. Enemy had infiltrated in strength seven miles south of the town, where they established a major roadblock. Eighth Army ordered the ROK 3rd and 7th divisions to attack in the Hongchon area and destroy the enemy in their sectors. The US 23rd Regiment of the 2nd Division now received orders to attack the North Korean roadblock below Hongchon. American intelligence estimated there were more than 10,000 enemy troops east and southeast of Hongchon and that they were a threat to start an envelopment of the Eighth Army from their penetration on its east flank.[13]

As the situation developed in the last days of December, it was clear that the US 2nd Division was again in a hot spot. It would be the principal unit responsible for stopping the North Korean penetration in the Wonju area, with action expected within days. On 30 December the division issued its Operation Order 15, directing the concentration of its entire strength in the Wonju area. The 23rd Regiment was to establish a strong blocking position south of Hongchon and attack and reduce the enemy roadblock south of the town. The 38th Regiment, with the Netherlands Battalion attached to it, was to go into blocking positions south of Hoengsong, 20 miles south of Hongchon, patrol all roads in that vicinity, and prepare to counterattack any enemy penetration in the area. The 9th Infantry was to be in division reserve at Wonju. The central-corridor road connecting Hongchon, Hoengsong, and Wonju was almost due north-south if one ironed out the numerous twists and bends in it. The 9th Regimental CP opened at Wonju during the day. On the thirty-first the French Battalion was shuffled around once again; this time it was reattached to the 23rd Infantry, and it stayed with that regiment throughout 1951.

Pursuant to orders, the 3rd Battalion, 23rd Infantry, moved north out of Hoengsong on 30 December and attacked the enemy roadblock south of Hongchon. The next morning the 2nd Battalion joined the 3rd Battalion in reducing the regimental-sized North Korean roadblock below Hongchon. The two battalions then held the road open while the ROK II Corps withdrew south from the Hongchon area. The 1st Battalion remained in its defensive position north of Wonju.[14] The 72nd Tank Battalion could not cross the icy mountain passes from the south and was not present with the 2nd Division at Wonju at the end of December.

With a new American X Corps front opening up in the east-central part of the UN line centering on the Hongchon-Wonju-Chungju corridor, it was now necessary to consider the logistics of supplying that part of the front. A railroad ran north from Pusan and Pohang-dong through Andong to Wonju, where it turned west-northwest to the Han River valley and hence on west to Seoul. A major vehicular road followed the railroad north to Wonju. Eighth Army made an inspection of the road and the rail line, especially the latter, as it would have to play an important role in carrying all kinds of military supplies to this part of the front in the future. The rail line ran through rugged mountainous terrain. The inspection revealed more than 200 bridges and 95 tunnels. Protecting this railroad from enemy guerrilla action would be difficult.[15]

On 30 December Eighth Army intelligence concluded that North Korean soldiers in the so-called Iron Triangle area (a triangular area north of the 38th Parallel described by the three point towns of Chorwon and Kumhwa on the base and Pyonggang at the northern point) had shifted eastward and that CCF had replaced them. This proved to be correct. Everything now indicated two major groupings for a major offensive clear across the peninsula: CCF were in the west, and North Koreans in the east-central part centering on Wonju. Geography and communication lines dictated that these two arms of an offensive would be relatively independent of each other and could be coordinated only as to the time of occurrence. The UN units in defense against these two emerging arms of an enemy offensive also would have to act largely independently of each other.

On 30 December elements of the ROK 7th Regiment, 6th Division, of the US IX Corps captured a Chinese officer from the 3rd Battalion, 339th Regiment, 113th Division, 38th Army. He talked freely. He said the 38th Army would attack with three divisions abreast late on New Year's Eve. He gave the alignment as the CCF 112th Division on the left, the 113th Division in the center, and the 114th Division on the right. The 38th Army's attack was to be part of a general Chinese assault coordinated with that of the CCF 39th, 40th, and 42nd armies. All these Chinese forces had been part of the enemy 2nd Phase Offensive that drove Eighth Army out of North Korea a few weeks earlier. The prisoner's information on the nature of the enemy's impending attack proved correct. Eighth Army had this information one day before the enemy struck, but an attack had been anticipated.[16]

That night, 30–31 December, the ROK 1st Division withdrew its outposts from the north side of the Imjin River, and ROK patrols reported enemy forces had occupied the high ground on the north bank. During the day, American air power hunted over the enemy lines for targets of opportunity. One of the significant aerial achievements of the day was the reported destruction of five large-caliber artillery pieces and thirteen smaller pieces 7 miles north-northwest of Yonchon, and four more artillery pieces and four vehicles 4½ miles east of the town. About ten more artillery pieces were seen in the area. Yonchon had been for weeks a center of first North Korean and then Chinese activity. It was situated just north of the Imjin River and 28 miles from Uijongbu on the main invasion road from Chorwon and the north, which led almost straight south to Seoul. It could be pinpointed at this time as a major enemy departure point for crossing the Imjin River and launching an attack down the Uijongbu corridor toward Seoul.[17]

At the south end of the Korean peninsula, activity at the port of Pusan was almost as hectic as it was at the front. The US 3rd Infantry Division, which had begun unloading on 26 December, completed it on the thirty-first. X Corps alerted the division to move to the Andong-Wonju area after 4 January. But there had been either a cross-up in communication or a very quick change of mind, because Eighth Army the same day, 30 December, alerted the 3rd Division to prepare for an early move to the western front and assembly in the Ansong-Pyongtaek area in army reserve and to expect immediate attachment to either I or IX Corps. Pursuant to this army alert, the division sent a reconnaissance party to Pyongtaek the next day to locate an assembly area. On 31 December all troops were ashore at Pusan, and 96 percent of the division's equipment had been unloaded and was in an assembly area.[18]

December 1950 had been an unusual month of port activity at Pusan and for the 2nd Logistical Command, which operated port military activity there for Eighth Army and the Far East Command. The evacuation of X Corps from Hungnam in northeast Korea, most of it through Pusan, was largely responsible for the extra burden. For instance, X Corps had approximately 17,500 vehicles, most of which were unloaded at Pusan. Virtually all the vehicles were moved out of Pusan on roads, leaving the rail lines for other use. Of vehicles, only tanks were generally moved forward by rail. Pusan had an estimated capacity to handle 40,000 long tons in a 20-hour day. In December it handled 846,000 measurement tons of cargo, in and out. In addition to X Corps shipping, organization and equipment evacuated from Inchon, and a large part of the 3rd Logistical Command evacuated from Ascom City, near Inchon, came in at Inchon. At the same time, the routine handling of army equipment, supplies, and personnel continued in and out of the port.

A total of 391 ships entered or left the port with their cargoes during December. On an average there were 162 officers, 25 warrant officers, and 1,018 enlisted men of the army engaged in port work.

On the last day of the year, the New Zealand 16th Field Artillery Regiment, with 1,231 officers and men, landed at Pusan. They waited at Pusan until their heavy equipment arrived, and then on 19 January 1951 moved to Miryang for additional training.[19]

The 2nd Logistical Command at Pusan also had to provide food for prisoners of war. The standard diet provided the prisoners consisted of a daily ration of three hops of rice, two and a half hops of barley, one-sixth pound of fish, and an allowance of 200 won per man that was used to purchase additional items such as seaweed, fruit, and vegetables, as these items were available in the local market. On 31 December 1950 the prisoner of war strength totaled 137,175.[20]

The last day of December saw a new Eighth Army program initiated to give rest and recreation (R&R) to combat personnel in Korea. This program would give men five days of leave in Japan, where arrangements had been made for 1,500 spaces in Special Service hotels. At first the daily quota was 200 men from Korea. The first troops to engage in this program, which immediately became popular, were 200 members of the US 25th Infantry Division, who arrived in Japan on 31 December 1950.[21]

On 30 December the G-4 of the 2nd Logistical Command received information that one regiment of the US 7th Infantry Division was to move north to join the X Corps at daylight and that the regiment was short about 17 truckloads of equipment and clothing. There were no details. The G-4 Section, however, ordered 17 trucks to stand by and the quartermaster to be ready to issue supplies. The list of clothing needed came that night at 8:50 P.M. All equipment, clothing, and quartermaster items required were loaded and departed from Pusan in a convoy at 4 A.M., 31 December. This type of action at the port was typical of rear-service activities called on to meet front-line requirements, and without prompt response would have vastly increased difficulties for the combat troops.[22] Without an efficient logistical organization an army cannot fight for long.

The last day of the year dawned with no great hope or expectation in Eighth Army. The war had been in progress now for six months and six days since the North Korean army had crossed the border of South Korea on 25 June. Now it seemed Eighth Army was back to the feeling of the Naktong perimeter days of late August, when the North Koreans threatened to drive all the way to Pusan.

Eighth Army ordered the X Corps to have an Advance CP in the Wonju area on the thirty-first, to establish communications with the 2nd Infantry Division, and then to assume operational control of it. The assistant division commander was forward with the 23rd Infantry. From there he reported that a large enemy column was moving from the east toward Wonju and that a major fight was imminent. He asked that maximum supplies available be forwarded to the regiment and that air support be alerted.

The 38th Infantry Regimental headquarters and its 2nd Battalion arrived at 8 P.M. that evening. After unloading, the trucks turned around and headed back to Chechon to load the 1st Battalion and bring it forward. Before the day ended, X Corps received orders to assume engineer maintenance of the Andong-Tanyang-Chechon-Wonju Main Supply Road (MSR). Intelligence reports now indicated that North Korean forces had penetrated the ROK lines southeast of Hongchon and were moving to envelop that place from the east. The troops available to meet the forthcoming attack were the partially assembled 2nd Infantry Division and the ROK II Corps 7th and 8th divisions.[23] X Corps started the 7th Infantry Division north to replace the 38th Infantry in the Chechon area. The 3rd Ranger Company joined the division at this time. Army policy now was to attach a Ranger company to each American division as quickly as they became available.

In the course of the Korean War, the flight of civilians from a front area usually indicated an enemy attack was at hand. The civilians always seemed to know when the climax of an enemy buildup had arrived, and they tried to escape just before they were engulfed in a battle area. Now, at the end of December, there was a great movement of refugees south from the 38th Parallel and the Seoul area. On 31 December, about 100,000 Korean refugees were causing great confusion in the Inchon area as they tried to pass through, going south. More than 400,000 refugees were reported fleeing from Seoul. About 1,000 a day were arriving at Taegu from the north, most of them probably from the east-central corridor area from Andong northward.[24]

On 31 December Eighth Army gave its final order of 1950: Eighth Army was to defend the Imjin River–38th Parallel line and secure Seoul for the maximum time, short of allowing an enemy envelopment that would prevent the army from withdrawing south, and to select and defend in successive positions south of the Imjin River line. The same order required the X Corps to take command of the 2nd Division and defend the Wonju corridor in the east-central part of the front. It might be noted that, in anticipating a withdrawal from the Imjin River, there were available for such a Han River crossing the low-level rail bridge, which had been decked and could be used for motor traffic, and three floating (pontoon) bridges, two at Seoul and one just east of the city. Eighth Army now ordered the return of the 1st Marine Division from X Corps to its control.[25]

By evening 28 December, General Ridgway had visited nearly all the Eighth Army front and had conferred with ROK commanders of the east-central front. He said later that, by that time, he knew the consensus from private to general was "Let's get the hell out of here!"—that Eighth Army probably could not be made to fight in its current position and frame of mind. He felt, he said, that the army could not hold along the Imjin River and 38th Parallel line with only two battered and understrength divisions (24th and 25th) on the line and one other American division (1st Cavalry) in a blocking position behind them.[26] But if General Ridgway had indeed formed the opinion by 28 December that he could not hold above Seoul and that the Eighth Army would not fight at that time, he did not disclose it to those around him. The records indicate that he did not openly and officially give up hope of holding a bridgehead north of the Han River

Korean refugees flee from Seoul across a dike in the rice fields, ahead of the advancing Chinese forces, 5 January 1951. *National Archives, 111-SC 355576*

until five days later, 2 January 1951. He knew that the enemy would strike at any moment – he expected the attack to begin on the night of 31 December, New Year's Eve.

The shocking lack of fighting morale that Ridgway found throughout Eighth Army and the lack of any real strength in the ROK troops must have been the cause of his taking a step that was known at the time to only a few persons high in the Defense Department and to General MacArthur, and subsequently known to relatively few persons. It was a message on 29 December to General Collins, the Army chief of staff, about the use of Nationalist Chinese soldiers from Formosa in an invasion of the South China coast, which might ease the pressure on the UN command in Korea.

In Ridgway's 26 December conference in Tokyo with General MacArthur, the latter had referred to Ridgway's recommendation that Chinese Nationalist troops on Formosa, offered by Generalissimo Chiang Kai-shek at the beginning of the war, be used in Korea, or in an invasion of South China. General Ridgway was familiar with this proposal and the Joint Chiefs' decision not to adopt MacArthur's recommendation, in which he apparently had concurred when he was still in the Pentagon.

It was something of a surprise, therefore, when General Ridgway on 29 December 1950, four days after he arrived in Korea, sent a message at 5:20 P.M. to General Collins in which he referred to his conversations with General MacArthur on 26 December and the possible use of Chinese Nationalist troops in the Korean War, that in particular the Chinese Nationalists on Formosa be permitted to operate on the Chinese mainland without limitation. MacArthur's reasoning was that, with the CCF making a major effort in Korea, and having moved the CCF Third and Fourth field armies to Manchuria from the Chinese coastal area in South China, opposite Formosa, that area was now wide open to invasion by the Chinese Nationalists, and if they opened a second front there against the CCF, it would relieve Chinese pressure on the UN forces in Korea.

Ridgway's message to General Collins said in part, "Viewed entirely within sphere of my responsibility to U.S. Government & UN allies for ground operations, logic of this recommendation is convincing to me and I feel it would be negligent were I not to state my full concurrence at once. CINCFE [MacArthur] has no repeat no knowledge of this message nor of my intention of sending it. I shall, however, repeat it to him promptly after dispatch. Request acknowledgment." Signed "Ridgway."[27]

General Ridgway confirmed to the author in an interview on 21 October 1975 that this message was correct. The American authorities in Washington never supported this proposal for Chinese Nationalists to invade South China, probably because of British and other UN opposition or fear it would result in Soviet intervention.

Later, General Whitney, an aide to General MacArthur, wrote that Ridgway had supported MacArthur's recommendation that Chinese Nationalist troops be used in Korea. Whitney was wrong. General Ridgway did not recommend that these troops be used in Korea, but only on the Chinese mainland. The author has found no evidence that General Ridgway ever recommended these troops be used in Korea itself. Only the desperate situation he found existing in the UN forces in Korea in late December 1950 when he assumed command of Eighth Army led him to support the use of Chiang Kai-shek's soldiers in South China as a means of helping to pull Eighth Army out of its near collapse as a fighting force.

Believing as he did that the enemy assault on the UN forces would begin on New Year's Eve, General Ridgway, now at Taegu, told Gen. Leven Allen, his chief of staff, on Sunday morning, 31 December, that he was returning to Seoul and his Advance CP at once, in anticipation of an enemy attack. If it did not develop by 2 January, he would return to Taegu. General Ridgway landed at the Seoul airport at 11:30 A.M. and went directly to Seoul. After a quick lunch he went by jeep to the I Corps and IX Corps CPs. From there he traveled along the front line and talked with unit commanders. The front lay in hilly, lonely, but attractive landscape. He may have had a moment's encouragement when, at the British 29th Brigade's position, he met a young British lieutenant who was helping prepare a ridgeline defensive position. He met Ridgway with a smile and a smart salute. Ridgway asked him if he thought everything was all right up there. He answered, "Splendid, sir. It is a bit drafty, though." Ridgway returned to Seoul just before dark.[28] Two hours later the CCF began their 3rd Phase Offensive, most commonly called by American soldiers, "the New Year's Eve Offensive."

On 8 January 1951, Ridgway wrote a personal letter to General Collins, chief of staff, explaining his feeling at the time.

My first visit to the combat area the day following my arrival found two of the Corps' forward elements occupying much of the original ground organizations on the south side of the 38th parallel in fairly close contact with the enemy who occupied the former North Korean organized positions on the north side. The latter had a great numerical superiority; had had two to three weeks to build up in that area; and enjoyed the advantage of strong positions. Both Corps commanders and all their Divisional commanders, who I visited in their own areas, were of the opinion that any major offensive action on our part would fail and probably with heavy losses.

I concurred in that estimate and put aside the hope I had entertained before the visit of offensive action to inflict losses and gain the initiative.[29]

The Chinese 3rd Phase Offensive

BY THE END of December 1950, the Chinese XIII Army Group of the Fourth Field Army, composed of six armies, having 19 divisions and 57 regiments, had moved south from the Pyongyang area to confront the UN forces grouped under Eighth Army in their defensive positions along the Imjin River near the 38th Parallel. This enemy force was the same one that had driven Eighth Army out of North Korea in the battles along the Chongchon River and forced the evacuation of Pyongyang, the North Korean capital, four weeks earlier. The Chinese divisions now held the western part of a new enemy deployment that stretched across the width of Korea, with reorganized old and newly formed North Korean divisions moving into place on the eastern part of the line. The dividing line between the Chinese and the North Korean troops was at the Iron Triangle. The Chinese force concentrated in the west was in position to strike directly south at Seoul and the lower Han River. The NK 8th Division, a screening force, was along the west coast, but it played no important part in the impending action.

From the Iron Triangle eastward to the Sea of Japan, North Korean rehabilitated divisions were being moved south from the Manchurian border almost daily to fill in the jagged line eastward. These new and rehabilitated old North Korean divisions were only one-third to one-half strength, and poorly trained. They could not be considered first-class troops, but they were nevertheless a dangerous threat in the vital central corridor of Korea, where the UN had almost no troops to oppose them and where Eighth Army and the UN command now had to scramble to improvise a defense. This defense took the form of new and rehabilitated South Korean divisions that were no better than the understrength and poorly trained North Korean divisions opposite them. The situation in the central corridor centering on Hongchon, Chunchon, Hoengsong, Wonju, Chechon, and Tanyang and leading south to both Taegu and Pusan offered the North Koreans opportunities to outflank the Eighth Army in the west. The UN command sent the X Corps piecemeal, just arrived from its evacuation

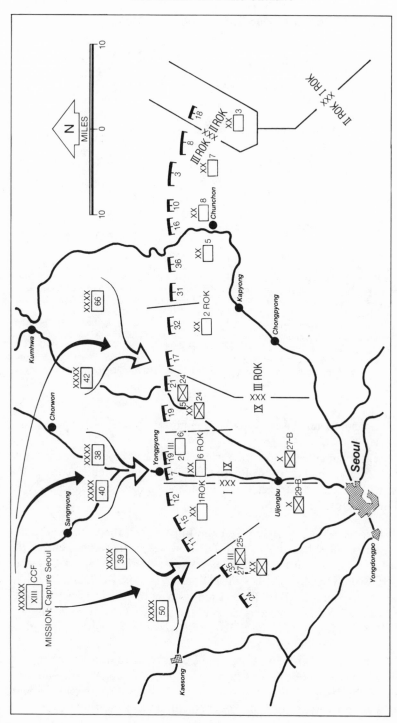

MAP 1. CCF and UN deployment 31 December 1950, at the outset of the CCF 3rd Phase Offensive

TABLE 1.   **UN Forces in Korea, December 1950**

Contingent	Average Daily Supported Strength
US Eighth Army	136,525
Korean augmentation	12,573
X Corps	79,736
US Air Force	13,605
British and Australian Army	12,269
Other UN forces	10,399
Subtotal	265,107
ROK Marines	2,374
ROK Army	206,182
Subtotal	208,556
Total	473,663[a]

Source: Eighth Army Comd. Rpt., December 1950.

[a]In the months from August through December 1950, the US forces in Korea received a total of 64,940 replacements from the zone of the interior (i.e., the US). But the American infantry divisions were far understrength on 1 January 1951, when the CCF 3rd Phase Offensive started. The authorized strength of a division was 18,935 officers and men. The 25th Infantry Division, however, had a total assigned strength of only 15,673 at the end of December. The 1st Cavalry Division, with an authorized strength of 18,940, had an assigned strength of only 14,578 officers and men. The 2nd Infantry Division after Kunu-ri had only approximately 10,000 officers and men, but it took in a few thousand replacements from the United States during December 1950. Rifleman was the classification most in demand. The need for riflemen was so great in December that, during the month, the 25th Division transferred 1,646 from surplus personnel in other categories to that of rifleman. See official reports of units cited. UN strength was relatively stable in January 1951, with a maximum strength of 444,336.

of Hungnam in northeast Korea, to the area as quickly as possible. (See table 1.)

The story of events happening in the central corridor at the same time the CCF unleashed their 3rd Phase Offensive against Eighth Army in the west will be told in later chapters. First, the Chinese attacks in the west require our attention.

When the Chinese arrived near the Imjin River, their reconnaissance units established that the US 25th Division was at the western end of the UN line, and eastward from it in succession were the ROK 1st Division, the ROK 6th Division, the US 24th Division, and the ROK 2nd Division. The US 25th and the ROK 1st divisions were in the US I Corps; the ROK 6th and the US 24th divisions were in the US IX Corps. Farther east was the ROK III Corps with the ROK 2nd Division at its western boundary with the US 24th Division.

The boundary between I Corps and IX Corps was a nearly straight road and railroad north from Seoul through Uijongbu to Yongpyong and Yonchon on the east side of the Imjin River, an ancient invasion road to Seoul. It was almost certain to be one of the main axes of Chinese attacks. On either side of this road and railroad were the ROK 1st Division on the west side and the ROK 6th Division on the east side. The experiences of Eighth Army in the Chinese 2nd Phase Offensive at the Chongchon River should have taught it that the Chinese nearly always tried to find the boundaries between enemy units and to direct their main penetrating thrusts at these known points of weakness. It seems a bit odd, therefore, that General Walker had chosen to place two ROK divisions adjacent to each other at this critical point of the line, when all experience should have required his strongest units to be there instead. General Ridgway had no opportunity after he arrived to make any shift of troops in the defense line before the enemy attack came.

The Chinese XIII Army Group deployed with its six armies lined up with the 50th on its western flank and, eastward from it in succession, the 39th, 40th, 38th, 42nd, and 66th armies. The 50th and 39th armies were opposite the US I Corps; the 40th and 38th armies were opposite the US IX Corps; and the 42nd and 66th armies were just east of IX Corps along its boundary with the ROK 2nd Division in the ROK III Corps sector. (See table 2.)

The Chinese XIII Army Group had an estimated strength of about

TABLE 2. **CCF and UN Troop Alignment, 31 December 1950**

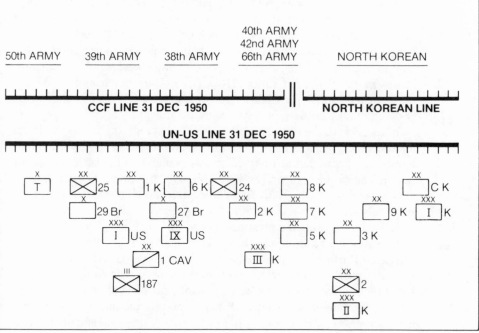

Source: ATIS reports, and Eighth Army and division Comd. Rpts., December 1950.

170,000 men on 1 January 1950, with most of its divisions having a strength of 7,500 to 8,000 men (see table 3). One division, however, the 124th, had an estimated strength of fewer than 3,500 men. In its battles with the 7th Marine Regiment on the road to the Chosin Reservoir in northeast Korea in November 1950, it had lost so heavily as to become almost combat ineffective. It must be remembered that a Chinese army was somewhat comparable to an American corps, and that an American division at or near full strength was equal to two Chinese divisions. Chinese divisions in the Korean War were nearly always understrength, as indeed were the American divisions also, especially in riflemen.

In the Imjin River battles that began on New Year's Eve and ended with the Chinese recapture of Seoul and the crossing of the Han River in the period 1 through 6 January 1951, the Chinese success had been so remarkable that the Chinese XIX Army Group, expecting soon to enter the Korean fighting, had made for it an exhaustive study of the XIII Army Group preparations and tactics in the Imjin River battles. This document was mimeographed in Chinese and widely circulated and studied by the Chinese officer corps after it was issued on 29 March 1951. At least one copy was captured at an unknown date by the US 25th Division. Eighth Army requested that the Allied Translation and Interrogation Service (ATIS) in Tokyo make a complete translation of it. It is the Chinese story of how they won the battle, and it is one of the most revealing Chinese documents captured during the war, showing the patience, the careful reconnaissance, and then all subsequent detail in preparing for the attack. This attack, like nearly all those that the Chinese launched, was a frontal attack for its initial penetration, contrary to the general belief that the Chinese always came around a gap or a flank to exploit their enemy's weakness. The account in this narrative of the Chinese 116th Division in preparing to make the initial penetration of the Eighth Army line in the ROK 1st Division sector is based almost entirely on this enemy document.[1]

It begins with the statement "As we had been preparing for over a month for the attack, we had plentiful information on the enemy situation and terrain and knew that artillery cover was available. The battle we fought was an attack from comparatively well prepared positions. The 116th Division broke through the ROK Army front in less than two and a half hours with only two of its regiments."

ROK units had laid a great number of mines along both banks of the Imjin River, near the surface, three meters apart and distributed in an area fifteen by thirty meters, such that "it was possible, at night, to discover the pattern by touch alone." Two or three rows of single apron and square barbed-wire entanglements were set up along the bank at possible crossing places. The height of the entanglements was approximately 1 meter, and the distances between the rows, 10 to 12 meters. Concealed and open bunkers were constructed at key defense points, at fords. The bunkers were 3

TABLE 3.   **CCF XIII Army Group Order of Battle, 1 January 1951**

Army	Division	Regiments	Estimated Strength
38th	112th	334th, 335th, 336th	7,728
	113th	337th, 338th, 339th	7,560
	114th	340th, 341st, 342nd	8,299
39th	115th	343rd, 344th, 345th	7,970
	116th	346th, 347th, 348th	7,970
	117th	349th, 350th, 351st	7,976
40th	118th	352nd, 353rd, 354th	7,961
	119th	355th, 356th, 357th	7,970
	120th	358th, 359th, 360th	7,721
42nd	124th	370th, 371st, 372nd	3,479
	125th	373rd, 374th, 375th	7,560
	126th	376th, 377th, 378th	7,218
50th	148th	442nd, 443rd, 444th	8,129
	149th	445th, 446th, 447th	8,135
	150th	448th, 449th, 450th	8,136
	167th[a]	499th, 500th, 501st	
66th	196th	586th, 587th, 588th	8,124
	197th	589th, 590th, 591st	8,127
	198th	592nd, 593rd, 594th	8,126
Total:			
6 armies	19 divisions	57 regiments	138,189[b]

Source: ATIS reports and captured order of battle.
[a] The 167th Division came originally from the 56th Army.
[b] In addition, the army group included an unidentified cavalry unit of 2,928 and also 5,000 cavalry for each of the six armies, for a total estimated strength of 171,117.

meters high and 2 meters thick, connected by communication trenches. Their main function seemed to be to protect personnel from cold. Machine gun emplacements were thick and stronger, but were still vulnerable to field-gun fire. In the mountainous areas in front of commanding heights from the river bank to Mugon-ni, a depth of 20 kilometers (12 miles), the ROK 1st Division had constructed a network of double- and triple-row communication trenches, emplacements, and covered trenches and shelters.

The ROKs were divided into two echelons, the first larger than the second. The first echelon of each regiment deployed two battalions, and each battalion deployed two companies. One battalion remained in the regiment's rear echelon, and one company was the battalion's rear echelon.

The captured Chinese document stated that "friendly forces penetrated the ROK 1st Division. Two battalions of the 12th Regiment, 1st ROK Division, were holding positions opposite T'ojong and two battalions of the 11th Regiment, 1st ROK Division were opposite Sindae. The point of penetration was the boundary between the 11th and 12th Regiments. The ROK

11th Regiment was on the left or west sector of the ROK line, the 12th Regiment was on the right or east sector, the 15th, or reserve, regiment was behind them." The area the Chinese chose for their penetration attack was five air miles east of Korangpo-ri. Between Korangpo-ri and the crossing site south of Sindae, the Imjin River had a number of large, deep loops in its course.[2]

The Chinese placed recoilless rifles and light and heavy machine guns in their forward positions. On their secondary line were the mortars and howitzers of two mortar companies and one howitzer battery. On their third line farther back were 100-mm and 150-mm howitzers [caliber questionable]. Their fire was intended to interdict villages, highways, ravines, and hilltops their infantry might seize.

The Chinese document said the ROKs did not wait in their positions prior to the Chinese attack but launched independent attacks of their own in platoon and company strength, eight times in seven days. These ROK attacks always started about 9 A.M. with air and artillery support and ended at dusk. The Chinese said they killed 89 ROKs, captured 14, and destroyed the entire reconnaissance squad of the ROK 12th Regiment.

In preparing for the projected action, the 348th Regiment of the 116th Division preceded the main body of the division and carried out a reconnaissance along 26 miles of the river front from Changdan to Majon-ni. Their most useful information on the ROK situation and the river came from interrogations of ROK prisoners. The Imjin River varied from 60 to 170 meters wide and from very shallow up to a meter deep. All the fords except the one at Sindae were frozen. Infantry and artillery officers and noncommissioned officers were assigned to study the terrain and select points for breakthrough. They found that the river could be waded about 700 meters from two breakthrough gaps in the ROK lines. They chose Hills 182 and 148, about two miles from the southern side of the river, to be occupied after the breakthrough. The two hills were to provide advantageous points where security forces could protect following attack forces that would be sent through the penetration gap in the ROK lines. The Chinese reconnaissance parties found the roads beside these hills good for the movement of artillery, and they also offered concealment. These roads also were used to exploit the breakthrough after the penetration. There was one disadvantage at the area chosen for breakthrough: the bends and folds of the Imjin River here offered the ROKs positions from which they could direct flanking enfilading fire into the Chinese as they crossed for their attack. This breakthrough point was seven to eight miles west of the main Seoul highway and the railroad running north to Uijongbu, Tongduchon-ni, Yonchon, and Chorwon.

Infantry and artillery officers and noncommissioned officers repeatedly reconnoitered the terrain to gain a comprehensive knowledge of the attack routes and objectives. Each of the two attack regiments established two observation posts from which they watched ROK movements and located their fieldworks and fire positions. Even high-ranking officers accompanied reconnaissance units to measure the depth of the water and the thickness of the ice. The "thrust" battalions in particular studied all aspects of their assigned mission thoroughly. They also prepared special equipment that their reconnaissance showed them to be necessary in the attack. The Chinese document describes many of their preparations:

The attacking regiment made twelve ladders, five to ten meters long, to aid in climbing the river bank.

The shock company made two mine clearing hooks, fitted on poles two *chang* long [trans: One chang equals 11 feet, 9 inches] for the clearing of mines on the southern bank of the river.

The river crossing units gathered planks, straw and chaff to cover holes in the ice made by enemy fire, and to prevent slipping. The river-crossing unit (consisting of over 500 men) cut the sleeves of their padded pants open so that they could be rolled up to avoid getting wet, and each of them made one pair of knee-length waterproof stockings. They also applied lard and suet to their feet to help prevent frostbite.

Each soldier made one or two straw sandals and one pair of "foot-binding," to increase speed while walking on ice and climbing snow-covered hills.

Each man carried three days' dry ration and one day's ordinary rations.

The meat and fat ration was increased before combat to increase the resistance of our troops to the cold.

Map reading was taught to eliminate the habit of depending on guides. This training was very effective.

Some of tactical training taught: Use of ladders in climbing steep banks, from 26 to 42 feet high.

Skiing and climbing snow-covered hills as an aid in river crossing and attacking over ice.

Destruction of barbed-wire entanglements and the clearing and capturing of mines.

Techniques of attacking bunkers, crossing open spaces and attacking along communication trenches.

Since we were to break through on a 1,500 meter front [nearly a mile], division headquarters decided that both the division and the regiments would use two echelons, but that before the breakthrough there should be three echelons. Thus, the 346th Regiment (T'ojong) and the 347th Regiment (Sindae) broke through side by side, with two battalions breaking through in each regiment. The division used four battalions and four "thrust companies" to effect the initial penetration. Because of the width of the breakthrough area, it was decided that after the breakthrough, 10 companies should be given the mission of penetrating the enemy rear, and that two companies should be used to "tear apart" [widen] the breakthrough gap and ensure the safety of three following units which would immediately enter combat. . . .

Our breakthrough was made at the point of contact between two adjacent regiments; the distance between the two breakthrough openings was 700 meters.

The 116th Division had amassed a total of 66 field guns, including howitzers, to destroy the ROK fieldworks at the breakthrough gap and also at the rear of the second line and to place neutralizing fire on the ROK artillery. The 116th Division would have had more regular howitzers for this use except for an air raid that had recently destroyed 9 of their 10 regular howitzers. The breakthrough infantry carried special equipment and were armed as follows:

The "thrusting company" consisted of four teams: An Engineer team (two squads for ladder handling, one squad for mine sweeping); an assault team (one platoon); a supporting team (one platoon); and a weapons team (with a 60 mm mortar and light and heavy machine guns). Besides the T/E number of automatic weapons, one heavy machine gun and one rocket launcher were attached to the company. In addition, it had five antitank magnetic mines, five Bangalore torpedoes, and four 5.5 pound blocks of explosive. Six hand grenades were issued to each man. . . .

In addition to the use of more than 1,000 meters of natural gullies, each regiment employed two companies for trench-digging along the route of attack. In two nights' work (about 10 hours) they completed 500 meters of longitudinal and cross communication trenches one meter wide and 1.5 meters deep, with antiaircraft shelters dug in on both sides. This, supplemented by natural gullies, was capable of taking care of four battalions keeping the strength of the regiment intact and its intentions unknown to the enemy before the penetration. Shelters near the firing positions of various weapons, ammunition bunkers, and regimental and battalion command and observation posts were also constructed.

A dense mine field laid by the enemy on both sides of the river constituted a menace to our troops. Three explosions caused 10 casualties among our probing units. The division sent out two engineer platoons and cleared 160 mines from the front of the four thrusting companies in two nights. During the attack that followed not a single man was lost on our side of the river. . . .

All artillery guns entered their emplacements on the night of the 30th and before daybreak were well camouflaged with black or gray branches or snow.

The first echelons of regiment combat teams and command organizations took up their positions. On the night of the 30th six infantry battalions, seven mountain and field artillery battalions and divisional and regimental command organizations, totaling more than 7,500 men and 70 artillery pieces, were well concealed within an area 1,500 meters (east to west) by 2,500 meters (north to south).

The success or failure of the attack depended upon concealment during the daylight hours of the 31st. Closest attention was paid by officers of all grades to the strict maintenance of antiaircraft discipline. The divisional commander personally inspected the condition of the troops at dawn. All personnel took cover in underground shelters and did not leave them for any reason before the attack began. Not a single man, horse, rifle, or one round of ammunition was exposed. Enemy planes circled at a low altitude all day long, but were unable to detect our intentions. We were thus able to achieve complete surprise, and when enemy planes returned in the evening we had already crossed the Imjin River and were driving into enemy territory.

At 1640 hours on 31st December 1950, our artillery initiated the attack by delivering a 20 minute covering barrage. When enemy positions were satisfactorily softened up, three flares were fired, the bombardment was intensified, and the movement, ladder operation and mine clearing activities of the infantry were begun.

After 3 minutes [trans.: presumably 1703 hours] five more flares were fired, the barrage was lifted, light and heavy MGs opened up, and the infantry started their attack, the ladders already having been properly set up.

After 5 minutes [trans.: 1705 hours], the thrusting company of the 36th [346th] Regiment signaled the occupation of an enemy position on the right wing.

After 11 minutes [trans.: 1711 hours], the thrusting company of the 37th [347th] Regiment, after fording the waist-deep river and climbing a 30 foot high cliff, also signaled the occupation of an enemy position. Within 40 minutes all enemy resistance along the river was ended.

At 1750 hours, Hill 192 and Hill 147 were simultaneously secured by the two regiments. The majority of the defending enemy were annihilated in their positions. The penetration was a success.

After the initial penetration, the 36th Regiment (ed.: 346th Regiment] assigned one battalion to cooperate with the 37th Regiment [347th Regiment] in its attack on Maji-ri while the main force of the regiment crushed enemy resistance to the east of Maji-ri and captured Hill 340 [ed.: probably Hill 314], mopping up all enemy defenses on hills along the route. It continued to drive to Mutal-ni and took Suchon-ni at 0800 hours on 1 January, advancing 20 km during the night. The 37th [347] Regiment occupied Maji-ri at 2200 hours, the remnants of the defending enemy fleeing southward. In pursuit, the 37th [347th] took hill after hill, and arrived Hwachon [ed.: possibly Hyoch'on-ni] at 0600 hours, having also accomplished 15 km during the night.

This advance during the first night after the penetration would give the 346th Regiment a gain of 12 miles and the 347th Regiment one of 9 miles. In further comments on this action, the 116th Division discussion stated that the Sindae penetration sector gave the enemy flanking positions and "the river bank was difficult to climb. Relying on this, the enemy did not anticipate an attack and could consequently offer only slight resistance." Shades of Wolfe surprising Montcalm on the Plains of Abraham at Quebec!

The 116th Division commentator also spoke of the value of feint attacks in making easier the real penetration. Feint attacks should be made where the enemy expects the main attack. In the case of the CCF crossings of the Imjin River on New Year's Eve, the ROK 1st Division expected the CCF main effort would be made in the Korangpo-ri area, five air miles west of where it actually was made. At Korangpo-ri the river configuration and the terrain favored the Chinese. There the ROK 1st Division had placed its greatest strength. Two regiments of Chinese made the feint there, the 344th Regiment of the 115th Division and the 348th Regiment of the 116th Division. While the 116th Division was secretly preparing its main attack five miles to the east of Korangpo-ri, these two regiments carried out active reconnaissance activity in the Korangpo-ri area and deceived the enemy as to the real center of projected attack. The CCF 116th Divi-

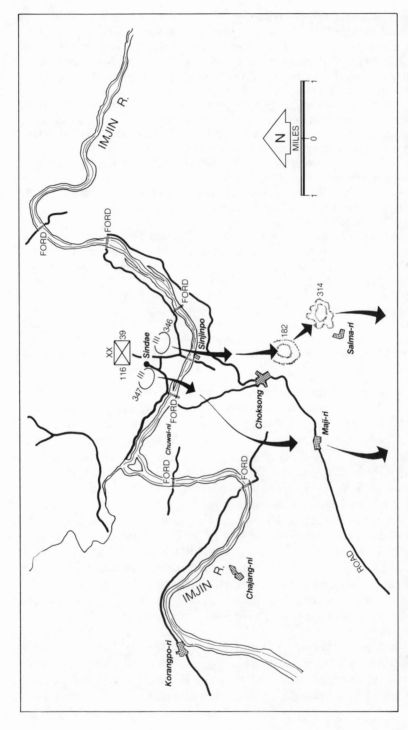

MAP 2. Initial crossing of the Imjin River and penetration of the ROK 1st Division by the CCF 347th and 346th regiments, 39th Army, 31 December 1950

sion analyst said the success of the Imjin River penetration "was largely due to the thoroughness of observation and reconnaissance."

At the same time the 116th Division penetrated the ROK 1st Division on the night of 31 December–1 January, the CCF 117th Division, also of the 39th Army, got behind the UN front line south of the Imjin River and intercepted the ROK 6th Division, which was in flight farther to the east in the IX Corps area. In forced marches during the night the 117th Division covered nearly 17 miles, repulsing five attacks en route and capturing 500 and wounding 300 of the ROK 6th Division.[3]

The UN line where the Chinese 116th Division made its initial, surprise penetration across the Imjin River was held by the ROK 1st Division, with its 11th Regiment on its left flank, the 12th Regiment on the right, and the 15th Regiment behind the other two in reserve. The 12th Regiment was at the regimental, division, and I Corps boundary all at the same time, with the ROK 7th Regiment of the ROK 6th Division of IX Corps to the east of it.

The Chinese 346th Regiment crossed the river at the corps boundary just south of the village of T'ojong and surprised the ROK 12th Regiment. The Chinese 347th Regiment crossed the river about 700 meters farther west, also into the lines of the ROK 12th Regiment. The south bank of the Imjin River here, and for several hundreds of yards farther west, was a narrow floodplain for a short distance back from the river, and then it rose in a 20- to 30-foot escarpment. The Chinese used ladders to scale it. Beyond were the minefields and barbed-wire entanglements of the ROK defenses. The Chinese were through and across these before the ROKs knew what was happening.

In the ensuing swift attack the Chinese cut the ROKs to pieces in their defensive works, and many fled. The CCF "thrust" companies, four in number, carried all before them, made a breach nearly a mile wide in the front lines, and then plunged on to several hills farther south, occupied them, and held them as gateways for the two or three CCF divisions that now poured through the gap. The penetrating Chinese did not stop to fight and reduce the several enemy back-up positions they encountered but bypassed them to move rapidly south. For the most part they followed secondary roads.

Within two or three hours after dark on 31 December, the ROK 12th Regiment was out of the fight, dispersed or destroyed. The ROK 15th Regiment hurried forward to replace it. On the ROK 1st Division left, near Korangpo-ri, the ROK 11th Regiment fought stubbornly and held its position against Chinese attack for several hours. But as the penetration on its east grew deeper by the minute, the 11th Regiment was ordered to withdraw. For the same reason the ROK 15th Regiment also had to withdraw.[4]

Later, it was alleged that many of the ROK officers and men of the 1st and 6th divisions were away from their front-line posts when the Chinese assault came, taking part in New Year's Eve parties, and that many were in various stages of drunkenness or in houses back of the line warming themselves.[5] Major Daly, KMAG advisor with the ROK 1st Division, said that Gen. Paik Sun Yup, commander of the division, held his head very low on the morning of 1 January and apologized to General Milburn of I Corps for the failure of his troops. Capt. Harley F. Mooney of the US 3rd Division said that two weeks later a staff officer of the ROK 1st Division told him at Chonan that General Paik tried and shot a battalion commander and a senior captain of the division for gross negligence.[6]

Eastward across its boundary with the ROK 12th Regiment, the ROK 7th Regiment of the ROK 6th Division was on that division's west flank. The ROK 19th Regiment was on the east side of the ROK 6th Division's sector, where it had a boundary with the 19th Regiment of the US 24th Infantry Division, both in the IX Corps. The Chinese 38th Army attacked the ROK 6th Division just after dusk at the same time as the 116th Division of the 39th Army hit the ROK 1st Division. Behind the 7th and 19th regiments, the 6th Regiment was in reserve. The ROK 6th Division sector was astride and east of the main highway leading north from Seoul to Yongpyong and Chorwon. The Chinese crossed minefields and the barbed-wire barriers without regard to casualties in penetrating the 1st Battalion, ROK 19th Regiment, in their initial surprise attack. This CCF penetration of the ROK 6th Division was not as quickly accomplished as was that in the ROK 1st Division because it was not as expertly prepared and executed. But by midnight, the 6th Division was in flight to the rear.[7]

On the eastern, right, flank of the ROK 6th Division, the US 24th Infantry Division was astride the road that branched off the main highway at Uijongbu and ran northeast to Kumhwa. Its 19th Regiment was on its west side next to the ROK 6th Division, and its 21st Regiment was on the eastern flank guarding the road from Kumhwa. Only the 19th Regiment of the 24th Division came under heavy enemy attack on New Year's Eve. At least part of the enemy penetrations there was accomplished only after very heavy fighting, according to a prisoner report later, and some of the battalions of an unidentified CCF regiment lost contact with each other and had to wait for daylight to reorganize. Furthermore, according to this prisoner report, their reconnaissance had been inadequate because they found themselves fighting an American unit instead of the ROK 6th Division, which had been their objective.[8]

The CCF attack on the 24th Division centered on the 19th Regiment. The enemy attack penetrated its 2nd and 3rd battalions, and they fell back. This caused the 1st Battalion to withdraw. Soon the entire regiment was moving to the rear. Apparently the Chinese that massed against the 19th Regiment suffered heavy casualties, as groups of them were seen to assemble and reorganize in minefields with mines exploding around them after daylight. Eventually, however, the Chinese found the boundary with the

ROK 6th Division as well as the 19th Regiment's eastern boundary and exploited both of them.[9] The US IX Corps identified one enemy division from the CCF 39th Army and two divisions of the CCF 38th Army on its front during the night's attack.

In their initial attacks the Chinese overran some artillery positions. One battery of 155-mm howitzers of the 9th Field Artillery Battalion, which was well forward firing in support of the ROK 1st Division, was captured during the night.[10]

The 21st Infantry Regiment, on the 24th Division's right flank, was untouched during the night, although heavy fighting continued during the night on both sides of it – on the left, in the 19th Regimental sector, and on its right, across the boundary in the ROK 2nd Division. On the UN front western flank, beyond the ROK 1st Division, in the Turkish Brigade and the US 25th Infantry Division sectors, there was no enemy action.

All night long, General Ridgway at his Seoul Advance CP received fragmentary reports of the Chinese penetrations of his front lines and of their deep thrusts behind them into rear areas, and of developing chaos, especially in the ROK sectors. At dawn he got in his jeep and headed north on the main Uijongbu highway toward the front. He tells the sequel:

Only a few miles north of Seoul, I ran head-on into that fleeing army. I'd never had such an experience before, and I pray to God I never witness such a spectacle again. They were coming down the road in trucks, the men standing, packed so close together in those big carriers another small boy could not have found space among them. They had abandoned their heavy artillery, their machine guns – all their crew-served weapons. Only a few had kept their rifles. Their only thought was to get away, to put miles between them and the feared enemy that was at their heels. [These soldiers were from the ROK 6th Division.]

I jumped from my jeep and stood in the middle of the road, waving them to a halt. I might as well have tried to stop the flow of the Han. I spoke no Korean, and had no interpreter with me. I could find no officer who spoke English. The only solution was to let them run – and to set up road blocks far enough back where they could be stopped, channeled into bivouac areas, calmed down, refitted, and turned to face the enemy again. I went back immediately to order these straggler posts set up.[11]

Ridgway included some additional information on this incident at another place. When he tried to stop the lead trucks of fleeing ROK soldiers, he said, "The first few dodged by me without slowing down but I did soon succeed in stopping a group of trucks all carrying ROK officers. The group in the advance truck listened without comprehension and would not obey my gestures. Soon the whole procession was rolling again. The only effective move now was to set up straggler posts far to the rear, manned by our own MPs under officer command, to try to regain control. This method worked."[12]

General Ridgway went to President Rhee and asked for his help—would he go with him to these troops and try to put some heart in them? Rhee readily agreed. The two of them with pilots took off in battered old canvas-covered cub planes of World War II in bitterly cold weather. Ridgway wrote:

I nearly froze, though I was bundled in my heavy GI winter gear. President Rhee flew in his native dress, in a long white cotton kimono and low shoes, without even a scarf at his neck. His wrinkled, brown old face seemed to shrivel with the cold, but he never uttered a word of complaint.

We found them, as I had anticipated, where the MP road blocks had stopped them. They had been fed. They were being rearmed. Their first great panic was over. The brave old President addressed them with fiery eloquence. I could not understand what he said, but the effect of his words was obvious.

As we left them, he placed his hand upon my arm. "Do not be discouraged," he said. "They will fight again."[13]

The Eighth Army Command Report, daily historical report for 1 January 1951, says of this incident merely, "1230 stopped ROK 6th Division convoy with soldiers enroute to Seoul. Ordered MPs to hold trucks and notify Gen. Church (CG of 24th Infantry Division). Trucks to be turned around and ROKs returned to their units."[14]

During daylight of 1 January there was no stemming the enemy tide. It continued to roll south. General Ridgway and the corps commanders now planned to occupy the beachhead line around Seoul. In the worsening situation I Corps sent the British 29th Brigade north from its reserve position to take over the sector originally held by the ROK 1st Division. This was to be the 29th Brigade's first action in the Korean War. Its commander, Brig. Thomas Brodie, issued his field order before his forces closed on its positions at 6 P.M. It read, "At last after weeks of frustration we have nothing between us and the Chinese. I have no intention that this Brigade Group will retire before the enemy unless ordered by higher authority in order to conform with general movement. If you meet him you are to knock hell out of him with everything you have got. You are only to give ground on my orders."[15] Anyone acquainted with the Scots brigadier or his reputation knew that he was considered a tough soldier, and not to be trifled with.

The British 29th Brigade had more different types of tanks than any unit of the UN forces—the 55-ton Centurion, the 40-ton Churchill infantry-support tank equipped with flamethrowers, and the 28-ton Cromwell reconnaissance tank. The Centurion was a wide tank and not suitable for use in Korea. Sometimes it could not negotiate narrow roads in mountainous country. In its new assignment, the 29th Brigade had one of the toughest roles of all the UN forces on 1 January—it was right in the heart of the main enemy thrust. As it went into place, the two US Corps on orders started a general withdrawal to a secondary defense line eight to ten miles north of Seoul.[16]

The other British brigade, the 27th, in IX Corps reserve, reverted to 24th Division control and was to take a similar position at the front to cover the gap left by the collapse of the ROK 6th Division and to cover its withdrawal and that of the 24th Infantry Division. The 5th RCT of the 24th Division was the last of the two divisions to pass through the British 27th Brigade. It became engaged with Chinese in a firefight while doing this. This fight then passed to the 27th Brigade. The Chinese cut off part of the brigade – the Australian Battalion, which had to fight its way out. The battalion commander, Lieutenant Colonel Ferguson, happened to be with Brigadier Coad below the cut-off Australians. The Australians went about their job in a businesslike way. They dismounted from their vehicles, and under the direction of Lieutenant A. G. Keys, A and C companies fanned out to the flanks of the road and cleared the enemy from their firing positions. The Australians had only four wounded in this encounter. They killed seven Chinese and captured the light machine gun that had caused most of the trouble. The Australian battalion then resumed its drive on into Seoul, where it took up a river-bridge guard assignment.[17]

On the Eighth Army's extreme western flank, I Corps had the Turkish Brigade on the south bank of the Han River at its mouth. The 25th Infantry Division held a line on the south bank of the Imjin River from its confluence with the Han until it met the ROK 1st Division eastward. Neither the Turks nor the 25th Division received any enemy action during the night. Opposite the 25th Division was the NK 8th Division, and farther back, one or two days' march away, was the CCF 50th Army. But this army took no part in the first night's attack. With a massive enemy attack taking place only a few miles northeast of it, the 25th Division could not be allowed the luxury of nonparticipation very long. By midafternoon of 1 January it was ordered to move to the north of Seoul. Col. William Kelleher now commanded the division's 35th Regiment, replacing an older but highly respected regimental commander, Col. John Fisher, who had left Korea for medical reasons. Kelleher had previously commanded the 1st Battalion, 38th Infantry, 2nd Infantry Division, and was a highly decorated officer. He was rough and acted rough; some thought him a martinet. He insisted on haircuts and shaves and enforced discipline, from the battalion commanders on down. He reasoned, "If you look like a soldier, you are a soldier."

The I Corps order to the 25th Division instructed it to take a blocking position on the Kaesong-Seoul road eight miles northwest of Seoul. The division was to hold its new defensive position at all costs. The 27th Regiment of the division held an outpost line across the same road about seven miles farther north toward Kaesong. The division started its move in midafternoon. General Milburn, the I Corps commander, told General Kean, the 25th Division commander, that he planned to commit the British 29th Brigade in a counterattack northeast from the old ROK 1st Division CP, and if the British encountered enemy on its left flank in this attack, the 27th Regiment of the 25th Division should be prepared to go into a blocking position and protect the British left (west) flank. The 27th Regiment also would cover the withdrawal of the 25th Division from its initial position to its new defense line north of Seoul. The 1st Battalion, commanded by Lt. Col. Gilbert Check, was to be the last unit, the rear guard, for this movement. Check was known to be a competent, steady battalion commander. Milburn ordered the movement to begin at 1:40 P.M. It actually began about 3 P.M.[18]

Stragglers from the ROK 1st Division had been entering the 25th Division's lines from the east since early morning. The 25th Division gathered them in its rear, and now that it had to move, it requested the ROK division to send someone to take charge of them.

Lieutenant Colonel Check's 1st Battalion, 27th Infantry, covered the 25th Division rear as it began its hurried move to its blocking position north of Seoul. It withdrew in heavy fire – not enemy fire, but that from burning villages. The division had been ordered to burn all buildings to prevent enemy use. Since the 1st Battalion, 27th Infantry, was the last unit, it moved through and burned villages most of the way. One village had very narrow streets, and buildings on both sides of the road were burning furiously. The division had no enemy action during the day, and it closed at its new positions at 1:05 A.M., 2 January. The 27th Regiment as a whole closed into assembly areas at 2:10 A.M. that morning.[19]

By the end of the day, 1 January, enemy action had reduced the ROK 1st Division to about half strength. The 12th Regiment amounted to about one battalion, the 11th Regiment to about two battalions, and the 15th Regiment was largely intact. The division was ordered to the rear, out of enemy contact. The big gap in the ROK 12th Regimental line was exploited all day long by the Chinese. At 10:20 A.M. a Mosquito plane saw 3,000 to 4,000 enemy troops crossing the Imjin River in the gap. The Chinese on 1 January did not seek cover at daylight, but in order to exploit their breakthrough immediately, they moved south all day, often being good targets for air strikes. They were willing to pay the price. By nightfall the Chinese had penetrated about eight to nine miles in general, and on the main road north from Seoul to Uijongbu they had reached the vicinity of Tokchon-ni, only six miles north of Uijongbu. At Uijongbu itself an aerial observer saw enemy moving south on a nearby ridge. All day long air sorties found enemy in the open, moving south. It would be impossible to make a close guess as to how many enemy were killed or wounded during the day by aerial strikes. At 11 A.M. an aerial strike destroyed six enemy self-propelled guns and two vehicles southeast of Yonchon.[20]

The Chinese New Year's Offensive was not confined to the US I and IX Corps front north and northeast of Seoul. The Chinese 42nd and 66th armies spilled over eastward into the zones of the ROK 2nd and 5th divisions and the Kapyong area. Maj. Harold H. Meisner, a US KMAG advisor, in the ROK 36th Regiment, won the Distinguished Service Cross on 1 January when Chinese ambushed the ROK 36th Regiment at Kapyong. The 36th Regiment was badly disorganized by the sudden attack. Major Meisner located the ROK regimental commander and instructed him on the deployment of his troops. He then went from unit to unit, under fire, to see that the instructions were being carried out. As a result, what promised to be a debacle was turned into a success. The ROK regiment repulsed the attack.[21]

Coincident with the Chinese New Year's Offensive in the west, the North Koreans deployed in the central corridor and the eastern part of the enemy line launched simultaneous attacks against the ROK divisions there and the newly arrived US 2nd Infantry Division. This story, however, is told later.

In the west, General Milburn issued I Corps Operational Directive 34 at 9 P.M. on 1 January for corps units to be prepared to withdraw to Defense Line C (the south bank of the Han River) and farther to Defense Line D, at a time to be announced. Thus, it appeared that at the end of their first day of the 3rd Phase Offensive, the Chinese had succeeded so well that Eighth Army was preparing to evacuate Seoul and retreat to points south of the Han River.

After the holocaust of 1 January along the Imjin River and south of it, the second was relatively quiet. The Chinese now were consolidating their gains, and the Eighth Army and UN troops were almost everywhere in retreat and, on Eighth Army's orders, were withdrawing to the Seoul beachhead line. Most of the army had withdrawn from immediate contact with the Chinese. The Eighth Army front now lay a few miles west, north, and northeast of Uijongbu.

Except for K Company of the 27th Infantry, the US 25th Division, northwest of Uijongbu, had no enemy contact during the day. The 27th Infantry held the outpost line across the road from Munsan-ni to Uijongbu and Seoul all day and at midafternoon had contact with the British 29th Brigade on its right. An enemy force overran K Company, but it had no casualties. Apparently, the company simply withdrew when the enemy approached, leaving behind three 57-mm guns, two light machine guns, three BARs, an SCR-300 radio, a 3.5-inch rocket launcher, and ammunition for all the weapons.[22]

Major General Kean of the 25th Division, in Instructional Order No. 39, shortly after noon, stated that enemy were operating in civilian clothes and mixed with refugees and that drastic action must be taken to prevent them from passing through the outpost line and into combat areas. Action to be taken included preventing all movement in front of the Outpost Line of Resistance (OPLR) and the Main Line of Resistance (MLR) during

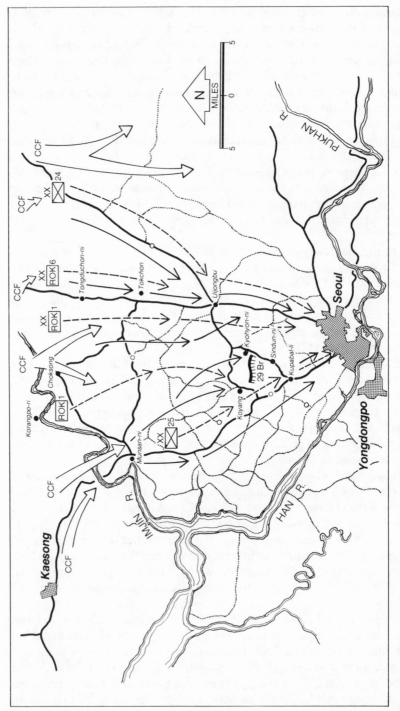

MAP 3. CCF 3rd Phase Offensive, 31 December 50–4 January 1951

darkness, by artillery and mortar fire, and during daylight denying all movement except that identified as friendly. This prevention was to be accomplished by placing barrages in front of refugee groups. If this action did not stop movement toward their lines, then they were to fire directly into the groups.[23]

In the ROK 1st Division sector an enemy force engaged the ROK 11th Regiment briefly just after daylight, but this fight did not last long, as the ROKs withdrew to a predetermined position. During the night the Chinese had built two bridges across the Imjin River in the Korangpo-ri area. About dusk the 12th and 15th ROK regiments, under attack, withdrew on orders to the Han River. Two battalions of the ROK 11th Regiment were attached to the British 29th Brigade and went into a defense position on the brigade's right flank in the Uijongbu area. The British brigade now held the defensive positions in the ROK 1st Division's former area.[24]

In the ROK 6th Division sector things were in a sorry state on 2 January. The two front-line regiments, the 7th and 19th, withdrew through the reserve regiment, the 2nd, headed for Seoul. At 9:30 A.M. only four battalions could be accounted for, and they had abandoned their artillery. At 6:30 P.M. 33 trucks, each carrying an average of 40 ROKs of the 6th Division, crossed the Han River to the south side. An estimated 1,000 to 2,000 more were crossing on foot. When the ROK 6th Division closed in an assembly area in the evening, it had about 3,000 troops; the 2nd Regiment had 1,800, the 7th Regiment, 140, and the 19th Regiment, 900. A later figure stated that IX Corps had moved 5,750 ROKs from the 6th Division across the Han River by truck and that 1,700 more were waiting to cross on foot. In any event, the ROK 6th Division by evening of 2 January was removed from the fighting sectors north of Seoul.[25]

Before daybreak of 2 January the 19th and 21st regiments of the 24th Division began to withdraw into the Beachhead Defense Line without enemy contact, covered by the 5th RCT and artillery fire of the 555th Field Artillery Battalion. In covering the withdrawal of the division, the 5th RCT had only brief enemy contact six miles north of Uijongbu. Lt. Col. Clarence E. Stuart, commanding the 555th, said his forward observers with the infantry adjusted fire by sight of exploding white phosphorus shells on enemy following the 5th RCT, effectively holding off pursuing enemy groups.[26]

Farther east in the ROK II Corps area, the 31st ROK Regiment of the ROK 5th Division had been under attack during 1 January and tried to withdraw during the night. But an enemy roadblock behind it, about four and a half miles north of Kapyong, stopped and disorganized it. Aerial observation the next day reported that the regiment had abandoned 15 of its 2½-ton trucks, five other vehicles, and six artillery pieces. Reduced enemy pressure during the day allowed the disorganized ROK 32nd Regiment of the ROK 2nd Division, on the west of the 31st Regiment, and the ROK

17th Regiment to make a withdrawal. But the enemy succeeded in surrounding the 31st Regiment north of Kapyong. An air report at 4:30 P.M. located the regiment and stated that it was surrounded by two Chinese regiments. An air strike was called for and planes dispatched to the scene. But this action was near dusk, and its effectiveness was not reported. An air observer said that at 5 P.M. he saw no activity at the former site of the 31st Regiment. Its status was unknown.[27]

Late in the afternoon of 2 January, General Ridgway made a last tour of the lines, traveling in an open jeep. He got estimates from all division and corps commanders. Both corps commanders advised him to withdraw the army south of the Han River. General Milburn told the author later that, when General Ridgway asked him for his view, he said, "I told him to get out. Coulter told him the same."[28]

On the afternoon or evening of 2 January, General Ridgway made up his mind to withdraw the army south of the Han River and to evacuate Seoul. He issued the order for this action the next morning, 3 January. In his own account of the reasons for his action he wrote:

In discussions with our two U.S. Corps Commanders, with the ROK Army Chief of Staff and with the Chief of KMAG, it became clear that a combination of enemy frontal attack and deep envelopment around our wide-open east flank, where the ROK had fled in panic, could soon place the entire army in jeopardy. I had not found sufficient basis for confidence in the ability of the troops to hold their positions, even if they were ordered to. Consequently I asked our ambassador, on January 3, to notify President Rhee that Seoul would be once more evacuated and that withdrawal from our forward positions would begin at once.

I also informed the Ambassador and what part of the ROK government still remained in Seoul that from 3 P.M. on, the bridges and main approach and exit roads would be closed to all but military traffic. All official government vehicles would have to clear before that hour and there would be no civilian traffic permitted from then on.[29]

4

The Third Evacuation of Seoul

THE NIGHT OF 2–3 January must have been a troubled and sleepless one for General Ridgway. That afternoon he had decided, after driving along Eighth Army's jagged front line and conferring with his division and corps commanders, that he must order the army to withdraw across the Han River and to evacuate Seoul. Perhaps in anticipation of such an order, he had instructed his staff and corps commanders during the day that army demolitions for necessary military destruction should combine a maximum hurt for the enemy with a minimum harm to the civilian population. He had stated that "destruction for destruction's sake will not be permitted, nor will anything approaching 'scorched earth' tactics be condoned."[1]

Now, on the morning of 3 January, Ridgway was up early. He had a host of duties to perform to set in motion the things he wanted done during the day. At 7:30 A.M. he instructed Muccio to inform the ROK government and all its agencies that, effective at 6 P.M., the use of all bridges over the Han River would be reserved for military traffic exclusively. Half an hour later he delegated to the I and IX corps commanders, General Milburn and General Coulter, complete authority to stop all civilian traffic in both directions, and to use weapons fire placed in front of civilians to stop their movement and to keep them in place.

At 10:00 A.M. he ordered Brig. Gen. Charles D. Palmer, commanding general of the 1st Cavalry Division Artillery, to report to him at once for detached duty for at least 48 hours and to bring with him a personal party. At 11:45 A.M. General Palmer reported to General Ridgway, who gave him his instructions. Palmer was to be responsible for control in I Corps of all traffic out of Seoul and across the Han River. Palmer had authority to come directly to Eighth Army for any assistance he might need. In short, Ridgway had handpicked Palmer to act in his name to control the all-important matter of both civilian and military traffic during Eighth Army's withdrawal across the Han River. He told Palmer that all civilian traffic should be shut off at 3 P.M. that afternoon, except for US Embassy and UN vehicles, which might use the bridges until 6 P.M.

At 11:50 he ordered the IX Corps to begin its withdrawal. Ten minutes later he ordered the 187th Airborne RCT to move east to Ichon, southeast of Seoul and south of the Han River, an important road center, to guard against any enveloping move of enemy forces in a breakthrough on the army's right or east flank beyond the US 24th Infantry Division. At 1 P.M. he ordered the army withdrawal to start at once. The corps commanders were to remove all sick, wounded, and dead; no usable equipment was to be left behind; and they were to use ruthless control of any slight break that might undermine troop morale during the withdrawal.

Ridgway himself stayed in Seoul on the north side of the Han River at the main bridge until 5:30 P.M. Then, after dark, he crossed in his jeep to the south side of the river and stayed overnight at the I Corps CP in Yongdongpo.[2]

Concerning enemy activity, 3 January was not a repeat of the day before. The pressing drive that characterized the Chinese attack on 1 January was resumed on the third. They had now regrouped deep behind Eighth Army's former front line and struck with full force southward. In addition to the Chinese divisions that had been in the attack on the first, the Chinese 50th Army, with its 148th, 149th, and 150th divisions, had now moved down from its position above Kaesong and was swinging southeast along the main highway from Kaesong through Munsan-ni toward Seoul. It formed the extreme right flank of the enemy attack and was on line with the Chinese 39th Army in the ROK 1st Division rear areas, now being held by the US 25th Division and the British 29th Brigade. All day of 3 January this area was one of Chinese attacks.

A second center of enemy action was down the main corridor through Uijongbu, directly north of Seoul. There the US 24th Division, one regiment of the ROK 6th Division, and the British 27th Brigade had to face the foe.

At the same time, farther east, in the area of the ROK 2nd Division and the other ROK forces that stretched on eastward to the central corridor and to the Sea of Japan, enemy forces (North Korean beyond the Iron Triangle) were in motion advancing south in general attack. The story of this central and eastern front will be told later.

As events developed during the afternoon and evening of 3 January, General Palmer did not have any serious trouble with the Korean civilian population trying to leave Seoul, and he did not have to exercise his authority to use weapons fire to control them. About half the population of Seoul had already left, and many of the others had gone to villages along the north bank of the Han. The increasingly cold weather, however, had frozen the Han River solid in some places, and the civilians in Seoul could cross on the ice away from the bridges if they wished – and thousands of them did. It was a matter of concern to Eighth Army also, that, with the river frozen over, enemy troops could cross the river on the ice if they were able to break through speedily on either flank while the withdrawal was in progress.[3]

A Chinese prisoner captured on 2 January in the ROK 6th Division sector revealed that the Chinese 40th Army, with its 118th, 119th, and 120th divisions, had arrived north of the Imjin River only the day before and had crossed the river in attack shortly before midnight. It had passed through Pyongyang on or about Christmas Day on its way to join in the 3rd Phase Offensive. The 40th Army on 3 January was crowding into the line between the 39th and 38th armies and helping in the push down the Uijongbu corridor.[4]

It appears, therefore, that by 3 January the Chinese 50th and 40th armies had reinforced the enemy forces that had made the initial assaults two days earlier. By this time the ROK 6th Division was nearly combat ineffective, with only one regiment, or about 30 percent of its strength, usable because of casualties, physical condition, and loss of equipment. The British 27th Brigade had been put into the line to take its place in the IX Corps sector.[5]

In the withdrawal plan, the ROK 1st Division of I Corps and the ROK 6th Division of IX Corps were the first major units to be withdrawn south of the Han River. This decision was made primarily because the Chinese attack had rendered both divisions, except the 11th Regiment of the ROK 1st Division, combat ineffective by the end of 2 January. The 11th Regiment, originally in the vicinity of Korangpo-ri, had fought well and had not suffered greatly. Its 3rd Battalion was attached to the 24th Infantry of the 25th Division, which was adjacent to it on the left, or west, and the 1st and 2nd battalions were attached to the British 29th Brigade, which had been moved hurriedly from its corps reserve position to fill the gap left in the line south of the Imjin by the enemy shattering the ROK 12th and 15th regiments.[6]

The US 24th Infantry Division held the right flank of the IX Corps sector, with its 19th Regiment on the left and the 21st Regiment on the right flank. The 5th RCT was in division reserve. Next eastward beyond the 21st Infantry and the IX Corps boundary, the ROK 2nd Division of the ROK II Corps was on line. On 3 January the Chinese 196th Division of the CCF 66th Army overran two of its regiments. This Chinese attack tore a great hole in the area on the east flank of the US IX Corps. Kapyong, a road center on the Pukhan River, fell to the enemy in this action. The 24th Division was now entirely exposed on its right flank. Threatening it at this point was the Chinese 126th Division of the 42nd Army, which was moving up for attack.[7]

The 21st Infantry was also under attack the morning of 3 January when the ROK 2nd Division on its right was being destroyed. Its 2nd Battalion outpost line, where each company had a platoon stationed, was driven in. From E Company's OPLR the E Company platoon withdrew to the MLR, but in the process they saw seven men in the G Company OPLR taken prisoner. The battalion did not fire on the G Company OPLR for fear of hitting some of their own men. In the action in the 21st Infantry sector during the morning, friendly aerial attacks strafed A and B companies of the 1st Battalion and G Company of the 2nd Battalion. At 1 P.M. General Church, the division commander, ordered Col. Richard Stephens to withdraw the 21st Regiment to Line D, south of the Han River. The regiment began this move at 5:25 P.M.[8]

Earlier in the morning, at 10 A.M., IX Corps had ordered the 24th Division to withdraw, but it could not disengage immediately from enemy contact for the move. Withdrawal order within the division was the 21st Infantry first, then the 19th Infantry, and lastly the 5th RCT. The 7th Cavalry Regiment and the British 27th Brigade were to follow the 24th Division.[9]

In the morning's attack by an enemy battalion on A Company of the 21st Infantry, near Uijongbu, Cpl. Billy Mosier of the Medical Company went out under enemy mortar and small-arms fire to assist some wounded. While treating one man, he heard a call for help from another some distance away. He went to that man and gave him first aid, with small-arms fire falling all around him. It made it impossible for him to evacuate this wounded man. Mosier picked up the wounded man's rifle and moved to the crest of a nearby knoll, from which he had good observation into the enemy position. He began to fire on the enemy and killed several, before he himself was killed by an enemy sniper.[10]

The 19th Infantry Regiment, on the left flank of the 24th Division, adjacent to the main road running north from Seoul, took the main blow of the large enemy force from the CCF 38th Army that now resumed the drive on Seoul. The attacks began before dawn on the third and continued all morning, forcing the 2nd Battalion to withdraw. The Chinese overran F and G companies four miles southeast of Uijongbu, and E Company was then moved to block behind F Company. During all these enemy thrusts artillery and air strikes were directed on them, with heavy enemy casualties reported, some strikes and artillery barrages reportedly inflicting 90 percent casualties on units. The 2nd Battalion estimated the Chinese suffered 700 casualties during the morning and saw them recovering many of their dead and wounded from the ground. Before noon, the 3rd Battalion, 19th Infantry, counterattacked the Chinese in the 2nd Battalion positions and restored part of the line. Enemy in large numbers were observed moving south around them on high ground. Just after noon the 2nd Battalion with fixed bayonets attacked Hill 389 against an estimated enemy company but found the Chinese had abandoned the hill, with enemy dead still in their positions. Late in the morning, the 24th Division reported the main road covered with enemy soldiers marching south. Artillery and air strikes were placed on them. During the morning of 3 January, the advance units of the Chinese 38th Army moved four or five miles southeast of Uijongbu and reached points only eight to ten miles from Seoul.[11]

Men of the 19th Infantry had numerous hand-to-hand encounters with Chinese soldiers in the almost-continuous combat on the morning of 3 January in the Uijongbu area. At 5 A.M. in the morning there was noise out on the road. A ROK soldier ran up to Lt. John W. Fahy, leader of the 3rd Platoon, F Company, 19th Infantry, and said Chinese had arrived on nearby high ground. The platoon withdrew. Even earlier, enemy approach was reported to 1st Lt. Edward L. Shea, commanding F Company. As he left his CP, he saw 10 people coming toward him. When he challenged them, they answered, "GI." Shea then realized they were enemy and fired three rounds from his M-1 at them before the rifle jammed. He got to the CP security force of about 20 men, and he started with them to climb up to the outpost position. There was snow on the ground, and it was cold. Shea was in the lead as they came to a huge boulder, as big "as two wall tents," he said. He went around its left side smack into a group of Chinese coming down the hill. Shea hit the first one over the head with his jammed rifle. His sergeant right behind him shot two more with his carbine. Shea fought with five Chinese who jumped on him. They got him to the ground and sat on him—one on his feet, another on his chest, and two others on his arms. Shea was a big, powerful man, 6 feet, 4 inches tall, 185 pounds. The Chinese stripped him of all his possessions and kept him on the ground. Three of the five Chinese then went away. One of the remaining two was unarmed, and the other covered Shea with a rifle. When the latter pointed his rifle at Shea's head, Shea kicked him in the groin, jumped up, knocked the unarmed Chinese to the ground, and started to run away. He got only 15 to 20 yards when a shot was fired and he fell unconscious.

Shea awoke some hours later, about 8 A.M. He saw nothing but heard Chinese talking. He lay there for a time, his head aching. He thought he had a chance to escape and began working his way downhill to a creek bed and then to the road. No enemy was in sight, and he walked along the road toward where he thought his battalion was located. He reached battalion lines at 9 A.M. He had a grazing bullet wound on the back of his head and pistol gashes on his head, where one of the five Chinese had pounded him with his pistol. Shea learned later that F Company had 63 casualties that morning.[12]

By noon of 3 January the 24th Division, east of the Uijongbu road, was increasingly under enemy pressure. Brig. Basil A. Coad, commander of the British 27th Brigade, attached to the division, received instructions to report to Gen. John Church, 24th Division commander. Coad, in reporting the incident, wrote, "I was sent for at 1415 hours by the Divisional commander, and I got the shortest order I ever had in my life. He just said to me, 'Coad, we are going to pull.' I was ordered to do rearguard to cover two American divisions."[13]

The rear-guard positions he was ordered to occupy were not the same he had previously reconnoitered, but he was supposed to have his brigade in them by dark. Coad gave credit to the initiative and experience of his battalion commanders for their ability to carry out the order. Of the withdrawal, he said, "During the night, the American divisions withdrew through us, and by 0430 hours we were in contact with Chinese [the 27th Brigade rear-guard positions were about six miles north of Seoul]. Both flanks were entirely open. . . . I was able to extricate my brigade over the river south of Seoul by 1000 hours."[14] It was now the morning of 4 January.

The Australian Battalion, one of the 27th Brigade's units, provides some additional information about the withdrawal of the UN forces of IX Corps. The Australian and Middlesex battalions of the 27th Brigade went into the rear-guard positions on the Uijongbu-Seoul road to cover the withdrawal of the 19th and 21st regiments of the US 24th Division. The Australian Battalion had the right-hand forward position astride the road about six miles north of Seoul, with D Company of the US 6th Tank Battalion attached to it for support. US artillery fire from the south side of the Han River fired in support. The Australians reported:

By 10 o'clock at night all retiring elements of the US Army IX Corps had passed through safely. By 11 o'clock D Company was engaged with the forward patrols of the enemy. Throughout the night D Company, the American tanks, and supporting artillery kept up defensive and harassing fire and, at 6 o'clock next morning, the Australians began "thinning out" back towards Seoul. As the last company (C Company) withdrew the enemy followed up and when the last Australian elements had mounted their trucks they could see the Chinese occupying the positions they had just evacuated. At 8:30 the Commonwealth Brigade withdrew from Seoul. The Australians were the last to cross the railroad bridge before US Army engineers demolished it. The Argylls were last out of the burning city, waiting for the 29th Brigade Ulsters who had struck trouble farther north, and when the last of the stragglers were through they blew the main supply route, leaving Seoul and the country north and east of the Han River to the Chinese and the North Koreans.[15]

West of the Uijongbu-Seoul main highway, and northwest of Seoul in the I Corps area, the US 25th Division, the British 29th Brigade, and the 11th Regiment of the ROK 1st Division had hard fighting on 3 January and were trying to coordinate their withdrawal with that of the 24th Division and the British 27th Brigade. When the Chinese made their surprise penetration of the ROK 1st Division on the night of 31 December, the 25th Division, on the west of the ROK 1st Division, received orders to move at once to block on the main highway running southeast from Kaesong through Munsan-ni to Seoul. The 27th Regiment of the division took up a blocking position on 1 January about 15 miles northwest of Seoul on the highway. It stayed there two days without any important action.

During the second, however, the 149th Division of the CCF 50th Army moved up from its reserve position, and by 3 January it formed the right flank of the Chinese forces bearing down on Seoul. When the 27th Infantry took up its original blocking position astride the Munsan-ni–Seoul road on 1 January, it established contact with the British 29th Brigade on its right, or northeast, at 3 P.M. in the afternoon. The British Brigade in effect had rushed into the void caused by the near destruction of the ROK 12th and 15th regiments in the first night and early the following morning of the Chinese offensive. The ROK 11th Regiment, in the vicinity of Korangpo-ri, had not suffered extensively in this opening phase of the battle and had been attached to the British 29th Brigade, still combat effective.

Thus, on 3 January, the Chinese 149th Division of the 50th Army, with the rest of the army behind it, advancing southeast on the Munsan-ni–Seoul road and the hills to the east and northeast of it, ran into the US 25th Division and the British 29th Brigade. These forces engaged in hard fighting and indeed in bitter battles all day long and on into the night of 3–4 January. During the day, the 25th Division withdrew in a series of movements down the highway toward Seoul, trying to coordinate its battles and withdrawals with those of the British 29th Brigade. Both forces were under I Corps orders to withdraw to the south side of the Han River. But these orders were not easy to comply with, given the repeated attacks and close pursuit of the Chinese confronting them.[16]

Maj. Gen. William B. Kean, commander of the 25th Division, is said to have exploded in wrath when he received the order on 3 January for his division to withdraw. Some on his immediate staff said he wanted to stay and fight it out, that he was upset upon receiving the order. Kean was considered a quiet, calm commander, and he gave confidence to his troops. He emphasized communication with all units of his command by voice radio. Research for this book indicated that Kean was the only division commander who wanted to fight it out north of the Han River.[17]

Action in the 25th Division sector began early on 3 January, when two enemy companies attacked K Company of the 27th Infantry at 2:55 A.M. with mortar, automatic, and small-arms fire. K Company was on the extreme right of the regimental line. It withdrew under pressure through the MLR to E Company, 35th Infantry. The 1st and 2nd battalions of the 27th Infantry were forced to withdraw through the 35th Infantry, beginning at 8:05 A.M. L Company, 27th Infantry, at 8:45 A.M. was ordered to establish a defensive position astride the MSR, behind the 35th Infantry, and to cover the expected withdrawal of the 35th Infantry and the British 29th Brigade.[18]

At 9:35 A.M. General Milburn informed General Kean that enemy dead had been identified as being from the 149th Division, CCF 50th Army, and ordered him to assume control of the British 29th Brigade immediately, stating that Kean would command all troops in the I Corps bridgehead. The Turkish Brigade was removed from 25th Division control and reverted to I Corps control.[19]

In the meantime, Lt. Col. Gordon E. Murch's 2nd Battalion, 27th Infantry, had taken possession of a dominant hill mass that covered an important road junction behind the 25th Division and the British 29th Brigade. A hundred laborers had arrived to dig in the position. At 11 A.M. the British 29th Brigade reported to the 25th Division that it had taken between 20 and 30 casualties on its right flank, including three officers killed, in the sector held by the Royal Northumberland Fusiliers. Tanks were sent to reinforce the British there.[20]

By 3 P.M. in the afternoon intense enemy pressure had developed on the 35th Infantry Regiment of the 25th Division and the adjacent British 29th Brigade. They were instructed to withdraw, with the 27th Infantry to cover them in this movement. An hour later, at 4 P.M., the 25th Division was officially ordered to withdraw south of the Han River, and it started the withdrawal. The 24th Infantry was to go first, followed by the 35th Infantry, and then the British Brigade. The 27th Regiment was to cover their withdrawal. By 7 P.M. the 1st Battalion, 27th Infantry, was in a blocking position near the village of Chungansa-ri, at the outskirts of Seoul.[21]

While all this activity was occurring south of it, the British 29th Brigade, on the north (right) flank of the 25th Division, was having one of the hardest series of battles in the entire Chinese 3rd Phase Offensive but was gradually withdrawing to keep in line with the 25th Division and with the 24th Division across the corps boundary in IX Corps.

When the British 29th Brigade was first committed on 1 January, after the Chinese assault across the Imjin River split wide open the ROK 1st Division, it was to counterattack against the Chinese in the area the ROKs had just lost. But that order was countermanded, and the brigade instead was ordered to take up a defensive position in the area just south and east of Koyang, eight air miles north and slightly west of the northern edge of Seoul. There it was two miles northeast of the main Kaesong–Munsanni–Seoul highway, on a secondary mountain road junction, the right fork of which ran northeast ten miles to Uijongbu and the main Seoul north–south highway. The brigade was also just east of the 25th Division, which was blocking along the Kaesong road to Seoul, the west coastal main highway leading from Seoul north to the border.

The 29th Brigade's defense position stretched about five miles eastward from just south of Koyang, where the Royal Ulster Rifles Battalion held the left flank and guarded the road junction. The Gloucestershire ("Gloster") Battalion was next to the east and in the center, with the Royal Northumberland Fusiliers Battalion on the right (east) flank near the small village of Chunghung-dong. The brigade, in effect, was in a line on a series of hilltops just south of the road running from Koyang toward Uijongbu, with its right flank anchored on high ground at a narrow, poor road track running through Kyohyon-ni south to Sindun-ni. This latter village was about the same distance from the main Kaesong-Seoul road at Kupabal-li as Koyang was from it.

Each of the three infantry battalions was supported by a mortar troop of the 170th Mortar Battery, Royal Artillery. The 45th Field Artillery Regiment and C Squadron of the 7th Royal Tank Regiment of Churchill tanks, which could operate on the narrow mountain tracks, were in general support of the brigade. The US 9th Field Artillery Battalion of 155-mm howitzers was also in support of the brigade. A reinforcing unit known as Cooper Force, consisting of the Reconnaissance Troop of the 8th Hussars, mounted on Cromwell tanks, and six other Cromwell tanks, under the command of Capt. D. L. Astley-Cooper of the 8th Hussars, supported the brigade. There were no large Centurion tanks present. All of these huge tanks were south of the Han River at Suwon, except for C Squadron, which was on an island of the Han River, south of Seoul. Brig. Thomas Brodie, an experienced professional soldier of World War II, commanded the 29th Brigade.[22]

Before daylight on 3 January, the 149th Division, CCF 50th Army, attacked the British 29th Brigade in its position near Koyang. The attack hit the Royal Ulster Rifles on the left (west) end of the line and the Royal Northumberland Fusiliers on the right (east) end of the line at the same time. The Gloucestershire Battalion, between the other two battalions and slightly back of the Fusiliers, was not involved. The 446th Regiment of the 149th Division seems to have been the leading Chinese element in the attack.[23]

The action started on the left in the Ulster Rifles sector about 4 A.M., when an American patrol, apparently from the 35th Infantry of the 25th Division, was driven from Koyang into the Ulster Rifles lines. The Ulster Battalion was dug in on Hill 456 southeast of Koyang. At first light the Chinese overran its B Company, and later they overran D Company. The battalion commander, Lt. Col. R. J. H. Carson, was ill at the time, and Maj. C. A. H. B. Blake, second in command, was the acting commander. In the fighting that followed during the morning, Major Blake counterattacked and restored the battalion's original positions.[24]

The Northumberland Fusiliers had a harder time of it during the early-morning attack. They held three hills, with a company on each hill; W Company was in reserve. There were gaps between the hills that could be well covered with fire during the daytime, but after dark it would be difficult to prevent enemy infiltration between them. The Chinese made a penetration in the Fusiliers position, and many snipers infiltrated in the gaps between the companies, and firing from high ground, they caused many casualties. The snipers were eventually eliminated or driven away by W Company and two troops of Churchill tanks of the 7th Royal Tank Battalion. These tanks were effectively handled by their crews on the narrow, icy roads. The Fusiliers position was reestablished by 4 P.M., with the Chinese in retreat to the north and bombarded in their flight by 4.2-inch mortar and 25-pounder cannon fire.[25] But the Fusiliers had lost 16 men killed, 45 wounded, and 3 missing in this action.

At 6 P.M. the 29th Brigade received orders to withdraw, but not to do so until after dark, at 9:30 P.M. The units made leisurely preparations for the withdrawal, because at the time the enemy had fled the scene. A night withdrawal was not customary in Eighth Army. Usually a daytime withdrawal was preferred, unless circumstances made it impossible. In daytime, aerial and artillery support could greatly facilitate a withdrawal from close contact with the enemy.

At 6 P.M. General Ridgway discussed the situation northwest of Seoul in the I Corps zone with General Milburn and told him that an American unit, not a British one, must be left as rear guard for the corps withdrawal. Milburn agreed.[26] General Kean of the 25th Division designated his 27th Regiment as the rear guard.

There are some discrepancies in the various reports in the official records as to just when the British 29th Brigade received and executed orders to withdraw from its positions south and east of Koyang. The brigade received orders to withdraw, apparently, at 6:00 or 6:30 P.M. and began the withdrawal perhaps as early as 8:30 P.M. or, at the latest, 10 P.M. The discrepancies may have arisen from the fact that not all the units of the brigade could have started at the same time. There necessarily would be a difference between the leading element and the last, or rear guard. They were to withdraw down the narrow mountain valley that ran southwest from their hill positions to the MSR, the Kaesong-Seoul road, a distance of about three or four miles, where they would be about five to six miles from the edge of Seoul. This mountain track seems to be the one that shows on the Korea 1:250,000-scale map of 1950 as running southwest, close beside a mountain stream, from Kyohyon-ni through Sindun-ni to the MSR at Kupabal-li. Kyohyon-ni is situated about four miles east of Koyang.[27]

Lieutenant Colonel Murch's 2nd Battalion, 27th Infantry, had established a roadblock on the MSR at the road junction about five miles northwest of Seoul, where the British and some other UN troops were expected to reach the MSR in their withdrawal. The withdrawal of these troops started at dark and included the 35th Infantry Regiment of the 25th Division, elements of the ROK 11th Regiment, and the British 29th Brigade. The 35th Infantry and the ROK troops and part of the 29th Brigade started coming out in a steady stream just after dark. They passed through

Murch's 2nd Battalion roadblock and then headed for Seoul with no difficulty. The Northumberland Fusiliers and the Gloucestershire Battalion of the brigade also passed through without trouble, as did the forward elements of the Royal Ulster Rifles. Near midnight the stream of withdrawing troops dwindled. Only the Ulster Battalion rear guard remained north of the MSR.[28]

The Ulster Rifles' withdrawal started about 9:30 P.M., and the leading elements made it out without incident down the narrow valley, the road through which was "a narrow track, slippery as glass, between frozen paddyfields." The Support Company, the Battle Patrol, and the tanks of Cooper Force were in the rear of the column. A short distance down the valley mortar and long-range small-arms fire began to fall on the Ulsters, and within a few minutes the column entered an ambush. The night was dark and cold. One of the tank commanders told Rene Cutforth later, "You couldn't see a damn thing through the tank slit, or even if you stood in the turret. We had men on foot showing us the way."[29]

Suddenly, Chinese soldiers swarmed down the slopes and overran the column. Fighting was very confused in the next hour or so, and its details differed, depending on just where one was in the column. It seems that most of the men in the front part of the column eventually escaped in groups. The rear echelon had it hard, and most of the casualties occurred there. One soldier caught in the melee of the initial rush of the Chinese said, "They came down the sides of the gully like a football crowd and some of them were laughing. They laid hold of our legs as we sat on the tanks — you couldn't keep them off, there were too many. They didn't seem to want to kill us when they got close up, but they tried to kill the officers. They dragged drivers out of their trucks by their arms and just took them away, laughing. We must have killed hundreds and hundreds."[30]

Another encounter in this ambush is instructive. Lance Cpl. Edward J. Phillips, apparently of the Ulster Rifles, but certainly a member of the ambushed force, told his story to a news correspondent within a few days after the event.

We were pulling back from our position northeast [northwest] of Seoul when we were attacked. At first everything went according to plan, but shortly after we had gotten under way we ran into mortar fire. As soon as the mortars began firing we heard a lot of whistles. Suddenly, on both sides of the road, hordes of Chinese got out of trenches and advanced on our trucks. Then we realized we were surrounded.

They were on us before we could get at our guns. I don't think it would have done any good if we had shot at them. They seemed like men who had been drugged [there is strong evidence that the Chinese did not drug their soldiers] — they were singing and moving sluggishly. Some of them fingered our clothing and uttered something that sounded like English. They motioned us off our trucks and marched us away.

I guess we went about 200 yards before I saw my chance to escape. I noticed

a hole and stumbled into it unnoticed. I was so relieved that I didn't mind sharing the spot with two dead Koreans I landed on.[31]

The rest of Phillips's story may be summarized. He remained in the
hole for about 20 minutes, when he conceived a bold way to escape from
the area. The Chinese who had captured him wore coats of the same type
he had on. He thought he might make his way through them unnoticed
in the dark, since he would look much like them. He turned up the collar
of his coat and rose slowly from his hiding place. With the light of burning fires aiding him, he passed through the Chinese unmolested and soon
rejoined his unit. It escaped.

In answer to a number of questions at I Corps, Phillips made the following comments: He and others had just gotten in the trucks and were waiting for the starting order when the enemy mortars began firing. Then they
heard whistles, which sounded like platoon leaders' whistles, and could
see tracer fire from their right. Among the Chinese who surrounded their
truck, there were very few small-arms or automatic weapons and no bayonets. Most of the soldiers carried only grenades. These men did not fire
on the trucks. The tracer fire showed that automatic or small-arms fire came
from some distance away. The Chinese soldiers paid no attention to this
or to the mortar fire. They came slowly toward them, walking with a rolling gait and singing and talking; some of the talk sounded like English.
They acted jubilant, gleeful. They climbed on the trucks and fingered the
UN soldiers' clothing with curiosity. They said, "Give up, Tommy?" In
the dark it was hard to estimate their number, but they were shoulder to
shoulder. Their grenades were of the weak concussion type. Phillips said
he had had one of them explode at his feet, but it did not hurt him.

In the chaotic battle the bulk of those in front got out to the MSR and
reached Murch's roadblock, where they got into waiting trucks and rode
on into Seoul. Murch, incidentally, held this roadblock until 5 A.M. on
4 January.

But cut off in the valley northward were some miscellaneous groups:
the Battle Patrol, some machine-gun carriers, a few mortars, a platoon of
C Company, and the tanks of Cooper Force. For them the fighting was
at close quarters. A small village on the road was ablaze. Captain Astley-
Cooper sent a tank to reconnoiter the adjacent stream bed to see if it offered
a better route of travel than the road. Mortar fire killed the tank commander.
Astley-Cooper in his tank moved down the stream bed, engaging enemy
there until his tank lost a track. His crew bailed out and scattered when
they found themselves in the midst of Chinese infantry. The British later
assumed that Astley-Cooper was killed there. The commander of A Echelon
on the main road had radio communication with him in his tank, and the
last message he received said, "It's bloody rough." Whether Astley-Cooper
was killed there may be questioned because a captured enemy document

later commented on this battle, saying that the 446th Regiment of the 149th Division, CCF 50th Army, in the vicinity of Koyang dealt the British 29th Brigade "a grave blow. More than 500 enemy were killed and wounded, and 193, incl a British Tank Bn. CO, were captured. Regt. also captured 35 tanks." This report would indicate that Astley-Cooper was captured.[32]

In this close fight, the Support Company made a bayonet charge, joined in by the tanks of Cooper Force, which resulted in a desperate hand-to-hand fight, in which the British estimated they killed "some 200 of the enemy." The British clubbed rifles when they ran out of ammunition. In this fight the acting commander of the Ulster Rifles, Major Blake, was killed. Several abandoned tanks lay across the road in the burning village, and others were knocked out or had slipped into the ditches. Trucks and other vehicles lay in the road and blocked it. Major Shaw of the Ulsters was able to assemble about 100 men of the battalion, and with three tanks he got through the village, driving the Chinese out, and continued on. A quarter of a mile farther the group came upon another tank, abandoned, that blocked the narrow road. Shaw decided their only recourse now was to destroy their three tanks, which they burned, and then he led his men over the hills to the MSR, where they passed through Murch's battalion lines about midnight.[33]

The British reported later that the Royal Ulster Rifles Battalion casualties were heavy – 230 killed, wounded, and missing; with 20 men and some tanks lost in the Cooper Force (8th Hussars). The Royal Northumberland Fusiliers had lost 50 men earlier, but not in the withdrawal ambush. The number of tanks lost in the withdrawal could not be determined in the course of this research, but it was significant. The figure of 12 Cromwell tanks lost or cut off in the ambush is mentioned frequently in US unit journal messages, especially in the 25th Infantry Division and its unit reports.

At his roadblock on the MSR, Lieutenant Colonel Murch had his first knowledge that a part of the Ulster Rifles had been cut off and were in a desperate plight when three British stragglers came into his E Company roadblock. They reported that the rear guard had been ambushed about a mile away and was trying to fight its way out. The 2nd Battalion S-3 Journal gives the time of the stragglers' arrival as 12:30 A.M. on 4 January. Murch immediately established radio contact with Brigadier Brodie and informed him that he would keep his 2nd Battalion in position at the roadblock as long as there was any possibility that the British rear echelon could get out. At this time the 2nd Battalion flanks were both open, and there were no friendly troops behind him.

Brodie was most appreciative of this offer but thought that nothing could be done to rescue the cut-off British troops, that they would have to fight their way out as best they could. At 3:50 A.M., 4 January, it appeared that the Chinese had closed the trap on those left in the ambush area and that no more would get out. By this time enemy had moved to the MSR in front of the 2nd Battalion. At 4 A.M. at least two companies of them moved down the MSR right into the 2nd Battalion. The battalion's massed automatic fire covering the road to the west cut down and virtually annihilated this enemy column. Artillery fire was called in to interdict the road and vicinity westward. The 2nd Battalion estimated that 400 or more enemy fell in this episode in front of E and G companies of the battalion.[34]

After this fight, the Chinese were free to flank the 2nd Battalion from both sides, to attack its rear, and even possibly to assault it from the front. There appeared to be no possibility that more British stragglers from the 29th Brigade would escape to Murch's position. He requested orders from the 27th Regiment, which instructed him to give up the roadblock and withdraw to Seoul. The 2nd Battalion began this movement at 5 A.M., marching rapidly. E Company formed the battalion's rear guard and was able to break enemy contact about 6 A.M. Trucks met the battalion at the edge of Seoul, where Lt. Col. Gilbert Check's 1st Battalion held a final roadblock, and in them the 2nd Battalion rolled through the deserted streets of Seoul to the Han River bridges.[35]

A report on 4 January added what appeared to be the last information the 25th Division and I Corps had about the British group cut off in the enemy ambush with little or no chance of escaping. This stated that the group included 11 tanks; 40 soldiers of B Company, Royal Ulster Rifles; and 40 men of the Heavy Weapons Company, Ulster Rifles.[36]

At 6:30 A.M., 4 January, General Ridgway learned at Yongdongpo that some elements of the British 29th Brigade, said to number some 30 men and four or five tanks, had been isolated by enemy attack and left behind in the withdrawal. He met immediately with Generals Milburn and Kean and asked for verification of the report. He told them he wanted every effort made to rescue these men. Then at 7:30 he instructed Colonel Unger to contact Brigadier Brodie and tell him the same thing. Ten minutes later he returned to General Milburn and told him it would be a disgrace to the United States forces if those British troops had been left behind.[37]

Later in the day, General Milburn informed General Ridgway that four 155-mm howitzers of the US C Battery, 9th Field Artillery Battalion, that had been supporting the British 29th Brigade and the ROK 11th Regimental units had been lost in the withdrawal. He said the third howitzer in line had skidded on an incline in the road and had blocked the way to the three howitzers behind it. While trying to free the blocking howitzer, CCF had attacked the battery crew members and driven them off. Ridgway wrote a second endorsement on Milburn's memorandum, saying, "Incomplete and unsatisfactory, make full investigation, and report to me."[38]

The Eighth Army Command Report for 4 January states that, at 6:30 A.M., General Milburn was instructed to verify the report of isolated British personnel and to take all possible means to retrieve them, short of losing an equal or greater number in the attempt. These instructions were also given to General Kean, 25th Division. At 7 A.M. Captain Lynch reported that he had obtained a Navy helicopter to assist in the evacuation of any British survivors found.[39]

The 25th Division, G-3 Section Journal, at 6 A.M. on 4 January carried a message that the British 29th Brigade, except for 12 tanks and 40 men that were lost, was south of the Han River. Brigadier Brodie of the brigade was reported to be en route north of the river in an attempt to locate the trapped units. Reports available to him indicated the group had been ambushed and cut off northwest of Sindun-ni, about five miles north of Seoul.[40]

Sometime after 1 A.M., 4 January, Brigadier Brodie came to Colonel Michaelis's 27th Infantry CP on word that some of his brigade had been cut off during its withdrawal. Lieutenant Colonel Murch had just told Colonel Michaelis that his 2nd Battalion and the 3rd Battalion were prepared to try to help extricate the trapped British. Brigadier Brodie told Michaelis that he appreciated beyond expression the gesture on the part of the two battalions but that such things were one of the tragedies of war and that he did not want the 27th Regiment to sacrifice any of its troops to bring out the British. He added that his trapped forces would have to "knock it out for themselves." But at Brodie's request, the I Corps provost marshal quickly provided him with an escort to his Tank Battalion's CP, from which he tried unsuccessfully, apparently at about 6 A.M., to contact his cut-off unit by tank radio.[41]

Meanwhile, after the 29th Brigade had withdrawn south of the Han River, at 8 A.M., 4 January, it reverted to I Corps reserve. The 3rd Battalion, 27th Infantry, at the north end of the bridge, reported the last of the British 29th Brigade cleared its K Company at the edge of Seoul at 4:15 A.M., 4 January. The 2nd Battalion, 27th Infantry, followed the British and cleared K Company and crossed to the south side of the river. K Company then crossed. The 1st Battalion at this time was trying to move from the edge of the city to the bridge.

But Chinese attacked B Company in its position at the northwest edge of Seoul, and only after a series of such attacks did the 1st Battalion reach the pontoon bridge. By this time, K Company had returned to the north end of the bridge to protect the engineers working on dismantling it. It remained there until 2:40 P.M. guarding the engineers, who finished their work on the M4-M4A2 bridge demolition charges ten minutes later.[42]

By 7:15 A.M. all the main units of the army had crossed the M4-M4A2 bridge in I Corps, and the engineers made ready to start its dismantling. But General Ridgway countermanded the order because part of the British 29th Brigade and a reported 12 tanks with it had not yet come through. After General Ridgway's early-morning order to Generals Milburn and Kean and Brigadier Brodie that every effort must be made to rescue the cut-off members of the 29th Brigade only five miles from Seoul, there was hectic activity to determine what could be done. At 7 A.M. a conference was held at the 27th Infantry CP on the MSR, attended by the commanding generals of the 24th and 25th divisions, with Brig. Gen. Palmer representing I Corps. Brigadier Brodie was present and also Colonel Michaelis of the 27th Infantry. Apparently no plan was formulated that gave promise of success in a rescue mission. Another conference was held at 9 A.M. In this meeting Colonel Itschner, the I Corps engineer, made a proposal that the bridge be held intact for an hour longer than agreed upon earlier. It was accepted. That meant the bridge would be held intact until 4 P.M. But at 1:30 P.M. General Ridgway decided the bridge should be demolished at once.[43]

Chinese appeared at the edge of Seoul from the west and northwest before daylight of 4 January and attacked B Company of the 1st Battalion, 27th Infantry, which was blocking in the city on the approaches to the Han River bridges. Artillery fire and air strikes helped B Company hold its position. A little later enemy attacked A and C companies. At 9 A.M. the division ordered the 3rd Battalion to help the 1st Battalion restore security. At 11 A.M., when all other friendly units had cleared Seoul and crossed the river, the 27th Regiment broke enemy contact and crossed the river. Only K Company, as previously stated, returned to the north end of the bridge to protect the engineers in their job of preparing demolitions.[44]

It would appear that, by daylight of 4 January, it was too late to do anything that would help the cut-off British troops. Most of them were already dead, wounded, or captured (and most of the wounded were captured). The Chinese were in control of the MSR from Seoul in the direction of Sindun-ni and Koyang; furthermore, they had reached the edge of Seoul from almost all directions except from the south. General Ridgway felt very badly about the losses in the British 29th Brigade. In an interview with the author some years later, General Ridgway said he felt that it was a disgrace to American arms to allow any other UN troops to be used as withdrawal rear-guard force in the face of the enemy. He reiterated he had made this viewpoint clear to all his commanders after the incident of 3–4 January 1951 northwest of Seoul.[45]

In this particular instance, General Ridgway had already made this point clear to both Generals Milburn and Kean, and the latter had designated the 27th Regiment of his division to be the rear guard along the Munsan-ni–Seoul road in the I Corps withdrawal. And indeed the regiment was the rear guard. Its 2nd Battalion was blocking at the point where the British 29th Brigade, two to three miles north of the MSR, was expected to withdraw safely to the MSR.

But in war the unexpected often happens. This time, a strong Chinese force was able to move undetected behind the British rear echelon and ambush the last units only a mile or two from safety. It must be remembered that Lieutenant Colonel Murch held his position five miles from Seoul in the face of enemy attacks until about 5 A.M. on the morning of 4 January to give the cut-off Ulster Rifles and Cromwell tanks of the 8th Hussars every possible chance to escape. The only known rescue of any British from this enemy ambush after daylight was by helicopter. The one Navy helicopter that was made available to help in any rescue effort made a reconnaissance of the Sindun-ni area and by 1 P.M. had brought out four men from the British brigade, and it returned to get three more.[46]

As early as 14 December 1950, Eighth Army gave I Corps responsibility for all Han River bridges and the MSR from Seoul south to Suwon. When the Eighth Army withdrawal began across the Han River on 2 January, there were three Class-50 military bridges across the Han River at Seoul, and three footbridges built by Korean civilians. The latter were used almost entirely by Korean civilians as a way of escaping from Seoul. They were built of 55-gallon empty gasoline and oil drums and a container known as Navy Cubes. They were an easily demolished form of pontoon bridge, with a makeshift narrow walkway. They were destroyed the morning of 4 January.

The three military bridges in I Corps need a brief description. They were known as the M-2 Treadway floating bridge, the combination M4-M4A2 floating bridge, and the Decked Shoo-fly (railroad) bridge. The US 14th Engineer (C) Battalion had responsibility for the security of these three bridges and was to be prepared to destroy them on orders from Col. Emerson C. Itschner, I Corps Engineers. After the initial order, there was a change during the evacuation of Seoul, and responsibility for the destruction of the Shoo-fly railroad bridge was delegated to the British 55th Field Squadron, Royal Engineers. Colonel Itschner established one-way traffic over the two floating bridges: south over the M-2 bridge, and north over the M4-M4A2 bridge. When the military evacuation began, there was no northbound traffic allowed—it was all southbound.

The Shoo-fly railroad bridge was a trestle of heavy wood decking construction, built as a temporary structure to replace the blown railroad bridge after the UN recapture of Seoul in September; the M-2 bridge was built with rubber pontoons supporting a steel treadway decking; the M4-M4A2 bridge used wood and steel boats as its pontoon-type supports for a wood planking deck. It was the stronger of the two floating bridges.[47]

The first military bridge to be dismantled was the M2 bridge, the farthest west of the three bridges. The 14th Engineer (C) Battalion and the 55th Engineer Treadway Bridge Company dismantled and salvaged its parts, except for a few pontoons that had been pierced by ice. Ice on the Han River was from four to five inches thick at this time. DUKWs (amphibious vehicles) towed the M-2 raft sections of four pontoon and decking sections to the shore, where they were further dismantled. The bridge had been removed by 9:30 in the evening of 2 January.[48]

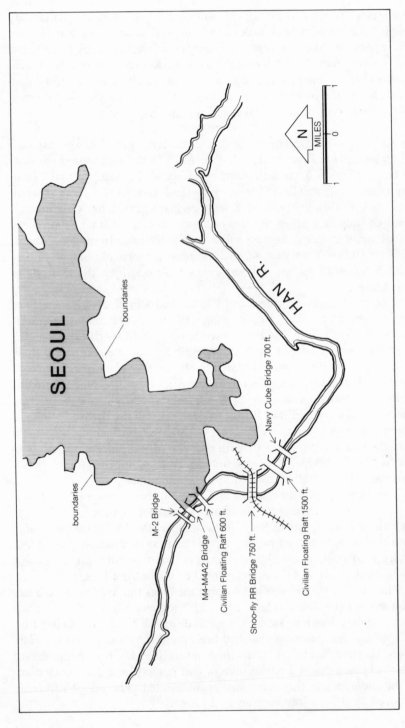

MAP 4. **Han River bridges at Seoul, January 1951**

This pontoon bridge was the last bridge across the Han River to be destroyed on 4 January 1951 after the last UN troops had evacuated Seoul. *National Archives, 111-SC 355547*

Before noting the use and destruction of the two remaining military bridges in I Corps's zone, a few words should be given concerning the IX Corps zone bridges and their use and destruction. In general, the IX Corps completed its crossing of the Han River ahead of I Corps. The IX Corps had a temporary pontoon bridge east of Seoul (called the Al Jolson bridge) that most of its troops used on 3 January, and there was a permanent bridge farther upstream, east of Seoul, that carried a major road to Ichon, south of the Han River, that some of the troops used.

There is some confusion in the various unit reports as to just what happened at the IX Corps bridge east of Seoul, just when all the troops had crossed it, and when it was blown. A briefing for General Ridgway on the morning of 4 January, according to the Eighth Army Command Report of that date, states that the 21st Infantry Regiment had cleared the bridge at midnight 3 January and that only the 19th Regiment was left to clear at 1:14 A.M. on the fourth. The 5th RCT, a covering force, was to cross during the morning in the I Corps zone. It appears, also, that at least part of the British 29th Brigade of IX Corps crossed in the I Corps zone on 4 January.[49]

The 7th Cavalry Regiment covered the withdrawal of the 24th Division to the Han River. The 8th Cavalry was to control the river crossings, and its commander, Lt. Col. Harold K. Johnson, gave the 3rd Battalion responsibility for destroying the bridge when the troops had crossed. According to the 1st Cavalry Division Command Report for January, the 3rd Battalion blew the bridge at 5:30 P.M. on 3 January and then marched on foot over the bridge leading to Ichon.[50]

At 9:35 A.M. on the morning of 4 January, however, Col. Richard W. Stephens, commander of the 21st Infantry Regiment, 24th Division, received information that the bridge had been blown prematurely while troops of his regiment were still crossing it, and men were seen floating in the river, some wounded. The IX Corps Command Report for the day stated simply that all bridges had been destroyed by 7:30 on 4 January.[51]

We now return to the two military bridges that remained in the I Corps zone of Seoul: the Shoo-fly railroad bridge and the M4-M4A2 bridge. The latter was west of, or below, the Shoo-fly bridge, which crossed the river near the partly destroyed permanent railroad bridge crossing the Han River into Seoul. The I Corps traffic-control point for crossing the river was at the south end of the M4-M4A2 bridge.

I Corps traffic officers at both the M4-M4A2 and the Shoo-fly bridges kept a tabulation of the organizations crossing, the number and type of their vehicles, and the time the first and last vehicles of each organization crossed. At 6 A.M. on 4 January 1st Lt. Donald K. Fetig, B Company, 14th Engineer (C) Battalion, reported for duty as traffic control officer at the Shoo-fly bridge. He checked units of the 24th Division (that had not crossed the IX Corps bridge) as they crossed the bridge at 9:30 A.M. Some units of the 1st Cavalry Division followed. The British brigades followed the 5th RCT. The last unit to cross the Shoo-fly bridge from Seoul was the Argyll Battalion of the British 27th Brigade. At noon the order was given to blow the bridge, which the 55th British Royal Engineers accomplished between 12:30 and 1 P.M. The plan had been that it would be the last one to be destroyed.[52]

At 7 A.M. that morning B and C companies, 14th Engineer (C) Battalion, had stood by at the M4-M4A2 bridge downstream from the Shoo-fly bridge to dismantle it. They chopped ice from between the boats and pontoons to free the sections. Tidal waters reached as high up the Han as Seoul, and as a result the ice was rough and irregular at many places, including at this bridge. They also removed cables, curbs, guide rails, and markers. But General Ridgway ordered that work should go no further, as he hoped the cut-off British tanks and 29th Brigade personnel north of Seoul might still be rescued, and they would need a bridge to cross the Han. A rescue force was never sent, however, and it was only at 11 A.M. that work began in earnest for the removal and salvage of the bridge. The engineer work force was given until 1 P.M. to complete their work. Chinese elements were beginning to appear in Seoul. Colonel Itschner, I Corps engineer, requested, as 1 P.M. approached, that he be given another hour to do the work. It was granted. But at 1:30, Eighth Army ordered the salvage work to cease, when it was only half finished, and the rest of the bridge to be demolished. At 3:05 P.M. everything seemed to be in order to blow the bridge, and the lieutenant in charge set off the explosives. But some of the charges had frozen, and the bridge was only partially destroyed. New explosives around the south abutment were recharged and the bridge blown a second time at 3:40 P.M. This time the job was completed, and the last bridge over the Han was down.[53]

At 12:10 P.M. 4 January the I Corps Headquarters closed at Yongdongpo and opened at Suwon, about 20 miles south of the Han River and Seoul.[54] General Ridgway joined the I Corps CP at 3:30 that afternoon.

Everywhere on the approaches to Seoul the Chinese followed closely the withdrawing rear guards of Eighth Army. On the northwest sector along the Munsan-ni–Seoul highway, where the 27th Infantry Regiment was blocking for the 25th Division and the British 29th Brigade, the 1st Battalion, 27th Infantry, had several holding engagements with Chinese units in the western part of the city, before and after daylight of 4 January. At 8 A.M. B Company fought off an enemy attack of an estimated two companies. An hour later A Company repulsed another enemy attack a little farther into the city. At 10:45 A.M., when the battalion was ordered to withdraw, A Company found dead and wounded Chinese in the stream bed in front of it. At 11 A.M. Chinese units attacked elements of the blocking 27th Regiment only two miles west of the Korean capitol building.[55] Air strikes during the morning reportedly killed several hundred enemy troops on the western edge of Seoul. At 10 A.M. aerial observation reported an estimated 200 enemy in mixed clothing entering the city from the west.

Perhaps the symbolically most significant enemy event that occurred in Seoul on 4 January was the arrival of an enemy platoon of 25 men at the Seoul City Hall about 1 P.M., where it raised the North Korean flag. A patrol from the ROK 1st Division into the city observed this event. An aerial observer also witnessed it.[56]

During the afternoon of 4 January there were several reports of enemy patrols entering the city, and enemy units were at the edge of the city on the west, north, and northeast. The CCF 39th Army was the main enemy force driving into the city from the north. The CCF 50th Army was on the immediate west and northwest of the city, and some of its elements followed the US 27th Infantry Regiment into the western part of the city.

The 50th Army's main role was to occupy the area west of the city. A Chinese three-man patrol crossed the river in the late afternoon, but withdrew at 8:45 P.M. under ROK 1st Division fire.

At 2 P.M., 4 January, K Company, 27th Infantry, guarding the engineers of the 14th Engineer (C) Battalion in their final minutes of work on demolition charges to blow the M4-M4A2 bridge, withdrew to the south bank of the Han. It seems to have been the last tactical army unit to leave Seoul and the north bank of the river.[57]

The story of the third fall of Seoul requires a few words about the scene in the city as all kinds of traffic, including civilian refugees, filled the streets leading to the M4-M4A2 bridge on the night of 3 January. A member of the 502nd Reconnaissance Platoon, the commanding general's guard at Eighth Army Headquarters at the University of Seoul, was in the mass of traffic that had lined up to get to the bridge. Cpl. Randle M. Hurst gives some idea of what it seemed like to him. The army headquarters had already left, and by evening the university area was deserted. At evening he and Barns, another member of his platoon, pulled out of the compound and got in the line of vehicles headed for the bridge.

Korean civilians were going past, carrying all their possessions on their backs or on carts. We saw one old woman being transported in a wheelbarrow. A youth was pushing the wheelbarrow, and the family was following. . . . We finally started to move. We did not move far. After three or four hundred feet we stopped and sat and sat. There was more and more movement of civilians and we did not see any ROKNP [ROK National Police]. It soon dawned on me that the only law and order now prevailing in Seoul was right where we were. . . . The rifle section was supposed to be behind the two M-24 tanks, and that was where we were. . . . Our jeep was the very last vehicle in the procession.

As dusk approached, people began building bonfires. Soon, we moved up to a bonfire. About this time some curious British vehicles caught up with us and attached themselves to our convoy. . . . They made hot tea at this bonfire and offered us some. Barns and I were on a hot cocoa jag in those days, and so we stuck to hot cocoa. . . .

When dark settled in, and we were still a long way from that pontoon bridge [the M4-M4A2] across the Han, another truck towing a 105 mm howitzer, manned entirely by blacks, caught up with us and got in behind the British tank. I do not recall what outfit they were from. I heard somewhere that their outfit had already crossed the Han, and they were all AWOL. . . . They stood around the bonfire with us, visiting and joking with the British. We were all enjoying the experience.

Slowly we moved from bonfire to bonfire. Duckworth [1st Lt. in command of the 502nd Reconnaissance Platoon] came back and told us not to let anyone pass the rear end of the convoy because people were cutting in ahead, making the line longer, and that we were not across the river yet.

To carry out this order, we uncovered our machine gun and I stood in the middle of the street with my rifle and tried not to let people pass. I had little luck until the British and blacks teamed up and parked the artillery truck alongside

the British tank. This effectively blocked the street. Civilian traffic piled up behind us. . . . Very pathetic. In fact, dreadful. . . . After crossing the bridge, our whole
convoy speeded up. The road south, one of the few paved roads in Korea, not
paved far, of course, was amazingly free of refugees.[58]

Some of the British and Australian war correspondents wrote afterward
of their experiences in the evacuation of Seoul during the night of 3–4
January. Ronald Monson, an Australian war correspondent, wrote:

When I left Seoul at 4 A.M. [4 January] the vast empty city was like a city of the
dead with flames that were devouring its heart turning it into a vast funeral pyre.
Fires were raging in all quarters of the city, but the biggest was burning just opposite the Chosen Hotel—headquarters of the United Nations Commission until
the previous afternoon. Now the hotel was empty. The last United Nations delegate had left for the south feeling that all the high hopes of creating a United Republic of Korea had gone up in the smoke wreathing the city even then. . . .
   Down in the streets looters were busy. Men with bursting packs on their backs
and guns or sticks in their hands slunk down side streets like alley cats or roamed
freely through shops and houses. Here and there along the way to the Han River
bridge a group of citizens crouched helplessly over one of their number too old
or too sick to travel. Once a woman, with an old man dead by her side, lifted her
arms in a dumb appeal to the passing column. "She stood extended like a crucifix
for a moment," wrote Cutworth, "before she let them drop to her sides with a smack
of finality." All that night refugee fires twinkled along the Han where the yellow
sand crunched with ice crystals and the dark waters froze into a sheet of green ice.[59]

In Monson's group when it left Seoul, Rene Cutworth, of the BBC,
wrote on the morning of the fourth after he had reached the south bank
of the Han:

On the far bank, Seoul towered up above the embankment in tip-tilted terraces.
There were ice crystals on them, too, and all along the embankment down river
from the pontoon bridge, a gaily coloured multitude swarmed along the edge of
the ice. They crossed it in families, the women staggering on the slippery ice, losing their bundles, falling down, peering wildly around for their children whose
hands had been snatched from theirs in some skid or fall. Some families pushed
handcarts of household belongings and half a dozen bullocks had been urged on
the ice. Two of them lay where they had fallen near my side of the river, with
their legs broken, bellowing dismally. The peasant who stood over them rained
shattering kick after kick into their ribs. A little girl, lost, stood on the ice five
yards out of the column, a small bundle on her head, her hands clasped across
her ribs, and gave scream after scream of terror, but the column shuffled past her
in silence. And then the dreadful sounds of the bullocks and the little girl faded
into insignificance as a great brazen voice began to speak from the sky. It was the
loud-speaker aeroplane, used for propaganda over enemy territory, and it had been
brought up to try to persuade the refugees to stay where they were, to stay in Seoul
and not to cross the river; for, not far south of the city now, the roads were impassable for the press of people.[60]

While the UN forces were evacuating Seoul and withdrawing south across the Han River, the Inchon tidal basin locks were destroyed to render the ship basin unusable to the Chinese and North Koreans. The plan for the destruction of these shipping facilities had been prepared earlier and issued as an instruction letter on 12 December 1950 by the 3rd Logistical Command.

1st Lt. Frank C. Casillas was the operations officer of the 50th Engineer Port Construction Company, and the information on the details of the plan came from his records and recollections.[61] The locks and tidal basin at Inchon were initially developed by Japan in the early 1900s. The entrance to the basin was 750 feet long and 40 feet deep. The lock chamber measured 450 feet by 60 feet. There was 14 feet of water at mean low tide. All walls were of masonry construction. The water depth in the chamber was controlled by two pairs of electrically operated steel gates, normally opened on rising tide at 23 feet and closed on receding tide at the same water elevation. Shipping could be released from the basin at any point in the tidal range that would accommodate the draft of a particular vessel.

Approximately at 1 P.M., 4 January 1951, Capt. Gordon L. Eastwood, commanding officer of the 50th Engineer Port Construction Company, received verbal orders from Lt. Col. E. O. Davis, 3rd Logistical Command, to carry out the demolition plan of the Inchon port facilities as given in the instruction letter of the 3rd Logistical Command headquarters, 12 December 1950. The principal items in the destruction plan were (1) tidal locks; (2) three 100-octane gasoline storage tanks, each of 100,000-barrel capacity; (3) two jet fuel tanks on the south side of the basin; and (4) the marshaling railroad yards in the vicinity of the basin.

Three demolition teams were organized to do the work. Team No. 1 was composed of one officer (Lieutenant Casillas) and 11 enlisted men to destroy the locks; Team No. 2 had 15 enlisted men to destroy the fuel tanks; and Team No. 3 had 15 men to destroy the rail frogs, switches, and locomotives in the marshaling yards.

Beginning at 3 P.M. on 4 January, First Lieutenant Casillas and his team of 11 men began placing explosives on the lock gates. They placed 100 pounds of TNT between the two turnbuckles of each gate, 70 pounds next to each anchor hinge pin, 50 pounds on each main bull gear next to the activation strut pin, and 50 pounds next to each ball-gear pinion section. The charges were primed with detonating cord and fired simultaneously with nonelectric blasting caps. The back gate was destroyed at 6 P.M. The demolition teams and four vehicles were taken aboard the USS *Lt. Bedoin*, standing in the harbor off Wolmi-do Island, and at 4:30 A.M., 5 January, the entire engineer company sailed for Pusan.

The utter futility of this destruction became apparent a month later. On 6 February 1951, the 2nd Logistical Command ordered Captain Eastwood of the 50th Engineer Port Construction Company to prepare plans for the rehabilitation of the Inchon locks – a tremendous task in terms of cost, technical labor, and time involved. The port facilities of the locks and holding basin were lost for Eighth Army use for nine months into the future once Ridgway got the army headed north again.[62]

The Chinese XIII Army Group spent the next three days, 5–7 January, moving up to the Han River, occupying Seoul, and sending elements of two divisions, the 149th and 150th of the 50th Army, across to the south side of the Han River to occupy some critical hills and positions there as an outpost line protecting them from the south. They always gave 7 January as the date when their 3rd Phase Offensive ended. The plan of that offensive, therefore, was to capture Seoul and drive the Eighth Army south of the Han. It should be borne in mind, however, that the 3rd Phase Offensive encompassed only their own troops and did not include the various efforts of North Korean troops in the central corridor and eastward of the Iron Triangle area. Those efforts assumed major proportions and continued throughout the month of January. We will pick up that action with the next chapter. The 3rd Phase Offensive was a tremendous success for the Chinese, and the weeks immediately following it marked perhaps the lowest point reached at any time by the UN forces in Korea.

Had the enemy forces been able to continue their attack south of the Han in full force following the capture of Seoul, they probably could have driven the UN back to the Pusan perimeter, and possibly out of Korea. But the Chinese were in no condition to continue a pursuit operation after their capture of Seoul. As usual with the Chinese after a major operation, even one lasting only a few days, they needed time to reorganize, and especially to prepare logistically for further offensive action. Resupply of food and ammunition was always a major undertaking for a large Chinese force, even after a decisive victory. And, too, the Chinese never moved into a new offensive without careful planning and reconnaissance of their enemy's positions and intelligence of UN intentions and preparations. In this instance, the Chinese did not pursue Eighth Army south of the Han River. That gave the army a chance to get out of immediate reach of the Chinese in the western part of Korea, to get its breath, and to calm down from another humiliating defeat. Most important, it gave General Ridgway a chance to get hold of the army and to gain some control over it, and gradually to change its mood and morale.

From Chinese sources, there is evidence that the commander of the Chinese Volunteer Forces, Peng Dehuai, ordered his forces to halt pursuit on the south side of the Han River after the fall of Seoul. A recent translation of a Chinese document published in *Kunlun,* the magazine of the Chinese People's Liberation Army, reflects what are thought to be Peng's views at this time. Peng had just moved into his new headquarters near Pyongyang (in Kunja-ri), in a stone cave that was entered through a wooden plank building that connected to the cave entrance. Here he received a telephone report that the Chinese ambassador to Korea had just arrived with Soviet ambassador Raguliev, who wanted to talk with Peng about the war situation. Shortly after 7 January 1951, the two ambassadors climbed the hill to Peng's command post, followed by an interpreter. Raguliev told Peng they had just received important information that "the Americans are prepared to completely withdraw following our retaking of Seoul." Peng replied, "I don't believe it. It's unreliable." Raguliev replied that it was "an indisputable fact that the enemy wavered along the entire line. . . . The enemy is now faced with an overall situation of total collapse. The Korean War can be over in one go at it. I can't understand why the Volunteers suddenly stopped their pursuit and aren't taking any action at the 37th Parallel."[63]

Peng's interpreter answered,

Concerning the matter of halting the pursuit, the commander carefully studied it over with us then made up his mind. The following are some of the reasons: First, the Volunteers have conducted three campaigns, one right after the other, since entering Korea, and have not had rest, reorganization, and replenishment. The troops are exhausted. Second, supplies are quite difficult. A large number of motor vehicles have been destroyed by bombing, and food and ammunition cannot be supplied. And third, perhaps the most important reason, if we continue pursuit, the supply lines are bound to become longer and supplies will become more difficult. The enemy could use the narrow, long terrain of Korea and his sea and air superiority to land in our rear at any time and that is extremely dangerous.

Peng continued, "What's more, the enemy is absolutely not going to make any overall withdrawal. This is a false impression that is to lure us southward. I, Peng Dehuai, am not MacArthur. I will not be taken in by this!"

This view of Peng's stopping the Chinese attack in the 3rd Phase Offensive is supported by a Chinese biography of Peng published in volume 3 of *Biographies of PLA Generals*. In section VI of this biography, relating to the Korean War, the statement is made,

After the Chinese and Korean forces followed up the victory and liberated Seoul on January 4, 1951, they crossed the Han River on the 5th and advanced to the 37th Parallel's Suwon, Chungju, and other areas. He [Peng] then on January 7 resolutely ordered the various units to stop their pursuit.

There were some comrades at the time, however, who believed that after the enemy had received three heavy blows from us, that he had been destroyed and was no longer an army and that he would flee at the sight of an oncoming force. They actively advocated taking advantage of the victory to pursue, to press on to the finish without letup, to drive the U.S. Army into the sea and liberate all Korea. Peng Dehuai believed that even though the enemy had suffered three heavy blows from us, his main force had still not been seriously damaged and moreover his followup forces were still very strong. The Volunteers, after going through three campaigns, were having serious difficulties with troops and material. He rejected their views because of this.

General Ridgway's first objective was to establish Eighth Army in what he thought was a strong defensive position on a series of hills, beginning west of Pyongtaek, 40 air miles south of Seoul and the Han River, astride the main highway and railroad running up from Pusan, the only port now in his possession, and continuing the defensive positions, known as Line D, in a continuous line running northeast to Wonju in the central corridor. At the time, there was nothing resembling a defensive line eastward from Wonju to the coast. But there were a large number of rehabilitated North Korean divisions there that were trying to break through scattered ROK divisions and the US 2nd Infantry Division, newly arrived in the Wonju area. Whether the Chinese XIII Army Group, or other new Chinese formations, would renew attack against Eighth Army in the west below the Han River was unknown.

On 5 January, with his Eighth Army now south of the Han River, General Ridgway ordered Operational Plan 20 into effect. At noon all army units were to withdraw to Line D, sometimes called the Pyongtaek line, because the army's left flank was anchored at that South Korean town astride the MSR and rail line that ran the length of Korea. For the immediate future, however, I Corps was to hold Suwon in order to evacuate extensive supplies held there and at the airfield. Ridgway also ordered the Eighth Army staff to study plans concerning the possible evacuation of Korea, including timetables, tonnage, shipping required, and many other factors. At the same time, he ordered General Church of the 24th Division to send the assistant division commander, Brigadier General Davidson, back south to resume work on the Raider Line, a perimeter defense line for Pusan, stretching across the southern tip of the peninsula from Masan on the southwest to Samnangjin on the Naktong River, 20 air miles north of Pusan. Ridgway discussed with Davidson what he wanted in the way of special defenses, including certain terrain features to be included in the line and the construction of lateral roads south of the line. Fortunately, after three weeks, Ridgway judged the crisis had passed, and he recalled Davidson to the 24th Division.[64]

General Ridgway at this time also brought another US infantry division into Eighth Army. The 3rd Infantry Division, formerly a part of General Almond's X Corps, was attached on 4 January to Milburn's I Corps and ordered to take defensive positions at once on Line D. It went into the army line east of Pyongtaek, in the Ansong area, with the British 29th Brigade on its left and the ROK 1st Division on its right. It started patrolling on 5 January.[65]

In Suwon the I Corps advance found an estimated 100,000 Korean civilian refugees blocking the rail yards. The huge mob prevented trains

US and ROK troops ride a tank of the 89th Tank Battalion through throngs of refugees retreating from Seoul on 5 January 1951, during the CCF 3rd Phase Offensive. *US Army photograph, SC 355570*

from moving. Korean police dispersed the refugees and, acting under Eighth Army orders, directed them away from the MSR to roads leading into the southwestern Korean provinces, away from the old Pusan perimeter area. The Korean police were empowered to use force of arms if necessary. The policy was rigorously followed and was successful in the days that followed. Meanwhile great crowds of Korean refugees gathered at Taegu and Pusan, farther south. Taegu was estimated to have 140,000 at this time, and Pusan 275,000.[66]

In the withdrawal from Seoul, Eighth Army major units went into Line D in much the same relationship to each other they had held in the defense line above Seoul. I Corps held the army left flank, and IX Corps was on its right, eastward. On 5 January the main function of IX Corps was to protect I Corps on its east from possible interference in the evacuation of supplies from Suwon. The ROK 6th Division performed this function at Suwon, and farther east the 187th Airborne RCT near Ichon performed the same function for the ROK 6th Division.[67]

Enemy patrols had crossed the Han River in a few places near Kimpo airfield and Yongdongpo during the night, and aerial observers reported two large enemy convoys moving south from Uijongbu, north of the river. One of the patrols reported four enemy antitank guns in position on the northeast outskirts of Seoul firing before dawn into former UN positions on the south side of the river. Aerial observers reported there were an estimated two enemy battalions at Kimpo airfield at 11 A.M., and other groups were moving south from there. Air strikes at noon hit these and other enemy groups in that vicinity with reported heavy enemy casualties. The ROK 6th Division I&R Platoon reported seeing an estimated 16,000 Chinese on the north side of the Han River, and two companies of them south of the river. UN planes strafed Chinese troops in the streets of Seoul and hit other enemy forces just northwest of the city. In Seoul two city blocks were on fire. A massive strike of 65 B-29s hit Pyongyang, the North Korean capital, and its rail yards. But during the day Chinese forces continued to enter Seoul, and some of them took up positions along the north bank of the Han River. The Eighth Army on the south side had no contact with them on 5 January.[68]

On 6 January, Ambassador Muccio sent to the secretary of state in Washington two messages that President Syngman Rhee asked him to dispatch in his behalf to the president of the United States about the situation in Korea. In one Rhee discussed the withdrawal from Seoul to Suwon and said he feared the worst if it continued. He asked for more arms for the South Koreans and asked that General MacArthur be authorized to use any weapon, including the atomic bomb. In the second message, Ambassador Muccio sent a copy of a letter that President Rhee had sent to General MacArthur the day before, 5 January. In the letter, Rhee had said that 250,000 trained South Koreans were now ready for service, better than those then at the front if given a rifle. He continued, "Another thing I want to suggest is that 50,000 or more of the Chinese Nationalist Army be allowed to land in Korea to join with the UN forces at once. I think that will be of great help at present. If you hesitate to request General Chiang Kai-shek directly, [I] will do so. Kindly let me know."[69]

General Ridgway discussed these communications with Ambassador Muccio. He did not favor use of the atomic bomb and did not seem to know for sure whether the nearest available atomic bomb was on Okinawa, Guam, or back in the United States. He stated later to Col. John M. Blair, USA, however, that if the Soviet Union had come into the war, there were plans to mine Vladivostok harbor.[70]

During the night of 5–6 January the Chinese crossed the Han River in regimental strength with tanks east of Yongdongpo. Their patrols had moved as far south as Anyang-ni by midnight. By that time part of the Chinese force, about seven miles below Seoul, had engaged elements of the ROK 11th Regiment, which was covering the south side of the Han

behind I Corps. This contact lasted until 2 P.M., when the Chinese withdrew and dug in just beyond artillery range. There were other reports of
enemy groups south of the Han on the sixth. Korean civilians reported
that from 5,000 to 6,000 Chinese had crossed the river during the night.[71]

All morning of 6 January, work was hectic to clear Suwon of supplies
and to prepare some facilities for demolition. The 27th Regiment of the
25th Division continued to form the 25th Division rear guard and, together
with the ROK 11th Regiment, constituted the rear guard for the I Corps
withdrawal. F Company, with a platoon of tanks, remained in Suwon to
protect the engineers while they completed their demolition work. When
the Chinese broke contact with them, the ROK 11th Regiment withdrew
south and cleared Suwon at 7 P.M. The Advance CP of the 25th Division
reached Chonan, 36 road miles south of Suwon, at 8 P.M., and the rest
of the division followed during the night. Suwon was evacuated during
the day.[72]

The first village south of Suwon was Osan, near which the first engagement of US troops with North Koreans had occurred at the beginning of
the war. Here the MSR crossed the Chinwi River on a 280-foot-long, two-
lane, four-span, concrete bridge. There must have been a failure to get information of the change in bridge destruction policy to the 65th Engineer
Combat Battalion, because it blew this bridge during the day. Four weeks
later the army needed that bridge. Lt. Sam Starobin, S-2 of the engineer
battalion, said of that event, "We believed we were withdrawing from Korea
and we did thorough work on our demolition."[73]

In the rail yards at Suwon during the day, there was a bad accident.
A southbound freight train had masses of refugees hanging on to its sides,
car tops, and on the engine. This train ran into the rear of a stationary
ROK hospital train loaded with wounded. The last car of the hospital train
was demolished, and the next car split into halves. Many Korean refugees
and ROK soldiers were killed or injured. The 25th Division surgeon sent
the Clearing Company of the Medical Battalion to the scene to give all
assistance possible.[74]

Evacuation of supplies from Suwon was completed in the afternoon of
6 January. Both I and IX corps then moved rapidly into Defense Line D.
Both the 27th and 29th British brigades were already there, as were parts
of the US 3rd and 24th divisions. For all practical purposes the Eighth
Army was in or ready to go into Line D by the end of 7 January. This
position could be called a line only from Pyongtaek on the west to Wonju
on the northeast. It crossed to the north side of the Han River some miles
south of Yoju. From its junction with the Pukhan River about 20 air miles
east of Seoul, the upper reaches of the Han River bent sharply to the
southeast into the Taebaek Mountains. From Wonju eastward to the coast
only a jagged series of ROK divisions offered any semblance to a defense
position. Enemy forces were able to penetrate these positions at will, and

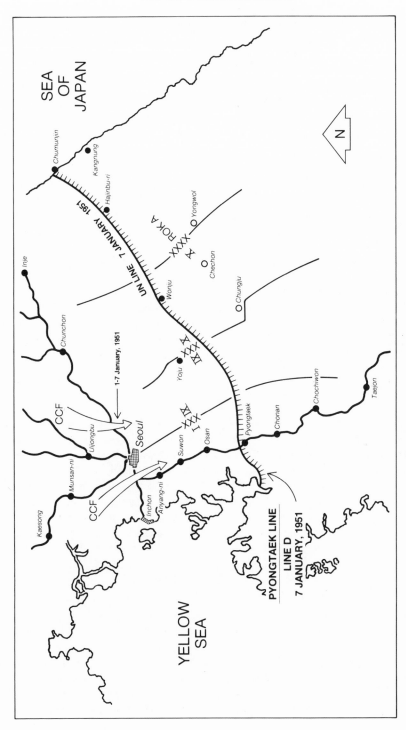

MAP 5. UN line south of Seoul and the Han River, 7 January 1951, at end of CCF 3rd Phase Offensive

as a result there was widespread enemy guerrilla action far south of the Wonju area. Only the recently arrived US 2nd Division at Wonju offered any real defense to the central mountain corridor, and a battle for control of Wonju in the X Corps area was in progress at the time I and IX corps of Eighth Army went into their Line D defense positions.[75]

General Milburn established his I Corps headquarters CP at Chonan, on the MSR, 15 miles south of Pyongtaek. The 25th Division also had its CP there as the main I Corps reserve force. General Coulter put his IX Corps CP at Chungju, about 15 miles southeast of the 24th Division on Line D, and almost due south of Wonju. General Almond had his X Corps CP there also, and this proximity gave the two corps commanders the opportunity to coordinate their future actions in the central corridor, which the IX Corps now bordered on the west. Chungju was an important road junction point, and it also was situated on the big bend of the upper Han River, where it turned sharply, from a generally southwestern flow from its source in the high Taebaek Range, not far from the east coast, to the northwest. The IX Corps CP now was 50 air miles from the I Corps CP, a drastic change in their geographical relationship. From Chungju, high mountain terrain spread eastward to the coast and the Sea of Japan.

General Ridgway had a very small group that stayed with him as an adjunct to the I Corps CP at Chonan. Ridgway did not go to the main Eighth Army CP at Taegu. He considered his situation with I Corps at Chonan as temporary. He felt that a battle CP does not belong in a city distant from the front, that such an arrangement tended to separate the command staff from the troops, making it all but impossible to establish confidence and mutual respect, which are essential factors in military success. He had with him, he has said, his two aides, Col. Walter Winton and Joe Dale, an orderly, a driver for his personal jeep, and a driver and operator for his radio jeep. He had, of course, access to all of I Corps communication equipment. He later wrote: "Knew it was no source of joy or comfort to General Milburn of the I Corps to have the Army Commander under foot at all times; but I felt as a stopgap arrangement it was best for my small group to camp and bivouac with his forward CP. And he was patient and generous with us."[76]

Enemy patrols reached Suwon during the morning of 7 January, several groups of company strength being seen by ROK 1st Division patrols. In the afternoon other ROK patrols north of Line D found Chinese reconnaissance groups up to company strength in the vicinity of Kumyangjang, a road center 12 miles east of Suwon. There was no sign, however, of any enemy pursuit south of the Han River.[77]

A lieutenant of the ROK 6th Division who had been a prisoner of the Chinese for several weeks and had escaped to his division reported that the Chinese to whom he had talked while a prisoner were confident, that they did not fear use of the atomic bomb, that they thought it would not be used because of American fear that the Soviets would retaliate. They also thought that, if they had tanks, planes, and a better food supply, they could quickly drive to complete victory, but they were badly handicapped by lack of these weapons and poor food. This same ROK officer said he had learned that the Chinese could not have moved at night effectively over mountain trails without local guides.[78]

We know that General Ridgway was displeased with the performance of Eighth Army in the CCF 3rd Phase Offensive, which forced the evacuation of Seoul and drove the UN forces south of the Han River. It became apparent early in the Chinese attack that the army was not going to make a fight of it. With his arrival as its commander only five days before the Chinese attack, he had no chance to get control of the army, change its already-formed opinion that it was on the way out of Korea, or make any changes in command of major units or of their disposition in the Imjin River defense line. His extreme displeasure with the army's performance was conveyed to his corps commanders on 7 January, when the army had reached Line D. His message read:

Reports so far reaching me indicate your forces withdrew to D line without evidence of having inflicted any substantial losses on enemy and without material delay. In fact, some major units are reported as having broken contact. I desire prompt confirming reports and if substantially correct, the reason for non-compliance with my directives. From here on, the enemy has but two alternatives; (A) a time-consuming coordinated advance offering us minimum opportunities for inflicting punishment, but at least giving us much time, or; (B) an uncoordinated rapid follow-up, perhaps even pursuit. The former permits accomplishment of part of our mission and the latter, unlimited opportunity for accomplishing all of it. I shall expect utmost exploitation of every opportunity in accordance with my basic directive.[79]

In the depth of his despair at the situation at the end of the first week of January 1951 in Korea, General Ridgway wrote on 8 January his most revealing comments of the period in a personal letter to Gen. J. Lawton Collins, Army chief of staff, in Washington.

During daylight of the first day following the hostile attack [1 January] my instructions were not complied with.

That night I repeated them in person and during the next daylight period both Corps, at my insistence, made an effort, but in my opinion, an inadequate one.

Again and again I personally instructed both Corps commanders to so conduct their withdrawal as to leave strong forces so positioned as to permit powerful counterattacks with armored and infantry teams during each daylight period, withdrawing those forces about dark as necessary.

These orders, too, failed of execution.

The next step was to point out to Corps C/Gs, which I did yesterday, that the CCF 4th Field Army . . . had two alternatives, (1) time consuming coordinated follow-up (2) uncoordinated follow-up — pursuit. Former, achieve maximum delay, latter, opportunities for severe punishment.

There is a marked absence of vaunted American Resourcefulness. [Ridgway said the army clung to creature comforts, was carried around by truck, and therefore stuck to roads.] Our infantry has largely lost the capabilities of their honored forefathers in American Military annals. They no longer even think of operating on foot away from their transportation and heavy equipment. *You and Wayne* [Mark W. Clark] *insist on attainment, by general officers of combat commands, of the highest standards of our military traditions.*

We have dropped far back on the military scale from the standards of our Civil War troops. The finest of our past infantry leaders must shudder in their graves, if their all seeing gaze now takes in the battlefield performance of some of their descendants.

I would say, let's go! Let's wake up the American people, lest it be too late. Let's pour on the heat in our training and, above all, let's be ruthless with our general officers if they fail to measure up.[80]

This was the period when the spirit of Americans was perhaps at its nadir in Korea. Most persons in the army thought it was on its way out of Korea. The letters and messages from MacArthur and the JCS reflect it. On 7 January, General MacArthur wrote to General Ridgway, "No use of chemicals in case of evacuation. Prohibition complete and drastic." The next day Ridgway informed MacArthur that Syngman Rhee and the ROK officials believed the UN was going to evacuate Korea and that a very dangerous atmosphere was developing. Already MacArthur had given his staff instruction to continue plans for the evacuation of Korea. His operations officer, General Wright, had asked Rear Adm. Arleigh A. Burke, the deputy chief of staff, US Navy, Far East, for advice, since the evacuation would be largely a Navy task. Burke, on 7 January, replied to Wright on the problems involved, saying that the evacuation from Pusan would be far more difficult than that from Hungnam and that advance plans should be pressed to completion. He also said the division that would hold the beachhead while the evacuation was under way should be designated, and he advised that it should be the 1st Marine Division. No division was designated immediately, however, and by the time another week had passed, General Wright formed the judgment that the Eighth Army could hold on in Korea.[81]

Mention was made earlier that President Rhee desired to have the United States arm more Korean divisions for the war and that Ambassador Muccio, at Rhee's request, had forwarded his proposals to the secretary of state. This subject had been under consideration in the Joint Chiefs of Staff and also in MacArthur's Far East Command for some time. In the crisis of defeat in Korea that now beset the UN forces, the Joint Chiefs of Staff on 4 January sent a message to General MacArthur tabulating the state of its weapons stockpile that might be used to comply with Syngman Rhee's request in part and asked for his recommendations. The JCS message said in part:

The problem of arming additional ROK manpower is under consideration. Fol info is furnished:

a. No machine guns, mortars, antitank guns or arty can be made available from the ZI [Zone of Interior, or the United States]; however, the fol can be made av in a reasonably short time: (1) 160,000 model 1903 rifles, with a backup of spare parts for 50,000. (2) 70,000 M3 submachine guns. (3) 150,000 M1 carbines. (4) 8,000 model Browning automatic rifles.

b. Ammo supply for the M3 submachine guns, the Browning auto rifles, 100,000 model 1903 rifles and 100,000 M1 carbines is feasible.

2. Based on av of above weapons it appears that ROK forces could be increased fr 200,000 to 300,000 men armed with rifles, auto rifles, carbines, and submachine guns. However, unless used in part to form new divs, which would be rel ineff due to lack of inf supporting weapons and arty, it is probable that only on the order of 75,000 can be eff utilized initially, with an ult buildup to approx 100,000 in the fol type organizations:

a. Augment the rifle str of ROK div and other UN forces.

b. For spec units for guarding lines of comm and for opns against communist guerrillas.

c. Conduct guerrilla opns in Communist-held territory.

3. . . . Arms should be issued only to org units under the control and discipline of the mil authorities in Korea.

4. Req your comments and rec to incl:

a. Total no of additional ROK personnel that can be profitably employed.

b. Method of employment, namely, new divs, additional str. in current divs, et cet.

c. Length of time req to org and train additional manpower.

d. Other points in connection with current problems.[82]

Two days later General MacArthur replied to the JCS dispatch. He said:

1. Considered here that influence of past and possible future events is of importance equal to or greater than material available in analyzing problem of arming additional ROK manpower.

2. Continued effort has been made since 25 June 50 to effect the most practicable utilization of Korean pers. In add to materially augmenting the ROK Army, members of the Youth Corps and other qualified males have been supplied with significant quantities of small arms for the purpose of strengthening police units, anti-guerrilla sec elements and creation of spec-organizations to operate in en held territory. Despite the relatively large number of non-army pers now under arms, en guerrilla units continue to operate effectively in many widely scattered regions of South Korea. Friendly guerrilla forces, however, have accomplished little in Communist rear areas – primarily due to lack of strong willed leadership.

3. In the combat areas withdrawal of UN forces, incl the curr retrograde movement from the Seoul vic, has been due in most instances to the inability of ROK units to maintain the integrity of their assigned sectors. This failure has been repeated in sit involving either NK or Chinese forces and, whenever determined en pressure is encountered, appears to have equal application to ROK divisions closely integrated in US corps zones as well as those operating directly under ROK

Army control. In consequence it now appears that any possibility of checking the en may be dependent upon the establishment of a defensive psn of such proportions that US divisions can be deployed in depth in mutually supporting locations. . . .

[Paragraph 4 says in effect that better use of the weapons available could be made to increase the security of Japan rather than arming additional ROK forces.]

5. In view of the past accomplishments of ROK armed forces, the probable restricted size of the battle field in which we may operate in the near future, and the high priority of NPRJ [Japan National Police] requirements, the value of attempting to organize train and arm additional ROK forces in the immediate future appears questionable. It is considered that the short range requirement can best be met by utilizing manpower to replace losses in existing ROK units rather than creating new organizations. The long range req for or desirability of arming additional ROK pers appears to be dependent primarily upon determination of the future US mil psn with respect to both the Korean campaign and the generally critical situation in the Far East.[83]

The position General MacArthur stated about putting more weapons in the hands of relatively untrained new ROK formations, without proven officer leadership, continued to be a bone of contention between Syngman Rhee's government and the Eighth Army and the Far East Command as the war continued. In too many cases it was a means of conveying American military equipment and supplies to the enemy, when the ROKs broke under enemy attack and abandoned their equipment.

By the end of the CCF 3rd Phase Offensive on 7 January 1951, enough information, part of it based on captured enemy weapons, had been accumulated by the UN command in Korea to know the type of weapons, other than handguns, that the North Korean and Chinese armies had used as

TABLE 4. **North Korean and CCF Support Weapons, 6 January 1951**

Weapon	Model	Max. Effective Range (yards)
76-mm antitank gun	1942	14,300
76-mm howitzer	1927	9,350
76-mm mountain gun	1938	11,049
82-mm mortar	1943	3,390
120-mm mortar	1943	6,562
122-mm howitzer	1938	12,900
122-mm gun	1931/1937	22,755
US 60-mm mortar		2,017
US 81-mm mortar (light ammo.)		3,290
US 81-mm mortar (heavy ammo.)		2,596
US 4.2-inch mortar		4,357

Source: Eighth Army Comd. Rpt. Intelligence Sec., 6 January 1951.

support weapons. This was important information and was summarized by the Intelligence Section for the Army chief of staff on 6 January 1951.[84] (See table 4.)

With the CCF 3rd Phase Offensive at an end and no sign of a projected Chinese pursuit of Eighth Army in the immediate future, Chinese screening forces of the 50th Army halted about 18 miles south of the Han River, in the vicinity of Suwon, which they held, as Eighth Army went into its Pyongtaek Defense Line D, 20 miles farther south. There was no contact between the two forces.

This lull in the battles in the west of Korea offers a good opportunity to turn to the central corridor and the eastern mountains, where large forces of newly reconstituted North Korean units were making a determined bid to brush aside the weak and ineffective ROK units hastily assembled there and to make an enveloping movement around the right flank of Eighth Army and penetrate deep into South Korea, possibly even to Taegu, threatening Pusan. Wonju was the focal point of the battles there. What happened in the central corridor at this time was crucial to all the UN forces in Korea and would determine whether Eighth Army in the west could long stay in its Defense Line D.

5

The Fight for the Central Corridor

ON 1 JANUARY 1951, as the CCF 3rd Phase Offensive opened in the west, the central corridor of Korea through the Taebaek Mountain Range lay open as a military prize of the first order. The side that could seize it first might find it decisive in the future course of the war. The situation reminded one of the dictum of Nathan Bedford Forrest, the Confederate general from Tennessee in the American Civil War who won fame as a raiding cavalry leader. He tried "to git thar fust with the mostest." The next two weeks in the central corridor saw that dictum as a test between North Korean forces on the one hand and a few untested ROK divisions and the US 2nd Infantry Division on the other.

The understrength North Korean divisions of the newly rehabilitated NK II and V corps moved south from near the border to seize control of the central corridor while it could be had for the taking. At the same time, the UN comand became aware of the threat and tried to get enough military strength there to contest control of the corridor. It would be disastrous to allow the enemy to move large forces south through it and get behind Eighth Army in the west. The only force the UN command had to move to the central corridor was three poorly trained and understrength ROK divisions, the 2nd, the 5th, and the 8th. When one or more of them broke at the first enemy contact, Eighth Army rushed the US 2nd Division to Wonju, a key crossroads point in the corridor.

For General Ridgway it was a touch-and-go situation. He ordered Gen. Edward M. ("Ned") Almond, X Corps commander, to hurry north to take command of the ROK divisions in the corridor and the US 2nd Infantry Division, which had just arrived there from Eighth Army reserve at Yongdongpo, where it had been taking in replacements and reequipping. For General Almond it was to be a test of his leadership and generalship. On the outcome rested no less than the decision whether the UN could remain in Korea. The fight for the central corridor demanded a decisive and aggressive commander. In Almond it had one.

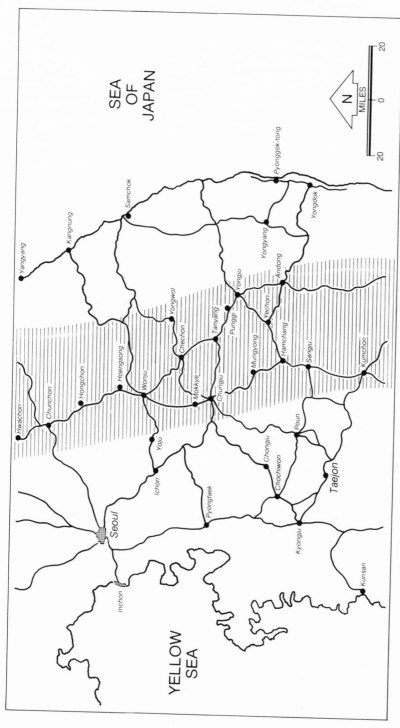

MAP 6. **Central corridor, January 1951**

Before the US 2nd Division reached the Wonju area, the ROK 2nd, 5th, 7th, and 8th divisions were scattered about in the Chunchon and Hongchon area, north of Wonju. The North Koreans split open the ROK 8th Division and all but destroyed it. They then had a clear run over the mountain trails deep into the south by a route that ran east of Wonju. Thousands of them had penetrated as far as 80 miles south of Wonju by this eastern route, while several of their sister units concentrated north of Wonju to mount an attack on it.

As a preliminary to such an attack, however, a North Korean division had established a regimental-sized roadblock between Hongchon and Hoengsong, which cut off virtually all South Korean troops in the area. The first task the 2nd Division had on its arrival at Wonju was to eliminate this enemy roadblock south of Hongchon so that the cut-off ROK troops could escape south. The 23rd and 38th regiments of the 2nd Division accomplished this mission at the end of December, destroying a North Korean division in the process.

General Ridgway considered Wonju the key to the central route, and he wanted General Almond to hold it and to make it the anchor on which the IX Corps of Eighth Army on Line D, running east from Pyongtaek, would be able to tie in with the X Corps and, it was hoped, in time to form a continuous UN line on the east coast. Wonju was the junction point of five main roads in this part of Korea; one ran north to Chunchon, another northwest to Seoul and Suwon, another to Kangnung on the east coast, and another south to Taegu and hence on to Pusan. The last, and perhaps the most important, ran southeast through Chechon, Tanyang, and Andong, to Pusan. The rail line from Pusan north to Wonju followed the latter route; after passing through Wonju, it continued on northwest to Seoul.

The North Korean forces were organized into two corps, the II and the V, for their planned attack. The II Corps was to penetrate deep behind the UN line, cut the X Corps line of communications and disrupt transport in the Chechon-Tanyang-Andong-Taegu area. This corps was to avoid major combat in its movement through and around the UN forward positions. The V Corps, on the other hand, was to constitute the assault force that would attack the UN forces in the Wonju area frontally along the Hongchon-Hoengsong-Wonju axis and force their withdrawal from Wonju at the same time the North Korean II Corps was cutting up the rear areas.

The NK III Corps may have been considered as a reserve or replacement pool for the II and V corps. It was known to be in the vicinity of Inje during most of January, although some elements of it may have been northeast of Wonju in support of the V Corps for a period. Generally, at least, it seems to have played no active role in the fight for Wonju and the penetrations into the US X Corps rear areas.[1] The strengths estimated in table 5 show that all the NK divisions were far understrength, some equivalent to only a regiment.

TABLE 5. **North Korean Troop Strength, 1 January 1951**

Corps	Division	Estimated Strength
II	2nd	2,800
	9th	3,300
	10th	3,500
	31st	4,600
Subtotal		14,200
III	1st	5,500
	3rd	4,800
	5th	5,000
Subtotal		15,300
V	4th	4,500
	6th	5,750
	7th	3,250
	12th	3,750
	27th	3,750
	38th	5,000
	43rd	3,000
	3rd Brigade	3,000
Subtotal		32,000
Total		61,500

Source: Eighth Army Comd. Rpt., January 1951.

At the end of January the NK II Corps was estimated to number only about 8,000 men; the NK V Corps about 20,000 men; and the NK III Corps was estimated to have increased to number from 22,000 to 24,000 men. During the month the NK II Corps was decimated in the mountain areas east and southeast of Wonju in their guerrilla-type operations, while the NK V Corps suffered crippling casualties in its attacks along the Wonju axis.[2]

Another factor influenced the initial performance of the 2nd Infantry Division and X Corps in their defense of Wonju during the first two weeks of January. Only three weeks after General Walker relieved Maj. Gen. Laurence Keiser from command of the 2nd Infantry Division in early December 1950, replacing him with Maj. Gen. Robert B. McClure, the new commander found himself suddenly sent with his division to the snowy, icy, mountainous area of Wonju. Now the 2nd Division was a part of X Corps. Not only did it have a new commander, but it was under a new corps and corps commander. And, of course, since 26 December it was also under a new army commander as well. The relationship between General Almond, the X Corps commander, and General McClure did not start off auspiciously. On 31 December 1950, Almond, accompanied by Lt. Col. William J. McCaffrey, deputy chief of staff, and Lt. Col. John H. Chiles, G-3, X Corps, left Suwon airfield at 1:35 P.M. in a snowstorm for General McClure's CP at Wonju. The 2nd Division was dispirited, Almond learned, and McClure was not sure how it would perform in combat.[3]

Upon request, Lieutenant General McCaffrey gave a full account of what transpired in the meeting with General McClure that day. He said that, when he bent over a situation map, studying it with McClure, he detected a strong whiskey breath on him. Almond ordered McClure to get his division together and to remove from it the miscellaneous ROK units that were interspersed in it, as they could not be counted on in a crisis and their presence might cause the sacrifice of some of the division's troops. The conversation between McClure and Almond became heated on this subject. Almond finally gave McClure a peremptory order to separate the ROKs from the 2nd Division American units, and to do it that day. The hour was late, and there was little time left for it.

When Almond returned to his CP, he asked McCaffrey to remain behind with McClure, and he told McClure to ask McCaffrey if there were any questions. Later in the evening, McClure told McCaffrey he could not separate the ROKs from the division that night and asked for the latter's approval. McCaffrey refused. McClure took no action concerning the ROKs that night. When he learned of the episode, Almond was displeased, but did nothing.[4]

During McClure's first days at Wonju, rail and truck transport was unable to bring up supplies for the division. At this time the 21st Troop Carrier Squadron C-47s landed 115 tons of cargo at Wonju's icy airstrip, and the 314th Troop Carrier Group C-119s dropped 460 tons.[5] In a conversation at the Wonju CP on 3 January, McClure told Almond he feared the 2nd Division was open to having its supply route cut by North Koreans from the east. Almond replied that he agreed, and he was having the 7th Infantry Divison move into position to prevent it.[6]

Almond visited the 2nd Division almost daily in early January. His X Corps Advance CP was now at Chungju, 30 air miles south of Wonju. Almond seems to have made it his CP beginning on 6 January. Chungju was also General Coulter's IX Corps headquarters. The boundary between IX Corps and X Corps ran on a north-south line at the edge of Chungju. Locating the IX and X corps CPs at the same place, at the western edge of the Taebaek Mountains, made for good cooperation between Coulter and Almond. At this time there were a bewildering number of X Corps CPs. The Main CP was still at Kyongju, the Advance CP was established at Chungju at 6 P.M. on 2 January, and at that time X Corps assumed operational control of the 2nd Infantry Division. On 7 January the corps established a Rear CP at Andong, which was in charge of antiguerrilla operations in the corps rear areas. It was almost as active and important in the X Corps operations as the Advance CP.[7]

The 7th Infantry Division's CP was now at Kyongju, but it would soon move north as the division was put into the X Corps line. The 17th Regiment, less one battalion, was the first of the 7th Division's regiments to enter the line. It closed on Chechon 1 January, southeast of the 2nd Division. The rest of the division rapidly followed it to that area, with the mission of helping to deal with the large number of North Koreans that had bypassed the Wonju area.[8]

The first important action of the US 2nd Division in the central corridor took place on 1–2 January near Changbong-ni. There Lt. Col. Charles F. Kane's 3rd Battalion, 23rd Infantry, attacked the North Korean roadblock six miles south of Hongchon. Lt. Col. James W. Edwards's 2nd Battalion attacked it a little later from the left (west) flank. The two battalions received heavy air and artillery support, and by midafternoon 2 January they had reopened the road. They held the path open for the ROK 5th and 8th divisions of the ROK II Corps to withdraw south. All day of 3 January masses of these ROK troops passed down the road. The US 2nd Division position now formed a salient, jutting north out of the lines, because ROK troops had withdrawn from both sides of it. Supply at this time was a critical problem, and airdrops had to be made. About one out of every five of the 55-gallon drums of gasoline burst open on hitting the frozen ground.[9]

Even though the 23rd Infantry had cleared the roadblock south of Hongchon by 2:15 P.M. on 2 January, it still was heavily engaged in the area, where an estimated 400 to 600 North Koreans still fought stubbornly in the mountainous terrain. On the second, in clearing this roadblock, Sfc. Junior D. Edwards, of E Company, 2nd Battalion, won the Congressional Medal of Honor, Posthumously. He destroyed two enemy machine guns in repeated grenade attacks on them and was mortally wounded in destroying the second gun and its crew. His action enabled his platoon to hold its strongpoint.[10]

At noon on 3 January the X Corps assumed operational control of the ROK 2nd Division. The division was down to almost no effective strength, not more than one or two battalions. Two of its regiments had been cut off and dispersed or destroyed by Chinese north of the Han River at Yangpyong on the right flank of IX Corps. For the present at least, the division did not add much strength to the X Corps, which now had three ROK divisions under its control—the 2nd, 5th, and 8th. The US 2nd Division itself was far understrength at 14,433 men, 3,800 below authorized strength. Nevertheless, the 2nd Division, in response to an inquiry, said it did not want more ROK troops attached to it, as their combat performance was poor unless they were given three to six months of basic training and unless the ROK officers and noncommissioned officers with them spoke English. Furthermore, the ROK officers enforced discipline often in brutal fashion. They might keep kicking an enlisted man in the shins while upbraiding him about some minor transgression, or strike him in the chest with the butt of a rifle, or beat him over the head and the body with a thick piece of wood.[11]

In a letter on 2 January to General Almond, General Ridgway again expressed his disappointment in the caliber of soldiers in Eighth Army. He said in part, "We still have far to go to attain the standards of toughness of body and soul of American troops, who, as you so well remember, in each of several Civil War battles, with fewer men engaged than we now have in line, suffered in a few hours double the number of casualties that this command has had in six months of fighting."[12]

The North Korean forces were moving south in great force from Chunchon on 3 January toward the Hongchon-Wonju area for a major battle with X Corps. An intelligence agent who traveled south from Chunchon toward Hongchon on the third encountered an enemy packtrain of horses carrying ammunition and food. The agent estimated the packtrain to consist of 6,000 horses. When the train halted for the night at 11 P.M., the horses were not unloaded but stood nose to tail all night long with their straw-camouflaged loads. The Chinese provided local security during the night for the packtrain from three-man foxholes, one soldier in each on alert at all times. The next morning after the packtrain had started to move on toward Hongchon, an American F-80 plane flew over the column at 9 A.M. As the plane approached, all soldiers walking alongside the horses, one to a horse, dropped to the ground behind each horse and held one of its back legs. The horse column remained perfectly quiet as the plane passed. From a height, the line of horses had the appearance of a fence line or of a straw-covered trail. Other groups and columns of enemy soldiers were observed on the move over mountains and in valleys. They disregarded roads.[13]

By 3 January word also came in to X Corps that the ROK 9th Division, in the ROK III Corps area east of it in the high mountains toward the coast, had been cut to pieces but that the American KMAG advisor was trying to reorganize the 2nd Battalion of the 28th Regiment. The 28th Regimental commander and most of his officers were reported killed. The location of the 30th Regiment was not known. This area in the mountains from the Wonju corridor to the east coast was all but terrain incognito. About all that was known of it was that large enemy forces were moving around the X Corps Line D to the corps rear areas and would try to cut off all transport and communications to the Wonju front. On 3 January word came that an enemy force had established a roadblock between Tanyang and Punggi, cutting both the railroad and the MSR. Tanyang was 35 air miles southeast of Wonju. Such deep penetration not only seriously threatened the X Corps, but it also made I and IX corps of Eighth Army uneasy because, by swinging farther west in the rear areas, the North Korean II Corps could threaten their supply lines. The NK 10th Division was the most aggressive and successful of all the NK II Corps in its guerrilla and combat record in the UN rear areas in January. It reached as far as the outskirts of Andong.[14]

Things were getting worse by the day in the central corridor as the North Koreans pressed south toward Wonju. On 4 January the 38th Regiment of the US 2nd Division, holding a blocking position north of Hoengsong, reported the ROK 5th Regiment was retreating through its position. (X Corps had authorized the 38th Infantry to let the ROKs through.) The weather had been extremely cold, going down to 25 degrees below zero. Many of these retreating ROKs had frozen feet.[15]

With the situation east of Wonju already critical, where the NK II Corps was bypassing the 2nd Division and large numbers of North Koreans were approaching frontally from Chunchon, IX Corps moved the 3rd Infantry Division and the 187th Airborne RCT to the Ichon front in a blocking mission to protect the Wonju area from the west, and at the same time protect the IX Corps area against a North Korean penetration from the northeast. East and southeast of the US 2nd Division, the US 7th Division and the ROK Capital, 3rd, and 7th divisions in the eastern mountains tried to intercept elements of the NK II Corps and prevent their further movements into the X Corps rear.[16]

In the fighting near Changbong-ni on 2 January, when the 3rd and 2nd battalions, 23rd Infantry, broke the enemy roadblock that had cut off the ROK divisions northward near Hongchon, North Korean prisoners taken said they were surprised to find they were fighting American troops. They claimed to have had no knowledge that the US 2nd Division had arrived in the Wonju area.[17]

After the 5th and 8th ROK divisions had escaped south from the Hongchon area, the 23rd Infantry withdrew to Hoengsong, which the 38th Regiment of the 2nd Division had held in support of the 23rd Regiment ahead of it. C Company of the 38th Infantry was in a roadblock six miles north of Hoengsong. At 5:30 A.M. on 5 January, well before dawn, a North Korean force estimated to number 300 to 500 men hit and overran it. The North Koreans turned the captured mortars on the Americans. Artillery fire helped to drive the enemy force away, but by 1 P.M. that afternoon only one officer and ten enlisted men of C Company could be accounted for.[18]

Air reports during the day stated that the area southeast of Hoengsong was alive with enemy troops, possibly as many as 15,000, and that all villages there were filled with supplies. A UN supply train from the south arrived at Wonju during the day, a week late, and brought rations and petroleum products. Military units were instructed to draw and carry with them all the gasoline they could carry. The Hoengsong-Wonju-Chungju MSR was clogged with thousands of refugees moving south. At 9 A.M. X Corps ordered the 2nd Division to withdraw to Line D. In accordance with this order the 23rd and 38th regiments withdrew to Wonju and blew all bridges north of Hoengsong. The 3rd Battalion, 38th Infantry, was the last out of Hoengsong. The 9th Infantry Regiment of the 2nd Division held a defensive position between Hoengsong and Wonju while this withdrawal was in progress, and then it, with a battalion of the 23rd Infantry attached, moved on division order nine miles southeast of Wonju on the Chechon road, where it was to coordinate with the 17th Regiment of the US 7th Division in attacking enemy in that area. This withdrawal left the 2nd Division with only two regiments, minus, for the defense of Wonju.[19]

The division, not expecting to hold Wonju, began evacuating supplies from it. General Almond, however, hoped to control Wonju by occupying the hills to the north and northeast of it.

Throughout 6 January, the 2nd Division held a horseshoe-shaped perimeter defense line around Wonju. A regimental boundary between the 23rd Infantry and the 38th Infantry ran generally north-south on the east side of the Wonju River, which divided the town. The 38th Infantry was on the east side of the boundary; the 23rd Infantry was to the west of it. The MSR from the north entered Wonju in the 23rd Infantry sector. The 2nd Battalion, 38th Infantry, was on the northeast tip of the inverted U-shaped perimeter; the 3rd Battalion was at the southeast corner of the curve; and the 1st Battalion, in reserve, was at the bottom of the curve, directly south of Wonju. The 2nd Battalion, 23rd Infantry, was at the northwest tip of the inverted U and covered the MSR from the north. The French Battalion, attached to the 23rd Infantry Regiment, was in an arc on a hill southwest of it, and the 3rd Battalion, 23rd Infantry, was at the southwest corner of the curve. The 2nd Division CP left Wonju during the day and reestablished itself about five miles south of the town. The 37th and 38th field artillery battalions supported the two regiments from firing positions two miles south of Wonju.

General McClure had decided that he would withdraw the 2nd Division from Wonju the next day and establish a defense line on high ground three to five miles south and southwest of Wonju. Colonel Freeman, commanding the 23rd Infantry, agreed with him that the open terrain in the immediate vicinity of Wonju was not suitable for a good defensive position and that it would be best to take the division to the hills and place it astride the road there to Chungju.

The MSR from Hoengsong and the north divided just south of Wonju, the eastern fork going to Chechon, the western fork going to Chungju. The division held the perimeter described above on the night of 6–7 January.[20]

North Korean soldiers started infiltrating Wonju about 2:30 A.M., 7 January, and continued until daylight, when perhaps a battalion of them may have been scattered throughout the town. It was a loose and poorly coordinated operation. It seemed to have had no precise objective in the town,

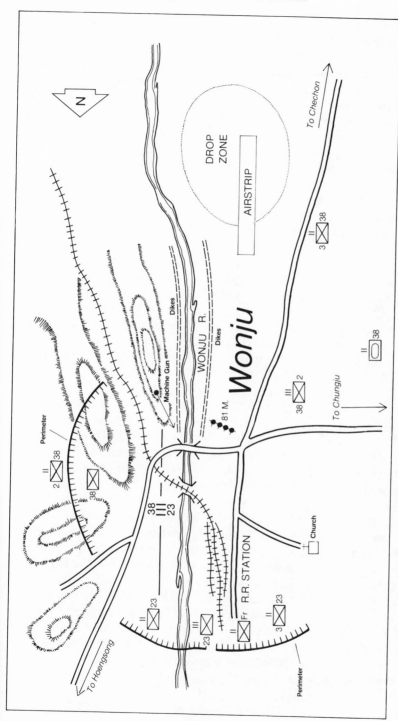

MAP 7. UN positions at Wonju, 6–7 January 1951

and the scattered enemy acted or reacted to situations entirely on their own on the spur of the moment. Apparently the presence of the enemy was first detected by outpost elements of G Company, 23rd Infantry. This outpost was under orders to withdraw without engaging the enemy. When they undertook to do this, they found other enemy between them and the town. They then moved laterally behind the OPLR to avoid these enemy. In this movement they were hit by friendly artillery fire and had three men killed and five wounded. They left behind a recoilless rifle. During the night several small groups of North Koreans were repulsed at different points in and around Wonju.[21]

Later, there was a controversy between Colonel Freeman, whose 2nd Battalion, 23rd Infantry, troops covered the road entering Wonju from the north, and Colonel Peploe, whose 38th Infantry, 2nd and 3rd battalions, were on the east and south of the road and south of Wonju. Freeman said the North Koreans did not come down the road into Wonju. Peploe said at least some large columns of them came down the road and passed 23rd Infantry positions without being fired on. He said prisoners related that they marched down the road in a column right into Wonju.[22] Some elements of the 2nd Battalion, 38th Infantry, on the east side of the road said they saw an estimated battalion of troops whom they thought were ROKs, marching two or three abreast down the road from Hoengsong, and did not fire on them. This column apparently had already passed the 23rd Infantry OPLR.[23]

At early light, riflemen of G Company, 38th Infantry, saw two platoons of Koreans, wearing US Army fatigues and moving in tactical squad formation, coming from the Wonju airstrip, which was on the southeast side of Wonju, toward the 3rd Battalion, 38th Infantry, CP. They heard some of this group shout, "Don't shoot, GIs," and one rifleman said they passed within 60 yards of him. This group increased its pace to a run as it neared a draw about 300 yards from the 3rd Battalion CP. From the draw these enemy started firing on the CP.

At this time, Lt. Col. Harold V. Maixner, 3rd Battalion commander, saw two companies ford the Wonju River and cross the field between the airfield and the battalion CP. Some of these enemy wore white parkas and were hard to recognize against the snowy background in the faint early morning light. They took shelter in a ditch along the side of the airfield and placed mortar and machine-gun fire on the CP area. Maixner ordered I Company, which was in reserve, to form a defense perimeter around the 3rd Battalion CP. From this position, I Company fired on and pinned down a force of from 100 to 200 enemy in the rice paddies only 50 to 100 yards east of the CP. Other 38th Infantry moved to surround this group of enemy, who surrendered at 7:30 A.M. Captain Debrook, 3rd Battalion S-2, said 77 North Koreans surrendered.[24]

The enemy force in the draw fought on until about 8:15 A.M., when the surviving soldiers there fled to the hills north of Wonju. I Company estimated there were 35 enemy killed, 25 wounded, and 25 taken prisoner. The 3rd Battalion in all this action lost only one man killed and six wounded.

In the town itself during the night, the S-2 of the 2nd Battalion, 38th Infantry, and a small wire crew in two jeeps were ambushed at the road and railroad underpass at the east edge of Wonju. They abandoned their jeeps and escaped. Later, at 4 A.M., a flare lighted the road and stream area at the bridge site and revealed two platoons of enemy coming down the Wonju River bed, one platoon on the dike path, and the other below near the stream. At 5 A.M. another flare apparently signaled, "Attack!" The 81-mm Mortar Platoon of H Company, 38th Infantry, located between the Wonju River and the MSR west of the river and slightly south of the bridge where the Hoengsong MSR entered Wonju, withdrew now to the 2nd Battalion, 38th Infantry, CP.

At 4 A.M. enemy had surrounded the E Company, 38th Infantry, outpost, which did not see or hear a signal to withdraw. Of the 36 men there, 12 made it back to the company CP. F Company, 38th Infantry, moving toward the railroad underpass on the east side of town to reduce the enemy roadblock there, saw 30 North Koreans coming from Wonju cross the bridge. The company opened fire, killing 11 of them and driving the rest back into town. A North Korean platoon now attacked from the underpass. An M16 quad-50, of the 82nd AAA AW Battalion, helped squash this attack. The North Korean platoon fled north, leaving nine dead behind. It was said that Lt. Col. James Edwards, commander of the 2nd Battalion, 23rd Infantry, from the porch of his CP in Wonju killed a North Korean soldier with .45 pistol about 5:30 A.M. But there was no group attack on his CP.[25]

The best estimate one can make suggests that the North Koreans infiltrated about a battalion into Wonju before daylight, and at least another enemy battalion fought at the defense perimeter. Most of those who entered the town seem to have done so by following the bed of the Wonju River, although at least one column came down the Hoengsong MSR. They entered the town generally where the railroad and the MSR crossed the Wonju River to the west side. They achieved surprise but did not exploit it. They were in dispersed groups, which were defeated and driven off in detail soon after daylight, with scattered remnants encountered thereafter, most of them trying to escape northward. The North Koreans never had control of the town, nor did they drive off any of the major units of the 23rd and 38th regiments and the French Battalion that formed the Wonju perimeter.

In such a case, why did not the 2nd Division continue to defend its perimeter at Wonju? The answer to that question seems to be that General McClure had already decided he could not defend Wonju and had given orders to withdraw from it on the seventh.

In order to carry out its orders in this decision, the 3rd Platoon, C Company, 2nd Engineer Combat Battalion, at 7 A.M. on 7 January started to prepare for its demolition work when the division withdrew from Wonju. Lt. William H. Champion commanded the 3rd Platoon. He and his 41 men were in support of the 38th Infantry. On the night of 6–7 January, they occupied the second floor of a concrete building in Wonju that was the 38th Infantry CP. At 5 A.M. on the seventh Champion and his men were awakened and told that an estimated three battalions of enemy had infiltrated the regimental perimeter and had entered Wonju. The men quickly got up and went to their foxholes outside the building. The weather was cold, a stiff wind was blowing, and snow covered the ground. They heard occasional firing and saw a few flares and tracers in the darkness, but when daylight came about 7 A.M., nothing had happened close to them in the two hours they spent in the foxholes. At 7 A.M. Lieutenant Champion and his crew of four demolition men loaded explosives in a jeep, and a ¾-ton truck was made ready with other demolition materials. First, he intended to prepare the railroad bridge for blowing. He did not get far from the CP when an enemy machine gun, located on higher ground about 150 yards to the east, opened fire on the road, and bullets hit ahead of him. The crew stopped and drove the jeep and truck under cover and then got into a ditch. From there they soon saw a rifle company of the 38th Infantry making a sweep through the town and joined it. The company split off a part that went after the enemy machine gun, and in a few minutes they had silenced it. Lieutenant Champion and his crew walked through Wonju with the rifle company, while their drivers brought the two vehicles along behind at a safe distance. In this sweep the riflemen killed several enemy soldiers. They then set up a machine gun near the highway bridge and fired at the huts on the other (east) side of the river. Champion and his crew, under the covering fire of the machine gun, carried their demolition charges to the bridge and began preparing them.[26]

Lieutenant Champion's mission in getting ready for the 2nd Division's planned evacuation from Wonju later in the day included preparing the destruction of the highway and railroad bridges across the Wonju River, 16 railroad cars of ammunition and small-arms supplies in the railroad yards (about 80 tons altogether), and about two tons of small-arms ammunition and Korean rifles in a church building on a hill west of Wonju. The 38th Infantry riflemen took their machine gun and left after about 15 minutes, when there seemed to be no danger to Champion and his crew. About 20 minutes later Champion saw five or six North Koreans walking single file along the river bank from the southwest. They apparently were trying to get back north to safety. The soldier in front had a burp gun, but the others had no small arms. The lead soldier was within 40 feet of the bridge. Champion, who had gone to an observation point to watch for enemy while his men worked, now without any security, shouted a warning to his men.

At this, the lead North Korean, instead of using his burp gun, reached into his shirt for a grenade. Champion could not fire on him for fear of hitting his own men. But one of the demolition crew at the bridge killed the lead North Korean. The rest scattered behind a river dike. Other enemy soldiers farther back joined the lead group there, and a firefight with the engineers at the bridge started. Some of the engineers left their places behind the bridge piers and succeeded in getting to a flanking position from which they could fire on the North Koreans behind the dike. After a short time they killed nine enemy soldiers there and took three others prisoner. The engineers then returned to the highway bridge and finished placing their demolition charges.[27]

Preparing the railroad bridge for demolition was a bit more difficult. It had about ten piers, the second and third of which were of wood and log cribbing; the rest were of concrete. They placed heavy charges on the first log-cribbing pier and on the first concrete pier, with a charge on top of the track between the piers. They also secreted a five-gallon can of gasoline in the cribbing of the third pier for emergency use. This work had been completed by 7:50 A.M. The engineers then went to the railroad station, arriving there at 8 o'clock. There the job was to wire the 16 cars loaded with 155-mm, 105-mm, and 75-mm artillery shells and small-arms ammunition. It was 10:30 when this job was completed. Champion then took his crew back to the CP. From there he took his demolition crew to the church west of town to prepare it. Upon arriving there he found the charges already set. He checked them for completeness and returned to the CP.

During Champion's trip to the church, the S-3 of the 1st Battalion, 38th Infantry, ordered Master Sergeant Grupe to take a squad of soldiers to the airstrip to destroy housing, gasoline, and other supplies there. At the airstrip Grupe found 200 drums of gasoline that had recently been air-dropped, 20 cases of rifle ammunition, and about 12 cases of rations. The squad shot tracer bullets into the drums of gasoline. The gasoline burned down to the levels of the rifle fire holes, and then the rest exploded. The cases of small-arms ammunition were piled around one of the drums of gasoline and the heat from the burning gasoline exploded them. The squad set fire to three or four buildings, and their job was done. They carried the C rations back to the 38th Infantry. Upon returning from the church the engineers mined the CP building. It was planned that the demolitions would all be set off at 6 P.M. that evening. The 38th Infantry had cleared Wonju of enemy by 10 A.M., and for the rest of the day the town was secure.[28]

At 4:30 in the afternoon, General Almond at his X Corps headquarters in Chungju received a telephone call from General McClure requesting permission to blow up all the ammunition in Wonju that could not be moved. Almond gave his approval. Then the two generals discussed McClure's plan for withdrawing the 2nd Infantry Division from Wonju.

Almond approved the withdrawal only on the condition that it be no farther than the first high ground south of the town (this was the series of
hills about three to five miles south of the town).[29] It should be mentioned
that, during the day, North Koreans south of Wonju succeeded in ambushing a train loaded with 150 tons of rice and carrying two artillery pieces
and some ammunition.[30]

The 2nd Division withdrawal began in an orderly way and with no enemy
opposition or harassment early in the afternoon, several hours in fact before General McClure telephoned General Almond about it. It seems clear
from the withdrawal time and subsequent events that McClure had made
up his own mind about it, and where he would stop, prior to his conversation on the subject with Almond.

The French Battalion led the withdrawal from the Wonju perimeter,
starting at 1 P.M. The 3rd Battalion, 38th Infantry, followed at 2 P.M.; the
2nd Battalion, 23rd Infantry, left at 3 P.M.; and the 1st Battalion, 38th Infantry, left at 4 P.M. Research for this book could not determine the departure time of the 3rd Battalion, 23rd Infantry. The 2nd Battalion, 38th
Infantry, was the last to leave Wonju at dark and later. The Netherlands
Battalion, attached to the 38th Infantry, was in position about a mile south
of Wonju and from there covered the division withdrawal by fire. The 38th
Field Artillery Battalion, in a firing position south of Wonju, also covered the withdrawal. The H Company mortar platoon, 38th Infantry, fired
a basic load on the hills northeast of Wonju during the withdrawal from
within the perimeter.

The bridges were to be blown at 6 P.M., but the last of the troops of
the 38th Infantry had not cleared the highway bridge and the town by then,
and that demolition had to be deferred. The authority to destroy the bridges
was then delegated to Lieutenant Colonel Skeldon, the 2nd Battalion, 38th
Infantry, commander. Things began to be hectic in Wonju when the S-3
of the 1st Battalion, 38th Infantry, informed the engineers that North Koreans had begun to infiltrate Wonju again at 5:30, or just about dark.

Lieutenant Champion had told the C Platoon of engineers to withdraw
with the 38th Infantry command group. Only Sergeant Johnson and he
would remain behind to set off the demolitions on Lieutenant Colonel
Skeldon's order, which came just before 7 P.M. It was now completely
dark. Skeldon and his driver went with Champion and Johnson to the highway bridge to make sure the area was free of friendly troops. He stopped
at the bridge, while Champion and Johnson drove up the bed of the Wonju
River 500 yards to the railroad bridge to blow it. They heard two or three
North Koreans talking as they approached the fuses. They hurriedly changed
course and went to the hidden can of gasoline in the log cribbing of the
pier. They dumped the gasoline on the logs, set them afire, jumped into
their jeep, and gunned it away. They were back at the highway bridge in
a few minutes, but Skeldon, driver, and jeep were gone. They learned la-

ter that Skeldon had discovered enemy soldiers approaching and had to leave.

When Johnson went to light the fuse for the highway bridge demolition, an enemy soldier ran out. Champion shot him. Johnson pulled the lighter on the time fuse, and both then drove fast toward the railroad station. Many buildings in Wonju were now burning, and all kinds of rubble littered the streets. On the way to the railroad station, Champion and Johnson met no enemy. They lighted the fuses there, staying only long enough to see the powder train start to burn. Then they were off to the church on the western edge of the town. Again they met no enemy, and they lighted the fuses. They hurried back to the Chungju road and drove rapidly south on it.

The old primacord in the wiring at the railroad station around the 16 boxcars burned very slowly, and the two men were five or six miles south of Wonju when, at 9 P.M., the sky suddenly lighted up brightly. When the 2nd Division returned to Wonju two weeks later, they found that all their demolitions had worked. The highway bridge had to be rebuilt, the log cribbing at the railroad bridge had burned, and the boxcars stood in the rail yard demolished. Two miles south of Wonju, Champion and Johnson caught up with F Company, the tail of the 2nd Battalion, 38th Infantry. There was a snowstorm during part of the withdrawal which left eight inches of snow on the ground, and that night the temperature dropped to 20 degrees below zero. The 2nd Battalion, 38th Infantry, left behind 36 wounded North Korean prisoners. Six miles south of Wonju a concrete highway bridge spanned a stream. This bridge was blown after all elements of the division had cleared it about 11 P.M. Already the division had withdrawn miles beyond the point General Almond had ordered General McClure to occupy. The column, including all the division artillery, kept on going several miles farther before it stopped for the night.[31]

It is not known with certainty what North Korean formations had infiltrated Wonju during the night of 6–7 January. More than 100 North Korean prisoners were captured during the night and the daylight hours of the morning. These prisoners came from the 15th and 16th regiments of the NK 6th Division, the 7th Regiment of the NK 27th Division, and elements of the NK 12th and 10th divisions. The NK 12th Division elements at Wonju apparently approached the town from the north. The prisoners from the 15th and 16th regiments of the NK 6th Division said they came through Hoengsong, to the north. Those of the 10th and 27th divisions seem to have approached and attacked Wonju from the east. The US 38th Regiment, which occupied most of Wonju, estimated that perhaps two battalions of North Koreans got into the town or fought within the 2nd Division perimeter at Wonju.

The 3rd Battalion, 38th Infantry, had the hardest fight of all the 2nd Division forces engaged, and at the height of the NK attack before and shortly after daybreak, the battalion was in some danger of being surrounded at the southeast sector of the perimeter. Prisoners from the 2nd Battalion, 15th Regiment, of the NK 6th Division, said they arrived at Wonju about 5 A.M. and entered the town but were forced to retreat. They said their battalion came through Hoengsong, to the north of Wonju, and between Hoengsong and Wonju met or passed many other NK units headed south. Those with rifles carried 50 rounds of ammunition, and the machine guns had been issued 500 rounds each. They carried four days of rations. The strength of the 2nd Battalion, 15th Regiment, 6th Division, on 7 January was 250 men; that of the 15th Regiment, 1,000 men.[32]

An officer from the 7th Regiment, 27th Division, captured at Wonju on the seventh, said the division had 2,100 soldiers, that it had left Hoengsong at 5 P.M. (about dark) 6 January with the mission of seizing Wonju by daybreak the next morning. At the time of his capture he said that two regiments had already bypassed Wonju, their destination unknown to him. Many of the prisoners captured at Wonju said they had picked up their weapons after Americans had discarded them. They also favored American weapons because it was easier to get ammunition resupply for them from that abandoned or discarded by American soldiers.[33]

After the loss of Wonju on 7 January, air supply for the X Corps shifted to Chungju, and the railhead was at Chechon. The attack on Wonju was only part of the North Korean attack in the central corridor at this time. Equally important perhaps, and certainly a definite part of the North Korean plan, was the spreading warfare far to the south of Wonju.

On the same day as the fight at Wonju, 7 January, three Koreans dressed in GI uniforms came to the police station in Tanyang, 38 air miles southeast of Wonju, and said their unit (presumably stated to be ROK) was in trouble and needed 30 men immediately. The three Koreans led a police force a short distance from Tanyang, where a guerrilla force opened fire on them and killed most of the police. A Korean refugee held by the 7th Infantry Division as a prisoner in the Chechon area said he saw NK guerrillas holding eight American prisoners naked, except for a blanket each.

About this time the 17th Regiment of the US 7th Division in the Chechon area engaged in a fight with 400 enemy, killing an estimated 50 of them. An enemy force ambushed the 7th Division supply train before dawn on 10 January and was driven off only after a two-hour fight with the train guards. The division estimated that, during the day, it killed 482 enemy and took 14 prisoners in several engagements with NK guerrilla forces.

The next day 200 enemy attacked G Company, 32nd Infantry, at a roadblock on the Tanyang-Yongwol road, surrounding it. E Company had to send a platoon to help rescue G Company. An estimated 52 enemy were killed in this fight. At the same time, 7th Division troops failed to reduce an enemy roadblock on the Tanyang-Chungju road. On 7 January NK guerrillas scored a coup when, three miles southeast of Tanyang, they disabled a tank of the 7th Reconnaissance Company. Eight enlisted men stayed with the tank overnight, and the next morning 2 men were sent to repair it. Captain Roberts, commander of the Reconnaissance Company, led 4 men out to investigate when he heard firing. In this encounter, a guerrilla force that attacked the group at the disabled tank killed Roberts and killed or wounded all of the other 15 men there. A Company, 17th Infantry, then went to the scene and, after a firefight, drove off the guerrilla force, suffering some further casualties. Similar incidents were daily events in the rear areas of X Corps at this time.[34]

It was clear to many participants and observers in the 2nd Infantry Division and in X Corps by the end of the first week of January that General McClure, the 2nd Division commander, and General Almond, the corps commander, did not see eye to eye and that there was a developing difference of opinion between them as to how to fight the battles around Wonju in the central corridor. In this developing difference, Col. Paul L. Freeman, commanding the 23rd Regiment, agreed with McClure most of the time. This fact was of some importance because the 23rd Infantry was the strongest regiment of the division, partly because it had not gone down the division gauntlet below Kunu-ri at the Chongchon River in late November and was thereby saved many probable casualties.

The fighting around Wonju brought out the differences between Almond and McClure quite clearly. Almond thought Wonju could be defended and wanted the 2nd Division to secure it by building up a position there on the basis of holding the hills to the north and northeast of the town. McClure thought Wonju could not be defended successfully, partly because it was in a bowl-shaped flat or semiflat area, surrounded by hills. Colonel Freeman agreed with McClure. Freeman was generally a pessimistic officer and not blessed with an aggressive spirit. He was something of an intellectual, perhaps, and might have been more suited to a role as a staff or planning officer. Freeman, however, when forced by higher authority to make a stand and fight, usually commanded his troops well. But as a consistent supporter of McClure's view, he was a constant irritant to General Almond in early January in the Wonju area.

Much depended on the X Corps's containing the resurgent North Koreans there who had already brushed aside incompetent ROK divisions. If the North Koreans were not contained and held off from gaining control of the corridor and its rear areas, Eighth Army itself in the west probably would have had to withdraw farther south. This development might have meant the United States and the UN would abandon Korea altogether. A great responsibility rested on Ned Almond at this time to hold the central corridor. Only if he did could General Ridgway have a decent chance to rekindle the esprit de corps of his defeated army that then had its collective will set on leaving Korea.

General Almond was a fighting man, and he meant to do his best to see that his crippled X Corps fought the North Koreans. In the month of January 1951, Almond earned laurels and should have the gratitude of all patriotic Americans. The events of 7 January seem to show that the 2nd Division was not hard pressed that day at Wonju and that the division should have been able to hold the place if aggressively led, instead of retreating far to the south. Some of those present that day felt Wonju should not have been evacuated. A few examples of the current thought among some of the officers and troops there will illustrate this feeling.

First Lt. Lee Ross Hartell was a forward observer with the 15th Field Artillery Battalion, 2nd Division Artillery. He was a veteran of World War II combat in Europe with the 43rd Infantry Division but had only recently rejoined the army. In the middle of December he and other replacements arrived in Japan. He was sent on to Korea with little delay. On arrival there he heard talk of the recent "bugout,"—the first time, he said, he had ever heard the phrase. Soon he was sent to the 2nd Division and was assigned to the 15th Artillery Battalion. He arrived just in time to be present at Wonju. In a letter to his brother in the United States written on 20 March, he said that a ROK unit on their east flank started to crumble, prompting the division CO to call for withdrawal. Hartell told his brother that this was wonderful news for the troops, who had their eyes on Pusan and possibly beyond Korea altogether.[35]

Col. Gerald G. Epley, chief of staff, 2nd Division, at Wonju, expressed the view later to the author that he thought Wonju could have been held by taking possession of the hills immediately south of it, the very position General Almond on the afternoon of 7 January had ordered General McClure to occupy, but which McClure ignored. Epley said that Col. George Peploe, commander of the 38th Regiment, held the same view as he did.[36]

Capt. Marvin L. Nance, commander of E Company, 23rd Infantry, told the author that he thought it was a mistake to pull out of Wonju on 7 January—that there had not been a strong North Korean attack. He said the orders he received to pull back came with no explanation. Only a few enemy troops had reached the 2nd Battalion CP, and their effort amounted to little. He said the enemy who did get into Wonju came through F Company of the 2nd Battalion, 23rd Infantry, which held a position on the north side of Wonju at the perimeter where the MSR from Hoengsong crossed it. Another member of the 23rd Infantry at Wonju, Maj. Sam D. Radow, said he thought McClure's withdrawal from Wonju was unnecessary, that it was a "bugout."[37]

Maj. Will G. Atwood, Jr., and Capt. Daniel E. Sullivan, Jr., of the X Corps historical section, told the author that it was well known among the X Corps staff at the time of Wonju that General Almond was very angry at Colonel Freeman's constant complaining and pessimistic attitude, that it got to the point that Almond would turn his back on him and walk away.

Almond was also critical of General McClure because he did not get Freeman to buckle down to his job and develop a better attitude.

Maj. Gen. Clark L. Ruffner, in a long interview at his 2nd Division Headquarters in Korea in August 1951, expressed his views of the situation at Wonju when he was Almond's chief of staff. Ruffner had been the X Corps chief of staff ever since it was organized in Japan for the Inchon landing the previous September, until he took command of the 2nd Infantry Division. Ruffner told the author that General Almond had been displeased by Colonel Freeman in the Wonju area and that he was having increasing difficulty with General McClure in the latter's handling of the 2nd Division. General Ruffner's comments indicated that he had only unalloyed admiration for Almond as a fighting soldier. He said of him, "His first instinct was to fight. He is the fightingest guy. Ned gets things done the hard way—a fighter, a hard man. He won both Distinguished Service Crosses many times over, for my money."[38]

In a letter to General Ridgway many years later, the author expressed his admiration for General Almond's leadership in the fight for the Wonju central corridor of Korea in January 1950. General Ridgway replied, "I concur on Almond's leadership in the Central Corridor. I rated him SUPERIOR as a Corps Commander on his Efficiency Report."[39]

Just as the North Koreans attacked Wonju during the night of 6–7 January and the 2nd Division hurried away south the next day, a period of extremely bad weather descended on this part of Korea. A storm moving south out of Siberia reached Korea and the central corridor area around Wonju on the evening of the sixth. It brought heavy snowstorms and low visibility, together with some of the coldest weather of the winter. For three straight days, 8–10 January, Task Force 77 carriers off the east coast of Korea had to cancel all flights because of ice on their decks. A break during part of the eighth allowed ground-based planes of the Fifth Air Force, however, to get 50 sorties to the Wonju area. But the weather closed in again, and the X Corps was without air support until the weather began to clear on 11 January.[40] This bad weather helped the North Koreans, and nothing changed much, although General Almond did his best to stir his units to drive north toward Wonju. This period of very cold weather and deep snow was not one in which to hope for great successes.

6

Almond's X Corps and the Recapture of Wonju

AT 2 A.M. 8 JANUARY, General Almond learned at his Advance CP at Chungju that Major General McClure had withdrawn his 2nd Infantry Division from 8 to 13 miles south of Wonju. Anyone who knew General Almond could have no doubt what his reactions would be to a subordinate who deliberately ignored an order that was critical to a military mission. Almond was furious upon learning that McClure had violated his specific order of only a few hours earlier to hold the hill position 3 to 5 miles south of Wonju, from which the artillery could bombard Wonju and the infantry could readily move back when there was an opportunity to regain the town. When Almond learned of the extent of the 2nd Division's withdrawal from Wonju and vicinity the night of 7 January, he woke General Ruffner at 3 A.M., 8 January, and told him that the 2nd Division was to attack back toward Wonju at 6 A.M. that morning with four battalions.[1] Almond's first overt reaction was to order General McClure to initiate a reconnaissance in force with not less than one battalion and to retake Wonju and its airstrip.[2]

Almond's diary for 8 January shows other steps he took at once to counter the 2nd Division retreat from the vicinity of Wonju. At 8:15 A.M. he flew by L-17 plane from Chungju to the vicinity of McClure's CP at Worhyon and completed the trip by jeep, arriving at the 2nd Division CP at 8:50. Accompanying him were Maj. Gen. Clark L. Ruffner, X Corps chief of staff, and Lt. Col. John Chiles, his G-3. At 9 A.M. Almond and his two staff officers had a conference with General McClure. In this brief exchange, General Almond reviewed the performance of the 2nd Division during the past few days and emphasized to General McClure the necessity for an offensive spirit in the division. He and his party then returned to Chungju. There he conferred with General Coulter of the IX Corps. Then at 9:30 A.M., accompanied by Lieutenant Colonel Chiles, he departed by L-17 plane for a conference at Taegu with General Ridgway. There is no record of the conversation between Almond and Ridgway, but there can be no doubt that the situation in X Corps and McClure's disobedience concerning an important military order was uppermost in Almond's mind. From Taegu, Almond and Chiles flew on to Andong after lunch, and then to the 7th Infantry Division's CP at Yongju, where Almond discussed the situation with Colonel Heath, the division chief of staff. Almond was back at Chungju at 4:25 P.M.[3]

Meanwhile, pursuant to Almond's order, Colonel Freeman started the 23rd Infantry back toward Wonju on 8 January. The 1st Battalion led off from the Chechon road and at 11 A.M. engaged an estimated enemy regiment 3,000 yards south of Wonju. The North Koreans counterattacked the 1st Battalion, trying to envelop it. Attacks by the 9th Infantry Regiment toward Wonju on the Chechon road and by elements of the ROK 8th Division from the southwest both failed.[4]

The main effort on the eighth, however, came from the 2nd Battalion, 23rd Infantry, on the Chungju road. The French Battalion followed the 2nd Battalion. Also, the 2nd Battalion, 38th Infantry, was attached to the 23rd Infantry for this counterattack. The 2nd Battalion, 23rd Infantry, led off in a line of companies with E, F, and G, in that order. After about three miles, E Company surprised a North Korean regiment asleep in a village and wrought considerable destruction on it, artillery fire killing about 200 of them. But the North Koreans rallied and, with the help of others, maneuvered to threaten to outflank the 2nd Battalion, which was then ordered to withdraw.[5]

The next day, 9 January, Colonel Freeman resumed his reconnaissance in force with two battalions abreast along the Chungju-Wonju road; the 2nd Battalion, 38th Infantry, was on the left (west) of the road, the 2nd Battalion, 23rd Infantry, was on the right (east) of the road. Lieutenant Colonel Skeldon's 2nd Battalion, 38th Infantry, was far understrength, its E Company having only 50 men, and F Company only 47 men. The weather was now bitter cold, and the troops did not have hot meals, their kitchen trucks being 40 miles to the rear. Only half the men had entrenching tools. The French Battalion, however, managed to have hot meals.

The two-battalion attack advanced north until it came to the village where the 2nd Battalion, 23rd Infantry, had surprised the large North Korean force the day before. There E Company, 38th Infantry, encountered enemy dug in at the foot of the next high ridge northward. Freeman's attack force made no further headway, and the two battalions pulled back to go into a defense perimeter for the night. The weather reached 30 degrees below zero that night. To add to the miseries of the troops, the shoepacs recently issued to the 23rd Infantry were of one size—large. Lieutenant Heath, a platoon leader of G Company, 23rd Infantry, said some men had to wear as many as four pairs of socks to fill the excess space in their shoepacs.[6]

In an order of 9 January to General McClure, General Almond stated the attack force was not to withdraw except on X Corps order. That morning Almond had a conference at 9 A.M. with General Coulter of IX Corps and Colonel Kunzig, Coulter's G-3, together with General Ruffner, his own chief of staff, and his G-2 and G-3, to review what they considered a serious worsening of the situation. Then, at 10:30 A.M., General Almond left his CP in a jeep to inspect the front line of the 2nd Division attack toward Wonju. Twenty minutes later General McClure joined him. They stopped briefly at Colonel Peploe's 38th Infantry CP and then continued on to Colonel Freeman's 23rd CP at Nichon. Freeman's S-3, Major Dumaine, briefed them on the current situation. Almond noted that Brig. Gen. Loyal Haynes, the 2nd Division Artillery commander, was not present, and he instructed that he come forward to control the artillery fire in the attack. He also ordered that Gen. Cho Yung Hi, commanding the ROK 8th Division, come up. Almond then got in his jeep and proceeded. He dismounted at the 81-mm mortar position and proceeded from there on foot 1,500 yards to the observation post of the 2nd Battalion, 23rd Infantry. There he talked with Colonel Freeman and Lieutenant Colonel Edwards, the 2nd Battalion commander.

Almond told Freeman and Edwards of deficiencies he had already noted: artillery pieces were not manned by their gun crews; some guns were even pointed in the wrong direction; the division artillery commander was not up to supervise the artillery fire; two rounds of artillery fire had fallen short in the right-hand company of the battalion sector; the senior battalion commander was supervising the attack instead of the regimental staff; and the battalion commander had not organized a forward CP and his companies were not following approved staff operations. Almond directed General McClure to take steps immediately to correct the deficiencies. At 1:40 P.M. Almond left the 2nd Battalion area for Chungju. On the way he met General Hi, the ROK 8th Division commander, and held a roadside conference with him on his attack toward Wonju.[7]

One of the low points in the Korean War had now been reached. In the west, Eighth Army had been driven out of Seoul and south of the Han River. In the vital central corridor the efforts to hold Wonju had failed because the 2nd Division withdrew from it, and thousands of North Koreans had infiltrated past it southward to rear areas of X Corps. The Far East Command military intelligence section estimated at this time that 7,500 North Korean soldiers were engaged in guerrilla-type operations south and southeast of Wonju in the Yongwol, Chechon, and Tanyang areas. This was the region to which the US 7th Infantry Division had been rushed to deal with the formidable enemy forces in the X Corps rear areas. The X Corps now ordered the 1st Marine Division to move at once to the Kyongju-Yongchon area to prevent enemy from crossing the Andong-Yongdok road in the eastern mountains. The 7th Division itself had posted its 17th Infantry Regiment in the Chechon area, the 32nd Regiment around Tanyang, and the 31st Regiment at Yongju, where the division had established its CP on 4 January.[8]

Only the NK 10th Division had successfully infiltrated in the first part of January through the 7th Division zone. It had succeeded in reaching the Chechon-Tanyang road in strength. But elements of all three NK corps, the II, III, and V, were in contact with the 7th Division in the rear areas. Hit-and-run tactics of guerrilla-type action characterized their operations. On 13 January General Barr moved his 7th Division CP from Yongju to Tanyang, the center of NK action at this time and near a vital mountain pass on the central corridor MSR. The 32nd Infantry Regiment had been heavily engaged and had suffered considerable casualties in the Tanyang area.[9]

At this time Maj. Gen. David Barr, 7th Division commander, lost his assistant division commander, Brig. Gen. Henry I. Hodes, on 12 January in transfer to Eighth Army as deputy chief of staff. General Barr himself had only a short time left as division commander, through 25 January, when Maj. Gen. Claude B. Ferenbaugh succeeded him. On 15 January, Col. Robert F. Sink succeeded Hodes as assistant division commander. For the present, two of the 7th Division's three regiments retained their commanders – Col. Herbert B. Powell, 17th Regiment, and Col. Charles G. Beauchamp, 32nd Regiment. Col. John A. Gavin commanded the 31st Infantry Regiment, succeeding Col. Allan D. MacLean, killed in the Chosin Reservoir campaign in northeast Korea in late 1950.

The terrain between Samchok on the east coast and Taejon to the southwest is the highest and the worst in central South Korea. It was in this area that the NK soldiers of the II Corps had infiltrated by 8 January in an effort to cut the main lateral roads and the more important north-south roads behind X Corps's front in the Wonju area. The mountain passes were the most important spots on the north-south roads, and on some of the lateral roads as well, because supplies for both IX Corps and X Corps would have to pass over them from the south and southwest. The two most important passes on north-south roads in the X Corps rear were those in the vicinity of Mungyong and Punggi. Two other passes near Poun, northeast of Taejon, were important in providing security against an envelopment around or through Chungju to the southwest MSR below Pyongtaek, the western anchor of the Eighth Army line. The NK forces would have to control all these passes to afford any chance of a successful movement to converge on Taegu. By 8 January the NK guerrilla forces threatened Tanyang and Punggi Pass. They were constantly harassing UN forces on the Tanyang-Punggi-Yongju road.[10]

The Eighth Army was so concerned about the safety of the Mungyong Pass that, on 8 January, it sent the 5th Cavalry Regiment from reserve to guard it, placing the 1st Battalion on the east side of the pass and the 3rd

Battalion on the north side of it to deny it to North Korean units. And on the same day Eighth Army issued Operation Plan 21, which would have the army withdraw on a date and hour to be announced to what it called Defense Line E and to prepare for further withdrawal to Line F. Line E ran from west to east through Kunsan on the west coast through Kyongju, Chongju, Chungju, and Yongwol. Line F ran from Hadong in the west to the Kum River, Yongdong, Sangju, Andong, and Pyonggok-tong on the east coast. Fortunately, Eighth Army was not forced to take up either of these defense lines farther south. But when Operational Plan 21 was issued on 8 January, the gap between the US X Corps in the central corridor and the ROK I Corps near the east coast was so great, even though elements of the ROK III Corps had begun to fill the void, and the Wonju salient stuck so far forward to the north, that Eighth Army thought the withdrawal would have to be made. It looked as if the NK II Corps was aiming to get control of Tanyang and Punggi Pass and go through the Southern Sobaek Range to join the guerrillas already south of the Chechon-Yongwol road.[11]

That such a linkup did not come to pass must be credited to the energetic action of Almond's X Corps in the central corridor and in its rear areas. Almond's determined action to goad and jolt his units to strong attack and successful defense and to hunt down the guerrillas in the rear areas halted the NK V Corps, and it cut up and defeated in detail the guerrillas and the NK II Corps in the rear areas. In the rear areas behind X Corps, General Ridgway threw in Eighth Army reserve forces such as the 187th Airborne RCT, the 5th Cavalry Regiment, and elements of the 1st Marine Division to turn back the deepest points of the North Korean penetrations. This victory in the first three weeks of January was a necessary achievement in allowing General Ridgway soon thereafter to turn Eighth Army around and begin his attack back north.

On the morning of 9 January, General Ridgway made an air reconnaissance of the Naktong River, from Taegu to Masan. He conferred with his engineers about their preparing a fordability chart of the river to cover from Taegu to the mouth of the Naktong. He also instructed that any divisions occupying the sector should mine every known ford. He was taking no chances; it might be necessary to withdraw soon into the Pusan perimeter.

At 9:50 A.M. Ridgway arrived at Masan, where Maj. Gen. Oliver P. Smith, commanding the 1st Marine Division, met him. Ridgway held a conference with all the Marine division's principal staff officers and the regimental officers. He told them that, upon arrival in Korea, he had hoped to take offensive action, but upon learning the true situation he had to give up the idea. He went on to say that the UN action now must be based on powerful local counterattacks and to inflict maximum losses on the enemy, consistent with keeping all major units intact. He told the Marine officers they must "Bleed China white. I have the fullest confidence that we can stay indefinitely when delay merges into defense."[12]

After leaving the 1st Marine CP, General Ridgway went on to Pusan, and then he returned to Taegu. There he had as dinner guests, at Eighth Army Main CP, ROK Defense Minister Sihn and General Chung, the ROK Army chief of staff. General Farrell, chief of KMAG; Maj. Gen. Leven Allen, Eighth Army chief of staff; and Colonels Collier and Landrum, deputy chiefs of staff, were also present.

On 10 January the US 2nd Division, under pressure from General Almond, continued its counterattack toward Wonju. It followed two main axes: the road from Chechon and Sillim-ni to Wonju on the east, where the 9th Infantry Regiment had established a series of roadblocks, and the road from Chungju to Wonju on the west, where the 23rd and 38th regiments tried to retrace in reverse their recent withdrawal.

On the tenth the 9th Infantry sent two company-sized patrols north from Sillim-ni. F Company, followed by G Company, moved out along the high ground west of the road to contact the enemy. F Company established contact with a North Korean force at 11:30, and G Company was committed to the fight immediately. The 2nd Battalion, thereupon, was ordered to use its entire force to destroy this enemy group, which then began to withdraw. The 2nd Battalion followed it, with F Company digging in for the night near Mundal. Sillim-ni was a patrol base for the 9th Infantry. The regiment's policy was to change battalions every day or every two days, thus allowing a battalion to fight one day, rest a day, and then return to active contact with the enemy. The patrol base, which became a regular type of operational base in the central corridor at this time, was successful in the very cold weather that prevailed at this time. The patrol bases were of a permanent defense type, with warming tents, special hardship kits, and washing facilities. Their use improved the spirit and well-being of the officers and men and contributed to successful operations against the North Koreans.[13]

General Almond ordered Colonel Freeman to use four battalions on 10 January in his attack toward Wonju along the Chungju road. The 3rd Battalion, 38th Infantry, and the French Battalion were to aid the 23rd Infantry, and the 38th Field Artillery Battalion was to fire support. Colonel Peploe and the bulk of the 38th Infantry were to provide defense for the attack. The attack met an estimated six battalions of enemy (one estimate was 7,000 North Koreans about three miles south of Wonju), and heavy fighting prevailed during the afternoon. F Company, 23rd Infantry, drove the North Koreans from Hill 247, and E Company, 23rd Infantry, secured Hill 216, which was three and a half miles southwest of Wonju, by late afternoon. The 2nd Battalion, 38th Infantry, took a ridge south of Wonju, and at one point the battalion was within one mile of Wonju on its southeast.

The fighting in the French Battalion area was severe southwest of Wonju.

At 3 P.M. a platoon from the 3rd Company, led by Lt. Gildas Leburrier, fixed bayonets as the North Koreans closed with it and charged the North Koreans. In the melee that followed the French killed 27 enemy, and those left fled in panic. Later in the afternoon, at 5:30, a similar bayonet fight took place between the 2nd Platoon of the French 1st Company, led by Lt. Ange Nicalai and Lt. Pierre Lainel. The platoon's ammunition was expended in the attack on enemy-held Hill 216, and it had to resort to fixing bayonets, together with E Company, 23rd Infantry, in holding its ground. In this close-in fight the North Koreans had 60 casualties, and Lieutenant Lainel was wounded. Again, the enemy fled in the face of the French bayonet assault.[14]

But the attack did not carry into Wonju. The North Koreans counterattacked and, with reinforcements, threatened to envelop both UN flanks. Artillery fire, however, broke up this effort, and Dutch and French troops reinforced the 23rd Infantry. At the end of the day, Freeman's attack force dug in on defensive positions about two and a half miles southwest of Wonju. American artillery, however, now had Wonju within range.[15]

General Ridgway was so impressed by the results of the French use of the bayonet on 10 January that he sent information about it to all Eighth Army division commanders on 13 January, adding that the only other use of the bayonet that had come to his knowledge was its use by the Turkish Brigade, who had been equally successful. He encouraged its use by American units. On 15 January Ridgway awarded the Silver Star to Lts. Gildas Leburrier and Pierre Lainel for their role in the bayonet attacks on the tenth near Wonju.[16]

On 11 January there was only patrolling in the Wonju area. The North Koreans apparently wanted nothing more this day than to rest in the Wonju area. In the fighting on the tenth, hundreds of North Koreans at Wonju were casualties, but it was impossible to arrive at any accurate figures. The weather cleared about noon on the eleventh, and the Fifth Air Force was able to get planes in the air. All civilian houses and structures of any kind in the immediate front of UN troops were destroyed. In the arctic weather that prevailed now in the mountainous Wonju area, it was quickly learned that the North Koreans crowded into all types of structures, especially houses in the villages, for some protection from the weather. It became an established policy to destroy all such havens for the enemy. It was almost a scorched-earth policy, but it was implemented to save American lives, which it did.

The 2nd Division now held the high ground just south of Wonju, and although Wonju was a no-man's-land, the supporting artillery from its firing positions south of the town, as one participant put it, "leathered the hell out of the Chinks [North Koreans] holding the high ground north of the town." Pilots who bombed Wonju reported seeing no enemy soldiers in the town. It had become too dangerous for them to use the remaining buildings as shelters. On 12 January ten B-29s bombed Wonju, but the pilots reported no enemy troops seen, and they believed it was unoccupied. The UN forces, including the 23rd and 38th infantry regiments and their attached French and Netherlands Battalions resumed their attack on the twelfth, estimating they destroyed 1,100 enemy during the day. The 2nd Battalion, 23rd Infantry, with heavy air and artillery support, captured Hill 247 southwest of Wonju. On reaching the crest of the hill, the troops counted 80 enemy dead there, and trails in the heavy snow showed that an unknown number of wounded or dead had been dragged off the hill.[17]

The weather during this part of January when the 2nd Division was trying to recapture Wonju was perhaps the worst of the winter. In the period 10 to 16 January, the temperature was down to 21 to 30 degrees below zero, with about 12 to 14 inches of snow on the ground. Frostbite cases were more numerous than battle casualties. The French escaped frostbite more than the Americans because they dug their foxholes better. Harold Martin, a writer for the *Saturday Evening Post,* visited the Wonju front at this time and wrote a laudatory account of the French Battalion. The French were all volunteers and led by three-star Général de Corps d'Armée Magrin-Vernerey, onetime inspector general of the French Foreign Legion. He had the highest decorations France could bestow on a soldier, and he had been wounded 17 times. In order to be allowed to command the French Battalion in the Korean War, he had adopted the name Ralph Monclar with the rank of lieutenant colonel. He was generally known in Korea as Colonel Monclar. Martin described the men of the French Battalion at Wonju as follows:

By any standards by which a soldier can be judged they are among the finest fighting men this war has seen. They truly go "to war as to a wedding." They keep their weapons clean. They endure cold, hardship, and the strain of ceaseless combat with an exuberance nobody else can. . . . The American soldier hates the cold and he hates to dig. He scrapes a hollow wallow for himself and then crowds into it, chilled and miserable. The Frenchman goes to earth like a fox. He digs a deep round hole just large enough for his body and his weapon to poke out comfortably. A few feet down he begins to widen out. He digs his subterranean chamber big enough to lie in it at his ease. He lays a deep carpet of rice straw on the bottom. He cuts a shelf into one side and here, as neatly arranged as a grocery display, he lays his grenades and his extra ammunition so that it will be close at hand. Lower down he cuts another shelf and here he builds a little fire and warms his food. . . . He places a poncho over the top to keep out the smoke and through the poncho he puts a cardboard container which serves as a stove pipe.[18]

The frigid weather of mid-January was enough to stall all military activity. During this period, and other cold spells during the winter, the Army's new cold-weather shoepac was demonstrated to be unfit for soldiers to wear if they were to be engaged in active marching, maneuvering, or climbing the hills and ridges to engage the enemy. They were good enough against cold and wet conditions if the troops were relatively inactive. But on long marches or maneuvering to contact the enemy, perspiration built up in the shoepac around the feet and then froze. The shoepac caused innumerable cases of foot frostbite. Most officers and men found that the regulation leather combat boot with cushion sole socks should be worn on foot marches and was the best general all-around foot gear, and if the four-buckle or other rubber overshoe was worn over the boot, it was the best cold and wet weather footgear available.

In the subzero weather of Korea in midwinter, everything was likely to freeze in a few minutes. One officer wrote that hot water poured into a car radiator was ice before it reached the bottom. To avoid frostbite men dried their socks twice daily when they were able to do it (the person had to be sitting in front of a fire). Water took an hour and a half to boil on small stoves. It often required two hours in boiling water to warm a can of frozen meat. Motors of trucks and tanks had to be started and run every 15 minutes or half hour to keep them operational. The bare difficulties of living, not to think of fighting at the same time, were enough to try men's endurance.[19] The expedient many men used to unfreeze a rifle or a BAR, and sometimes a machine gun, was to urinate on its bolt. At Wonju, in one instance, the trails of two artillery pieces cracked from the cold weather one night with the temperature at 21 degrees below zero and 18 inches of snow on the ground.[20]

In patrol actions in the Wonju campaign, the antiaircraft vehicles—the M16 quad-50 and the M19 dual-40—were invaluable. They were mobile bases of fire. The quad-50, with its four heavy .50-caliber machine guns, and the dual-40, with its two 40-mm Bofors guns, provided an unrivaled mass of fire that could be quickly directed to any point of the compass and gave to small patrols of platoon and company strength the firepower to move farther from its patrol base in daylight than would otherwise have been possible. There was some criticism from the antiaircraft artillery commanders of splitting up their units and spreading a single or a few of the weapons carriers (the M19s and M16s) with the infantry, but their effectiveness in such use could not be denied. The infantry wanted them more than any other type of support. Lt. Col. Charles E. Henry of the 21st AAA AW Bn (SP) stated the case very well:

The infantry either attacks or defends every day and night. Why should the tremendous amount of fire-power represented by 64 M16s sit back with the artillery idly awaiting attack. . . .

We hear the argument advanced by AAA commanders, "You can't turn 'em over to the infantry, you wouldn't have any control over them." Why not? Who is more capable of planning the part a machine gun plays than the infantry battalion commander? The M16 is nothing more than a mobile base of fire. When an AAA officer higher than a platoon leader attempts to control his outfit tactically while supporting the infantry, he's throwing a monkey wrench into a smoothly operating machine.[21]

Ridgway complained after he arrived in Korea that the Eighth Army often did not use more than a third of its firepower in the early phase of the war – that it was sitting back in column on a road, unused. He cited the quad-50 as a prime example of a weapon with a wonderful capability for overhead fire support for infantry in the narrow Korean valleys.[22]

Both Generals Ridgway and Almond, in developing the defended patrol bases, from which patrols ranged far and wide in pursuit of North Korean units and guerrillas and gradually destroyed them in the rear and flank areas of the X Corps in the central corridor in January 1951, used the antiaircraft M16s and M19s as a potent part of the patrols.

First Lt. Lee R. Hartell was a participant in these daily patrols in the Wonju area and told in a letter to his brother how General Ridgway's system of maintaining contact with the enemy and engaging small groups worked. Hartell was an artillery forward observer attached to B Company of the 1st Battalion, 9th Infantry, 2nd Division. His account of a typical long-distance patrol told much about the tactics used in the 2nd Division's action, and in that of the 7th and 1st Marine divisions and the 187th Airborne RCT.

Hartell's division had reached the high ground just south of Wonju, in the action of 8–12 January, and the 9th Infantry was attacking toward Wonju from Sillim-ni, southeast of town. He wrote to his brother that an infantry company mounted on tanks and quad-50s would move forward, destroy as many enemy as possible, and move back, such that the main body would always be moving forward and mopping up. Each day Hartell and his team were in small firefights, and by radio they learned that Wonju had been retaken. B Company, in hand-to-hand fighting, cleared a hill of enemy without sustaining a casualty.

Hartell and his patrol group operated north and northeast of Wonju for the next few days with indifferent results and much trouble with a blown bridge and damaged roads. On 16 January his patrol was given a destination at a village two miles southeast of enemy-occupied Hoengsong. On this patrol they encountered an old man and a boy who told them an enemy regimental headquarters and several hundred enemy troops were just over the hills. Being cautious about intelligence from civilians, Hartell radioed an artillery plane overhead for information and got a report of activity in the villages of Sugol and Pausil.

The scout for Hartell's team then pointed out two enemy moving south on the road. Instead of halting on command, the two began firing, and Hartell's team returned fire, killing one and mortally wounding the other. The wounded soldier told them the dead man was a dispatch carrier taking top secret information from Chinese headquarters to the North Korean front-line commander in Sugol. Remembering the civilians' tip, Hartell radioed for an air strike on the Sugol-Pausil sector. The patrol then pulled back through the dark until they were south of Wonju again, where the contents of the briefcase were inspected and then sent on to top headquarters.[23]

The patrols in which Hartell participated were typical of 2nd Division activity, as well as that of the 7th Division, 187th Airborne, and elements of the 1st Marine Division, all of them thrown into the scattered but numerous battles around and below Wonju in the central corridor of Korea at this critical time. Except for the efforts of the 23rd and 38th infantry regiments of the 2nd Division and their attached French and Dutch allies in direct attack on Wonju, these platoon, company, and sometimes battalion actions were typical of the UN tactics in fighting the North Koreans and guerrilla forces over a vast expanse of central and southeast Korea as far south as Andong, and almost reaching the edge of Taegu, where Eighth Army's Main CP was located. It was the sum of these many small-unit actions that defeated the North Koreans and guerrillas in the central corridor in January and sent the remnants reeling back northward in defeat. But much of this result was not apparent at the time from day to day, and the crisis seemed real.

On 13 January, General Almond spent the entire day in a personal inspection of the forward 2nd Division troops engaged in the attack on Wonju. He left his CP at Chungju at 8:30 A.M. and did not return to it until 6:30 that night, well after dark. Almond stopped first at Colonel Peploe's 38th Infantry CP. There, Peploe told Almond that his high battle casualties resulted primarily from trench foot and frozen feet. Peploe thought the recent receipt of 2,700 pairs of socks should reduce a critical shortage he had in the regiment. General Almond advised Peploe to insist on daily inspection of the men by company commander and his officers to ensure that they would change and dry their socks. Almond then hurried on to Colonel Freeman's 23rd Infantry CP, where Freeman's staff and many of Almond's X Corps staff awaited him. Freeman gave an account of the heavy fighting during the night, when his troops received "three banzai attacks," beginning at 4 A.M. In the final stages, fighting was close in. The enemy hit E Company hardest, and that company inflicted more than 100 casualties, suffering only two killed and four wounded themselves. Freeman said that, on 12 January, the 23rd and 38th regiments had driven the enemy northward. He thought there were about 10,000 North Koreans massed in front of him at Wonju. He complained about the inadequate air support he had received on the twelfth and said jet fighters were not effective on strafing missions. They did little damage to the dug-in enemy. He wanted more napalm and general-purpose bombs. Almond fired off a radio message to Eighth Army on the subject. In discussions with the assembled staffs Almond stressed the need to get more hot food to the troops, to provide better indoctrination of the men in foot care, and to identify enemy units by aggressive patrolling. He said he intended to visit all front-line battalions during the day and then left by jeep to do just that.

He went first to the 2nd Battalion, 23rd Infantry, where Lieutenant Colonel Edwards outlined his battalion's situation. Almond then went on foot to inspect E Company's front-line positions. He talked with Captain Saegar there, and upon looking at the foxholes, he thought they were poorly prepared, and the providing of hot food poorly organized. Then on to the 2nd Battalion, 38th Infantry. There he met Lieutenant Colonel Skeldon, the battalion commander, and continued on foot to its E Company's front line, where he talked with Captain Allen. He also saw the bodies of 14 enemy dead killed in front of E Company that morning. Almond thought the company's morale was good but their positions poorly dug in.

Just after noon Almond reached the French Battalion's front line. There he conferred with Colonel Monclar and his executive officer, Major Lemire. They then went to the 2nd Company's front-line positions. Almond found morale good and the weapons locations and the foxhole construction excellent, the best of any positions he saw all day. From the French sector he went to the 3rd Battalion, 23rd Infantry, and then on foot to K Company's front-line positions. He found fields of fire deficient and supervision inadequate.

He continued on to A Company, Netherlands Battalion, on foot, accompanied by Lieutenant Van Sdest, a platoon leader. He found morale high. A village lay just in front of the Netherlands line. Almond requested an artillery fire mission to destroy it. He had ordered that all such villages and buildings be destroyed, as they provided shelter to the enemy. As he watched, eight rounds of 105-mm white phosphorus started several fires in the village. He timed the response to the request as 11 minutes.

Almond returned to his jeep and went back to the 23rd Infantry CP. There he engaged in a lively discussion with Brig. Gen. Loyal Haynes, the 2nd Division Artillery commander. Almond had not been satisfied with his performance in the Wonju area and was critical of Haynes's lack of front-line supervision of the artillery support.

Almond next went on to Lieutenant Colonel Kelleher's 1st Battalion, 38th Infantry, CP, and then to its A Company's front line. He proceeded to the positions on foot, accompanied by Lieutenant Gardner, the company executive officer. Almond pronounced the foxholes poorly prepared, the 57th Recoilless Rifle crew inefficient, and company leadership poor.

From the 1st Battalion, 38th Infantry, CP, General Almond started back to Chungju by jeep at 4:30 P.M. He arrived there two hours later. All in all, Almond's inspection found the 2nd Division's front-line positions in front of Wonju wanting in leadership control and careful preparation and inefficient in weapons use.[24]

The most important event of 13 January, however, was General Almond's relief of Maj. Gen. Robert McClure as commanding general of the 2nd Infantry Division. The next day, 14 January, General Ridgway designated Maj. Gen. Clark L. Ruffner, X Corps chief of staff, as the new division commander. In a longhand ink entry that Almond made at the end of his personal diary for 13 January 1951, which he added to his personal copy on 31 March 1953, Almond stated: "On this date the Division Commander (Gen. Robt. McClure) was relieved for poor leadership of his division. CG Eighth Army designated Maj. Gen. Clark Ruffner my Chief of Staff as the new C.G. 2nd Inf Div (on my recommendation). A wiser move, I never made." This entry was initialed "A" and dated "3/31/53."[25]

While General Almond's diary entry of 13 January 1951 says he relieved McClure of his command on that date, it was probably the next day that the change actually became effective. General Ridgway says he relieved General McClure of command of the 2nd Division on 14 January. In a communication to General MacArthur on 17 January, Ridgway said that, on the recommendation of General Almond, "I relieved Maj. Gen. Robert B. McClure of command of the 2nd Infantry Division on 14 January 1951." Ridgway, again on the recommendation of Almond, appointed Maj. Gen. Clark L. Ruffner, on 14 January, the new commander of the 2nd Infantry Division.[26] On the same day Col. John S. Guthrie, commander of the 7th Infantry Regiment, US 3rd Infantry Division, succeeded Ruffner as chief of staff, X Corps.[27]

It is apparent that General Almond had decided prior to 13 January to relieve General McClure. It seems likely that he reached the decision on the morning of 8 January, when he learned that McClure the day before had violated his explicit instructions that, if McClure believed he had to evacuate Wonju, McClure should not withdraw farther than the first row of hills about two to three miles south of Wonju. When McClure ignored that order and withdrew the 2nd Division as far as 13 miles south of Wonju, his fate was sealed as 2nd Division commander. Almond would never accept such violation of his explicit orders. Nor should he have. Almond faced some risk in his brusque relief of McClure. McClure had been Gen. J. Lawton Collins's chief of staff, when Collins commanded the 25th Infantry Division in the South Pacific in World War II.

In a letter to the author, General Almond had the following to say about his relief of General McClure:

I know all about the relief of General McClure. He was relieved by me after I watched him operate in a haphazard manner for some 12 days, from January 1 to 12, in the Wonju area, and finally, through a failure of his to maintain a position in defense of area of Wonju after I had ordered him in compliance with 8th Army Commander's order, specifically to do so. He issued a withdrawal order in spite of my direct order to him, and I took the action necessary to make a full report to General MacArthur, but demanded that McClure be relieved and another Division Commander appointed.[28]

Almond has more to say about McClure's relief and General Collins's interest in it. The Joint Chiefs of Staff sent General Collins to Korea in mid-January to report on the precarious situation of Eighth Army and the UN – would Eighth Army have to leave Korea? On 15 January General Collins visited the X Corps HQ at Chungju to form an opinion of its situation. Collins asked Almond to ride with him from the CP in Chungju to the airstrip. During that ride Almond learned that General Collins was more interested in the reasons for McClure's relief from command than he was in the immediate situation in the X Corps area. In his personal diary, Almond wrote on 15 January 1951:

General Collins asked me the question: "Did you have a certain reason for relieving General McClure from command of the 2nd Division?" My reply was "I had so many reasons to relieve McClure for failure to carry out my orders, which were in consonance with those of Gen. Ridgway, for the defense of the important road center at Wonju that I found a number of certain reasons." General Collins made no further remark, but I further told General Collins that General MacArthur had a three page letter from me giving a full account of why McClure was relieved, which appeared to satisfy both him and the then Eighth Army Commander, General Ridgway.[29]

It would appear that the three-page letter Almond sent to MacArthur on McClure's relief was forwarded through Ridgway, Eighth Army commander. Ridgway's comments on this letter are not known, although it appears he supported Almond's action.

During the period 10–17 January, the situation appeared most desperate to Eighth Army in the X Corps area east of Chechon and in an arc swinging south and west of Chechon. In that area the North Korean II Corps had infiltrated thousands of soldiers, while the North Korean V Corps held the bulk of the 2nd Infantry Division in the Wonju area under an ongoing frontal attack. Perhaps this middle part of January 1951 was the low point of the war for all American echelons – and certainly it seemed so for the Far East Command, where General MacArthur reached the depth of gloom and indicated to the Joint Chiefs of Staff that the UN forces might have to vacate Korea altogether.

But in the mountains and valleys of the central corridor, the ever-moving fight to destroy the North Korean infiltrators and guerrilla bands went on day after day, and often into the night, in the far-reaching tactic of platoon- and company-sized long-distance patrols from a series of patrol bases. Some of these have already been mentioned. On the morning of 13 January, B

Company, 9th Infantry, sent a 30-man patrol to the northwest from its base to reconnoiter enemy approach routes. When it reached the vehicle dismount point, it left five men to guard the vehicles; the rest of the patrol continued on foot eastward toward the suspected enemy approach route. When the patrol reached the suspected enemy-used route, Lieutenant Schmidt, in command, sent 7 men south, while he took the remainder of the patrol northward. Civilians warned Schmidt and his 18-man patrol that enemy occupied a village only a mile to his front. Schmidt continued north. When he approached the village he deployed his men and opened fire on the cluster of huts. He had surprised an estimated 150 enemy sleeping. In the sudden chaotic action the enemy had an estimated 20 killed, 9 wounded, and 2 were taken prisoner. Schmidt's patrol had no casualties during the action. It was late at night when Schmidt's patrol arrived back at its base.[30]

On 13 January the 7th Infantry Division lost Yongwol to North Koreans. The 3rd Battalion, 17th Infantry, encountered about 200 dug-in enemy and withdrew, breaking contact. The battalion then called in air strikes and artillery fire on the enemy force. Aerial observers at the Yongwol area reported an enemy concentration of approximately 2,000 troops there, moving from east to west. These observers directed artillery fire on them, and most scattered to nearby hills. Two days later, the 1st and 2nd battalions, 17th Infantry, sent patrols into Yongwol in the early afternoon, but they were fired on and withdrew. Artillery fire and air strikes continued on enemy in the Yongwol area. On the seventeenth, General Almond directed General Barr, the 7th Division commander, to reoccupy Yongwol as soon as possible.[31]

On 13 January, the 187th Airborne RCT left Andong at 6 A.M. and moved north to the heart of the guerrilla fighting, closing near Punggi at 1:30 P.M. There the 3rd Battalion relieved the 2nd Battalion, 31st Infantry, 7th Division, and assumed responsibility for protecting the mountain pass southeast of Tanyang, halfway between Tanyang and Punggi. The 3rd Battalion of the airborne RCT that afternoon saw an estimated 200 enemy on a ridgeline in front of its I Company. It opened fire with artillery and mortars. The 187th Airborne RCT had traveled 243 road miles from Suwon in the west to reach the Punggi-Tanyang area in the central corridor. On the fifteenth its I&R Platoon had a brief firefight with an estimated 200 enemy, who fled to the northeast. This force was identified as the 1st Battalion, 703rd Regiment, of the NK 9th Division.

The next day the 2nd Battalion had a firefight with an estimated 500 enemy, whom it dispersed toward the south. Within two days the 187th RCT intelligence officer, by interrogating prisoners, refugees, South Korean security police, and local agents, learned the routes used by the enemy and their methods of operation. He estimated enemy forces operating in the Tanyang area as the NK 2nd Division with 2,500 men, the NK 10th

Division with 3,000 men, and four guerrilla groups totaling 2,000 men – in all, about 7,500 enemy. The 187th Airborne RCT carried out an effective campaign, and within a week of its arrival it had pretty much eliminated the enemy threat to Tanyang and Punggi Pass. It counted 53 enemy killed, 205 more estimated killed, 436 wounded, and 71 prisoners captured. Prisoners taken at this time and in the subsequent week said the 187th Airborne's unexpected attack had destroyed much of the NK 2nd Division, that the NK 10th Division had lost heavily, and that only about 1,500 of their troops had moved around the left flank of the 187th Airborne RCT toward the south, where the 1st Marine Division then engaged them.[32]

On 22 January a patrol of A Company, 187th Airborne, found 12 American bodies from the 32nd Infantry and notified that regiment. At this time, the 2nd Battalion, which relieved the 3rd Battalion, 187th RCT, at Punggi Pass southeast of Tanyang, reported weather at 27 degrees below zero and winds from 15 to 25 miles an hour.

The 5th Cavalry Regiment, on similar duty in the Mungyong area, southwest of Punggi, reported frigid weather of 22 degrees below zero at night and not more than 10 degrees above during the day. The 5th Cavalry stated that they started the motors of their vehicles every hour, day and night, and that they had a critical shortage of antifreeze fluid. Since sugar gave them more energy in the cold, the men wanted chocolate and cookies to take with them on patrols. During this period, a battalion of the 21st Infantry, 24th Division, west of Chungju in the IX Corps zone, had to make a night motor march and had 90 frostbite cases in a 15-hour period. These men were wearing shoepacs. Removal of shoepacs to change socks in the open or while riding trucks in 20 degrees below zero could not be done successfully. The 21st Infantry at this time was issuing two chocolate bars daily to its troops.[33]

At the middle of January, then, the X Corps, with the bulk of the 2nd Division, was holding the vital area from Chungju north to the edge of Wonju and west to the IX Corps boundary and the Han River. The 7th Division, still trying to fill in its 31st and 32nd regiments with replacements, held the Chechon area southeast of Wonju. The Eighth Army moved the 187th Airborne RCT from reserve to halt the guerrilla attacks and the NK flanking and encircling movement to the south of X Corps in the Tanyang-Punggi area; it sent the 5th Cavalry Regiment to hold a vital mountain pass and lateral route through the Mungyong area southeast of Tanyang toward Taegu; and it ordered the 1st Marine Division to the Andong area. There NK troops had made their farthest penetration, and there the NK 10th Division was finally stopped and put on the ropes. Fortunately, at this time, the Chinese in the west were unable to follow up their capture of Seoul and mount a pursuit of Eighth Army south of the Han River and attack the new Pyongtaek line.

At this time Eighth Army seemed to have become overly concerned about the so-called Wonju salient that jutted many miles to the north of the Eighth Army Pyongtaek line. At the same time, North Koreans were bypassing it on the east and controlled most of the mountainous area between it and the east coast. Also, the CCF began to shift troops eastward along the Han River in the IX Corps area toward the X Corps boundary. There was fear the Wonju salient was a weak point in the army line that the enemy might pinch off. This fear led Eighth Army to authorize the 2nd Division to pull back from Wonju a distance of about ten miles.

Before Eighth Army gave this order, however, General Ridgway on 12 January requested the Fifth Air Force and the Far East Air Force Bomber Command to send a saturation bomber strike by B-29s against Wonju. The Air Force responded on that day with ten B-29s from the 98th Group. At this time the bombers made their first operational use of proximity-fused 500-pound general-purpose bombs, which burst in air just above the ground and showered steel fragments in blanket-type coverage over the ground below. The pilots had trouble identifying snow-covered Wonju but finally found their target and then blanketed it with showers of steel bomb fragments.[34] Not much could survive that strike. Radio Peking, however, two days later, on 14 January, announced that its 3rd Phase Offensive (the New Year's Offensive) had been successfully concluded with the capture of Wonju.[35]

At midnight 14 January, General Ruffner, now commanding the 2nd Infantry Division, received orders to withdraw his troops from the Wonju area to a new line farther south and give up the Wonju salient, which would even out and shorten the army defense line. The movement was to start at 10 A.M. on 15 January and be completed on the sixteenth.[36]

The withdrawal took place on 15–16 January, moving the line about ten miles south of Wonju, straightening the army line from the IX Corps flank near Yoju eastward to a point north of Chungju and Worhyon (2nd Division CP), eastward toward Chechon and Yongwol. At 8 A.M., 15 January, X Corps ordered the Chungju-Wonju road closed to northbound traffic so that the southbound traffic of the 23rd and 38th infantry regiments from the Wonju area could withdraw without interruption. The 3rd Battalion, 38th Infantry, covered this withdrawal.

On the way south from Wonju, Colonel Freeman met Brig. Gen. George C. Stewart, assistant 2nd Division commander, who had new orders for him. Freeman was to hold a sector west of the Chungju-Wonju road to the Han River with two battalions. He diverted the 3rd Battalion from the column to take positions west of the road; the 1st Battalion of the 23rd Infantry Regiment had already been released from control of the 9th Infantry Regiment in the Chechon area and was taking a position along the Han River that would tie in on the X Corps west flank with the IX Corps east flank and from there extend eastward, where it would meet the 3rd Battalion position. Each battalion had about five miles of front in mountainous country devoid of lateral roads. The positions taken in this formidable country were generally platoon positions on mountain peaks and crests of high ridges that dominated possible enemy routes of advance. But no enemy appeared. The 2nd Battalion, 23rd Infantry, and the French Battalion continued on to 2nd Division reserve positions near Mokye-dong. Their reserve status lasted only one day.[37]

The X Corps now had the ROK 2nd and 8th divisions and the 1st and 3rd battalions, 23rd Infantry, on line west of the Chungju-Wonju road westward to the Han River and the IX Corps boundary. East of the Chungju road the 38th Infantry Regiment went into position, and the 9th Regiment extended to the boundary with the 7th Infantry Division, near Chechon. After one day in 2nd Division reserve, the 2nd Battalion, 23rd Infantry, moved to the Chechon area to help the 9th Infantry and the 7th Division there. The French Battalion was at the same time assigned to long-distance motorized patrols in front of the 2nd Division.

On 15 January enemy in the Yongwol area resisted the effort of the 3rd Battalion, 17th Infantry, to enter Yongwol. The 3rd Battalion withdrew, then called in an air strike on the enemy. In the same general area a North Korean was captured a mile southeast of Yongwol. He said he was a runner from the NK II Corps to the NK 31st Division, eight miles south of Yongwol. He said the NK II Corps CP was west of Yongwol.[38]

At this time, the 7th Infantry Division, with its 17th Regiment in the Chechon area, the 32nd Infantry in the Tanyang area, and the 31st Infantry in the Yongju area, was in contact with elements of all three enemy corps operating in the central corridor and on its right flank and in the rear of the 2nd Division—the NK II, III, and V corps. With the Tanyang area becoming the center and critical point of enemy guerrilla action at the middle of the month, the 7th Division CP moved from Yongju to Tanyang on 13 January. The 32nd Infantry, in the Tanyang area, had a lot of enemy contacts and much fighting. On 13–14 January there was infiltration of the 32nd Infantry. On one occasion, an enemy force let flank guards of the 1st Battalion, 32nd Infantry, pass and then struck the main body of the battalion with all weapons, forcing it to withdraw. The next day enemy posing as ROK troops attacked B Company, 32nd Infantry. In this fight, B Company lost 6 men killed and 6 wounded. The enemy force lost 16 dead within B Company's position and an estimated 40 to 50 outside it.[39]

Rail service opened from Tanyang to Chechon on 13 January, which was a great boon to the 17th Infantry. By the end of the month Chechon had become the railhead for the 7th Division, and its supply levels for the first time became adequate.

There was serious enemy activity deep behind the X Corps front at the middle of January in many areas at the same time. This activity was the crest of the North Korean effort in the Eighth Army rear areas. With action in the Chechon and Tanyang areas at a high point, another large enemy infiltrating force threatened the road and mountain pass between Chungju and Mungyong, 20 air miles to the southeast. Two battalions of the 5th Cavalry Regiment and the Greek Battalion attacked on 15 January to wipe out this enemy group, but the 35th Regiment of the ROK 5th Division, which was to block its escape, failed to arrive at its blocking position in time. This enemy force escaped to the northeast, where it is believed it joined the NK 10th Division near Tanyang. On the same day, the I&R Platoon of the 187th Airborne RCT engaged 300 enemy only a mile north of Andong, forcing their withdrawal.[40]

While this irregular warfare was in progress behind the X Corps front, and the bulk of the 2nd Division had withdrawn from south of Wonju and shifted its strength west and northwest toward the Han River and the IX Corps boundary, the 9th Infantry still maintained its patrol bases on the Chechon road and near Sillim-ni leading northwest to Wonju. It was destined to be the unit that recaptured Wonju.

On 17 January Captain Walker took his E Company, 9th Infantry, accompanied by two tanks, and went all the way from its patrol base to Wonju without encountering opposition. It stayed in the town all night without hostile enemy contact, but it returned with a few straggler North Korean prisoners. Another patrol of an officer and 20 men, in five jeeps from G Company, 9th Infantry, accompanied by two M16 half-track quad-50s, was stopped by a minefield, where they captured 9 North Koreans. The patrol left its jeeps there and continued on foot to a point northwest of Wonju. There it met two squads of enemy, and it then withdrew.[41]

During the evening of 18 January, Lt. Col. Cesibes V. Barberis, commander of the 2nd Battalion, 9th Infantry, called a staff meeting outside Wonju and told his officers that the 2nd Battalion was going into Wonju the next day. On the nineteenth the battalion, with two tanks and two 105-mm howitzers, reached the south end of the Wonju airstrip by 10 A.M. It continued on into the town and at its northern edge received enemy small-arms fire. The 2nd Battalion returned to the south end of the airstrip for the night. The next afternoon, at 3 P.M. 20 January, Generals Ridgway and Ruffner landed on the airstrip.[42]

The 9th Infantry established its main patrol base at Wonju on 24 January and sent the regimental tank company and attached AAA M19 dual-40s and M16 quad-50s there also to provide supporting fire for its patrols. This action was the final step in securing Wonju once again. That morning the 9th Infantry sent out three patrols from its newly established Wonju base. Each patrol had about 100 men altogether—a rifle platoon with tank and M19 and M16 support. Patrol No. 1 went north up the road toward Hoengsong; Patrol No. 2 went west on the road to Yoju to contact friendly forces there; Patrol No. 3 went northeast toward Saemal, which was a likely approach from which enemy forces might strike at Wonju. By the afternoon of 27 January, all three patrols had reported no enemy contacts. Upon receipt of this information, the 9th Infantry decided to send the 1st Battalion (−) to Hoengsong to establish a patrol base there from which to support even deeper patrols to the north. The 1st Battalion reached Wonju the next morning.

A task force comprising A Company, tanks, M19s and M16s, and four 105-mm howitzers from B Battery, 15th Field Artillery Battalion, was then organized and sent north toward Hoengsong. When this task force reached Hoengsong just before noon, an unknown number of enemy in the town fired on it. A Company, supported by its heavy firepower, attacked at once and drove the enemy from the town. On the north side of Hoengsong, A Company reformed and continued the attack northward. Two miles north of the town it again met enemy troops, and a sharp firefight developed. The enemy gave way eventually and fled north. The 9th Infantry, 2nd Division, at the end of the month had control not only of Wonju but also of Hoengsong.[43]

The tables had turned. The NK II Corps was in full flight to sanctuary in the north from its deep envelopment around the east side of X Corps, in which it was mostly destroyed. The NK V Corps was so badly hurt in its frontal attacks against the 2nd Division in the Wonju area by this time that it too was virtually combat ineffective and had moved away from the fight northward to recuperate.

One of the single most severe setbacks the NK II Corps must have suffered in its envelopment movements undoubtedly was on 15 or 16 January, when 40 Navy planes flying off a carrier along the east coast caught about 3,000 North Korean troops, possibly an entire understrength division, in a narrow valley southeast of Yongwol and virtually wiped it out in a series of strikes lasting an hour and a half. The radio report of this incident came from the Tactical Air Support Party Controller with the ROK III Corps, through the ROK 18th Regiment of the 3rd Division. The report stated that an actual ground count showed 2,200 North Korean dead. This incident was in the almost roadless, high mountain area of the ROK Army sector of the ROK III Corps. The western boundary of the ROK III Corps passed on a northwest-to-southeast line just east of Yongwol.[44] A few days later the ROK III Corps reported that enemy activity and resistance north of Yongwol and overlooking the upper Han River valley was almost gone.

At the far southern end of the NK II Corps penetration below Tanyang, the 187th Airborne RCT patrolled constantly and encountered only small enemy groups between 16 and 27 January. These patrols burned all villages used by the enemy and others that might be used. Where they found no enemy, they evacuated the civilians. On the twenty-seventh the RCT burned 12 villages; the next day, 10 more. On the last day of January the 187th I&R Platoon patrolled from Tanyang to Yongju-dong. At the latter place it found 36 North Korean bodies the civilians said had been killed by an air strike on 10 January. The Korean civilians at Yongju-dong said they had already disposed of the bodies of more than 100 other North Koreans killed in the air strike.[45]

In the patrol movements north after 16 January in the 2nd Division front from the Chungju and Sillim-ni area that resulted in the recapture of Wonju, not everything was a model of soldierly conduct and valor; it never can be. The platoon leader of the P&A Platoon, 1st Lt. Walter Hurtt, Headquarters Company, 2nd Battalion, 38th Infantry, has mentioned some of his own observations and experiences at that time. The supply problem in the movement back north from Chungju to Wonju was made especially difficult because of the bridge that engineers had destroyed a few miles south of Wonju on the night of 7 January. There was no bypass built around it for 2½-ton trucks, and they had to unload there on the way back, hand-carry the supplies to the north side of the bridge, and reload them there on jeeps and weapon carriers.

On the morning of 7 January Hurtt was taking two trucks of ammunition to Wonju. Approaching Wonju, he came upon 50 or 100 stragglers, about 30 of whom had no weapons—they had either lost them or thrown them away. They yelled to him that there was an enemy roadblock just ahead. When Hurtt got to the roadblock, he found it was one made by some of his own platoon and 10 attached ROK soldiers. In the meantime, the ammunition sergeant on the second truck had deserted and was later found in Chechon. And Hurtt's own shotgun guard on the back of his truck was gone. Hurtt stopped the stragglers going south and rearmed those without weapons from weapons in his two ammunition trucks. Some of these men deserted him as his group continued north.

On 20 January Hurtt was with the patrol that entered Wonju. He and his 15-man patrol were attached to E Company, 9th Infantry, and went with it into Wonju. According to him, the evidence there showed that the 7 January demolitions at the railroad station had not gone off. He found two railroad cars at the railroad station intact, but it looked as if the Air Force had strafed the area. He said 11 of the 16 cars in the Wonju railroad yard still had usable ammunition—80 tons of it.[46]

Anyone who has long been with or around combat troops sooner or later hears stories of men who have shot themselves in the hand or foot in order to claim a wound in action and to be evacuated and escape the war with a minor injury. M. Sgt. Olen MacGregor of F Company, 38th Infantry, said several men in the Wonju battles shot themselves through the hand. He also alleged that three men from the Outpost Line of Resistance went AWOL at a time when there was no enemy attack.[47]

On 20 January, General Almond conferred with General Barr of the 7th Division, which had been busy trying to contain and stop enemy activity in the Chechon and Yongwol areas on the X Corps's right flank, next to the mountainous no-man's-land of the ROK III Corps. Barr thought his division had eliminated enemy from the area except for some remnants in the Yongwol vicinity. But the next day the 3rd Platoon of L Company, 17th Infantry, sent a 31-man patrol to Yongwol, led by a master sergeant. An enemy force ambushed the patrol near Yongwol before noon. Communication had broken down, and the 3rd Battalion did not send a rescue force until the next day, when L Company went to the scene. There it found 11 men of the patrol killed and 4 wounded, with 16 men missing. There were 22 enemy dead also at the scene. Fifteen days later the 17th Infantry learned what had happened when the enemy released five prisoners from the ambushed platoon and they returned to their unit. They said the platoon had run out of ammunition in its creek-bed position with the North Koreans on higher ground around them. At dark the remaining 16 men surrendered. They said their radio antennae had been ripped off and they had lost communication. Liaison planes, however, saw them and dropped messages.[48]

Even though the 9th Infantry held the Wonju airstrip and had gone to the north end of the town on 20 January, there was really good security in the Wonju area only on the day when Generals Ridgway and Ruffner landed at the airstrip. F Company, 9th Infantry, had returned to the northern edge of the town, with enemy following closely behind it. There the rest of the 2nd Battalion joined in the fight and drove the North Koreans away. But that evening after dark the patrol base was moved out of Wonju to the southeast of the town. It expected to return to the town the next morning. During the next day, enemy held positions on hills north and northeast of the town. A platoon of E Company, 38th Infantry, had attacked one of the hill positions but had not secured it.

The next day, 22 January, there seemed to be increased enemy strength on the hills north of Wonju. The 2nd Battalion attacked Hill 233, 1,000 yards northeast of the town. Its E Company had cleared the hill by 12:30. On this day, as well as on the several preceding days, air strikes in the Wonju area greatly harassed and damaged enemy efforts to hold on to the town. The next day, the 1st Battalion, 9th Infantry, entered Wonju. It had contact with a North Korean force in the afternoon on Hill 273, north of the town, but succeeded in driving the enemy off the hill. A strong armored patrol then advanced up the Hoengsong road against only light resistance.[49]

The following day, 24 January, the 1st Battalion, 9th Infantry, continued its advance toward Hoengsong. It encountered an enemy company two miles south of the town, and in a firefight there it dispersed the enemy force in midafternoon. The patrol then entered Hoengsong. The bulk of the 1st Battalion, 9th Infantry, remained in Wonju overnight.[50]

It was now apparent that the NK II Corps that had infiltrated during the month deep behind the X Corps front by passing it on the right (east) flank had been defeated in detail and decimated. Its remnants were turning back north in the hope of escaping. The NK 10th Division had been the most successful of all enemy units, reaching a point southeast of Andong. But it was now isolated from the rest of the NK II Corps. Its remnants had turned back and, hoping to avoid enemy contact, were trying to escape. The big threat to UN forces in the central corridor was now over for the time being. This fact, apparent to the CCF, which had remained quiescent on the west flank of the North Korean effort during January, now necessitated some action from it. In the latter part of January there had been some movement of Chinese forces eastward along the Han River in the IX Corps sector toward the central corridor. Perhaps they intended to try again where the North Koreans had failed.

During the latter half of the month there had been meetings two or three times a week at Eighth Army headquarters, attended by Generals Almond and Coulter of X Corps and IX Corps, in preliminary planning for implementing General Ridgway's concept of resuming the offensive as soon as the situation in the central corridor was brought under control. The X Corps, with important help from Eighth Army reserve forces in its rear areas, had now accomplished that objective.

At midmonth, General Almond had instituted a practice that he had long wanted to see established in army units at battalion levels. In his northeast Korean campaign in late 1950, he had seen the Tactical Air Control Party (TACP) system work in the 1st Marine Division in the Chosin Reservoir campaign and in a more limited way in Army units. He was an enthusiastic supporter of the TACP in every infantry battalion for direction of close air support in infantry combat. On 16 January he had sent a letter to General Ridgway requesting additional TACPs for the 7th Infantry Division because that division had many battalion actions that could not be supported by artillery because of terrain factors. Only close air support could help fill the void. The same day, in a telephone call to General Ruffner, he ordered Ruffner to organize at once a TACP for each battalion in the 2nd Division. This party would consist of one officer, one SCR-300 radio and operator, and one jeep and driver. By using the SCR-300 radio, this TAC Party could contact pilots of Mosquito and liaison planes overhead and give them instructions about enemy targets below in combat with the infantry. These pilots in turn would communicate with the fighter and bomber planes at the scene as to the targets to attack. These TACPs did not have a VHF radio, in use by the Marines and Air Force TACPs, by which the ground controller could communicate directly with the attacking strike pilots. But it was a first step toward that desired goal, which in the meantime gave valuable aid to the ground combat forces in action with the enemy.[51]

With a new phase of the war now about to take place, in which the UN forces would turn north again in attack, gingerly and carefully at first, we turn to the western part of the UN line, to the I Corps and IX Corps sectors, where General Ridgway had been planning to locate the southernmost advance enemy formations and to strike them. It would be a test for what he hoped and believed would be a new Eighth Army spirit.

Transition: Eighth Army in the West

IN THE THREE AND A HALF WEEKS after 7 January, when General Ridgway settled in with his very small Advance CP with I Corps at Chonan, the enemy did not attack the army position on what was then called Line D, the Pyongtaek line. It was a period of rest and some patrolling for the troops, and for Ridgway a period of intense thought and planning toward turning Eighth Army around and heading north. He decided quite early that his main task was somehow to change the spirit of Eighth Army, among both its officers and its rank-and-file, so that it would change from the defeatist attitude that had generated the desire to hurry on toward Pusan and out of Korea, and had led it to give up its positions north of Seoul and cross the Han River without ever really making a fight of it. During the period from 7 January to the end of the month, Ridgway alternated between being at Chonan and being at Taegu, the Eighth Army Main CP.

The last three weeks of January were the low point of Eighth Army, and of the UN effort, in Korea. During this time most of the army expected to leave Korea forever, and the pendulum of debate in Tokyo and Washington swung back and forth as to whether the army should be ordered out of Korea. It seemed that only one man, General Ridgway, remained constant in his view that the army would stay in Korea, and, furthermore, that it would face north again and drive the enemy before it.

Ridgway's basic plan for such an operation was to get a firm line established, and when the advance began it would be solid; no one unit would be permitted to get very far ahead of the rest of the line. A thorough search of all the ground would be made to make sure no enemy had been left behind the advance, and the troops would climb the hills and intervening terrain between roads. This army would not be roadbound. Advances would not be primarily to gain ground; they would be to find and destroy the enemy, bit by bit.

Logistically, Eighth Army now had no port on the west coast north of Pusan after it abandoned Inchon and Seoul in early January. But the Navy improvised one 25 miles north of Kunsan at the town of Taechon, which lay at the head of a drying bay. From this town a single-track railroad and a dirt-gravel road ran to Chonan, now headquarters for I Corps and General Ridgway's Advance CP. There the branch railroad joined the main-line railroad. In December, Admiral Thakrey swept an anchorage area at Taechon as a precaution against the loss of Inchon. In January, therefore, the LSTs that had loaded out at Inchon in the evacuation of that place were able to unload their supplies at Taechon. On 8 January a convoy arrived from Ulsan on the east coast with artillery and tanks for the US 3rd Infantry Division. This anchorage was used in January to bring in petroleum products and other supplies for Eighth Army, and it greatly relieved the overburdened main-line railroad.[1]

On 8 January, the day after Eighth Army settled into the Pyongtaek line, Brig. Gen. Sladen Bradley, formerly assistant commander of the US 2nd Infantry Division, joined the 25th Division as its assistant division commander. It was understood at the time that he would become commanding general of the division when Maj. Gen. William B. Kean, its commander, was rotated back to the United States, which occurred on 25 February 1951. Kean then became commander in the United States of the III US Corps at Camp Roberts, California. Kean may have been the ablest army division commander in Korea up to the time of his departure. (But Oliver Smith's superb performance with the 1st Marine Division in the Chosin Reservoir operation must not be forgotten.)

On 8 January the last Eighth Army soldiers left Suwon after the last bridge there was blown. The next night there was heavy snow, and the weather turned bad and very cold. The Air Force had planned a strike on Osan the next day, but it had to be postponed. Six CCF deserters from the 148th Division of the 50th Army, now in the vicinity of Suwon, were captured south of Osan on the tenth. They gave information about the CCF 50th Army, which was now south of the Han River. Since Eighth Army had broken contact with the enemy after it crossed the Han, little was known about enemy front lines and intentions.[2]

During this period at Chonan, and after 31 January at Suwon, General Ridgway was hard to please. Lieutenant Colonel Read, of the I Corps G-2 Section, said he used to brief Ridgway daily. Ridgway wanted exact information on men, weapons, vehicles, kind of mines, and terrain covered by fire; he was sharp and hard to satisfy, but he did not use profanity. He was interested in all details, minutely so. Read said, "He got us out of the bug-out fever and put offensive spirit into us."[3]

Ridgway had by now established his command relationship with the ROK soldiers. President Syngman Rhee had given General MacArthur complete command of the ROK Army. MacArthur delegated this authority to Ridgway, who gave his instructions to Gen. Chung Il Kwon, the ROK Army chief of staff, and at the same time to Brig. Gen. Francis W.

Farrell, chief of KMAG at Eighth Army Headquarters. Ridgway also delegated his authority to the several corps commanders in Eighth Army. Through this dual channel of orders he was able to get incompetent ROK commanders relieved. Ridgway also refused to authorize weapons and military equipment to ROK divisions until he was satisfied their division staffs were as competent as they could be made.[4]

From the beginning, Ridgway was sensitive to the need to reassure the South Korean people and their government and army that he was in the fight to help them win. There was the danger at this time that Syngman Rhee and his ROK army would think the US Army was on the point of deserting them and that they would desert the UN force and not obey its orders. General Ridgway from the outset had established good working relations with General Chung Il Kwon, chief of staff of the ROK Army. On 11 January he sought to strengthen this personal tie by writing the following to General Chung:

Now that I have had sufficient time to see the situation as it now exists, to view the terrain, and personally talk to the principal Commanders, I deem it opportune to share my personal basic conclusions with you.

First, there is here but one ultimate objective – freedom for your people. To attain that objective, there is only one force – our combined Allied Army.

Second, there is but one single common destiny for this combined Allied Army. It will fight together and stay together whatever the future holds.

I would like you to feel free to convey to all ranks this simple statement which I send to you with complete sincerity and all the emphasis I can command.[5]

At the very moment Ridgway wrote these words to General Chung, the issue of whether the United States Eighth Army and the UN forces attached to it stayed in Korea was riding the ball of a pendulum, swinging back and forth in every telecon and communication between General MacArthur in Tokyo and the Joint Chiefs of Staff in Washington. The outcome was a toss-up, although General Ridgway himself was dedicated to staying in Korea. He believed he could drive the Chinese and North Korean forces out of South Korea, if given a little time. He did not believe they could drive him into the sea.

About this time a British military critic, Cyril Falls, Chicelle Professor of the History of War, Oxford University, wrote a piece for the *Illustrated London News* that he entitled "Theory and Practice in Korea." His understanding of the Korean War, as expressed in that article, was seriously flawed. For example, he said, "The Chinese have never launched a frontal attack on the main body of the Eighth Army in force bearing any relation to their numerical strength." He was very wrong, for their attack was *always* a frontal attack, but with penetration and envelopment in mind. Despite his misunderstanding of the nature of Chinese tactics, he voiced a feeling at the end of his piece that was widely held on both sides of the Atlantic.

As for the tactical situation, I cannot avoid fearing that the attribution to the Chinese of power so great and military qualities so high as to necessitate retreat, whenever they come to close quarters, may create the danger which it suggests by exercising a harmful effect on the spirit of the troops. Perhaps my doubts are excessive and will be falsified by a happier ending to the undertaking than I am inclined to fear. I only hope it may be so. It would be a serious matter if the land forces of the two greatest nations of the western world could not deal with Chinese, armed with what they can carry in their hands, even at long numerical odds.[6]

General Ridgway at this time expressed his views in a personal letter to Gen. Wade H. Haislip in the Defense Department in Washington. He wrote: "My one over-riding problem, dominating all others, is to achieve the spiritual awakening of the latent capabilities of this command. If God permits me to do that, we shall achieve more, far more, than our people think possible – and perhaps inflict a bloody defeat on the Chinese which even China will long remember, wanton as she is in the sacrifice of lives."[7]

Although this is a combat history of the Korean War, and not one of political and diplomatic events, a few remarks are necessary at this point to relate the combat situation on the ground to the political and military-command view of the situation. On 10 January 1951, General MacArthur sent a long message on Korea to the Joint Chiefs of Staff in Washington stating that, if China concentrated its military potential on the Korean border, it would render his command's military position in Korea untenable. He added, "Under these conditions in the absence of overriding political considerations the Command should be withdrawn from the Peninsula just as rapidly as it is tactically feasible to do so."[8]

Actually, the day before, on 9 January, the Joint Chiefs of Staff had told MacArthur, "Should it become evident in your judgment that evacuation is essential to avoid severe losses of men and material you will at that time withdraw from Korea to Japan."[9] The secretary of defense and President Truman approved these instructions.

On 12 January the matter was discussed at length by the Joint Chiefs of Staff. Secretary of Defense Marshall sent the JCS memorandum to the National Security Council for its consideration. At the same time, the Joint Chiefs of Staff sent Gen. J. Lawton Collins, Army chief of staff, and Gen. Hoyt Vandenberg, commanding general of the Air Force, to Korea to assess the situation. They reported back to the JCS on 17 January in Washington. Marshall said Collins reported that Eighth Army was "in good shape and was improving daily." He added that "the Communist Chinese had not made any move to push south from the Han River. Thereafter, the situation of our forces in Korea continued to improve and during the latter half of January the enemy forces remained on the defensive."[10]

In his testimony in the MacArthur hearings, General Marshall revealed one of the many instances in which the American military view of what should have been done was not concurred in by the UN and which curtailed American military operations. Senator Russell, chairman of the Senate and House Joint Committees, asked General Marshall about the issue of bombing Chinese bases in Manchuria – how had that policy evolved? Marshall answered:

There was initiated in the JCS a proposal about Dec 7 or 8 to authorize Gen. MacArthur to institute a procedure in the air called "hot pursuit," which meant that our planes could follow theirs for a stated distance over the Yalu River into Manchuria. That was considered, concurred in by me, as a matter of fact I had urgently recommended it – and was concurred in by the Sec of State and approved by the President, and the Sec of State was directed to take that up with the 13 nations involved with us in fighting in Manchuria [Korea]. They voted solidly against it, so for the time being we had to drop that.[11]

The JCS directive to MacArthur of 9 January 1951, approved by President Truman, therefore stood as its policy directive. The Joint Chiefs of Staff's detailed draft of further instructions in its 12 January document, sent to the National Security Council for final action before submittal to the president, was never issued. General Collins's report to the JCS on 17 January made it a moot point for the present, because he had said it was unlikely, with conditions improved relating to Eighth Army and the failure of the Chinese to press on south of the Han River, that UN forces would be pushed out of Korea. General Marshall, defense secretary, said in the MacArthur hearings, "We were at our lowest point, I might say, about January 9 to 10."[12]

All through the Chinese 2nd Phase Offensive, beginning in late November, and continuing through the 3rd Phase Offensive, in January 1951, the UN forces, including the US Eighth Army, seemed to have acted under duress of fear of the Chinese armies. Several of Gen. Karl von Clausewitz's axioms in his *Principles of War* seem to describe the situation. "Not only are we uncertain about the strength of the enemy, but in addition rumor (i.e. all the news which we obtain from outposts, through spies, or by accident) exaggerate his size. The majority of people are timid by nature, and that is why they constantly exaggerate danger. All influences on the military leader, therefore, combine to give him a false impression of his opponent's strength, and from this arises a new source of indecision."[13]

Likewise, one can find in Clausewitz the precise manner in which the CCF seemed always to act in attacking the UN forces: "We must select for our attack one point of the enemy's position and attack it with great superiority, leaving the rest of his army in uncertainty but keeping it occupied. This is the only way that we can use an equal or smaller force to fight with advantage and thus with a chance of success." One of Clausewitz's axioms seemed to describe Ridgway's personal approach to generalship: "Theory leaves it to the military leader, however, to act according to his own courage, according to his spirit of enterprise, and his self-confidence. Make your choice, therefore, according to this inner force; but never forget that no military leader has ever become great without audacity."[14]

But one cannot deny that plain common sense must be used in conducting warfare. Perhaps Marshal Chuikov expressed it best in his *Battle for Stalingrad,* in saying, "The most important thing that I learned on the banks of the Volga was to be impatient of blue-prints. We constantly looked for new methods of organizing and conducting battle, starting from the precise conditions in which we were fighting."

One has to consider always the type of men who form the rank-and-file at any given time. In Korea, after December 1950, the US Eighth Army took in many replacements. After his disastrous Russian campaign, Napoleon raised 350,000 new soldiers. His Grande Armée was all but destroyed. Of his new soldiers, Napoleon said, "We must act with caution, not to bring bad troops into danger, and be so foolish as to think that a man is a soldier. . . . Poor soldiers need much artillery."[15]

On the subject of morale of a soldier, Gen. Sir Ian Hamilton in his *Soul and Body of an Army* has said, "Patriotism – Morale – Religion – Fanaticism; a force without a name – fire stolen from Heaven, in virtue of which naked, half-armed, undisciplined Fuzz-Wuzzy may break, has at least penetrated, that arch-essence of organization, discipline and training – a British Infantry Square."[16]

Restoring Eighth Army morale, "a force without a name," was of high priority in Ridgway's objectives. Without it he could accomplish little. How he did accomplish that objective will be unfolded gradually in the story that follows. It did not come suddenly, in one fell swoop, but was the result finally of a patient, consistent, plan of action, aided by the undefined strengths that emanated from his own character.

One of Ridgway's common remarks to commanders at this time when he visited their CPs was, "Don't want to see your defense plans – want to see your attack plans." Knowledge of this attitude worked its way down to the rank-and-file. They soon sensed that a different attitude prevailed, and it spread gradually to them. But the old feeling died hard. When Colonel Kelleher, commanding the 35th Infantry, said to his men, "We are going to attack," the comment from many out of his hearing was, "Bull——, who does he think he is kidding?"[17]

Evidence of continued movement of military matériel south is found in the British 29th Brigade's loading 21 Centurion tanks on flatcars at Taejon on 11 January for shipment to Pusan, and the remaining squadron of the 8th Hussars Tank Battalion was to start for Taejon not later than 12 January. On this same day, 11 January, the 19th Engineer Combat group was to reconnoiter and prepare plans for the demolition of key bridges and tunnels southward, including the railroad bridge at Waegwan and highway bridges over the Naktong River.[18]

The weather cleared on 11 January, and aircraft again took to the air and flew over no-man's-land north of Chonan in the west. Snow lay three feet deep in some places. Pilots in one flight saw an estimated 2,500 enemy soldiers moving south, paralleling the Osan-Pyongtaek highway. The planes attacked, and the pilots estimated they destroyed half this force. Later, American ground troops took a document from a dead Chinese soldier in the Osan area, a diary with the last entry dated 11 January, stating he was a member of the 450th Regiment of the 150th Division, 50th Army. The entry stated that an American air strike on his unit in the vicinity of Osan on the eleventh had killed 45 men and wounded another 19. The strike also destroyed one mortar and two machine guns. The diary entry blamed the losses on white-clad Korean civilians who jumped into the Chinese shelters and foxholes with the soldiers and made the positions conspicuous from the air. It said that in the future all civilians would be excluded from areas troops occupied.[19]

In this phase of operations in Korea, the ROK II Corps was deactivated on 10 January. Its divisions had been so nearly destroyed in the CCF 3rd Phase Offensive in early January, where the ROK corps held the part of the line immediately east of the US IX Corps, that it was considered combat ineffective. Henceforth the US X Corps filled the line east of the IX Corps and continued Line D eastward to the ROK III Corps, which held ragged positions in the mountains on the east side of the central corridor. Beyond it eastward to the coast, the ROK I Corps held a loose and disjointed line at first, with many gaps through which enemy could pass almost at will.

On 12 January, a guerrilla force pulled off one of the boldest coups of the war behind the lines, south of Taejon. Six prisoners said there were 80 guerrillas involved in the attack. They were armed with some submachine guns, 18 Soviet rifles, and 40 grenades. They also had some improvised mines that they planted on the tracks of the main-line railroad about two miles south of Okchon. The mines were fused for delayed action. The locomotive and three cars of the 23-car train passed over the mines before they detonated. On detonating, the mines set several of the cars burning, and eight ammunition cars exploded. The guerrillas opened fire from their positions on the nearby hill, wounding several of the train crew. All rail and vehicular traffic on the nearby highway was stopped because of exploding shells. A South Korean police force went to the scene and drove off the guerrillas, capturing six of them. The 15th Explosive Ordnance Disposal Squad cleared the tracks. Many ROK guards on the train, wounded in the ambush, were taken to an Okchon hospital. It is not known how many of the guards were killed. That same night another northbound train was fired on in this same vicinity, but it got through.[20]

After this disaster, the army arranged that all supply trains in the future would have flatcars or gondolas, front and rear, mounting machine guns. Hospital trains had two gondola cars – the first in front would detonate mines, and the second carried two machine guns, three US military police, two ROK military police, and from eight to ten South Korean National Police as guards. Another gondola car at the rear of the train carried the same number of armed personnel and two machine guns. Consideration was given to mounting a light tank on a flatcar to give all-around fire protection.

The need to use more Koreans in the front lines led General Ridgway to ask all major commanders for their opinion on a proposal to add 100 KATUSA (South Koreans attached to the US Army) to each company. The reply was strongly negative. Most commanders considered the KATUSA, with their limited training and the language barrier, as more of a detriment than a help at the fighting front.[21]

In mid-January, when the prevailing opinion among the rank-and-file of Eighth Army and most of the officers was still for getting out of Korea as quickly as possible, Ridgway had to try to stem this spirit almost alone. His Eighth Army general staff was against him; the most pessimistic and negative of them all was Col. John Dabney, his G-3 operations officer. Ridgway was so disturbed by Dabney's views that he decided to relieve him of his duties but was persuaded by his chief of staff, Maj. Gen. Leven C. Allen, not to do it, in deference to Dabney's long career. But Dabney was eased out in another month or two, promoted to brigadier general.[22]

Col. Richard W. Stephens, commander of the 21st Infantry, 24th Division, said at the time, "There was a lot of foot-dragging by Eighth Army officers on staying and fighting in Korea." Lt. Col. LeRoy Lutes, a member of the Far East Command staff, told the author that Colonel Dabney had requested that Lutes be sent to Korea to help draw up an Eighth Army evacuation plan because he had had experience in the evacuation of X Corps from Hungnam in northeast Korea in late December 1950. Lutes said this plan, completed about 1 February 1951, had been requested by the Far East Command in Tokyo. Col. Robert Halleck, who had served as I Corps Artillery officer and commander of the 24th Infantry Division Artillery, said the Eighth Army staff did not support Ridgway in his efforts to get the army turned around in January 1951. The staff officers were busy planning a series of successive lines of withdrawal from Line D. These were to be Lines Easy, Fox, George – and all of the officers were convinced that the army would not be able to move forward northward but would be going south. He said ammunition was not issued to Eighth Army, as some requested, because the logistics staff did not want it forward, as another withdrawal was expected and a "bugout" feared. Colonel Halleck told the author he felt that Ridgway's getting Eighth Army turned around in the face of all the opposition he had was one of the marvels of military history. Halleck said he was not given to hero worship, "but Ridgway has it."[23]

On this subject, Ridgway has an informative comment in his book *The Korean War.*

I was shocked, some time in late January, at the results of a Staff study I had requested concerning "the desirable location of major elements of the Eighth Army for the period February 20 to August 31, 1951." You must understand that I was thinking as I had right from the start, in terms of attack. The worst of the winter would be over by March and the heavy rains and heavy cloud cover normally expected in June, July, and August would turn large areas into mudholes, make many roads impassable, wash out culverts and bridges in the mountains and reduce the effectiveness of close air support. We would need to improve our positions markedly to enable us to move back toward the 38th parallel.

But the recommendations I received in a G-3 authenticated document, reported as having been cleared with G-2, G-4, the Engineers, and a representative of COMNAVFE and the Weather Section, Fifth Air Force, were for phased redeployment to positions south of the Sobaek Range. In effect, the study (still in my possession) urged that we should abandon all thought of going on the offensive, that we should hold our present positions until the winter was over, and then, before the summer rains came, withdraw to the very lodgment area from which the Inchon victory had set us free—the old Pusan Perimeter. To have approved it would have been to surrender all initiative, an unthinkable course of action. I disapproved it at once.

. . . I made my immediate plans for a coordinated phased advance by both US Corps—the I and the IX—for the purpose of developing the enemy situation on their front. . . . They were to be ready to advance to the Han if so ordered, and there to hold.[24]

In the summer and autumn of 1951, the author talked in Korea with hundreds of officers and men of all ranks about Ridgway's influence on the Korean War. Almost without exception, all who had any opinion at all (and most of them did) said that Ridgway made the difference in the outcome of the war—that he had prevented the Eighth Army from marching out of Korea, that he had singlehandedly given it a new spirit in two months after he assumed command and had turned it around to face the enemy and then driven that enemy north out of South Korea. He led the American troops in retrieving the military honor of the United States.

Aerial reports on 12 January said no enemy had been observed in the Osan area, but enemy had been observed ten miles northward in Suwon and east of Suwon. The next day aerial observers saw enemy moving east of Suwon. Col. John Michaelis of the 27th Infantry, 25th Division, sent patrols to Osan on the thirteenth and reported it free of enemy. They went some distance beyond it without enemy contact, but they did not go as far as Suwon. The temperature stood at zero at daylight but had been 11 degrees below zero during the night.[25]

On 14 January agents reported there were from 50 to 100 dead Korean refugees in Osan, killed by the air strike there on the eleventh, but there were no enemy dead in Osan. The agents reported the enemy had left before the strike, and about 1,000 CCF in the hills west of the town had returned to it after the strike ended. On the fourteenth a flight of B-26 bombers hit Suwon with bombs and left a gift for the enemy in a strange mishap—when the bombs were released, a notebook fell out containing information on the location of the US 25th, 24th, and 2nd divisions and their CPs.

January 14 was a notable day in another respect. At noon General Ridgway issued an operational order to I and IX corps. It stated that intelligence indicated an enemy buildup between Osan and Suwon, and I Corps was to attack it with a strong armor force, not less than one tank battalion and appropriate reinforcements. It was to inflict maximum destruction on the enemy and then withdraw to its present position. The attack was to start at daylight 15 January. Research for this book pointed to this attack as the first offensive action in the west that Ridgway had ordered since Eighth Army went into Line D, the Pyongtaek line, following the withdrawal from Seoul and crossing of the Han River.

On the same day that Ridgway ordered his first offensive action in the west from Line D, he received reports giving him current troop strengths in major units of Eighth Army and the miles of Line D they occupied. (See tables 6 and 7.) These figures indicate that Ridgway at the middle of January had approximately 216,000 men on Line D, which extended 140 miles across the breadth of Korea, slanting to the northeast slightly in the western half, increasingly so in the eastern half, where it was a more broken and ragged line held entirely by ROK troops.

TABLE 6. **Eighth Army Troop Strength, 14 January 1951**

Unit	No. of Inf. Bns.	Total Personnel	Tanks	Miles of Front
US I Corps	18 (ROK 9, 7 Unk)	48,964	254	19
US IX Corps	18 (ROK 9, 4 Unk)	45,183	114	24
US X Corps	21 (ROK 27, 2? Unk)	60,753	193	47
Subtotal		154,900		
ROK I Corps	10	24,800	0	15
ROK III Corps	27	35,940	0	33
Subtotal		60,740		
Eighth Army Reserve	9 (ROK 13)	20,566	109	–
Total	103	236,206	670	138

Source: Folder S-Z, Box 17, Ridgway Papers; Col. Edgar G. Conley, Eighth Army G-1, to Ridgway. The "Unk" in the tabulation of the battalions in the I, IX, and X US corps apparently means that number of ROK battalions were scattered by the CCF in the 3rd Phase Offensive, and their status unknown.

TABLE 7.   **KATUSA with US Combat Forces, 14 January 1951**

Unit	Number of Personnel
1st Cavalry Division	1,355
2nd Infantry Division	1,103
3rd Infantry Division	2,740
7th Infantry Division	2,835
24th Infantry Division	1,306
25th Infantry Division	1,136
1st Marine Division	187
I Corps	311
IX Corps	1,081
X Corps	302
Subtotal	12,356
Signal	465
Ordnance	1,115
Engineer	1,680
Subtotal	3,260
Total	15,616

Source: Col. Edgar G. Conley, Eighth Army G-1, to Ridgway, Folder D-L, Box 17, Ridgway Papers.

On 14 January General Ridgway issued orders to all commanders to conserve supplies. He said there had been a reckless abandonment of critical and valuable property in the past. He asserted that command failure to take punitive action had encouraged carelessness and a complacency that could not be tolerated.[26]

The operation that Ridgway had ordered to begin on 15 January was code-named "Wolfhound," probably because it was to be carried out largely by units of the 27th Infantry Regiment, 25th Division, known throughout the army as the "Wolfhound" Regiment. As a preliminary to the attack, 24 B-26 bombers and 126 fighter planes were to report to TACPs in the Suwon-Osan area between 8:00 and 8:40 A.M. Ridgway's directive to General Milburn, I Corps commander, on the reconnaissance in force was specific.

Personal for Gen Milburn (0900) Ridgway. I expect that by dark today, or at latest on 16 January, this operation will be completed and participating forces pulled back to within close supporting assistance of your corps.

I desire to caution you against permitting a situation to develop which would demand commitment of additional major elements to extricate your forces. The preventive for this is reconnaissance, ground and air, but particularly ground. Large scale exploitation, if opportunity occurs, will be on Army order only. Acknowledge by phone or clear radio.[27]

The Wolfhound operation was a two-day affair. It started at daylight, 7 A.M., on 15 January and was concluded after dark on the sixteenth. The task force comprised the 1st, 2nd, and 3rd battalions, 27th Infantry; the 89th Tank Battalion; the 8th Field Artillery Battalion; and a company of the 65th Engineer Combat Battalion. Cooperating on its right (east) flank, two battalions of the 3rd Infantry Division, the 90th Artillery Battalion, and one battalion of the ROK 1st Division were to protect that flank and its rear. Still farther east in the IX Corps zone, the ROK 6th Division sent a battalion north to Kumyangjang-ni, southeast of Suwon, in cooperative support of that flank.

In the Wolfhound attack, the 1st Battalion, 27th Infantry, with D Company, 89th Tank Battalion, took a road west of the MSR toward Osan and Suwon; the 3rd Battalion with the rest of the tank battalion advanced north up the MSR. The 2nd and 1st battalions of the regiment advanced abreast. Their point of departure was Sojong-ni, about five miles north of Pyong-taek. Col. John Michaelis commanded the regiment.[28]

The 3rd Battalion attacked north from Sojong-ni with L Company on the MSR with a company of tanks. I Company screened the right side of the road, and K Company screened the left side. Many civilian bodies littered the MSR, the result of the large air strike three days before. A squad of civilian Korean police with L Company removed the bodies ahead of the tanks, gathering 50 between Sojong-ni and Osan. They also found 35 wounded civilians in Kalgon-ni alone. Blown bridges north of Sojong-ni and at Osan delayed the 3rd Battalion's advance. By 5:30 the engineers had completed a bypass of one blown bridge north of Osan. The 3rd Battalion went into a perimeter defense there for the night, where the reserve battalion joined it. Neither had encountered enemy during the day. The 1st Battalion with D Company of the tank battalion on the western road also had no enemy contact during the day. It stopped at Pyong-ni at 4 P.M.[29]

Over Suwon and in its vicinity there were 107 air sorties on 15 January. This massive air activity resulted in an estimated destruction of 15 carts, a petroleum dump, 112 buildings, 2 camels, 18 other pack animals, and 990 enemy troops. Another 116 buildings were damaged. The 1st Battalion traveled a distance of about 20 miles on the fifteenth; the 3rd and 2nd battalions, moving on a more direct line, advanced about 8 miles.

The next morning at 8 A.M. the 2nd Battalion, 27th Infantry, passed through the 3rd Battalion and led the advance toward Suwon. E Company swept the high ground east of the road; F Company swept the ground west of it. Snow and ice covered the MSR. All villages were screened. Aerial observers reported an enemy company dug in on a ridge east of the road and directed an air strike on it, but the ground task force thought the position too far away for immediate foot reconnaissance. On the western leg of the advance, the 1st Battalion and D Company of the 89th Tank Battalion moved parallel with the 2nd Battalion but encountered no enemy during the morning. Both battalions received radio orders to expedite their advance toward Suwon and to return before nightfall.

At 11:30 A.M. the 2nd Battalion on the MSR received a message to "send an armored spearhead ahead to Suwon." Capt. Jack Michaely commanded G Company, then in battalion reserve. He took his company, less one platoon, and loaded his men on five tanks. By noon he was on his way. The five tanks were within 800 yards of the south edge of Suwon by 2 P.M. There, still undiscovered by enemy, he unloaded his infantry, and G Company deployed to protect the tanks. The tanks and infantry then advanced 300 yards farther up the road. The lead scout at that point saw a single Chinese soldier break from a house ahead and run for a machine-gun position on a low ridge to the east, about 200 yards away. A single shot brought him down, but this noise alerted the rest of the enemy in Suwon. The Chinese had been surprised, expecting no attack of any kind, except perhaps aerial. Ever since crossing the Han River they had experienced no hostile effort by the UN forces. They had grown careless and were enjoying the comparative comfort and warmth of the buildings in Suwon.

The Chinese now poured from the houses and other buildings in the town and ran for their defense positions on the ridges southeast and southwest of the town. None made it at first. Small-arms fire and machine-gun fire from the tanks cut them down. But enemy fire came on the column from both sides of Suwon and from the roofs of buildings, where an estimated 200 enemy had taken positions. Tank fire destroyed some enemy emplacements, and 60-mm mortar fire also hit some on the eastern ridge. Cub planes in the air over Suwon radioed to the artillery forward observer with G Company the location of enemy positions. The Chinese soldiers at Suwon on 16 January were dressed in white camouflage uniforms. An aerial report informed Captain Michaely, in command of the task force now at the edge of the town, that two enemy forces, numbering about 250 men, were moving on his right (east) flank to get into his rear. An air strike hit the larger group of about 200 but did not stop it.

Michaely radioed for instructions at this juncture. He was ordered to withdraw and told that he had accomplished his mission. Accordingly, his advance task force from G Company and the five tanks of B Company, 89th Tank Battalion, withdrew 3,000 yards at 4 P.M. and escaped contact with the flanking force of Chinese to the east. The rest of the battalion and accompanying tanks had stopped south of Suwon and were not engaged. By this time air strikes, totaling 201 sorties, were hitting Suwon and all known enemy positions east and southwest of the town. Michaely's task force estimated it had inflicted about 200 casualties by ground fire on the enemy in this engagement. It estimated that air strikes at the same time had caused at least 300 more enemy casualties. In its overall estimate, I Corps claimed a higher number – 195 killed and 5 prisoners from ground action, and 1,180 enemy casualties from air action as far east as Yoju.

The 1st Battalion secondary 27th Infantry column on the western road turned toward Suwon in the afternoon and reached a point close to the town's western edge, but it was not engaged. At 5 P.M. both columns were ordered to withdraw to Osan.[30]

The Wolfhound task force had extremely light casualties in the advance to Suwon and in the firefight there at the southern edge of the town. It had three killed and six wounded, and one ROK soldier wounded. On 17 January, the task force, on orders received the night of the sixteenth, returned to its former positions on Line D, north of Sojong-ni.

On 18 January Gen. Frank Milburn submitted a report to General Ridgway on the operation. He listed the units involved as (1) one infantry battalion (an error, since there were three), one field artillery battalion, one tank battalion, one engineer company, 25th Division; (2) two battalions infantry, two tank companies, and supporting artillery, 3rd Infantry Division; and (3) one battalion, 1st ROK Division. He said the task force found no enemy concentration south of Suwon. The 3rd Division and ROK 1st Division elements found no enemy concentration south of a line from Suwon east to Kumyangjang-ni. The enemy, in establishing his screening line, apparently had turned east from Suwon instead of pressing farther south.[31]

The prisoners, five in number, were all taken behind the G Company advance group that reached Suwon. They apparently were stragglers, as two of them were from the CCF 40th Army, two were from the 50th Army, and one was from the 55th Army.[32] At this time only two divisions of the CCF 50th Army were south of the Han River.

On 16 January, at the same time the 2nd Battalion, 27th Infantry, was approaching Suwon, the 1st Battalion, 15th Infantry, of the US 3rd Division, on the next road eastward, moved north to Kumyangjang-ni, entered it without enemy resistance, and cut the lateral road from Suwon to that place. It turned west on the road toward Suwon but encountered enemy mortar fire northwest of Kumyangjang-ni. It then turned back for the night. The 2nd Battalion, 65th Infantry, 3rd Division, followed the 1st Battalion, 15th Infantry, part way toward Kumyangjang-ni, then turned northwest toward Osan, where it halted for the night. Following the two battalions of the 3rd Infantry Division, the 2nd Battalion, 12th Regiment, ROK 1st Division, approached Kumyangjang-ni and secured a village south of it for the night.

From the IX Corps sector, still farther east, the ROK 3rd Battalion, 2nd Regiment, of the ROK 6th Division moved to Kumyangjang-ni and established contact with the 1st Battalion of the 15th Infantry. Beyond it, Lieutenant Colonel Perez, commander of the 2nd Battalion, 21st Infantry, 24th Division, in the Yoju area, at noon informed Colonel Stephens, his regimental commander, that his F Company patrol had a firefight with 50 to 60 Chinese in the village of Iho-ri. Perez sent the rest of F Company to the patrol's aid and then requested an air strike. Perez ordered the patrol out of the village. Six flights of planes came in, including 4 jets, 12 Navy Corsairs, and 12 F-51s. They rocketed, napalmed, and strafed the village, setting it afire. The lead patrol saw 33 enemy soldiers rush out of the village toward the east. At 2 P.M. in the afternoon the patrol went back into the village, where it found 6 enemy dead in the streets, 10 dead in burning buildings—all of these badly burned by napalm. Identification of the enemy unit caught here was impossible from the bodies. F Company encountered no enemy in another village and in the nearby area.[33]

All these movements north by several divisions of I and IX corps, east of the Suwon MSR, were designed to be diversion actions to help the 27th Infantry reach Suwon and to gain information about the forward screening line of enemy forces north of UN positions on Line D. All of them taken together showed that there were no North Korean units in the area, which had been widely rumored, and that the Chinese were not there in force.

While these successes lifted the spirits of men on Line D, there was another setback in rear areas. Nine enlisted men of A Company, 76th Engineer Combat Battalion, were killed by a guerrilla force while working near Kunsan on the west coast.[34]

Also on 16 January patrols from the Australian Battalion entered Ichon, an important crossroads junction town on the lateral road running east from Suwon to Kumyangjang-ni, Ichon, and then to Yoju on the Han River. They had no opposition, but that night one of their outposts saw 40 to 50 enemy approaching along the Seoul-Ichon road. The outpost killed about 20 of this group. Korean civilians informed the Australians that a Chinese force was located about three or four miles north of Ichon. Air strikes were directed on this area.

This period of January was very cold, and the Australians suffered from it as much as the American units. Some men were found frozen to death in their foxholes, and others had to be lifted out of their holes. For a time the Australians had an average of 12 cold-weather casualties a day.[35]

The increasing success of X Corps in the central corridor and at Wonju in the middle of January against the massive North Korean infiltration operation, and the success of Operation Wolfhound to Suwon in the west, could not have come at a better time, because they coincided with the visit of Army Chief of Staff Gen. J. Lawton Collins and Commander of the US Air Force Gen. Hoyt Vandenberg to the Far East. The Joint Chiefs of Staff had sent them on 15 January to form an opinion on the ground, and after discussions with General MacArthur, whether Eighth Army could stay in Korea.

Ridgway spent most of 17 January with notables from Washington, D.C. At 8 A.M. he, together with Brig. Gen. Francis Farrell, chief of KMAG, Eighth Army, accompanied General Collins to Yongju, where they had a conference with Brigadier General Bowen, commander of the US 187th Airborne RCT; Major General Yu, commander of the ROK III Corps;

and Brigadier General Mim, commander of the ROK 5th Division. At 10:40 A.M. the party returned to K-2 airfield, Taegu, where they met President Syngman Rhee and Defense Minister Sihn of South Korea. General Collins departed Taegu at 11 A.M.

Then, at 1 P.M., Lt. Gen. Walter Bedell Smith, chief of the CIA; Maj. Gen. Alexander R. Bolling, US Army G-2; and Maj. Gen. Willoughby, Far East Command G-2, arrived at Taegu. After an hour and fifteen minutes' discussion they left. Generals Collins and Vandenberg reported to the Joint Chiefs of Staff that they found Eighth Army in an improved condition, and they believed it could hold in Korea. The crisis seemed over.[36]

In order to put in perspective the battles with the North Koreans and Chinese in the harsh winter weather of 1950–51 and the situation at the front in mid-January 1951, it would be well to give an enemy view of their situation at this time. Not only the UN forces suffered. A diary, presumably written by a Chinese company commander in the CCF 50th Army, covering the period October 1950 to 17 January 1951, tells their story well, and no doubt accurately.

Difficulties: 1) We have been troubled on the march due to icy roads. 2) We are exhausted from incessant night marches. To make matters worse, when we should be resting during the day, we cannot take a nap due to enemy air activity. 3) Due to a shortage of large-head shoes, almost all the soldiers are suffering from frostbite. 4) We have had to cross rivers with our uniforms on during combat, which has resulted in severe frostbite. 5) The fighting is becoming critical due to lack of ammo and food. 6) Lack of lubrication causes untimely rifle jams when firing. 7) As we have had to carry heavy equipment on our backs, we are always heavily burdened when marching. 8) The physical condition of the soldiers has been getting worse as they have to hide in shelters all day long, and fight only at night or during enemy air assaults. 9) When reconnoitering at night disguised in civilian clothing, it is very difficult to carry out the mission because of language difficulties.

Morale of the soldiers of our unit: Enemy air strikes frighten the soldiers most of all. The most unbearable labor they have to endure is to carry heavy equipment on their backs when climbing mountain ridges. Their conviction that they will win the war is wavering.

How our company should act toward enemy PsW: Our PW policy will influence the war and we have done our best. Observe the regulations when you take enemy PsW. Do not follow the policy the NKA used against enemy PsW which, naturally caused desperate resistance by the enemy. Our company captured more than 100 US PsW but we didn't kill any of them.[37]

On 17 January the Joint Chiefs of Staff replied to President Syngman Rhee's suggestion that the US should arm the Korean Youth Corps. The Joint Chiefs turned down the proposal, saying that the most effective utilization of members of the Korean Youth Corps and other qualified Korean males was to replace losses in existing ROK units.[38]

Kumyangjang-ni, 12 miles southeast of Suwon, continued to be an object of interest for UN patrols because it was the first sizable village east of Suwon on the main lateral road eastward and was a crossroads for important north-south and east-west communications. On the morning of 17 January the company commander of the 3rd Division Reconnaissance Company received orders to make a reconnaissance northward to include Kumyangjang-ni. His mission was to determine enemy strength in the region, enemy movements if any, obtain prisoners, and return. The company was ambushed in Kumyangjang-ni and extricated itself only with great difficulty and considerable loss of life and equipment.

The one prisoner taken in the fight said he was from the 449th Regiment, 150th Division, CCF 50th Army. The Reconnaissance Company estimated it had killed or wounded about 25 enemy. But it had lost 9 men killed and 11 wounded (including 3 ROKs) and had lost 7 jeeps, 3 jeep trailers, and 2 of their 81-mm mortars.[39]

It was relatively quiet on the western part of the army front on 19 January. One change took place following the return of the 27th Infantry from its advance to Suwon. The 35th Regiment of the 25th Division began relieving it on the division OPLR, and Colonel Kelleher of the 35th Infantry assumed responsibility for the line the next day at 3:45 P.M. The 27th Regiment then went into 25th Division reserve. The 25th Division's official report for 19 January noted an increase in rape, robbery, and murder in Chochiwon after the 24th Infantry had been stationed there.[40]

Numerous patrols in I Corps and IX Corps zones during the previous three days resulted in a report on 20 January that there were no enemy tanks south of the Han River and that there were no large enemy formations south of the Yoju–Ichon–Kumyangjang-ni lateral road. Prisoner information indicated that, in some CCF units, up to 40 percent of the men had no individual arms but did have grenades. They also said there had been no resupply of rifle ammunition since they had first crossed the Manchurian border into Korea. Task Force Johnson, composed of the 3rd Battalion, 8th Cavalry Regiment, and the 70th Tank Battalion, IX Corps, on 20 January failed to uncover any enemy force in strength close to the I and IX corps front.[41]

On 20 January General Ridgway took action designed to correct a tactical flaw in the deployment of Eighth Army major units that had in the past cost it dearly. He ordered I Corps to change line formation to avoid having two ROK divisions adjacent in the line. A prime example of the error of such deployment was afforded in the CCF 3rd Phase Offensive on New Year's Eve north of Seoul along the Imjin River line. There the ROK 1st Division of I Corps was adjacent to the ROK 6th Division of IX Corps at the corps boundary. The CCF struck hard at both ROK divisions at this boundary and made major penetrations in each, virtually sweeping aside two ROK regiments. The UN line then crumbled.[42]

The 5th RCT of the 24th Division, IX Corps, on 21 January sent a patrol all the way to the Han River at Chonyang, the farthest north of any UN force in Korea that day. Another patrol of the 5th RCT encountered enemy, and in a firefight had seven men wounded. During the day, General Church of the 24th Division ordered the 5th RCT to send its reserve battalion and all tanks and one battery of 105-mm artillery to Ichon, and for them to stay there until driven out.[43] At this time the Ichon–Kumyangjang-ni area was considered one of the most strongly enemy-held regions south of the Han River.

General Ridgway's G-2 estimated at this time there were 20,000 North Korean troops west of Seoul along the Han River, 174,000 Chinese troops of the Fourth Field Army from Uijongbu east to Hongchon (including those south of the Han River to Suwon and Ichon), 30,000 Chinese of the 37th Army south of Chunchon, 22,000 of the NK V Corps between Chunchon and Wonju, 30,000 of the NK III Corps in the mountains west of Yang-nang, and about 32,000 guerrillas scattered in the rear areas south of the army front line.[44] Of these troops only the 37th Army was a major new Chinese force that had not previously been engaged in the battles from the Chongchon on south since the end of November 1950. This now placed seven instead of six Chinese Armies of the Fourth Field Army in Korea. There was some evidence that Chinese forces were shifting to the east toward the X Corps, and a newly arrived force, the Chinese 37th Army, was apparently concentrating in the Chunchon area, north of Wonju, and headed for the X Corps front.

In the nearly four weeks that Ridgway had been in Korea and in command of Eighth Army, he had learned that the army did not know what it was fighting for and that it had little motivation to fight. This was a cause of great and continuing concern to him. He realized that, unless he could give the men some motivation, a reason for risking their lives daily, and inculcate some "fire from Heaven" in their effort, the army would fall short of his hope and expectation. He wanted to give the men some of the same motivation he had. This thought came to a driving impulse when on 21 January he went to Eighth Army Main Headquarters in Taegu. Upon arriving at Taegu, he dictated a statement to the Eighth Army entitled "Why We Are Here? What Are We Fighting For?" After Ridgway had dictated the statement, Eighth Army during the day reproduced it and sent copies to all commanders, with instructions that all men in all ranks should be given a chance to see it. Part of his statement was as follows:

During my first few weeks in Korea it seemed to me two questions were uppermost in the minds of the members of the Eighth Army. These were: "Why are we here?" and "What are we fighting for?". . .

The second question is of much greater significance, and every member of this command is entitled to a full and reasoned answer. Mine follows.

To me the issues are clear. It is not a question of this or that Korean town or village. Real estate is, here, incidental. It is not restricted to the issue of freedom for our South Korean Allies, whose fidelity and valor under the severest stresses of battle we recognize; though that freedom is a symbol of the wider issues, and included among them.

The real issues are whether the power of Western civilization, as God has permitted it to flower in our own beloved lands, shall defy and defeat Communism; whether the rule of men who shoot their prisoners, enslave their citizens, and deride the dignity of man, shall displace the rule of those to whom the individual and his individual rights are sacred; whether we are to survive with God's hand to guide and lead us, or to perish in the dead existence of a Godless world.

If these be true, and to me they are, beyond any possibility of challenge, then this has long since ceased to be a fight for freedom for our Korean Allies alone and for their national survival. It has become, and it continues to be, a fight for our own freedom, for our own survival, in an honorable, independent national existence.

The sacrifices we have made, and those we shall yet support, are not offered vicariously for others, but in our own direct defense.

In the final analysis, the issue now joined right here in Korea is whether Communism or individual freedom shall prevail; whether the flight of fear-driven people we have witnessed here shall be checked, or shall at some future time, however distant, engulf our own loved ones in all its misery and despair.

These are the things for which we fight. Never have members of any military command had a greater challenge than we, or a finer opportunity to show ourselves or our people at their best—and thus do honor to the profession of arms, and to those brave men who bred us.[45]

A high-ranking officer has said he never saw the memo and never heard it discussed. It is doubtful if most men in Eighth Army knew of it. Some years later, in response to a query concerning the origin of this statement to Eighth Army, General Ridgway wrote in response, "It came from the heart, at a critical time in the evolving transformation of the spirit of the Eighth Army. It came from the soul. It was not a long-studied carefully written statement. It was dictated within a few moments during a quick visit to my rear echelon command post from my battle command post 200 miles to the north. It was dictated in about ten minutes."[46]

On 22 January Task Force Johnson, comprising the 3rd Battalion, 8th Cavalry Regiment; the 6th Tank Battalion, minus one platoon; C Battery, 99th Field Artillery Battalion; the 3rd Platoon, C Company, 8th Engineer Battalion, continued its reconnaissance in force on the Kumyangjang-ni–Ichon road. Other UN units to the east and west of it gave flank protection. An I Corps patrol to Osan on Task Force Johnson's west flank reported no enemy contact, and a IX Corps patrol on its east flank to Yoju reported no enemy contact. Task Force Johnson, however, encountered enemy at three places, all north of the Ichon road, and inflicted an estimated 75 enemy casualties in firefights. The Air Force flew 44 sorties during the day in support of the task force. Task Force Johnson came under fire one mile west of Kumyangjang-ni. An air strike killed most of this enemy group. The air estimate stated the strike killed about 180 out of 200 with napalm, 500-pound bombs, and strafing. This encounter occurred between 3:00 and 3:45 P.M. The task force suffered only three wounded during the day. Its reconnaissance in force revealed there were no strong enemy forces close to the I Corps and IX Corps fronts. The task force units returned to their former positions in the line at 7:30 P.M. But aerial reports indicated there were 3,000 enemy troops north of the Kumyangjang-ni–Ichon road.[47]

The favorable reports of nearly all the patrols from I and IX corps in the past week caused General Ridgway on 23 January to issue secret, fragmentary orders for what he called Operation Thunderbolt. It was to be a strong reconnaissance in force combat operation into the Suwon-Ichon-Yoju area south of the Han River. Both I and IX corps were to use not less than one infantry division, reinforced with armor, and one ROK regiment. Advance would be by phase lines only after determining that no major enemy force had been bypassed in the hills. The operation was to begin 25 January.[48]

In the Eighth Army conference on 23 January at Taegu, in which the Thunderbolt operation was planned, General Ridgway said all bridges and culverts that had been blown in the early January withdrawal from Seoul would be rebuilt as they were recaptured and secured. His notes of the conference indicate that Eighth Army did not know with certainty what was northeast of the Han River and had no positive identification of CCF units there. He stated he did not believe the CCF could launch a major offensive prior to February. He announced to the conferees that Thunderbolt would start on 25 January, and he emphasized to all present, "We must clean out everything on the way whether it is a company or a battalion. . . . We must establish by ground reconnaissance that no hostile enemy forces have been by-passed that will jeopardize our columns."[49]

In the afternoon, General Ridgway went aboard the USS *Mt. McKinley*, where he held a conference with Admiral Radford, commander in chief Navy, Pacific; Admiral Struble, commander 7th Fleet; Admiral Boyle, commander Amphibious Group 1; and Admiral Joy, commander, Navy Far East. They reviewed plans for the evacuation of Eighth Army and Korean allies in the event the United States made a decision to evacuate Korea. Ridgway emphasized to the Navy group that he had no intention of implementing any evacuation plans, only of anticipating that possibility.[50]

Some days earlier, Ridgway had informed all command units of Eighth Army and the ROK Army of the great success French units had achieved in bayonet charges against North Korean troops at Wonju on 10 January and urged them to consider it as a combat tactic. Now he received a letter from Maj. Gen. Chung Il Kwon, chief of staff of the ROK Army, saying that the ROK Army had issued a directive to all units that bayonet training was to be given to the troops and bayonet use in combat was to be enforced. He said one drawback, however, was that only one-fifth of the ROK Army had bayonets.[51]

The day ended on a somewhat comical note that might easily have been a tragic one. A liaison plane over the Osan area in the late afternoon saw a 2½-ton truck with US marking traveling north into Osan at high speed, well into enemy territory. Assuming that it was an enemy truck because of the speed it was traveling, the plane notified an Australian fighter plane in the vicinity. The fighter plane strafed the truck with one gun on three passes at 5 P.M., and hit and stopped the truck. Two hours later a report came in that a driver from the 64th Field Artillery Battalion had been out looking for spare parts he could salvage and had paid little attention to where he was going. After the strafing, he fixed a tire that had been hit and returned to his unit. He had seen no enemy in Osan.[52]

On 24 January General Ridgway went to his Advance CP at Chonan to be near the front as Operation Thunderbolt jumped off the next morning. He also had a conference with the commanding generals of I Corps and the 3rd Infantry Division, Generals Milburn and Soule, in which he instructed them to start planning to exploit an advance and to hold on a general line following the high ground overlooking the Han River.[53]

What did no-man's-land, enemy territory, look like as seen from overhead, as the troops of I and IX corps prepared to jump off the next morning at dawn, 7:30 A.M.? Army G-2 had estimated that the enemy strength in front of Eighth Army was 174,000 men, but their location could not be determined with any certainty. General Partridge, commander of the Fifth Air Force, offered to fly General Ridgway over enemy territory to see for themselves what they could discover. General Ridgway recorded the results.

On January 24, with Lt. General Partridge, Commander of the Fifth Air Force, at the controls of a two-seat trainer plane, I flew twenty miles into enemy territory. For two hours we flew over that lonely, empty land, skimming the ridge tops, ducking into the valleys, circling over the little dead villages. Over all this snowy land, which covered our entire battlefront, we saw no sign of life or movement. No smoke came from the chimneys, and nothing moved either on or off the roads, neither vehicles, men nor animals. In only one little village, that lay at the head of a valley, did I see faint signs that troops were there. From this huddle of thatched houses a thin line of cart tracks led from the outskirts of the village into the dense pine woods on the hills above. It was clear that here, in this village, the enemy was taking shelter against the bitter cold by night, moving out before sun-up to hide in the woods, for with our bomber aircraft hunting targets like hungry hawks hunting mice, a village was no safe place to be by day. I flew back to my headquarters pondering what I had seen. The information I had gathered was negative. But I was satisfied in my own mind that, if I should order an attack, I would not be sending Eighth Army into a trap in which it could be destroyed.[54]

The countryside that looked so empty to Ridgway and Partridge on 24 January was not in reality so empty. There were thousands of Chinese troops hidden there under their skillful camouflage, exercising their extreme patience in hiding their presence.

Before daylight on 25 January, General Ridgway was on the telephone and in the next hour and a half had made nine different calls to the operation and staff officers of Eighth Army and I Corps. Then he took a light plane and landed at the 25th Infantry Division's airstrip. There he told General Kean to get the Suwon airstrip ready for use as soon as possible—to sweep it for mines and have engineer equipment grade it free of snow. He wanted a railhead established at Suwon quickly. He planned an airdrop of a ranger company and part of the 187th Airborne RCT north of Suwon to cut off enemy, but this move was canceled in the days ahead. Ridgway visited the Turkish Brigade, which was attached to the 25th Division, and had a fine impression of them. Ridgway stressed that he wanted aerial reconnaissance over the attack during the day and constant surveillance of the Han River crossings. He wanted, also, maximum use made of all antiaircraft automatic weapons, especially the quad-50s, in support of the ground troops. He said civilian dead should be cleared from the roads in advance, and traffic discipline rigidly enforced.[55]

The 21st AAA AW Battalion (SP) docked at Pusan on 10 January. Its M16s alone had a capacity of 140,000 rounds of .50-caliber machine gun fire a minute. Its commander, Lt. Col. Charles E. Henry, had a good appreciation of how his battalion could be used for ground support, and he knew that General Ridgway expected to use it primarily in that way. The 21st AAA AW Battalion made a three-day forced road march of 300 miles from Pusan to Chonan, where it joined the 25th Infantry Division on 25 January. It had made it to the front for the opening day of the Eighth Army attack. The next day, Gen. George B. Barth, commander of the 25th Division Artillery, announced the battalion's mission. He said, "The Army commander has directed that the 21st give direct ground support to infantry operations."[56]

The attack units assigned to Thunderbolt moved to their line of departure, Osan–Chon-ni–Yoju, during the night of 24–25 January. The I Corps attack on the army left jumped off on schedule 25 January with the 35th Infantry and the Turkish Brigade in the advance, the former on the left aimed at Suwon, and the latter on the right, headed for Kumyangjang-ni. For most of the day enemy resistance was light to medium. In midafternoon the 35th Infantry encountered 200 enemy, who withdrew after a firefight. On the west, the 27th Infantry of the 25th Division occupied Osan and began establishing permanent defenses there. The 35th Infantry, meantime, approached the Suwon airfield.[57]

The 1st and 3rd battalions of the Turkish Brigade had stiffening resistance as they neared Kumyangjang-ni. At 4 P.M. an estimated enemy regiment counterattacked the Turks, and an estimated 300 to 400 CCF troops made a partial penetration in the Turks position. Aided by heavy artillery fire, the Turks counterattacked after dark, about 7:30 P.M., and forced the enemy forces to withdraw northward. The 2nd Battalion of the Turks reached the edge of Kumyangjang-ni at 9 P.M.

The boundary between I Corps and IX Corps on their 30-mile front ran just east of Kumyangjang-ni. Into that area the 1st Cavalry Division of the IX Corps advanced on the morning of 25 January, with its 8th Cavalry Regiment on the left (west) and the 7th Cavalry on the right. The 8th Cavalry met opposition, as expected, at the same places earlier patrols had encountered enemy. By 7:30 P.M. the 8th Cavalry had 17 men wounded from enemy action and one killed by friendly artillery fire. Three 105-mm howitzers fired 500 rounds by an incorrect deflection reading. There was an estimated enemy regiment in front of the 2nd Battalion, 8th Cavalry, and it ran into heavy resistance and a series of counterattacks. These overran a platoon of E Company and penetrated between E and G companies. Three companies, E, F, and G, were cut off from the rest of the regiment. The regimental S-3 instructed the cut-off companies to keep a tight perimeter and told them that artillery and mortar fire would protect them during the night. B-47 bombers dropped friendly flares over their position and the surrounding enemy. At such times the enemy stopped firing. The regiment maintained communication with the surrounded companies. They buttoned up their defenses and calmly beat off all enemy attacks during the night. This action took place near Yangji-ri, five miles east of Kumyangjang-ni. The night aerial action and continuous artillery support fire gave the men the confidence they needed to remain collected and hold firm through the night. The 8th Cavalry had 8 men killed and 42 wounded during 25 January and that night, most of them in the 2nd Battalion.[58]

On the morning of 26 January the 35th Infantry, 25th Division, was at the edge of Suwon and ready to clear the town. Advance elements of the 2nd Battalion were in Suwon at 11 A.M., and they continued on to its northwest edge. By 1 P.M. the battalion had secured the town without enemy contact, except for a few stragglers. In securing Suwon, E Company had trouble in getting tanks across the river in the town. The Suwon airfield was occupied without enemy opposition and found to be in better condition than expected. The 1st Battalion remained in the town.[59]

At Osan, I Company of the 27th Infantry sent a platoon to hold Hill 134, north of the town. They found 35 CCF bodies there and took 3 prisoners.

Adjacent to the 35th Infantry on the southeast, the Turkish Brigade had a much harder time on 26 January. It was headed right into the heart of enemy strength south of the Han River, the village Kumyangjang-ni and the hills ringing the crossroads town. The CCF were well dug in on two strongpoints, Hills 156 and 185, and one company occupied the village with strong defense positions in many buildings there.

Hill 156 became known as "Turks Ridge" because of the fierce hand-to-hand fighting there when the Turks engaged an estimated regiment in close-in bayonet fighting. On the twenty-sixth, the Turks had hard fighting all day at Kumyangjang-ni and on the hills to the northwest and northeast of the town. When the Turks finally took possession of Hill 156 at 5:30 P.M., about dark, and occupied the town against its defense by a company of enemy in buildings, the Chinese who still survived at 7:30 P.M. withdrew northward. Subsequently, according to the Eighth Army G-3 Journal for 26 January, 475 Chinese dead were counted on Hill 156.[60]

After the Turks had won their bloody victory at Hill 156, Brig. Gen. Tahzin Yazici, their commander, told how he aroused his men to a fighting pitch. He said he told his men that the Chinese units holding Hill 156 were the same as those that cut them up in their first battle of the Korean War at Wawon, east of Kunu-ri, in late November (he actually did not know the identity of the units), and here they could take revenge. He ordered an attack at 1 A.M. up the 400-yard icy slope of Hill 156 with bayonets fixed. He said his "men went up that slope as if they were running in an Olympic sprint." According to several versions of this attack, it was one chiefly of slashing bayonets and long knives, and most of the Chinese dead had bayonet and knife wounds.[61] The Turks were widely known in Eighth Army for bothering little about minor wounds. Sometimes they just put a dab of Mercurochrome over a flesh bullet hole and stayed in the line.

It has been mentioned earlier that the 21st AAA AW Bn (SP) joined the 25th Division on 25 January. Here we learn that one of its platoons was involved with the Turks in the attack on Hill 156 at Kumyangjang-ni the next day. The antiaircraft battalion commander gave an intimate account of how and why all this occurred, and it shows Ridgway's taking decisive action. Lieutenant Colonel Henry's personal account is worth including.

What's that scrap iron doing back here? That's all it is when you don't fire it, scrap iron. "It's defending the artillery, Sir" was the answer. "Defending against what?" was the next explosive comment. You want to kill some Chinese, don't you, Captain? Then get your guns up with the infantry where they belong. Go back and tell your division commander to do something about this.

This was the conversation between General Ridgway, 8th Army commander, and one of my battery commanders. The date: 26 Jan 51, the day the 8th Army started its "limited offensive" after two and a half months of steady withdrawals. It was also the day that the 21st AAA AW Bn (SP) joined the 25th Div, where according to the book and time honored custom, they were assigned the mission of defending the Division artillery against ground attack. The place: a field artillery battalion emplaced in firing position in a frozen rice paddy across the road from Suwon Airstrip. The occasion: Gen Ridgway was at the airstrip . . . and had observed the M16s of C Battery emplaced on the artillery battalion perimeter. . . .

The result: within an hour, C Battery was on its way to join the 35th Inf; B

Battery was on its way to join the 27th Inf; and I was conferring with Col. Kelleher, the CO of the 35th Inf, trying to persuade him to use D Battery in addition to C Battery. . . .

I hunted up Gen. Barth again at the airstrip, who spoke to the div commander, who in turn spoke to Col. Kelleher and the halftracks of C Battery were again on their way to the 35th Inf. Gen. Ridgway had spoken. . . . Battery A joined the Turkish Brigade the same afternoon.[62]

Five miles from the Turks, the 2nd Battalion, 8th Cavalry, survived the night of 25–26 January, although completely surrounded. The regiment continued the attack, but for the two days it had 38 killed and 141 wounded. The 7th Cavalry took over part of the 8th Cavalry sector, and the 5th Cavalry went through the 8th Cavalry on the morning of 27 January. Attached to the 7th Cavalry Regiment was a battalion of the Greek Expeditionary Force. It defended Hill 381.[63]

On 26 January General Ridgway had to interrupt his attention to Operation Thunderbolt to take part in a ceremony at the X Corps CP. At 10 A.M. Ridgway reconnoitered the front from Suwon to Ichon by air and then flew down the Han River to Chungju, where he landed on the X Corps C-47 airstrip. At 11:35 a ceremony was held for Generals Barr and Church, who were leaving their commands of the 7th Infantry Division and the 24th Infantry Division, respectively, to return to the United States for reassignment there. General Barr was to be assigned command of the Armor Center at Fort Knox, Kentucky; General Church was to be assigned to command of the Infantry Center at Fort Benning, Georgia. The Department of the Army had decided upon these reassignments some months earlier on the theory that senior officers acquainted with the Korean War should be in charge of the two schools and training centers. Maj. Gen. Claude B. Ferenbaugh replaced General Barr in command of the 7th Infantry Division, and Maj. Gen. Blackshear M. Bryan replaced General Church in command of the 24th Division. This was the beginning of the change in division commanders in Eighth Army. Generals Kean and Gay and General Smith of the 1st Marine Division would also be rotated back to the United States in the next few months.

After the good-bye ceremonies, the assembled dignitaries had lunch at General Almond's X Corps mess, and General Ridgway afterward, at 2 P.M., flew back to the I Corps liaison airstrip at Chonan to see General Soule of the 3rd Division and the 7th Infantry regimental staff. There he presented two Silver Stars and 11 battlefield commissions. That evening at 8 P.M. General Ridgway ordered the 3rd Infantry Division into the line.[64]

When the author was with Eighth Army in 1951, he heard numerous comments about the great change in Eighth Army after Ridgway assumed command of it, including the allegation that he changed many battalion and regimental commanders. Asked if this charge was true, General Ridgway answered that it was not, that after Church, Barr, Gay, and Kean left the division commands, their successors had the responsibility of changing battalion and regimental commanders if they thought it desirable. Ridgway said what he did to get better officer material into Eighth Army "was to ask Collins to secure me the Regt and Bn commanders . . . who had fine combat records in WW II. He did and I made them available to Divisions."[65]

A major problem in obtaining good replacements affected especially the rank-and-file of noncommissioned officers and infantrymen in rifle companies. Of the replacements that came to Eighth Army from the United States at this time, less than 20 percent of them had infantry or artillery MOS (Military Occupational Specialty) numbers. It was in the rifleman category that replacements were most needed. Most of the replacements that were called to active duty at this time came from the reserve corps, and most of them were sent to the infantry companies, even though they did not have infantry MOS numbers. Such assignment caused a lot of resentment among these men. They had expected to be placed in their specialties, and it did their morale no good to find that in Korea they went directly to rifle companies.

We return to the third day of Operation Thunderbolt, 27 January. The 35th Infantry, 25th Division, consolidated its hold on the Suwon area and extended its line three miles westward from the town. Just after midnight of the twenty-sixth, an enemy patrol penetrated briefly the boundary between L and E companies, but there was no important action. General Ridgway put the 3rd Infantry Division into the line between the US 24th Division and the 1st Cavalry Division. This reinforced the army line there, in case enemy strength in the Kumyangjang-ni area increased.[66]

In the Kumyangjang-ni area, where the Turkish Brigade had hard fights in the preceding two days, the 2nd Battalion, 5th Cavalry Regiment, moved west to enter the town and hold it and fought a continuing battle with Chinese troops in the hills north of the town. It estimated it inflicted 300 casualties on the enemy, and it took three prisoners. The 1st Battalion, 5th Cavalry, suffered five men wounded, one of whom later died from his wounds, when an F-82 fighter plane strafed a village that B Company occupied.[67]

In the west, a captured enemy combat order, dated 27 January, issued by the commanding officer of the NK 1st Infantry Regiment, stated, "Enemy forces have pushed forward along a four km northwest sector of Suwon, and are contacting Chinese Communist forces. At the same time, the enemy fleet consisting of seven ships, is approaching Inchon harbor. In estimating the above enemy situation, it appears that the enemy intends to land in the vicinity of Inchon. I hereby give you the following orders: Assemble all units and prepare for combat by 2400 hours 28 Jan 51."[68]

By 27 January Eighth Army intelligence was able to state that the 50th CCF Army was deployed along the Suwon–Kumyangjang-ni–Ichon line.

This was a line of about 30 miles, following a main lateral east-west road between Suwon and Ichon. On average, the road ran about 20 air miles south of the Han River. From Ichon a main road ran northwest to Seoul and the Han River, which it crossed by a bridge five miles southeast of Seoul. The villages of Kumyangjang-ni and Yangji-ri, about 5 miles apart (Yangji-ri east of Kumyangjang-ni), were at the southern ends respectively of two ridges of high ground that ran south from the Han River, from near the junction of the Pukhan with it, to the lateral road that marked in general the CCF 50th Army's defense line. This lateral road followed the lowest and best route and east-west south of the Han River and was of vital logistic support to any Chinese force south of the river. It now seemed certain that the Chinese XIII Army Group of the Fourth Field Army had only one of six of its armies south of the Han River.

The failure of the North Korean refurbished and reorganized divisions of the NK II and V corps, which had attacked ROK divisions and the US X Corps in the central corridor, to gain control of the key passes through the Sobaek Range of South Korea and to capture Chungju had denied to the CCF any possibility it might have had to exploit that axis south. It now was apparent to the Chinese command that they would have to open that route themselves with a major offensive if it was to be available to them. This perception was probably the reason for the beginning of a movement of Chinese units eastward from the Seoul area. At the same time, indications were that the divisions of the Chinese Third Field Army that had conducted the Chosin Reservoir campaign in northeast Korea were still resting, rehabilitating, and reorganizing in the Hamhung, Hungnam, and Wonsan areas of the east coast and were not ready to reenter combat operations. It seemed apparent that the Chinese XIII Army Group of the Fourth Field Army did not plan on meeting Eighth Army in a major engagement south of the Han River below Seoul in the Suwon-Ichon area.[69]

The NK V and II corps, which had been almost constantly engaged in combat and infiltration tactics in the Wonju-Chungju-Chechon area and elsewhere in the central corridor throughout most of January, were now reported to have assembled their survivor remnants and to be resting and refitting north of X Corps and the ROK III Corps. This favorable enemy situation in the east-central front at the end of January caused General Ridgway to ask the ROK Army chief of staff and General Almond of X Corps if they could recommend a reconnaissance in force attack in front of their sectors of the Eighth Army line to cause further disruption of enemy plans.[70]

In the I and IX corps sectors at this time, the Chinese continued to build up their forces in the Kumyangjang-ni area, along the boundary between the two US corps. The boundary ran north-south from the eastern side of the town. The 1st Cavalry Division moved west along the road from Ichon to this area, with the Greek Battalion attached to its 7th Cavalry Regiment. On 28 January the 1st Battalion, 5th Cavalry Regiment, turned north at Kumyangjang-ni and moved against the row of hills on the east side of the road.

That night Chinese attacked the 1st Battalion, 7th Cavalry Regiment, nearby, drove in its outposts, and then moved around the battalion's right flank. Another enemy assault group at the same time hit the 2nd Battalion, 7th Cavalry, position. In this fight there was much noise, including considerable blowing of bugles. Just before midnight a flight of B-27 planes came over the enemy in front of the 2nd Battalion and dropped flares, and with the area lighted they dropped bombs and napalm on the Chinese. When the planes ran out of flares and left, artillery fire replaced the air strikes.

An hour after midnight, the Chinese renewed their attack, this time against A Company, 7th Cavalry, and penetrated the company CP. Elements of the Greek Battalion with a platoon of tanks from C Company, 70th Tank Battalion, came to the relief of A Company and at 3 A.M. engaged the Chinese. An hour later, helped by the continued defense of the 1st Battalion, they repulsed the enemy attack. The 1st Battalion lost 2 men killed and 21 wounded in this night battle. The next morning the 1st Battalion, 7th Cavalry, counted 75 dead CCF soldiers within its perimeter and 12 dead just outside it.[71]

The main force of the Greek Battalion at this time was located on Hill 381. Enemy first attacked the Greeks there shortly before 1 A.M., 29 January, driving straight against the hill from the north. Then they sent another force against the hill up a draw on its west side. The latter force reached to within hand-grenade range before its presence was known. It was estimated later that about 3,000 Chinese tried during the night to drive the Greeks from Hill 381, as it was a vital position that protected the 1st Battalion, 7th Cavalry. Enemy assault forces reached the top of the hill three times. Each time a counterattack drove them off. In this close-in fighting the Greeks used bayonets, rifle butts, and fists when their ammunition had been expended. Personal heroism among the Greeks was common during the fierce night battle. The Greeks won the outspoken praise of the 7th Cavalry. The very small area on the crest of Hill 381 (said to be only 16 square yards) had 15 dead Chinese on it, most of them killed by bayonet or clubbed rifle. This was the Greeks' first battle in Korea.

At 4:30 A.M. a Chinese red flare signaled the Chinese withdrawal. Artillery fire then killed more on their withdrawal route. Three Chinese prisoners, all mortally wounded, were captured that night at Hill 381. Before they died, they told interrogators that the entire Chinese 334th Regiment, 112th Division, 38th Army, had made the attack on Hill 381.

Lieutenant Colonel Arbousiz, the Greek battalion commander, estimated the Chinese suffered 800 casualties on Hill 381. The bloody evidence covered much of the hillside. The Greeks reported 12 killed, 17 wounded, and 1 missing. But there had been many more wounded who never stopped fighting and never reported to an aid station – they refused to be evacuated. Throughout the night battle, the 1st Battalion, 7th Cavalry, supported the Greeks with their artillery, mortars, and machine guns, but because of the terrain and their own situation, they were unable to move reserves to Hill 381. The Greeks won the fight on their own. The battle at Hill 381 established the enviable reputation the Greek Battalion held from that time on.[72]

About midafternoon of 29 January, C Company of the 5th Cavalry moved against Hill 312, north of Kumyangjang-ni, on the right of the road, by advancing along a ridge approaching it from the southwest. An air strike and an artillery barrage against the hill allowed the company to get to within 75 yards of the crest. Then, when the artillery barrage lifted, the Chinese came from their hidden positions to their firing line and hit and stopped the C Company men with a heavy concentration of small-arms, automatic-weapons, and mortar fire. It was ordered to fall back and dig in for the night. The company captured a mortally wounded prisoner who said 300 enemy held the hill and had orders to stay there at all costs. This clash was the prelude to very heavy fighting in the Kumyangjang-ni area the next day, involving both the Greek Battalion and the 1st Battalion, 5th Cavalry.[73]

The enemy soldiers in front of the 1st Cavalry Division, north of Kumyangjang-ni, were from the CCF 38th Army, a part of the XIII Army Group, which was now committed to battle south of the Han River. A prisoner said that his unit had been put into the line hurriedly and ordered to attack immediately and that his unit was outside UN artillery range until 7 P.M. on 28 January. It was ordered then to advance in a dogtrot, which it maintained for two hours to reach the front, where it halted to reorganize before attacking.[74]

An equally fierce struggle took place not far from Hill 381 at the same time on 30 January. This fight involved the 1st Battalion, 5th Cavalry, at Hill 312. The previous afternoon the battalion had approached the hill and had sent C Company, reinforced, to attack it. We have mentioned that enemy fire had forced it to withdraw under the covering fire of A Company, 70th Tank Battalion. Tactical aircraft dropped napalm and 500-pound bombs on the hill that night, and this action probably prevented an enemy attack then.

At 9 A.M. on the thirtieth, B and A companies moved out in attack on Hill 312. B Company took the route C Company had used the previous afternoon, up the slope from the southwest; A Company moved north parallel with the road until it came opposite Hill 312. It then turned east toward the hill from its west flank. The Chinese in the meantime had engaged B Company and were absorbed in that fight and failed to notice the approach of A Company. The latter got to within 75 yards of the enemy line before it was noticed. The plan had worked – B Company was to pin down the Chinese while A Company attacked from another quarter. Both companies now fixed bayonets. The 1st and 2nd platoons of A Company got to within 10 yards of the enemy trench line, the ground now becoming very steep to the crest. The Chinese from their bunkers and connecting trenches rolled and tossed a shower of grenades on the 2nd Platoon, commanded by 1st Lt. Robert M. McGovern. The men kicked the grenades aside or farther down the hill, or in many instances they threw them back on the enemy.

McGovern had been wounded in the first enemy fire when his and the 1st Platoon were 75 yards down the slope, but he assured his platoon that he was able to stay in the fight, and he led them on up the hill. Now, with the grenades causing several casualties in his platoon, it stalled 30 feet from the enemy. McGovern by personal example had led the assault of A Company thus far. Now he went for a machine gun that he had spotted only yards away firing at his platoon. A burst of fire tore his carbine from his hands. He pulled his .45-caliber pistol, and firing it he closed on the machine-gun emplacement, throwing a grenade into it as he got near. At almost the same instant a bullet hit McGovern again, this time mortally wounding him. He fell in front of the machine gun that was now silent. It was calculated later that he had killed seven Chinese at the machine-gun emplacement. The 2nd Platoon men now rushed to the crest, followed by the 1st Platoon, and there engaged enemy in their trenches with bayonets and rifle butts. Wounded men from both sides staggered away. B Company hurried up the hill and joined the fight near its end. The 3rd Platoon of A Company, initially in reserve, had been committed when the fight reached the crest. Some accounts say that Corporal Klein and Private First Class Sanchez of the 3rd Platoon helped Lieutenant McGovern silence the machine gun where he fell. First Lt. John Kader commanded A Company in its successful attack. Lieutenant McGovern received the Congressional Medal of Honor, Posthumously, for his part in capturing Hill 312 on 30 January.[75]

Lt. Col. Morgan B. Heasley commanded the 1st Battalion, 5th Cavalry, and Maj. James M. Gibson was its executive officer during the fight for Hill 312. They coordinated the night air strike and all supporting tank and artillery fires in support of the infantry action.

Immediately after the capture of Hill 312 on 30 January, Capt. William C. Dobson, Jr., commanding B Company, took two platoons of his company toward Hill 300, the next high point 1,000 yards north of Hill 312. The enemy on Hill 300 counterattacked. A force had crawled to within 40 yards of Dobson's group when he was alerted to the enemy's proximity by an observation plane that made two passes very low to indicate the presence of the enemy. Dobson's two platoons then repulsed this attack. The observation plane led in four jets for an air strike on enemy only 100 yards north of B Company.

An examination of the enemy defenses on Hill 312 showed that the bunkers were log lined, that a four- to five-foot-deep communication trench ran around the crest of the hill, that wounded could be evacuated to the reverse slope by means of this trench, and that mortar emplacements had been dug in 100 yards down the reverse slope. Two prisoners captured during the battle said that 300 Chinese soldiers were on Hill 312, some 200 more were on Hill 300 to the north, and an unknown number were hidden in the low ground between the two hills. One prisoner said that he had climbed Hill 312 with a platoon of 22 men at 5 P.M. on 28 January and that this advance group had been followed immediately by two companies, bringing the total strength on the hill to 250 men. He added that from 600 to 700 reserves were in the vicinity.

The official 1st Cavalry Division Command Report says that, in the entire Hill 312 operation from 29 through 30 January, the 1st Battalion, 5th Cavalry, incurred casualties of 10 killed and 63 wounded. Hand grenades and small-arms fire caused most of them.

A brief note, not so praiseworthy and not recorded in the official reports of the engagement, was revealed by Lieutenant Blumenson's interviews in C Company. In the C Company attack on Hill 312 on the afternoon of 29 January, 1st Lt. James F. Eismann, 1st Platoon leader, said his platoon came under enemy small-arms fire. He tried twice to get the platoon to move forward, but the men would not respond. He then took his rifle and set out alone, hoping this action would prompt his men to follow. But it did not. Eismann moved to the left extremity of Hill 312 and got to within 25 yards of the top, he said, and could see the Chinese in their trenches. He had four hand grenades. He threw one into the trench. It did not explode. The second one he threw also did not explode. A Chinese soldier threw the third grenade back at him, and his fourth grenade exploded. His rifle did not fire when he tried to hit an enemy machine-gun emplacement. He motioned his men up, but they did not come. Now, without an operational weapon, he started back down. On the way, shrapnel hit him in the leg. He told the company commander the hill could be taken from the left side. He said that only about 25 to 30 men in the company were working and that, if the men had done their job, he thought the hill could have been taken on the twenty-ninth. Eismann had joined the company only a short time before this action as a replacement called up from the reserve corps.[76]

Much was said and written about the bayonet fighting in the battle for Hill 312. The extent of it, however, is a matter of speculation, if not of dispute. That there was some is certain. The platoon leaders of A Company, however, said they saw none. Some men of both A and B companies fixed bayonets; some did not. First Lt. John Kader, A Company commander, said he thought about ten men in his two assault platoons used the bayonet, either in fighting or in killing wounded but still dangerous enemy soldiers. Another officer told of seeing knife fighting. Still another soldier said he saw one man jump into a trench on top the hill and kill a Chinese grenade thrower with his bayonet.[77]

The capture of Hill 312 and the other battles in the vicinity of Kumyangjang-ni on 28–30 January opened the road north of that town for a distance of seven miles. On 31 January, the 8th Cavalry Regiment passed through the 5th Cavalry Regiment at Hill 312 and took up the advance north toward the Han River.

At the west end of the Eighth Army line, in the Suwon area, important changes were taking place at the end of the month. The Turkish Brigade and the 35th Infantry of the 25th Division had advanced north of Suwon and were engaging enemy forces that were trying to check further UN advances there just below Seoul. The Turkish Brigade encountered the NK 8th Division on the extreme left. The 35th Infantry found the 148th and 149th CCF divisions of the 50th Army holding defensive positions on high ground along the main highway and the railroad leading to the Han River and Seoul. On the right (east) of the 25th Division, the 3rd Infantry Division, which had been inserted into the Eighth Army line between the 25th and the 1st Cavalry divisions, faced the CCF 150th Division of the 50th Army. Next eastward came the 1st Cavalry Division, which faced the strength of the CCF 38th Army, which the Chinese command had hurriedly sent south of the Han River toward Kumyangjang-ni to reinforce the CCF 50th Army. The NK I Corps continued its coastal defense duties in the Inchon area.

On 30 January some changes were made in posting security forces around Suwon. The 3rd Battalion, 27th Infantry, moved from the airfield to positions northwest of Suwon. In its place at the airfield, the 3rd Battalion, 24th Infantry, assumed responsibility for airfield security. The next day, K-13 airfield at Suwon started evacuating wounded to rear hospitals and to Japan. At Taejon, also, wounded were being evacuated from its K-5 airfield.[78]

Perhaps most significant of all occurrences at Suwon and vicinity at the end of January was the removal of the I Corps CP from Chonan to Suwon on 31 January. General Ridgway moved Eighth Army's Forward CP to Suwon at the same time. This change in itself was a great leap forward.[79]

The 2nd Battalion, 15th Infantry, of the newly committed 3rd Infantry Division had one important, and at the same time tragic, engagement with CCF of the 150th Division at the end of January. On the thirtieth, General Soule brought pressure to bear on the 15th Regimental commander to drive enemy from Hill 425, where they were holding up the regimental advance. The highest ground in the 15th Regiment's zone of attack, Hill 425, had stopped the advance on 29 and 30 January. Its capture would also help the 5th Cavalry Regiment, on the right flank in the vicinity of Kumyangjang-ni, to capture its objective. The supporting artillery fire mission was assigned to the 999th Field Artillery Battalion, a 155-mm self-propelled howitzer battalion in general support of the 3rd Division. The forward observer with the 2nd Battalion registered one howitzer on the crest of Hill 425 and then called for a battery volley on the forward slope of the hill. The howitzers in the battery apparently fired low-angle fire, and their shells failed to clear the top of a lower hill in front of Hill 425. They exploded atop the two leading platoons of F Company and the leading platoon of G Company just as F Company's leading platoon with bayonets fixed had gained the crest of the lower hill and the enemy there had left it in flight for Hill 425. The concentration of 155-mm howitzer fire killed, wounded, or dazed most of the men of the three platoons. The artillery forward observer with F Company and the F Company commander, Capt. Caleb A. Cole, both of them with the leading platoon, tried desperately to call off the fire before a second volley came in. Captain Cole finally found an undamaged SCR-300 radio and established contact with the 2nd Battalion S-3. But the second volley was already on its way. It completely destroyed any remaining organization in the two platoons of F Company and the one platoon of G Company. Six uninjured survivors of the leading platoon of F Company lay flat on the ground, hugging the earth, while enemy overran them. When the Chinese had passed, the radio platoon operator first, and then the others, rose and shot the Chinese in the back.

Early the next morning a patrol from B Company of the 15th Infantry learned that the enemy had withdrawn. The infantrymen of the 2nd Battalion by maneuver and assault fire and use of hand grenades had accomplished their mission by early 1 February. The battalion had a loss, however, of 23 killed and 146 wounded. The records do not disclose how many of these casualties were inflicted by the friendly erroneous 155-mm howitzer fire.[80]

The 65th Infantry, another regiment of the 3rd Division, had some hard fights in the three days at the end of the month, when it was put into the line northeast of Suwon. The 1st and 2nd battalions had hand-to-hand fighting on Hills 149 and 172 there before they won them.[81]

At the right flank of the IX Corps, the US 24th Division in the Ichon area, and west of Ichon, had increasing enemy contacts as the CCF began shifting eastward at the end of the month. Near Hyonbang-ni, five miles northeast of Ichon, Cpl. Gerald L. Dilley of B Company, 19th Infantry, won the Distinguished Service Cross on 30 January by his extraordinary bravery and leadership when he took over command of a squad. Although already wounded, he led the squad in neutralizing two enemy positions. Then a grenade explosion knocked him down a steep cliff. He climbed back up to his squad and led it against two strong enemy emplacements; one held two machine guns, the other contained Chinese with two submachine guns. Jointly these weapons held up the advance of B Company. Dilley worked his way forward under enemy machine-gun fire and a shower of grenades to reconnoiter the best approach to the enemy emplacements. While doing this, he was wounded again by machine-gun fire. When he returned to his waiting squad, he organized them for an assault. He himself went against one of the machine-gun emplacements, entered it, and killed the crew of four with bayonet and rifle butt. His squad cleared the other emplacement in a hand-to-hand fight. Enemy resistance on the hill ceased, and B Company moved forward. On the summit, Dilley reorganized his squad. At this time the company commander noticed his wounds and ordered him to the medical aid station.[82]

On 29 January the 5th RCT of the 24th Division closed on Ichon. The 1st and 2nd battalions immediately went into attack on enemy positions nearby in the next two days, using air and artillery support. Second Lt. Carl H. Dodd, a platoon leader of E Company, 5th RCT, was assigned the point position. Heavy enemy fire caused his platoon to falter. He charged the closest enemy machine gun and killed or wounded the crew. His men, stirred by his example, fixed bayonets and, tossing grenades into enemy positions, swept forward. Dodd then reorganized his platoon for an attack on Hill 256. He led his platoon, using rifle and grenades as he climbed along a narrow approach. Still 200 yards away from the crest, he moved ahead of his platoon and destroyed an enemy mortar and killed its crew with his last grenade. Dodd returned to his halted platoon, rearmed himself, and then led the platoon up the slope through heavy fog against remaining enemy. The fog helped him to reach the crest, where he and his men with bayonet and grenades in close fighting won the objective.[83]

As the month closed, the 21st Infantry Regiment of the 24th Division, on the IX Corps's right flank, was joining in patrol action with the 23rd Infantry of the 2nd Infantry Division, X Corps, just eastward across the Han River and the corps boundary. Two corps joined in such action because enemy buildup in this isolated and very mountainous sector was on the increase, and active, large-sized patrols were necessary to find out what was taking place in enemy deployments. Chinese were now moving into this boundary area of the IX and X Corps sectors, where formerly only North Korean units had penetrated to the central corridor. At the same time, the 2nd Division of X Corps shifted somewhat to the northwest. Its 23rd Infantry on its left flank was in the hilly terrain bordering the Han River. This was ground that soon was to become known as the Twin Tunnels and Chipyong-ni area.[84]

At the end of January the CCF screening force of the 148th, 149th, and 150th divisions of the 50th Army had crossed the Han River after the capture of Seoul on 4–5 January and taken up a defensive position along the Suwon–Kumyangjang-ni–Ichon line, roughly 20 miles south of the Han River. In the last few days of January, the 50th Army had been reinforced at the eastern end of the screening line by the Chinese 38th Army, composed of the 112th, 113th, and 114th divisions. The Chinese defensive line in front of Eighth Army by divisions, extending from the west coast inland along the I and IX corps fronts to the central corridor, now was as follows: NK 8th Division, then Chinese forces west to east — 148th, 149th, and 150th divisions of the 50th Army; and 112th, 113th, and 114th divisions of the 38th Army.[85]

The month ended with the arrival at Pusan on 31 January of two other units of UN forces for commitment in Korea: a Belgian infantry battalion of about 540 officers and men, with a detachment of 60 officers and volunteers from Luxembourg, under the command of Lt. Col. Pam Crahay. Maj. Gen. David G. Barr, formerly commander of the US 7th Infantry Division, and Maj. Gen. John H. Church, formerly commander of the US 24th Division, left Korea for the United States on 31 January 1951.

Eighth Army to the Han River

THE WAR in Korea changed in February 1951 from what it had been in January. After General Ridgway started his reconnaissance in force against Suwon in mid-January and ordered Operation Thunderbolt with at least two infantry divisions on 25 January, prisoners captured early in that operation and the encounters themselves showed that the enemy initially had only two Chinese divisions of the 50th Army south of the Han River below Seoul as a screening force.

A week later, at the beginning of February, the enemy had reinforced these two divisions with the third division of the 50th Army, three divisions of the 38th Army, and the NK 8th Division. Instead of two enemy divisions south of the Han confronting I and IX corps of Eighth Army, there were now seven enemy divisions. As a result, the fighting in February was no longer a reconnaissance in force; it was a full-scale attack. Enemy resistance north of Suwon increased dramatically. At the same time, there was a regrouping of North Korean forces in the central corridor and a shifting of several Chinese divisions to that sector to reinforce the North Korean divisions that had failed in January to open up the route south of Wonju as a major axis of attack against Eighth Army. We will first follow the actions of I and IX corps in the west before moving eastward to the central corridor, which rapidly became a theater of heavy battles in February.

By the first of February the front line, now one of contact, was about 20 miles north of Defense Line D that Eighth Army had held during the second and third weeks of January. It was now an infantry war again, but different from that previously. There were daily engagements, platoon, company, and battalion level mostly, virtually all of it fought on hills or mountains, difficult and precipitous country, and a lot of it some distance from a major road. Korean porters carried ammunition and supplies to the troops. Vehicles could not make it to the point of contact. Frequently the initiative in combat fell on junior officers. There was less high-level decision making involved in the outcome of most engagements. It was a fight involving minor tactics of squad, platoon, and company. The initiative and daring of a sergeant or of a second lieutenant platoon leader often made the difference between winning and losing. The Chinese and North Koreans showed a strong disposition to stay and fight it out at close quarters on hilltops. When one considers the total UN control of the air and the fearsome weapons, such as napalm, that rained down on the enemy, the great volume of artillery fire that saturated their positions, and the large number of tanks that supported the infantry advances, one must acknowledge the courage and fortitude of these light infantry, mostly peasant, soldiers who engaged UN troops.

General Ridgway's tactics of slow and methodical advance, constant patrolling into enemy-held territory, a mutually supporting front line of adjacent units, and perimeter defense positions at night, with a stronger morale in rank-and-file that increased as the days passed, now were bringing victory to the UN units and defeat to the enemy. January was a month in which Ridgway started to leave his imprint on Eighth Army. Although General Almond wrote a letter three months later in which he expressed his sentiments on the change wrought in Eighth Army in January, it is appropriate to quote from it here, as we begin the story of the heavy battles in February 1951.

As I have told you several times before, and expressed again in my last letter, your revitalization of the spirit of Eighth Army at the time when it was at a very low ebb in late December has been a revelation to me in the potentialities of leadership. I have always tried to act along the lines that you so ably demonstrated but I had never seen it develop so quickly as during the month of January 1951. . . . It was an inspiration to all who had the responsibility of leadership in Eighth Army, not the least of whom were the Corps commanders concerned.[1]

In New York on 1 February, the United Nations adopted a resolution naming the Chinese Communists in Korea as the aggressors. Back in Korea the month of February started off with a new commander in IX Corps. On the first, General Coulter received an assignment as deputy commander of Eighth Army, a new position, and Maj. Gen. Bryant E. Moore succeeded him in command of IX Corps. General Ridgway outlined General Coulter's new duties as deputy commander of Eighth Army: "As my deputy, I want you as your primary and principal responsibility, to represent me and EUSAK interests with the Government of the Republic of Korea. Your happy relations with the President and his Ministers fit you. I should like you to work in the closest harmony with Ambassador Muccio."[2] Because President Rhee's government now had its headquarters at Pusan, General Coulter stayed at Eighth Army Rear Headquarters in Pusan so that he was near President Rhee and could be at his side at a moment's notice.

Henceforth, General Coulter was President Rhee's almost constant companion whenever the Korean president went to visit his troops or to attend a military conference. General Coulter told the author that President Rhee would go anywhere and do anything he thought would help the South Korean cause but that, when the two of them flew in a plane together, Coulter usually had to hold Rhee's hands the entire trip.

In a conference on 1 February at the X Corps CP, General Ridgway told President Rhee, his ROK Army chief of staff, his defense minister, and General Almond that both American and ROK intelligence was inadequate and must improve. He also urged that every effort should be made to influence South Korean guerrillas to stop fighting for the enemy and to change sides.[3]

Ridgway felt that air support for Eighth Army was good but that it could have been better. The Air Force in Washington, he said, insisted on retaining control of operations and would not release it to the Far East Air Force. The Washington Air Force concept was that the full Army Air Force should be used to gain air mastery in the area of combat. Close support of ground forces had to take second place. Accordingly, the Army ground forces did not have anywhere near the volume of, or effectiveness of, air close ground support given the Marines. Army units were always envious of the tremendous help given by the 1st Marine Air Wing to the troops of the 1st Marine Division. The Marines had about 225 Corsairs of combat aircraft in Korea for close support in their combat with enemy. This close support was fantastic. Even if the Air Force had endorsed such support for Army ground troops, the cost of providing combat planes on that scale could not have been met immediately. Ridgway, and also Almond, were dedicated supporters of air close support of ground troops. As overall commander of the Eighth Army forces in Korea, General Ridgway could not allow the Marines always to have exclusive use of the 1st Marine Air Wing combat planes for themselves alone. On occasion he had to allot some of this close support to Army units of the other six American divisions in Korea.[4]

As Eighth Army's major units lined up on 1 February to continue the attack toward the Han River, I Corps was on the army's left astride the MSR leading to Anyang and Yongdongpo, with the Turkish Brigade in the lead on the east side of the road. Next eastward, the US 3rd Infantry Division, with the 65th and 15th regiments on line, extended I Corps to its boundary with IX Corps. The boundary was at Kumyangjang-ni and slanted slightly west of north from there toward the Han. This put the 15th Regiment on the high ground north of Kumyangjang-ni and west of the road northward. The town and the road were in the IX Corps zone of responsibility.

The 1st Cavalry Division advanced up this road and swept the line of hills on its east side. Both the 3rd Division and the 1st Cavalry Division had a succession of hard battles on their lines of advance. The 1st Cavalry Division and the US 24th Division carried the IX Corps lines eastward to where it met the X Corps boundary at the Han River. Here the river made a big bend, so that, between X Corps and IX Corps boundaries, it ran almost south to north. Yoju was on the Han River in the IX Corps area, but only three miles eastward was the X Corps boundary. Elements of the 24th Division's 21st Infantry held the boundary for IX Corps, and elements of the 23rd Infantry of the US 2nd Division held the boundary position at the Han River for X Corps.[5]

The NK 8th Division and the CCF 50th Army faced I Corps in the west; the CCF 38th Army, recently hurried to the south side of the Han River to reinforce the 50th Army, faced IX Corps. The CCF 42nd Army was east of these forces and seemed headed for contact with the US 2nd Division at or near its boundary with IX Corps.

The UN advance began on the morning of 1 February with the I Corps mission that of taking the high ground on the south side of the Han River from the west coast of Korea east to a line running north from Kumyangjang-ni. In that sector the Turks faced the NK 8th Division; the 25th and the 3rd divisions faced the 148th, 149th, and 150th divisions of the CCF 50th Army. Everywhere I Corps met stubborn and unyielding resistance. It gained scarcely a mile during the day. The CCF 149th Division held the 65th and 15th regiments of the 3rd Division on the I Corps right flank near Kumyangjang-ni to no gain. At nightfall the 2nd Battalion, 65th Infantry, was still only five to five and a half miles northeast of Suwon, and the advance 15th Infantry troops were only eight and a half miles northeast of Suwon, farther east near the corps boundary.[6]

In the IX Corps sector, the 8th Cavalry Regiment was on the division left, the 7th Cavalry and the Greek Battalion were on the right, with the 5th Cavalry in reserve. There was some fall-off in the stubborn enemy resistance there from previous days, but still no easy advance. There were reports that the enemy here was abandoning some wounded, and even in some cases that they had shot seriously wounded whom they were unable to move. Part of the 450th Regiment of the CCF 50th Army and the 38th Army were in front of IX Corps. Enemy resistance was strong enough to hold the 1st Cavalry Division to small gains, and at nightfall it was only four and a half to five miles north of Kumyangjang-ni.

The worst fighting of the day was in an area about ten miles north of Yoju, just across the boundary in X Corps at a place along the Wonju-Seoul railroad and east of the Han River that became known as the "Twin Tunnels," five miles southeast of Chipyong-ni. The Twin Tunnels battle will be described in the next chapter. Here it is mentioned to indicate that Chinese formations were moving in great strength north of the Han River eastward toward the central corridor, where the possibility of a Chinese offensive in the days ahead neared reality.

During the first days of February the 21st Infantry Regiment of the 24th Division, on the right flank of IX Corps, under its new commander, Lt. Col. Gines Perez, held a blocking position astride the Han River near Yoju, with the 1st and 3rd battalions west of the river, and the 2nd Battalion east of the river near Koksu-ri.[7] This position was south of the Twin Tunnels area in the X Corps sector. There had now developed great concern that the CCF might undertake a major offensive along the upper Han River valley to penetrate behind the Eighth Army line.

Enemy resistance continued on 2 February to Eighth Army attacks, and in one place an enemy attack penetrated the 2nd Battalion, 65th Infantry, 3rd Division, to the battalion CP. Counterattacks restored the line before daybreak.

On 3 February General Ridgway wrote a letter to General MacArthur that he hand-delivered to MacArthur personally at 11 A.M., 4 February. It summarized what the I and IX corps of Eighth Army had done during the last half of January and gave his plans for operations east of the Han River to the Sea of Japan. He outlined what his strategic concept was for operations in Korea in the immediate future.

I and IX Corps coordinated a phased advance under Army control for the purpose of developing the enemy situation in their front, inflict maximum losses with minimum sustained, and prepare to exploit on Army order to Han, and there to hold.

Planning a coordinated operation by US X Corps and ROK I and III Corps to commence next few days, objective of advance to and holding general line Yongpyong-Hoengsong-Kangnung with the three corps in relative order west to east as now constituted.

Plan as far east as Yongpyong sound unless enemy resistance strong. East of Yongpyong to Sea of Japan, 90 airmiles a different prospect. Very rugged, well wooded, deficient in roads. Prolonged effort to hold such a line vs strong enemy effort requires greater forces than now available, and entail heavy attrition, with little gain.

No great advantage in advancing beyond Han commensurate with risks unless China decides to withdraw N of 38th Parallel. 38th Parallel as such an indefensible line with forces now available.

No good defensible position north of the Han and thence extending east across the Peninsula which would justify the losses required to take and defend it, and in fact defense of any such line would be unsound for the same reasons as mentioned above. . . . attempt to capture Seoul unsound unless it incidental to opportunity for trapping and destruction of a major part of enemy forces, although prepared plan for capture of Seoul if opportunity offers.[8]

In connection with the possible capture of Seoul, Ridgway on 26 January had instructed the Eighth Army chief of staff, Maj. Gen. Leven Allen, to prepare plans for crossing the Han River and the capture of Seoul.[9]

General MacArthur replied to Ridgway's letter without delay, saying,

Ref Ltr 3 Feb. In accord with your general plan. If you reach river (Han) without serious resistance, probe farther until you develop his line, or absence of line. Reoccupation of Kimpo AF and of Inchon Harbor of value—should be taken if easy prey. Relieve supply difficulties and increase power of air support. Occupation of

Seoul of diplomatic and pyschological value, but military practically negligible. Your performance of the last two weeks in concept and in execution has been splendid and worthy of the highest traditions of a great captain. My best to you as always.[10]

Lt. Col. G. I. Malcolm, writing in *The Argylls in Korea*, described the February fighting: "Barrelling down the road was off . . . simply the old tactical story of making sure of one position before attacking the next." It was company through company; battalion through battalion in succession.

On the army left, the only North Korean troops south of the Han River that engaged the Turks and elements of the 25th Division were the NK 8th Division. Four prisoners from it on 3 February said that a large proportion of its troops were ill with typhus, as high as 50 percent in some companies, one entire platoon in another company, and that the 83rd Regiment had only about 60 men to a battalion. Obviously, this NK division on the extreme west end of the line was hardly combat effective.[11]

On 3 February an enemy strongpoint on Hill 431, southwest of Anyang, changed hands several times during a day of bitter fighting. The Turks initially had taken the hill in the afternoon of the second. That night two enemy companies counterattacked and, in a two-hour fight, recaptured the hill and forced the Turks back half a mile. On 3 February the Turks attacked the hill again, which an estimated enemy battalion now held. By midafternoon the Turks had the hill. But they could not hold it, and by 5 P.M., just at dark, an enemy-reinforced battalion counterattack from Hill 427 drove the Turks off Hill 431 once again. A part of this enemy force hit the adjacent 2nd Battalion, 35th Infantry, to the east but were there repulsed. The Chinese withdrew from Hill 427, losing an estimated 100 men killed by artillery fire. The enemy still held Hill 431.[12]

East of the Turks and the 25th Division, the US 3rd Division also had hard going on 3 February. Its 65th Regiment had lost some ground to the enemy on the second but had won it back and then on the third had attacked against stubborn resistance. The 25th and the 3rd divisions were opposed by the CCF 50th Army.[13]

Although there was bitter opposition by the 50th Army along the MSR from Suwon to Anyang and on the row of hills on each side of the highway, where the Chinese had established their strongpoints, there appeared to be no enemy reinforcements there, which would have been the case had the Chinese been intent on holding a bridgehead south of the Han River near the west coast. Perhaps the naval bombardment that was now in progress in the Inchon area, including 8-inch shellfire from the *St. Paul* as early as 25 January, caused the Chinese to think they could not hold south of the Han River in the coastal area. The fleet built up day after day on the west coast in the Inchon region, and on 9 February the battleship *Missouri* arrived there with its 16-inch guns. It had come all the way around the peninsula from Kangnung, where it had been helping the ROK Capital Division along the east coast. The concentration of naval ships on the west coast in the Inchon area had been planned by Ridgway and the naval command to help the ground troops at the western end of the Eighth Army line.[14]

The Chinese were in a precarious position south of the Han River in the Inchon region and below Seoul. All the bridges across the Han had been destroyed, and none had been rebuilt; the ice on the river would soon be breaking up, and combined naval gunfire, air power, and the ground forces might isolate any enemy troops south of the river. As the enemy slowly withdrew north toward the Han after stubborn resistance at chosen strongpoints, it began to appear that their efforts were more of a delaying type of operation south of the river rather than a fight to hold the ground. It is likely the Chinese plan was to defend strongly south of the river only for the time being but to hold indefinitely north of the Han.

But certainly the 1st Cavalry Division on 3 February found that its 8th Cavalry Regiment was opposed by organized resistance on both flanks. Enemy mortar fire was heavy at times. The regiment also had some other bad luck that day. The breechblock blew out of a 155-mm howitzer of C Battery, 82nd Field Artillery Battalion, killing two and seriously wounding three other men.[15]

On the IX Corps right flank, the US 24th Division held an increasingly important sector as the Chinese forces north of the Han began moving formations eastward. There, north of Ichon and on toward Yangpyong on the Han River, and where the course of the Han turned west and northwest toward Seoul from a previously general northern course from the Chungju area, Chinese troops of the 112th and 113th divisions, CCF 38th Army, had by now dug in on favorable high ground, a long ridge south of the Han River. The 24th Division had its 5th RCT on the left and the 19th Infantry on the right. The 21st Regiment was to the east of the 19th Regiment on a screening mission along the X Corps boundary, where the irregular course of the Han River split the regiment's zone. In some places terrain east of the Han River was in IX Corps and the 21st Infantry's sector.[16]

Into this formidable terrain, and against the 38th Army's MLR, the 19th Infantry attacked on 3 February. The 3rd Battalion led off, with the 1st Battalion following. This initial movement was after dark. The Chinese counterattacked during the night with a large force. It drove the 1st Battalion back and cut the supply line to the 3rd Battalion. Both battalions were forced back to their jump-off initial points of departure. The 19th Infantry's attack failed. The Chinese continued to hold their positions against further efforts of the 24th Division to advance in this sector. It was apparent that, at least for the present, the 38th Army was not going to give up its strong defense positions between Ichon and Yangpyong at the bend of the Han River.[17]

The fight, begun on 3 February, continued that night. Capt. Charles T. Bailey of A Company, 19th Infantry, sent Sgt. Stanley T. Adams with a platoon to establish an outpost about 200 yards ahead of the company. At 1 A.M., 4 February, an estimated force of 250 Chinese, employing small-arms, machine-gun, and mortar fire, hit this outpost, forcing it back on the company's main position. Adams at this point saw an estimated 150 enemy silhouetted against the skyline approaching his platoon. Sergeant Adams fixed bayonet and urged his platoon to do the same. At the head of 13 of his platoon, Adams charged the approaching enemy. A subma-chine gun slug hit Adams in the leg, knocking him to the ground, 50 yards from the enemy. Adams jumped to his feet, ignoring the wound, and closed with the Chinese. Four times grenades bounced off him before they ex-ploded, each time the concussion knocking him momentarily to the ground. Closing with the foremost enemy, Adams used his bayonet and clubbed rifle butt, swinging viciously in every direction. Many fell before the blows of the tall and powerful Kansan. Others who had followed him fought in the same way. The close-in fight continued spasmodically for more than an hour. Then the Chinese force withdrew. A count later showed 50 dead enemy at the scene. Many of them had bayonet wounds and suffered crushed skulls from rifle butt blows. Adams was a veteran of the North African and Italian campaigns of World War II. Captain Bailey had observed part of this fight at the outpost. It is not strange that Sergeant Adams was soon a master sergeant, and five months later he was awarded the Congressional Medal of Honor for his heroic performance and leadership on the night of 3–4 February near Sesim-ni, Korea.[18]

In a related action, another enlisted man, Cpl. Bobby G. Stuart, also of A Company, 19th Infantry, earned the Distinguished Service Cross that same night. When a machine gunner was wounded that night, Stuart took the place behind the gun and continued a destructive fire against the enemy. Then the company was ordered to withdraw. Stuart picked up the gun, cradled it in his arms, and continued to fire it as he covered the company's withdrawal. The company reorganized and then counterattacked. Stuart, still carrying the machine gun, took part prominently in the counterattack. When the company had retaken its former position, Stuart set up the gun in a good but exposed position and continued effective fire. He aided ap-preciably in helping repulse two Chinese counterattacks. During this ac-tion he was wounded by mortar fire, but he would not leave his gun until a replacement gunner arrived. He was then evacuated for medical treatment.[19]

Meanwhile, at Suwon, General Ridgway held a corps commanders con-ference. In it, he stressed several things: he wanted greater attention given to the training level of troops, artillery fire should be coordinated better between adjacent units, more stress should be placed on taking ridges of high ground, it was undesirable to use generals' sons as aides, and he said he was trying to get more night battlefield illumination. General Almond of X Corps reported that preparations for his corps's jump-off in an offensive to begin the next morning were completed. General Ridgway discussed his consideration of relieving the 2nd Infantry Division by the 1st Marine Division.[20] But it was not ordered.

Meanwhile, the CCF 38th Army forced the 5th and 19th regiments of the 24th Division to withdraw from their advance positions. Two battalions of the 21st Infantry covered the 24th Division withdrawal. The Chinese did not follow up their advantage in this success. The next day Eighth Army attached the ROK 19th Regiment to the 24th Division to strengthen its overextended line. The Chinese 38th Army held to the high ground in the IX Corps sector at this time and immediately counterattacked if driven from any of its positions. Hill 514, now in the ROK 19th Regiment's sector, was bitterly fought over for several days before it was finally gained by the ROK regiment.[21]

West of the 24th Division, the 1st Cavalry had an equally hard battle. The 2nd Battalion, 7th Cavalry Regiment, attacked Hills 481 and 512 on 4 February. On Hill 512, the Chinese waited on the crest until F Company was nearly within grenade range before they reacted. In effect, they had set up an ambush. It was forced into disarray when a Mosquito plane discovered the situation on Hill 512 and brought in an F-51 fighter plane, which flew at treetop level through heavy small-arms and machine-gun fire to drop a napalm tank on the key enemy position. The napalm tank ignited within 50 yards of F Company's assault troops. This kind of close air support enabled the company, being already almost on the crest, to take the hill. Subsequently it held the hill against three consecutive strong enemy counterattacks. Counted on Hill 512 were 105 CCF dead. E Company relieved F Company on Hill 512 after it had been secured.[22]

At this time it appeared the battalion of the 5th Cavalry Division that earlier had been sent to guard the Mungyang Pass in the central corridor in the X Corps sector was more badly needed in its own division's sector. It was ordered to rejoin its regiment.

By now some combat intelligence regarding the CCF 38th Army had been acquired from prisoners. It revealed that 40-year-old General Liang Pe Ye commanded the 38th Army and that Lt. Col. Chong Liem Sung, 33 years old, commanded the 335th Regiment of the 112th Division.[23]

On 5 February the 1st Cavalry Division had some important changes in its command structure. Maj. Gen. Hobart R. Gay, who had commanded the division since its landing at Pohang-dong the previous July, left Korea. A farewell ceremony for him was held at the division schoolhouse CP, attended by 1,000 members of the division. Brig. Gen. Charles D. Palmer, the division artillery commander, was promoted to command of the division. At Suwon airport, General Ridgway said farewell to General Gay. At the same time, Col. Harold K. Johnson, commander of the 8th Cavalry Regiment, was transferred to chief of staff, I Corps Headquarters.

Col. Peter D. Clainos, long a battalion commander in the 7th Cavalry, succeeded to command of the 8th Cavalry Regiment.[24]

During 5 February, enemy resistance was heavy in virtually all sectors of the I Corps and IX Corps fronts. Two armor-infantry task forces, Task Force Dolvin and Task Force Bartlett, were formed to lead the advance to the Han River along the MSR toward Yongdongpo and another road to the west of the MSR. Task Force Dolvin comprised the 1st Battalion, 27th Infantry; the 89th Tank Battalion (– D Company); C Company, 64th Tank Battalion; one platoon of the Heavy Mortar Company; the 1st Platoon, C Company, 65th Engineer Battalion; the 1st Platoon, B Battery, 21st AAA AW Battalion; and a TACP.

Task Force Dolvin moved through the 35th Infantry on the Suwon-Anyang road at 7 A.M. Enemy resistance along the road proved to be light, and the task force was in Anyang at 8:20 A.M. But a force of 300 to 400 enemy troops held the high ground northeast of Anyang. Air strikes and artillery and mortar fire were brought down on this force, and after the position had been well saturated by this heavy attack, B Company, 27th Infantry, attacked and secured Hill 300. In the meantime C Company secured the town of Anyang. The combined air and ground action at Anyang resulted in an estimated 600 enemy casualties for the day. At 2 P.M. General Ridgway visited the town to congratulate Lt. Col. Welborn G. Dolvin, commander of the task force.[25]

In the rugged hills three miles southwest of Anyang, however, fighting was intense on and around the Hill 431 area. There elements of the 27th Infantry, the Turkish Brigade, and the ROK 15th Regiment of the ROK 1st Division attacked an enemy force that had fought stubbornly for several days to hold this ground. On 5 February, however, the attacking infantry were helped by the 2nd Platoon of M16s (quad-50s) of B Battery, 21st AAA AW Battalion. The enemy had pinned down the infantry. Air strikes and artillery seemed to help little – the dug-in enemy still stayed in their positions. The M16s were then ordered to take position on a hill 1,000 yards distant. That was as close as they could get to the enemy and still cover the entire enemy-held area. Capt. John Popovics placed his five quad-50s on a razorback ridge and from there directed his concentrated automatic fire on the enemy – 75,000 rounds of .50-caliber machine-gun fire on the enemy at ranges of from 1,000 to 1,800 yards, according to Popovics. This fire was so effective that the infantry captured Hill 431, incurring only a few casualties themselves in their final success.[26]

On the next road west of Task Force Dolvin, Task Force Bartlett set out at the same time as Dolvin to clear the ground of enemy in the direction of Inchon. This task force comprised the 2nd Battalion, 27th Infantry; the 64th Tank Battalion (– C Company); the 2nd Platoon, 27th Heavy Mortar Company; the 1st Platoon, A Company, 65th Engineer Battalion; a platoon from A Battery, 21st AAA AW Battalion; and a TACP.

Task Force Bartlett had less success during the day than Dolvin. It engaged two enemy companies and overran them, but 4,000 yards farther north the task force encountered a tank ditch trap, protected by enemy mortar and automatic-weapons fire. In the late afternoon the entire task force withdrew, relieved by elements of the Turkish Brigade, but the tanks joined the infantry on the perimeter for the night.[27]

One of the many actions of Task Force Bartlett on 5 February, before it turned back from the tank trap, involved E Company, 27th Infantry, which was screening the hills on the right (east) side of the road. Sudden enemy fire from a low ridge there hit along the road. Capt. Lewis L. Millett, commanding E Company, deployed his platoons to sweep the hill on the right. Millett had long been a very daring and successful artillery forward observer for the 8th Field Artillery Battalion. In that job he had to be up at the front line of infantry or slightly ahead of it, and he had long been fascinated with the danger and thrill of close infantry combat. Preceding him in command of E Company had been Capt. Reginald Desiderio, who had been killed in a heavy battle north of Ipsok in North Korea, north of the Chongchon River, in the opening days of the CCF 2nd Phase Offensive at the end of November 1950. Desiderio won the Congressional Medal of Honor, Posthumously, in that battle. His was an honored name in E Company. Meanwhile, Millett had asked to be transferred to the infantry, and on 1 January 1951 he was given command of E Company.

During the month he had his company reissue bayonets (they had thrown away the original issue). E Company had also discarded their helmets. Millett fixed a bayonet to his M-1 rifle, and he had his company do the same. He gave them only a basic instruction on bayonet use but told them toward the end of January that the next fight they were in they were going to use the bayonet. So, on 5 February, he led his 1st Platoon in a charge up the slope of Hill 180, a lower part of Hill 440, with bayonets fixed. Chinese on the crest saw the men coming and did not wait for a close encounter. They ran from Hill 180 down the back slope. This was just the beginning, as Task Force Bartlett moved back and forth along this road, unable to overcome the tank trap and make real progress north. This stalemate continued through 6 February on into the seventh. E Company and Millett then came into the action again. Their story will be picked up later.

On 5 February the 25th Infantry Division received the first Provisional Searchlight Company to become operational in Eighth Army. It was attached to the Turkish Brigade. They reported that direct lighting of the front lines exposed them as much as the enemy, and that it was more useful to the friendly forces they were supposed to aid if their beams could be reflected off cloud cover as indirect light to fall on enemy-held areas.[28]

On the right of the 25th Division, the 3rd Infantry Division continued to have hard fighting, but it reported on the fifth that the 149th Division of the 50th CCF Army to its front was falling back slowly and in an orderly fashion, following ridgelines, which were unsuitable for close pursuit by tanks, and using automatic weapons to cover its withdrawal.[29]

On 5 February the I Corps Engineers began work on plans for crossing the Han River, making aerial studies for sites for two Class-50 M-2 bridges. In the advances made thus far toward the Han, I Corps Engineers found former supply areas and abandoned materials in them had been little disturbed or destroyed by the enemy.[30]

On the sixth, Task Force Bartlett advanced again from its perimeter and was soon engaged with two enemy companies in a hard fight. Even though the task force claimed it inflicted 100 casualties on the enemy, it returned to its MLR for the night. All its patrols met and were engaged by enemy forces. Pfc. Paul L. Strickler of G Company, 27th Infantry, covering his company's withdrawal, was killed in close combat.[31]

East of Task Force Bartlett, companion Task Force Dolvin had better success on 6 February. It captured more of the high ground east of Anyang. The Turkish Brigade, at the same time, a few miles southwest of Anyang in the hills near Ansan, fought a bitter battle for Hill 226.[32] These enemy positions in the high ground northeast and southwest of Anyang were the best defenses the enemy had left south of Yongdongpo and the Han River.

The ice of the Han River was now breaking up. Two of three enemy-built temporary bridges across the river in the Seoul area washed out, and other crossing sites eastward were under water. A lack of military bridges across the Han placed the CCF and the NK 8th Division, still south of the river, in an increasingly precarious position. It was rapidly becoming a question of how long the enemy could afford to keep troops south of the Han without risk of sacrificing them to the advancing Eighth Army.

The 1st Cavalry Division in the IX Corps sector found stubborn enemy resistance on 6 February. An enemy attack overran L Company, 7th Cavalry, in hand-to-hand fighting. At the same time, prisoners said their units had a shortage of food and the cold weather had lowered morale. About half the enemy prisoners taken had to have amputations because of severe frostbite. They said air and artillery attacks had been very effective against them. They also said they were now finding what had been lacking in previous engagements — the American troops were showing a willingness to engage in close combat, even to use the bayonet.[33]

Major General Palmer, now commander of the 1st Cavalry Division, ordered the division provost marshal to pick up all men in the division without helmets and to send word to their commanding officers that they were to wear web equipment.[34] This condition of enlisted men's having discarded not only their bayonets but also their steel helmets and other equipment as an encumbrance during the winter and their withdrawal from North Korea was endemic in Eighth Army. Ridgway had noted it and was aghast at its prevalence. It was a condition so bad that many units had to be virtually reequipped with some of the weapons and equipment considered necessary for combat.

In the western part of IX Corps, action during this time was especially severe in the 24th Division sector. There the 38th Army proved a stubborn foe and did not easily give up positions that had been dug in on high ground. In four days of attack, the 5th RCT, despite heavy artillery support, had not taken its objective near Subuk. On 6 February, the ROK 19th Regiment relieved the 5th RCT and continued the attack there. Farther east, enemy attacked B and L companies of the 21st Infantry and forced L Company from Hill 296. The 2nd Platoon of K Company counterattacked this enemy force, and supported by air strikes, artillery, and mortar fire, it regained the hill. The 21st Infantry had an unknown number killed and 49 wounded in this action. It was estimated that an enemy battalion had lost 280 killed and 305 wounded by all arms in the action. No doubt this estimate was a bit high, as that number normally would leave no able-bodied survivors in a CCF battalion. Two days later, General Ridgway sent word to the 21st Infantry that he wanted its patrols to go "as far and deep as necessary to know where and in what force the en."[35] This area along the Han River at the boundary between the US IX Corps and X Corps was rapidly becoming a hot spot. It was feared the enemy was building up there to launch a major offensive.

In the 19th Infantry sector of the 24th Division, there was also continued severe action on 6 February. Capt. Anthony Dannucci, Jr., commander of G Company, was killed leading a bayonet charge that broke up an enemy attack.[36]

Although Task Force Dolvin had captured the airport at Anyang and had occupied at least part of the town earlier, it was not until 7 February that it really had control of the place. Elements of the task force entered Anyang about daybreak at 7:14 A.M. and found it booby-trapped. Most of the task force passed through or around the town and was then heavily engaged with enemy just north of it. Meanwhile elements of the 35th Infantry reached the town in a flanking attack from the west. In truth, it was hard to say just when during the day Anyang was completely controlled by UN troops, as there were enemy forces all around the town. At 3 P.M. the 35th Infantry Regiment officially relieved Task Force Dolvin in the town, and the task force continued its attacks north of the town. Southwest of Anyang, Task Force Bartlett had not yet secured the high ground and come abreast of Task Force Dolvin. All day of 7 February that task force encountered the same resistance that had held it up for two days.[37]

North Korean prisoners captured at and in the vicinity of Anyang revealed that the NK 47th Division had relieved Chinese units there and had at least one regiment engaged in the defense of Anyang. The NK 17th Division had moved from Seoul to Inchon to relieve the NK 47th Division there so that it could move east to the I Corps front at Anyang. On 8 February, prisoners from all regiments of the NK 47th Division were taken in the vicinity of Anyang.[38]

On the morning of 7 February, Task Force Bartlett left its night perimeter for the third day in a row to attack north. The 2nd Battalion, 27th Infantry, crossed the line of departure at 7:45 A.M. Capt. Lewis L. Millett, commanding E Company, took the east side of the road. At Hill 180, Millett and his company again met enemy that proved to be a mixed force of Chinese and North Korean soldiers. They were dug in on the hilltop, actually a ridgeline, in a series of foxholes that were so heavily camouflaged with tree branches that, on approaching them, one could not see what was in them.

Millett's company received fire from the hill and moved out toward it. Millett ran across a stretch of flat paddy land at the western base of the hill and there stopped to organize his 1st and 3rd platoons—the 1st Platoon had already been pinned down by enemy fire. He ordered his men to fix bayonets and said they were going to assault the hill with grenades and bayonets. He led the advance.

What followed has been described variously by different reports and in press articles. All of them refer to the close-in fighting on the crest and along the ridgeline. The reports and press articles all mention prominently the extent of bayonet fighting, in which Millett led the way, but some other individuals apparently killed more of the enemy by bayonet than he did. It seems that those wielding the bayonet tried either to strike the throat of an enemy or to plunge the bayonet in the chest. Most of the bayonet killing was done while the enemy soldiers were in their camouflaged foxholes, but some encounters were outside the foxholes. Many E Company men were shot in the back of the head, indicating that they had passed unseen enemy, who killed them from their covered holes after they had passed. It was a weird and wild battle. The alleged number of enemy killed by bayonet varies widely in different accounts, ranging from 18 to 47. There is no way one can determine precisely what the figure was, but the battle on Hill 180, which led to its being called Bayonet Hill, certainly was one of the close-in engagements in which the bayonet was extensively used. Most reports of bayonet fighting in the Korean War are grossly exaggerated. The account presented here relies basically on the report of the 2nd Battalion, attached to the 27th Infantry's Command Report for 7 February 1951, as it was the infantry unit actually a part of Task Force Bartlett and in command of the infantry action that day. It says that, after Hill 180 was gained, there were 47 enemy dead counted on the hill, of whom 18 appeared to have been killed by bayonet.[39]

Enemy survivors on Hill 180 finally fled and left behind and in good working order considerable equipment, including two heavy machine guns, one light machine gun, three "Buffalo-type" guns (frequently used as anti-tank weapons), two Thompson submachine guns, and numerous rifles and grenades. Captain Millett was awarded the Congressional Medal of Honor for his leadership and "conspicuous gallantry" in the action at Hill 180 on 7 February 1951. The award says that he "bayoneted two enemy soldiers."[40]

The next day Task Force Bartlett moved on north and came to a small village two miles north of Hill 180. The day before, the Chinese and North Koreans had established a first-aid station there to which wounded from the Hill 180 battle were brought for treatment. According to villagers, 60 enemy wounded had been brought there from Hill 180.[41]

On 13 March 1951, I Corps published and distributed Armor Combat Lesson Bulletin No. 11, "Notes on Task Force Bartlett, 5–11 February 1951" [mimeographed copy in author's possession erroneously gives date as 5–11 January], reproduced from "Memo, 64th Hvy Tk Bn, dated 27 Feb 51." This document gives a critique of the actions on 5–7 February, with extensive criticism of the tank part of the operation. In the course of its summary the document says, "Intense fire was received on the 5th, 6th, and 7th. During the period 8th through 11th, the task force received light fire and advanced rapidly to take its objectives."

By 7 February the US 3rd Division considered the 149th Division of the CCF 50th Army in its front as combat ineffective, estimating it had then less than 3,000 effectives. These troops were in fact engaged in defensive action primarily in order to let the survivors fall back in an orderly way to the Han River.[42]

East of the 3rd Division, the 1st Cavalry Division made a good advance during 7 February of up to 9,000 yards against moderate resistance, and it found evidence that some enemy to its front had withdrawn during the night. But the Greek Battalion, attached to the 7th Cavalry, failed in an attempt to take Hill 402, where enemy held out strongly. The advance of the division was spotty, relatively easy at some places, but none at all at others. The division estimated it had killed 193 enemy and wounded 400 during the day.[43]

One of the highest-ranking Chinese officers to fall into Eighth Army's hands surrendered to the 8th Cavalry Regiment on 7 February. He was a member of the former Chinese Nationalist Army of Chiang Kai-shek and proved to be a valuable informant. Lt. Col. Chen Chung was 34 years old and was a G-4 staff officer of the 50th Army. In the Chinese Nationalist Army he had been deputy chief of staff of the 60th Army, which surrendered its 35,000 men en masse to the Communists in Manchuria during the Chinese civil war. The CNA 60th Army was redesignated the CCF 50th Army and given political training. He said the commanding general and all of the regimental commanders of the 150th Division, 50th Army, were former CNA officers. Chen said their food in Korea was obtained locally, that a planned withdrawal was in progress in front of the US IX Corps, and that the CCF believed they must fight until the UN had been driven out of Korea if they ever were to return home.[44]

Another high-ranking prisoner, Chong Liem Sung, commander of the

335th Regiment, 112th Division, 38th Army, said there was little frater-
nizing between the CCF and South Korean civilians because of the language barrier. On the other hand, he said, the civilians seemed to show
no resentment toward them.[45]

It may be speculated that, because the CCF 50th Army largely comprised former Chinese Nationalist Army soldiers, it had been chosen by
the Chinese Communist Army command to be the screening force that
stood between the UN forces and their own well-indoctrinated units and
that, if any units were to be sacrificed in renewed fighting south of the
Han River, the loss or decimation of the 50th Army would be less costly
to them than that of any other in the XIII Army Group.

The enemy delaying action at Anyang was particularly troublesome to
real advance. The town did not seem to be wholly in friendly possession
at night as the tank forces withdrew at dusk to a safe perimeter outside
the town. Enemy soldiers, for instance, entered Anyang during the night
of 7–8 February and placed many mines on the main road. Fortunately,
their camouflage was carelessly or hurriedly done, and the mines were easily detected. The continued fighting around Anyang and in the town itself
in the sector of Task Force Dolvin's advance, and also the successful enemy
defense of the high hills on the secondary road west of the MSR in the
vicinity of Ansa, three to four air miles southwest of Anyang, in the sector
of Task Force Bartlett, caused General Ridgway on 8 February, at a meeting
of corps commanders at the IX Corps CP, to tell General Milburn of I
Corps that the high ground in front of the 25th Division was the key to
the situation in I Corps, and he hoped the corps would push harder there.
He also announced that I Corps would get ten new artillery battalions,
which would include most of the new heavy weapons to arrive, two self-
propelled 155-mm howitzer battalions, and one 8-inch howitzer battalion.
Ridgway felt the heavy artillery could be used to best advantage on the
army's west flank.[46]

On this day, Ridgway sent a letter to General Almond at X Corps, where
heavy fighting had been in progress, that shows some of the thoughts that
were going through his mind at this time. Almond reproduced the letter
on 14 February and distributed it to his X Corps units. He quoted from
Ridgway's letter about the manner of man George Washington was and
how he had met more difficult problems during the American Revolution.
Ridgway urged that, on 22 February, Washington's birthday, he be remembered for "faith in God, and for his unswerving devotion to duty, and for
his nobility of nature, his integrity, his courage, and his wisdom: Compared to the problems and uncertainties which he confronted and conquered,
ours seem small indeed. Compared to the means available to him, ours
are abundantly adequate."[47]

An hour of artillery and air bombardment preceded Task Force Dolvin's attack on the morning of 8 February northeast of Anyang. A tank

company of the 64th Tank Battalion crossed the rice paddies and reached the base of a hill the infantry was to attack. A squad of infantry preceded each of the two platoons of tanks that then started up the incline of the hill. One man in each squad had a bright recognition panel fastened to his back. This panel enabled supporting tank and artillery units to know exactly where the front of the attacking force was at all times. It was a success and became a rather common practice in joint infantry and tank action. In this case, the two platoons of tanks and their squads of infantry took the hill without resistance. But in a similar attack on Hill 178, north of Anyang, enemy left the hill and moved from its back slope to an adjacent hill where they had good observation of the attacking force and where they had enfilading fire on them. The tanks had failed to take flanking positions to cut off such enemy action and avoid friendly casualties. A Company, 27th Infantry, took Hill 178. There it was relieved on position by K Company, 35th Infantry.[48]

In the course of this action, A Company on Hill 178 observed troops on a neighboring hill and asked the task force headquarters if they were friendly or hostile. The answer came back that they were not friendly. The A Company commander then brought them under fire by his 57-mm recoilless rifle, and he called for artillery fire to be laid on them. Fortunately, before this artillery fire could be delivered, headquarters sent word that these troops on the hill southwest of Hill 178 were friendly. In fact, they were K Company, 35th Infantry, which relieved A Company on Hill 178. So another disaster was avoided. Every commander of attacking forces, and especially a headquarters that is coordinating the actions of separate units, must know at all times by radio communication, if they are not visually under control, where the friendly forces are located. In this temporary snarl-up luckily there were no casualties. But there could have been many.

In the IX Corps sector eastward, the 1st Cavalry Division did not have much success on 8 February. The 1st and 3rd battalions of the 5th Cavalry passed through the 8th Cavalry and took over the attack north. That night the 2nd Battalion, 5th Cavalry, attacked Hill 202. Enemy on the hill repulsed G Company's attack. Then F Company attacked and was on the hill at 5 A.M. But an enemy counterattack confused F Company, and it was soon out of control. G Company withdrew, leaving the Chinese of the 38th Army again in control of Hill 202. Plans were made to send the 3rd Battalion, 5th Cavalry, through the 2nd Battalion on 9 February and try to gain the hill. The Greek Battalion during the day was also frustrated in its attempt to gain a knob 6,500 yards north of Hill 202 that it had been trying to seize. The Chinese simply would not let them have it and drove them off.[49]

A Chinese prisoner captured during 8 February in the IX Corps sector explained why it was so difficult to make headway against the 38th Army units. He was a member of the 2nd Battalion, 339th Regiment, 113th Division, of the 38th Army. He said the troops had suffered heavily from air and artillery bombardments. Nevertheless, they had been ordered not to withdraw in any circumstances. He said he saw three fellow soldiers commit suicide (probably after being wounded). The prisoner himself, when captured, had been wounded. He said at the time of his capture his company was down to 12 men. He estimated that 85 percent of his unit's casualties had been caused by artillery fire.[50]

On the night of 8–9 February the dam broke. During the night the NK 8th and 47th divisions, the CCF 50th Army, and the CCF 38th Army troops in front of I Corps withdrew silently northward and crossed the Han River. By the end of day elements of the UN Eighth Army stood on the south bank of the river and looked across to Seoul. They were now 40 to 50 miles north of where General Ridgway had launched his Wolfhound reconnaissance in force on 25 January.

Task Force Scott, which included a rifle platoon of K Company, 24th Infantry, and a platoon of tanks from A Company, 79th Battalion, on the morning of 9 February went all the way to Inchon without opposition and then returned. Navy units had already been to Inchon briefly. Inchon was silent; the enemy had evacuated it completely. The last enemy troops there were apparently elements of the NK 47th Division, which had relieved the NK 8th Division, so that the latter could go into the line near Anyang to help the Chinese 50th Army. The NK 47th Division troops had left Inchon for Yongdongpo, where they crossed to the north side of the river. The NK 8th Division was next in line eastward. It apparently was the last enemy unit in the I Corps sector to withdraw across the Han River, covering the crossings of the CCF 50th Army during the night.[51] The NK 8th Division released 22 American and 15 ROK prisoners during the night who came into the lines of K Company, 35th Infantry, 25th Division, 2,000 yards north of Anyang.[52]

On 9 February Task Force Bartlett of the 25th Division finally advanced, passing the abandoned enemy positions in the hills southwest of Anyang, and was only two and a half miles south of Yongdongpo at dark. It encountered no enemy. What a change from the previous three days! The 3rd Battalion, 27th Infantry, relieved the 2nd Battalion when the task force returned to its assembly area. Other elements of the task force were also relieved there by other units.[53]

East of Task Force Bartlett, Task Force Dolvin on the Yongdongpo MSR reached Hill 600, six miles south of Yongdongpo, at 9 A.M. At 5 P.M. it was six miles southwest of Seoul.

The 65th Infantry of the US 3rd Division had been engaged for several days in a methodical push against stubborn enemy in rough ground east of the 25th Division. This action carried them on 9 February the 30 miles to the Han from their starting point. The regiment formed Task Force Myers, named after Capt. A. W. Myers of the tank company, 65th Infantry, to push to the Han that day. The task force included the 65th Infantry's Tank Company; G Company, 65th Infantry, 3rd Division; one platoon of the 3rd Engineer Battalion; D Battery of the 3rd Antiaircraft Artillery Battalion; an artillery forward observer; and a TACP. The task force was formed at noon 9 February and started north two hours later. At 5:10 P.M. it reached the Han River at the village of Karang, seven miles southeast of Seoul. The village of Sokchon-ni was about 1,000 yards distant from Task Force Myers. This task force was the first unit of I Corps to reach the Han. Everywhere on its route enemy had vanished. A sergeant commanded the lead tank that pulled up at the river bank. It was not quite dark. He got out of the tank and looked around at the peaceful scene. Captain Myers munched a doughnut. He said only one rifle shot had disturbed them on their run to the river.[54]

Things were not so easy on 9 February at the IX Corps extreme right flank. Chinese from the 38th Army were still there. The enemy had not evacuated during the night the area along the Han River adjacent to the X Corps. Every indication there still was that an enemy offensive would soon engulf that part of the front in a series of bitter battles. The scene of action was changing. Large troop movements on 9 February had been observed leaving the Pukhan bridge area, headed southeast. A platoon-sized patrol from E Company, 21st Infantry Regiment, 24th Division, went deep into enemy territory on the ninth. An estimated enemy company ambushed it, and only a few men escaped. Two officers, the platoon leader and the artillery forward observer, 13 enlisted men, and 5 ROK soldiers were either killed, wounded, or captured.[55]

In a letter to General MacArthur on 9 February, General Ridgway showed that he was thinking many months ahead as to the nature of his operations in the future and how they might be affected by the weather. In the letter he said, "Weather and its effect on terrain will condition military operations during the next 6 months. The period of good weather for operations by 8th Army and supporting naval and air services expires about 31 March; a period of fair weather for such operations about 31 May. South and Central Korea in a normal year described as 'quagmires of mud' during June, July, and August."[56]

On 9 February the US IX Corps received a sizable reinforcement to its infantry forces. The Princess Patricia's Canadian Light Infantry, consisting of 45 officers and 873 enlisted men, had started disembarking at Pusan on 18 December 1950. From there the battalion had moved to a training area and now was considered ready for attachment to combat troops. The Princess Patricia Battalion was attached to the 27th British Commonwealth Infantry Brigade, US IX Corps, on 9 February. This gave the 27th Brigade four infantry battalions.[57]

General Ridgway held a conference on 10 February with Col. Pascal

Strong, Eighth Army Engineer, on the problems of logistic supply of Eighth Army, now that it looked as if the army might move still farther north than its recent advances. Ridgway wanted the rail capacity improved to relieve the strain on road and air facilities in delivering the needed tonnage. Colonel Strong said that he was in the process of double-tracking the western main-line railroad as far as Suwon but that the eastern line to support the X Corps and several ROK divisions in the central corridor and east of it, as well as the eastern part of IX Corps in some places, presented many difficult bridging problems, and it would be impossible to advance its railhead north of Chechon for at least another two months. It looked, therefore, that for at least until the middle of April, the railheads would be Suwon in the west and Chechon in the center and east-central areas.[58]

In one of their gestures of generosity to prisoners, the CCF on 8 February released in Seoul 48 UN prisoners. On reaching the UN lines on the ninth, the returnees told how they had seen about 5,000 to 8,000 CCF soldiers moving southeast on a trail north of the Han River, two miles east of Yangpyong, in the eastern part of the IX Corps sector. This large group apparently was an entire CCF division. Air reports also indicated there was a large movement of CCF forces moving from west to east, north of the X Corps in the central corps area, especially in the area around Hongchon.[59]

On 10 February, both Task Force Dolvin and Task Force Bartlett, their initial missions completed, were made a part of a new task force, Task Force Allen, which had the mission of moving rapidly to the Han River opposite and below Seoul. Task Force Bartlett seized Sosa and then went on to Kimpo during the day. Task Force Dolvin, part of Task Force Allen, bypassed Yongdongpo on the south and west to seize Kimpo airfield by 3:30 that afternoon. Only enemy minefields on the runways were found. The task force had moved along the MSR from the vicinity of Anyang to the south side of Yongdongpo and there had turned to Kimpo. The Task Force Bartlett part of Task Force Allen had moved generally parallel to and west of Dolvin, also without enemy contact. Task Force Dolvin went into an assembly area west of Kimpo for the night, and Task Force Bartlett stayed near Sosa. The next day both forces patrolled to the Han River without incident. That evening both Dolvin and Bartlett returned to Anyang and dissolved, reverting to their parent units. It was estimated they had inflicted 2,700 casualties on the enemy.[60]

The US 35th Regiment, following in the wake of Task Force Dolvin, captured Yongdongpo on 10 February and then went on the short distance to the Han River, opposite Seoul. There, Col. Gerald C. Kelleher, the regimental commander, was able to bring his tired men to a halt for the time being. The 35th Regiment had had several severe fights on the way from Anyang to Yongdongpo along the MSR, even though it had followed Task Force Dolvin.[61] The 1st Battalion, 24th Regiment, of the 25th Division secured the Kimpo area on 10 February, after Task Force Allen troops had gone on to the Han.[62]

The Navy had preceded Eighth Army to Inchon, but on 10 February Eighth Army ground forces reached and secured Inchon. At 5:50 P.M. a tank unit of the 24th Regiment, 25th Division, reached Inchon without firing a shot. The port city was deserted but had been largely destroyed by the UN forces during the evacuation in early January, with rubble and barbed-wire entanglements piled up everywhere. The next day at 10:15 A.M. the 25th Reconnaissance Company entered and searched the town.[63]

A ROK 15th Regiment patrol of the ROK 1st Division reached the Han River south of Seoul at 10:15 A.M., 10 February. Fifteen minutes later a patrol crossed the river and entered the south-central part of Seoul. It apparently did not go far into the city, although it reported meeting no enemy. Two hours later another ROK patrol crossed the river and entered the city 2,000 yards west of the first one. Enemy small-arms fire hit it, whereupon it returned across the river. Two battalions, the 2nd and 3rd, of the ROK 15th Regiment were now on the south bank of the river, opposite Seoul. Most of I Corps moved north during the day to the Han River. Patrols to the north side of the Han into Seoul on the eleventh and twelfth encountered enemy, and they were forced to withdraw.[64]

One off-beat incident occurred at Yongdongpo after the 35th Infantry captured the town without opposition and secured it. Elements of the regiment took control of the Oriental Brewery and confiscated 4,000 gallons of flat beer – flat, but welcome nevertheless. One bearded sergeant was encountered carrying a keg of it on his muddied shoulder. He commented, "My outfit ain't had any beer for weeks, and here's where they get at least one day's ration. But I hope the UCTU doesn't hear about it. They'd probably want us to put it back."[65]

Some distance east of Seoul, Task Force Fisher of the 3rd Infantry Division, named after the commander of the tank company in it, pushed north to the Han River on 10 February. Enemy fire on it from the north bank told it the other side was defended. There was still enemy opposition in front of the eastern part of the 3rd Division. An enemy force held the top of a high hill overlooking the river. Tanks and antiaircraft weapons carriers, the M16s and M19s, took up firing positions on the road against the enemy-held position, at a distance of 1,500 yards from it. In a period of less than a minute, Captain McCallum, commander of D Battery, 3rd AAA AW Battalion, said the M19s put down 762 rounds of 40-mm shells on the position, killing 41 and wounding 17 enemy. The survivors ran for the reverse slope, where fighter planes struck them with machine-gun strafing, rockets, and napalm.[66]

On 10 February the 1st Cavalry Division captured a Chinese captain who talked freely about a big CCF offensive to start on 12 February. The attack would be two-pronged, each prong comprising three divisions. The purpose was to split the UN sector. One prong would attack from Yang-pyong along the Han River toward Chungju; the other would attack south from the Hoengsong-Chunchon area through Wonju, with the two prongs forming a double envelopment of the UN forces caught between them.[67] This information was on the mark.

With the recapture of Inchon a big task loomed ahead for Eighth Army, or more precisely, the 2nd Logistical Command – the repair of the destroyed Inchon harbor and locks. Just one month after Eighth Army engineers had destroyed the harbor and locks when the army was on the point of with-drawing south of the Han River on 4–5 January, they had the much more difficult task of rebuilding them. The harbor had been destroyed under plans that almost certainly envisaged a future in which the UN forces and Eighth Army would never again need the use of the port. There had been strong opposition to this policy, but it had not prevailed. Colonel Strong, Eighth Army engineer, for instance, had pointed out that the Chinese would be unable to use the port facilities in any event, in any great degree, be-cause they did not have the shipping and naval forces to do so. General Ridgway had not yet had time after his arrival in Korea to catch up with all Eighth Army plans relative to further withdrawal, and it seems he was not aware of the plans to destroy the Inchon harbor facilities.

On 6 February 1951, the commanding officer of the 2nd Logistical Com-mand ordered Capt. Gordon L. Eastwood of the 50th Engineer Port Con-struction Company to prepare plans for the rehabilitation of the Inchon locks. On the ninth, Eastwood went to Japan to help in preparing a list of materials needed to accomplish the task. On 15 February the 50th Port Construction Company arrived at Inchon from Pusan by LST for begin-ning the long and difficult task. Nine months later the work had not been completed, although part of the locks progressively became operational.[68] Their destruction certainly was one of the most foolish things done by Eighth Army in its withdrawal in December 1950 and early January 1951, and for nearly a year later adversely affected the operations of the UN forces in Korea.

In February the 3rd Infantry Division took 522 prisoners, 418 of them from the 81st Regiment of the NK 8th Division, which had been stationed on the enemy's right flank in the Seoul area. When the CCF 149th Divi-sion of the 50th Army began to pull back toward the Han River in an or-derly retreat beginning on 5–6 February and crossed to the north side of the Han River, the 81st Regiment of the NK 8th Division launched a suicide-type attack on 13 February. The regiment crossed the Han River near Tukto to penetrate the 3rd Division and cut its lines of communication. Elements of the 15th Regiment of the US 3rd Division first established contact with it near Suso-ri. The North Korean regiment had occupied Hill 291. The 1st Battalion, 15th Regiment, attacked the hill and had driven the North Koreans from it by 5:45 P.M.

After dark of 13 February the NK regiment penetrated a gap between the 15th and 7th regiments of the 3rd Division and gained the division's rear by 2:55 A.M., 14 February. It attacked the 1st Battalion, 65th Infantry, the division's reserve. The battalion repulsed the attack and then, after daylight, began to sweep the area of the enemy's penetration. A and B companies, 65th Infantry, followed a ridgeline and captured 100 North Koreans and killed another 114. Light planes helped in this fight with the NK regiment by marking their location with smoke grenades. The remaining enemy surrendered when caught between the 15th Infantry and the pursuing 65th Infantry. The NK 81st Regiment was destroyed. It suffered 1,000 killed and 418 captured; only 300 to 400 escaped back across the Han River.[69]

During February 1951, General Ridgway continued to have his small Advance CP with the I Corps CP at Suwon. During this time it was a common sight to see the general walking up and down in the road in front of his tent, deep in thought. But he was alert enough to what was going on around him to stop anyone who did not salute him and to remind him of military custom. And at the daily briefings in the I Corps CP, he asked the briefer a constant stream of "Why?" and "How do you know that?" The I Corps staff during January and February became well acquainted with Ridgway's character and his wanting to know the facts. He did not remain silent in the presence of a lot of generalities.[70]

Several months after the Suwon-area battles in February 1951, the author discovered at the I Corps CP an anonymous document entitled "Lament of Suwon" (see the appendix for the complete text and explanation). Written in the style of a medieval war chronicle, it told of the feats and defeats of "Matthew the Good" and "Ned the Anointed" and others and suggests that the unknown writer sensed an epic quality in the events around Suwon. The next chapter focuses on the "troubled waters of Ned the Anointed" or General Almond's battle-tossed X Corps in the central corridor.

9

Twin Tunnels: Prelude to Chipyong-ni

THE PRECEDING CHAPTER has shown that enemy pressure was increasing as January 1951 drews to a close, at the right boundary of IX Corps with the X Corps, east of the big bend of the Han River. Intelligence placed the CCF 42nd Division somewhere in this area, but UN forces had not established contact with it. Since Eighth Army feared the CCF were moving forces eastward to launch a major offensive down the Han River corridor toward Chungju and in the central corridor past Wonju, extensive patrolling along the IX and X corps boundary in the rough and almost roadless area there near the bend of the river was in progress. The X Corps had responsibility, generally, for the area east of the Han River and in the central corridor. The US 2nd Division's 23rd Infantry Regiment was on the division's west flank there along the Han River and had contact with the 21st Regiment of the US 24th Division, which was on the west side of the Han River, at the corps boundary. At the end of January, this was the only area in X Corps that felt continuing pressure, and it was the point of greatest concern. Division and corps intelligence needed to establish contact with the CCF 42nd Army and to discover the direction of its movements.

The 2nd Battalion of the 23rd Infantry, 2nd Division, now reverted to regimental control. It relieved the French Battalion in the latter's advanced position at Munmang-ni, about 8 miles southwest of Wonju, on the road between that place and Yoju, which was 10 air miles southwest of Munmang-ni on the south bank of the Han River. The battalion sent its patrols to the west and north, going ever farther as it failed to contact enemy forces. Ice on the Han River became treacherous, and in some places it broke up. The patrols from the 21st Infantry Regiment, 24th Division, in IX Corps, no longer could cross the river on the ice in light vehicles, but the men could still walk across. Snow flurries and haze often made aerial observation difficult. These motorized patrols of light vehicles, jeeps, and weapons carriers, of reinforced platoon and company size, on occasion made round trips of 50 to 100 miles over narrow trails and roads. The time given the patrols to complete their missions seldom allowed them to proceed with deliberate caution. It was dangerous and nerve-straining work.

On 28 January a motorized patrol from K Company, 23rd Infantry, reinforced with weapons from the Weapons Company (M Company) was ambushed at Anchang-ni, north of the Wonju-Yoju road. The patrol consisted of 1 officer and 16 enlisted men in five jeeps. The patrol had traveled over the same road the day before and had encountered no enemy. On the twenty-eighth, however, an enemy force lay in ambush, and fire came in on the patrol from three sides. The first indication of trouble was a single rifle shot at a curve in the road. The patrol dismounted, and at once a hail of small-arms and automatic fire hit it, killing 8 enlisted men. Then an estimated 200 enemy charged down to the road. It appears that they captured the platoon leader and 6 enlisted men; only one man, wounded, was let go. Another patrol of 24 men heard the firing and came to the scene. It rescued the wounded man and opened fire on the enemy force, but the patrol withdrew in the face of superior force.

Learning of the ambush, Colonel Freeman, the regimental commander, sent Capt. Stanley C. Tyrrell and his F Company to the scene. Tyrrell drove the enemy force north and brought back the bodies of eight dead men, and four of the five jeeps.[1]

The same day, 28 January, the 1st Battalion sent a reinforced platoon on a dangerous patrol to the Twin Tunnels area on the railroad that ran from Wonju west and northwest to Chipyong-ni. The Twin Tunnels were from three to four miles south of Chipyong-ni. The small village of Sinchon lay about a mile southeast of the eastern tunnel. The Twin Tunnels by road were 40 miles from the 1st Battalion's CP and 20 miles from the nearest friendly regimental force. A weakened bridge on the road precluded the use of tanks in the patrol, restricting it to jeeps and weapons carriers. Intelligence surmised that enemy forces were in the area. Battalion, regimental, and division headquarters were surprised when the patrol reached its objective and returned before dark without enemy contact.[2]

General Almond, the X Corps commander, was not satisfied with the result of the 1st Battalion, 23rd Infantry, patrol to the Twin Tunnels area on the twenty-eighth, and at 10:40 P.M. that night he ordered the 2nd Infantry Division to repeat the patrol on the next day, in conjunction with a patrol contingent from the adjoining 21st Infantry, of IX Corps, at the boundary along the Han River. Because the 21st Infantry could not get its jeeps across the Han River at Iho-ri, the 23rd Infantry was to supply five jeeps for the 21st Infantry contingent. The two units were to join at Iho-ri, on the east bank of the Han, at 10:30 A.M. on 29 January. The 23rd Infantry received the order at 11 P.M. on the twenty-eighth. Col. Richard Stephens of the 21st Infantry, 24th Division, received an order after midnight to send an officer with 14 enlisted men across the river to meet the 1st Battalion, 23rd Infantry, patrol at Iho-ri at 10:30 that morning, 29 Janu-

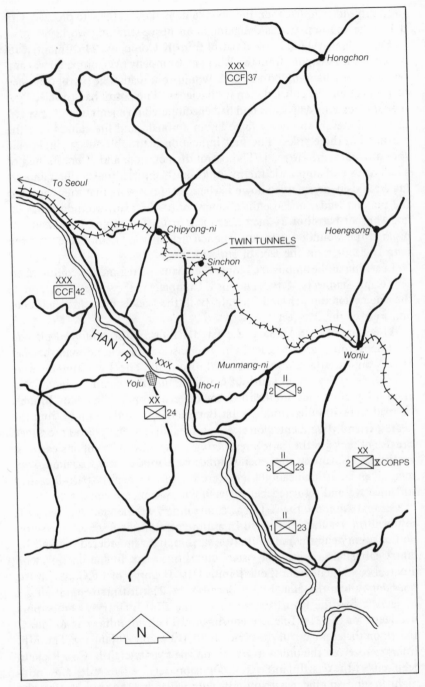

MAP 8. **UN positions in Twin Tunnels area, January–February 1951**

ary. Lt. Harold P. Mueller, a platoon leader of F Company, 21st Infantry, was to lead the 21st Infantry part of the patrol.

Lt. James P. Mitchell, a platoon leader of C Company, 23rd Infantry, was the leader of the 23rd Infantry contingent to the patrol and in command of the joint patrol. The 1st Battalion Headquarters had instructed him that his mission was to make contact with enemy forces believed to be in the Twin Tunnels area, but not to engage any sizable force. He assembled his men, most of them from C Company, but Lt. William C. Penrod, a platoon leader of D Company, and eight of his platoon were also part of the patrol.[3]

The two parts of the patrol met at Iho-ri at 11:15 A.M. Lieutenant Mueller and his men were well armed, including a light machine gun and six BARs. They gave his part of the patrol tremendous firepower for their numerical strength. They played a decisive role in the Twin Tunnels fight. According to Russell A. Gugeler's study of the patrol, Lieutenant Mitchell's contingent of 44 men had two BARs and rifles and carbines, but it also had a 75-mm and a 57-mm recoilless rifle, a 3.5-inch rocket launcher, and two light machine guns with tripod mounts. It also had two .50-caliber and three .30-caliber machine guns mounted on its vehicles. As a motorized patrol it was well armed. But in its battle at Twin Tunnels, these heavy weapons and the machine guns were left behind at the road, except the 3.5-inch rocket launcher and one .30-caliber machine gun, which was left on the hillside and never reached the patrol's perimeter. The heavy weapons of Mitchell's part of the patrol, left behind at the vehicles, therefore played no role in the fight. Lieutenant Mueller's one .30-caliber machine gun and his six BARs provided the dominant firepower of the joint patrol.

Mitchell had two weapons carriers (¾-ton trucks) and nine jeeps. In Mitchell's contingent were 20 men who had joined C Company only four days earlier. They were about to experience their first combat action. They were assigned as infantrymen, although they were from specialist groups and had little infantry training.[4]

Capt. Melvin R. Stai, the 1st Battalion assistant S-2, accompanied Mitchell's patrol to Iho-ri to make sure it met the 21st Infantry contingent. When it did so, he decided to continue on with the patrol. He did not return to his battalion as he had been instructed to do. Stai had an enviable record as a company commander (A Company, 23rd Infantry) during the Chongchon River battles with the Chinese in late November 1950. He was an experienced and capable combat commander.

Lieutenant Mitchell led the combined patrol north from Iho-ri in a jeep with four other men. His jeep mounted a .50-caliber machine gun. This group of five men constituted the advance party. The main force, under Lieutenant Penrod's control, followed at what seems an excessive distance, allegedly 1,500 yards, or almost a mile. The liaison plane provided to fly over the column left the patrol at Iho-ri when it lost visual contact there because of haze. The entire patrol, including Captain Stai, numbered 60 men, 4 of them officers. Twin Tunnels lay about 15 miles due north of Iho-ri.

Hill 453 dominated the terrain in the approach to the Twin Tunnels from the south. The hill was on the left (west) side of the narrow road that led to the tunnels. The road followed a narrow valley just east of Hill 453, crossed a shallow ford near its base, and proceeded a little farther to a point where a fork to the right led to the small village of Sinchon. The road then bent west for a short distance and turned north up the little valley to the railroad, which it crossed at a saddle between two ridges. Hill 333, the crest of a ridge on the east side of the little valley, dominated the immediate area of the tunnels and the road that continued north toward Chipyong-ni. The Twin Tunnels carried the railroad on an east-west course between the two ridges flanking the little valley. Hills 453 and 333 were the dominating and controlling terrain features at the scene of the patrol action. Chipyong-ni was about four miles northwest of the two tunnels.[5]

Lieutenant Mitchell stopped after crossing the ford when he passed Hill 453. He waited there for Lieutenant Mueller and Captain Stai, who were riding in the next two jeeps. In the discussion between them, Stai offered to go up the right-hand fork to investigate the village of Sinchon. The patrol was late, and this would save some time. Stai and his driver turned up the dirt road toward Sinchon. That was the last seen of Stai. Stai's driver, who stopped to let Stai enter the village on foot, soon turned around and was killed on his way to rejoin the patrol.

The two jeeps with Lieutenants Mitchell and Mueller continued on to the railroad track between the two tunnels. The remainder of the patrol began to close up. At this time, about 12:15 P.M., some members of Mueller's party saw enemy on the hill north of the railroad crossing and opened fire on them with small arms. Very quickly these opening shots were answered by a dozen mortar shells that landed near the road where the patrol's jeeps were now assembling. A liaison plane with Maj. Millard O. Engen, executive officer of the 1st Battalion, now appeared overhead (the haze that had turned it back at Iho-ri had now cleared), and he saw the scene below. He could see several large groups of Chinese soldiers on the hills surrounding the tunnels area. He tried to send a radio message to Mitchell to turn the patrol around and to leave the area immediately, but Mitchell's radio did not pick up the message.[6]

Lieutenant Mitchell by this time had seen enemy from Hill 453 crossing the road south of the ford and at once suspected he had been caught in an ambush and that the enemy was cutting off his exit. Meanwhile, the remainder of the patrol had crossed the ford and were bunching up with him at the railroad crossing. Mitchell decided he had to make a run for it back south past Hill 453. He shouted to the men to turn the jeeps around. Lieutenant Penrod was in the lead jeep. He tried to run past Hill 453 but could not make it. He called back to Mitchell that they could not get through.[7]

When the enemy were seen in large numbers, just prior to this, there seems to have been an argument between Mitchell and Mueller over what course of action the patrol should take in its critical situation. A contemporary document, time-dated 1500 (3 P.M.), 30 January 1951, giving an oral report of events, reflects information given to the S-2 section of the 21st Infantry Regiment. This document would have had to come from Lieutenant Mueller and members of his part of the patrol. It is worth including here because it is a summary given shortly after the survivors of the patrol escaped, and it is the earliest one discovered in the course of this research.

At 291245 Jan [members of the 23rd Inf. part of the patrol] encountered 3 enemy cooking rice. They fled to the north and were killed immediately. At the same time the patrol recd sml arms and MG fire from the rear. Patrol ldr fr 21st observed approxi 500 to 700 enemy on the high ground in vic of CS830430 and CS835440. The 2 Lts from 2nd Div wanted to turn vehicles around and attempt to run through the road block. Patrol ldr from 21st Inf insisted on setting up a defensive position until relief could reach them. It was decided they would destroy the vehicles and dig in on the high ground vic of CS836447. Patrol destroyed vehicles [apparently they did not] and moved into defensive positions 291330. At approximately 291345 Jan patrol was attacked by approximately 100 en fr the south. Enemy fired MGs into positions fr high ground in vic of CS825441 and CS835443 at the same time fr 12 to 15 grenadiers would advance up to the perimeter and throw hand grenades then the grenadiers would fall back and the MG fire would lift and approx 100 men would attack w/ rifles and SMGs [submachine guns]. Five such attacks took place at 1 hour intervals. At approx 291500 Jan an air O/P flew over and patrol put out panels (radio had been knocked out). The L5 plane flew over and dropped MG carbine and rifle ammunition and some grenades. Shortly afterwards another L5 dropped a message that said a relief column was on the way. At 291800 the enemy launched the 6th & final attack fr the south with approx 500 men. Attack was preceded by usual long range MG fire and grenadiers and many bugle horns and whistles blown. Attack was beat off just prior to darkness. During the attack some green flares were observed. Fr last atk until 300300 Jan, when relief reached patrol no enemy attacks were launched, some sporadic long range MG fire was received in positions. . . . Patrol casualties broke down 2 EM KIA, 1 SK interpreter KIA, 6 EM 1 Off WIA, 5 EM OK (21st Inf only).[8]

The action described took place at the joint patrol perimeter established on one of the knobs of the ridge that slanted down south from Hill 333 on the east side of the valley. The patrol occupied a knoll on the ridge about 900 yards south of the crest of Hill 333. The perimeter was about 400 feet above the road in the valley. Chinese troops from Hill 453 had climbed the south end of the spur ridge and got to the next knob south of Mueller's knob, about 150 to 200 yards south of it and a few feet higher in elevation, at the same time Mueller and his 14 men had taken possession of their knob. The main fight area was between these two knobs on the Hill 333 spur ridge.

When the firing started in the valley and Mueller had seen the large number of Chinese on high ground, he believed there was no chance of escaping by trying to exit on the road they had followed coming in. He wanted to get on defensible high ground as soon as possible. That lay immediately east of the eastern tunnel and where he and the joint patrol were on the road. He started up a side spur of the ridge that began almost at the road's edge and called for his men to follow him. The ridge was covered with low brush, and on the northern side there was about a foot of wet snow. Part way up the slope, Mueller stopped to examine the surroundings with his binoculars. Southward he saw Chinese soldiers running from Hill 453 for the same ridge and high ground he wanted to reach. He called back to Lieutenant Mitchell, telling him the patrol had to hurry to the high ground. Mitchell and Penrod abandoned their heavier weapons at the vehicles, and hand-carrying one .30-caliber tripod-mounted machine gun and the 3.5-inch rocket launcher, they loaded down their men with their small arms and as much ammunition as they could carry and started to climb the ridge, following Mueller's course in general in the snow but sometimes veering north of it.

Mueller and his 14 men raced for the knob ahead of Mitchell's group. They got there at the same time a group of Chinese reached the next knob south of them on the ridge, about 150 to 200 yards away. Mueller's men wore the white camouflage uniform; Mitchell's men from the 23rd Infantry wore the regular dark uniform and were conspicuous targets against the snowy background. Several of them were injured or wounded on the way up, as they came under enemy fire from the north. At one point, three Chinese riflemen appeared only 15 feet from where Lieutenant Mitchell was resting from exhaustion and wounded his companion. (Mitchell was weakened because of a spinal wound in World War II.) Mitchell was able to get his carbine working and killed all three enemy. When Mitchell's part of the patrol started for the high ground, seven of his men stayed in the roadside ditch, refusing to join in the climb. They were among the recent replacements in the company. Chinese killed all seven of them there.

It was a little while before any of the 23rd Infantry part of the patrol joined Mueller on the high ground. The knob had very little usable surface on its top, which tilted slightly to the east. There a steep drop-off gave protection from that side. After C Company men got to the knob, Mueller and Penrod put some of them in the saddle north of it. There simply was not enough room to place all the men on top. No holes were dug – the ground was frozen, and there was not time for it, as the enemy to the south of the perimeter attacked almost immediately.

The approach from the enemy-held knob to the south was along a very narrow hogback, which permitted only a few of them at a time to move along its crest. It was the critical point for both the Chinese and the embattled patrol, which had to defend that approach if it was to survive. Mueller realized the situation as soon as he saw the Chinese had reached the next knob just south of his position. Accordingly, he placed his one .30-caliber machine gun at the southern edge of his perimeter. He also posted several BAR men there with their killing fire. The first enemy attack came from the southern knob, with grenadiers getting to within grenade-throwing range. Enemy mortar fire covered their approach, together with flat trajectory machine gun fire from the enemy-held southern knob. From there the enemy machine gun could fire over the heads of grenadiers in the saddle as they moved toward the patrol's perimeter. Mueller's men stopped this first attack just short of the rim of their perimeter with concentrated machine-gun and BAR fire at close range.[9]

Mueller's .30-caliber machine gun and the BARs kept the Chinese at bay. Mueller's major concern during the afternoon was to keep these weapons in operation. Seven men among those who operated them were killed or wounded in the afternoon, all hit in the head. When a gunner on these weapons at the southern edge of the perimeter was hit, others would pull him back by his feet, and a replacement would crawl into position. At one point, a daring Chinese soldier crawled near to the perimeter, stood up, and fired a stream of automatic fire from his burp gun into the crowded perimeter. He hit five men, including Lieutenant Mueller, before he fell dead from return fire. All enemy attacks, except two after dark at the end of the fight, came from the south along the narrow hogback.

Meanwhile, Major Engen of the 1st Battalion and the liaison pilot who had witnessed the battle scene at the Twin Tunnels had to return to a refueling point. There he immediately informed Col. Paul Freeman, commander of the 23rd Infantry, of the situation. Freeman at once requested air strikes on the Chinese, and he informed the 2nd Battalion, the closest of his forces to the scene of battle, to send a relief column to the surrounded patrol. At 1 P.M. Lt. Col. James W. Edwards, commander of the 2nd Battalion, instructed Capt. Stanley C. Tyrrell to take his F Company, reinforced, to the Twin Tunnels. The company was ready to go when it received the order, but even so it took two hours to assemble the vehicles, weapons, supplies, a section of 81-mm mortars and a section of heavy machine guns from the Weapons Company, and an artillery forward observer party with its special radio for communication with liaison plane pilots to direct fighter-plane strikes. The total strength of the reinforced company was 167 officers and men. Tyrrell's mission was to rescue the surrounded patrol and to recover bodies and vehicles. If darkness came before he had accomplished the mission or established communication with the patrol, Edwards instructed Tyrrell to form a perimeter defense for the night and continue his mission the next morning. Tyrrell and F Company started forward at 3:15 P.M. The liaison plane and Major Engen had estimated two enemy battalions surrounded the patrol and were pressing attacks on it.[10]

The air strikes that Colonel Freeman requested were hurriedly arranged, and one report alleges six flights of four planes each, all using napalm, rockets, and strafing came over the enemy positions at the tunnels. According to the X Corps G-3 report, the men at the perimeter had no identification panels out, and the strikes were of limited effectiveness because they did not hit close enough to it. But the 21st Infantry report as well as Gugeler state that panels had been placed at the perimeter. Maj. Sam Radow, S-3 of the 1st Battalion, 23rd Infantry, told the author a few months later that the patrol had no air-marking panels with it—they had been left in the vehicles on the road. There is confusion also in the records about the number of sorties. Instead of six flights of four planes each, Gugeler's interview with some of Mitchell's party in the joint patrol stated there were only two sortie strikes, each of four planes. They said the planes came in low over the perimeter just before dark, about 5:30 P.M., and that their strikes were effective. The first strike strafed and rocketed the enemy; the second one dropped napalm. The 21st Infantry Command Report says the strikes were effective and that there were two of them.[11]

Captain Tyrrell's F Company reached the Twin Tunnels area just before dark, about 5:35 P.M., while the air strikes were in progress. His column consisted of 8 weapons carriers and 13 jeeps. Some of the vehicles pulled trailers loaded with extra mortar and recoilless-rifle ammunition. While Tyrrell was en route to the tunnels area, the pilot of the liaison plane dropped a message to him giving a rather precise location of the patrol and of the Chinese positions surrounding it. Two vehicles formed his point, about 200 yards in front of the rest of the column. Captain Tyrrell rode in the third jeep. When the point neared the ford, enemy small-arms fire and two machine guns fired on it from Hill 453. The two jeeps stopped, and their occupants scrambled into the roadside ditch.

Tyrrell soon came up. He dismounted from his jeep, took in the situation, ignored the enemy fire, and walked back toward his 2nd Platoon. He decided he could not proceed farther toward the patrol until he had silenced enemy fire from Hill 453. He ordered his 2nd Platoon to dismount and organize a base of fire against Hill 453, while his other two platoons attacked the hill. All three platoons were carrying out their instructions within a few minutes. The 81-mm mortars also got into action against enemy on Hill 453. The attack quickly achieved its purpose. The enemy abandoned their positions part way up the hill within half an hour. Darkness had now fallen. The 1st Platoon continued its climb and reached the crest of Hill 453 in two hours. On Tyrrell's orders it formed a defense perimeter there, and it sent a squad south to contact the 3rd Platoon, which was coming up another spur ridge. The two platoons made contact at 10:30 P.M. There were no Chinese now on Hill 453 offering any resistance.

Tyrrell was now ready to continue on toward the surrounded patrol's perimeter. Although the 21st Infantry report on the action, based apparently on information provided by its part of the patrol, said that there were no enemy attacks against the perimeter after dark but that long-distance enemy fire came in from time to time, Gugeler says that enemy attacks against the perimeter continued after dark and until shortly before the relief force arrived. His interviews with Lieutenant Mitchell and 23rd Infantry men in the patrol support this statement. Tyrrell's relief force also stated they heard firing in the direction of the patrol's perimeter after dark.

After F Company secured Hill 453, Tyrrell moved two of his platoons to positions northward on its slopes from which they could support his 2nd Platoon, which he intended to order into attack north toward the patrol's position. He coordinated these movements with the 2nd Platoon so that all elements of his force knew what was being planned. He also displaced his 81-mm mortars northward to support the 2nd Platoon. It was about 9 P.M. when he had completed these arrangements.

In the course of these preparations, three wounded men from Lieutenant Mitchell's 23rd Infantry contingent to the patrol came in to Tyrrell's position at the road and told him that all the other men in the patrol were dead. But a little later, 1st Lt. Leonard Napier, platoon leader of the 1st Platoon on Hill 453, called Tyrrell on his radio to tell him a man from the patrol had just come in to his position and had told him the patrol was still holding out. This information came from Lieutenant Mueller's aid man, who had worked his way back down the hill to try to get medical supplies from one of the vehicles. He had missed his way, however, and had ended up in Napier's position. Tyrrell got on the radio with the aid man, who repeated that the patrol still held out in its perimeter, even though three-fourths of them were casualties. Tyrrell felt that the aid man's testimony was reliable, and he at once ordered his 2nd Platoon to move out toward the patrol's perimeter. He had been on the point of ordering his company into a night perimeter, as the battalion commander had instructed him to do, but now he felt he must continue his effort to relieve the patrol.

Lt. Albert E. Jones, 2nd Platoon leader, took his platoon along the Hill 333 spur ridge northward, passing several small knobs and humps on the way, without opposition. About 10:30 P.M. his platoon was challenged as it neared the patrol's perimeter. It identified itself as part of Fox Company, 23rd Infantry, and then moved into the perimeter.

According to Gugeler, the last two attacks after dark came from a small knob on the west of the patrol's perimeter. This small hump was located on the path Mueller had traveled in the early afternoon in climbing from the road to the knob he chose to defend. The Chinese apparently abandoned the ridgeline as Lieutenant Jones's platoon was moving north along it. Two red flares that rose in the west may have been the signal to withdraw. There were no further enemy attacks during the night after Jones's platoon reached the patrol's position.

Those in the patrol able to do so assisted F Company in carrying litter cases down the hill to the road. There were about 30 wounded men in the perimeter when relief arrived, but some were able to get off the ridge on their own power. It was 3:30 A.M., 30 January, before all the wounded were off the hill and down at the road.

Some of the patrol's dead in the perimeter had been hit four or five times before they died. One man who had a mortal wound in his stomach loaded magazines for BARs and carbines for an hour and a half before he died. Another man, who fought as bravely and determinedly as any, was one of the recent replacements and now in his first combat action. He died of four wounds. Perhaps every man in the patrol who made it to the perimeter on the ridge was a hero at some time in the battle.

After the wounded in the perimeter had been taken off the ridge and placed in F Company's vehicles on the road below, Captain Tyrrell, at 3:30 A.M., 30 January, gave the order to move out. He placed one platoon of F Company in the lead on foot ahead of the vehicles. Another platoon on foot followed the vehicles. His company escorted the vehicles out, past Hill 453, fully prepared for any enemy action that might develop. None did. Tyrrell and his column reached Iho-ri, 15 miles away, at daybreak.

The patrol's casualties seem to have totaled about 39, although there are various figures in the records for those in the 23rd Infantry's contingent. Mueller's group of 15 men from the 21st Infantry, 24th Division, had 3 killed, 7 wounded, and 5 enlisted men unharmed. Mueller himself was wounded twice, the second time in the head. The author has not found a specific, reliable figure for the casualties in the 23rd Infantry part of the joint patrol. The X Corps gives a total of 4 men killed, 30 wounded, and 5 missing in action, for a total of 39 casualties. The 23rd RCT After Action Report states 5 killed were left on the hill. It appears that 51 men in all started from the road and eventually reached Mueller's perimeter. If the corps figure is reliable, then the 23rd Infantry had about 29 casualties, most of them wounded, with only a few killed, and 5 missing in action counted as part of the casualty figure. It seems only about 12 men of the 60-man joint patrol escaped unharmed. Captain Tyrrell did not have a single casualty in F Company. Enemy casualties were estimated to have been as high as 200 killed and 175 wounded. These figures are, of course, highly speculative.[12]

In considering this important engagement of the CCF 42nd Army and patrol elements of the US 2nd and 24th divisions, it seems reasonably certain that Lieutenant Mueller and his 14-man contingent from the 21st Infantry, with their immediate seizure of a high point on the eastern ridge as a defense position, together with the presence of their automatic weapons — the one .30-caliber machine gun and their six BARs — provided throughout the engagement the decisive defensive fire at the perimeter. These were the dominant factors that prevented the Chinese from destroying or capturing the patrol before Tyrrell's relief force arrived. It is also to be said that Captain Tyrrell, after his arrival at the scene, gave a classic example of a company commander's mastery of small-unit tactics, steady leadership, and cool judgment in an exacting command situation, that he knew what had to be done and how to do it, and that he did it.

This patrol action and Tyrrell's relief of the patrol answered a long-standing question in Eighth Army. Where was the Chinese 42nd Army? Events of the next few days showed that, while neither the patrol nor Tyrrell's relief force identified the enemy units they fought, they were in fact the advance elements of the CCF 42nd Army that had just moved into the Chipyong-ni area and were pushing south.

Concurrent with the Mitchell-Mueller patrol engagement with the Chinese at the Twin Tunnels on 29 January, the 2nd Division ordered the 23rd Regiment to move two battalions to a line along the Munmang-ni–Yoju road to block any enemy attempt to attack up the Han River valley. Colonel Freeman started this move at noon on the twenty-ninth, ordering the 3rd Battalion down from its mountainous position. The battalion came down from its snow-covered positions carrying heavy loads of extra ammunition and supplies. The French Battalion moved next. Transportation was not available beyond the unit transportation, and the riflemen walked. The division order required the two-battalion movement to be completed by 6 P.M., 30 January, and one battalion was to be across the Som River by dark of the twenty-ninth. Late that afternoon, a barely passable ford was found across the Som River, a tributary of the Han from the northeast, and the 3rd Battalion crossed it.[13]

During the night of 29–30 January the 2nd Division changed the orders to the 23rd Infantry, formalizing it the next day at noon. General Ruffner ordered Freeman to move with two of his battalions to the Twin Tunnels area immediately, find and destroy the enemy there, occupy the high ground, and get prisoners for identification of the enemy units. Freeman chose his 3rd Battalion and the French Battalion to move north into an assembly area for the attack at the Twin Tunnels. Their assembly area was near Chongam-ni, about four air miles almost due south of Sinchon and the Twin Tunnels.

The road from Chongam-ni ran along a narrow valley, generally north to Sinchon and the Twin Tunnels, the last four miles of which was the same road the Mitchell-Mueller joint patrol had followed. The 1st Battalion was to defend the Munmang-ni–Yoju road, and the 2nd Battalion was to remain at Munmang-ni, under 2nd Division control. The 1st Battalion moved most of its force to Korun-ni, at a ferry crossing of the Han River, about two miles east of Yoju. The 37th Field Artillery Battalion joined it there. Colonel Freeman and the regimental advance group, with the regimental mortar and medical companies and B Battery, 82nd AAA

AW Battalion, joined the two-battalion column headed for the Twin Tunnels. The attack force in the late afternoon assembled in a defensive perimeter without incident. At midnight the leading platoon of the regimental tank company arrived at the perimeter. It had come by forced march from Chechon through Wonju. Freeman issued orders for the attack to start the next morning, 31 January, at 7 A.M.[14]

On 31 January the attack formation left its assembly area at 6 A.M. and moved north up the valley three and a half miles to its departure point. The four-company French Battalion was on the left of the road, with responsibility for the road; the 3rd Battalion, 23rd Infantry, was on the right of the road. The more difficult terrain was in the French sector, including Hill 453. Crossing the line of departure at 9 A.M., the two battalions started their slow and tiresome climb up the slopes on either side of the road. Aerial observation disclosed no enemy on the ground ahead. All day the advance was in this fashion, the two battalions coordinating their advances along the high ground to stay roughly opposite each other. As soon as one hill was occupied, a force remained there with a base of fire to cover another group that advanced to the next high point. The slopes were snow covered and slippery. Artillery and mortar fire was directed on the high ground ahead of each advance.

The French Battalion reached the crest of Hill 453 at 1 P.M. It dominated all the surrounding area, and especially that to the north toward the Twin Tunnels. Colonel Freeman would have preferred not to occupy the hill, as it would make a perimeter including the Twin Tunnels stretched thin at some points, and in fact left some gaps in it. But the hill was so important for control of the terrain that he had to occupy it. With the French Battalion in possession of Hill 453 and with tanks, AAA AW M19s and M16s, and artillery on the road prepared to support the infantry at a moment's notice, the deployment of the attack force progressed faster.

The 3rd Battalion occupied the ridge running north that culminated in Hill 333, east of the tunnels. The French Battalion left its 1st Company on Hill 453, where it was isolated from the 2nd Company on Hill 279 across a valley northward. This gap had to be covered by fire. The French 3rd Company held the northern end of the French line west of the road and curved eastward to the road running north to Chipyong-ni. The Twin Tunnels and the railroad crossed the perimeter east-west near its center. The French 4th Company held a position at the southeastern curve of its line, near the road, and north of Hill 453.

On the east side of the road, where a roadblock was established between the French 4th Company and K Company, 23rd Infantry, the 3rd Battalion, 23rd Infantry, carried the east side of the perimeter northward with K, I, and L companies in that sequence. I and L companies jointly held Hill 333. But at one point there was a gap of 500 yards between I and L companies on the northeast arc of the perimeter. About two miles south of

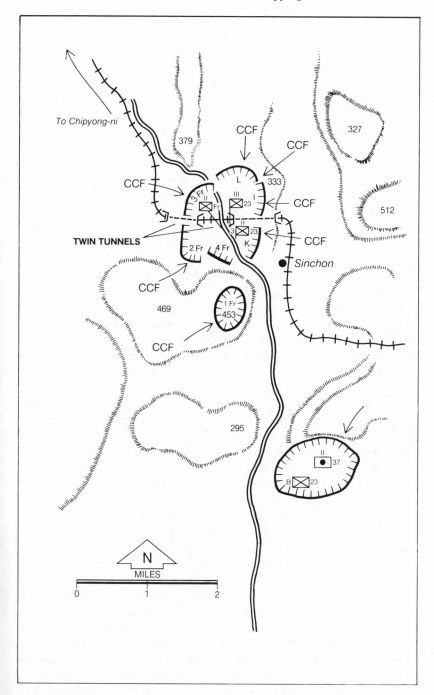

MAP 9. **Twin Tunnels battle, 31 January–1 February 1951**

the main perimeter a separate one was established for the artillery emplace-ments, and all the vehicles not immediately required within the infantry and command headquarters area were placed there and their drivers added to its defense force. The 23rd Regimental Headquarters and French Bat-talion Headquarters were placed close together near the center of the en-closed main perimeter at the Twin Tunnels on the railroad. Tank and AAA AW roadblocks were established at each perimeter.[15]

The night passed quietly until two hours before dawn. At 4:50 A.M. (Freeman says 4:30 A.M.), 1 February, the 374th Regiment of the 125th Division, CCF 42nd Army, struck at the roadblock at the north end of the perimeter between the French 3rd Company and L Company, 23rd Infantry. After a few minutes of heavy firing, both the tank and the M19 40-mm dual-40 at the roadblock came back down the road, each partially disabled by Chinese 2.46-inch rockets. Some of the crew members were wounded. The tank commander said a long column of enemy had marched right up the road to the roadblock. Both the tank and M19 had fired on the column, inflicting heavy casualties, but the enemy then deployed on both sides of the road and attacked the tank and M19 with rocket launchers and grenades. When these vehicles limped away, the enemy forces concen-trated their attack on L Company, east of the road. Artillery and mortar forward observers called in defensive barrages against the enemy, and the sky was illuminated by an eerie light as the shells exploded among the en-emy. This destructive fire caused the enemy to pull back. Then there was a lull.

Later two prisoners were taken, and a copy of the enemy attack order was found on a dead Chinese officer. Information from the prisoners and the attack order indicated that the 125th Division of the 42nd Army, which had been concentrating for attack in the Chipyong-ni area, had hurriedly struck the 23rd Infantry after a night march to the perimeter area. The 374th Regiment, the first to hit the perimeter, had marched down the road from Chipyong-ni.[16]

As the battle developed during the morning, the other two regiments of the 125th Division entered the attack against the perimeter. The Chi-nese 375th Regiment and 125th Headquarters units were located two miles north of the perimeter at Sanggosong. Some of these troops apparently ad-vanced south along the ridge that led into L Company. The 373rd and 374th regiments had been in the Hajin area, three miles west of Chipyong-ni. The 373rd Regiment moved across country during the night to reach the western part of the perimeter, at the French Battalion positions. As stated, the 374th Regiment from Hajin, moving on the road through Chipyong-ni, had been the first to reach and attack the perimeter on the north. The Chinese division had a strength of about 7,000 men.

At 6 A.M. the 373rd Regiment opened its attack against the French Bat-talion on the west side of the perimeter at Hill 453. For several hours it concentrated its attack down the narrow ridge that led from Hill 543 to Hill 453. (Hill 543 was southwest of Hill 453.) Artillery and mortar fire hit the Chinese here and took very heavy casualties among them. Despite the casualties, the Chinese pressed their attacks for three hours in an attempt to seize this dominating hill. The French 1st Company was very hard pressed on Hill 453 and had to engage in hand-to-hand fighting and itself suffered heavy casualties. Its ammunition supply ran low. In desperation the 1st Company launched a bayonet attack at 10:20 A.M. With victory almost in their hands, the Chinese fell back. While fighting continued here throughout the day, the Chinese did not again come that close to taking the hill.

When daylight came that morning, the weather was hazy. This condition quickly turned into a dark overcast with low visibility, which made air support impossible. Other bad news also came soon after daybreak. An armored patrol from the 2nd Reconnaissance Company coming north from Korun-ni reported an enemy force had cut the road between the 1st Battalion and the artillery. It reported it was engaged with this enemy. By radio Freeman ordered the 1st Battalion to send a company to open the road and to be prepared to move the rest of the 1st Battalion forward on order. B Company started at once for the enemy roadblock and dispersed the enemy there but reported other enemy on the ridges east of the artillery. Freeman needed B Company badly but felt the artillery even more had to have protection, so he ordered B Company to dig in around the artillery. The CCF on the eastern ridge soon attacked the artillery and B Company, but they were driven off. Freeman left B Company there under the command of the artillery battalion commander.

Enemy mortar fire slackened, fortunately, during the morning. It developed later that the enemy had not had time to bring up more than a few rounds each for the mortars. The Chinese commander also apparently felt they could win the battle with their numerical superiority, using only small-arms, grenades, and machine-gun fire.

When the Chinese failed to dislodge the French 1st Company from Hill 453 in their early attacks, they struck at the valley gap north of Hill 453 and between the French 1st and 2nd companies. There the French Heavy Weapons Company bore the brunt of the attacks and took many casualties, including their commander killed. Nine more tanks of the 23rd Regimental tank company arrived at the perimeter, and a platoon of them was placed in this valley gap. They helped to prevent an enemy breakthrough there.

It will be recalled that, at the beginning of the Chinese attack at 4:30 or 4:50 A.M. at the northern edge of the perimeter, L Company was the object of their first assaults. Observed artillery and mortar fire broke up these attacks, and a lull followed at that part of the perimeter. But soon the Chinese 374th Regiment resumed an assault on the east side of the perimeter and drove hard against L and I companies. Some Chinese penetrated the gap between the two companies, and I Company had to withdraw from its east-flank position. This attack was accompanied by many bugle calls and various whistles. I Company counterattacked and regained its position. It also extended its lines northward to close the gap between it and L Company. The Chinese 374th Regiment persisted in attacking from the east straight up the steep ridge slope into the center of I Company, although it could have centered its attack from higher ground north of L Company. This bad tactic cost it very heavy casualties, and Chinese dead lay in large numbers on the slope east of I Company. Second Lt. Thomas K. Craig of I Company particularly distinguished himself throughout the day in the I Company battles.[17]

Before noon, Major General Ruffner of the 2nd Division realized the attack force at the Twin Tunnels was in a very hard fight and needed the rest of the regiment. He released the 1st and 2nd battalions to 23rd Infantry control. The 1st Battalion gathered in its outposts and hit the road about 2 P.M., but lack of transportation mandated that most of it had to march on foot. The 2nd Battalion and Regimental Headquarters Company were to shuttle forward as quickly as possible. None of these troops was expected to reach the perimeter before dark, except E Company, which was sent forward at once. With these two battalions moving up, the division ordered the 9th Infantry Regiment to continue holding Wonju but to extend its responsibilities to the Yoju–Munmang-ni road.

While these moves were being initiated, the Chinese at noon hurled an intensified attack against the French 3rd Company and L Company at the northern end of the perimeter. Chinese units seized a high, rocky hill on the northwest arc of the French 3rd Company's position. This enemy success exposed L Company's flank, but worse, it opened up the inside and center of the perimeter area to enemy fire. The Chinese emplaced at least one machine gun on this hill, which opened fire on the regimental headquarters and trains area. This fire hit the regimental command post, the aid station, and vehicles there. The French 3rd Company tried repeatedly to regain its position, but the Chinese drove it back with heavy losses. At this time action was heavy nearly everywhere on the perimeter, and no units could be shifted to aid the French 3rd Company. Drivers, clerks, cooks, and mechanics everywhere had now been committed to the battle. Colonel Freeman recorded a final desperate effort to restore the position and destroy the enemy machine gun or guns on the rocky crest.

A final effort was made to restore the position. A twin-40 flack wagon, the sweetest weapon possible for vacuum cleaning a ridge, and two tanks were put into position. All available mortars and artillery were directed to concentrate on the hill. After the enemy had been given ten minutes of this treatment, the French, with bayonets fixed, started on the run up the hill, screaming like mad men. Again the enemy, with victory just within his grasp, turned and ran. The French and mortar fire pursued. When the French regained the hill there were hundreds of dead enemy piled up to testify to the accuracy of the tremendous concentrations of fire placed against them.[18]

The crisis of the battle was reached at 2 P.M. Although the French 3rd Company had just regained the rocky heights overlooking the interior of the perimeter and the automatic fire from that point had ceased, the enemy was hitting hard at the French 2nd Company across the saddle on the next high ground to the south. The French were being slowly pushed from their position there. At the same time, the Chinese were pressing equally hard against I Company of the 23rd Infantry on the other (east) side of the perimeter. One platoon with only 12 men left there was fighting with grenades and bayonets to hold the razorback ridge. Chinese had pushed between L and I companies to hold high ground that overlooked the interior of the perimeter and were firing down into it again. The battalion commander had shifted L and K companies as much as he dared to help I Company. Enemy pressure was renewed on Hill 453. Ammunition was nearly exhausted, and American and French casualties were increasing. In his manuscript Freeman said of the situation at midafternoon: "At three o'clock it looked like we were going to cave in in the center of both battalions. We had already designated an inner perimeter over the east tunnel to which we would fall back and defend if necessary, although it would have been a last stand—nothing more."

Ground haze had begun to clear at noon, and by now the skies had cleared enough to permit aircraft to rise from the nearest airstrips, where they had been waiting all morning. This change in the weather came for the Americans and French just in time. The first flight to come through the lifting clouds was a group of four Marine Corsairs. The ground controller of the TAC Party directed them to attack the Chinese in front of I Company on the east side of the perimeter. The Corsairs circled the designated strike area four times to make sure they could distinguish friend from foe. Then they climbed for the strike. They came down with 500-pound bombs right into the middle of the closely packed Chinese, came back down again with rockets, and finally strafed with their 20-mm guns.

The second flight came in right behind the Corsairs and was directed to hit the Chinese attacking the center of the French Battalion position on the opposite (west) side of the perimeter. There the planes caught the Chinese massed on a bare ridge where they were fully exposed. They fell in great numbers. These air strikes lifted the pressure on the French and the 23rd Infantry defenders. The Chinese attacks were largely halted by the continuing air strikes, involving 24 planes in all. They now concentrated on trying to dig in to escape the terrible punishment from the air. At the same time, artillery and mortar fire continued. For the first time during the day, air observers came in overhead and directed observed artillery fire on enemy masses hidden behind screening high ground.

The Chinese broke contact about 5:30 P.M. and tried to get away. Tanks ran up the main road to cut off the withdrawing enemy northward, and aerial observers directed continuing artillery fire on them. Quad-50s (M16s) hurriedly moved to points from which they could mow down escaping Chinese with their four machine guns. That ended the furious day-long battle at the Twin Tunnels. The night did not bring a renewal of the battle.[19]

The 23rd Infantry in this battle had 18 men killed, 110 wounded, and 1 missing in action; the French Battalion had 27 killed, 97 wounded, and 4 missing in action—a total of 257 casualties, out of the approximately 1,500 men engaged. It was estimated the Chinese 125th Division suffered 1,300 dead and 3,600 wounded, for an estimated total of nearly 5,000 men altogether. On 2 February a count of the enemy dead around the perimeter gave 600 enemy dead in front of the 23rd Infantry and 700 in front of the French Battalion (300 on Hill 453 and 400 in front of the 2nd and 3rd companies), for a total of approximately 1,300 counted dead.[20]

Before the fighting had stopped late in the afternoon, 14 C-119 Flying Boxcars came over the perimeter and dropped supplies of all kinds in a drop zone west of the road within the perimeter. Ambulances began the task of carrying loads of wounded to Yoju.

The 1st Battalion, 23rd Infantry, arrived at the perimeter on foot, very weary after its long march and now assigned the added task of clearing the road back toward Yoju of enemy roadblocks on its way. The 2nd Reconnaissance Company had joined in the roadblock fights. The 1st Battalion went into the line at the north end of the perimeter, between L Company east of the road and the French 3rd Company west of it. The line was now greatly strengthened by this reinforcement. E Company of the 2nd Battalion arrived at dark. Most of the company was placed in the valley saddle between the French 1st and 2nd companies, thus plugging a weak spot that had been troublesome all day long. The remainder of the 2nd Battalion arrived at the 37th Field Artillery position at midnight. Freeman ordered it to remain there. The 37th Field Artillery had done a heroic job of firing in defense of the perimeter throughout the day, and it merited infantry protection from possible enemy attacks. Colonel Freeman expected the enemy to renew their assaults during the night. But they did not come, and at daylight of 2 February there was no sign of enemy.

With no enemy threatening the artillery or the perimeter on 2 February, Freeman brought the 2nd Battalion forward into the main perimeter. He now had the entire 23rd Infantry (except B Company, which remained with the 37th Field Artillery Battalion), the French Battalion, B Battery of the 82nd AAA AW Battalion, and the 2nd Reconnaissance Company concentrated at the Twin Tunnels.

The 23rd RCT remained in its perimeter during 2 February. There was no enemy action against it. On 3 February, the RCT advanced over the low pass north of it and began a systematic screening of the ridges on either side of the road, the French Battalion on the west and the 1st Battalion, 23rd Infantry, on the east, as the RCT moved on Chipyong-ni, four miles away. The road all the way to Chipyong-ni was littered with bodies of Chinese who had been killed by air strikes and artillery and mortar fire two days before.

The 23rd Infantry occupied Chipyong-ni in the late afternoon of 3 February, with only sporadic fire from enemy on Hill 506. By 8 P.M. the RCT had occupied defensive positions on the high ground surrounding the town. From that time until 12 February the 23rd RCT and the French Battalion consolidated its defensive positions around Chipyong-ni, with the mission of holding it. During this period the force had patrols out daily to a distance of at least three miles to maintain contact with the enemy. Company-sized patrols during this time had several severe engagements with enemy forces to the north and northwest.[21]

On 3 February, Generals Ridgway, Almond, and Ruffner accompanied Under Secretary of the Army Earl P. Johnson to join Colonel Freeman and his staff on Hill 453, where they saw the Chinese dead the French 1st Company had left littering the hill.

The story must now shift to the central corridor, to the east of the Twin Tunnels and Chipyong-ni area, where enemy forces had concentrated to threaten the X Corps position there.

10

The Chinese 4th Phase Offensive

AT THE BEGINNING of February 1951, both Eighth Army and the CCF in Korea were planning offensives against each other. General Ridgway's plan called for an Eighth Army general limited-objective attack across the breadth of Korea. He gave the name "Roundup" to his operational plan. The major action was planned for General Almond's X Corps in the central corridor and was intended to advance from Wonju to Hongchon, where a double envelopment of an increasing concentration of enemy forces there was to be executed. The X Corps attack force comprised the ROK 8th and 5th divisions. The US 2nd Division would support the ROK Division on the left (west), and the US 7th Division would support the ROK 5th Division on the right. The jump-off date for Roundup in X Corps was 5 February.

Already by that that time the US 23rd RCT, with the French Battalion attached, had occupied Chipyong-ni on 3 February, following the severe battle at Twin Tunnels, four miles southeast of Chipyong-ni. The presence of the 125th Division there of the CCF 42nd Army confirmed UN intelligence that large Chinese units were shifting from the west of Korea near Seoul toward the central corridor and probably preparing for a major offensive.

At the same time, but unknown then to the UN, Chinese General Peng Dehuai, commanding the joint North Korean Army and the Chinese forces fighting in Korea, gave an address on 4 February 1951 in which he discussed the Chinese plan for resuming the offensive in Korea. A document captured on 14 February contained excerpts from this address, including the following:

We are obliged to begin the 4th phase of operations. The battle begins under unfavorable conditions. Our period of rest is interrupted and now, when we are not yet ready to fight, the 4th phase is underway. Between 25 October 1950 and January 1951, three phases of this war were completed. The 1st phase ranged from the south bank of the Yalu River to the line along the Chongchon River. The 2nd phase ranged from the Chongchon River line south to the line south of the Tae-dong River. The 3rd phase ranged from the line south of the Taedong River to the line south of the Han River. We did not pursue the enemy (during the 1st phase) quickly because the main force of the enemy still remained intact. If we had pursued the enemy immediately at that time, we might have gained complete victory, but we lacked mobile equipment to do so.[1]

General Peng apparently considered the engagement of the 23rd RCT and the attached French Battalion with the CCF 125th Division at the Twin Tunnels on 31 January as the beginning of the 4th Phase Offensive. His remarks indicate that the advance of the US 2nd Division troops into the area near Chipyong-ni and Piryong, while his forces were still in the process of concentrating there and elsewhere in the Hongchon area, forced the Chinese to begin their 4th Phase Offensive prematurely. In the previous three major Chinese offensives, they had chosen the dates to begin their attacks to their own liking, uninterrupted by their enemy. Now their preparations had to be hurried beyond their expectations, but even so they did not strike until nearly two weeks later.

Meanwhile, on 1 February, General Almond held a planning conference at his X Corps CP at Chungju for the X Corps part of Roundup. All his division commanders were there, including Brigadier Generals Min, ROK 5th Division; Chae (or Choi), ROK 8th Division; and Ham, ROK 2nd Division. Major General Yu, ROK III Corps, also attended. Brig. Gen. Frank S. Bowen, commanding the 187th Airborne RCT, was present because his RCT was scheduled to move to the Wonju area. General Ridgway arrived at the X Corps CP at 11 A.M. Ridgway subsequently conferred with Almond on his plan and approved it.[2]

The X Corps plan, issued on 1 February, was to become effective 5 February. All units were ready on that date. The ROK 8th Division on the left (west) was to attack from the Hoengsong area northward toward Hongchon; the ROK 5th Division on the right (east) was to attack toward the same objective. From the US 2nd and 7th divisions and the 187th Airborne RCT, artillery, infantry, and armor teams were to be formed that would support the two ROK divisions. The ROK I and III corps on the right of the X Corps to the east coast were to protect the corps's right flank. North Korean divisions were known to have massed in that area. A major change in the attack plan was made on 8 February, when Eighth Army attached the ROK 3rd Division to X Corps, and it moved into the attack line between the ROK 8th and 5th divisions. This assignment gave added strength to the center of the line south of Hongchon and enabled the ROK 8th Division to shift slightly westward where, if its attack was successful, it would be in a position to cut the Hongchon-Yongpyong road, a lateral east-west road along which the Chinese were moving large numbers of troops eastward to the X Corps's left flank. Three special support forces were created from the US 2nd and 7th divisions and attached to the ROK forces for the attack: Support Force 21, Support Team Charlie, and Support Team Baker.[3]

It should be noted that this idea of American support forces of combined infantry, artillery, and armor – *attached* to ROK units and under *their* command – was novel in the Korean War, and this is the first time they were used in that command relationship. It made for a very precarious use of American forces, given the previous performance record of South Korean divisions when attacked by Chinese forces.

As the first week of February passed, enemy opposition was generally light on the east side of X Corps but became increasingly heavy on the west side in the vicinity of Chipyong-ni, which was being held by the US 23rd Infantry RCT and the French Battalion. From there the 9th Infantry Regiment formed a connecting link between them and the Roundup attack forces now moving north of Wonju toward Hoengsong.

On 5 February artillery fired on air sightings of a concentration of an estimated 600 enemy troops six miles north of Hoengsong, killing a large number. The next day air reports continued to report numerous enemy groups north and northeast of Hoengsong, moving south or southeast. At this time the ice on the Han River was weakening, the river was rising, and crossing sites east of Seoul were under water. Two of the three CCF temporary bridges at Seoul were washed out. Large cracks began appearing in the ice. The increasing lack of usable crossing places at the Han River placed all CCF troops south of it in a precarious position. Only elements of the NK I Corps and of the CCF 50th and 38th armies were still fighting south of the river in the western zone. This was part of the intelligence picture that showed enemy forces moving from the west to the east and concentrating in the Piryong-Hongchon area, with the potential of driving south in the Han River corridor toward Chungju and down the central corridor past Wonju.[4]

When the X Corps Roundup attack forces jumped off in their attack on 5 February, the ROK 8th and 5th divisions were just north of Hoengsong. Their line of advance was north along the main road toward Hongchon. Between Wonju and Hoengsong the road was over mostly level or semilevel ground. Once across the Twinnam-Mul River a quarter mile north of Hoengsong, the road entered a mountainous area that extended all the way to Hongchon, reaching a culminating height in Hill 930, halfway between Hoengsong and Hongchon.

In the ROK III Corps area east of X Corps, the ROK 7th and 9th divisions meanwhile were unable to keep abreast of the Roundup attack divisions in the X Corps. They gradually fell behind, so that the Roundup force formed a salient protruding northward toward Hongchon. This made it vulnerable to an enemy attack, especially from its right (east) flank. By 8 February, when General Almond visited both the ROK 8th and ROK

5th divisions and held a conference with General Ridgway, it had become clear that the X Corps Roundup attack plan could not be carried out unless North Korean forces in front of the ROK III Corps could be blocked off from a potential flank attack against the main attack force. This consideration led the next day to shifting the ROK 5th Division eastward to protect against the massing North Koreans in the ROK III Corps sector and bringing up the ROK 3rd Division in its place in the main attack force on the right side of the ROK 8th Division. The main attack force now consisted of the ROK 8th Division on the left (west) and the ROK 3rd Division on the right, together with their American special support forces of infantry, artillery, and armor.[5]

Meanwhile, active patrolling took place on the right of the Roundup attack force and behind its line west from Wonju toward Yoju. On 5 February the 2nd Division Ranger Company made a night surround at 1 A.M. of Changal, a village 11 miles west of Hoengsong, where it surprised a sleeping enemy force. In the ensuing action most of the enemy were shot down as they rushed out of the buildings, still half asleep. The 9th Infantry Regiment of the 2nd Division had repeated encounters with enemy forces in its blocking positions between Wonju and Yoju, actually behind the UN line, as its patrols moved constantly to keep the Wonju-Yoju road open.[6]

Far to the east, the ROK Capital Division captured Kangnung on the coast, many miles north of the UN line in central Korea. Capt. Frank W. Lucas, KMAG advisor with the 2nd Battalion, ROK 26th Regiment, played the key role in routing a large North Korean force that for three days had held the dominating ground just north of Kangnung. The South Korean commander and many of his men were wounded in an effort to take Mosan Hill. Captain Lucas crawled to within 100 yards of the main enemy position and from there directed air strikes on the enemy. These strikes destroyed four machine guns and two mortars and inflicted 50 casualties. Lucas then led the ROK company in an assault on the disorganized enemy position and captured it. This action allowed the rest of the battalion to enter Kangnung.

On 8 February an important piece of information came into American possession. Documents taken from the body of a Chinese soldier north of Hoengsong identified the soldier as being from the 594th Regiment, 198th Division, CCF 66th Army. Although there had been many civilian and NK prisoner reports that Chinese were there, this was the first and, thus far, the only solid identification that CCF were in the Hongchon area.[7]

By 9 February enemy opposition had increased measurably, and the X Corps attack gained little. During the day trucks from the 187th Airborne RCT shuttled the ROK 3rd Division to Hoengsong. At Hoengsong the Netherlands Battalion constituted its main defense force. Support Team Charlie, which consisted of two infantry platoons from C Company, 17th Infantry, 7th Division, and a platoon of heavy tanks, joined the 36th Regiment of the ROK 5th Division. To the west of Hoengsong and Wonju, the 9th Infantry of the 2nd Division reported on 9 February that there was heavy enemy infiltration between Chipyong-ni and the X Corps attack force where the ROK 8th Division formed the western flank. The 9th Infantry at this time had several heavy fights with these infiltrating forces and succeeded in capturing several key hills from the enemy.[8]

On 10 February Brigadier General Chae (or Choi), commanding the ROK 8th Division, told General Almond that, in the ROK 10th Regimental sector shortly before midnight, a unit of the division's 21st Regiment had contact with a Chinese company of 70 men, in which it killed 20, wounded 30, and captured 7. This seems to have been the first battle encounter with Chinese the ROK 8th Division had in the X Corps attack. An agent, as well as Korean civilians, reported that the NK 7th Division was screening the advance of CCF and that the Chinese 66th Army would launch a major counteroffensive in a few days.[9]

The X Corps attack continued on 11 February. The ROK 11th Field Artillery Battalion supported the 22nd Regiment of the ROK 3rd Division north of Hoengsong. Elements of the ROK 8th, 3rd, and 5th divisions were now from five to eight miles north of Hoengsong, aligned from west to east in that order. The ROK 8th Division was attacking towering Hill 930, the crest of which was about halfway between Hoengsong and Hongchon, and east of the main road between the two places. The ROK 8th Division was several miles in advance of the 3rd and 5th divisions, which were in the hills northeast and east of Hoengsong. Everywhere the American support forces followed closely behind the ROK infantry and expended large amounts of artillery and mortar fire in aiding their attacks. At 11 A.M. the 1st Battalion, 38th Infantry, part of Support Force 21 and attached to the ROK 8th Division, moved north from Haktam-ni to Changbong-ni in support of the ROK 21st Regiment, which was leading the ROK attack.[10]

Changbong-ni is six air miles and eight road miles north of Hoengsong. Of the American support forces, only Support Team Baker was farther north, about four miles on the main Hoengsong-Hongchon road during the daytime, but it pulled back two miles at dark. Support Team Baker was in firing position there almost directly west of the crest of Hill 930. The ROK 21st Regiment had not yet captured the hill, but it was nearing the crest at dark on 11 February.

Throughout daytime of 10 and 11 February, aerial observer reports to the X Corps told of thousands of enemy troops in the open, moving east toward Hongchon and south toward Hoengsong. One pilot said he had never before seen so many enemy troops moving in the open. The morning had been overcast, but the skies had suddenly cleared in the afternoon of the tenth. Many of these enemy concentrations seemed to be moving toward Chipyong-ni; others toward Hongchon and Hoengsong. Two new bridges

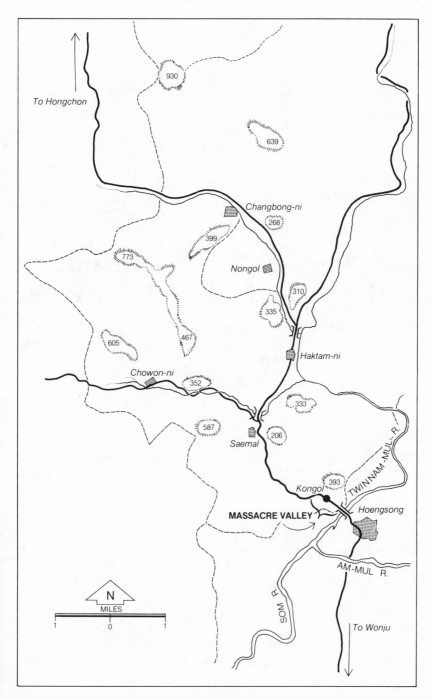

MAP 10. **Hoengsong area, 11–12 February 1951**

Hill 930, midway between Hoengsong to the south and Hongchon to the North (beyond the mountain). At the base of the mountain in the foreground is Changbong-ni, where Chinese hit the 2nd Division Support Forces that were aiding the ROK 8th Division, which was overrun. *US Army photograph, SC (unnumbered)*

were seen across the Hongchon River half a mile east of the town. One aerial report stated a large enemy concentration included 1,200 horses. At 6 P.M., 10 February, 32 planes strafed and napalmed this buildup area, and all the American artillery in range fired on it. That night B-26 bombers hit the area four times.[11]

The formations of support forces and support teams to assist the ROK 8th and 5th divisions with armor and artillery in their attacks north from Hoengsong was in the nature of an experiment to see if in this way they could get better performance from the ROK troops. It was to prove a costly experiment.

These support forces were as follows:

Support Force 21
15th Field Artillery Battalion, Lt. Col. John W. Keith, CO
1st Battalion, 38th Infantry, Lt. Col. William P. Kelleher, CO
A Battery, 503rd Field Artillery Battalion (155-mm how.) (this was a segregated unit of black troops)
D Battery, 82nd AAA AW (SP) Battalion, Capt. Simon J. Stevens and 1st Lt. Paul G. McCoy.

Lieutenant Colonel Keith, the artillery commander, commanded Support Force 21. The 1st Battalion, 38th Infantry, US 2nd Division, provided the infantry force for protection of the Support Force 21 artillery. Support Force 21 was attached to the ROK 8th Division.

Support Team Baker
L Company, 38th Infantry, Lt. Elmer J. Kallmeyer, CO
One platoon of tank company, 38th Infantry, Lt. James Mace, CO.

Support Team Baker was essentially from the 3rd Battalion, 38th Infantry, US 2nd Division. It specifically supported the ROK 21st Regiment, ROK 8th Division.

Support Team Charlie
Two platoons, C Company, 17th Infantry, US 7th Division
One platoon, heavy tanks.

Support Team Charlie was attached to the ROK 5th Division and specifically supported the ROK 36th Regiment. Another team, Support Team Easy, supported the ROK 35th Regiment, ROK 5th Division. It apparently had no enemy contact in the ROK regiment's attack toward Hill 527.

After the ROK 3rd Division was ordered up to go into the attack line between the ROK 8th and 5th divisions, Task Force White was formed to support it. The ROK 3rd Division moved to Hoengsong on 11 February, and during the day it advanced six miles north of Hoengsong to come abreast of the right flank of the ROK 8th Division.

Task Force White
2nd Battalion, 17th Infantry, US 7th Division
49th Field Artillery Battalion.

This force was attached to the ROK 3rd Division and specifically supported that division's 22nd and 23rd regiments.

The ROK 8th Division's CP was at Hoengsong. Its regiments were farther north during the early night of 11 February than those of the other two ROK divisions. The ROK 21st Regiment, 8th Division, was eight or nine miles north of Hoengsong on the southern slope of Hill 930. Support Force 21 was two to three miles behind and east of it, and about seven miles north of Hoengsong. It was in position on the hills immediately around the village of Changbong-ni, on the main road and at the base of Hill 930. The 3rd Battalion (minus L Company), 38th Infantry, was in position at Saemal, four miles south of Support Force 21 and three miles north of Hoengsong on the main road north toward Hongchon. The ROK 5th Division, on the right of the ROK 3rd Division, was about seven miles northeast of Hoengsong.[12]

Col. John G. Coughlin, commander of the 38th Infantry Regiment, had his CP at Hoengsong. Lieutenant Colonel Skeldon's 2nd Battalion was at Wonju, acting as security force for X Corps's Advance CP. Coughlin, accordingly, on 11 February did not have command of his regiment. Lt. Col. Harold Maixner, commander of the 3rd Battalion, 38th Regiment, at Saemal, behind the ROK 8th Division and Support Force 21, was under 2nd Division command. Only the 38th Regiment's special troops and the Netherlands Battalion were with Coughlin at Hoengsong. The Netherlands Battalion was the Hoengsong defense force.

On 11 February General Almond made a detailed aerial reconnaissance of the X Corps front, from Chipyong-ni on the left to the 31st Infantry, 7th Division, on the right at Pyongchang. He ordered the 7th Division to prepare to move the 32nd Infantry to Yoju to block there if the enemy launched an offensive up the Han River valley. He also conferred with the commanding generals of the ROK 3rd and 5th divisions.[13]

Kelleher's 1st Battalion, A Company, had its three platoons in perimeters on three hills just east of the village of Changbong-ni and east of the north-south road running through the village. First Lt. George W. Gardner commanded A Company. His 2nd Platoon held the northernmost hill, his 1st Platoon was south and a little east of the 2nd Platoon, and the 3rd Platoon was south of both and southeast of Changbong-ni. B Company was west of the road and southwest of A Company. C Company was south of both, astride the Hoengsong road.

Gardner said that, as dusk came on 11 February, the ROK 21st Regiment, ahead of him on the slope of Hill 930, seemed to have the situation under control, although it had advanced less than a mile during the day. To his front and flanks he could see a great number of soldiers that he thought were ROK troops. He went out with his Korean liaison officer to make sure they were friendly troops. He then established, on orders from Lieutenant Colonel Kelleher, a combat outpost on Hill 633, leaving there three forward observers, one for artillery, one for 81-mm mortars, and one for 60-mm mortars.[14]

The ROK 21st Regiment continued its attack during the night. About 9:30 P.M. a Chinese force counterattacked it, forcing it to fall back. Half an hour later, Support Team Baker, in direct support of the ROK regiment, withdrew from its advanced position to join Support Force 21 at Changbong-ni. Half an hour before midnight, Lt. Col. John W. Keith, commanding Support Force 21, informed it that the ROK 21st Regiment had orders to withdraw. Major Blackwell, the 1st Battalion S-3, contacted the ROK regimental commander and his KMAG liaison officer asking that they hold the regiment in place until the 21st Support Force could load up and be ready to move. Lieutenant Colonel Keith contacted General Haynes, the 2nd Division Artillery commander, requesting that he ask General Chae, ROK 8th Division commander, to direct the 21st Regiment to remain in place until the support force could load up. These efforts availed nothing. ROK soldiers from the 21st Regiment were streaming south through the 21st Support Force positions at this time. Keith then, at 2 A.M., 12 February, ordered the support force to load up as quickly as possible so it could move back to a former position at Haktam-ni.[15]

Already Chinese had overrun the ROK 20th and 50th field artillery battalions and had captured their howitzers. Consequently, they played no part in the ensuing action.[16]

Kelleher ordered a section of tanks and a platoon of infantry from L Company, Support Team Baker, now joined with Support Force 21, to proceed to a bridge south of Changbong-ni to hold and protect it for passage of the support force. But short of the bridge an enemy hand grenade blinded the tank driver, and the tank went out of control, ran off the road, and turned over. An enemy bazooka knocked out the second tank, and it went off the right side of the road. Lt. Elmer J. Kallmeyer, L Company commander and commander of Support Team Baker, received word of this occurrence. It never was learned what happened to the tanks' crew members or the platoon of infantry. Before attacking Support Force 21 frontally, the Chinese had already cut the road behind it.

The enemy force that launched this powerful counterattack the night of 11–12 February north of Hoengsong included four Chinese divisions: the 117th Division from the CCF 39th Army and the 124th Division from the 42nd Army, and two divisions, the 197th and 198th, from the 66th Army.[17] An enemy document captured later, referring directly to the attack on the night of 11–12 February north of Hoengsong, gave this report:

In the fourth campaign [the CCF 117th Division] received a similar mission [in the 3rd campaign it had crossed the Imjin River north of Seoul and had cut off the ROK 6th Division], together with other friendly units. Again, by covering over 70 Li [1 li = 1,890 feet, or a little over ⅓ mile] in a single night of forced marching, and climbing several mountains, it advanced to a predetermined line extending between Pyok Hak Mt and Ha Il, blocking the enemy's retreat from Hak Kok ni to Hoengsong. Enemy reinforcements from Hoeng Song and enemy forces breaking through the envelopment at Hak Kok met with total annihilation. A major part of the ROK 8th Division and a part of the US 2nd Division were killed and captured and wounded.[18]

This document further identifies a regiment of the 117th Division that played a role in intercepting reinforcements coming to the scene from

Hoengsong. It says, "Comrade Hsueh Fu-li, Assistant Regimental Commander of the 349th Regiment, personally inspected positions, made troop adjustments, and by commanding the strategic positions and intercepting enemy reinforcements coming from Hoeng Song, the fleeing enemy was intercepted."[19]

A document issued on 12 February by the CCF 115th Division, 39th Army, stated, "Our 4th Offensive phase of the war began yesterday (11 Feb). All friendly units began to attack the enemy emplaced N of Hoengsong at 10 o'clock last evening and are advancing fairly rapidly. Tung Laie Pu attacked the ROK 8th Div . . . where they annihilated part of the enemy, captured 200 vehicles and more than 30 howitzers. The 17 Pu (117th Division) slashed into . . . 7 li (2.5 miles) nw of Hoengsong, damaged the enemy partly and captured more than 300 US and ROK PsW."[20]

The CCF 198th Division made the frontal attack against the ROK 21st Regiment and Support Force 21 just before midnight. It quickly broke through the ROK 21st Regiment. Another enemy force, the CCF 117th Division, hit the ROK 16th Regiment of the ROK 8th Division on its southwest flank some miles south of the CCF 198th Division, and the same CCF division hit the ROK 10th Regiment east of the ROK 16th Regiment. While this attack was in progress, confusion in the ROK ranks was heightened by the ROK 16th Regiment's moving west on the road from Saemal, four miles south of Changbong-ni. It met enemy resistance near Chowon-ni. The ROK 10th Regiment moved west and eliminated the initial resistance. It then crossed the 16th Regiment and moved north. The ROK 8th Division was soon an entangled mess.[21]

A large gap developed between the ROK 10th and 21st regiments, with the ROK 10th Regiment now west of the 21st. The 2nd Division Reconnaissance Company was diverted westward from its movement toward Changbong-ni to close the gap between the two ROK regiments at Chowon-ni, two miles west of Saemal. The 8th ROK Division units were already beginning to lose their identity and drifting southeast toward Hoengsong. A column of marching troops emerged from the darkness. The Reconnaissance Company thought it was enemy and opened fire on it. The column kept moving on without returning the fire. The Reconnaissance Company now thought it was a friendly force. But in fact it was elements of the CCF 197th Division marching through the gap between the 10th and 21st regiments of the ROK 8th Division. It was virtually unopposed. Enemy troops overran the ROK 10th and 16th regimental CPs. By 1 A.M., 12 February, there was no communication between the ROK 8th Division and its three regiments, and there were numerous roadblocks behind all of them. Enemy destroyed a key bridge at Chowon-ni. Units of the ROK 8th Division were defeated in detail.[22]

In the preceding few pages we have digressed from the enemy attack on the ROK 21st Regiment and Support Force 21 to show what was happening simultaneously behind them a few miles to the southwest. We now return to the Changbong-ni area, where the retreating ROK 21st Regiment had left the American Support Force 21 alone and fully exposed to the Chinese onslaught along the Hoengsong-Hongchon north-south road.

At 2 A.M., 12 February, Major Blackwell, the 1st Battalion, 38th Infantry S-3, ordered Lieutenant Gardner, A Company commander, to load out his kitchen and to make arrangements to secure the withdrawal of Support Force 21. In a few minutes, however, the platoon leader of the 3rd Platoon reported he saw several flares of various colors to the northeast of A Company's position. In a very short time Chinese attacked the 3rd and 1st platoons from the north and the northeast. ROK 8th Division troops supposedly in front of Support Force 21 at this time had fled without firing a shot. Chinese grenades, light mortar fire, and automatic and small-arms fire hit A Company. By radio Gardner ordered his forward observer outpost personnel to withdraw to the company perimeter, but they reported that they were surrounded and could not. None of these forward observers was ever seen again. A Company held its position until the support-force column began to move out. A Company covered the rear and fought the rear-guard action for Support Force 21.[23]

Support Force 21 left its Changbong-ni position about 4 A.M., 12 February. Gardner had two tanks of Support Team Baker and two M16 quad-50s with his company. Enemy were along the road in front of the company and along its sides, as well as behind it. Gardner's company came to a stop to fight a delaying action. He placed his infantry platoons at the rear (north) and left (east) flank, set up his mortars and 57-mm recoilless rifles, and placed a security force on the northwest of his position. He said, "Had it not been for the cold steel nerve and high efficiency of the two tank crews, my company would surely have been wiped out by this time. As it was, we had held the enemy off; we had resupplied our ammo from the company jeeps, and were about out of ammo again. We fixed bayonets."

It was beginning to get light. In the dawn off to the southwest, Gardner saw a bunch of howitzers in rice paddies. He was amazed, for he had assumed that the artillery of Support Force 21 had already withdrawn. He described the scene.

I saw three (3) 155 mm howitzers already march-ordered to their prime movers; 155 mm ammunition stacked all over the area; one 2½ ton truck full of ammunition, but not in running order, several jeeps and trailers, most of them inoperable; and my Executive Officer reported that two more 155 mm howitzers were still in position, ready to fire. I sent some of my men over to the prime movers and they fired two 50 cal MGs that were ring-mounted on the prime movers until they had used up all the ammunition. The enemy was still persistent; so we cast about, trying to find someone who could fire any type of howitzer; and there were no artillerymen to be found—also, my men stated, that they could not fire the howitzers. Then I sent my Executive Officer to find someone who could drive the prime movers, so that we could evacuate them; but he reported there were no artillery-men around, and that our men could not drive the tractors. All of this equipment belonged to "A" Battery of the 503rd F.A. and it had been wantonly abandoned. Also, we had no way to destroy it, nor the time. When B and C Companies made it possible for the motor column to move, Company A was fighting on three sides, and was sustaining heavy casualties. When the columns moved, we fought a delay-ing action, and brought our wounded along; picking up the wounded delayed us, and we became cut off from the Bn; so we had to fight forward, too. By this time I figured that at least two fresh reinforced companies were engaging my relatively small force.[24]

The front of the column, a considerable distance ahead of Gardner's rear guard, had heavy fighting at several places. Perhaps the worst spot for the point and cutting edge of Support Force 21 was at Haktam-ni, where the Chinese had established a strong fireblock soon after penetrating the ROK 8th Division and lay in wait for the arrival of the American support force. Tanks led the support advance, and they were immediately engaged there. The antiaircraft weapons carriers, the M16s (quad-50s) and the M19s (dual-40s), were always brought up for their terrific firepower in breaking enemy fireblocks. The Haktam-ni fireblock was a strong one of mortar, machine-gun, and small-arms fire covering an improvised roadblock. D Bat-tery of the 82nd AAA AW Battalion sent some M16s and M19s to the head of the column at once, which joined the tanks in fighting the fireblock.

The Chinese concentrated their efforts on the tanks and the antiaircraft weapons at the head of the column, hitting them with preregistered mor-tar fire and heavy automatic fire. And they also resorted to their usual tactic in fighting these weapons by sending special teams with bangalore torpe-does and hand grenades for close-in attack. Meanwhile, Chinese infantry swarmed off the hills close to the road and closed with the mixed Ameri-can and ROK troops in the column. The M16s and M19s took a heavy toll of Chinese killed and wounded, but they suffered heavy losses them-selves. Lt. Col. Walter Killilae, commander of the 82nd AAA AW Bat-talion, said that in this fight "in several instances the infantry troops assisted in manning the weapons as the original crews were hit. UN troops at times lined up on one side of the road and tossed grenades at the enemy attacking from the other side of the road." He especially commended the action of the D Battery fire unit leaders in this action: Sgts. Roy P. Wood, Julius Hawkins, Robert L. Wood, and John Cervellone. The D Battery commander, Capt. Simon J. Stevens, and the second-in-command, 1st Lt. Paul G. Mc-Coy, gave outstanding leadership, the latter being among the wounded.[25]

When the leading elements of Support Force 21 and Lieutenant Colo-nel Kelleher passed the position of A Battery, 503rd Field Artillery Bat-talion, shortly after 4 A.M., he saw the 155-mm howitzers there and activ-ity indicating the artillerymen were preparing them for march order. The 105-mm howitzers of the 15th Field Artillery Battalion were already on the road. The 155-mm howitzers were supposed to have moved out first. Kelleher said, "The entire FA personnel of Support Force 21 passed this prime mover and howitzer [only one of five] without attempting to move it. . . . 17 of the 105 mm howitzers from the 15th FA Battalion reached the 3rd Battalion."[26] The 18th 105-mm howitzer and its 2½-ton truck mover were lost in some unrecorded manner before it reached Saemal. When Gardner's A Company rear guard of the column came to the firing position of the 155-mm howitzer site some time after Kelleher and the front of the 1st Battalion, 38th Infantry, had passed it, there were no artillerymen there, and the five howitzers and their tractor prime movers had been entirely abandoned.

As Gardner fought his way forward to a cliff area overhanging the road opposite the village of Nongol, a little more than a mile south of Changbong-ni, he saw two artillery prime movers and one 155-mm howitzer blocking the road. This was the only 155-mm howitzer to get on the road, and it did not get far. A Company moved the howitzer out of the way by hand, but could not start or move the prime mover for lack of experienced drivers. Gardner got his vehicles around the two prime movers, and the company continued on 2½ miles to the crossroads junction of Saemal, where the 3rd Battalion (− L company), 38th Infantry, had held fast in its perimeter. The rest of Task Force 21 had already arrived there. It was 10 A.M. Gardner reorganized his company and put it in a perimeter defense position around A Battery, 15th Field Artillery, which was in position and firing. Gardner made a quick count of his company at this point, and found that he had lost 2 officers and approximately 110 men. He also told Lieutenant Gleason, the 105-mm howitzer battery commander, that the people he could see on all the knolls and ridges from the southwest in an arc to the north and then down to the southeast were enemy soldiers. Gleason had his howitzers fan their fire and put it point-blank on any enemy group that showed itself. Some of the A Company infantry helped by carrying ammunition to the artillery. Some Chinese, however, got to within 800 yards of the howitzers and wiped out all but two men of a squad Gardner had placed on a ridge to the east. ROK troops that had reached the Saemal position would not fight and were only in the way. Gardner said, "Most of their officers were dead or wounded (or had fled) and try as we did we could not get them to fight."[27]

When Support Force 21 began to move south from Changbong-ni at 4 A.M., Lieutenant Colonel Kelleher had it deployed in a column of companies, with B Company leading, then C, Headquarters, and D companies following. A Company brought up the rear. Two miles south of Changbong-ni, where a steep hillside came down to the road on its east side, the column encountered very heavy enemy automatic and small-arms fire. In reporting this encounter, Kelleher wrote, "Several of the lead vehicles were knocked out and drivers and other personnel of the vehicles were killed by bayonets, or taken prisoner and in a few cases they were stripped of their valuables and released."[28]

Kelleher now ordered C Company to take the lead, with C Company on the east side of the road and B Company on the west side. Their mission was to clear the high ground flanking the road closely so that the vehicular column could move. The two infantry companies moved out to sweep the high ground at 5:45 A.M. Fifteen minutes earlier Kelleher had ordered his artillery and the antiaircraft weapons to fire point-blank into the enemy concentrations on the east side of the road. Kelleher took direct control of the artillery at this time because he could not locate Lieutenant Colonel Keith, the support force commander. He saw him only once after leaving Changbong-ni until he reached the 3rd Battalion at Saemal. Chinese bugles sounded calls that resembled taps and mess call. One of them was located only 200 yards east of the road. White phosphorus artillery shells silenced it. In its drive forward, C Company had a hard fight in clearing the ridgeline, but on the west side B Company had only light resistance until it came to Hill 335. There one of its platoons was annihilated, with only two men escaping.

One problem Kelleher had was in finding drivers for the leading 12 to 14 vehicles. Disabled vehicles were pushed to the roadside, and the road column kept abreast of C and B companies on the ridgelines. Two miles north of Saemal, where the 55 grid line crosses the road and high ground closed in on both sides, heavy mortar fire hit the column. C Company successfully swept this area on the east and forced enemy there to pull back to higher positions. Then the Chinese placed intense automatic-weapons fire on the road column. Kelleher had to commit his Headquarters Company here, which silenced this fire. Only a short distance farther, when the column once again moved forward, it came to a concrete bridge, which the Chinese covered with fire from east, south, and west. This bridge was located where two streams came together, forming the Kumgye-chon, a mile and a half northeast of Saemal. B Company deployed to cover the bridge while the rest of the column crossed. From there, Support Force 21 proceeded on to the 3rd Battalion perimeter at Saemal. On the way it received heavy fire from the high ground south of Haktam-ni about half a mile north of Saemal. Quad-50s with the column were largely responsible for silencing this fire. All these positions where heavy enemy fire was encountered south of Changbong-ni had been occupied by enemy forces before Support Force 21 started its withdrawal. Kelleher's battalion arrived at Saemal about 10 A.M., 12 February.[29]

By the time Kelleher's battalion reached Saemal, members of the ROK 21st Regiment were scattered through the column, disorganized and in complete rout. They made no effort to help in any way, and attempts to get them in the fight were unsuccessful. In reaching Saemal, the 1st Battalion had suffered approximately 290 casualties. At Saemal, Kelleher received orders to go into a perimeter to help the 3rd Battalion defense. But soon thereafter, at 11 A.M., another order came for the 1st Battalion to attack toward Hoengsong, clearing the ground on both sides of the road as it came.

Before continuing with the advance of the 1st Battalion, 38th Infantry, toward Hoengsong from Saemal, it is necessary to mention events that occurred in the vicinity of the 3rd Battalion, 38th Infantry, during the night of 11–12 February at its crossroads junction position near Saemal. Mortar fire and small-arms fire fell in front of K Company's position shortly after midnight, but it was not itself under fire. At 1:30 A.M. men from K Company, 9th Infantry, a task force that was attached to the ROK 16th Regiment, 8th Division, came into the 3rd Battalion perimeter. This task force had been engaged with enemy in front of the 3rd Battalion. Captain Jones, commander of K Company, 9th Infantry, soon came into the perimeter slightly wounded. Lt. Col. Harold V. Maixner, commander of the 3rd Battalion, 38th Infantry, questioned Jones about the condition of the ROK 16th Regiment. He said the regiment had been overrun and his own K Company badly hurt, with most of his men lost in the action, and he did not know where his survivors were. At this time ROK soldiers from the 16th and 11th regiments of the 8th Division were streaming past the 3rd Battalion CP, going south. Maixner ordered a checkpoint established at the road junction at Saemal where the road from the west joined that from the north to continue on south as one road toward Hoengsong. He wanted to put the ROKs in his defense perimeter, but he had no command authority over them, so he had to hold them until he could get in touch with ROK commanders.

About 2 hours later, at 3:30 A.M., an enemy concentration was reported at Chowon-ni, two miles west of Saemal. Maixner ordered his artillery officer to request artillery fire on the area. He did not get this artillery fire, because Brigadier General Chae, commander of the ROK 8th Division, would not give clearance for it. Maixner ordered his Weapons Company (M) and K Company to fire all available mortars, recoilless rifles, and machine guns on the Chowon-ni area. Just before giving this order, Maixner received radio information from Lieutenant Colonel Kelleher that his 1st Battalion had received orders to withdraw from Changbong-ni to Haktam-ni, about a mile and a half north of the 3rd Battalion.

Maixner now received word from the 2nd Division Artillery command that it had not been able to obtain clearance for artillery fire in his area, because the commander of the ROK 8th Division said he had sent an engineer unit to help the ROK 16th Regiment. Captain Tate, S-3 of the 3rd Battalion, told division artillery that the 3rd Battalion had already taken Chowon-ni under fire and that enemy held the area. This information had no effect because the division artillery again stated it could not give artillery support until the ROK 8th Division cleared it.[30] One is bound to wonder why Major General Ruffner, 2nd Division commander, did not raise the issue with General Almond, X Corps commander.

By 3 A.M., 12 February, the 3rd Battalion, 38th Infantry, at Saemal was under heavy enemy attack. M Company was hard pressed in its perimeter and received orders to withdraw from Hill 300, one of the perimeter high points. During this withdrawal, Sgt. Charles R. Long, a forward observer for the mortar platoon, remained in his forward position and continued to direct mortar fire by radio on the closing enemy. He used his carbine and hand grenades to keep the foremost enemy from closing on his foxhole. But he quickly was surrounded, and it was then only a question of how long he could continue his lone stand. In his last radio message the 27-year-old sergeant said that he had exhausted his carbine ammunition and thrown his last grenade, and then he called for a concentration of 40 rounds of high explosive fire on a map coordinate that included his own position. Sergeant Long was killed at his post, but his company successfully withdrew under the protection of his directed mortar fire. Long received the Medal of Honor, Posthumously.[31]

I Company, 3rd Battalion, began to receive fire about 3:30 A.M. from Hill 333, Pyokhak-san, a mile northeast of the 3rd Battalion CP. At this time some members of the KMAG group attached to the ROK 16th Regiment came in to the 3rd Battalion perimeter. They gave Lieutenant Colonel Maixner permission to use the retreating ROKs as he saw fit. He immediately issued orders they were to help hold the line. As they were being made ready for that duty, K Company sent a message to him that a ROK engineer unit, presumably the one that had been sent to help the ROK 16th Infantry, had arrived and taken a position on its right flank. Maixner instructed K Company to send the ROK engineer officer to him. When he arrived, he said the ROK 16th Regiment had been overrun. Maixner attached his unit to K Company.

At 4 A.M. the 2nd Division Artillery again informed Maixner that it had been unable to obtain clearance to place artillery fire forward of the position of the 3rd Battalion, 38th Infantry, at Saemal. Maixner told division artillery that the ROK engineers unit was now in his perimeter and that there was no reason artillery fire could not be placed forward of him. But this argument did no good; there still was no artillery fire forthcoming.

During the latter part of the night, the 3rd Battalion received enemy mortar fire. By daylight, I and K companies were receiving heavy small-arms fire. At this time some Chinese were able to get within K Company's perimeter by following close behind some retreating ROKs. An artillery officer arrived in the perimeter and stated that the enemy had established a roadblock south of the perimeter, thereby cutting the road between Saemal and Hoengsong. By 7 A.M. the Chinese had succeeded in overrunning the CPs of both K and M companies. The perimeter held fast, however, in spite of the infiltration of enemy to the two CPs, and measures were prepared to destroy these infiltrators. By 7:30 A.M. the left flank of the 3rd Battalion was heavily engaged by enemy. Mortar fire continued to fall throughout the battalion area, and some enemy were infiltrating to within the perimeter from the southwest. This development caused Maixner to reinforce the observation post in his rear to the south with headquarters personnel. The CP then received enemy small-arms fire from the south. There was every indication that Chinese now surrounded the 3rd Battalion. This was the situation at Saemal when the advance elements of Support Force 21 and Support Team Baker began to arrive at the 3rd Battalion perimeter a little after 9 A.M. The support forces closed in the perimeter just before 10 A.M. The two infantry battalions were now united in one defense position.[32]

Closer to Hoengsong, almost at its northern edge, there was fighting. A bloody encounter took place with Chinese just north of Hoengsong beginning at 7:30 A.M., 12 February, at the same time Support Force 21 was trying to fight its way south from Changbong-ni and the 3rd Battalion, 38th Infantry, was fighting hard to hold its perimeter at Saemal. If any proof were needed that Chinese in great numbers had already penetrated to the edge of Hoengsong and that everything north of that place was in the midst of a Chinese surround, this morning battle near Hoengsong gave it.

The Chinese in fact had executed one of their most successful operations of the war in the initial phases of the attack. They struck frontally at weak points and at the same time sent large numbers of their forces through quick penetrations far into the rear, carrying out flanking operations simultaneously. They had done the same thing at Tokchon against the ROK II Corps in the 2nd Phase Offensive in late November 1950, and again against Eighth Army in their 3rd Phase Offensive in crossing the Imjin River on New Year's Eve. In this case, the Chinese penetration of the ROK 8th Division had resulted in the destruction within four hours of its 21st, 16th, and 10th regiments as effective fighting forces. The American support forces were entirely engulfed in the Chinese penetrations and advances thereafter. At daylight their escape route back to Hoengsong was entirely in Chinese possession. How could they possibly fight out?

In an attempt to help Support Force 21 and the 3rd Battalion, 38th Infantry, a relief force of six tanks and the Security Platoon of the 38th Infantry left Hoengsong at 7:30 A.M. and proceeded northward toward Saemal. The 2nd Platoon, 38th Infantry, tank company provided four tanks, and the 9th Infantry added two more, for the total of six. Lt. James Howden of the 38th Tank Company commanded the force. Second Lt. Francis Uzzo commanded the Security Platoon.[33]

The road north to Saemal left the northern edge of Hoengsong and crossed a flat river-basin bottom a quarter mile to the Twinnam-Mul River, which it crossed on a concrete bridge. This river flowed west only a little more than a mile when another stream, the Am-Mul, joined it from the southeast, forming the Som River. The Som River played an important role in the heavy actions between Hoengsong-Wonju and the Chipyong-ni area to the west. It flowed through very mountainous country, eventually to empty into the Han. The terrain north of the Twinnam-Mul was mountainous, and the road threaded its way north in a twisting gorgelike route, following minor drainages with steep ridges and hills rising on both sides. High ground dominated the road all the way to Hongchon, north of Hill 930.

As Lieutenant Howden's relief force was crossing the river north of Hoengsong, the men noticed a lone Chinese soldier walking toward them. They did not fire on him, as they expected him to surrender. When they met, the Chinese soldier put up his hands in the fashion of a boxer, indicating he wanted to fight Lieutenant Uzzo, the Security Platoon leader. Then he tried to unsling a weapon that hung on his shoulder, but Uzzo shot him with his pistol before he could do this. The relief force continued on toward Saemal.

The group soon met 5 more enemy, who fired on it. They returned the fire and killed them all. After proceeding about 150 yards, the force saw about 200 to 400 (eyewitnesses vary in their estimate) soldiers in ROK uniforms standing in a group in the road. They were actually Chinese soldiers, who, when they saw the approaching Americans, waved their hands as if they were friendly. ROK troops had passed south all night in this area, and, for all the men knew, it was possible these were more of them. Lieutenant Uzzo stood by the lead tank as this group approached. One of them said in English, "We are friends." Everyone in front now began to shake hands. While this was going on, Uzzo noticed that many more men were appearing on the hills to their front and on both flanks. The foremost of the supposedly friendly group on the road were within six feet of Uzzo and the lead tank. The crew in the sixth and last tank in the column had watched a group of men that had moved around their right flank on the road and had now gotten into their rear. Up front, one of the "friends" threw a piece of paper to Uzzo which read, "Surrender: Give up your arms and cartridge belts and we will allow you to keep your personal effects and lead you back to your lines unharmed." This was the first intimation Uzzo had that the group of men in front of him were enemy, not ROKs. Uzzo told his platoon sergeant to have his men withdraw and take firing positions, and at the same time the lead tank opened point-blank machine-gun fire at the group in front of it. An enemy bugle sounded, and the group on the road opened up on the lead tank and Uzzo. The rear tank opened fire on the enemy group that had infiltrated to its right rear. They hit the ground, and tank fire held them there, unable to move.

Individual Chinese from the group on the road tried to drop grenades through the hatches of the two lead tanks, but the crews had just closed them. The tanks, in reverse gear, tried to back down the road. The second tank driver misjudged the edge of it and turned over. Both forces were now firing all guns, and it was thought there were at least 500 Chinese on the road and the hillsides around the column.

An enemy machine-gun burst hit Lieutenant Uzzo in the back, and he fell into the ditch alongside the lead tank. The tank crew members tried to rescue him, but he told them he was badly hit and could not move, and they should withdraw. His Security Platoon members could not get to him because of the curtain of enemy fire that covered this entire spot. Another burst of enemy machine-gun fire was seen to hit Uzzo on the chest, but he still was able to fire his weapon from his prone position in the ditch when Cpl. James J. Lee of the Security Platoon last saw him.

The tanks reached a point where they could turn around, covered by fire from each other and the Security Platoon. All this time the enemy force on the high ground on the east side of the road was trying to out-flank the relief column and get behind it. One tank got across the bridge at the river and took a position from where it could fire on this enemy force. Also, a part of the Netherlands Battalion, in position at the north edge of Hoengsong, placed fire on this enemy force. Howden's tank had been hit in the withdrawal, and it slid off the road. Lieutenant Howden had been pinned under its gun and was wounded, but a hazardous rescue effort by his men freed him. His relief force now withdrew into Hoeng-song, without further enemy fire, under the protective barrages laid down by the one tank and the Netherlands detachment.[34]

Meanwhile, three miles north of Hoengsong, Lieutenant Colonel Maix-ner at Saemal received an order relayed by the 38th Infantry from X Corps that Support Force 21 should continue on to Hoengsong but that his 3rd Battalion should remain in its defense perimeter until 6 P.M. This order was given to Lieutenant Colonel Kelleher about 11 A.M. He and his 1st Battalion were to clear both sides of the road as he advanced. Kelleher put his C Company on the west side of the road, B Company on the east, and A Company in reserve, sweeping the road itself and protecting the vehicu-lar column. Kelleher's infantry jumped off in the attack at 11:45 A.M. C Company fixed bayonets before it charged the first ridge, but the Chinese there vacated it rather than face the steel.

Before the Support Force 21 advance began, Lieutenant Colonels Kelle-her and Maixner discussed the situation of the wounded. The 3rd Bat-talion aid station was now full of wounded, and it seemed impossible to take care of them all. Maixner and Kelleher decided they would load the wounded on all available transportation and place these vehicles at the head of the Support Force 21 column. Upon reaching Hoengsong, these wounded would be delivered to a Medical Collecting Station. While the work of load-ing the wounded was in progress, a helicopter came in through a hail of enemy small-arms fire to evacuate a seriously wounded soldier. Two men were killed in helping to get the wounded soldier to the helicopter, but the helicopter got out.

As Support Force 21 was preparing to resume its fighting withdrawal toward Hoengsong, Maixner decided to shorten his 3rd Battalion perimeter at Saemal. He pulled in the left flank of K Company from Hill 587 west of Saemal. The ridge running south from Hill 587 was a center of enemy fire, and Hill 206, on the east side of the road opposite Saemal, was also heavily infested with enemy troops. Enemy fire from both these locations now increased on the Saemal perimeter. Maixner replied with artillery and M16 and M19 automatic fire and succeeded in silencing a large part of it.[35]

In its attack from Saemal southward on the ridgeline east of the road, B Company gained almost a mile before enemy opposition increased to the point where it could go no farther. In this advance, Corporal Wall threw a grenade at an enemy machine gunner but forgot to pull the pin. The unexploded grenade hit the enemy on the head, stunning him temporarily — long enough for Wall to rush the emplacement and finish the job. When enemy strength stopped B Company, Kelleher committed A Company to take the lead from B Company, but it had to fight its way to the company, taking many casualties in the process. Kelleher now formed his Headquarters Company and various service troops into a composite company and committed them to the west side of the road opposite but behind A Company, and it destroyed four machine guns and a mortar that had moved up behind B and A companies on the east side of the road. There seemed to be no vacuum behind the 1st Battalion after it swept the ridges. Other enemy filled in behind as fast as it moved forward and attacked from the rear. This was a very severe action for A and B companies. When the situation had been stabilized, the two companies found that they had only 40 men altogether, and they reorganized into a composite company.

In this fight, Lieutenant Gardner of A Company had again tried to get ROK troops to help. He found the commanding officer of the ROK 21st Regiment and told him to get his cowardly troops into the fight. He tried, said Gardner, but could do nothing, since he could not find any subordinate ROK officers. With the help of his first sergeant, Gardner beat some of the ROKs and, at gunpoint, forced them into the line. Gardner had only 14 men left in his company. He said the ground all about was littered with dead Americans, ROKs, and Chinese. By using the improvised Headquarters Company and his own men, Gardner was able to get the high ground on his flanks and to establish two outposts. His shaky skirmish line was only 30 yards ahead of Kelleher's observation post.

Gardner sent a runner back to the rear to bring up any reinforcements he could find. When he returned, the runner reported that there were many artillerymen to the rear, sitting on their vehicles, some securing their flanks, but most cowering in the ditches. Gardner went to the rear and, walking along the road column, organized some of these men into groups and sent them to his skirmish line and also to the west of the road, where a fight was going on for possession of a hill. Some of these men, Gardner said, gave a good account of themselves, but most found a secluded spot and helped not at all, hoping that one of their officers would not find them, and seemingly waiting for the enemy to find them. Gardner said five of the artillerymen told him they were not fighting men and had no desire to fight as infantry. At this juncture, word came that the 3rd Battalion at Saemal was moving out to join them in the fight.[36]

About 3:30 P.M., when a Chinese counterattack from the southeast had forced A and B Companies back about 500 yards, there were at least 200 ROK soldiers in the road column. Kelleher said, "All efforts to get these people organized and to help us were in vain. They would hide in trucks, ditches, some were observed to throw away their belts, ammunition and posing as wounded to avoid combat. One ROK soldier was caught breaking his M-1 rifle."

At 3 P.M. the 2nd Division authorized the 38th Infantry at Hoengsong to instruct the 3rd Battalion at Saemal to assist the 1st Battalion in its efforts to withdraw Support Force 21 to Hoengsong. Lieutenant Colonel Kelleher coordinated the joint attack with Lieutenant Colonel Maixner. The plan was for the 1st Battalion to take the left (east) side of the road, and the 3rd Battalion the right (west) side. The Saemal-Hoengsong road would be the boundary between them. This action called for C Company on the west side to move to the east side to join the 1st Battalion there when Maixner's 3rd Battalion came up and moved through it. Each battalion would sweep the high ground on its side of the road so the road column could move ahead abreast of them. The 3rd Battalion put K Company in the lead, followed by I Company. As each hill was taken, one platoon would remain on the hill to secure it until all friendly elements had passed. L Company and Headquarters personnel of the 3rd Battalion formed the rear guard. The 3rd Battalion vehicles would follow closely behind Support Force 21 vehicles. The 1st Battalion planned to have its A and B companies attack abreast of each other. C Company, when it crossed the road to the east side, would be behind them. By this time A and B companies were only one small composite company.

At 4:30 the 1st Battalion infantry jumped off in attack on the east side of the road. Two tanks of the 3rd Battalion were sent to aid this attack. The 1st Battalion gained the next high ground, knocking out six enemy machine guns and killing 90 enemy. When they passed over the crest of this enemy position and started down the next little valley, they came upon two groups of 25 Chinese each, eating a meal. They quickly killed these enemy.[37]

All day Support Force 21 had been trying to form a sleeve protecting the road vehicular column from enemy on the sides of the road and had succeeded thus far in doing so, but by now it and the 3rd Battalion that had joined it south of Saemal were nearly exhausted. The enemy fireblock along the entire road was nearly a solid one.

Col. John G. Coughlin, commander of the 38th Infantry and at his CP in Hoengsong all through the fighting, thus far had no command authority, except for logistic support. The chain of command from the X Corps to the fighting men of the support forces had been a nightmare of confusion from the beginning. The relief force that started from Hoengsong in the late afternoon was composed of the 1st Battalion, 18th Regiment, ROK 3rd Division; G Company, 187th Airborne RCT; and a platoon of tanks, C Company, 38th Tank Company. Research for this book did not bring to light the identity of its commander.

The ROK 1st Battalion, 18th Regiment, moved out in the lead, attacking north across the bridge from Hoengsong at 5 P.M. It did not continue the attack up the road but climbed the hill just northeast of the bridge at Hoengsong. The rest of the relief force never even crossed the bridge and at nightfall was still on the south side of the river at the northern edge of Hoengsong.

During the afternoon, General Almond had come to Hoengsong, looking for General Chae, commander of the ROK 8th Division, long since a disintegrated and useless combat formation. He found him, but there is no record of what passed between them. But as a result of the situation Almond found at Hoengsong and the knowledge he gained of the situation of his support forces caught in the hills northward in an enemy vise, he sent Lieutenant Colonel Willems, an assistant G-1 of X Corps, to Colonel Coughlin at 6:15 P.M. to tell Coughlin that he was now in command of all the troops in the Hoengsong area as the senior officer present. Coughlin told the author that Almond blamed him for not taking command of the troops in the Hoengsong area when the disaster descended, because he was the senior officer there (not counting Brigadier General Chae of the ROK 8th Division). In the command structure that had been set up, which bypassed Colonel Coughlin completely, this was an odd charge to make and one which Coughlin resented at the time. Later, though, he said, he came to admire Almond.[38]

But now, since he had been invested with command of all the forces in the Hoengsong area at a belated hour, Coughlin took the relief force in hand. He went down to the bridge, turned the infantry and tank troops around, took them back the short distance to Hoengsong, and reorganized them. He placed Capt. Reginald J. Hinton, commander of the 38th Tank Company in command of it and ordered it to move out. It was now 6:30 P.M., and darkness had fallen.

When the relief force crossed the bridge, it found the ROK 1st Battalion, 18th Regiment, had abandoned the hill just east of it. Hinton's force had moved north only 1,000 yards beyond the bridge when it came under heavy enemy mortar, automatic, and small-arms fire. It pressed ahead for about a mile, incurring 30 casualties. Hinton by radio requested permission to withdraw. He was ordered to go forward. So his tanks and G Company, 187th Airborne RCT, fought slowly northward. Either they did not clear the enemy from the hills alongside the road thoroughly, or the Chinese let them through without heavy resistance at some places, or the CCF came back to their fireblock positions as soon as the relief force had passed, because when the united forces fought back south later, the enemy held all the high ground in great strength.

Hinton's tanks met two tanks of the 3rd Battalion at 7:45 P.M. Hinton's tanks and infantry now joined Kelleher's and Maixner's 1st and 3rd battalions, and the combined force prepared to continue the fight south through the enemy fireblock. M. Sgt. Vite E. Perrone, 2nd Platoon, 38th Tank Company, brought up the rear of the road column.

Lieutenant Gardner of A Company, 38th Infantry, said, "When G Company of the 187th RCT reached us, they turned around and started fighting out with us; and again, the enemy was unrelenting; he cut the company to ribbons and wounded and killed more of our foot-sloggers. Also he knocked out more vehicles. I put a security force on the high ground to the left of the road, with a M/Sgt in charge, and told them to deny this ground to the enemy until the column had passed; which they did, but the enemy had too many other strong points."[39]

When the two forces joined, they were about a mile and a half from the bridge at the north end of Hoengsong. Two tanks took up firing positions at the side of the road, and quad-50s of the 82nd AAA AW Battalion added their automatic fire to suppress enemy machine guns firing from the west side of the road. Gardner's A Company held the hill opposite on the east side. The help given by the M16s during the entire withdrawal can hardly be overstated. And so it was now in the final phase. In this action six gunners were successively wounded on one M16 and four on another.[40]

One mistake was made, however, at this time. Because Hinton's relief force had just fought its way north on the road, it was thought the way back would be relatively free of an enemy fireblock. Accordingly, the infantry on the high ground were called in and placed on the road for a rapid run the short remaining distance to Hoengsong. When I Company started down the road, there was no longer the slow-moving and fighting screen on the high ground bordering it; the fireblock in fact was still there and in great strength. The 38th Infantry Special Report on Hoengsong sums up the last chaotic run through the gauntlet they now had to run from where the relief force met the support forces.

As leading elements of the column started down the road, they encountered heavy mortar, small arms, and machine gun fire from points previously physically secured. It became necessary for the column to run a gauntlet of fire the remaining distance to Hoengsong. The fire was being delivered at point blank range. In numerous instances, friendly forces would hold one side of the road and the enemy the other. Hand grenade duels were fought all along the route. According to Sgt.

Perrone, at Kungol, map reading coordinate 0950, only 500 yards north of the Hoengsong bridge, an enemy mortar round struck a prime mover [a 2½-ton truck], causing the 105 mm howitzer which it was towing to jackknife, forming a block on the road, making vehicular movement past this point impossible. All vehicles behind this prime mover were abandoned.

This and other delays enabled the enemy to pinch off portions of the column. L and Headquarters Companies, at the rear of the column, were receiving murderous fire and their casualties were mounting very fast. In order to get through, some of the men broke up into small groups and fought their way across country. Others bulled their way through firing their weapons at pointblank range. When a weapon was rendered useless, another one would be picked up along the route and the firing would be resumed. Even though the men knew they were fighting against terrific odds, they were fighting superbly. Finally, the column arrived at the river west of Hoengsong; however they were still subject to mortar fire. At this point, the 3rd Battalion was met by Colonel Coughlin, Commanding Officer, 38th Regiment. Colonel Coughlin directed the 3rd Battalion to continue on to Wonju.[41]

Lieutenant Colonel Maixner of the 3rd Battalion and Master Sergeant Perrone, commanding the 2nd Platoon, 38th Tank Company, at the rear of the column, gave specific testimony before the Stewart-Duvall inspector general investigation concerning the jackknifed 105-mm howitzer and its 2½-ton truck. Maixner said a mortar shell struck the howitzer, which jackknifed and blocked the road to all wheeled vehicles behind it. Tanks were unable to budge the heavily loaded truck and howitzer. First Lt. Paul L. Meyer of the 3rd Battalion said that about 100 men came running down the road saying they had been ordered to abandon the trucks behind the howitzer. He then went forward about 50 yards and found the 2½-ton truck and the 105-howitzer it had been pulling jackknifed across the road and an enemy machine gun firing into the cab of the truck so no one could approach the truck and try to move it and clear the road.

But Sergeant Perrone gave the best information of what happened after the howitzer blocked the road. When he arrived at an assembly area two miles south of Hoengsong soon after midnight, he said that a large number of vehicles, he estimated to number about 30, had been abandoned at CS 0950 (that is, at Kungol), approximately 500 yards north of the river at Hoengsong, and that the lead trucks were burning. All personnel had fled. He passed this silent column of trucks and the roadblock with his tanks and had come on through.[42] This part of the withdrawal route was later named "Massacre Valley" by elements of the 1st Marine Division, which were the first American troops to see the scene a month later.

In one of the numerous episodes that occurred after the howitzer jackknifed just north of Hoengsong on the twisting, narrow road, Capt. Harold F. Hogan with about 30 men crawled down the ditch on the east side of the road in a firefight with enemy on the other side of the road, which

Aerial view over Saemal looking south over the road into Massacre Valley. Hoengsong, not visible in this photograph, is at the other end of the valley. *US Army photograph (unnumbered)*

they won. A truck passed Hogan and his men but came to a halt a short distance ahead. When Hogan came up to it, he found those riding in front were in the ditch, dead or wounded. A load of wounded men were in the back of the truck. Hogan obtained a driver who took the truck on out.

There are many variant statements from different sources as to just when the first of the survivors reached Hoengsong. It seems that 9 P.M., 12 February, would be near the mark. Colonel Coughlin said the last 2nd Division vehicles to get through had cleared Hoengsong by 10 P.M. Stragglers and small groups kept coming in after that up until midnight.

First Lt. Lee R. Hartell was in the air all day of 12 February over the support forces, reporting their situation and trying to get artillery fire sup-

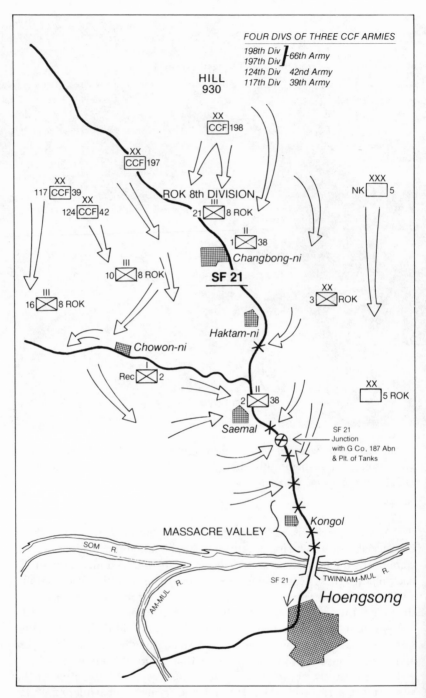

MAP 11. **CCF attack on the ROK 8th Division and US Support Forces (38th Infantry), 11–12 February 1951**

port for them. In a letter he later wrote to his brother "Chic," he described how, late that afternoon, Chinese mortar fire hit jeeps only 2,000 yards from Hoengsong, blocking the road as hundreds of enemy descended onto it and engaged in a furious hand-to-hand fight that left hundreds of bodies lying everywhere. Most of the jeeps' surviving occupants were dragged into the woods and the vehicles set ablaze. An enormous roadblock was established, with a thousand enemy on either side of the road. Napalm and air strikes could not budge the roadblock, and the massacre continued all night as unit integrity broke down and every man fought his own fight.[43]

After some weeks, when American troops won back the area north of Hoengsong, 1st Lt. John Mewha walked through Massacre Valley with company commanders of the 1st Battalion, 38th Infantry. At that time, Lieutenant Gardner, commander of A Company, said of that stretch of road just north of Hoengsong, "There were so many wounded, that you had to step between their legs in order to move forward."[44] One wonders how many American and other wounded there were run over by vehicles in the darkness. In a precipitous retreat, drivers of vehicles, intent on getting forward at all cost, often did not pay much attention to bodies on the road.

Later on 3 March, when elements of the 1st Marine Division moved up the road from Hoengsong, the 2nd Division formed a salvage and recovery team under the command of Lt. Col. Richard O. Gordon to accompany the 1st Marines to recover bodies and equipment. In the period from 3 to 12 March, this team recovered more than 250 bodies. All had frozen and were in good condition for identification except for a few that had been burned or crushed by tanks. Most showed multiple bullet wounds. Mortar and artillery fire had killed a few. Personnel of the 38th Infantry and 15th Field Artillery Battalion helped in the identification.

Recovery of equipment was nearly complete. All five of the 155-mm howitzers of A Battery, 503rd FA Battalion, were recovered, and six M-5 tractors, only two of which were repairable, and four of six tanks were evacuated. Most of the trucks were badly shot up and of value only for some spare parts.[45]

While four Chinese divisions attacked and virtually destroyed the ROK 8th Division in four hours, beginning about midnight of 11 February, other Chinese units at the same time struck the ROK 3rd and 5th divisions to the east of the 8th Division. The ROK 5th Division suffered heavily and was partially destroyed. This left open a large area east of Hoengsong for enemy movement toward that place and to the road south of it. About the same time that the leading elements of Support Force 21 and the 3rd Battalion, 38th Infantry, fought their way through to Hoengsong, at 9 P.M., enemy from the east were approaching Hoengsong. The main defense force there all day had been the Netherlands Battalion and elements of the 187th Airborne RCT. The Netherlands Battalion now came under attack in Hoengsong. From noon of the twelfth on, the Netherlands Battalion saw groups of enemy soldiers on the hills to the north and northwest across the river and fired on them. The battalion was deployed astride the main road going north and on either side of it. From its position, the Netherlands Battalion fired in support of the American troops trying to fight their way south to Hoengsong. C Battery, 82nd AAA AW Battalion, supported the Netherlands Battalion. After dark, enemy soldiers infiltrated across the river, sometimes mixed in with retreating ROK soldiers, and passed around the right (east) flank of the Netherlands defense position and approached directly toward the Netherlands CP from the northeast.

At 9:15 P.M. a column of about 60 men were seen approaching the CP from the northeast. The security guard fired on it and stopped the column. Someone in the column shouted, "OK, ROKs; OK, ROKs." A grenade hit a Netherlands jeep in the vicinity and set it on fire. In the glare of this light, Netherlands soldiers saw ROK unit colors on the sleeves of some of the men in the column. Lt. Col. M. P. A. den Ouden, the Netherlands commander, ordered Sergeant Pakkar from the S-2 section to take an interpreter and find out definitely who these men were. Pakkar and the interpreter approached the stopped column. As they got close to it, the interpreter heard the men talking among themselves and recognized the language as Chinese. He shouted to Pakkar, "They're Chinese!" Pakkar called the warning back to the security guards. The Chinese opened fire. Pakkar was never seen again. The Chinese with their first fire rushed into the CP perimeter. Lieutenant Colonel den Ouden was giving orders to his men when a grenade exploded at his feet. Its fragments killed him. Four of his men tried to pull his body over an embankment to the CP, but heavy enemy fire prevented it. The Chinese gained control of the CP area temporarily because, other than its security guard, all the rest of the battalion — A, B, and the Heavy Weapons companies — was on the perimeter line inside Hoengsong. From high ground near the CP area, the Chinese fired on other parts of the Netherlands positions. By this time other Chinese had entered Hoengsong in different parts of the town.

Captain DeVries of A Company, Netherlands Battalion, assumed command of the Netherlands fight. At 9:45 P.M. he said the last of the Americans retreating from the north had passed through Hoengsong, and the Netherlands Battalion itself could now withdraw. A Company left first, then B Company, and finally the Heavy Weapons Company left at 10:30 P.M. The battalion assembled at the bridge south of Hoengsong on the road to Wonju, and its survivors arrived there without further action. In this attack on the Netherlands CP area in Hoengsong, the Chinese killed 10 and wounded 28, and 9 were missing in action. Captain DeVries commanded the battalion the remainder of the night. Lieutenant Colonel den Ouden was buried in the UN Cemetery at Pusan on 8 March 1951. Lt. Col. W. D. H. Eekhout succeeded him to command of the Netherlands Battalion.[46]

The ROK 3rd and 5th divisions, to the east of the ROK 8th Division, narrowly escaped the same fate that overtook the 8th Division. A Chinese division hit the ROK 3rd Division at the same time during the night of 11–12 February, while farther east several North Korean understrength divisions of the NK V Corps struck the ROK 5th Division. At 4:30 A.M., 12 February, an artillery forward observer with the 1st Battalion, 22nd Regiment, ROK 3rd Division, arrived at Hoengsong with word that enemy had overrun the 1st Battalion CP and the battalion supply point and that enemy had also surprised and overrun the ROK 35th Regiment of the ROK 5th Division on its right. The ROK 23rd Regiment of the 3rd Division was under attack, and the 11th Field Artillery Battalion had gone into a perimeter defense, expecting an attack. By 6:15 A.M. enemy were within 200 yards of the artillery position and firing small arms into it. The 11th Artillery fired machine guns and 75-mm guns into the enemy force, causing it to withdraw to a nearby hill. Colonel Song, commanding the ROK 11th Field Artillery Battalion, asked the ROK 35th Regiment, 5th Division, for reinforcements. That regiment could give none, but it did give supporting fire. Colonel Song decided at noon that he would have to withdraw his artillery, which he began doing at 12:30 P.M. B Battery was the last to leave and covered his withdrawal. The 11th Artillery left only one destroyed gun behind.

The ROK 22nd Regiment was the lead element of the ROK 3rd Division. In the night attack, elements of the CCF 198th Division soon isolated it, and it was considered lost, but later in the day it broke out and withdrew south. Task Force White, composed of the 49th Field Artillery Battalion and the 2nd Battalion, 17th Infantry, 7th Division, supported the ROK 3rd Division and was heavily engaged near Hoengsong in helping the division to withdraw. After the ROK 3rd Division had withdrawn south from the battleground northeast of Hoengsong, only its 18th Regiment was considered combat useful. The 17th Infantry was ordered to assemble at Sillim-ni, north of Chechon, and Task Force White withdrew to that point on 13 February. Task Force White had 4 killed, 39 wounded, and 7 missing in action.[47]

In the ROK 5th Division sector, enemy quickly enveloped both flanks of its 35th Regiment, its lead unit. Team Charlie, consisting of two platoons of C Company, 17th Infantry Regiment, 7th Division, and one platoon of heavy tanks, supported the 5th Division. X Corps ordered the ROK 5th Division to withdraw south and defend the road leading east into Hoengsong. But enemy followed the ROKs so closely that the division had to abandon its mission and continue withdrawing rapidly farther south. In the course of this withdrawal enemy overran the tank destroyer battalion and three engineer companies, and the entire division was pushed on toward Chechon. On 13 February X Corps ordered the ROK 5th Division to assemble near Sillim-ni, about nine miles north of Chechon, on the road from

Wonju. It appeared that elements of the North Korean 6th, 7th, 9th, and 12th divisions had attacked the ROK 5th Division.[48]

As daylight of 12 February wore on, with the only catastrophe reported from the area north of Hoengsong, General Almond and his X Corps staff placed priority attention on the defense of Wonju. It seemed certain that the enemy would overrun Hoengsong. During the afternoon, Almond had started the 2nd Battalion, 38th Infantry, from Wonju to go north to help in the rescue of the support forces and 38th Infantry troops caught behind the ROK 8th Division, but he countermanded the order and brought the battalion back to Wonju. He wanted to hold a line from Chipyong-ni on the west through Wonju, Saemal (not to be confused with the town of the same name north of Hoengsong), and hence northeast toward the coast. Finally, at long last, General Almond issued X Corps Operational Order No. 104 at 8 P.M., 12 February, which dissolved all American artillery, armor, and infantry elements of the several support forces and teams he had formed earlier to help the ROK 8th, 3rd, and 5th divisions in the Roundup attack and returned the units to their parent US organizations.[49]

The ROK 8th Division withdrew on south, and at 8 P.M. on 12 February it established its CP at Chupo-ri. In a night and a day, the enemy had cut off the X Corps salient that had extended north of Wonju.

General Almond now intended to establish a defense line on high ground about 2½ miles north of Wonju. At 2:45 P.M. on the twelfth, the X Corps G-3 section sent a message to the 3rd Battalion, 38th Infantry, at Saemal, three miles north of Hoengsong, to withdraw to a point 4,000 yards north of Wonju. This order applied to the entire regiment, which was to carry it out as soon as possible. There the X Corps planned its defense line. It would have the Netherlands Battalion on the left (west) of the line, with the 2nd, 3rd, and 1st battalions of the 38th Infantry next eastward in the center, and the 187th Airborne RCT on the right (east) flank. The 2nd Battalion, 187th Airborne RCT, would be in reserve. The ROK 18th Regiment would block on the east of the line, and the ROK Ranger Company would block on the west. The 2nd Battalion, 17th Infantry, 7th Division, would be responsible for the rear of the position.[50]

During the day X Corps brought the 187th Airborne RCT north to reinforce the Wonju defenses. Almond placed Brig. Gen. George C. Stewart, assistant commander of the 2nd Division, in charge of the Wonju defense forces. Stewart called a meeting of the unit commanders and told them there would be no withdrawal from the Wonju defenses. He placed all available artillery to fire on all approaches to Wonju. Aerial observers were in the sky over Wonju and the vicinity during all daylight hours.[51]

The losses of personnel and equipment on 12 February north of Hoengsong were appalling. In a meeting at Suwon on 13 February with General MacArthur and other high officers of the Far East Command, General

Partridge of the US Fifth Air Force took General Ridgway aside and said to him, "It's none of my business, but you're in trouble north of Wonju. It looks like Kunu-ri again." "I said little," Ridgway wrote, "except to indicate we were aware of what was happening and would take care of it. No other person was within hearing."[52] Partridge was right—it did look like another Kunu-ri, on a smaller scale.

On 14 February General Almond sent a personal message to General Ridgway at Eighth Army Headquarters. He wrote, "Loss of ground on counterattack due principally to complete collapse of 8 ROK Division and portion of 5th ROK Division—collapse of 8 ROK led to heavy personnel and material losses in 2nd Div Arty and in 2 Bns of 38th Inf protecting it. Est. 4 enemy divs in front of 8 ROK Div." In another personal message the same day to Ridgway, Almond gave him a summary of the losses incurred 11–13 February at Hoengsong. His best estimate as of that date gave personnel losses as in table 8.

TABLE 8. **UN Losses at Hoengsong, 11–13 February 1951**

Unit/Item	Casualties/ Number Lost
2nd Infantry Division	1,136
7th Infantry Division	139
187th Airborne RCT	45
Netherlands Battalion	112[a]
96th Field Artillery Battalion	14
ROK 3rd Division	4,330
ROK 5th Division	4,060
ROK 8th Division	8,524
105-mm howitzer (US)	14
105-mm howitzer (ROK)	27
155-mm howitzer	6
Liaison plane	1
M-4A3E8 tank	6
2½-ton truck	67
¾-ton truck	41
Jeep	91
SCR-300 radio	22
SCR-608 radio	10
Entire signal equipment, US 15th FA Battalion	–
Greater part of vehicles, weapons, and organizational equipment, ROK 8th Division	–

Source: Almond, letter to Ridgway, 14 Feb 51, Hoengsong, 11–13 Feb 51, Unclassified Binder, Ridgway Papers.

[a]The total includes the CO killed.

On 9 March, when figures on the Hoengsong debacle were apparently considered final, General Ridgway sent a message to General MacArthur in Tokyo saying that current reports gave 2nd Division personnel losses at Hoengsong as 99 killed, 490 wounded, and 948 missing in action, for a total of 1,537 casualties. (Many of the missing in action must have been unidentified killed.) He gave the best estimate of heavy equipment losses at 5 155-mm howitzers (6 were actually lost), 14 105-mm howitzers, 6 tanks, 40 2½-ton trucks, and 40 ¾-ton trucks.[53]

General Ridgway had been much concerned when the first reports came into Eighth Army headquarters about the disaster in the making north of Hoengsong. When this disaster had been confirmed, he wrote on 13 February to Almond, "Dear Ned, While there is nothing sacrosanct about a piece of artillery, compared to the loss of the lives of men, I don't expect to hear again of such loss as reported to me this morning of five 155 Hows of Battery A, 503rd. It is primae facie indication of faulty leadership of serious import in some echelon [Ridgway indicated he was sending his G-3 to him for a discussion of the subject]."[54]

On the same day, General Almond sent a message to General Ruffner, commanding the 2nd Infantry Division, asking why the commanding general of the 2nd Division Artillery had not moved the support units involved between 11 A.M. and 3 P.M., 12 February, although the 7th Division did so and got through Hoengsong from east of the 2nd Division and concentrated at Wonju with the loss of only one 155-mm howitzer and its prime mover, two wire trucks, and a minimum of personnel losses.[55]

The explanation of why the 7th Infantry support force, or Task Force White, as it was generally called, got away with so little loss when the ROK 3rd Division withdrew was not superior command performance but a series of flukes and the common sense and good judgment of its commanding officer. It had been ordered to join Support Force 21 after the ROK divisions crumbled under the Chinese attacks, but enemy action between it and Support Force 21 prevented that—it could not reach the MSR from Hoengsong to Changbong-ni. Only then did its commanding officer determine to improve a trail that led east and south from its position. The 7th Infantry Division support force of the 49th Field Battalion and the 2nd Battalion, 17th Infantry, had not been attacked in its position—the enemy at this time was concentrating on Support Force 21 and the 3rd Battalion, 38th Infantry, on the MSR. Capt. Guy P. McMurray, executive officer of C Battery, 49th Field Artillery Battalion, has said of 12 February,

All during the day of the 12th my battery, with the other two batteries of the battalion, sat in a valley with air strikes on our flanks, our front, and our rear waiting for word to move out of the position. At about 7 o'clock on the night of the 12th, we started moving out by "goat trail" to the east and south—heading toward Hoengsong and Wonju to the south of that. At approximately 2130 we reached the outskirts of Hoengsong, ran into a Chinese roadblock in a location formerly held by a Dutch Battalion, and came under heavy mortar and machine gun fire. . . . We were halted in the area for approximately 3 hours.[56]

Colonel Coughlin, CO of the 38th Infantry and now commander of all American and ROK forces in the Hoengsong area by Almond's verbal order, saw this column coming into Hoengsong from the north. He estimated the time as being about 7 P.M. He said it turned out to be the 7th Division support force. He located the infantry battalion commander of the force, informed him of his command of all troops in the area, and told him of his plan to return all troops to Wonju. Since Coughlin had no need for the 49th Artillery Battalion at Hoengsong, he told the CO that it could proceed directly on to Wonju but that he needed the infantry battalion desperately to try and hold off the Chinese until all of Support Force 21 had cleared the vicinity. The infantry officer left to inform the 49th Artillery commander of what Colonel Coughlin had said, with the understanding that he would return immediately with his infantry and Coughlin would show him what he wanted done. Coughlin did not see the officer again until 10 P.M., after all vehicles of Support Force 21 had cleared Hoengsong.[57]

With B Company of the Netherlands Battalion in position at Hoengsong and the 2nd Battalion of the 17th Infantry, 7th Division, also now in Hoengsong and all the vehicles of Support Force 21 that had escaped cleared through Hoengsong, Colonel Coughlin thought he had the situation under control. His biggest fear was another enemy fireblock on the road south to Wonju. With that possibility in mind he held four tanks on the road south to Wonju just south of Hoengsong until all wheeled vehicles had cleared on the way to Wonju. B Company of the Netherlands Battalion and the 17th Infantry battalion then broke contact with the Chinese and moved toward Wonju.[58]

The catastrophe north of Hoengsong caused General Almond, commander of X Corps, to request an investigation. He appointed Brig. Gen. George Stewart, assistant commander 2nd Infantry Division, to head the investigation panel, and named Lt. Col. Herman C. Duvall, the 2nd Division inspector general, to be a member with Stewart. Major General Ruffner, commander of the 2nd Division, told the author that a member of Eighth Army Inspector General Section sat in with the investigating panel and approved its report. General Stewart and Lieutenant Colonel Duvall held hearings and took testimony and affidavits during the period 15–19 February and submitted their report, dated 23 February 1951, to General Almond. This report brought out a great amount of information on the Hoengsong operation from survivors, most of it never publicized. Its main finding and recommendations were the following:

The cause for the heavy losses in equipment and personnel from the forces provided by the 2nd Division to support the attack of the 8th ROK Division was the sudden and complete rout and disintegration of the 8th ROK Division which came with little or no warning to the 2nd Infantry Division forces. . . .

No US units be intermingled with ROK units in the future.

Due recognition be given to the many brave men, living and dead, who heroically fought to rectify an impossible situation brought on solely by the panic ridden flight of those they had supported.[59]

Lt. Col. Milton G. Norum, executive officer, 38th Infantry Regiment, at the regimental CP in Hoengsong during 11–12 February, testified that he acted as a relay agent for messages from X Corps to Support Force 21 and the 3rd Battalion, 38th Infantry, at Saemal. Colonel Coughlin stated that he had informational copies of all such orders but no control or operating authority over Support Force 21 or any of his battalions until Lieutenant Colonel Willem, the personal representative of General Almond, gave him oral orders from Almond in the evening of 12 February to assume command of all forces in the Hoengsong area and send them to Wonju. There was great confusion about who commanded the artillery in the various support forces, especially that in Support Force 21. General Ruffner, commander of the 2nd Division, told the author that "he could not move a single . . . thing." He thought the X Corps Artillery commander, Col. William P. Ennis, had control of the artillery through the ROK commanders, that the 2nd Division Artillery commander, Brigadier General Haynes, had no authority, and that General Chae, ROK 8th Division commander, gave the orders as long as he was at Hoengsong (night of 11–12 and all morning of 12 February).[60]

Colonel Ennis, commanding the X Corps Artillery, testified before the Stewart-Duvall investigating panel that "about 12 1130 Feb 51, the X Corps Commanding General asked me where the 2nd Division task force was located. I replied that the 3rd Battalion, 38th perimeter was at DS 075518 [Saemal]. He directed that I initiate action to have the two task forces withdraw to Hoengsong without delay and to fight their way out if necessary. I telephoned Col. Niel M. Wallace, X Corps Artillery Executive Officer, and ordered him to pass on the orders to Brig. Gen. Haynes and Lt. Col. Barney White." The X Corps Artillery S-3 Journal, 12 February 51, shows he telephoned the order to Haynes at 121200 February 1951.[61] So, it was noon 12 February before X Corps stepped into the picture, despite several earlier pleas that the artillery be free to fire into attacking enemy in the ROK sector south of Changbong-ni.

General Almond left the X Corps headquarters at 10:30 A.M., 12 February, to go north to Hoengsong to find out what had happened in the ROK 8th Division sector, and at the same time he sent the corps G-3 to the ROK 3rd Division sector to find out what the situation was there.[62] Almond found that, by 11:20 A.M., large numbers of ROK soldiers were streaming south on the road from Hoengsong to Wonju and by noon the

ROK 36th Regiment of the ROK 5th Division was fleeing south. The 187th Airborne RCT stopped these men and turned them around.

Lieutenant Colonel Keith, commander of Support Force 21, is known to have been wounded twice and was missing in action south of Saemal, Many, many officers of the support force were killed or wounded. Lieutenant Gardner of A Company, 38th Infantry, was the only officer who, with 12 men of his company, reached Saemal in his rear-guard action for Support Force 21 from Changbong-ni. K Company, 9th Infantry, part of Support Force Able, could muster only one officer and five enlisted men on 13 February. The commander of A Battery, 503rd Battery, was missing in action. These are only examples of what happened.

Several things stand out in the Hoengsong action. The past experience of Eighth Army with ROK units in combat against the Chinese formations did not warrant the command action of General Almond in placing American units under ROK division command, and it is surprising that General Ridgway approved the plan. Upon reading the draft of this chapter, General Ridgway said that he did not recall that anyone called his attention to this aspect of Almond's plan.

At the beginning of the action the soldiers of A Battery, 503rd Artillery Battalion, near Changbong-ni, ran off and abandoned 5 of their 6 howitzers; only 1 and its tractor got on the road. The 15th Field Artillery Battalion, also near Changbong-ni, performed well at the beginning of the action and got to Saemal with 17 of 18 of their 105-mm howitzers. The infantry battalions in the action, Lieutenant Colonel Kelleher's 1st Battalion, 38th Infantry, and Lieutenant Colonel Maixner's 3rd Battalion, 38th Infantry, in a defense perimeter at Saemal during the night of 11–12 February and most of the day of the twelfth, until it joined the 1st Battalion in fighting out to Hoengsong, performed heroically and in the best traditions of the US Army. The 1st Battalion fought the enemy off the hills from Changbong-ni to Saemal, a distance of five miles, forming a "moving sleeve" for the passage of the vehicles on the road. And the 1st and 3rd battalions did the same thing from Saemal to within a mile of Hoengsong in the face of superior numbers of Chinese stationed in prepared positions on every piece of high ground on the road south. This was no bugging out down the road; it was a controlled and disciplined performance of officer and noncommissioned leadership and sacrificial fighting by rank-and-file. Praise and homage for these men are their due and cannot be too high.

In March 1951, elements of the 1st Marine Division, the first American soldiers to pass over the road north of Hoengsong after the 11–12 February action, reported startling facts of the carnage they saw there. At that time, Lt. Col. James T. Quirck, the Eighth Army information officer, admitted to General Ridgway that he had not given full information to the press corps on the disaster that had taken place. The Marines called the hill-gorge road section immediately north of the river at Hoengsong, the last half mile of the withdrawal route, Massacre Valley, and the Valley of Death. They found the frozen bodies littering the road everywhere, in trucks and under them and on both sides of the road. They erected a sign there that read, "Massacre Valley, Scene of Harry S. Truman's Police Action. Nice Going Harry!"[63]

In 48 hours CCF and North Korean divisions had pushed the X Corps back south 15 miles in the central corridor. The X Corps and Eighth Army rushed the British 27th Brigade and the ROK 6th Division into a line alongside the 2nd Division and the 187th Airborne RCT between Chipyong-ni on the west and Wonju on the east. On 13 February the Air Force flew 867 sorties, 286 of them in close support, against enemy forces. Already four Chinese divisions and the North Korean 2nd, 7th, and 27th divisions of the North Korean V Corps on the northeast of the attack zone had moved down to the Wonju defense area.

On 13 February large enemy forces had all but surrounded Chipyong-ni, 20 air miles northeast of Wonju. A battle there was already beginning that would decide the fate of the X Corps line centering on Wonju. Hoengsong was merely the opening battle, a bloody and disastrous one to be sure, of the Chinese 4th Phase Offensive. Much more was to come in the days ahead that would test X Corps and Eighth Army to the utmost. Combat at both Chipyong-ni and Wonju went on simultaneously, beginning on the thirteenth at Chipyong-ni, and starting on the fourteenth at Wonju. The outcome at Wonju depended in a large degree on the battle at Chipyong-ni.

11

The Key Battle: Chipyong-ni

THREE DAYS after its tense battle with the 373rd and 374th regiments of the Chinese 125th Division at the Twin Tunnels, the 23rd RCT of the 2nd Division on 3 February cautiously entered the village of Chipyong-ni, five miles up the road from the Twin Tunnels. The Chinese 125th Division headquarters troops and its 375th Regiment, together with survivors of the other two regiments, had withdrawn to the northeast to Hill 506, a mountain stronghold, two miles northeast of Chipyong-ni. This forbidding mountain mass had many abandoned tunnels from earlier gold mines, and it had been the concentration point earlier of the 125th Division prior to the battle at the Twin Tunnels. It now became a haven for the decimated division, one that the 23rd RCT soon found was still strong enough to be immovable from its mountain redoubt. The CCF 125th Division in its haven there was far from finished as a combat force.

The mission of the 23rd RCT after 3 February was to control the road center of Chipyong-ni, to occupy high ground in its vicinity, and to protect the right flank of IX Corps and the left flank of X Corps. It might also serve in the future as a planned departure point for an Eighth Army offensive northward. Colonel Freeman, the 23rd RCT commander, considered the low hills around Chipyong-ni suitable for a good defense perimeter by a force of his size—four infantry battalions, including the French Battalion, and supporting weapons. There was an outer ring of higher hills around the low hills that immediately surrounded the town, but they were too far away for effective enemy use of small-arms fire but yet were in range of Freeman's larger mortars, artillery, and tanks, for harassing and supporting fires. Also, air strikes could bring all the higher ground under attack.

Freeman established outpost forces each morning at dawn about 1,000 yards in front of his position to the north, west, and south. At dusk they withdrew, leaving their forward observation posts heavily mined, booby-trapped, and with trip flares set. Combat patrols each day went beyond these positions. For eight days Freeman's force was relatively undisturbed as they brought in large supplies of ammunition, rations, barbed wire, mines, and supplies of all types. B Company of the 2nd Engineers came to Chipyong-ni and built a liaison plane airstrip at the southwestern edge of the town. Colonel Freeman told the author that he established his CP behind F Company in the perimeter defense, just north of the railroad.[1]

Freeman had about 5,000 men altogether in his Chipyong-ni perimeter. The 2nd Reconnaissance Company and the 3rd Battalion of the 9th Infantry patrolled the supply road to the south and east toward Wonju. Eight miles to the south, a battalion of the 24th Infantry Division moved to the north bank of the Han River, and the British 27th Commonwealth Brigade at Yoju in the IX Corps zone daily sent patrols north that maintained contact with Freeman's patrols southward.

In this interval of relative quiet, Freeman tried to rid Hill 506, northeast of Chipyong-ni, of the remnants of the CCF 125th Division, which had occupied the mountain after the battle at the Twin Tunnels. At first he gave the task to his 1st Battalion, but it got mired down in deep snow near the top and had to be relieved by air strikes. Next the 2nd Battalion tried its hand on an eastward attack through Sanggosong, where a narrow road ended, but it had to withdraw before darkness. Then the 3rd Battalion tried to do the job, with all the support that tanks and AAA AW vehicles could give. But the Chinese with automatic-weapons fire stopped every effort. They were determined and would not give an inch. Air strikes seemed to have no effect on them. The terrain was almost impassable. It required four-man parties as long as eight hours to carry out a wounded litter case. The 1st Battalion, 9th Infantry, joined in the attack from the south, but it met equally stubborn resistance. At this point, with hardly a dent made in the Chinese defense of Hill 506, the effort was halted. Other events now claimed priority attention.

Enemy activity had increased on massive Hill 583, four air miles southwest of Chipyong-ni. Beyond it toward the Han River, a battalion of the 24th Division on the north side of the river was being infiltrated by enemy troops. Freeman sent company-sized patrols from the French Battalion to clear out the enemy on Hill 583, but they had no success after two days of effort. The 2nd Battalion, 23rd Infantry, was ordered to make a sweep of the area on 12 February, but that order was canceled when an attack on Chipyong-ni seemed imminent. As it chanced, all the 23rd RCT troops were back at Chipyong-ni when the big enemy assault hit the perimeter.[2]

Aerial observers noted very large troop movements during the day of 11 February. A large body of troops, following mountain trails to the northeast of Chipyong-ni, was estimated to be a full division. After bypassing Chipyong-ni later in the night, this enemy division hit the ROK 8th Division north of Hoengsong, several miles eastward. Other enemy units swung east of Chipyong-ni, then turned back west and cut the 23rd RCT main supply road at Wonchon and Chaun-ni, north of Korun-ni, where the road from Wonju came to the Han River and turned north to Chipyong-ni. This cutting off of the 23rd RCT's exits to the rear occurred before the Chinese launched their main frontal attack at Chipyong-ni.[3]

It is not clear just when General Ridgway made up his mind unalterably that the 23rd RCT and the French Battalion would remain in their perimeter defense at Chipyong-ni and fight it out there with large Chinese forces that had nearly surrounded it by the night of 11 February. It is known, however, that, in a conference at the X Corps Tactical CP at Wonju at noon, 12 February, he ordered General Almond to keep the 23rd RCT at Chipyong-ni.[4] At the same conference, Ridgway informed General Almond and his staff that he was attaching the 187th Airborne RCT to the corps for operational control and that ROK I Corps was placed under X Corps, with responsibility for the control of the ROK 3rd and 5th divisions. Serious difficulties were being experienced with the ROK troops at this time, as their leaders complained bitterly about the way X Corps was treating them, and they objected to the command structure that controlled them. Their poor performance, at the same time, made the issue tense and unpredictable. It greatly concerned General Ridgway.

At the conference on 12 February at the X Corps Tactical CP, it was known that about 12 miles of the mythical Eighth Army line between Wonju and Chipyong-ni was virtually undefended, at the very time that Chinese formations had just destroyed the ROK 8th Division, put the ROK 3rd and 5th divisions into hasty withdrawals southward with heavy losses, captured Hoengsong, were advancing on Wonju, and had surrounded Chipyong-ni. The 9th Infantry Regiment and the 2nd Reconnaissance Company had been patrolling this part of the X Corps line. They had several skirmishes and company-sized fights with enemy along the road through this area. There were clear indications, however, that division-sized enemy formations had entered this no-man's-land east of Chipyong-ni. Their destinations were then unknown. But they had entered a big gap in the army line, and if they chose, they could race south with little opposition and split the X Corps line wide open and reach its rear.

General Ridgway hurriedly ordered the British 27th Commonwealth Brigade and the ROK 6th Division from IX Corps to move into this gap and attached them to X Corps. Had the Chinese decided to exploit their penetration by continuing to move south, the IX Corps units would have been too late. But, perhaps fortunately, the two Chinese divisions that had entered the gap, the 115th and 116th, had other plans. They turned west after getting past Chipyong-ni and cut the two roads leading south toward the Han River that offered escape routes for the trapped units at Chipyong-ni. This was a typical Chinese maneuver.[5]

Meanwhile, at Chipyong-ni, Colonel Freeman wanted to withdraw his forces at once. General Ruffner, 2nd Division commander, agreed. So did General Almond when the request was passed on to him. But he said he could not order the withdrawal because General Ridgway had just ordered him to keep the 23rd RCT at Chipyong-ni and fight the battle there.

At 4:10 P.M. on 12 February, the G-3 of the 2nd Infantry Division, in response to a request from Colonel Freeman for permission to withdraw his forces from Chipyong-ni, fearing they would be cut off and lost, sent a radio message to Freeman that read, "8th Army CG has decided you stay where you are. Other two regiments pulling back south. I am trying to get this changed as soon as CG gets back." Freeman had by this time decided he could not pull out at night and responded, "I do not want to pull back tonight as it will leave me wide open. If I get hit too bad tonight though I will need help. I have two choices if I am badly pushed – 1, toward 24th Division, and other back to where I was [apparently meaning the Twin Tunnels area], and if I move it will have to be under an air umbrella."[6]

At 2:22 P.M. on 13 February the 2nd Division G-3 recorded a message just received from Colonel Freeman that read, "Almond here about 1½ hours ago, asked my recommendation when I could move back to Yoju. I told him in the morning. I have changed my recommendation to as early as possible this evening due to conditions relating to the 2nd Reconnaissance and around my area. Pass this request to CG X Corps and relay answer to me as soon as possible." The 2nd Division G-3 replied to Freeman that he would pass the request to Almond, but that he had to get the answer from the commanding general, Eighth Army.[7] When this request was given to Almond, he said that he had already transmitted Freeman's request to General Ridgway and that the latter would not approve the request.[8]

The author has discussed this order to hold at Chipyong-ni with both Generals Ridgway and Almond. Ridgway said he was determined to hold Chipyong-ni, the hinge between IX Corps and X Corps, even if he had to send all of Eighth Army reserves and part of the IX Corps into the battle there to do so. Almond wrote, "Your query as to Ridgway's insistence on holding at Chipyong-ni is very easily explained, I think. 'He wanted to hold firm' what he had gained and saw avalanche of the enemy pressing his right flank. I agreed but did not have the reserves to stand firm as he desired. When he assured me that he would 'rescue' Combat Team 23 I assured him we would hold."[9]

General Ridgway's orders to stay at Chipyong-ni and fight a perimeter battle against what appeared to be great odds was a mark of his eminence as a general. Chipyong-ni in several ways turned the war around.

Colonel Freeman had the following major units in his 23rd RCT at Chipyong-ni on the eve of battle:

23rd Infantry Regiment, 2nd Infantry Division
37th Field Artillery Battalion, 105-mm howitzers
French Battalion, UN Forces
B Battery, 82nd AAA AW Battalion, SP

B Battery, 503rd Field Artillery Battalion, 155-mm howitzers
B Company, 2nd Engineer Battalion
2nd Clearing Platoon, Clearing Company, 2nd Medical Company
1st Infantry Ranger Company

Altogether he had about 5,000 troops in his command.

The 23rd RCT did not at first dig in much at Chipyong-ni, but as the enemy buildup there developed and it finally appeared that a battle would be fought there, more attention was given to this need. American troops did not like to dig much, especially in frozen ground. The artillery batteries, however, did a good job of getting their guns dug in. The ground was frozen down to a depth of 8 to 10 inches. On top it was all pick work. A shovel would not make a dent in the ground until the hole had reached about 12 inches in depth. The artillerymen used a sledge to drive a crowbar into the frozen ground and then put a winch on it to pry a break in the ground. The infantry did not, in general, do a good job of digging in. The author walked around the perimeter of the UN forces at Chipyong-ni in August 1951 and saw very few foxholes. There were some at K Company's position above the road that entered Chipyong-ni at the southeast corner of the perimeter. There were numerous piles of ration cans and related debris that marked troop positions, and there were endless lines of field telephone wire that had connected company and platoon positions but were later never taken up. In some places loose rocks were piled up in low parapets at some infantry positions. The most dug-in positions were on G Company's hill, and many of them were made on its reverse slope by the Chinese when they got possession of the hill.[10]

Chipyong-ni was an elongated village, about half a mile long on an east-west axis, a block or two wide on each side. Only a few buildings were of brick and frame construction; most of them were the typical mud-thatch construction. The single-track railroad ran northwest from Wonju and passed Chipyong-ni at its southern edge on its way to Seoul. The newly prepared airstrip lay at the southwestern edge of the village, running on a northwest-southeast axis, parallel to and just north of the railroad.

The Chipyong-ni perimeter defense line encompassed an area about two and a half miles long (east-west) by two miles (north-south) at its widest part in the middle, narrowing to about a mile wide at its eastern end and a little more than that at its western end. The village of Chipyong-ni lay entirely within the perimeter toward its southwestern arc. The western end of the airstrip coincided with the southwestern edge of the perimeter. The 37th Field Artillery Battalion and B Battery of the 503rd Artillery Battalion were emplaced at the southwestern part of the perimeter, south of the village and the railroad.

The infantry units were on line, with the 1st Battalion on the north, the 3rd Battalion on the east, the 2nd Battalion on the south, and the

View to the southeast showing the railroad curving around the south side of Chipyong-ni. *Photograph by the author, August 1951*

French Battalion on the west. Beginning at the northwestern corner of the perimeter, the rifle companies were in the following order, clockwise: C, A, L, I, K, E, F, G, French 1, French ROK, French 2, French 3. Freeman at the beginning had a reserve force of B Company, the 1st Ranger Company, and the Headquarters Company Band. They were stationed behind A and C companies. A mobile reserve was maintained at all times. Each unit on line could give fire support to units on either side of it.[11]

Five roads entered the perimeter. The main north-south road entered the perimeter on the north through C Company's sector and exited on the south at the boundary between G and French 1 companies. Two roads from the east and southeast entered the perimeter at the southeast corner at the boundaries between E and F companies and exited on the west side in the sector of the ROK company attached to the French Battalion. The main road south from Chipyong-ni, running through Koksu-ri to Yoju, exited at the boundary between G and French 1 companies, passing through the small village of Masan, which lay about half a mile south of Chipyong-ni.[12]

Chipyong-ni was just inside the X Corps boundary, with the IX Corps boundary passing it on the west side. The five roads passing through it, gateways to the Hongchon valley to the east, the Han River valley to the west, and the Wonju corridor to the southeast. Because of its road-center position, it was important to both sides. Its possession threatened all enemy forces still south of the Han River to the west and southwest, while at the

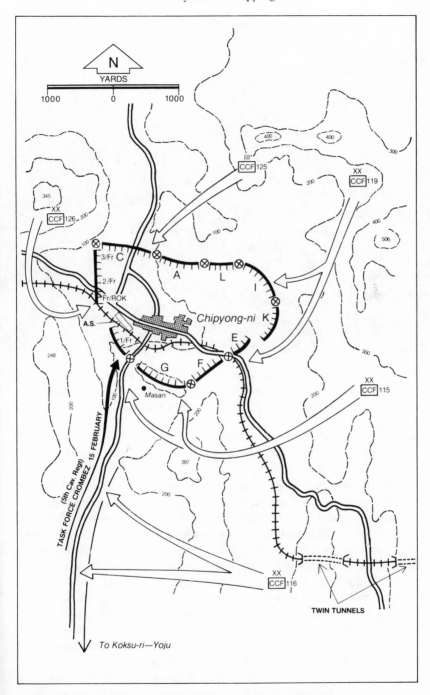

N
YARDS
1000   0   1000

400   400   300

III
CCF 125

XX
CCF 119

345

XX
CCF 126   200   400

506

100
⊗
3/Fr C   ⊗   ⊗   ⊗
2/Fr   A   L   I   ⊗
Fr/ROK
A.S.   Chipyong-ni K

1/Fr   E   300
248   G   F   ⊕   ⊕
⊕   XX
• Masan   CCF 115

TASK FORCE CROMBEZ 15 FEBRUARY
(5th Cav. Regt)   200

200

397

200

200

XX
CCF 116   TWIN TUNNELS

To Koksu-ri—Yoju

MAP 12. **23rd Infantry, 2nd Division, and French Battalion perimeter defense at Chipyong-ni, 13–15 February 1951**

View south from George Hill, showing the road through the Pass (where the road first passes from view) from Chipyong-ni to Koksu-ri. Task Force Crombez came up this road. *Photograph by the author, August 1951*

same time it afforded a possible jump-off point for a UN attack into the enemy's concentration area at Hongchon.

The troops at Chipyong-ni had a quiet night on 12 February, except for light probing attacks against C Company on the north end of the perimeter and against the 3rd Battalion on the east side, all of which were easily repulsed. Enemy flare activity was in evidence from the perimeter. American artillery at Chipyong-ni delivered harassing fires on probable enemy approach routes and assembly areas during the night, and there was some night bombing of enemy areas by radar-controlled B-26s.

After daylight 13 February, Freeman sent patrols out in all directions, some of them as far as 5,000 yards from the perimeter. They reported increased enemy activity to the north, east, and west. Aerial observers farther away from the perimeter reported large enemy groups moving toward Chipyong-ni from the north and east. Artillery and 40 air sorties hit these groups while they were still some distance from the perimeter. Some of the patrols were pinned down by enemy fire and had to be extricated by artillery fire and by air strikes. As darkness came on in the evening of

View of the critical area at the east end of Chipyong-ni where the railroad from the east passes over the road from Twin Tunnels. *Photograph by the author, August 1951*

13 February, the Chinese put flares into the sky to help guide them to their assembly areas.[13] All signs pointed to the last phases of the enemy's moving into their assembly areas around the perimeter for a night attack.

During the day, General Ridgway had issued orders for the 1st Marine Division to prepare for movement toward the battle area, with one RCT to be at Chungju, the Headquarters CP area for both IX and X Corps, by 15 February. The division was to be attached to the IX Corps. Its initial mission was to block the mountain passes leading east and southeast from Chungju to the enemy.

At 8 o'clock, by which time it was fully dark, Chinese bugles blared and whistles blew at the northwest and southwest of the perimeter. The troops in their positions waited. They were not going to shoot at noises in the dark. The next two hours were quiet at the perimeter. But at 10:15 P.M. the enemy troops were ready for their attack. First came an enemy mortar and artillery barrage from the north, northwest, and southwest that hit the perimeter and inside it at the center. At the same time, enemy infantry ran into the outer defenses of trip flares, antipersonnel mines, and booby-

trapped areas in front of C Company at the north end. The waiting soldiers did not fire a shot until the Chinese got to the barbed wire in front
of them. Then C Company called for 155-mm illuminating shells over its
position, and they were delivered at once. The C Company machine guns
then cut loose with heavy fire on the fully lighted enemy assault forces.
The quad-50s and tanks near the road on the west, next to the French Battalion, joined in the heavy automatic fire on the exposed Chinese. The survivors of the first attack wave disappeared.

Now, Soviet-built 120-mm heavy mortars, which the Chinese had emplaced behind Hills 345 and 248, about two and a half miles northwest
and two miles west, respectively, of the center of the perimeter, began to
drop their shells in the center of the perimeter. Two of the shells started
fires and lighted up the area for enemy-adjusted fire. This accurate mortar
fire began to take a toll of personnel in the CP, the nearby mortar and artillery positions, the supply dumps, and the aid stations within the perimeter. Enemy pack howitzers and the Soviet-built 76-mm guns now joined
in the bombardment.

About midnight a fragment from a mortar shell that hit the 23rd RCT
CP gave Colonel Freeman a flesh wound in the leg. He insisted it was not
important and refused evacuation. But the next day General Almond sent
Lt. Col. John H. Chiles, X Corps G-3, to Chipyong-ni to replace him in
command of the 23rd RCT. Freeman insisted on remaining at Chipyong-
ni another 24 hours and did not leave in a helicopter until noon of 15 February. He thought the flesh wound in his calf would heal in a short time.
In the interval he caught a courier plane ride to the United States. He never
returned to Korea.[14] There is no evidence that Lieutenant Colonel Chiles's
presence changed the battle in any way.

There was a brief calm along the perimeter just before midnight, but
Chinese attacks again soon hit all of the 1st Battalion, with A Company
receiving the strongest attack. At 2:15 A.M. enemy hit K Company in a
desperate attack at the southeast corner of the 3rd Battalion line, and attacks spread from there to the 2nd Battalion on the south side of the perimeter. There, in the G Company sector, the Chinese made their first
penetration, at 3:45 A.M., 14 February. This attack came from Hill 397,
south of the perimeter. A squad from the 3rd Platoon, F Company, and
additional help from K Company helped G Company repel this initial
penetration and restore its line. The enemy withdrew at 5:30 A.M. Capt.
Russell A. Gugeler, in his *Combat Actions in Korea*, has a detailed account
of G Company's action in the Chipyong-ni battle.[15]

The Chinese decided sometime after midnight that perhaps the best
places on the perimeter to center their attacks were on the French Battalion sector on the west and the 2nd Battalion area on the south, at least
partly because they had good avenues of approach to the perimeter in those
parts. Hill 345 was heavily occupied by the enemy. It lay only 1,200 yards

northwest of the northwest corner of the perimeter and provided an easy downhill approach to the French Battalion. The greatest difficulty there for them, however, was the open area beyond the barbed wire in front of the French Battalion, which the French covered with grazing machine-gun fire. Also, Hill 248, which was actually a long narrow ridge running north-south, southwest of the perimeter, was only another 1,200 yards from its south end. A large enemy force had assembled in the safety of its reverse slope. From the northern end of this ridge, the Chinese tried to over-run the French but again were stopped by automatic grazing fire placed just in front of the barbed wire.

In the 2nd Battalion sector, and especially that of G Company, the Chinese 115th Division found that Hill 397 provided a natural approach from the south into the perimeter. The crest of Hill 397 was only 1,200 yards south of G Company's positions, but more important, a long nose of the hill slanted northeast to end only 400 yards from the east boundary of G Company. This was the enemy's approach route. As the fighting progressed through the night of 13–14 February, the G Company position became the perimeter's most critical point. Because the most intense fighting at Chipyong-ni over a longer period of time took place at the G Company sector than anywhere else on the perimeter, it is useful to draw on an enemy document captured later to show how the Chinese operated there against the south side of the perimeter.

The 115th and 116th Divisions, 39th CCF Army, were further commanded to cut off other enemy forces stationed at Chipyong-ni in order to prevent the enemy from escaping and to intercept enemy reinforcements. . . .
     At dawn on the 14th of February 1951, the 116th Division, pushed forward to [Chaum-ni], annihilated two companies of the US 23rd Regiment, [actually they were the 2nd Reconnaissance Company and L Company, 9th Infantry, 2nd Division]. The 115th Division also arrived at Kudon without encountering any forces en route. On the same night the 115th Division commenced an enveloping maneuver, pushing forward toward the enemy forces in Chipyong-ni, and surrounded the area in cooperation with the 119th Division, 126th Division, and a regiment belonging to the 125th Division.[16]

The quoted comments mean that the CCF 115th and 116th divisions of the CCF 39th Army moved south past Chipyong-ni on the east during the night of 13–14 February to get into its rear. The 115th Division turned west at Kudun, just south of the Twin Tunnels, four to five miles southeast of Chipyong-ni, and arrived at the southern part of the 23rd RCT perimeter during the night. The CCF 116th Division continued two and a half miles farther south from Kudun to Chaum-ni, where it encountered the 2nd Reconnaissance Company and L Company of the 9th Infantry Regiment and annihilated them. The 116th Division then sent some elements farther west to Koksu-ri to cut off the road running south from Chipyong-ni to Yoju. Part of the division remained behind to occupy hill positions along the 23rd RCT MSR north of Korun-ni and the Han River, running through Chaum-ni, Kudun, and the Twin Tunnels area to Chipyong-ni. Thus, during the night these two enemy divisions completed the investment of Chipyong-ni on the south, one division joining in the assault on the perimeter, the other cutting the two roads leading south and southwest from Chipyong-ni and establishing extensive fireblocks on them. The CCF 116th Division thus closed the escape exit to the 23rd RCT, and at the same time was ready to oppose any rescue force. In connection with the movement of the CCF 116th Division, Major Dumaine, the 23rd RCT S-3, received a radio message at 6:30 A.M. on 14 February from the 2nd Reconnaissance Company saying that it and L Company, 9th Infantry, were being attacked on three sides at Chaum-ni, about ten road miles southeast of Chipyong-ni, on the 23rd RCTs MSR.[17]

During the night of 13–14 February, the four M19s (dual-40s) and six M16s (quad-50s) of B Battery, 82nd AAA AW Battalion, SP, were distributed around the perimeter to help the infantry repel enemy attacks. B Battery of the antiaircraft artillery had 100 men and two basic loads of ammunition – and it needed all of it. Capt. Clyde T. Hathaway commanded the battery, assisted by his executive officer, Capt. James C. Wilson; 1st Platoon leader, 1st Lt. Joe W. Seymour; 2nd Platoon leader, 2nd Lt. George Hair; and assistant 2nd Platoon leader, 2nd Lt. William Faulkner.

The first heavy action of the AAA gun carriages was in defense of K Company, at the southeastern corner of the perimeter. There the MSR from the southeast entered Chipyong-ni, and the single-track railroad passed through a tunnel and then crossed the MSR over a trestle about 600 yards from the eastern edge of Chipyong-ni. The enemy attack there from Hill 397 hit K Company at 2:30 A.M. Within half an hour an M19 there fired 580 rounds of 40-mm shells, and two M16s fired 2,200 rounds of .50-caliber ammunition. The Chinese made a penetration of K Company, nevertheless, and established a roadblock behind the 3rd Battalion. Some units of K Company were cut off. An attempt to evacuate wounded by an M16 and a tank with a squad of infantry and a litter jeep had to be abandoned temporarily when an enemy satchel charge knocked out the tank and destroyed the litter jeep. An M19 with a full load of ammunition ran through the enemy at this penetration and joined two M19s and an M16 in the surrounded area. The AAA gun carriages with the 3rd Battalion in the cut-off area now placed heavy fire on an enemy concentration trying to advance along the road into Chipyong-ni west of the tunnel and railroad trestle.[18]

By 3 A.M., 14 February, enemy were attacking the perimeter almost everywhere. The French had counterattacked the Chinese with a bayonet charge at the northwest corner of the perimeter when their ammunition was exhausted. The Chinese ran away in precipitous flight. C Company, at the north side of the perimeter, repulsed another attack; G Company, at the south, regained its positions, but K Company was still in a close-in fight to hold on. The enemy kept pouring through the railroad tunnel and over the railroad trestle in this approach to the perimeter at its southeast corner. At the western side of the perimeter, the French repulsed new attacks, which were directed at C Battery, 37th Field Artillery, and B Battery, 503rd Artillery. Fighting reached within 20 yards of one of the two M16s in the French sector. The French finally repelled this attack at 7 A.M. One of the quad-50s had fired 2,000 rounds in this action. But for intensity of close-in fighting, perhaps no sector of the perimeter was more closely contested than G Company's hill, where, for a time, enemy occupied some of the 155-mm howitzer positions of B Battery, 503rd Artillery, behind the G Company line. One M16 quad-50, supporting G Company and the 155-mm howitzers, fired 10,000 rounds of ammunition.[19]

In his account of the battle of Chipyong-ni, Colonel Freeman told of the intensity of fighting in the early hours of 14 February: "At three in the morning, February 14th," he said, "the enemy was trying to break through down the road between the French and Second Battalions, and under the railroad trestle between the Second and Third Battalions. Here he ran into our road blocks composed of tanks and flack-wagons. He tried desperately to eliminate these vehicles with high explosive charges tied to the end of long poles and with grenades, but while two were damaged the terrific volume of fire they put out forced him to abandon his effort." At 5:30 A.M., February 14, enemy pressure had relaxed along most parts of the perimeter, except that K Company was still having a desperate struggle with Chinese at the roadblock. Later, at daylight, the enemy prepared for another assault on the French position. Freeman wrote, "The French coming out of their foxholes charged down the slope with bayonets, broke up the attack before it could be formed, grabbed fourteen surprised Chinese by the back of their collars and dragged them in as prisoners. These prisoners, including an officer, confirmed that we were being attacked by elements of five Chinese divisions with a total force of about 30,000. These prisoners identified themselves as being from the 359th Regiment, 120th Division, 40th Army."[20]

At dawn 14 February, the Chinese broke off their attack and withdrew behind hills to the east and west. At daybreak there were approximately 100 wounded men within the walls of the two squad tents that composed the Medical Collecting Station. Six tents in all were erected during the battle, buttressed by railroad ties and rice bags. On the morning of the second day, there were about 200 wounded men in the five battalion aid stations and in the Collecting Station. At the end of the battle, by evening 15 February, there were about 300 casualties in them. There were in that time approximately 50 to 60 helicopter evacuations of the more critically wounded. Finally, at noon 16 February, a 5th Cavalry escorted convoy, Task Force Stewart, of 28 ambulances and seven 2½-ton trucks, carried 250 casualties to the 5th Cavalry Clearing Station at Koksu-ri.[21] Only two of the wounded at Chipyong-ni died of their wounds after they reached the 23rd RCT Clearing Station within the perimeter.

During 14 February, only three air strikes came in to hit enemy areas around the 23rd perimeter. The situation was considered so critical in the Wonju area east of them that nearly all available aircraft were sent there. The three strikes that did arrive were directed to hit the Twin Tunnels area, where large numbers of enemy had taken shelter during daylight. Air delivery of needed supplies, however, came in to the perimeter during the day, as 24 C-119 Flying Boxcars dropped their cargoes. But these supplies did not include heavy mortar and illumination shells, and rifle ammunition was not packed in clips. The latter was a serious problem for infantry in night fighting. The day was spent in mending damaged defense features, cleaning weapons, distributing ammunition, maintaining close-in reconnaissance, and serving hot meals.

In the morning of 14 February, the 2nd Division G-2 informed the 23rd RCT that IX Corps had ordered the British 27th Commonwealth Brigade to move from Yoju to clear the 23rd RCT MSR so that it could connect perimeter forces with the 9th Infantry Regiment to the east toward Wonju. At first the British Brigade met no resistance as it started toward the 23rd RCT at Chipyong-ni. Soon, however, it ran into Chinese units constituting an enemy roadblock behind the 23rd RCT, and it was all but halted. That morning, also, the IX Corps alerted the 5th Cavalry Regiment to move from Yoju on the road through Koksu-ri to open that road, west of the one the British Brigade was following, to Chipyong-ni for evacuation of casualties and to resupply the 23rd RCT. Like the British Brigade, it did not get far before it found its way blocked by Chinese units that had already taken positions along the road during the previous night.[22]

On the night of 14–15 February, the Chinese seemed to have a better overall plan for their attacks than on the first night. At dark they delivered an hour-long heavy barrage of mortar and artillery fire on the perimeter. At 7 P.M. the always-disconcerting bugle calls sounded to the south, soon after which the enemy infantry attacks began. They concentrated on the two roads entering the perimeter on either flank of the 2nd Battalion. One entered from the south through Masan at the right flank of G Company. There they attacked G Company in a column of companies from Hill 397. On the other side they came from Hill 506 to the northeast, where thousands of enemy troops had hidden during the day, and hit the 3rd Battalion, especially K Company, where the road entered the perimeter in the vicinity of the tunnel and railroad trestle.

The large airdrop of supplies during the day had not included illuminating shells, and at night their lack was felt. Freeman sent urgent radio calls for a "Firefly" to come to their help. A Firefly was a C-47 plane that flew over a friendly position at night and dropped large flares that burn about 15 minutes, changing the scene below to one of almost daylight. These Fireflies came in relays so that one replaced another when its flares were spent. On the night of 14–15 February, these planes stayed over the perimeter most of the night. Freeman later wrote of them that they "helped save our skins as much as any other gadget of the grim business of night fighting."

By 1:30 A.M., 15 February, the enemy attacks had spread to the 1st Battalion, at the north of the perimeter, and it had intensified in front of the 3rd Battalion. Chinese penetrated I Company's position, but the battalion commander declined offered reinforcements and instead moved a platoon from his L Company, adjacent to I Company, to help I Company restore its position.

Again the fighting was extremely heavy in the hours after midnight in G Company's position, at the middle part of the southern arc of the perimeter. G Company suffered so many casualties that there no longer were enough men left to hold the position. At 3:15 A.M., 15 February, a few survivors straggled down the north side of the ridge. The fight had been hand-to-hand for each foxhole. Lt. Col. James Edwards, 2nd Battalion commander, sent a platoon of the 1st Ranger Company and F Company's reserve platoon to the scene to win back the critical G Company hill. The adjoining left end of the French Battalion position was forced to pull back when G Company lost its hill.[23]

Lt. Robert Curtis, an officer on the 2nd Battalion staff, led the F Company platoon and the Ranger Company platoon, together with a tank, at 3:30 A.M. toward the G Company position. The Ranger Company commander accompanied his platoon. When Curtis reached 1st Lt. Thomas Heath, the G Company commander, and started to get his force of rangers and F Company men organized for an attack on the enemy-held ridge, he got resistance from the Ranger Company commander, who said his men would obey only the regimental commander's orders, not Curtis's. The latter called Lieutenant Colonel Edwards of the 2nd Battalion and explained the situation. Edwards sent Capt. John H. Ramsburg of his staff to the scene to take command. Ramsburg left the battalion just before 4 A.M. for G Company. He tried unsuccessfully to explain to the Ranger Company commander that he was in command of the infantry assembled to counterattack. He separated the now-intermingled men, finding he had 36 men in the Ranger Platoon, 28 men in the F Company platoon, 4 to 5 men from G Company, 6 to 7 mortarmen, and two machine-gun crews. He placed the Ranger Platoon on the right and the F Company platoon on the left of his skirmish line. The two machine-gun crews were to give them covering fire by raking the ridge crest as they climbed upward.

While Captain Ramsburg was preparing to launch his counterattack against the Chinese on G Company's hill, Capt. John A. Elledge, liaison officer from the 37th Field Artillery Battalion to B Battery, 503rd Artillery, set about getting an M16 quad-50 that had slid off the trail at the bottom of the G Company hill out of a ditch and back into operation. Its crew had abandoned what they thought was a useless weapon. Elledge induced a nearby tank crew to take their tank to pull the quad-50 back onto level ground, where it would no longer partially block the trail, and turned it so that its four machine guns could be directed readily at the enemy-held hill. He found that the multiple gun mount mechanism worked. Elledge decided he could fire the guns himself and got permission from Captain Ramsburg to fire on the crest of the hill. Under the protection of this covering fire, a tank got to the abandoned B Battery artillery position and evacuated 16 wounded men from a supply tent there. He also destroyed an enemy crew on the hill that was preparing to fire a 75-mm recoilless rifle (which G Company had left there) at his quad-50. Elledge and three tanks tried by their fire to keep the Chinese at bay and help Ramsburg's counterattack, but in the end the Chinese all but annihilated the F Company platoon and the Ranger platoon.[24] They remained in control of G Company's hill and started to dig in there.

There was a mixup of some undetermined source that resulted in friendly fire hitting the Ranger platoon on the right side of the line (coming, it was thought, from the adjacent French Battalion) and also in fire hitting it from tanks at the foot of the hill, which caused several ranger wounded. The Rangers reached the top of the ridge first, and then men from F Company got there. But they could not stay. Casualties in both platoons were heavy, and the survivors had to slide back to the bottom. Both Ramsburg and Heath were wounded, the latter critically.[25] The counterattack was a complete failure. The Chinese at this point might have plunged after the survivors down the hill and wrought havoc there, but they did not leave the hill crest.

In a captured enemy document we have the story of this counterattack, which failed and left G Company's position in enemy hands, the most serious enemy penetration into the Chipyong-ni perimeter during the two-day and two-night battle, and which the enemy continued to hold the rest of that night and all the following day until the Chinese withdrew from the battle late in the afternoon. The Chinese document mentions two place-names, Ma San and Kap Chon, in its discussions. Masan was a small village of about 15 to 20 huts just south of the G Company position in the perimeter. Kap Chon is not identified on any American map the author has seen, but from the context of the narrative it would seem to refer to a cluster of houses near the southern edge of Chipyong-ni.

The 1st Battalion of the 344th Regiment [39th Army] arrived at its line of departure, from which two unsuccessful attacks had been already made by the 356th Regiment [119th Division, 40th Army] at 1900 hours. The 1st Battalion also started to attack at 2400. Our fire power was not adequately organized, because of the enemy's superior fire power and open terrain. For this reason we attacked three times, and each time we failed, with our troops suffering heavy casualties. At 4 o'clock on the 15th, the battalion moved to the mountain areas on the east, on command of the Regiment facing the enemy. At 2100 [14 Feb.], the 3rd Battalion [344th Regiment, 115th Division] arrived at its line of departure. At that time our 377th Regiment [126th Division, 42nd Army] was organized and launched three attacks on a small hilltop 300 m [meters] to the southeast of the railroad station, but was unsuccessful, losing more than half of its forces. The 3rd Battalion [344th Regiment, 115th Division] was more successful, starting to attack at 1 o'clock; it occupied the first hilltop within 40 minutes, taking the second and third hilltops in succession. It was half past four o'clock before any further progress into the enemy area was made. The Regiment gave an order to cease attacking, reconstruct the field works immediately, and hold the occupied positions firmly in preparation for continuing the attack on the night of the 15th.[26]

Thus, it was the 3rd Battalion, 344th Regiment, 115th Division, 39th Army that captured and held G Company's position on the Chipyong-ni perimeter, repulsed the several counterattacks to regain it during the predawn hours of 15 February and during the following daylight hours, and continued to hold it with stubborn defense until the tanks of Task Force Crombez arrived in the late afternoon.

When news came to Lieutenant Colonel Edwards that the two-platoon attack by the rangers and F Company had failed, he sent the rest of the Ranger Company to continue an effort to regain G Company's position, but it did not make any effort until B Company from the regimental reserve joined it later in the morning. Even then, the two joined forces made no headway during the morning. Artillerymen from the 37th Field Artillery Battalion also failed to regain the hill. Three tanks and a quad-50 covered the withdrawal of the artillerymen from B Battery, 503rd Artillery, and remnants of Captain Ramsburg's counterattack force back to the positions of the 37th Field Artillery Battalion and to the 2nd Battalion headquarters area and elsewhere in the CP area at the southern edge of Chipyong-ni.[27]

The effort of the composite Ranger platoon and the F Company platoon finally ended at 8 A.M., 15 February, with complete failure. From then on G Company was out of the fight. Lieutenant Colonel Edwards committed B Company from the regimental reserve to try to recover and restore the G Company position at the south end of the perimeter. The regimental reserve was reestablished by making B Company, 2nd Engineer Combat Battalion, the reserve.

While the intense fight was going on at G Company's position, other units on the perimeter held or restored their positions, so that, with the coming of daylight on 15 February, the perimeter was intact except at G Company's sector on the southern arc. When the haze had cleared on the morning of 15 February, fighter planes came in and worked over all known enemy positions close to the perimeter and cleared them, except on Hill

397, directly south of the enemy's penetration at G Company's sector, only 1,000 yards south of the perimeter. There "the most stubborn, fanatical unit in the Chinese army must have been pitted against us and was determined to die to the last man. They disdained cover and fired their rifles and machine guns at the attacking fighter planes."[28] On this day 131 sorties flew to Chipyong-ni in support of perimeter defense.

The main effort in the perimeter after daylight on 15 February was to regain from the Chinese the G Company position that they had captured and held during the latter part of the night. Lieutenant Colonel Edwards, 2nd Battalion commander, had most of the Ranger Company and B Company from the regimental reserve for the task. He took charge of the plans for the counterattack. Edwards went up to the position at dawn, but B Company did not arrive until 9:30 A.M. because it had to gather itself and its equipment together and move from its reserve bivouac area across the perimeter. Edwards attached the Ranger Company and the remnants of G Company, less the 3rd Platoon, to B Company in preparing for the attack and ordered the B Company commander, Captain Pratt, to attack as soon as possible. The 3rd Platoon of G Company and the B Battery men of the 503rd Artillery had withdrawn to a secondary line and were to support the attack with fire from there. The French had also pulled back in that part of their line adjacent to G Company and were in a secondary line.

Edwards did not give the B Company commander specific instructions as to the attack, since he usually left the details to his company commanders, but in this instance he should have been more explicit in his instructions. When B Company made its first attack at 10 A.M., it was in only platoon strength, whereas Edwards had intended that a coordinated attack with the entire force would be made. The Chinese easily threw the B Company platoon back down the hill with casualties. This failure was repeated by another platoon attack that met the same fate. The 1st Ranger Company was held in reserve and never participated in these efforts. It was a futile and ill-conceived counterattack. The morning attacks accomplished nothing.[29]

Both the American sources and the Chinese captured document relating to the action at the G Company position make frequent mention of the three hills or knobs at the position. Perhaps a few words as to the physical features of G Company's "hill" will be useful in understanding events there. It really was not a hill but an elongated low ridge that had three knobs. The ridge was the southern side of a U-shaped terrain feature that ran east-west at the south side of Chipyong-ni. The open end of the U faced west. The highest part of the southern side of this U-shaped ridge was at its center, and this feature generally is referred to as the "hill." There the highest of the three knobs dominated the area south toward the village of Masan. G Company had organized its defenses on this low ridge, which lay entirely within an area encompassed by the 100- and 200-meter contours. G Company initially placed a platoon on each of the three knobs, with the 1st Platoon on the right-hand, western, knob next to the French Battalion boundary, the 3rd Platoon on the highest knob in the center, and the 2nd Platoon on the left-hand, eastern, knob, adjacent to its boundary with F Company.

A long spur ridge from Hill 397, which the Chinese held with a large force, sloped down from its crest northeasterly to a point near the eastern edge of G Company's position. This spur ridge offered a good approach to G Company, and it was from Hill 397 that the Chinese came and attacked G Company during the Chipyong-ni battle. While the precise elevation of the middle knob of G Company's position is not known to the author and is not shown on maps, one may guess that it did not reach 200 meters, because the entire position lay within an area encompassed between the 100- and 200-meter contour lines.[30]

At noon Lieutenant Colonel Edwards received word that air strikes he had called for would arrive about 1 P.M. He pulled back the parts of B Company's two platoons that were still on the north slope of the hill, as he expected napalm drops and did not want to expose the troops to this deadly weapon. The air strikes came in beginning about 1 P.M. and continued in relays to 2 P.M. Many sorties dropped napalm tanks on the Chinese—the 3rd Battalion, 344th Regiment, of the 115th Division—that held G Company's position. After the air strikes, Edwards sent B Company with all three platoons abreast up the hill again, but Chinese resistance was still adamant, and a hail of machine-gun and small-arms fire from the reverse slope knocked them off the crest.[31]

First Lt. Donald O. Miller, of the 2nd Battalion, 23rd Infantry, was present and familiar with the fighting on G Company's hill 14–15 February and F Company's role in it. After F Company sent a platoon to join with a Ranger Platoon to counterattack the Chinese on the hill in predawn darkness 15 February, he wrote that the enemy repulsed the attack with mortar, machine-gun, and small-arms fire; "the casualties were so high it forced the 3rd Platoon and the Rangers platoon to withdraw; the 3rd Platoon had 22 WIA, 1 MIA, and 5 men were left. The Ranger Platoon casualties are unknown, but it was apparent that they were ineffective due to heavy casualties." After daylight G Company had only its 2nd Platoon left. It had escaped enemy attack. Miller said,

This platoon was then attached to F Company at this time. During the daylight hours of the 15th of February, I was on F Co. O.P. and could with no trouble look down upon the enemy on G Co. old position. .50 M/G, 60 and 81 mortar and artillery was directed on the enemy from Fox Co. O.P. The air corps appeared and it was found that the Fox Co. OP was the only place the air strikes on the enemy could be directed most effectively. Thus F Co. O.P. directed all of the air strikes on the enemy with excellent results. At approximately 1430 lead tanks from the 5 Cav Regt. came in behind the enemy and total confusion fell on the enemy breaking up the enemies attacks, the enemy started to withdraw under terrific fire from the tanks, artillery, mortars, M/G and small arms. The enemy withdrew towards Hill 397 and to the west suffering heavy casualties.[32]

The 100-meter contour line extends as an elongated ridge formation from Chipyong-ni to the southeast to a point just north of the eastern end of F Company's perimeter sector. The observation post must have been on the point of this ridge, and from there one could look to the southwest along G Company's hill and see the crest and part of the reverse slope. It was an ideal place from which to direct all kinds of observed fire on enemy holding the G Company sector, and especially from which a TACP could direct air strikes. The observed fire from this observation post undoubtedly had an important effect in destroying Chinese strength there and, together with the approach of Task Force Crombez in the enemy's rear in the late afternoon of 15 February, broke up the enemy's hold on this position and sent enemy all around the southern arc of the perimeter in panic flight to the hills.

It is incredible that the Chinese had still held out on the hill. Annex 8 to the 23rd RCT Command Report for February on air support during the battle of Chipyong-ni states: "At times during these strikes napalm was dropped as close as 75 yards in front of the friendly troops. The enemy was so concentrated that one (1) napalm bomb killed 60 (counted) enemy in one position. Such close support was only possible through direct communication with the platoon leaders by phone and direct observation of the target area by the TACP."

Coincident with the directed artillery fires and air strikes from the F Company observation post, Edwards now decided the key to the reduction of the hill was to get tanks down the road that passed south just west of the enemy-held G Company's position so that they could fire into the enemy on the reverse slope. He sent the P&A (Pioneer and Ammunition) Platoon out to remove antitank mines in the road, but Chinese close to the road drove them back. Edwards then sent two tanks to cover the P&A men, but Chinese bazooka teams close to the road drove the tanks back.

In this impasse, Edwards decided to use the Ranger Company to protect the tanks and to destroy the enemy bazooka teams. He put Lieutenant Perry in charge of the tanks and the P&A Platoon and ordered the commander of the Ranger Company to get the Chinese bazooka teams. The Ranger lieutenant objected to being used in that way, saying he was not trained "for attacking and defending like ordinary infantry." According to him, he was only a hit-and-run specialist. Edwards then responded:

I told him by God that he now was an infantryman and would do what I told him to or report to the rear under arrest. So they started out with the tanks. I had to go with them as the minute they moved out they started to the west side of the road to hide behind the tanks. I chased them over to the east side so they could shoot at the Chinese bazooka men when they popped up out of their holes. I never thought much of the special units as Rangers, Special Forces, etc. I think good old infantrymen can do any of their jobs. . . . With Perry and Von Tom in front and me near the rear of the Rangers, we kept them on the east side of the road and from hiding behind the tanks. The bazooka men tried to shoot at the tanks, but the P&A, Perry, Von Tom and the tanks with their .50 cal. MGs got all of them. Von Tom was hit here while shooting at a bazooka man with his .45.[33]

The P&A Platoon now removed the mines from the road, protected by tank fire. The tanks then ran rapidly down the road to points from which they could fire on the reverse slopes of Hills B, C, and D (G Company's position knobs). Edwards says their fire killed about 200 Chinese, that B Company then reached the crest of these knobs, and that the rest of a Chinese regiment, numbering about 800 men, broke and ran with everyone shooting at them. This happened about 4:30 P.M. This flight of the Chinese was caused by a combination of the successful tank action against the reverse (south) slope of the enemy-held hill and the arrival within sight around a bend of the road southward of Col. Marcel Crombez's lead tanks in a column of 24 tanks that had been fighting their way northward to relieve the Chipyong-ni defenders. The devastating air strikes earlier also had been a potent factor in terrorizing the Chinese. About 250 Chinese soldiers were running in front of the 1st Cavalry Division tanks. Edwards wrote:

Immediately I ordered two tanks, under Swede, to meet them. Between the two forces, all of the 250 Chinks were slaughtered. This panicked the whole Chinese Army and they all got out of their holes and ran away from us. I never saw a sight like that and never expect to see another like it. Every hill around the perimeter had running chinks on it. . . . The Air corps was striking, the artillery shooting, the flack wagons barking, every mortar and recoilless firing and every rifleman shooting! There were more targets than we had weapons! What a day! That broke the siege.[34]

The 1st Cavalry tank column from the south entered the Chipyong-ni perimeter at 5:15 P.M. The battle of Chipyong-ni was ended.

It will be well to include here an account of the end of the battle as seen from the enemy's point of view in the culminating events at the southern arc of the perimeter. It differs somewhat from that of the perimeter's defenders. The account quoted below refers to the CCF 115th Division, which on the morning of 15 February held the area south of the 23rd RCT perimeter.

On the 15th . . . after daybreak, our troops, because of the surrounding terrain and overconcentration, suffered heavy casualties from enemy air and artillery attacks. However . . . the enemy failed to take our positions. At 1600 more than 20 enemy tanks coming to reinforce Chop-Pyong-ni from the direction of Koksu-ri, surprised us; by being almost at the door of the Regimental CP before they were discovered, seriously threatening the flanks and rear of the 2nd Battalion. The Regiment immediately ordered the displacement of the 2nd Battalion to the positions occupied by the 3rd Battalion. The tanks coming up to charge our rear and flanks were subjected to cross fire launched by our 1st and 2nd Battalions laying in ambush, which completely annihilated a company of enemy infantry up on the tanks. Twenty others, from the battalion commander [Lt. Col. Treacy] down, were captured. We also destroyed four tanks and one motor vehicle. The 3rd Battalion of the 344th Regiment, after occupying three hilltops situated on the southeast of the railway station, was prevented by daybreak from making any further exploitation of its success and ordered its 9th Company to hold the occupied positions. The company in turn ordered one of its platoons to hold the positions, leaving it a heavy machine gun while the main force of the company took cover at the base of the hill. The enemy launched four counterattacks with small units (platoons) between 0800 hours and 1300 hours, supported by mortar fire. Each of these attacks failing, the enemy again attacked after 1300 hours with air support strafing, bombing, and dropping gasoline can. With the position in flames, the troops still remained firm, beating back another two enemy counterattacks. At 1500 hours, enemy tanks arrived [apparently these were the two tanks Lt. Col. Edwards got down the road to the reverse side of the G Company hill]; the company, after suffering heavy losses, was unable to cope with this new situation. The entire battalion moved to concentrate at positions surrounding Sin Tae below Mang Mi-ri Hill [Sindae on US map, three-fourths of a mile southeast of the perimeter on the MSR toward the Twin Tunnels].[35]

It is now necessary to drop back a few days and pick up the story of Task Force Crombez, whose tank column had reached Chipyong-ni in the midst of a hectic battle at the perimeter in the late afternoon of 15 February. Before the battle of Chipyong-ni began, enemy troops of the CCF 116th Division had cut the road south of Chipyong-ni to Yoju at Koksu-ri. From there northward they had troops on all the high ground along the road to the edge of Chipyong-ni, and when the time came they were prepared to attack any effort of UN troops to advance north on that road from the Han River to help or relieve the 23rd RCT. On 12 February enemy troops surrounded a UN outpost force at Koksu-ri, which drifted back south to escape. The next day a 21st Infantry patrol tried to reach Koksu-ri, but it was repulsed and driven back. Again on the fourteenth still another patrol with tanks tried to enter Koksu-ri, but the Chinese there fought them off, disabling one tank and holding the infantry in the patrol at arm's length. The patrol received orders to break contact and withdraw. It destroyed the disabled tank and a jeep. It estimated there was a battalion of enemy in Koksu-ri. During the night the 5th Cavalry Regiment was to attack through Koksu-ri toward Chipyong-ni.[36]

Ten days earlier, on 4 February, the British 27th Brigade had moved to Yoju, an important Han River ferry crossing point, but had no enemy contact at the time. On 14 February, however, the Middlesex Battalion of the brigade started up the MSR toward Chipyong-ni to open the road to the 23rd RCT. A Company took the center along the road, while C and

D companies swept the hills on either side. After two hours the Middlesex advance platoon saw enemy ahead who were digging in on a hill overlooking the road. There followed a battle to control this high ground, which the battalion finally won. The next morning, 15 February, the Australian Battalion took over the lead, but it was then only four miles northeast of Yoju. It had become evident in the fighting on the afternoon of 14 February that the British 27th Brigade was not going to have an uncontested march to Chipyong-ni; the evidence was that it would have to fight all the way there, and might not get there for days.[37]

This British 27th Brigade situation in the late afternoon of the fourteenth caused Maj. Gen. Bryant E. Moore, commander of the US IX Corps, to order Lt. Col. George B. Pickett, the armored officer of IX Corps, at 5 P.M. to move D Company, 6th Tank Battalion, immediately to join Col. Marcel G. Crombez, commander of the 5th Cavalry Regiment of the 1st Cavalry Division. General Moore at the same time had told Crombez he would have to take the 5th Cavalry to Chipyong-ni to relieve the 23rd RCT, which had been surrounded there. Moore had informed Crombez, "You'll have to move tonight, and I know you will do it." The British Brigade, he said, was on the other more direct and better road to Chipyong-ni, but they had run into enemy heavily entrenched and were unable to make a rapid advance. Moore had told Pickett he wanted D Company to be on the move within half an hour. Pickett suggested that the entire 6th Tank Battalion should join Crombez. But part of it was with the 24th Division and, it was thought, could not be assembled quickly. General Moore would listen to no suggested change in his order, and he reiterated that D Company was to be on the move within half an hour. Pickett had it on the road in 28 minutes.[38] General Moore was the author of the Task Force tactical plans to relieve the surrounded Chipyong-ni defenders.

Crombez's force consisted of:

5th Cavalry Regiment
A Company, 70th Tank Battalion (Heavy)
D Company, 6th Tank Battalion (Medium)
61st Field Artillery Battalion
A Battery, 92nd Armored Field Artillery Battalion

This task force made a night march 14 February from the vicinity of Yoju to Chupo-ri, where a destroyed bridge halted the march. During the night the engineers repaired the bridge, and the next morning, 15 February, the 1st Battalion, 5th Cavalry, had contact with Chinese soldiers. Colonel Crombez then committed the 2nd Battalion, keeping the 3rd Battalion in reserve and blocking in the rear. Large numbers of Chinese were in front of the regiment and slowed its advance to a crawl. By 11 A.M. it was apparent to Crombez that he would never get to Chipyong-ni before nightfall at that rate. The CCF 116th Division in front of him made any infantry advance slow and costly. During the morning, General Moore visited Crombez and noted the heavy enemy resistance, with the 1st Battalion trying to advance on the east side of the road, and the 2nd Battalion on the west side.

In the early afternoon, Major General Ruffner, commanding the 2nd Division, came to Crombez and asked if he could reach his 23rd RCT that day. Crombez replied that he would do so and would personally lead a force to it before nightfall. When Major General Palmer, commanding the 1st Cavalry Division, arrived at the task force in the early afternoon, Crombez borrowed his helicopter to fly a reconnaissance over the road to Chipyong-ni. Colonel Crombez had decided that, with his task force bogged down at noon near the village of Maduri, a little more than a mile south of Koksu-ri and six miles south of Chipyong-ni, he would have to break through with an armored force and leave the rest behind to fight their way northward. For this punch-through force he selected the following units:

D Company, 6th Tank Battalion

A Company (less two platoons), 70th Tank Battalion

L Company, 5th Cavalry, infantry to ride the tanks

1st Squad, 1st Platoon, A Company, 8th Engineers (C) Battalion

one 2½-ton truck with four or five ROK soldiers to follow the tank column (added later by Lt. Col. Treacy, CO, 3rd Battalion, 5th Cavalry, without Crombez's knowledge)

There is some discrepancy as to whether the total number of tanks in the armored force numbered 23 or 24. Crombez himself said there were 23. Members of the 23rd RCT at Chipyong-ni said there were 24 tanks in Task Force Crombez when it neared Chipyong-ni. It was thought that the L Company infantry, riding the tanks, would give protection to the tanks by killing or driving off enemy soldiers that got close to them. The squad of engineers was to remove from the road any mines encountered. The 2½-ton truck that followed the armored column was to pick up wounded that might fall on the road.

Marcel Crombez, who was to lead the armored breakthrough force, was a quiet officer and not given to flamboyant self-promotion. Brig. Gen. Frank A. Allen, assistant 1st Cavalry Division commander, said that Crombez hid his light under a basket, that he was a student of warfare and a fine leader of troops in combat. His personal behavior in the drive through to Chipyong-ni proved at least the latter. General Ridgway arrived at the scene before Crombez set out. He said Crombez's personal leadership of the armored force was an act of great courage.[39]

Colonel Crombez apparently decided on his own that he would take the armored attack through to Chipyong-ni and that he would command it personally. He placed Lt. Col. Edgar J. Treacy, Jr., commander of the 3rd Battalion, 5th Cavalry, in command of the supply column and ordered him to bring it forward only when he gave word that the road was clear.

The squad of four engineer soldiers was to ride on the second tank and observe the road for mines and lift them if any were discovered. Otherwise there were to be no troops riding on the first five tanks in column. The 160 L Company infantry rode about 10 to a tank, one of each group being selected to fire the tank top machine gun. Colonel Crombez rode in the fifth tank in column and from it issued radio orders to the tank column as it moved toward Chipyong-ni. Capt. John C. Barrett, commanding L Company, rode in the sixth tank. Lieutenant Colonel Treacy, the 3rd Battalion commander, rode on the same tank with 10 enlisted men. Barrett said the first four tanks in line, instead of five, as stated by other sources, did not have infantrymen riding on them. He also said that Lieutenant Johnson, executive officer of L Company, rode the last tank. Capt. John M. Hiers, commander of D Company, 6th Tank Battalion, rode in the fourth tank in column. His M46 tanks mounted 90-mm cannon and had better armor protection than the 70th Tank Battalion M4A3 tanks, which mounted 76-mm guns. D Company tanks were in the lead. Lt. Lawrence DeSchweinitz commanded the lead tank.

Captains Hiers and Barrett agreed on a plan for the infantry to dismount from the tanks if the column stopped and, on a signal, to remount when the tanks were ready to resume the advance. This plan did not work, as it seldom did elsewhere. The tanks would start up without the infantry getting on board first. When the tanks started up the infantry would run from the ditches and try to clamber aboard, on any tank they could catch up with. Some made it, but many did not, and they were left in enemy territory to shift for themselves. Those not wounded usually banded together under officer or noncommissioned officer leadership and worked their way back to the 1st Battalion, 5th Cavalry, lines near Koksu-ri.

It should be mentioned that the idea for a 2½-ton truck with some ROK soldiers in it to follow the tank column and pick up wounded was not in Colonel Crombez's plan but was improvised by Lieutenant Colonel Treacy, who ordered Captain Barrett to take the L Company service truck with four (some said five) ROKs of the L Company 5th Platoon to ride in it as litter bearers.[40]

Crombez ordered his tanks to keep about 50 yards apart. At 3:45 P.M. 15 February he started the column forward from its initial point just south of Maduri, where it passed through the lines of the 1st and 2nd battalions, 5th Cavalry. Colonel Crombez described the start of the task force.

I organized and personally took the Task Force to Chipyong-ni. Immediately prior to my departure, I had radioed the C/O [Lt. Col. Chiles] of the 23rd RCT that we were about to take off. Lt. Col. Chiles requested we come up immediately with or without the supply train. I decided to break through with the Task Force, tanks only, and have the supply train brought up later. I had made plans with Colonel Treacy for him to bring up the supply train for the 23rd Inf with an escort of 2 tank platoons and 2 rifle platoons when the supply road was cleared of the enemy and safe to proceed thereon, and had instructed Colonel Treacy to await my instructions by radio when I deemed the road safe as to travel, he nevertheless, unknown to me, joined L co. with the tanks.

Near the small village of Koksu-ri, the Task Force came under intense enemy small arms fire, the tanks stopped, and some of the infantry were forced to dismount from the tanks. Colonel Treacy who had been operating a machine gun on a tank was one of these.

A wounded soldier, Corporal Carroll G. Everist . . . of Co L, states that when the tanks moved on, that he, some other members of his company and Colonel Treacy were captured by the Chinese; that Colonel Treacy was very slightly wounded, and that Colonel Treacy carried him on his back to a near-by village where they were questioned by their captors. The Chinese recognized Colonel Treacy's rank and treated him with respect.

While we were approaching the pass, I radioed to my Operation Officer to hold the supply train until further orders from me personally. I further stated that the going was too rough, we were having tough slugging and that the supply train would not get through.[41]

In an interview with the author, Colonel Crombez did not criticize Treacy for violating an order, in joining L Company and the tank column. He said Treacy was a fine battalion commander and wanted to be part of any action that involved his battalion.[42] Since L Company was part of his battalion, his aggressive nature simply compelled him to join what he knew would be a very dangerous mission, with his riflemen fully exposed to enemy fire. It proved fatal for him. One might say of him as Oliver Goldsmith did of Auburn's village preacher in *The Deserted Village:* "E'en his failings leaned to virtue's side."

When Task Force Crombez started north up the road, the 5th Cavalry artillery did not fire direct support for it, because of the danger to the infantry riding the tanks, but did direct artillery fire on the hills flanking the road, where enemy troops had strong positions, trying to pin them down and to keep them from rushing the tanks on the road.[43] Major Humphrey, S-2 of the 5th Cavalry Regiment, was able to monitor the progress of the tank column by radio. Three times he heard questions from tank commanders to Colonel Crombez when enemy fire was especially heavy, as to whether they should go on. Each time Crombez calmly replied, "Continue forward."

The tanks proceeded for perhaps a mile before they received enemy fire. It first began to come in on them just south of Koksu-ri. The road going north made a sharp turn into the village. Enemy fire here hit several men on the tanks, and the tank gun turrets swinging to fire on enemy knocked other infantrymen off the tanks. The lead tanks stopped in Koksu-ri after making it around the road bend. M. Sgt. Lloyd L. Jones, platoon sergeant of the 3rd Platoon, L Company, ordered the men on his tank, two of whom were now wounded, to dismount from his tank, the 15th or 16th in line. The traversing turret and gun knocked Jones off. Many infantrymen dismounted at Koksu-ri and its vicinity.

After a brief halt, the tanks started up without a tanker inside unbuttoning the hatch and signaling the dismounted riflemen, as had been agreed upon, that they were about to continue forward. Lieutenant Johnson, executive officer of L Company, was wounded here. Many men from the 2nd Platoon of L Company had dismounted 300 to 400 yards ahead and were in roadside ditches. When the tank column started up, about 30 men were left behind in the vicinity of Koksu-ri. Cpl. Hubert M. Cobb, of the 4th Platoon, L Company, made it all the way to Chipyong-ni, but he said it was almost impossible to get back on a tank once it had started to move.

Capt. Joe W. Finley, F Company commander, in the 2nd Battalion, saw from his company observation post the tank column stop at Koksu-ri and then continue. Half an hour later he saw 10 men from L Company in a dry stream bed coming back toward his company position. Others came in later, about 30 in all. Some of them asked for litter teams to go out and rescue wounded.[44] Sergeant Jones said he saw the ROKs in the 2½-ton truck following the column pick up 3 wounded from the road and put them in the truck. He would not put his two wounded in the truck. Maj. Charles J. Parzial, S-3 of the 5th Cavalry, who had radio contact with Crombez during the attack, sent some tanks out from A Company, 70th Tank Battalion, to recover L Company infantrymen near Koksu-ri. He said these tanks went only as far as the bend in the road south of Koksu-ri.

M. Sgt. Jessie O. Giddons, a platoon leader in D Company, 6th Tank Battalion, thought enemy fire was severe in Koksu-ri. He said it wounded First Lieutenant Lahey, an L Company platoon leader riding his tank, and then subsequent fire killed him. Enemy in company strength was on the hills on either side of the road just beyond Koksu-ri. Here, where most of the infantry dismounted, they fought from the ditches and killed many Chinese trying to reach the tanks. The Chinese attacked the tanks with grenades, bottles of gasoline, pole charges, and bazooka fire. Some of the fighting, he said, was hand-to-hand in the roadside ditches.

M. Sgt. Joe Kirland commanded the fifth tank in line, the one Colonel Crombez rode in. Kirland said Crombez directed the fire of the tank gunner and commanded the entire column from the tank. When the lead tank slowed down and showed an inclination to halt, Crombez ordered the second tank to crowd it and keep it moving.[45] Kirland said, "Throughout the attack, Colonel Crombez was very calm and controlled the forces in an outstanding manner."

Cpl. Paul Campbell, a rifleman in the 4th Squad, 2nd Platoon, L Company, rode on the sixth tank in line all the way into Chipyong-ni. He operated the .50-caliber machine gun mounted on top the tank and fired it on enemy throughout the four and a half miles of the enemy fireblock from Koksu-ri to Chipyong-ni. On the way he saw several enemy satchel and pole-charge crews, but no bazooka teams. Nor did he see any enemy fleeing from the tanks. The Chinese fired burp guns and machine guns on the tanks, and tried to reach them with satchel and pole charges. Often, he said, they were only 50 yards away.

Cpl. Wayne O. Kemp of the 1st Platoon, L Company, was riding on the eighteenth tank in line when he had to dismount at Koksu-ri. He was unable to remount when the tanks started up. He ran along the tank for a while but finally was picked up by the 2½-ton truck following the column, which then was carrying five wounded. Five ROK soldiers accompanied this truck, which was under enemy fire all the way. The truck made it all the way to the cut about a mile south of the 23rd RCT perimeter at Chipyong-ni. There enemy stopped it, and all the ROKs with it were either killed, wounded, or missing in action.[46]

The worst spot of the four-and-a-half-mile-long fireblock between Koksu-ri and Chipyong-ni was about a mile south of the 23rd RCT perimeter at the south side of Chipyong-ni. There Hill 248 on the west side sent a long finger ridge southeast toward the road, and Hill 397 on the east side sent a steeper and shorter finger ridge west to the road, where they met in a saddle. There a 50-foot cut had been made for the passage of the road. Here it was possible for satchel charge crews and enemy bazooka teams to lie in wait on top the embankments and drop their explosive charges or fire their rocket launchers directly down on the tanks. It was a perilous point of passage.

Before entering upon some details of the passage of Task Force Crombez through the "Pass," as it was called, a mile south of the Chipyong-ni perimeter, it might be well to give Colonel Crombez's terse comment about the end of the task force's run up the road.

The last 4½ miles to Chipyong-ni we encountered constant enemy fire, small arms, automatic weapons fire, mortar, bazooka 2.36 and some 3.5; fanatical Chinese attempted with pole and satchel charges to stop the tanks. The bow gunner in my tank killed off two 2.36 bazooka crews.

We hit them at the most psychological moment while another enemy force was launching an attack on the 23rd Inf RCT attempting to drive the 23rd RCT from the south to the north. The enemy group on the ridges along both sides of the mountain row from Koksu-ri to Chipyong-ni had been carefully emplaced with the forethought of preventing any troops coming to the rescue of the 23rd RCT. Judging by the bazooka crews, the enemy had carefully planned a firm defense of the road. However, the Chinese were decisively defeated and crushed. This fact is borne out by the fact as proven later that all enemy forces withdrew during the night.

During the period of this operation, 5th Cav was under the operational control of IX Corps.[47]

Colonel Crombez estimated there were 2,000 Chinese soldiers along the road and nearby hills as the tank column approached the Pass. When the lead tank got into the Pass, enemy forces stationed atop the embankments on both sides attacked it with rockets, antitank rifles, pole charges, satchel charges, and intense small-arms fire. Lieutenant DeSchweinitz's lead tank was hit by a rocket, apparently a 2.36 inch, on its turret. It did not disable the tank, but it wounded all members of the tank crew.

Captain Hiers, commanding D Company of the 6th Tank Battalion, was in the fourth tank in line when it entered the Pass. A 3.5-inch rocket fired from above hit it on the left side, penetrated the armor there, and exploded amidst the ammunition on the ready rack. The explosions and fire there killed Captain Hiers and the tank gunner at once and set the tank on fire. Corporal Calhoun, the driver, was badly burned, but he gunned the tank through the Pass and then pulled it off to the side of the road, allowing the rest of the column to pass. No one had seen Hiers's tank hit, but they had seen sleeping bags and packs on the turret burning before the tank entered the Pass. The driver and assistant driver escaped from the tank and were subsequently rescued by Lieutenant Boydson of A Company, 70th Tank Battalion. Lieutenant Colonel Growden, commander of the 6th Tank Battalion, visited the scene at the Pass later and found the tail fins of a 3.5-inch rocket beside Hiers's tank. The launcher location was also found on the hillside, with evidence that three or four rockets had been fired. The 3.5-inch rocket was an American weapon, and it had to be a captured one that knocked out Hiers's tank.[48]

Just before 5 P.M. Crombez stopped the tank column at Masan, the small village just outside the south side of the Chipyong-ni perimeter, and cleaned out enemy there by tank fire. Enemy groups of 50 to 100 were running into draws trying to escape, and other enemy were running from the reverse side of the G Company position of the 23rd RCT perimeter. The 90-mm high explosive fire of D Company's tanks cut down an unknown number of these fleeing enemy. Two tanks from the Chipyong-ni defenders that had been helping Lieutenant Colonel Edwards and B Company, 23rd Infantry, and the Ranger Company drive the enemy from the G Company position went down the road to meet the incoming Task Force Crombez. When the task force entered the Chipyong-ni perimeter at 5:10 P.M., there were still 23 infantrymen of L Company and 4 engineer troops riding its tanks, 13 of them wounded. One died of his wounds that evening.[49]

Sfc. James Maxwell, in the second tank in line, said that, when he entered Chipyong-ni, "some of the men of the 23rd Infantry and some of the French troops came out and kissed my tank."[50] Altogether, about 100 of the L Company infantry, dismounted from the tanks, made their way back to the 5th Cavalry lines at Koksu-ri that day and night, so their loss was not as great as had been at first feared.

Captain Barrett said L Company's casualties on the drive to Chipyong-ni from Koksu-ri were about 20 killed, 40 wounded, and 20 missing in action. He did not favor having infantrymen ride tanks in an armor attack — they were sitting ducks for enemy fire. Also, the swiveling of the turret and the tank cannon would knock riders off and of itself might injure them severely. Another matter of concern was that the deck of a tank got too hot to stand on for any length of time. The fire concussion of a 90-mm tank gun also was great enough to knock a man off a tank if the tank was not firing straight ahead or nearly so. Finally, there was no way of controlling the movement of tanks in an enemy action to make it certain that they would inform the infantry of the intention to move and give them time to remount the tanks. Most observers of tank-infantry combined action, and persons with experience in the matter, agree that it is a mistake fraught with fatal results to place infantrymen on tanks going into action.[51]

Captain Barrett said that Lieutenant Chastaine, an L Company platoon leader, was killed before they reached the Pass. Barrett had his personal revenge in the Chipyong-ni action when he shot and killed, at 50 yards range, three Chinese carrying a bangalore torpedo as they ran across an open area toward the tanks.

Before closing this account of Task Force Crombez's run to Chipyong-ni from Koksu-ri to relieve the 23rd RCT on 15 February, a further word should be said about Lieutenant Colonel Treacy, commander of the 3rd Battalion, who was wounded and missing in action. We have mentioned earlier that he was one of the dismounted men who was left by the tanks near Koksu-ri. According to other testimony by members of L Company, he caught up with a tank other than the one he had been riding, clambered aboard, and for a time operated its top machine gun. Later a turning of the tank turret knocked him off the tank, and he was picked up by the 2½-ton truck following the tank column. Farther north, a soldier said he saw Treacy's name scratched on the side of a building along the roadside together with several other names. Captain Barrett said that, the next day after they had reached Chipyong-ni, 16 February, he talked with a wounded man who had been on the 2½-ton truck when it stopped in the Pass. He said that Sergeant Kerzan, the driver and wounded, had driven the truck to the Pass after the tanks had gone on. Chinese there closed in on the truck and took prisoners, all who were able to walk, including Treacy.[52] Nothing further was ever learned about Treacy's fate, as far as the author was able to determine. The 2½-ton truck was later recovered. It had two flat tires. On 16 February, 876 enemy dead were counted along the route of Task Force Crombez.[53]

Colonel Crombez had intended that his tanks would return to the 5th Cavalry RCT that night with a convoy of wounded. But the events of the day made a night return seem a risky venture. In the discussion about whether the tanks should return that night, the men of L Company not wounded, about ten of them, volunteered to ride the tanks back as infantry protection. Crombez decided not to make a night march back but to wait for daylight on the sixteenth. The next day when Crombez gave them the choice of accompanying the tanks, Captain Barrett said he ordered the men not to go. But he himself went and, with a driver and a jeep, immediately returned to Koksu-ri, picking up four wounded men lying along the road. He put them in an ambulance when Task Force Stewart caught up with him at the Pass just south of Chipyong-ni, where he had stopped at the 2½-ton truck that had followed Task Force Crombez and had stood there since Chinese had stopped it. It was still operable.[54]

Contrary to expectations in the 23rd RCT, there were no enemy attacks against the Chipyong-ni perimeter during the night of 15–16 February. An enemy document captured later explained the reason.

On the 15th, the 115th Division intended to continue the attack at night, but received orders from the 39th CCF Army in the afternoon, ordering it to continue the attack on the night of the 16th, in cooperation with the 40th Army, and to make other troop adjustments. Further orders were given to the 117th Division to take over the defense of the [two words unreadable] as surrounding Chaun-ni CS 8339 and the 116th Division to advance south of Koksu-ri CS 7742 to intercept army reinforcements coming from the south. The entire 42nd Army was distributed around Iho-ri, north of Munmak to intercept enemy reinforcements coming from Wonju. . . .

The 115th Division made the following adjustments

The various regiments distributed their forces as follows: The 343d Regiment ordered one platoon of its 1st Battalion to Masan CS 7947; the main positions of the Regiment were the ones then occupied by its 1st and 3rd Battalions. The 344th Regiment dispatched the 1st Company of its 1st Battalion to hold the enemy, its 2nd Battalion to the mountain areas west of Chowang-ni CS 8345, the 3rd Battalion to Sindae CS 8146, with its main force remaining at Mangmi-san, and the regimental CP at Sokpul.

D. Disengagement: At 160330 February 1951, the 115th Division received a coded order from ——— [trans. illegible] ordering immediate displacement. However, due to confused conditions of the troops, having fought for 24 hours without rest, the many casualties, and obscurity of the situation, it was not possible to carry out the displacements immediately upon receiving the order. However, considering the coming daybreak, and fearing envelopment by the enemy if and when other friendly units withdrew, it was decided to order the various regiments to carry out the displacement. . . .

B. Critique.

1. In the conduct of the entire campaign, or the battle command, we have underestimated the enemy. In view of their past characteristics in battle, *we expected the enemy to flee at Chipyong-ni, after the enemy at Hoengsong was annihilated.*

2. Unfamiliarity with the situation. We thought the enemy had merely field works when they had organized key points of defense and other such defense work as bunkers, wire entanglements, et cetera, with tanks, acting as mobile fortresses. We not only did not organize, coordinate, and have the attacking units under a centralized command, but even two regiments of the same division failed to coordinate their movements, resulting in a "You fight, I rest" attitude.[55]

It will be seen from this unusually forthright and generally correct statement of the Chinese army group on actions at Chipyong-ni that the Chinese had expected the American and French forces there to flee the place after the enemy's complete victory north of Hoengsong and the occupation of Hoengsong. Such, indeed, had been the experience with UN forces previously in the Korean War, if one substitutes the more euphemistic term "withdraw" for "flee." But Chipyong-ni changed the nature of UN actions for the future. It was the first time the Chinese had been defeated since their intervention in the war in late October 1950. It was the first time an American and UN force of regimental or larger size had stood in a perimeter defense and defended itself successfully, turning back a much larger Chinese force. It was the signpost in the Korean War that marked what was to be the American practice in the future. It was the event that solidified morale of the American and UN Eighth Army to one of confidence that it could meet the enemy and hold its own. After Chipyong-ni, the war entered a new phase.

A light snow on the morning of 16 February obscured the scene, and Colonel Crombez decided to delay his start back to the 5th Cavalry positions until the weather cleared. At 12:15 he started back with 22 of his original 24 tanks. Questions in his mind were, Would the road be mined? Would the enemy still be in place along the road? A barrage of 4.2-inch heavy mortars was placed on the Pass area just south of Chipyong-ni before he started. Then he was on his way. Not a single enemy was seen on the journey back. Not a single shot was fired. His task force reached the 2nd Battalion, 5th Cavalry, lines at 12:45 P.M., about a quarter of a mile south of Koksu-ri.[56]

The 5th Cavalry Regiment captured Koksu-ri after two days of combat against elements of the CCF 116th Division. Early on the sixteenth an estimated enemy regiment could be seen two and a half miles eastward from Koksu-ri, moving north and northeast carrying wounded on litters. The 2nd Battalion, 5th Cavalry, entered Koksu-ri at noon, with the rest of the regiment east and west of the town. It had secured the town by 2 P.M.

Since 15 February Capt. Keith M. Stewart had held what was now called Task Force Stewart—trucks loaded with supplies for the 23rd RCT at Chipyong-ni and ambulances to receive the wounded there—behind the lines of the 5th Cavalry Regiment awaiting word from Colonel Crombez that it would be safe for him to bring the convoy on to Chipyong-ni. That word came only when Crombez arrived at Koksu-ri in the afternoon of 16 February with his tank force. Crombez at that time ordered Captain Stewart to proceed at once to Chipyong-ni. Tanks escorted 28 2½-ton trucks loaded with supplies and 19 ambulances from Koksu-ri at midafternoon. They arrived at Chipyong-ni without event. The wounded there were immediately loaded into the ambulances and 7 additional 2½-ton trucks and started back under escort for Koksu-ri, where they arrived during the evening. At Chipyong-ni, a night drop from 19 aircraft resupplied the 23rd

RCT with small-arms and mortar ammunition. The last drop was made at 11:40 P.M. The RCT was again ready for what might come. But there were no more enemy attacks in the next two days while it remained at Chipyong-ni.[57]

A casualty report for the 23rd RCT at Chipyong-ni from 3 to 16 February gives the figures in table 9. There are varying intelligence statements in the official records at X Corps, 2nd Division, and 23rd RCT levels of the enemy units involved in the Chipyong-ni battle and of Chinese casualties there. Most of them were made at the end of the battle or shortly thereafter. A few months later significant Chinese documents were captured that, with surprising frankness, gave the Chinese order of battle, some of their unit movements to the battlefield, their actions there by battalion, regiment, division, and army, their mistakes at Chipyong-ni, and the heavy casualties suffered. A study of these is essential for any credible approximation of the enemy situation at Chipyong-ni. Any UN or American estimate of enemy losses at Chipyong-ni, most of them on the order of 5,000 casualties in killed or wounded and 79 or 80 prisoners, are only educated guesses, as there was never any comprehensive count of dead bodies for the entire perimeter and its vicinity. The number of wounded can be only an imprecise estimate based on a ratio count in relation to dead, as the enemy took away most of its wounded. It can be stated, however, that the Chinese suffered heavy casualties, by their own admission, and the massive artillery, mortar, and the murderous air strikes, especially those of napalm drops, exacted appalling costs to the enemy.

There is more specific information about the enemy divisions involved in the attack. Enemy documents captured later give battalion, regiment, and division identification in many cases for actions at different parts of the Chipyong-ni perimeter. This information is especially specific for the Chinese 115th Division of the 39th Army at the southern side of the perimeter. One can reasonably conclude that elements of four divisions in three Chinese armies were involved at the Chipyong-ni perimeter, and a

TABLE 9. **UN Casualties at Chipyong-ni, 3–16 February 1951**

Unit	KIA	WIA	MIA	Nonbattle	Total
1st Bn., 23rd Inf.	14	70	2	25	111
2nd Bn., 23rd Inf.	9	82	37	8	136
3rd Bn., 23rd Inf.	18	35	3	2	58
Special units	2	25	0	7	34
Total 23rd Inf.	43	212	42	42	339
French Bn.	9	47	0	9	65
Total	52	259	42	51	404

Source: Freeman, "Wonju through Chipyong-ni."

fifth division was used in cutting the roads south of Chipyong-ni to the Han River (see table 10).

The 115th Division of the 39th Army had two regiments in the fight and probably was the most intensively engaged of all the enemy divisions. It made a sweeping bypass of Chipyong-ni initially on the east, turned south for a few miles, and then at Kudun turned west to come in on the south side of the Chipyong-ni perimeter. Its companion 116th Division took essentially the same route as to points of departure, movements east and then south of Chipyong-ni, but proceeded some four or five miles farther south before turning west. It came to the 23rd MSR at Chaum-ni and had an engagement there with American troops patrolling the MSR between Wonju and Chipyong-ni. Part of the division took positions along this road, and part of it went on farther west to cut the other road from Yoju through Koksu-ri to Chipyong-ni. The third division of the 39th Army, the 117th Division, was on an axis of advance farther east of the 115th and 116th divisions and went to the Hoengsong front, where it participated in that action.

The 119th Division of the CCF 40th Army came to the Chipyong-ni perimeter from the northeast and was engaged chiefly on the eastern side of the perimeter.

The CCF 125th Division, as noted earlier, had fought in the intense battle at Twin Tunnels with its 373rd and 374th regiments, which were pretty much decimated there. The remnants of the division had then taken refuge in massive Hill 506 east-northeast of Chipyong-ni. Only its third regiment, the 375th, was combat effective, and it is believed it is the only one that fought extensively at Chipyong-ni, although a prisoner from it said that the division's 3,000 men were divided into three provisional regiments.

The 126th Division of the 42nd Army approached the perimeter from the northwest and fought on the western and southwestern parts of the perimeter with its 377th Regiment, at the same time its sister division, the 125th, struck the northern part of the perimeter. One cannot say that

TABLE 10. **CCF Forces at Chipyong-ni, 13–15 February 1951**

Armies at Chipyong-ni	Division	Regiments
39th	115th	343rd, 344th, 345th
40th	119th	355th, 356th, 357th
42nd	126th	376th, 377th, 378th
	125th	375th
Army cutting the road south of Chipyong-ni		
39th	116th	346th, 347th, 348th

all the battalions and regiments of these Chinese divisions were actively or extensively engaged at Chipyong-ni. These divisions did not coordinate their actions, and in this respect the Chinese attack on Chipyong-ni was a poor performance in overall command.

The 116th Division of the 39th Army fought the battles along the two roads coming into Chipyong-ni from the south and southeast. It fought Task Force Crombez on the road from Yoju, beginning at Koksu-ri and hence northward. And it also fought the advance of the British 27th Commonwealth Brigade on the MSR eastward toward Chipyong-ni.

It remains to notice that the 116th Division met a UN force at Chaum-ni about dawn on the morning of 14 February when it was moving into its blocking positions on the two roads just mentioned. This action was in reality part of the Chipyong-ni battle.

It has been mentioned that the 2nd Reconnaissance Company and the 9th Infantry Regiment of the US 2nd Division had the task of patrolling and trying to hold open the MSR of the 23rd RCT between Chipyong-ni and Wonju. This area came to be a no-man's-land as the Chinese 4th Phase Offensive developed. First the enemy captured Hoengsong and then drove rapidly south to the edge of Wonju. And immediately following the fall of Hoengsong, Chinese divisions surrounded and attacked Chipyong-ni. On 13 February, the 2nd Reconnaissance Company could not establish contact with patrols from Chipyong-ni, and it found a large number of enemy troops blocking its way between Korun-ni and the 23rd RCT. (Korun-ni was the village on the Han River where the MSR from Wonju turned north from its previous westerly direction to a northerly one to run through Chaum-ni to Kudun and there bear northwest through the Twin Tunnels area to Chipyong-ni.) Enemy troops on 13 February blocked the Reconnaissance Company six miles southeast of Chipyong-ni. L Company of the 9th Regiment, 2nd Division, went up the road to join it, and the two companies engaged the Chinese in a continuing battle. At some point during the night the Reconnaissance Company and L Company withdrew southward. On the fourteenth, IX Corps started the British 27th Commonwealth Brigade from Yoju to help keep open this MSR and to advance along it toward Chipyong-ni. But the British Brigade met enemy only a few miles from Yoju and made slow progress.

On 17 February, after stubborn resistance to the Australian Battalion, the Chinese blocking force abandoned its high-ground position during the night for another one a little farther north. Before withdrawing, the Chinese released 30 American prisoners they had held for three days. They were from the 2nd Reconnaissance and L companies.[58]

On 13 February the 2nd Reconnaissance Company held Hill 112, two miles south of Chaum-ni on the MSR. During the night of 13–14 February the CCF 116th Division was on the move from north of Chipyong-ni

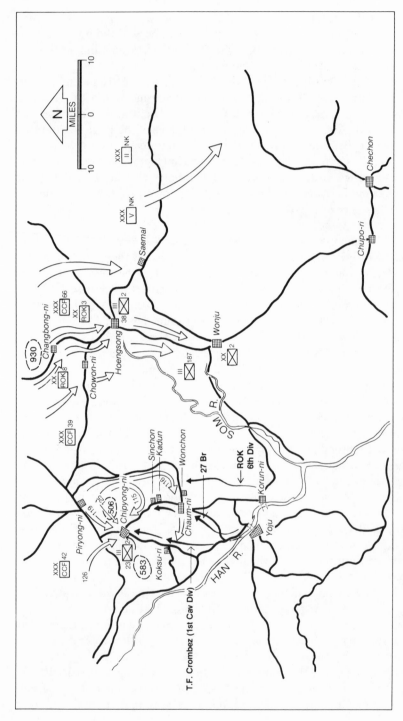

MAP 13. **CCF 4th Phase Offensive, 11–16 February 1951**

in an eastward flanking movement to cut the roads south of Chipyong-ni. What happened that night was not known for many days, or if it was known to a few, it did not get into the official military journal messages and records. But an uproar suddenly erupted when a Canadian newspaper in Toronto published a dispatch from Bill Boss, a war correspondent who was traveling with the Canadian Princess Patricia regiment when it arrived at the small Korean village of Kudun, on the MSR, four air miles southeast of Chipyong-ni. According to the report, Boss counted 68 bodies of US soldiers there. He said that they went to sleep with only one sentry and that some of the bodies were found naked and some lay where they had been trying to get out of their sleeping bags. They had not dug any foxholes or other defensive positions. The Chinese who had come upon them had killed them easily. General MacArthur flung this news upon General Ridgway and asked for an immediate report of the incident, and he asked why the story had "passed your censor."[59]

General Ridgway at once, on 1 March, asked his Eighth Army Inspector General's section to investigate the Boss story. Nearly two weeks later, on 13 March 1951, Lt. Col. Roy W. Horton, of the Eighth Army Inspector General's section, made his report. He said the incident centered at Chaumni, three road miles south of Kudun on the 23rd RCT MSR. He said the 2nd Reconnaissance Company had been patrolling the MSR from Chipyongni, to Ipo-ri, the left flank of X Corps, and establishing there contact with the IX Corps. On 13 February, L Company (a unit of black soldiers in the 3rd Battalion, 9th Infantry) had joined the 2nd Reconnaissance Company to establish a blocking position. Major Stine, the executive officer of the 3rd Battalion, 9th Infantry, was with L Company, and in command. At 6 P.M. 13 February the combined force withdrew to Chaum-ni. He said they spent the night preparing a perimeter defense, as they expected to be attacked. Between 5 A.M. and 6 A.M. the next morning, 14 February, an estimated 1,000 Chinese soldiers attacked them with small-arms, mortar, and machine-gun fire, but casualties were light. Sometime between 8 A.M. and 10 A.M. the two companies decided to withdraw. They loaded their wounded, and with a tank in the lead and others at the rear, eight jeeps, and two M-39 personnel carriers, they started to run a gauntlet of enemy fire. The report said the greatest losses were at a blown bridge on the south side of Chaum-ni, where they lost six jeeps with nonambulatory wounded. Some who got through said they tried for two days to get back to the scene, but failed. The first information on the bodies came from the British 27th Brigade, which had reverted to IX Corps control on 19 February.

The Graves Registration Officer, 9th Infantry, 2nd Division, and the assistant G-4, 2nd Division, went to the scene to recover the bodies. The largest group was three-fourths of a mile south of Chaum-ni; there were others nearer the village within ten feet of the road, and there were some in the village. Many had ring fingers cut off, their outer garments removed, clothes and boots taken. The Graves Registration unit took out 114 bodies. The 2nd Division casualty section gave a total of 212 killed, wounded, missing, and died of wounds. Captain Baca of the 2nd Reconnaissance Company was killed.[60] The captured booklet (in Chinese) "A Collection of Combat Experiences," issued by HQ, CCF 19th Army Group, 29 March 51, in its critique of the Chipyong-ni operation says of this incident, "At dawn on the 14th of February 1951, the 116th Division, pushing forward to Chaum-ni, annihilated two companies of the US 23rd Regiment."

On 16 and 17 February the 23rd RCT remained at Chipyong-ni but had no further enemy action there. The 5th Cavalry Regiment continued fighting its way north from Koksu-ri, and the British 27th Commonwealth Brigade slowly fought its way north toward Chipyong-ni. In a sense, Chipyong-ni for a short time was an island of victory in a sea controlled by the Chinese. Only 20 air miles to the southeast Wonju was under siege from Chinese and North Korean forces on all sides. And farther east and southeast of Wonju, the North Korean II and V corps had made a deep penetration on the X Corps eastern flank that reached almost to Chechon. Had there been no victory at Chipyong-ni, it seems hardly likely that UN forces could have held Wonju. It is now necessary to move the narrative to the Wonju area to see how the Chinese 4th Phase Offensive fared there.

12

The Third Battle for Wonju

THIS CHAPTER considers the CCF 4th Phase Offensive east of Chipyong-ni. On 14 February Wonju was threatened by massive movement of Chinese south of its vicinity after their great success in routing the ROK 8th, 3rd, and 5th divisions north and northeast of Hoengsong and in occupying Hoengsong. The decision at Chipyong-ni still hung in the balance for another day. The situation was fluid on 14 February everywhere on the CCF 4th Phase Offensive 20-mile front. Indeed, the situation was considered so precarious at Wonju that nearly all the tactical airplanes available were sent there, and almost none were directed to Chipyong-ni. As part of the CCF 4th Phase Offensive, the North Korean II and V corps turned back from their withdrawal and resumed a heavy attack on the east side of the Chinese formations, threatening the east flank of X Corps, where there were only weak ROK troops standing in their way. Only the US 7th Division, which had recently been moved north and committed in the Chechon region to help hold that communications center in the eastern mountains (which now served as the railhead for all rail-carried supplies from the port of Pusan for the troops in the central corridor), offered some reliable strength.

As a result of the Hoengsong disaster of 11–13 February, the ROK 8th Division had been rendered combat ineffective and had been sent to Chupori, south of the battle area, to try for reassembly and reorganization to give it some, although reduced, fighting capability. The ROK 3rd and 5th divisions still had some usefulness but were far from division strength. The ROK troops in the eastern front at this time were of doubtful stability and combat strength. Without the victory at Chipyong-ni, which became apparent on 15 February, the CCF 4th Phase Offensive might have rolled on to at least partial victory. Their formations may have reached Yoju and the Han River and there turned southeast along the Han River corridor.

At this critical time a serious accident at the Chechon railhead occurred in the rail yards that affected supply capability in some categories of ammunition and other supplies for the immediate future. On 11 February civilian laborers were loading boxes of ammunition from a railcar to a truck that had pulled up alongside. The driver of the truck soon heard a popping sound and observed smoke from the truck. Within half a minute, ammunition in the truck exploded and set the adjoining railcar on fire. From there a chaos of exploding ammunition and burning cars spread to others in the crowded railyard. A bulldozer and a tank retriever pushed or pulled 45 to 50 loaded cars away from the explosions and burning cars. About 75 percent of the ammunition in the railyard was saved, as well as some cars of rations and POL (petroleum) products. About 20 to 25 railcars were destroyed or badly damaged, along with their contents. The fire was not completely out until the next day. A final tally showed that 10 to 15 ammunition cars were destroyed, 17 or 18 cars of quartermaster supplies were destroyed, 43 soldiers were injured, 6 of them seriously, and 20 percent of the Chechon railyards were damaged. At this time the Chechon Ammunition Supply Point (ASP) 40 had on hand only 900 rounds of high explosive 105-mm howitzer shells, 525 rounds of 155-mm shells, and no propelling charges or M55 fuses. By 19 February 155-mm howitzer ammunition was so low at ASP 40 that three battalions of X Corps were unable to refill their basic loads.[1]

At the same time, pilferage of supplies from the docks at Pusan and from trains going north to the front reached such a high level that General Ridgway ordered the Eighth Army inspector general to investigate it. Military Police and Korean police had to guard all supply trains at every stop they made going north.

General Ridgway spent all of 14 February going from command post to command post, receiving the latest information there pertinent to the battle situation and giving orders for immediate response to the CCF and NK threat. The crucial area at the moment was in the X Corps.

At 7:30 A.M. he telephoned his chief of staff and told him to send the Eighth Army inspector general to investigate the great loss of personnel and equipment in the 2nd Infantry Division in the Hoengsong area during the past three days. Three hours later Ridgway arrived at the X Corps CP at Chungju and conferred with General Almond. He told Almond that the CCF were attacking on a 20-mile front, with their greatest concentration against Eighth Army and not the ROK Army units east of X Corps. He told Almond the shoulders of the enemy penetration must be held, and he wanted a better performance from the ROK III Corps, which had been attached to Almond's command. Units must maintain their integrity, and equipment must not be abandoned. He said the greatest priority was to open the MSR north and west to the 23rd RCT at Chipyong-ni. Ridgway next conferred at 11:45 A.M. with Maj. Gen. B. E. Moore, commanding the IX Corps, at its airstrip. He told Moore that three CCF divisions of the CCF 66th Army and one division each from the 40th and 42nd armies had been identified in the ongoing battles—they were fresh troops recently thrown into the Chinese offensive. He explained quickly the disaster at Hoengsong and the knockout of the ROK 8th Division. He said the hill mass north and northeast of Chungju must be held. He told Moore he had insisted to Almond that the 23rd RCT must hold at Chipyong-ni. He also said that he was starting the 1st Marine Division north toward the battle area and that he expected it to concentrate in the Chungju area within the next seven to ten days.

At 1 P.M. Ridgway telephoned his chief of staff that the road south of Chipyong-ni must be watched closely, and if the IX Corps had to attack north to open the road, it must be done before dark to prevent CCF Forces from building strength across it during the night. Finally, at 4:30 P.M. Ridgway returned to the Eighth Army Main CP at Taegu, where he called a conference of his principal staff officers. Ridgway estimated that the CCF had about 100,000 men committed to the 4th Phase Offensive, and against them the UN had about 75,000 men—not an unfavorable situation, in his opinion. He told his assembled staff that "the force which holds Chungju has the situation in hand." Then he continued, "Take the artillery away from the ROK Corps if they can't take care of it—they will not get any more equipment until they have demonstrated that they can take care of what they have." At this point, General Farrell, chief of KMAG, joined the group. Ridgway told Farrell that he must stay with the ROKs where they were moving back and emphasize to them that they were fighting North Koreans and not Chinese, that this fact would lessen their fears and disposition to panic, which they manifested when they thought they were facing Chinese. The ROKs on the east coast, he said, were disposed on adjacent ridges and high ground when their vehicles were on the road, and their record was good. He wanted more of that performance from the ROKs in the east central front. He told his staff that he was starting the first unit of the 1st Marine Division northward the next morning. He ended by saying that, if the Eighth Army had to give ground at Wonju, the US 2nd and 7th divisions and the 187th Airborne RCT there should withdraw their left flank to cover the Wonju-Chechon road. Ridgway ended the meeting by pinning three stars on General Milburn of I Corps.[2]

The X Corps line on 14 February was roughly east-west through Wonju and then curved to the southwest through the 9th Infantry to the ROK 6th Division, the British 27th Brigade, and the US 23rd RCT at Chipyong-ni. In the high country at the northwest corner of Wonju, a heavy Chinese attack was in progress against the 38th Infantry Regiment of the 2nd Division and the 187th Airborne RCT in an attempt to break through to Wonju. An estimated enemy division was in the attack. The Chinese attack made a penetration of the 38th Infantry and compelled the Netherlands Battalion to withdraw from its position, but it failed to break the UN defenses of Wonju. The enemy attack seemed to be veering off to the southwest. The weather was generally bad, and the Chinese apparently gambled on an over-cast sky to persist during the day and protect daylight movement, because there was an unusually heavy movement of concentrated masses of enemy to the north and west of Wonju on the morning of the fourteenth.[3]

But the cloud cover was thin—in spots, no clouds at all—and the morning weather offered the Air Force a good chance to catch large forces of enemy in the open, northwest of Wonju. The first observation report of large numbers of enemy just north of Wonju came into receiving radios at 7:15 A.M. on 14 February. Air strikes and artillery VT fuse shells began to hit this enemy group, and other aerial reports were now coming in of widespread enemy movements trying to cross the Som River, a large tributary of the Han that rose in the mountains above Hoengsong and then twisted its way southwest through a tangle of mountains to enter the Han, seven air miles a little north of west of Wonju. Mountain trails from the north and northwest came down to the Som all along its course, crossed to the south side at fords and ferry sites, and then continued on south to strike the main road (the 23rd RCT MSR) between Wonju and Chipyong-ni. At several of the big bends of the Som River, large areas of flat, open land had developed. Here were natural crossing sites, and they provided good assembly areas for large Chinese formations on the move. One of these flat, open areas was at a mile-long big U-bend of the Som, five and a half air miles northwest of Wonju.[4]

First Lt. Lee R. Hartell was serving as an aerial observer along the Som River northwest of Wonju on the morning of 14 February. At the U bend of the river he and his pilot saw what looked like a heavy tree line in the sandy beach. At second thought it seemed strange to see a heavy tree line in midwinter, and at second glance they realized that the "tree line" was moving. Huge columns—an estimated two enemy divisions with pack animals—were moving into an assembly area. Hartell and his pilot Valdez called for fire, and the 38th FA responded with a round of white phosphorus. A further request for fire was received with more caution, but finally a full range of explosive fire was directed on the area, actually turning the river red with blood. Hartell told his brother that he, Valdez, and Capt. Brady, S-3 of the 38th FA Battalion, were forgotten in the press releases about the "Wonju Shoot" but that at least the official records included their names and the estimated number of enemy casualties inflicted—3,000 to 3,500.[5]

Lee Hartell later went back to his old job as an artillery forward observer with B Company, 9th Infantry, 2nd Division. On 26 August 1951 he went up on Hill 700, an approach to Bloody Ridge, near the Punchbowl area in the high mountains of eastern Korea. That night an enemy attack overran his position, and he died there, remaining at his post and to his last breath calling to his artillery battalion for adjusting fire. He received the Medal of Honor, Posthumously.[6]

As many as four artillery battalions joined in the barrages on the enemy bunched in the Som River valley northwest of Wonju. Some who had crossed the Som seemed headed for the Netherlands Battalion in the line northwest of Wonju. One column, speculated to be the 120th Division of the 40th Army, was massed for half a mile in the open river flat, its tail about six miles northwest of Wonju. This apparently was the enemy mass Lee Hartell described. Other aerial observers reported large groups crossing the Som and heading south. It was apparent that two or more divisions, or large elements of them, were attempting to get behind Wonju, or were in the act of by-passing the town on the west to attack other objectives. Aerial reports in the afternoon reported that many enemy from these troops had turned around and were trying to escape to the north.[7] The "Wonju Shoot" became a byword among artillerymen in Eighth Army and the X Corps. The event was described with some choice rhetoric in many newspapers and most of the nationally circulated weeklies in the United States.

Not all the enemy were north and northwest of Wonju on 14 February. At 3 P.M. the ROK 23rd Regiment, 3rd Division, attacked and eliminated an enemy roadblock seven and a half miles southeast of Wonju. The next day an estimated 2,000 enemy attacked the same ROK regiment near the same spot.

The main fight for Wonju on 14 February, however, centered on the high ground three to four miles northwest of Wonju. The enemy had driven the 38th Infantry from Hill 325, and it tried all day to recapture the position but failed. The Chinese also drove back the Netherlands Battalion, which was attached to the 38th Infantry. Late in the afternoon a flight of South African UN aircraft strafed the Netherlands Battalion at 6 P.M., and napalm drops also hit its A and B companies. The 2nd Battalion, 187th RCT, also was hit by napalm. The South African fliers said they were guided by the ground controller. But he said he did not control the mission. Some speculation arose that Chinese might have controlled the flight and strikes through use of captured equipment. The Netherlands Battalion had 16 casualties from the air strikes—1 killed and 15 wounded. The extent of the casualties in the 2nd Battalion, 187th Airborne RCT, was not immediately reported. The commanding officer of the 3rd Battalion, 38th Infantry, went to the Netherlands Battalion to help it reorganize.[8]

Interesting information was obtained on the fourteenth from interrogation of a Chinese prisoner captured at Chipyong-ni. He said he was inducted into the Chinese Army in China on 21 December 1950, that he and 3,000 other replacements received ten days of basic training north of Seoul, and that this group was the first replacements sent to Korea. He said this replacement group arrived at a point 12 kilometers north of Chipyong-ni in the night of 13 February, and the group was assigned to the 359th Regiment of the 40th Army. They were told they were to try to get weapons on the battlefield. The majority had four grenades each, but they had no rifles.[9] Numerous prisoners captured at this time stated in their interrogations that, while still in Manchuria before leaving for Korea, they were told that they could pick up abandoned American arms at the front.[10]

In response to these disclosures, and on the basis of its own knowledge of the fact that American and ROK soldiers often abandoned their weapons in battle and retreat, the X Corps on the afternoon of 14 February sent a message to the 2nd Division stating: "In spite of repeated instructions, it appears that all echelons of command are not yet fully aware of the gravity of permitting the enemy to acquire usable weapons and equipment. Investigation will not be satisfied by the mere conclusion 'loss due to enemy action.' Facts must show that the item was in no manner lost by failure to perform to the utmost so as to protect the property. Disciplinary action against violaters will be immediate and severe."[11]

Hill 342, held by the 187th Airborne RCT only a little more than a mile west of the Wonju-Hoengsong road and two and a half miles north of Wonju, and Hills 255 and 325 southwest of 342, held by the Netherlands Battalion and the 38th Infantry, were the focus of strong enemy attack all day of 14 February. These hills, and others, under attack were on a line only an air mile or less north of the MSR that ran west from Wonju to the Han River at Korun-ni, and there turned north to Chipyong-ni. The fighting was at times desperate, and several outstanding deeds of courage and leadership at platoon and company level won the Distinguished Service Cross for men who were individually responsible in large part for winning back lost positions or for holding firm against strong attack. The 2nd Battalion, 187th Airborne RCT, counterattacked to restore the positions the enemy had won from the 3rd Battalion, 38th Infantry, at Hills 342, 213, 325, and 255. Hill 325 changed hands several times. Capt. John H. Nelson, commanding officer of F Company, 38th Infantry, and his company fought all night of 14-15 February to regain Hill 325, failing three times. At dawn of the fifteenth, he personally led another counterattack and engaged enemy troops in their entrenchments in close combat with hand grenades and carbine. He inspired his men to follow his example, and the company regained the hill. They then came under enemy mortar fire, already preregistered on the crest. Nelson went from man to man in organizing the hilltop position. At this time enemy mortar fire killed him.[12]

At 4:45 A.M. on 15 February Chinese attackers drove K Company, 187th Airborne, from Hill 342. The company rallied on the south slope of the hill, and from there by early afternoon had recaptured the hill. I Company of the 187th Airborne RCT then continued the attack, passing through K Company. There were about 100 counted dead Chinese on the slope.

Perhaps the most spectacular company action in this fighting north and northwest of Wonju on 14 February was the action of E Company, 187th

Airborne RCT, in capturing Hill 255, which was in the center of a string of hills the enemy had captured overlooking Wonju and the MSR from there westward. The crest of Hill 255 was less than one air mile from the Wonju MSR and only three air miles from Wonju. First Lt. James H. Nix, 1st Platoon leader of E Company, had his platoon on the left, and 1st Lt. William J. Dolan, 3rd Platoon leader, had his platoon on the right of a two-platoon frontal attack against the hill, held by an enemy battalion. The 2nd Platoon formed a base of fire to support the attack. The attack on the left began at 2 P.M. and on the right a half hour later. In his attack on the left, Lieutenant Nix and his platoon came to within 20 yards of the crest. From there, with their ammunition nearly exhausted and under very heavy enemy fire, the platoon withdrew to reorganize.

During this platoon attack, Lieutenant Dolan with the 3rd Platoon on the right reached the crest of Hill 255, but enfilading machine-gun fire from a higher knob to the right, Hill 392, forced him to fall back. After several successive failures to regain the crest, Dolan decided the only hope for success was to storm the enemy's position. Dolan by now had been wounded in the thigh by a grenade, but he refused medical attention and continued in command of the platoon. Dolan instructed every man in his group regarding what he intended to do. His force in the 3rd Platoon was down to 8 men, but he received 17 reinforcements from G Company, and 2 men carried up a resupply of ammunition. Enemy had reoccupied a bunker. Dolan's 3.5-inch rocket-launcher man, although wounded twice, crawled to a spot from which he destroyed the bunker with one rocket. Dolan then led his men over the top, and they engaged in hand-to-hand fighting. Dolan was credited with killing over 30 enemy with grenades, carbine fire, and rifle butt.

Approximately simultaneously with Dolan's final action, Lieutenant Nix from his position on the left observed the 3rd Platoon's progress, and he resumed his attack with the 1st Platoon. He reached the crest from his side with a part of his platoon, and at once noted a ravine on the reverse slope that was full of enemy. Exposing himself, he emptied his carbine into the massed enemy, killing ten of them. He then drew his pistol and led his men in an attack on enemy foxholes, and when the pistol was empty, he picked up an automatic weapon to use. Both platoons in their close-in final attacks swung rifle butts and crushed skulls. The two platoons had possession of the hill just at dusk. They had been in the fight 3 hours and 40 minutes.

E Company had 63 casualties in this fight, the 1st Platoon had 9 killed and 17 wounded, but 450 enemy dead were counted on the hill and its reverse slope. In writing a report of his platoon's action, Lieutenant Dolan commented, "All of my men and I noticed an important fact concerning the Chinese. In close combat, invariably the Red Chinese take time to decide whether to throw a grenade or to shoot. He would shoot without aiming and miss, or take too much time aiming. The few seconds that it took to make this decision gave us time to kill him."[13]

E Company, 187th Airborne RCT, received the Presidential Unit Citaticn for this action, and First Lieutenants Nix and Dolan each received the Distinguished Service Cross for their leadership and courage in capturing Hill 255 on 14 February.[14] Wonju remained in American possession.

The battle losses of the ROK 3rd Division in the Hoengsong action of 9–12 February had now been counted, and it was placed at 3,000 men on 14 February. By the sixteenth, however, 1,000 of them had returned to the division. The ROK 3rd Division at that time, badly disorganized, still had its artillery, but half its crew-served weapons were gone. From the remnants of the ROK 8th Division, reorganized at Chupo-ri, two provisional battalions were formed and put back into action.[15]

A mile northeast of Hill 255, the 2nd Battalion, 187th Airborne, on 15 February found fighting just about as hard as it had engaged in the day before on Hill 255. Two Chinese prisoners said that the 360th Regiment, 120th Division, 40th Army, was on the hill and on Hill 342. Its mission was to secure the high ground there and to take Wonju. Hill 342 was the closer of the two dominant hills to Wonju and the MSR north toward Hoengsong. On the fifteenth the enemy still held Hill 342, both the crest and the reverse slope. First Lt. David N. White, a platoon leader in G Company, 187th Airborne, was given the task of attacking the hill. As White's platoon started up the forward slope, enemy stopped it with machine-gun and small-arms fire. White located the nearest machine gun and crawled to within 20 yards of it. He killed the gun crew with carbine fire. A second machine gun, 50 yards from the first, opened fire on White and wounded him in the chest, but he crawled toward it, getting to within 15 yards of it. He threw a white phosphorus grenade into the emplacement but was wounded in the act by enemy fire and died there. The enemy still held Hill 342.[16]

On 15 February the 38th Infantry and the attached Netherlands Battalion had heavy fighting again, first losing and then regaining their positions. The greatest menace on the fifteenth, however, shifted eastward from Wonju to Chechon. There North Koreans penetrated to within six miles of Chechon. The X Corps hastily had to form a defense line north of the town with remnants of the ROK 3rd and 5th divisions. Elements of the US 7th Infantry Division moved up behind them. On orders from General Ridgway, the competent ROK commander of the ROK I Corps from the east coast had arrived with his staff at Chechon to take command of the ROK 3rd, 5th, and 8th divisions in defense of the vulnerable area east of X Corps. The NK II, III, and V corps were massing there and pushing south.[17]

In the midst of all the enemy threats to X Corps on 15 February, the day was still a notable one for General Almond. General Ridgway went to Chungju for a conference with Almond, and while there he pinned the third star of a lieutenant general on him. Ridgway had begun to worry that the French Battalion and the Netherlands Battalion might be on the verge of becoming battle weary, and he told Almond to pull them out of the line at the first opportunity. There were reassignments in the higher commands of Eighth Army also that day. Maj. Gen. William Kean, commander of the 25th Division since it had arrived in Korea, was released to the Department of the Army; Brig. Gen. Sladen Bradley was appointed to command the 25th Division; and Col. John Michaelis, commanding officer of the 27th Infantry Regiment, was made assistant division commander, 25th Division.[18]

Although Chinese were still strong on some hills west of the Hoengsong road, there were very few on the road itself. Two ROK soldiers walked all the way from Hoengsong to Wonju that day without seeing any enemy along the road or being fired on, but they could see Chinese on hills to the west.

Ever since the ROK debacle in the fighting north and east of Hoengsong 11 to 13 February, the situation between their commanders and the X Corps staff had grown constantly worse. The ROKs felt humiliated at the blame put at their door as the enemy success spread eastward through the zone of their responsibility, east of Hoengsong and Wonju. Their resentment boiled over, and their attitude approached one of hostility and possible defection from General Almond's X Corps control. This growing trouble in the UN command in the east-central front at a moment of crisis worried General Ridgway.

On the morning of 16 February, General Ridgway met Col. John S. Guthrie, the new X Corps chief of staff, at the X Corps advance airstrip at Wonju. Ridgway told Guthrie that the ROK commanders of the ROK 8th, 3rd, and 5th divisions, which were attached to X Corps, "were very resentful of the way they are treated in the Corps." Ridgway reminded Guthrie that the UN command was heavily dependent upon the ROK units as battle partners. Their loss of cooperation would be a serious and critical disaffection, and their feeling must be corrected at once. Ridgway told Guthrie it was a responsibility of command to foresee and eliminate causes of friction and to absorb it and prevent its spread. He said to Guthrie, "This is a heart to heart talk which I want conveyed to Gen. Almond, and a situation I want promptly corrected."[19]

A perennial question in coalition warfare is, How can one praise a failing partner, especially when the failure is so great as to jeopardize one's own security and that of thousands of one's own troops? One can have sympathy for General Almond in this matter. The South Korean Army remained a problem for most of the Korean War.

At the Taegu CP on 16 February, General Ridgway began a conference at 4 P.M. with the highest military officials of the ROK Army. Present at this conference were Gen. Chung Il Kwon, chief of staff, ROK Army; South Korean defense minister Sihn Sung Mo; Ambassador Muccio; General Coulter, deputy Eighth Army commander and liaison to President Syngman Rhee; and Maj. Gen. Leven Allen, chief of staff, Eighth Army. General Ridgway began the meeting by saying he was glad to have seen General Chung the day before at the scene of battle crisis, that he thought a senior commander should always be present at the crucial moment. He said the Chinese now had elements of four armies – the 39th, 40th, 42nd, and 66th – in their attack, that the attack was a strong one, and that it would take the best effort of all to check it, contain it, and then destroy it. He asked for such help from all present.

Ridgway continued that he was not going to try now to fix responsibility for mistakes made recently (apparently referring to the Hoengsong debacle, and possibly to the ROK III Corps' failure to the east of X Corps), that it was too early for that, but as soon as possible he wanted to see what they all could learn as a lesson and what could be done immediately and also as a long-range objective to improve the situation.

He emphasized the importance of maneuver and use of firepower and the importance of continuous reconnaissance, with reporting of it to the proper authority. If this were done, there could be no excuse for enemy destruction of the unit.

Ridgway bore down on the recent loss of great quantities of military equipment. He reiterated that he had told all commanders that the loss of or abandonment of usable combat equipment was a grave offense against everyone in the army and would not be tolerated. Chinese troops went into battle armed only with grenades, for the sole purpose of capturing UN weapons and using them. When a soldier came back without his weapon, the unit commander should investigate and find out why the soldier lost it.

One of the complaints the ROK generals apparently had made concerned the removal from General Yu, commander of the ROK III Corps, of some of his divisions. Ridgway asked the ROK chief of staff, General Chung, to do everything he could to ensure that General Yu understood the gravity of the situation and promised that he would get back the ROK 3rd and 5th divisions, since they preferred to be under their own corps commander (they had been placed in X Corps under General Almond's command). But Ridgway said it could not be done at the moment, as there was evidence that the enemy was launching an attack eastward against the Pyongchang-Yongwol corridor, and it was essential that all units there be under a single commander. He further said to General Chung that he should impress on General Yu that even minor offensive moves often paid large dividends, that he should not continue falling back, and that every effort should be directed toward getting increased resistance to the enemy from the ROK 7th and 9th divisions in the ROK III Corps zone.

At this point, Defense Minister Sihn and General Chung said the ROK division commanders were resentful of the way they were being used in X Corps. General Ridgway replied that all must use every resource to resolve that difficulty, that there must not be friction between corps commanders. He then took the opportunity to commend the ROK 1st and 6th divisions on their gallant actions. He asked Minister Sihn and General Chung to consider his remarks and to make any suggestions or comments they desired. Sihn and Chung at this time withdrew from the meeting.

General Ridgway told Ambassador Muccio that he had instructed his army commanders there would be nothing in the nature of a scorched-earth policy in their operation – waterworks and power plants would not be harmed, only designated bridges would be destroyed, and minimal damage to others would be inflicted in the interest of delaying enemy movements. Ridgway then went into a conference with Generals Allen, Hodes, and Dabney and Colonels Stebbins and Ferguson of his Eighth Army staff concerning the current situation and planned operations.

Later that day Ridgway conferred with General Moore, the IX Corps commander. He wanted Moore to be sure there was no lapse that would jeopardize the 23rd RCT at Chipyong-ni and run the risk of losing it or any part of its forces. He told Moore that it was important that he hold the high ground 4,000 yards southwest of Chipyong-ni for use as a line of departure, but not to risk the loss of any major unit. He said the boundary between IX Corps and X Corps would be changed to move the IX Corps eastward, and it might have to assume responsibility for the 23rd RCT at Chipyong-ni for a short time, but it would revert to control of the 2nd Division.

Ridgway then conferred briefly with Colonel Guthrie, chief of staff, X Corps, about the situation at Wonju. He told Guthrie to leave the 187th Airborne RCT in its present position (across the MSR north of Wonju on high ground on either side) but said that holding Wonju and the flat bowl in which it sat was unimportant, that the high ground south of Wonju should be held if enemy pressure forced a movement away from the present positions the 2nd Division and the 187th Airborne RCT held there.[20]

It is worthy of note that naval activity had continued heavy in the coastal area of northeast Korea where the coastal highway and the railroad from Siberia ran close to the coast, the railroad passing through many tunnels, and in most places within range of the guns of American heavy naval vessels. This was an important axis of supply from the Soviet Union to the battlefields of central and eastern Korea. There, naval ships surpassed the Civil War record for continuous days of successive naval bombardment. The old record of 42 days' bombardment by Union gunboats at Vicksburg was broken when the US Navy on 16 February 1951 began its bombardment of the port of Wonsan and again when it started on 7 March 1951 the bombardment from offshore of Songjin, 140 miles south of the Siberian border. Naval fire was concentrated on interdiction targets, such as bridges, tunnels, and road and railroad junction points. There were also targets of opportunity, anything discovered to be of military value to the enemy.

It was a target of opportunity at Wonsan on 15 February that provided one of the most devastating events of the war. In less than eight minutes the gunfire of a light cruiser and three destroyers obliterated 8,000 Chinese troops. These troops worked at night and slept by day. For some time the Navy had intelligence of this concentration of enemy troops on labor detail sleeping in Wonsan but did nothing, in the hope that the enemy would gain confidence in their security and bring in more and more for accommodation. When the maximum target was calculated to have accumulated, the USS *Manchester,* a light cruiser, and two destroyers opened fire on the predetermined targets at 11 A.M. on 15 February. Intelligence estimated that their continuous fire for five minutes killed 6,000 enemy troops in two areas. Two hours later, the destroyer USS *Wallace L. Lind* fired for three minutes on a third predetermined target of sleeping men and killed another estimated 2,000 enemy troops.[21] In the east coastal bombardments in support of the war, the battleship *Missouri* and the *New Jersey* took part, closing several railroad tunnels.

Many miles south and inland from the naval actions against the coastal military facilities of the enemy, American troops defending Wonju at the same time felt the battle tide had turned on 16 February. The 187th Airborne RCT reported that day that the CCF 360th Regiment of the 120th Division, 40th Army, had been decisively defeated in the mountains northwest of Wonju, and that it was withdrawing toward Hoengsong. But it also reported that these troops still had their clothing, equipment, weapons in good shape, excellent discipline, and were capable of powerful assaults and strong resistance in defensive positions. With the withdrawing of the CCF 120th Division from the northwest edge of Wonju, many members and stragglers of the US 38th Infantry began coming through the lines. Some of them were released prisoners. They reported their captors had treated them with respect and compassion. One of them, Pfc. Michael Killio, D Company, 38th Infantry, captured on 13 February north of Hoengsong, said he had walked down the road from Hoengsong to Wonju, during which several small groups of Chinese had stopped him but allowed him to go on.[22]

In the mountains west of Wonju things had not gone very well. The British 27th Brigade and the ROK 6th Division had made only slow advance against stubborn Chinese resistance in the gap between Chipyong-ni and Wonju. On 16 February a gap of nearly two miles existed between them. With each passing day, it became clear that, if Task Force Crombez, the tank relief force from the 5th Cavalry Division on the Koksu-ri road, had not reached Chipyong-ni on 15 February, the infantry elements of the

5th Cavalry and those of the British 27th Brigade and the ROK 6th Division eastward would not have reached Chipyong-ni for several days, with possibly disastrous results. The enemy fireblocks south of Chipyong-ni would have served their purpose, and the 23rd RCT would not have been relieved quickly. Chinese attack on the 23rd RCT at Chipyong-ni, according to enemy documents, would have continued.[23]

On 16 February the 38th Infantry, which had fought long and hard at the northwestern arc above Wonju, was ordered out of the line into 2nd Division reserve at Munmang-ni, ten road miles southwest of Wonju on the MSR to Yoju. Its 1st Battalion, however, had to secure the road.[24]

The 5th Cavalry Regiment did not relieve the 23rd RCT at Chipyong-ni until 18 February. In the meantime, 23rd RCT patrols failed to make enemy contact around Chipyong-ni and only occasionally had to endure some harassing mortar fire from distant hills. The enemy plainly was shifting Chinese strength west and north. But in the eastern part of X Corps, North Korean forces of its V and II corps rapidly pushed back the ROK 5th and 3rd divisions toward Chechon. Two provisional battalions of the ROK 8th Division were sent into a gap between the other two ROK divisions. The North Koreans now threatened to break through the Chechon-Yongwol road in the east. General Ridgway ordered General Almond to use US troops to stop the NK penetration northeast of Chechon and to establish contact with the ROK troops of the III Corps eastward, north of Yongwol.[25]

The US 7th Infantry Division now became an important part of the UN deployment east of the US 2nd Division to help stop the North Korean drive north of Chechon. Maj. Gen. Claude B. Ferenbaugh had succeeded in command of the division when General Barr had rotated back to the United States a few weeks earlier, and he had two new regimental commanders, Col. William N. Quinn, formerly the G-2 of X Corps and now in command of the 17th Infantry, and Col. John A. Gavin, commanding the 31st Infantry. The 31st Regiment had been trying to regain regimental strength after its near destruction at Chosin Reservoir in early December 1950. Col. Charles G. Beauchamp remained as the experienced commander of the 32nd Infantry Regiment, which had lost its 1st Battalion at Chosin. The NK 17th Regiment of the NK 2nd Division was in contact with the division on the eastern front on 15 February. The 31st Infantry had the mission of protecting the mountain pass between Tanyang and Andong. The other two regiments were to block enemy passage in the Chechon and Yongwol areas against further enemy penetration from the north and the east.[26] The 7th Division was now the easternmost American division on the line across Korea.

The next day, the 187th Airborne RCT released the 2nd Battalion, 17th Infantry, to the US 7th Division, which replaced it with the 1st Battalion. On 17 February the 187th Airborne had no enemy contacts in its patrols north of Wonju, and it released the 3rd Battalion, 17th Infantry, to the 7th Division, and the battalion left for Chechon.

There was little significant action on 17 February. Patrol action and intelligence from the civilian population indicated the Chinese were making at least limited withdrawals in the Chipyong-ni area and in front of Wonju. Only in the east-central front north and east of Chechon, in the North Korean sector of the front, was there strong resistance to UN and ROK patrols and limited advances. The enemy seemed intent on holding a line from Hoengsong westward to Yangpyong at the bend of the Han River. Hoengsong seemed to be the dividing line between Chinese and North Korean sectors, the North Koreans being east of Hoengsong. The 5th Cavalry Regiment made contact with the 23rd RCT at Chipyong-ni on the seventeenth and scheduled to relieve it there. But General Palmer, commanding the 1st Cavalry Division, told his subordinates there was to be no unseemly haste in occupying Chipyong-ni. He said he wanted to get the commanding ground around it first, and he let the 23rd RCT remain in its perimeter at the village in the meantime. A patrol from F Company, 5th Cavalry, received enemy grenades and small-arms fire near the crest of Hill 583 and withdrew. Another patrol found Hill 482 deserted. It seemed on 17 February that the 1st Cavalry Division might take over Chipyong-ni on the eighteenth. The 23rd RCT would be under control of the 5th Cavalry Regiment until it was ordered to withdraw from Chipyong-ni. Operation Roundup obviously had failed in its objective in gaining its geographical objectives, but it did succeed in killing and wounding vast numbers of the enemy. In that sense only was it a success.[27]

Heavy snow fell on the morning of 18 February. But extensive UN troop movements were in progress nevertheless. The 1st Cavalry Division moved north of the Han River from Yoju. The 5th Cavalry Regiment was already north of the river as far as Koksu-ri. The 8th Cavalry on the left, or west, of the 5th Cavalry found the ford at Yoju shallow enough to cross the river, except for ¼-ton trucks. The 5th Cavalry advanced on Chipyong-ni without enemy opposition and arrived there without difficulty, relieving the 23rd RCT of responsibility for the area. The last of the 23rd RCT cleared the 1st Cavalry Division lines there at 5:45 P.M. on the eighteenth. Thereafter the 1st Cavalry Division had responsibility for Chipyong-ni and vicinity, and the 2nd Division boundary was moved eastward. The 8th Cavalry Regiment was to secure the high ground south of the Hukchon River.[28]

That morning, General Moore, IX Corps commander, telephoned General Ridgway to say that the 5th RCT of the 24th Division, east of the Han River, had advanced without enemy opposition. Along its line of advance the 5th RCT had found 600 CCF dead in foxholes, with cooking equipment and weapons abandoned. Line-crossers and straggler returnees reported the CCF in front of X Corps were withdrawing to the north and west. General Ridgway ordered X Corps to exploit this situation by attacking east into the North Korean troops in the east-central corridor.[29]

General Almond now recommended to General Ridgway that the IX and X corps attack north and west in an enveloping movement calculated to cut off the salient formed by the NK V and III corps in their drive on Chechon. These NK troops were to the east of X Corps. General Ridgway approved the proposal, and an Eighth Army plan to implement it, called "Killer," was issued on 18 February. This plan required the X Corps to move its boundary eastward, so that its left boundary was east of Wonju. The 1st Marine Divison of IX Corps then occupied the zone from Wonju westward formerly held by the 2nd Division. The 187th Airborne RCT was on line east of the 2nd Division; the ROK I Corps, with the 3rd and 5th ROK divisions, was in the center; and on the right flank, elements of the US 7th Infantry Division were in place. The British 27th Brigade and the ROK 6th Division reverted to IX Corps control.

Operations Order No. 14, issued on 19 February, called for the 1st Marine Division to attack north and northeast through the 2nd Division at 10 A.M., 21 February. At the same time, the US 7th Division was to attack north along the Pyongchang–Pangnim-ni road and at Pangnim-ni to turn west to make a junction with the 1st Marine Division. A day after the 1st Marine Division and the 7th Division had launched their attacks, the 2nd Division was to attack north and compress the enemy, now caught in the three-sided attack. Meanwhile the ROK I Corps would resist enemy pressure farther east, and the ROK III Corps would protect the right flank. This planned pincer movement was expected to surround the enemy in the Hoengsong-Pyongchang-Wonju triangle, cut off their escape route northward, and destroy them.[30]

On 18 February, the day the 1st Cavalry Division relieved the 23rd RCT at Chipyong-ni, the British 27th Brigade, attacking just east of the 1st Cavalry Division, celebrated its own red-letter day. In a blizzard, it welcomed the arrival of the 2nd Battalion, Canadian Princess Patricia's Light Infantry. The British 27th Brigade now consisted of a Canadian battalion, an Australian battalion, a New Zealand field regiment, an English battalion, a Scottish battalion, and an Indian field ambulance, all commanded by an Englishman, Brig. Basil Coad.[31]

On 19 February General Almond decorated a platoon of the ROK 18th Regiment for unusual valor in holding its position north of Wonju against superior odds. At the 187th Airborne CP he gave Silver Stars to five members of the platoon and Bronze Stars to eight others—all of the survivors of the platoon. The remainder of the platoon, who had been killed or wounded, he decorated "in absentia" with Silver Stars. General Almond expressed his personal appreciation of the platoon's outstanding valor. General Almond directed Colonel Yim, commander of the ROK 18th Regiment, to continue to hold its position north of Wonju.[32]

The day before Operation Killer was to get in motion, 20 February, General MacArthur and his chief of staff, Gen. Doyle Hickey, and Generals Whitney and Partridge from the Far East Command flew into Wonju. They were joined there by Generals Ridgway, Almond, Ruffner, Ferenbaugh, and Bowen. MacArthur held a press conference for about ten press correspondents, in which he said he approved the pending operation. After the conference, Ridgway telephoned Major General Allen, Eighth Army chief of staff, instructing him to order the ROK Capital Division to continue holding the Kangnung area on the east coast and the lateral road from it west, even if the division was cut off in doing so. It could always be evacuated by sea, if necessary. General Allen was to inform the ROK III Corps commander of this decision.[33]

Operation Killer jumped off on schedule at 10 A.M., 21 February. Opposition was light, and, in succeeding days, lessened even more. On 24 February, the 7th Division reached Pangnim-ni on the road from Chechon, and 2nd Division elements occupied high ground overlooking the Pangnim-ni road, arriving there by its cross-country route.

On 22 February it was evident that the North Korean elements in the Chechon salient were withdrawing northward, thereby evading the pincer movement started by the US IX and X corps. The NK 7th Division covered these withdrawal movements. The North Koreans seemed to be taking up a new defense line east of Hoengsong, where they apparently had a boundary with Chinese forces west of there. The NK III Corps, consisting of the 1st and 15th divisions, entered the line in the Pyongchang area to reinforce the NK V and II corps. Every indication pointed to the North Koreans' planning a strong defensive position north of the Hoengsong–Pangnim-ni lateral (west-east) road.[34]

The last week of February was characterized by heavy rains and warming weather, which melted snows in the mountains. Streams went out of their banks, bridges were swept away, mud was everywhere, slopes were slippery, railroad tunnel cave-ins were common on the rail track north of Andong to Chechon, and military operations generally were slowed.

A disturbing discovery during these last days of February was that the enemy possessed new M-1 American rifles with new sniperscope sights. These weapons were found alongside some of the enemy dead. Cosmoline showed on some parts of the weapons, indicating they had only recently been unpacked. This equipment enabled enemy snipers to pick off targets at long range.[35]

The bad weather that set in simultaneously with the Operation Killer jump-off slowed down its forward progress, but even so, it is apparent that the operation would not have succeeded in its objectives. The enemy had foreseen the intent and withdrew from its forward penetrations in the east-central front in time to escape. With the failure of Operation Killer, the 187th Airborne RCT, which had played a yeoman role in stopping the CCF

Heavy rain or melting snow turned roads into quagmires. These troops are from the 17th Regiment, 7th Division. *National Archives, 111-SC 368504*

drive on Wonju, moved from the Wonju front on 21–22 February to Chechon, reverting there to corps control. From Chechon it went to Taegu, closing there on 28 February.[36]

Although the Chinese withdrew from the immediate vicinity of Chipyong-ni and from in front of Wonju in the period of 18–22 February, they did not carry out this withdrawal everywhere. In the high mountains only a few miles southeast of Chipyong-ni, for example, the Australian and Canadian troops of the British 27th Brigade on 24 February were held at Hill 614 for four days of hard fighting. The mountain slope was so steep that stretcher bearers had to slide wounded off the ridge.[37]

At another place, Hill 514, the enemy was found to have been dug in so well with carefully cleared fields of fire that it was never captured. But when the enemy abandoned it, large amounts of ammunition were found

On sloping ground, heavy rains could wash out a road. US Army engineers set about repairing this one near Inje. *National Archives, 111-SC 376086*

at gun positions, and many weapons were found there. These included a miscellaneous lot – 6 Bren guns, 12 BARs, 5 US light machine guns, 2 US heavy machine guns, 30 or more US M-1 rifles, about the same number of carbines, many foreign-made rifles, and an estimated 2,000 potato-masher grenades. There were no wounded there, but from 400 to 500 enemy dead were on the military and topographic crests of the hill.[38]

The IX Corps Engineers finally completed a bridge across the Han River at Yoju on 25 February, and it was a significant factor in improving the supply situation for troops now north and east of the river. But by now many roads everywhere in east-central Korea were impassable because of mud. During the last week of February the Air Force was called on for an unusually large number of airdrops of supplies. There was no other way they could be brought into the high mountain country, with streams overflowing banks, bridges out, fords too deep, and every trail a slithering path of mud.[39]

Does an individual sometimes make the difference in battle? Certainly – in fact, commonly so. A convincing example is provided by the action of Cpl. Einar H. Ingman, E Company, 17th Infantry Regiment, 7th Infantry Division, on 26 February. In Operation Killer, then nearing its end, the 7th Division, it will be recalled, was to attack north on the right flank along the Pyongchang-Champyong axis, and upon reaching Pangnim-ni, it was to turn west at the road junction on the Saemal-Hoengsong road. The little village of Maltari is about three road miles west of the road junction. Sharp hills come down to the road from both sides. The two leading squads of the assault platoon of E Company attacked a strongly held ridge but were almost immediately pinned down by heavy automatic fire that wounded both squad leaders and several other men. Ingman assumed command of the two squads, reorganized and combined them, and led them in continuing the attack. He located an enemy machine gun that was firing on his men. He charged it alone, threw a grenade into the position, and then killed the remaining crew members with rifle fire. A second enemy machine gun only 15 yards away fired on his squad, inflicting casualties and stopping it. Ingman now charged this gun position and was hit by grenade fragments and small-arms fire. He was wounded about the face and neck and knocked to the ground. With remarkable stamina and courage he rose from the ground and, using only his rifle, killed the entire machine-gun crew before he fell unconscious from his wounds. His men secured the ridge position, as more than a hundred enemy troops abandoned their weapons and fled.[40]

In the midst of Operation Killer, on 24 February, IX Corps lost its commander, Maj. Gen. Bryant E. Moore, who had commanded it for only 12 days. On 25 February, Colonel Conley, the Eighth Army G-1, gave General Ridgway a memorandum that described the death of General Moore. Conley's memorandum said that General Moore's helicopter was flying low over the Han River near Yoju, close to the 24th Infantry Division CP, when, at 10:30 A.M., 24 February, its rotor blade hit an unseen cable. The helicopter flipped over and fell into shallow water at the edge of the river. Some troops nearby helped General Moore out of the helicopter. He seemed at that time to have suffered only a twisted knee. Moore took a hot bath, seemed uninjured, and telephoned his corps headquarters at 10:45 A.M. He died 15 minutes later in the van of Brig. Gen. H. J. D. Myers, 24th Division artillery commander. A coronary thrombosis caused his death. A teletype message from IX Corps to Eighth Army at 5 A.M., 25 February, added a detail or two. It said a tractor pulled Moore's helicopter to shore when it fell into the Han River, that Moore bathed, pulled a blanket around himself, had hot coffee, and collapsed in General Myers's van at 11:05 A.M. Moore was highly esteemed by those who knew him. He was a veteran of

World War II in both the Pacific and European theaters. He was quiet and self-effacing but very competent. The 56-year-old officer had commanded the 164th Infantry Regiment of the Americal Division at Guadalcanal, and the 8th Infantry Division at the Rhine in Europe. He had also served as superintendent of West Point just prior to being sent to Korea.[41]

The Department of the Army called Maj. Gen. William M. Hoge, of Remagen Bridge fame in the European theater of World War II, to succeed Moore. But for the immediate future and until Hoge's arrival, Maj. Gen. Oliver P. Smith, commander of the 1st Marine Division, assumed command of IX Corps, and Brig. Gen. Lewis B. Puller, assistant division commander of the 1st Marine Division, assumed command of the Marine division.

On the same day as General Moore's death, 24 February, General Ridgway sent a private letter to Gen. Wade H. Haislip, vice chief of staff, US Army. Ridgway wrote of the limits of his intelligence about the enemy in Korea and reiterated his concept of his mission and purpose.

We have a curtain beyond the range of our immediate combat intelligence activities which I find extremely difficult to pierce. The location, strength, composition, status of supply and equipment, morale, and intentions of the major groups of hostile forces reported to be in Korea, presently outside of the immediate combat zone, but capable of intervening in a matter of days, remain largely undetermined.

Since assuming command, I have given but one truly basic directive to this army. . . . That directive seeks the objective of the maximum destruction of hostile forces and the maximum conservation of our own. Terrain, except as a weapon to facilitate the attainment of this objective, has no significance to me. General MacArthur has fully approved.

I believe that nothing short of Divine guidance could have brought us results so far achieved. I have implicit faith in its continuance.[42]

The same day, Ridgway confided to his personal papers a memorandum for record, expressing his surprise at General MacArthur's behavior on 20 February in a press conference MacArthur called when he visited the X Corps Tactical CP at Wonju. This was the day before Operation Killer was to jump off, and the operation had been considered a matter of utmost secrecy. General MacArthur and his staff in Tokyo had had no part in conceiving or planning the operation. Yet, in the press conference, General MacArthur said, "I have just ordered a resumption of the initiative." Ridgway stated, "Operation Killer was planned by me on Sunday evening 18 February." He had briefed the commanding generals of the IX and X corps and the 1st Marine Division the next day and had ordered it executed not later than 21 February. This episode, on MacArthur's third visit to Korea since Ridgway had taken command of Eighth Army, alerted Ridgway to the fact that General MacArthur had not lost his interest in being in the limelight when a promising military operation was about to take place.[43]

On 24 February General Ridgway finally received from Colonel Tarkenton of Eighth Army staff an answer to his question in mid-January about the ROK II Corps. He had asked, "Which divisions do we consider as destroyed?" Tarkenton's answer was, "None completely destroyed. The combat effectiveness of the corps is not more than 20%." He listed the divisions' estimated strength as follows:[44]

2nd Division	2,500
9th Division	1,700
10th Division	2,100
27th Division	1,300
31st Division	3,300
	10,900

Fighting flared at given points during the last week of February in Operation Killer, although it was not general throughout the zone. On 23 February the rain stopped before dawn, and the day cleared enough to allow the Air Force to take to the air. In the Chipyong-ni area the 2nd Battalion, 5th Cavalry Regiment, finally took Hill 467 after previous stubborn resistance from the Chinese defenders. Seven air strikes using 250-pound and 500-pound VT fuse bombs, and artillery concentrations, in the afternoon broke the enemy's spirit. B Company, attached to the 2nd Battalion, was the first attacking unit to gain the crest. G Company followed, and the hill was secured by 4:45 P.M. In one episode during the almost continuous air strikes, approximately 500 enemy came off the hill to the paddy ground on the north side of the hill, seeking some safety from the strikes. But a 500-pound VT fragmentation bomb exploded directly over them. Colonel Crombez, speaking of the fight for Hill 469, said, "Infantry must follow close behind air strikes and artillery barrages. The infantry must have the determination to close for the final kill."[45]

After capturing the hill, a patrol from F Company, 5th Cavalry, found large amounts of supplies there, including 15 cases of 81-mm mortar shells, 5 cases of 60-mm mortar shells, 6,000 rounds of M-1 rifle ammunition, several rounds of US 3.5-inch and 2.36-inch rockets, 2 cases of Chinese grenades, 20 boxes of mines, and 439 bags of husked rice.

At the end of the month Eighth Army was testing a piece of new equipment. Five armored vests were sent to each division and two to each corps and were to be worn in combat. The vests weighed 14 pounds and were designed to protect the torso against shell fragments and small arms. General Ridgway had also asked for life belts for patrols crossing rivers. He obtained ten for each rifle company.

In the course of Operation Killer, the 1st Marine Division attacked from Wonju toward Hoengsong. On 23 February it reached Hoengsong, and press dispatches from correspondents with them were filed on the twenty-seventh telling of some of the grisly spectacles to be seen in the destroyed town and along the road between Wonju and Hoengsong, dating from the CCF 4th Phase Offensive of 11–14 February. Worse was to come when the 1st Marine Division entered the Massacre Valley area north of Hoengsong in the first days of March.[46]

What might reasonably be considered to be a representative viewpoint of the Chinese soldiers in late February is disclosed in the translation of some entries in a Chinese notebook captured in the IX Corps zone and received at Eighth Army on 26 February.

Difficulties: Roads coated with ice and slippery. Soldiers exhausted from night marches. In day cannot sleep because of air strikes. Because of shortage of winter boots almost all soldiers suffer frost bite. Have to cross rivers in uniform in combat – severe frost bite. Lack ammunition, and food critical. Physical condition of soldiers getting worse, heavy burdens in mountains. Reconnaissance at night difficult because of language.

Morale: Unbearable labor carrying heavy equipment on backs in Mts. Air strikes frighten worst. Conviction win the war is wavering. Wonder if ever return home. Not as willing to fight in S. Korea as in N. Korea. Most soldiers not informed of present unfavorable conditions.[47]

As Operation Killer drew to a close, there was a sharp counterattack by the NK 6th Division against the ROK 3rd Division on the eastern front, which probably was made to help the NK 12th Division escape northward.[48] Even though Operation Killer, for all practical purposes, was ended by 28 February, it was necessary to continue a form of offensive to keep the enemy off balance and to prevent further strong counterattack. Eighth Army planned that the IX and X corps would continue to advance toward the 38th Parallel in their zones, and in the west the I and IX corps would threaten Seoul from the east and try to seize the area north of it as far as the Imjin River. The plan to do this was called Operation Ripper. It was to be issued 1 March.

With the heavy action in the central and east-central corridor of Korea during February 1951 now easing and the Chinese 4th Phase Offensive defeated, it is necessary to turn back to the western part of Korea to follow what had happened along the lower Han River and in the Seoul area.

13

Eighth Army's Crossing of the Han and Capture of Seoul

WHILE FURIOUS BATTLES of the Chinese 4th Phase Offensive characterized the central front during the middle part of February 1951 – in Hoengsong, Chipyong-ni, and Wonju – the western part of Eighth Army front remained generally quiet. The western part of the line in the I Corps sector had already reached the south bank of the Han River, and the troops there looked across the river to Seoul. On the right, the line east of Seoul to Yangpyong had only limited and sporadic action. But in this area the Chinese still had a bridgehead south of the Han River.

In the I Corps sector opposite Seoul and west to Inchon and the Yellow Sea, the first part of February was characterized by frequent exchanges of tank and artillery fire across the river from the Eighth Army positions and mortar and artillery fire from the Chinese and North Koreans. At this time, ROK patrols from the ROK 1st Division that crossed into Seoul were driven back by enemy action, but enough intelligence was obtained to inform the UN command that Seoul was full of troops, and there was no indication that the enemy was abandoning the city. Enemy strength in Seoul in the first part of February consisted of 18,000 men of the CCF 50th Army that had recrossed to the north side of the river and another 19,000 to 20,000 soldiers of the NK 8th and 47th infantry divisions, and the 17th Mechanized Division. Between 37,000 and 38,000 enemy soldiers, therefore, about half of them CCF, still defended Seoul. The enemy bridgehead south of the river and eastward to Yangpyong and the bend of the Han, eight air miles west of Chipyong-ni, would have to be eliminated before Eighth Army could undertake a river crossing. And also, no crossing of the Han in the Seoul area would be feasible until the Chinese and North Korean offensive in the central corridor had been defeated and turned back. Preceding chapters have shown that this objective was accomplished by early March.

In following the ground action in Korea at this time, one may be tempted to forget the considerable contribution that naval and air action made to success on the ground. To do so would give a distorted picture. Before proceeding with an account of the elimination of the enemy bridgehead south of the Han River in the west, some attention must be given to the naval situation on both coasts, to air interdiction efforts that slowed enemy resupply to the front from Manchuria and Siberia, and to air resupply of Eighth Army units in the mountainous regions of the central and eastern sectors. Also, the active guerrilla situation in the Eighth Army rear must be mentioned.

Naval forces were active, in cooperation with ground forces, in the reoccupation of Inchon, the most important port on the west coast of Korea. The battleship *Missouri* and other naval forces bombarded enemy positions around Inchon on 9 February and simulated a landing in the area. Chinese and North Korean forces in the area abandoned the immediate coastal area there, and during the afternoon of 10 February a force of ROK Marines from the island of Tokchok-to, in the Yellow Sea approach to Inchon, landed and occupied Inchon. Simultaneously, Eighth Army troops arrived on the south bank of the Han.[1]

At the same time in February on the east coast, the Navy concentrated on the bombardment of Wonsan and the capture of islands in the harbor. ROK marine troops occupied many of the islands in Wonsan harbor and elsewhere at strategic points on the northeastern coast of Korea under cover of US naval bombardment. Some of these islands, such as Yo-do and Ung-do, guarded the entrance to Wonsan harbor. These actions forced the Chinese and North Koreans to keep large enemy infantry and artillery forces at Wonsan and in its vicinity to protect against a threatened amphibious landing there, although with each passing month more fieldworks and enemy fortifications in the Wonsan area increased the difficulty and risk of any landing there. On 12 February minesweepers entered Wonsan harbor to check the channel. US destroyers four days later entered the harbor and bombarded Wonsan. On 18 February, enemy artillery fire from Sin-do island hit the destroyer *Ozbourn*. This brought an air strike from naval Task Force 77, and a naval bombardment of the island the next day and an amphibious assault force landing of 110 ROK Marines. After a two-hour naval bombardment of the island, under aerial observation, the ROK Marines landed on the island unopposed and secured it.[2]

During January and February, with increasing movement of ammunition, weapons, and general supply to the front lines in east and east-central Korea, there was a large increase of rail traffic from the Chinese border over the Hoeryong-to-Wonsan railroad. Hoeryong was a key transportation center at the Chinese border, with rail connections to the Soviet Union. This very important supply line from the border to the front line ran south 50 air miles to Chongjin, on the Sea of Japan, and then followed the coastal line south and southwest to Hungnam and Wonsan. At some places the rail line bent inland some miles, but for long distances it followed closely the coast line to avoid the high mountains that generally came down precipitously to the Sea of Japan. There were repeated aerial and other intelligence reports of heavy movement of traffic on the Hoeryong-Wonsan rail line. Because of the mountainous terrain traversed by this rail line, there were numerous tunnels and bridges on it. On 15 February General Stratemeyer requested Admiral Joy to use naval air power to help the Fifth Air Force Bomber Command interdict this rail line, concentrating on bridges and tunnels. Admiral Joy agreed to use 7th Fleet carrier planes for ten days in a concentrated attack on the Hoeryong-Wonsan railroad.

On 20 February Admiral Joy had a list of rail and highway bridges and tunnels on the east coast that would be within range of naval gunfire and naval air attack. There were many targets in the Wonsan area; 23 were north near Kyongsan Man, and 25 south of Songjin. The battleship *Missouri* had by now returned from the Inchon area to the east coast, and it began shelling the double river multiple bridges at Tanchon, about 20 air miles south of Songjin. This bombardment continued on 22 and 23 February, breaking down these overwater bridges. Meantime, the fast carrier planes struck at rail interdiction. This effort had been planned to end on 25 February, but it was extended indefinitely. Naval Task Force 77, in effect, took over responsibility for continued interdiction in northeast Korea, while the B-29s of the Fifth Air Force Bomber Command assumed the same responsibility for northwest Korea.[3]

UN air control of the skies declined in January and February over northwest Korea below the Yalu. American planes had to fly from bases too far from the target area, and the number of MiG fighters increased in number, flying from Antung, just across the Manchurian border from Sinuiju. Successful attacks on Pyongyang airfield and at Sinuiju, however, were made on 23 January. But the Fifth Air Force avoided air combat over northwest Korea generally during February. In the area between the Yalu and Chongchon rivers, it was usually not profitable. The enemy MiGs came to dominate that region, and it soon was called MiG Alley, a name that stuck through the remainder of the Korean War. During this time the enemy had large labor contingents busy repairing and improving their airfields in North Korea at Sinuiju, Sinanju, Sunan, Pyongyang, Yonpo, Wonsan, Ongjin, Sinmak, and Kangdong.[4]

The Fifth Air Force also was a vital factor in keeping X Corps and the ROK III Corps troops resupplied with ammunition, food, medical supplies, and clothing during February in the mountainous central corridor and eastern Korea. Late February was a period of heavy rains and melting snows in this region, and vehicular transport could not keep the front supplied. Airdrops and hand carry from the drop sites was the order of the day in many places. As an example of the magnitude of the air effort in resupply of the combat troops, between 23 and 28 February the 314th Troop Carrier Group dropped 256 C-119 loads of supplies, amounting to 1,358 tons, to ground troops in the central corridor north of Wonju.[5]

Behind the lines, especially in the Andong area of South Korea, 75 air miles southeast of Wonju, an estimated 15,000 to 18,000 guerrillas fought repeated small-unit actions to disrupt rail and road transportation of supplies to the Eighth Army central front, often with considerable success. All trains had to have guards. The 1st Marine Division for many weeks was committed to this area to check traffic disruptions and, if possible, to destroy or scatter the guerrilla forces. The Marines succeeded in destroying some of the guerrilla bands, but when the division was hurriedly moved north in mid-February to the Wonju area to join an attack northward, many thousands of guerrillas still remained active in Eighth Army rear areas. South Korean National Police now took over the task of reducing guerrilla activity behind Eighth Army lines where their activity was most troublesome. It was never wholly suppressed.

During the night of 13–14 February, the 81st Regiment, NK 8th Division, crossed the Han River and infiltrated deeply behind the US 3rd Infantry Division opposite Seoul, some of them almost reaching Suwon. Most of this enemy force was behind the US 65th Infantry and the 3rd Division CPs by dawn of 14 February. The 3rd Division mounted an all-out attack during the day. The 2nd Battalion, 65th Infantry, and the 1st and 3rd battalion, 15th Infantry, engaged the enemy between 10 A.M. and 5 P.M., as did elements of the 7th Infantry Regiment. The 81st NK Regiment was all but annihilated during the day. The Eighth Army Command Report claimed that the 3rd Division killed 1,152 by count and captured 353. The G-2 Section of the army gave a somewhat different figure of enemy casualties, estimating that 200 prisoners were taken and the rest killed or driven back north across the river. Aerial observers late in the afternoon estimated that about 300 survivors of this enemy force crossed back to the north side of the Han. This attack, apparently designed as a diversion at the time the attack on Chipyong-ni was in progress, accomplished only its own destruction.[6]

In this fighting on 14 February, Cpl. Albert V. Erickson, C Company, 7th Infantry Regiment, won the Distinguished Service Cross for saving a squad of the 1st Battalion from probable destruction when a numerically superior force of the infiltrating 81st NK Regiment attacked. The squad, on outpost duty, was brought under heavy fire, which wounded all but one member. It started to withdraw and was about to be cut off when Erickson, in the perimeter, saw its difficulty. Although under enemy attack himself, Erickson shifted his line of fire from his own protection to cover the withdrawal of the outpost squad, which got out safely. In this exchange, enemy fire hit and mortally wounded Corporal Erickson.[7]

During the night of 14–15 February the 445th Regiment of the 149th CCF Division, 50th Army, waded the Han to the south side to help survivors of the NK 81st Regiment. This activity resulted in some sharp engagements on the fifteenth with the 2nd Battalion, 15th Regiment, 3rd Division. Elements of E, F, and G companies, with tank support, drove the Chinese from their strongpoint, Hill 87. In withdrawing toward the river, the Chinese came under tank crossfire that resulted in a slaughter. In this fight the 2nd Battalion took 9 Chinese prisoners and killed 266. The prisoners said the 445th Regiment had waded the Han the night before to help the NK 81st Regiment.[8]

By the middle of February, both Chinese and North Korean prisoners reported that most of their units had 20 percent casualties from frostbite and that there were many cases of stomach ailments. The North Koreans also reported that typhoid was rampant in many units.[9]

On 14 February, Eighth Army gave control of and responsibility for the Han River corridor above the big bend to the US IX Corps. Eighth Army intelligence now stated that all three divisions (the 124th, 125th, and 126th) of the CCF 42nd Army, the 120th Division of the 40th Army; and the 197th and 198th divisions of the CCF 66th Army—six in all—had been identified as being in the central corridor zone.

It is of interest that Radio Peking, in a broadcast on 14 February, celebrated the first anniversary of the "Sino-Soviet Treaty of Friendship and Alliance and Mutual Assistance." It quoted Chou En-lai as writing in an article for publication in *Pravda* that "in the event of one of the contracting parties being attacked by Japan or states allied with it and thus being involved in a state of war, the other contracting party will immediately render military and other assistance with all means at its disposal."[10] This statement seemed to be a threat to the UN and its forces in Korea that the Soviet Union might intervene in the Korean War.

On 15 February Maj. Gen. John B. Coulter, long the commander of the US IX Corps, was promoted to lieutenant general and transferred to Eighth Army headquarters, with assignment to the army liaison office in Pusan, to be near the South Korean government offices and President Syngman Rhee.[11] At the same time, Col. George B. Peploe was promoted to brigadier general. This able commander of the 38th Regiment of the US 2nd Division became chief of staff, IX Corps. Another proven combat commander, Col. John H. Michaelis, commander of the 27th (Wolfhound) Regiment, 25th Division, was transferred to the division headquarters and on 26 February became assistant division commander.

Coincident with these changes in personnel ranks and duties, I Corps closed its CP at Suwon at 2 P.M., 15 February, and opened it at a point eastward, just north of Kumyangjang-ni. General Ridgway, who had maintained his small Advance Tactical CP with I Corps at Chonan and subsequently at Suwon, was planning to establish his CP at Yoju. When I Corps moved its CP near Kumyangjang-ni, the 25th Infantry Division relieved the 1st Cavalry Division, and the latter moved east to the Chipyong-ni area, then held by the US 2nd Division of X Corps.[12] The enemy offensive in mid-February in the central corridor caused these shifts in division and corps positions.

On 15 February the 2nd Engineer Special Brigade moved from Pusan to Inchon to start the tremendous work of reopening that port. The next day a force of ROK Marines landed at Inchon to provide security in the port area. Inchon was used in only a limited way for logistic purposes in February. The Eighth Army G-4 advised General Ridgway that the army did not need to use the port for bringing in supplies to support planned tactical operations in the near future and that no more than two days of supplies should be accumulated there because, with the heavy daily tidal variations, supplies could not be quickly evacuated. General Ridgway at first allowed only one day's supply to be held at Inchon. Just as Inchon was reoccupied by Eighth Army, the first train to arrive at Suwon from the south came in on the sixteenth. Supply by air remained the major source of maintaining the Suwon area army front for some time, however, as from 10 to 160 planeloads of rations and lubricants arrived there daily. The 25th Division closed out of its positions on the south bank of the Han River opposite Seoul on 16 February and moved eastward. The 3rd Division now held the river line opposite Seoul, with the ROK 1st Division extending west from its boundary to Inchon and the Han estuary.[13]

Although the 3rd Division reported that an estimated 3,000 to 4,000 enemy remained in its sector south of the Han River, there was increasing evidence that the enemy in I Corps's zone was withdrawing to the north side of the Han. Only near the big bend of the river near Yangpyong, in front of the 24th Division in IX Corps, did the enemy seem strong and intent on giving no ground. A little farther east in the Chipyong-ni area, there were still strong Chinese forces all around that site of recent heavy battle. UN progress was slow anywhere only a few miles from the town.[14]

By the third week of February it was well known in X Corps and elsewhere in the army that the heavy battles of mid-February in the central corridor had resulted in very heavy enemy casualties and that the CCF 4th Phase Offensive had thus far failed in its objectives. A British correspondent, Arthur Moore, who had just come from Peking, reported from New Delhi, India, that Manchurian hospitals had been unable to care for the Chinese wounded and that Peking and Tientsin were drained of gasoline. He said, "The war in Korea . . . is already somewhat of a surprise to the Chinese. . . . Casualties are much greater than they anticipated. Hospitals in Peiping are heavily denuded of their nursing staffs, as they have gone to the front."[15] Arthur Moore was believed to have been the only non-Communist correspondent allowed to enter the Chinese capital since the

Chinese entrance into the Korean War. He wrote his dispatch datelined "at sea off the China coast," after his departure from China.

Patrols on the right flank of I Corps south of the Han River on 18 February reported no enemy contact during the night of the seventeenth, and it appeared that enemy in front of their sector had withdrawn across the river during the night. But one large group of enemy was known to be still in front of the 3rd Division.

On the left flank of IX Corps, Lt. Col. Gines Perez, commander of the 21st Infantry (Col. Richard Stephens of the regiment had recently rotated to Japan), had his regiment astride the Han River in a blocking position, with the 2nd Battalion east of the river. On 18–19 February, the 21st Infantry made a limited-objective attack to the bend of the Han, near Yangpyong. The next day it crossed to the east side of the Han, relieved the 8th Cavalry Regiment there, and sent out patrols to establish contact with the enemy.[16]

On 20 February, line crossers reported to General Almond that enemy troops in front of his X Corps were withdrawing to the north and west. Ridgway ordered the X Corps to attack to its east to cut off North Korean forces in a deep salient there.[17] The next day the 5th RCT reached the Han River. West of Seoul, Eighth Army ordered the 3rd Battalion, 35th Infantry, 25th Division, to relieve the Turkish Brigade at Ascom City and to assume responsibility for patrolling the Kimpo peninsula on the south side of the Han River estuary.[18]

On 20 February the 3rd Battalion, 15th Regiment, 3rd Division, received authority to send patrols across the Han. A patrol crossed the river but was driven back by enemy fire. Intelligence agents in Seoul reported to I Corps on this day that Chinese troops in the city had withdrawn from Seoul two or three days earlier to the vicinity of Uijongbu but that, outside the city, enemy positions still defended the north bank of the river. Large Chinese 120-mm mortars on the north bank still fired into the 3rd Division zone on the south side.

In I Corps zone, however, by 21 February there were no organized groups of enemy south of the Han River. On the north bank of the Han, Korean civilians jammed all the villages along the river on the approaches to Seoul, getting ready to reenter the city. There were some North Korean soldiers in these groups trying to rejoin their military units. On 26 February a 3rd Battalion patrol from the 15th Infantry captured a North Korean soldier on the north bank. A Chinese captain from the 38th Army said the Fourth Field Army was to protect the Han River line at all costs, except for the city of Seoul. The city was to be abandoned. He said the Chinese armies that had engaged in the Chosin Reservoir campaign in November and December 1950 and that had been reorganizing and reequipping in the Hungnam-Wonsan area since then were now ready to reenter combat and

were prepared to execute a wide envelopment move around Eighth Army
if the UN forces tried to encircle the Chinese Fourth Field Army divisions
north of the Han River and eastward as far as Hongchon. Another prisoner report said that one of these armies, the 26th, had already relieved
part of the 38th Army at the left flank of the central front. And a document captured at Wonju referred to the 20th CCF Army. Other reports
placed the 24th Army of the Third Field Army at Chorwon. Taken together, these reports indicated that the Third Field Army was beginning
to arrive at the central front from the Wonsan area.[19]

Intelligence from many sources, agents, escapees, and Korean civilians,
on or about 20 February, reported that Seoul was being evacuated but that
large enemy forces were assembled about a day's march north of the Han
River and Eighth Army. The Far East Command intelligence report at
this time concluded that the enemy feared the UN might undertake amphibious landings simultaneously on the west coast at Chinnampo and at
the Hamhung-Wonsan areas of the east coast, behind their front lines, remi-
niscent of the Inchon landing in September behind the North Korean lines.
Strong enemy forces within fieldworks had been held in both places to meet
any such threat.[20]

For its part, Eighth Army on 20 February ordered the ROK 8th Division, which had been all but destroyed at Hoengsong on 11 February, to
assemble at Taegu for reorganization and reequipping. On 17 February
the division had been reported as having 4,400 men. But apparently some
of its fragmented remains had been used to form two provisional battalions,
which were placed on line between the ROK 5th and 3rd divisions, for
on 21 February the three regiments of the division together had only about
2,500 men. It was expected it would be a month before the division could
once again be ready for duty.[21]

By 22 February the enemy's heaviest concentration seemed to be in the
Yangpyong-Piryong area at the bend of the Han River and just east of it.
From there the Chinese defense line ran east to Hoengsong. At Hoengsong there seemed to be a boundary between Chinese and North Korean
troops, with the latter east of Hoengsong on to the coast.[22]

At noon on 21 February the weather intervened in operations all across
the front. It began to rain, and the downpour continued through the afternoon and the night. Aerial observation stopped. Most units remained where
they were. By morning of the twenty-second, water was rising in the Han
River and all its tributaries. Ford crossings were unusable. The Han River
rose from 22 to 32 inches in a day and was getting higher. Most roads near
the river had washed out. Supply traffic virtually stopped across the front.
Melting snow made matters worse. There were washouts, bridge collapses,
and tunnel cave-ins on the railroads. Traffic on the Andong rail line had
to be suspended. From 22 to 24 February the rain continued intermittently.
Supplies were moved in some cases by oxen and horses, but mostly it was

hand and back carry. Everyone was miserable. It was so bad that K Company of the 5th Cavalry Regiment took prisoners a Chinese platoon leader and his 28 shivering men who had been flooded out of their foxholes.[23]

The roads in mountainous central and east Korea in the best of times often quickly degenerated into trails. The UN forces by now had learned in that terrain that only human carriers could be depended on to get food and ammunition resupplies to the sharp ridges and the high peaks. Both sides fought for the high ground, and once obtained they defended it. Vehicles became all but useless, and it became necessary to use large numbers of Korean civilian carriers. In mid-February, for instance, the 19th Infantry Regiment of the 24th Division employed 1,000 such laborers and carriers. They were divided into groups of 200, each with a Korean leader, who then selected section leaders, mess personnel, and a supply clerk. These groups functioned as a unit. They assembled at the battalion supply officer's section, who put a noncommissioned officer in charge of each group. Each battalion had about 300 of the Korean laborers and carriers assigned to it. The usual practice was for 100 of them to work while the other 200 rested, and then they rotated on the work assignments. Sometimes, in a bad situation the parties might work three days, nine hours a day, without rest. Two pounds of rice was allocated daily for each worker. It was common for anyone climbing to a forward platoon or company position by trail to meet one of the parties coming or going, and often join them for the trip. The carrier parties were unarmed.[24]

During 1951, most American units had these Korean civilian labor and carrier groups, in varying numbers, depending on the terrain they were fighting in and the circumstances of their mission. A Korean man with a gee-ga, a wooden backpack common all over Korea, can carry 100 to 150 pounds at one and a half miles an hour across country for ten hours a day. An ox can carry, in grasspack saddles, one-half its weight, about 500 to 600 pounds, at one mile an hour up to eight or ten hours a day for periods up to 30 days before it needs rest. But when the UN and ROK Army institutionalized the carrier companies, they did not impose such a grueling daily performance requirement on the Korean carriers. The North Korean Army also made use of human carriers extensively throughout the war close to the front.

The 1st and 2nd ROK Army replacement centers, with confirmation from the Korean officers at the Ground General School and KMAG Headquarters at Seoul, agreed on the capability of the average Korean carrier as being 60 pounds for a distance of 15 miles in one working day or night, or 900 pound-miles. Horse- or ox-drawn carts usually transported 1,000 to 2,000 pounds a distance of 10 to 12 miles, depending on terrain and the conditions of roads.[25]

Systematic procurement of civilian labor for use in forward areas was undertaken by the EUSAK Civil Assistance Section. It was agreed that

carrier companies under the supervision of the EUSAK transportation officer should be formed. The Civilian Transport Corps (CTC) was formed,
initially to be organized in 82 carrier companies of 240 men each—a total
of 19,680 men. Within each company, 24 men were involved in administrative overhead and 216 were carriers, each capable of carrying 50 pounds
for ten miles a day. At first, most of the personnel for these companies were
drawn from the Korean National Defense Corps.

American regiments soon came to depend on the energy and loyalty with
which these carrier companies worked with them, and when the division
had to move to another front, they wanted the same carrier companies
transferred with them. Another Korean carrier regiment just would not
do. Troops on the defensive lines, and especially those on high ridges and
peaks, often gave their verbal or silent thanks to the Korean carriers for
bringing them food and weapons and ammunition needed to hold their
positions. This civilian carrier service began in March 1951. By November of that year Eighth Army stated, "Military operations in Korea could
not continue one day without the indigenous labor effort."[26] This depen-
dence was due in large part to the fact that, in the previous nine months,
the army had changed by the type of fighting required; it became a ridge-
and hill-climbing force that sought to hold the high ground, often miles
from the nearest vehicular road or trail.

The use of American artillery increased in the late winter of 1950–51
and the spring of 1951, both in number of pieces and the type of ammunition used. On 21 February 1951 a memorandum to the ordnance officer
of IX Corps covered the use of the VT fuse (vicinity time, or variable fuse
proximity detonation) in high-explosive shells. It contained a type of minia-
ture radar in the nose which was set to explode the shell at a certain distance above the ground and to scatter sharp steel fragments below. It was
so sensitive that often one could see shell bursts in the sky when such a
VT fuse was triggered by a cloud that was in or near the course of the
shell's trajectory. On one occasion the author saw so many of them at one
time in the Bloody Ridge area of eastern Korea that they looked like puffs
from exploding antiaircraft artillery shells. But the VT fuse shell was deadly
to troops on the ground. On 19 February the IX Corps issued a directive
to its artillery battalions that they must use the VT in 50 percent of their
basic loads. The directive said its use would increase the firepower of the
corps by a factor of five. It defined "firepower" as the total number of high
velocity fragments over a given area. The VT fuse gave the most effective
use of high-explosive shell fragments against prone, standing, or entrenched
enemy personnel, especially in the rough Korean terrain. It was estimated
that the VT fuse projectile was ten times more effective against entrenched
enemy than an impact shell.[27]

In mid-February the IX Corps, near the bend of the Han River, was

South Korean porters in the CTC carry food and ammunition to a Marine regiment on a mountainous position in central Korea. *US Marine photograph, A 9857*

up against the CCF 38th Army, which undoubtedly received many of the VT fuse shells. This army had been a crack enemy organization since the CCF intervention in October 1950. A Chinese soldier captured on 20 February stated he had heard a political officer say that the 38th Army was no longer combat effective because of casualties and that it was being replaced by the CCF 26th Army.[28]

At this time many reports came to Eighth Army of a typhoid epidemic that was ravaging enemy units, especially North Korean, and one American unit moved its bivouac area because of a rumor that typhoid had appeared in a nearby village. One agent reported that he had seen signs posted on nearly every village behind the enemy lines between Uijongbu and Kumhwa reading, "Do not enter—epidemic." But there were also other agent reports ominous for the future, indicating that the enemy was bringing to the front large numbers of artillery pieces. One agent reported he had seen an enemy formation of 20,000 men, with 20 large artillery pieces drawn by teams of eight horses, and about 100 other smaller artillery pieces, also horse drawn on the road to Kumhwa. This same large formation included 80 truckloads of ammunition and many horse-drawn carts or wagons of ammunition. A civilian laborer agent said it was the CCF 14th Field Artillery [CCF 2nd Field Artillery Army]. The identity of this huge artillery force was not definitely known at the time. It was new to the Korean War.[29]

If the UN forces had difficulties, so did the Chinese and North Koreans. The Chinese faced the same terrain and weather, and by many accounts suffered more from these factors than did the Americans because the latter had better clothing and shoes, doctors and medical facilities, food, and shelter. And the UN troops did not have to be in hourly fear during daylight of tons of napalm, rockets, and endless strafing, and a mass of mortar and artillery shells falling in their midst, guided to the target by aerial observers.

The aerial attacks were most feared by the enemy forces, and they went to endless trouble to avoid their worst effect. A few examples that occurred in February will illustrate. On 22 February Mosquito planes working with the US 25th Division east of Seoul brought in 11 flights of fighter planes through an overcast sky to attack enemy troops and destroyed about 1,000 of them. Three days later other Mosquito planes located large bodies of enemy dug in west of Hoengsong. One enemy battalion held up the entire ROK 6th Division. The Mosquito pilot called for seven flights of fighter-bombers at 45-minute intervals. After the last flight had left, a conservative estimate reported 200 enemy had been killed and 300 wounded. And during a three-day period between 24 and 26 February, 15 Mosquito missions assigned to the US 7th Division in the eastern mountains greatly helped that division in taking Pyongchang, its objective.[30] It was much the same elsewhere.

The CCF 38th Army, one of the best-trained armies of the Fourth Field Army and boasting an enviable combat record in the Chinese civil war, was in the first large formations of CCF to intervene in October 1950 in the Korean War. It had been in the midst of every Chinese campaign in Korea thereafter. In February 1951 its remnants were at the hinge of the UN line in the vicinity of the big bend of the Han River and the enemy concentration and assembly area there around Yangpyong. It had had nearly four months' experience with UN air power in Korea and possessed a realistic awareness of its deadly effect on troops. The CCF 112th Division of the 38th Army issued a directive, in February apparently, a copy of which was captured and translated in full for UN units' information.

Its provisions demonstrate the seriousness of air-defense measures for the Chinese. Among its strictures to troops were the following:

1. Morning meal must be cooked before dawn (0600). All personnel must be up by 0600. At 0630, eat breakfast. All must be in the air-raid shelter by 0700. At 1700, all units will move out from the shelter, and the mess details should immediately start cooking. During rainy weather, or under enemy air-attack, the schedule can be altered; and the personnel be so divided that half can take shelter in the village houses and the other half hide in the open area.

2. In the day time, all fires of any kind must be strictly prohibited. At night, all windows will be closed and especially windows of kitchens and offices will at least be curtained with straw mats if the windows are not provided with blackout cloth.

3. All units must provide air observation posts so that the sentry, upon spotting or hearing any enemy aircraft approaching, will blow alarm whistles. Thus all personnel who are not on essential duty can take shelters in the holes and even those on essential duty can be relieved to hide and remain motionless. . . .

4. All individuals will carry their weapon and ammo as well as other equipment whenever they take shelters in the holes. . . .

5. [Measures to be taken to hide and camouflage horses]

6. Those going outdoors for business will all be camouflaged, and all the guards will have authority to stop any non-camouflaged person.

7. In the daytime, large-scale hauling of equipment or food stuffs will be restricted.

8. Anti-aircraft firing positions should be set upon well selected points (equipped with light or heavy machine guns). When our anti-aircraft positions are discovered by enemy aircraft and are strafed, they must return the fire immediately with determined resistance. . . .

10. Make [civilians] understand that one individual carelessness can cause disaster to many and, further, that any defection by one household will invite devastation to the whole village. Therefore, everyone must cooperate to attain the best air-raid security.[31]

Because of the high waters of the Han River and the drowning out of ford crossings, the 1st Cavalry Division on 24 February requested amphibious tractors, or DUKWs, to get supplies to its troops east of the Han in the Chipyong-ni area. Two days later 20 DUKWs were attached to the division. Meanwhile on that day, 26 February, 36 C-119 Flying Boxcars dropped 20,000 gallons of gasoline and other supplies to these troops. Not surprising to many, examination of the Chinese dead that littered the hillsides east of the Han showed that they carried more entrenching tools than did American troops.[32]

A new and effective weapon, huge searchlights, now was introduced into the Korean War. On 25 February the 1st Provisional Searchlight Company was attached to I Corps for operational control. These searchlights illuminated the battle front at night. I Corps sent the first company to the 25th Division. The searchlights each had a 60-inch-wide reflector, were 14 feet, 2 inches tall, and weighed 9,000 pounds. Their light range was 35,000 yards. Each one had a crew of six men and required a truck and trailer to move it. The US 2nd Division first used searchlights for battle illumination on 12 April 1951. It became standard practice to issue six of them to a division, three to a front-line regiment. Before long, all infantry units were calling for them. They were especially desired at night in defensive positions. An object the size of a man could easily be seen at 100 yards, and it was learned that, when beamed at low clouds, they reflected the light back down and illuminated a large area.[33]

Maj. Gen. William B. Kean, commander of the 25th Division for three and a half years, was rotated on 25 February back to the United States, where he was to take command of the US III Corps at Camp Roberts, California. Kean had been an able and steady commander in Korea. Brig. Gen. J. Sladen Bradley succeeded him in command of the division.

The completion of a bridge across the Han River at Yoju on 25 February by the IX Corps Engineers promised relief in handling the logistics and supply problems for troops fighting east of the river, especially the 1st Cavalry Division, the British 27th Brigade, and the ROK 6th Division.

By the end of February it was apparent that enemy troops were leaving Seoul. Eighth Army planning for crossing the Han River to the north side had already begun. A feint to be executed early in March had been worked out and agents sent to the north bank to spread misinformation about it. Meanwhile, the US 25th Division began planning for the real crossing at the confluence of the Pukhan and Han rivers. I Corps had been overlooking the Han River now for two weeks.

There had been repeated reports near the end of February that at least two Chinese armies, the 24th and 26th of the Third Field Army, had moved to the central front from the Wonsan area, where they had been regrouping and reequipping after the Chosin Reservoir campaign of late November and December 1950. On 27 February Eighth Army intelligence finally accepted these armies as being in the Chorwon–Iron Triangle area, in reserve, ready for commitment to battle.[34] This enemy buildup of reserves centered on Kumhwa and Chorwon, where it was estimated that 33,000 troops, new to the central and western fronts, had assembled.

The six CCF divisions that had first entered Korea in October from Lin Piao's Fourth Field Army were beginning to show inevitable deterioration because of heavy casualties and the wear of winter weather and excessive fatigue. New formations were now necessary to keep the Chinese forces battle worthy. A Chinese captain, Zou Su Un, 378th Regiment, 126th Division, 42nd Army, captured on 25 February by the 8th Cavalry Regiment, said that the Chinese 38th Army had been reinforced three times because of continuing heavy casualties since October 1950 and that only 50 percent of the original troops remained. The other 50 percent were from the 163rd and 169th Independent Home Guard divisions in Manchuria. They had only basic training and no combat experience, he said.[35] Captain Zou stated that his own army, the 42nd, had 200 vehicles when it entered

the JCS requesting instructions before proceeding further. Until this determination had been made, the JCS are of the opinion that a decision to cross the 38th parallel or one to halt south of the line would be unsound, from the military point of view.

10. Any decision not to cross the 38th parallel, which is taken on the political level in consultation with other UN members, would inevitably result in disclosure to the enemy of this decision. Such a disclosure would permit the enemy to select his course of action based upon the known intentions of the UN ground forces and thus could jeopardize the military position of the UN in Korea.

11. In view of the above consideration, the JCS strongly recommend that the present military courses of action in Korea be continued at least until: . . .

12. Until this governmental decision (as to our future politico-military policy toward Korea) is reached there should be no change in that part of the directive to Gen. MacArthur which now permits him so to dispose his forces either north or south of the 38th parallel as best to provide for their security.

13. In light of all of the foregoing, the JCS strongly recommend that the draft memo on the subject of the 38th parallel, prepared by the Dept of State, not be submitted to the Pres; but instead that the Dept of State be urged to initiate action in accordance with paragraph 11 above.[38]

Perhaps nothing that happened on the field of battle in Korea in the first half of March hastened the approach of UN troops to the 38th Parallel as much as the crossing of the Han River on 7 March by the US 25th Division and the capture of Seoul on 16 March by the ROK 1st and the US 3rd divisions of I Corps. General Ridgway has stated that, once the CCF 4th Phase Offensive had been contained in February in the central corridor, he planned to move across the Han River in the Seoul area. He wrote, "I had planned this action personally on Sunday evening, February 18, . . . and had outlined it to the Commanding Generals of the US IX and X Corps and of the 1st Marine Division. It may be noted that this resumption of the offensive was the final implementation of the plan I had nourished from the time of my taking command of the Eighth Army – and had done so, it may be said, in the face of a retreat-psychology that seemed to have seized every commander from the Chief on down."[39]

Ridgway was not certain at the time whether the reported presence of four CCF armies at Pyongyang was indeed fact. If it were, then the Chinese had a very large force in reserve that could reinforce their frontline units in a few days. Ridgway's thinking was still dominated by the factors that had guided his actions thus far. He said, "It remained the infliction of maximum damage on the enemy with minimum to ourselves, the maintaining of all major units intact, and a careful avoidance of being sucked into an enemy trap – by ruse or as a result of our own aggressiveness – to be destroyed piecemeal. We were to pursue only to the point where we were still able to provide powerful support or at least manage a timely disengagement and local withdrawal."[40]

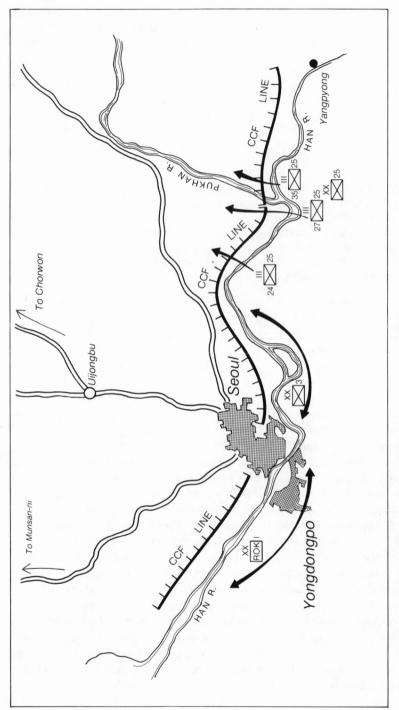

MAP 14. 25th Division crossing of the Han River, 7 March 1951

The crossing of the Han was planned to be east of Seoul, contrasting with historic past crossings which for centuries of Korean history had been northwest of Seoul. The 25th Division of I Corps was to make the crossing 14 to 18 miles east of Seoul. Recently it had moved east in the line to the right flank of I Corps to a sector between the 3rd Division of I Corps and the 24th Division of IX Corps. On the 25th Division's left, I Corps was to carry out deceptive actions in the Kimpo peninsula area west of Seoul, simulating preparations for a crossing there. At the same time, naval forces would demonstrate in the Chinnampo area to prevent the enemy from moving reinforcements south. Agents were also sent across the Han to circulate stories and to scatter leaflets to aid deception. Boat drills were carried out within enemy observation west of Seoul, and aerial attacks were made in coordination with the other deceptive actions.[41]

By 1 March the 25th Division was in positions along the south bank of the Han at its crossing sites. The 24th Infantry Regiment was on the division left flank; the Turkish Brigade held the right flank. The 27th Infantry, now in reserve, was to make the main crossing and gain the dominant terrain on the north side that was vital to success. It was massed on the south side of the Han just west of its junction with the Pukhan River. The 35th Infantry, also in reserve, was in position just east of the junction of the Pukhan with the Han and was to cross there on the east side of the river junction. D day had originally been set for 6 March, but it was set back one day to 7 March. Operational orders for the Han crossing were issued on 3 March.

The bridge that crossed the Pukhan River just above its junction with the Han had been blown. The only primary road in the crossing area ran on the north side of the river and closely followed the river bank. A high mountain mass ran north-south in the 27th Infantry sector on both sides of the Han. This range reached its peak in Hill 683, Yebong-san, on the north side. From it and subordinate Hills 587 and 610, the enemy had good observation southward over the crossing sites. Hill 658, seven air miles east of Hill 683 and east of the Pukhan River in the 35th Infantry crossing sector, also gave the enemy a good panoramic view of the two rivers' junction area. The Han River was from 460 to 800 feet wide in the 25th Division sector and was generally from seven to ten feet deep.[42]

The greatest massing of firepower thus far in the Korean War was planned to support the crossings. Ten artillery battalions were concentrated to cover the crossing sites, and 63 tanks and 36 4.2-inch mortars reinforced the artillery. Each tank carried 60 rounds of shells. Four engineer battalions supported the crossings.

The major units of I Corps on 1 March on line from west to east in the Seoul area and the crossing sites were, in order: ROK 1st Division, US 3rd Division, and the US 25th Division, with the Turkish Brigade attached. On the right of the 25th Division and guarding the I Corps right flank were the divisions of IX Corps, beginning with the US 24th Division.

At the beginning of the month the 24th Infantry Regiment and the Turkish Brigade held the 25th Division's line. The new searchlights illuminated enemy positions on the north side of the river.

It should be borne in mind that the Eighth Army Operation Ripper involved the US IX Corps in the center, where its main objective was the capture of Hongchon and Chunchon, and the X Corps, which was to advance on line with the IX Corps; east of it, the ROK III Corps was to carry the line forward to the coast near Yangyang. The rest of this chapter, however, will deal with action on the I Corps front, where the Han River crossing was to be made, followed, it was expected, by the capture of Seoul. The UN line on 1 March was about halfway between the 37th and 38th parallels. The objective of the entire operation was to advance to what was called the Idaho line, located just south of the 38th Parallel.[43]

In front of the UN forces in early March were six CCF armies, four North Korean corps, and one North Korean brigade. The major units of these forces, lined up from west to east, were the NK 1st Corps; the CCF 50th, 38th, 42nd, 39th, 40th, and 66th armies; the NK V, III, and II corps; and on the east coast near Kangnung, the NK 69th Brigade. Eighth Army estimated there were about 160,000 Chinese and 15,500 North Koreans, for a total of 175,500 enemy troops, in immediate contact on the line from coast to coast. Nine more CCF armies were believed to be in rear areas in reserve, as well as a number of NK brigades, and finally, and not to be forgotten, there were about 15,000 to 18,000 guerrillas in rear areas.[44] Of these enemy forces the NK 47th Division was in Seoul, and the 148th, 149th, and 150th divisions of the CCF 50th Army were just east of Seoul, opposite the ROK 1st Division and the US 3rd Division.

Two activities dominated I Corps and Eighth Army during the period 2–7 March: the logistic buildup of supplies near the front to support the river-crossing attack, and deception practices to mislead the enemy as to the actual purpose of the UN forces. On 2 March General Ridgway ordered the ROK 1st Division to make assault crossings of the Han River on 6–8 March in the Seoul area and west of Seoul as a diversionary feint, at the same time the 25th Division made the crossings 18 miles upstream. Beginning on 2 March, Ridgway ordered two front-line regiments (the 24th Infantry and the Turkish Brigade) to send daily tank-infantry reconnaissance patrols across the river at the chosen crossing sites. At first these drew enemy fire, but in a few days the enemy became used to these crossings and did not waste ammunition on them. On 7 March, when the real crossings began in a manner similar to the earlier crossings, except that the tanks now had assault boats hitched to them as they approached the river, the enemy was off-guard.[45]

While these deceptive activities were in progress, General Ridgway on 3 March conferred with Vice Adm. I. N. Keland, commander of Task Force

90, and promised him that, if events should dictate the evacuation of Inchon in the projected attack, he would give the Navy 48 hours' notice of such action. The Navy was concerned that CCF and North Koreans might make a surprise assault on Inchon, where work began on 15 February to rehabilitate the destroyed harbor. The 50th Engineer Port Construction Company returned on that date by LST from Pusan to undertake the work. Capt. Gordon L. Eastwood, commanding the company, had established a priority of raising Gates 3, 4, 1, and 2, in that order. On 20 February a 30-ton crane began raising Gate 3 and then Gate 4. Both gates were raised that day. Then, because Chinese and NK forces were still in Seoul and vicinity in large numbers, work was halted, and the port construction company for two weeks went on ship and sat in the harbor. When intelligence indicated that the evacuation of Seoul was beginning on 3 March, the Port Company resumed work and began raising Gate 1.[46]

In preparing for the attack across the Korean front to begin on 7 March, it was necessary to establish a five-day level of supply in rations, petroleum products, and ammunition. These supplies were scheduled to be at forward dumps by 5 March, but the buildup in fact was not completed until 7 March. The Eighth Army G-4, Colonel Stebbins, decided that I Corps supplies would be concentrated at Osan and Pyongchon and augmented over the beaches from ships at Inchon; IX Corps supplies would come from Suwon; the 1st Marine Division supplies would be held at Wonju; and X Corps supplies would be held at the Chechon railhead. In addition to these places, Eighth Army also used the ports of Kunsan and Ulsan. Rail traffic during this period was congested. Anticipating that the roads and railroad facilities north of the Han River would be in bad shape, General Ridgway had engineer units concentrate near the Han River crossing sites to be ready to start repair work on 250 bridges and 320 miles of important highways between the Han and Imjin Rivers to aid the infantry advance once it had crossed the Han River.[47]

One sign of General Ridgway's confidence that the attack would be successful was his instructions to I Corps on 4 March to start work on grading, ditching, and preparing the surface of an Eighth Army Tactical CP site at Yoju. He expected to direct future Eighth Army operations from there. When he moved to Yoju, it would be his first CP not associated with that of I Corps since the loss of Seoul on 4 January.[48]

On the night of 4–5 March, A Company, 65th Engineer Battalion, moved assault boats to within 100 yards of the Han River, where they were left in a concealed position. That night and the next day was one of great activity for the 25th Division units, as they displaced forward as inconspicuously as possible. On 5 March General Ridgway held a conference at the Eighth Army Main CP at Taegu. He told his staff he would not accept an extravagant request for artillery ammunition just to shoot more, that the supply situation was difficult, but that he thought an estimate of

50 rounds per gun daily was reasonable, and that, for I Corps, 65 rounds per gun daily was not unreasonable. The next day, 6 March, in a press conference, General Ridgway asked for press silence on the attack for 48 hours. He praised General MacArthur for his support and for having given him freedom of action.[49]

On 5 March General Ridgway announced to the army that D day was 7 March and H hour was 6:15 A.M. There had been some concern that, when the attack began, the enemy might destroy the Hwachon Reservoir Dam upstream on the Pukhan River and flood the crossing sites, destroy the infantry footbridges, and generally play havoc with the river-crossing equipment. Such action would leave advance units on the north side stranded and make further supporting crossings impossible. The Eighth Army engineer, Col. Pascal Strong, however, thought that destroying the Hwachon Dam was beyond the enemy's capability and that the best they could do would be to open the sluice gates and penstocks, which would result in minor flooding of the river southward to the Han. He calculated that this would not raise the water more than two feet. It would not, he thought, interfere with the bridge and ferry services but would drown out the fords on the Pukhan River near the reservoir.[50]

By the night of 6 March all preparations had been completed for the predawn attack across the river the next morning. On 4 March the 25th Division had asked for 200 assault boats for making the Han crossing. On the morning of 7 March, 254 of them were available. The 25th Division expected to cross in three places: the 24th Infantry would make a crossing farthest downstream on the left, near its boundary with the 3rd Division; the 27th Infantry would make the main crossing in the center; and the 35th Infantry would make a crossing farthest upstream, near its boundary with the 24th Division of IX Corps, to place it on the east side of the mouth of the Pukhan River where it joined the Han. While the 25th Division was making these crossings, units of the 3rd Division, downstream near Seoul, would demonstrate in the river with LTVs (landing vehicles, tracked). It was expected that the IX Corps attack on the right, or east, of I Corps would not advance rapidly, as it was operating in very rough terrain.

In its final arrangements the 27th Infantry concealed its assault boats near the river, and the 35th Infantry used tanks to pull trailers carrying its boats to the river during darkness. Footbridges for the two regiments were concealed in a stream bank about two miles from the river.[51]

At 5:55 A.M., 7 March, the planned heavy artillery preparation began to fall on enemy positions across the river from the 27th Infantry, 148 artillery guns firing from 5,000 to 7,000 rounds in the next 20 minutes. The 8th, 64th, 159th, 17th, 555th, 9th, 90th, and 45th (British) artillery battalions massed their fire on the enemy positions. At the same time, tanks fired their 90-mm guns, and three batteries of the 21st AAA AW Battalion moved up to the south bank and saturated the north bank of the Han with M16 quad-50 heavy machine-gun fire. At 6 :15 A.M. the artillery barrage lifted northward, and, still in the dark, the infantry crossing began at the three planned sites. After lifting behind its initial barrage, the artillery maintained its fire for another two and a half hours, during which the guns fired another 45,000 rounds. It was the greatest massing of artillery fire thus far in the Korean War. The effect was devastating on the enemy. Prisoners taken early in the morning were suffering from severe concussions.

The 65th Engineer Combat Battalion had assembled the necessary assault boats and related equipment for the infantry crossing, including rafts for vehicles and footbridge construction materials for later infantry crossings. A Company of the 65th Engineers was to carry the 27th Infantry assault battalion across the Han, B Company was to carry the 35th Infantry assault battalion to the north bank, and C Company was to build rafts and footbridges for the two regiments. The engineer battalion had 14 DUKWs attached to it for carrying immediate resupply across the river. The 77th Engineer Battalion was to carry the assault battalion of the 24th Infantry across the Han and then build a footbridge and rafts for the regiment. In addition, the 14th Engineer Combat Battalion was to build two 50-ton pontoon floating bridges across the Han for the 27th and 35th regiments' use. These two bridges were to be completed on the eighth.

The 3rd Battalion, 27th Infantry, with L Company leading and I Company following, had the first troops across. They had only slight resistance, some mortar and small-arms fire. The terrific artillery bombardment had killed, wounded, or stunned just about every enemy soldier opposite its crossing site. L Company started crossing at 6:16 A.M. in semidarkness and was on the north side by 6:30 A.M. L and I companies crossed at the sharp U-bend of the river where the Pukhan joins it. There, for more than 1,000 yards, they had to cross a huge sand beach without cover before they reached vegetation on the north side. Although fully exposed in this first stretch after reaching the north bank, darkness gave them some protection. The 3rd Battalion overran the dikes north of the Han in only a few minutes. They captured prisoners here, and weapons and equipment were taken in large numbers. K Company now crossed and joined I and L companies in the advance into the high, rough ground beyond the sand beach. K Company formed on the left flank of the battalion, then came L Company, and I Company was on the right flank. When the 1st Battalion, 27th Infantry, crossed later, it formed a line on the right (east) of the 3rd Battalion, with B, A, and C companies eastward. During the day, K Company took the dominant terrain in front of the 3rd Battalion.[52] Col. Gilbert J. Check, commander of the 27th Infantry, and Brig. Gen. George B. Barth, commander of the 25th Division artillery, watched the crossing from dug-in observation posts.

The 342nd Regiment of the 114th Division, CCF 38th Army, was opposite the 27th Infantry in the enemy's front defensive line, and it took a terrific pounding in the predawn artillery barrage. The 340th Regiment of the same division was north of the Han but east of the Pukhan opposite the 35th Infantry. The third enemy regiment, the 341st, at first was in reserve behind and north of the 342nd Regiment, both west of the Pukhan River. The 38th Army at this time was in effect a delaying force covering the withdrawal of other enemy formations in Seoul and north of the river.[53]

During the day the 3rd Battalion, 27th Infantry, captured 99 Chinese prisoners, and itself suffered 5 killed and 33 wounded. There was no enemy counterattack against it during the night.[54]

The crossing training program prior to 7 March had been geared to give at each step the exact time needed, spaced backward from dawn, to allow movement of all elements in the attack to their crossing sites under darkness and for the lead units to arrive on the north side at dawn. This training resulted in an almost exact timing of movement, which the lead elements achieved in the operation. In the movement of the 3rd Battalion, 27th Infantry, and in that of the lead elements of the 24th and 35th infantry, the enemy did not know the movement was under way until the attack forces were on the north side of the river. This schedule called for the 3rd Battalion, 27th Infantry, to leave its assembly area at 1:30 A.M., and the 1st Battalion at 2:15 A.M. The 2nd Battalion, the regiment's reserve battalion, was not to leave until 6:10 A.M. All the attack battalions, two to a regiment, were in their attack positions at 6 A.M. The assault boats were there awaiting them, having arrived at their positions at 5:30 A.M. The ground was frozen, the roads hard, but only a thin crust of ice was on the river. The morning before it had been snowing; now the weather was clear.

After the 3rd Battalion crossed the river in assault boats under cover of a rolling barrage of machine-gun fire from the 17 M16 quad-50s of Capt. Jack Harry's C Battery, 21st AAA AW Battalion, then C Company, 65th Engineer Battalion, began work under enemy small-arms and some mortar fire to get a footbridge established across the river in the 27th Infantry zone. It had the footbridge in by 9:15 A.M., and the 1st Battalion crossed the river on it. The battalion closed on the north side at 10:30 A.M. and went into position on the right flank of the 3rd Battalion. The 2nd Battalion was then ordered up to the river from its reserve position, and it began crossing on the footbridge at 1 P.M. In the afternoon the 3rd and 1st Battalions, 27th Infantry, were attacking abreast northward on the west side of the Pukhan River.

About the time the 1st Battalion was crossing the river, C Company, 89th Tank Battalion, crossed the Han 800 yards east of the infantry crossing, using a large island at the mouth of the Pukhan River for a ford-crossing site, and outflanked an enemy position in its surprise crossing. It then joined the 1st Battalion in an attack; the tanks routed the remaining Chi-

M4 tanks, 89th Tank Battalion, US 25th Division, crossing the Han River,
7 March 1951. *National Archives, 111-SC 359910*

nese, who abandoned their position and equipment, and overran a Chinese
artillery position.

Thus, when dusk came at 5 P.M., two battalions of the 27th Infantry
and a company of tanks had advanced from 4,000 to 5,000 yards north
of the Han, with A Company of the 1st Battalion anchoring the right end
of the line on the Pukhan River. Meanwhile, the 2nd Battalion of the 35th
Infantry had crossed the Han successfully and was up abreast of the 27th
Infantry on the east side of the Pukhan.[55]

In his 35th Infantry zone of crossing, Colonel Kelleher had a somewhat
different situation than did Colonel Check of the 27th Infantry. His 3rd
Battalion was to make the assault crossing on the right of the 27th Infantry,
just east of the mouth of the Pukhan River. The Han River there was not
quite as deep as below the junction of the two streams. Enemy forces held
high ground—Hill 658, overlooking Check's crossing site from the northeast at a distance of three to four miles—but a spur ridge ran west from
its crest to his crossing site at the east side of the mouth of the Pukhan,

giving the enemy complete visual control of the 35th Infantry crossing area.

East of the Pukhan, a single-track railroad ran along the north bank of the Han River, with six tunnels, in the 35th Infantry's zone. There were also three vehicular roads in its zone on the north side. One ran east-west along the bank of the Han to the blown bridge across the mouth of the Pukhan, another ran north along the east side of the Pukhan, and a third cut across the angle between the two rivers, starting five air miles up the Pukhan at the Munho-ri ferry site, to reach the Han at Okchon-ni, only a few miles west of Yangpyong. This third road, however, degenerated into a trail five or six miles from the Pukhan River. The Han was not fordable for vehicles in the 35th zone.

The 19th Infantry of the 24th Division was on the right flank of the 35th Infantry, at the IX Corps boundary. An idea of the roadless condition east of the 35th Infantry is revealed by the fact that, until the two regiments established contact north of the Han, the only vehicular route between them was 40 miles to the south.[56]

Four battalions of 105-mm howitzers, one battalion of 155-mm howitzers, and a British regiment of 25-pounders were in position to support the 35th Infantry crossing. They began their preparation at 5:55 A.M., at the identical time the artillery barrage for the 27th Infantry began. Previously, at 3:15 A.M., the 2nd Battalion, 35th Infantry, started for its forward assembly area, and 45 minutes later L Company led the 3rd Battalion on a three-mile march to the crossing site. K and L companies loaded into waiting assault boats and started across at 6:15 A.M.; the leading elements were ashore at 6:35. They made the crossing unopposed, but when only 300 yards inland they came under enemy small-arms fire. All the battalion was across the Han by 7:35 A.M. but came under mortar fire from nearby Hill 182.[57]

Lt. Col. Welborn G. Dolvin commanded the 89th Tank Battalion, which supported the crossing. He had made repeated reconnaissance trips both by light plane over the crossing site just east of the Pukhan River and also afoot along the south bank of the Han, searching for a place where some of his tanks might cross the river right after the infantry and support them quickly in expanding a beachhead. He concluded finally that it might be possible for the tanks to cross at a carefully chosen route and suggested to Capt. Herbert A. Brannon, commander of A Company, that he consider it. Brannon decided to try crossing with one tank, attached to a tow cable to the winch of the tank-recovery vehicle, which might pull it back to the south bank if it got into trouble. Lt. Thomas J. Allie, commanding the 3rd Platoon of A Company, volunteered to take the tank across. Colonel Kelleher at 7:15 authorized the tank commander to make the effort. If the one tank got across, the rest could follow, and their early presence on the north side would be of greatest value to the infantry.

The route Captain Brannon and Lieutenant Allie selected was to take the tank into the water from the sand beach just east of the junction of the Pukhan with the Han and go to the west (downstream) end of a small sand island there near the middle of the river, dividing it into two channels. He intended to cross the sand island and then try for the north bank. Allie found the water not quite as deep as he expected it to be, only about three feet deep, and had nearly reached the sand bar island at midstream when the tow cable broke because the winch fouled on the recovery vehicle. The tank driver gunned the tank ahead, and it reached the island. Once there, Allie could see some old earth footings for a former bridge at the east end of the island. He drove up to that point and dropped the tank into the water, aiming for the north bank straight across. Although the tank was in water up to the turret ring briefly, it made it to the north side. Other tanks in the platoon then followed in order. The third tank's escape hatch jarred loose, and the tank flooded out and stalled near the west end of the island. The other four tanks of the platoon were all on the north side by 8:20 A.M., however, and joined the infantry battalion, now stopped by enemy automatic fire. The four tanks moved ahead and destroyed three enemy machine guns along the railroad. The infantry then advanced to its objective.[58]

Colonel Kelleher now ordered a tank platoon attached to each of the three battalions, and at 1:15 P.M. he ordered the 2nd Battalion to cross the river in regimental reserve. The 2nd Battalion was delayed in its crossing because the footbridge, just installed, broke loose from the north bank and had to be reanchored. Once across, the battalion assembled at the point of land between the junction of the Pukhan with the Han, on the east side of the Pukhan. The 35th line, formed by the 3rd and 1st battalions, had moved inland about 2,000 yards by evening, with the 3rd Battalion facing north next to the Pukhan and the 1st Battalion curving from its right flank to face east and anchored on the Han. K Company had a two-hour fight to capture Hill 106 near the Pukhan River. All tanks of the 89th Tank Battalion had crossed to the north side of the Han in the 35th zone by 4 P.M.[59]

The 35th Infantry established an advance aid station on the north bank of the Han just as soon as the assault waves had formed their beachhead. It saved many lives. In the first two hours of operation it treated 57 casualties, many of whom would not have survived if they had not received immediate medical treatment. All the casualties were brought from there to the south side of the river in DUKWs. A 25th Division G-3 Journal message at 11:25 A.M. on 7 March indicated the 35th Infantry had reported 1 killed and 14 wounded by that time.[60]

Downstream, in the 24th Regimental sector, the 2nd Battalion began its crossing at 6:15 A.M., the same time as the others. F Company was the first across, at 6:35 A.M. Firing from the south bank of the river, B Company, 89th Tank Battalion, as well as A Company, 79th Heavy Tank Battalion, supported the crossing, which was west of Cho-ri, over a sand island in the river, to flat ground on the north side. At 9:05 A.M. five tanks forded the river to the north side. The 2nd Battalion received some long-range fire from Hills 568 and 683. From these high points enemy guns could reach the 24th Infantry landing areas to their southwest and west. Between 6:15 and 10:20 A.M. on the seventh, the two tank companies from the south bank fired more than 900 rounds of 90-mm shells into the enemy river-line positions, 3,500 to 4,500 yards away. The 2nd Battalion made rapid progress after its crossing. By 8:05 A.M. its leading elements were 2,500 yards inland. Planning had provided for the 24th Infantry to pass through the 27th Infantry if the latter faltered and to continue the attack in the high ground. But this did not happen.[61]

The first day of the Han River crossing was a great success. The beachheads on the north side had been easily established, and all units reached their first-day objectives. The tremendous artillery barrage had killed, wounded, and stunned the Chinese of the 38th Army defending the north side, and the crossing itself had achieved surprise. The 25th Division took 213 prisoners on 7 March, the largest number taken in any one day by any division in the ongoing offensive.[62] On the first day, both the 24th Infantry and the 35th Infantry had hard fights after the crossings, but the 27th Infantry, which was the only one mentioned in the *Stars and Stripes* story, had very little action. The reason was at least partly the complete devastation wrought in its sector by the massive artillery and mortar bombardment of the morning.

The Eighth Army surgeon reported on 7 March that there was an increase in head wounds because so many of the soldiers did not wear helmets. General Ridgway at once ordered that all troops in range of enemy guns had to wear helmets—a command more easily ordered than implemented. The next day the 25th Division alone reported that it was short 8,500 helmets, which meant that only one man in two had a helmet. The plain fact was that the troops had thrown away their helmets during the winter simply because they preferred to wear the warmer pile-lined cap. And they also threw away their entrenching tools because it was hard to dig with them in frozen ground. When the ground began to thaw in the spring, most of the troops did not have an entrenching tool. From the time he had taken command, General Ridgway had spoken out against this waste of equipment needed in combat, but the situation had not greatly improved by the time of the Han River crossing in March.[63] But by 29 March, General Ridgway's order of the seventh had begun to get results. The 25th Division on that date informed its units they could now draw helmets and liners and suggested that the pile caps be turned in.

On 8 March an estimated battalion of Chinese counterattacked the 2nd Battalion, 24th Infantry, from the northwest, forcing E and F companies back nearly a mile. This attack halted about 10:30 A.M. however, and with

K Company attached to it, the 2nd Battalion slowly pushed the enemy back during the day and by dark had regained most of what it had lost.[64] In this fight the 24th Infantry lost 7 men killed and 46 wounded.

In the center the 27th Infantry had only light opposition during the day, but it advanced only enough to keep abreast of the troops on its flanks. In its sector, the 14th Engineer Construction Battalion had continued work during the night using the new searchlights attached to the division. The heavy 50-ton floating pontoon bridge was finished on 9 March, and vehicles began to cross on it.[65] During the first 24 hours of the crossings, DUKWs attached to the 25th Division proved invaluable in getting food and ammunition resupply across the river to the troops.

By 9 March Chinese prisoners had identified all three regiments of the 114th Division, CCF 38th Army, as being in the 25th Division crossing area. They continued to resist west of the Pukhan River, but on that day enemy opposition to the 35th Infantry east of the Pukhan all but vanished. Captured enemy diaries from the bodies of Chinese dead echoed an entry for 8 March in one taken from an officer, which stated, "The enemy is already aware that our troops are not getting sufficient supplies or replacement of personnel. . . . The enemy is attacking us, taking advantage of these two conditions of our troops."[66]

In a memo for the record, 8 March 1951, General Ridgway made some entries concerning General MacArthur's visit to the front the day before and of some of their conversations. Ridgway at one point had mentioned some action he had taken. MacArthur had replied, "Matt, you do what you think is right every time, and never anything just because you may think I want it done. If you do that and make mistakes, I will back you 100 percent." At another point MacArthur told Ridgway he wanted a strong stand made south of the Han, not to give up there, whatever the result of the current attack should be. He also said he wanted an east-coast port established. Ridgway responded that he planned to use the lateral road from Kangnung westward for supply of the ROK I and III Corps and as much of the US X Corps as the road would support. He said he would bring in supplies to the ports of Samchok or Chumunjin as soon as they were secured, or over the beach at Kangnung itself.[67]

An event, long anticipated by General Ridgway, was his moving of the Eighth Army Advance Tactical CP from Suwon to Yoju on 7 March, which coincided with the beginning of the Han River crossing.[68]

On 9 March the 3rd Battalion, 24th Infantry, with tanks attached, attacked Hill 62, where enemy resistance persisted. In this attack, which won the hill and ended enemy resistance there, 17 prisoners were captured from the 9th Company, 449th Regiment, 150th Division, of the CCF 50th Army, and 75 enemy dead were counted. The 24th Infantry seemed to straddle the boundary between the CCF 50th and 38th armies.[69]

Also on the ninth, the 35th Infantry 1st and 3rd battalions diverged in their advance, and this move made it necessary for the regiment to insert the 2nd Battalion between them. Each battalion was ordered to hold one company in reserve. The main enemy activity was in the 3rd Battalion sector, adjacent to the Pukhan River. The next day the 3rd Battalion continued to advance up the bank of the Pukhan with tank-infantry teams.[70]

After the Han River crossings on 7 March, the Chinese defended some positions on the north side tenaciously until forced out or killed by grenade, bayonet, or flamethrowers. They defended many high points with long-range automatic-weapons fire, laid mines, and then withdrew before the UN forces came into close contact. As the 25th Division advanced farther north daily, the distance in the big V-shaped area between the Pukhan and Han rivers widened. The 27th Infantry line thus lengthened so greatly that, by 13 March, it had to insert its 3rd Battalion on the right of the 1st Battalion for a three-battalion line, instead of the two-battalion line that it had used from the crossing until then. At the same time, the 35th Infantry on the east bank of the Pukhan River had been tending westward and narrowing until on 11 March it had only a two-battalion line, the 2nd and 3rd battalions, and on 12 March the regiment was pinched out entirely on the east side of the Pukhan by the 19th Regiment of the 24th Division and went into division reserve.[71]

On 13 March the 27th Infantry, in the middle of the 25th Division line, was slightly in advance of the 24th Infantry on its left and had advanced about 10 miles in eight days through very rugged terrain on the west side of the Pukhan River. In that time the 27th Infantry had had 9 men killed and 98 wounded. It had captured 178 prisoners and estimated enemy casualties in front of it as 916. On 14–15 March the 2nd and 3rd battalions, 24th Infantry, on its left made a good advance before the division veered sharply to the left, or northwest, on 17–18 March.[72]

While the 25th Division was making the Han River crossings 14 to 18 miles east of Seoul on 7 March, and advancing north from the crossing in the week that followed, the US 3rd and the ROK 1st divisions had been sitting on the south bank of the Han, making diversionary actions in the river at times, or just waiting the outcome of the river crossings upstream. After the crossings succeeded and a good beachhead was established on the north side of the Han, agents and other intelligence indicated that the enemy was withdrawing north from the Seoul and Han River area. The two divisions then expected to enter Seoul unopposed within a few days. They just waited until they could cross the Han and enter Seoul without having to fight for the city.

On 12 March aerial observers reported to the 3rd Division that 600 enemy soldiers were moving away from Seoul to the northwest. That night 3rd Division patrols to the north bank of the Han just east of Seoul reported no enemy contact. Previously heavily defended positions were deserted. On the fourteenth, elements of the division crossed the river without opposition. Attack plans were filed away, not needed. On 15 March patrols advanced 5,000 yards north of the river without contact with an enemy.[73]

The best river-crossing site in the 3rd Division sector was the place where the Al Jolson bridge was later built. The enemy had defended that crossing site up until now. Although the north bank was now deserted by the enemy, they had left behind many mines. On 16 March the 2nd Battalion, 65th Infantry, of the 3rd Division crossed the river in DUKWs and occupied Hill 348 and established a formal, defended beachhead.

Patrols from Gen. Paik Sun Yup's ROK 1st Division, which held the south bank of the Han opposite Seoul, had patrols crossing the river at night for weeks. Their reports and other intelligence indicated that the Chinese had begun an organized withdrawal from the city on 12 March. ROK patrols crossed the river again into the city on the thirteenth, and I Corps received reports that South Korean flags were raised on some buildings. General Paik, however, did not yet assume the city was safe for unlimited crossings, and he sent his patrols deep into the hills on the west and north sides of Seoul toward Uijongbu. On 14 March the ROKs again crossed into the city and covered it in a thorough reconnaissance. They made no significant enemy contact. General Paik telephoned I Corps that there were no enemy in uniform in the city, but he believed some North Koreans were there in civilian clothes. Paik left several platoon-sized patrols in the city overnight. The 3rd Division also sent a platoon-sized patrol from the 2nd Battalion, 15th Regiment, into the southeastern edge of Seoul to stay there overnight.[74]

The next day, 15 March, there were increased crossings into Seoul. A ROK patrol captured a North Korean soldier who said his unit had received orders three days earlier to withdraw from Seoul and to assemble at Munsan-ni, and from there go to Chorwon. Air observers reported seeing no enemy in the city or its northern environs. The 2nd and 3rd battalions of the 15th Regiment, ROK 1st Division, crossed the river and screened the city without enemy contact. Most of the regiment returned to the south bank for the night. General Paik then ordered the 15th Regiment to cross the river at 8 A.M. on the sixteenth and to protect the bridge-crossing site west of the city, to patrol to the northwest, and to coordinate its actions with elements of the US 3rd Division on the southeast outskirts of Seoul. The 3rd Division had ordered a battalion to cross the Han and also to protect the bridge-crossing site east of the city and ordered the entire division to be prepared to cross to the north side on order. Hourly reports of the situation in Seoul on 15 March were sent to Eighth Army. A few ROK patrols drew limited enemy fire north of the city. But there was no organized resistance in the city. Many enemy prisoners were taken during the day, but they were mostly deserters who had little current information. One ROK patrol raised the ROK flag over the capitol building.[75]

At this time, 15 March, the US 25th Division had progressed in its attack after the river crossings to a point nine or ten miles north of the Han and seven or eight miles northeast of Seoul. There it was in control of the Seoul-Chunchon road, west of the Pukhan. East of the Pukhan River the US 24th Division had control of the road for some miles. On 15 March the 21st Infantry of the 24th Division at nightfall could see the Pukhan River and was approaching the Hwachon Reservoir on it upstream. This reservoir provided electricity for Seoul. Here the 24th Division passed in front of the 25th Division, crossed to the west side of the Pukhan, and continued its attack toward the reservoir. Farther east the IX and X corps had made advances in the Chunchon area. All these happenings made it necessary for the Chinese and North Koreans to withdraw from the Seoul area or risk being cut off. The enemy forces carried out an orderly and successful withdrawal toward the 38th Parallel.[76]

On 16 March UN forces occupied Seoul. The city had now changed hands for the fourth time, and it was to be the last time in the Korean War. The ROK 1st Division sent its 2nd Battalion, 15th Regiment, across the river between 7:00 and 9:20 A.M.; the 3rd Battalion crossed at 10 A.M., and the ROK 15th Regimental CP crossed at 11 A.M. Parts of the regiment went to the northern edge of the city. During the day Eighth Army redrew the unit boundaries on the Seoul front, giving all of the city to the ROK 1st Division as its responsibility. The I&R platoons of the ROK 12th and 15th regiments patrolled north and northwest of the city. The ROK 1st Division's responsibility for the Seoul area extended from the northwest corner of Yongdong-po on the south side of the river to an arc that circled the city on its north side.

At the same time the ROK 1st Division was occupying Seoul, the 2nd Battalion of the 65th Regiment, US 3rd Division, with a platoon of heavy mortars, an engineer unit, and a TACP, crossed the Han at 9:20 A.M. to the southeast edge of the city. General Ridgway accompanied the battalion across the river. An hour later, he watched ROK units crossing the river west of the city. The rest of the 65th Regiment crossed the river two days later. This regiment was composed of members of the Puerto Rican National Guard, commanded by Col. W. W. Harris.[77] On the evening of 16 March, the closest points of enemy contact around Seoul were five miles and ten miles northwest of the city and at the north and northeast outskirts of the city, where small enemy covering forces were encountered.[78]

Before leaving Seoul, the CCF, according to civilian and other intelligence, had issued orders that all males in the city between the ages 15 to 35 and all females 16 to 25 years of age would have to move north with them. South Korean police later estimated that 41,000 South Koreans were taken north when the enemy evacuated the city. The police found 1,500 unburied bodies in Seoul when they returned to the city, some of them CCF and NK soldiers who had starved. The population of Seoul was estimated to be about 135,000 when UN forces reoccupied it on 16 March, compared to a peacetime population of more than a million. For a considerable period of time, reaching into April, 5,000 to 10,000 former residents returned to the city daily after it returned to South Korean control.

In the period from 6 to 16 March, which saw Eighth Army cross the Han River successfully and recapture Seoul, the 25th Infantry Division and its supporting artillery and armor forces were virtually the only ground units involved in combat in the Seoul region, accomplishing a brilliant stroke at a modest cost in casualties. The division had 58 men killed, 333 wounded, and 7 missing in action for a total of 398 combat casualties. During the same period there were more than 3,000 counted enemy dead and an estimated 8,338 enemy casualties overall in the 25th Division sector.[79]

We know from captured documents dating from the middle of March 1951 that the CCF and the NK expected a UN landing in the Chinnampo and the Monggumpo-ri west coastal areas of North Korea at this time, and they also prepared for a UN landing in the Wonsan area on the east coast. It looked to them that the situation was similar to that of the days just prior to the Inchon landing, and they feared something like it might be attempted.

On 16 March General Ridgway wrote a most unwarlike letter to an old friend, Col. R. P. Eaton, at Headquarters, Caribbean command, Canal Zone. "You would be very much interested in the bird life here. . . . Magpies are everywhere, as they are in North China. They are larger than those of our Pacific Northwest, a bit more brilliantly colored, and more noisy and impertinent. Their nests are huge untidy masses of twigs and sticks roughly circular and some 18–24 inches across. I have flown over many in light planes and helicopters, and can't see any entrance on the top. It must be on the side."[80]

When Ridgway entered Seoul on 15 March, he found the city nearly demolished, but still many thousands of South Koreans there to greet him and troops who made the initial entrance. The shopping district had been destroyed by artillery fire and aerial strikes, all the lights were out, the light poles were down and wires dangling, and streetcars were destroyed or standing deserted and idle haphazardly around the city. Nearly all the destruction had been wrought by American artillery and aerial might. But the city gradually rebuilt its utilities and quickly became a center of activity, especially after President Syngman Rhee and the South Korean government moved back from Pusan.

To anyone at all familiar with the Korean War and General Ridgway's strategy, leadership, and moral force in regenerating the Eighth Army, which brought it back from defeat to move north of the Han River and regain Seoul during the first half of March, it is something of a shock to read in Dwight D. Eisenhower's book *Mandate for Change, 1953–1956,* the following account of these events:

On January 25 the UN forces attacked to the north, and by April 27 were in possession of Seoul and, along the entire front, had reached a line near the 38th Parallel. At this time the Chinese Communists, in their turn, launched a counteroffensive which drove UN forces once more to the south of Suwon, and Seoul fell into Communist hands for the third time.

Ten days earlier, General Ridgway had departed from Korea to assume the position of UN commander in Japan, because of General MacArthur's relief by President Truman. Named to succeed Ridgway was another soldier with no superior as a stout fighting man, General James A. Van Fleet, a West Point classmate of mine.

Following the Communist offensive, the last attack of which was made on May 16, General Van Fleet launched a final assault, recaptured Seoul, and established a line extending along the Han and Imjin Rivers north of Seoul on the west, to Kosong on the east coast.[81]

One would have to search long and hard to find a more garbled and incorrect statement of a military action than this one. One wonders, Who wrote the book? Could a military man of Eisenhower's long experience, and presumably intense interest in the Korean War at a time he was running for president in 1952, display such ignorance of the events? And if he did not write the passage himself, could he have failed to see the errors when he presumably read the manuscript before it was published? Many thousands of readers of his book were certainly misinformed, and the history of the war in March 1951 and later was grossly distorted from the statements in a book that one would expect to be factually correct.

With victory in the west accomplished for the present, and the South Korean capital at last again in South Korean and UN possession, the related action of IX and X corps and the ROK Army eastward to the Sea of Japan in Operation Ripper will concern us in the next chapter.

14

Warfare in the Mountains

WE HAVE NOTED in the previous chapter that I Corps had begun preparing a site at Yoju for an Eighth Army forward CP in the first days of March and that General Ridgway wrote on 7 March 1951 in his daily record that "8th Army Tac CP moved from Suwon to Yoju." The I Corps Command Report for March 1951 gives 10 March as the date for the establishment of the Eighth Army Tactical CP at Yoju. Both dates, 7 and 10 March, may be technically correct from different points of view. In any event, General Ridgway wrote to Gen. George C. Marshall, secretary of defense, on 12 March from his new CP:

At last I have a tactical CP, on a river bank, some little distance removed from the earthy, fruity smell of a Korean town. The Engineers ditched and sanded a bit of rice paddy. On that they put a tent floor, some straw mattings and two little command tents, each about 8 × 12, and one opening into the other. So I have a combination living room and office, and a bedroom. We are on a 25-foot bluff, facing north across the Han, with an indescribable view, rimmed in by mountains and which, as Spring now rapidly approaches, will yield more and more of the beauty of God's outdoors, which I know means as much to you as to me.[1]

Yoju was the ruins of a town on the south bank of the Han River, 40 air miles southeast of Seoul. Army engineers had recently installed a pontoon floating vehicular bridge across the Han at Yoju, which gave easy access to any of the roads to the front. At this new CP Ridgway had more time than he had had elsewhere to rethink the principles of war as they applied to Korea. His thinking was now taking into consideration the fact that he had more responsibility now and a larger force of men, by far, to take care of and to guide than he had ever had in Africa or in Europe in World War II. "The larger the command, the more time must go into planning; the longer it will take to move troops into position, to reconnoiter, to accumulate ammunition and other supplies, and to coordinate other participating elements on the ground and in the air," he wrote.[2]

The date of March 1951 is a good point at which to reassess the status of certain troop assets, their weapons, the efficiency of ROK units, and the contribution of the Korean Military Advisory Group (KMAG) to ROK performance. The war had been in progress now for about eight months, with widely varying degrees of success and failure, but by March 1951 the UN forces, under the leadership of General Ridgway, were beginning to gain the ascendancy for the first time since the massive Chinese intervention in October 1950.

On 11 March 1951, the Eighth Army made its first official statement on a rotation plan for troops to return to the United States or Japan after a length of service in Korea. The plan was to go into effect in April 1951. This announcement was a morale booster, and few Americans in combat units in Korea did not thereafter look forward to the date of their rotation.

Also in March 1951, the Army approved a new table of distribution for KMAG officers to the ROK divisions, and it amounted to a considerable increase over previous assignments. Beginning in March 1951 the following KMAG personnel were to be provided for ROK divisions:

ROK division:

1. 5 lieutenant colonels, to be assigned as 1 for senior advisor to ROK division commander, 1 as an assistant division advisor and executive officer, and 3 senior regimental advisors, 1 to a regiment.

2. 14 majors – 1 to advise division G-1 and G-4, 1 to advise division G-2 and G-3, 1 as senior artillery advisor, 1 as senior engineer advisor, and 1 as senior signal officer, and 9 battalion advisors, 1 to each of 9 infantry battalions.

3. 2 captains – 1 as assistant artillery advisor, and 1 as ordnance advisor.

4. 11 enlisted men to be assigned necessary administrative, mess, communications, and maintenance functions. This gave a total of 32 KMAG personnel to a ROK division.[3]

At the beginning of the war in June 1950 an average division KMAG group consisted of five officers and three enlisted men. The KMAG personnel were often great distances from headquarters in Seoul or other Eighth Army headquarters, sometimes in almost inaccessible locations, and they were largely on their own in establishing themselves with the ROK commander and unit to which they were assigned. It was generally a tough assignment. During the first year, KMAG personnel spent a lot of time in trying to improve the training of the junior ROK officers and enlisted men.

One of the regrettable oversights of ROK divisions during the first part of the war was their failure to plot and locate vehicular and antipersonnel mines. When they moved for any reason, there was no record of precisely where their mines might be, and since their previous positions were often reoccupied later, many American and ROK soldiers were killed by inadvertently exploding these mines. Steps were taken to improve drastically the recording of such minefields.[4]

Of all the ROK divisions, only the ROK 1st Division, under the command of Brig. Gen. Paik Sun Yup, at first had a tank battalion attached to it, the 73rd Tank Battalion. The 1st ROKs protected their tanks devotedly. Most of the ROK divisions were essentially light infantry units, without attached armor or artillery support; later, they had usually only one battalion of light artillery.

By March the 25th Infantry Division had developed an armored shield for the gunners of the M16 quad-50 antiaircraft weapon. It guarded against small-arms and mortar fire and was avidly sought by the antiaircraft units supporting the infantry. These gunners also wore an armored vest, which added to their protection, but it was too heavy to be worn by dismounted personnel. The shield developed by the 25th Division for its antiaircraft gunners was quickly adopted by Eighth Army and put into production for all its antiaircraft units.[5]

Artillerymen seemed to favor using white phosphorus shells initially against an enemy force in a dug-in defense system, because it was effective in flushing them from their foxholes and trenches, and the artillery then shifted to VT fuse shells, which cut the enemy down in great numbers once they were outside bunkers or foxholes.

An overlooked factor in keeping American units going in the first year of the war in Korea was the great contribution made by Japanese industry to the war effort. The Japanese made parts for GMC trucks, rebuilt World War II radio sets, rebuilt trucks and artillery mounts, and even manufactured locomotives for the Korean railroads. In one instance, Japanese manufacturing undertook to build 19 locomotives in 75 days—and delivered the first one in 31 days. General Yount, commander of the 2nd Logistical Command at Pusan, which provided the logistic support for Eighth Army, held the view that, without the Japanese industrial support and contribution to Eighth Army's needs in the first year of the war, the army would have collapsed.[6]

Another conclusion had emerged by March 1951: it was undesirable to accept United Nations offerings of forces less than a reinforced battalion of at least 1,000 men. The commander in chief, United Nations command, made it a policy that units should be basically infantry with their own supporting artillery.

The Army Field Forces Headquarters at Fort Monroe, Virginia, had by now assembled a large amount of data and reports from Korea about American troops in action there, and in a training memorandum, dated 13 March 1951, it set forth its evaluation of this data. It was critical of many things in the performance of the troops in Korea. It listed findings and some needs in further training, including the following:

1. There was a weakness in knowledge and use of hand signals. Leaders became casualties when they had to expose themselves to give orders.

2. Increasing use of the bayonet in close-combat by American troops had produced good results – fear in the enemy and confidence in American troops.
3. Both day and night foot patrols were defective; they failed to penetrate to the depth required and to gain contact and locate enemy forming up areas, to observe areas they were to patrol, and were often incapable of describing what they had seen.
4. Battlefield intelligence was far from satisfactory.
5. American soldiers were indifferent to, and poor at camouflage.
6. Too many casualties occurred because of failures of automatic or semi-automatic weapons at critical times. Known to be due to excessive dirt or dust on moving parts, and this due to failure to check condition of weapons constantly.
7. Success of North Korean and Chinese night fighting and attacks requires more training in night fighting and use of all possible night illumination. Usually enemy has completely surrounded a position's perimeter before his presence is known.
8. Troops are more wasteful of individual and organizational equipment than in World War II. They leave it on battlefields in large quantity, including tanks and vehicles.[7]

It was widely known that, in contrast to the generally uniform type of weapons used and type of ammunition resupply needed in the UN forces, the weapons and ammunition used by the North Korean and Chinese forces were burdensomely diverse. Weapons captured from Chinese units since their intervention showed the degree of this nonstandardization. An analysis of a large collection of such weapons showed that they originated in ten different countries – China, Japan, Soviet Union, United States, Great Britain, Canada, Germany, Belgium, Switzerland, and Czechoslovakia. The study showed further that 57 percent of submachine guns, 10 percent of rifles and carbines, 27 percent of heavy machine guns, 35 percent of mortars, 19 percent of field artillery, and 75 percent of rocket launchers came from the United States. Considering the weapons as a whole, the analysis stated that 26 percent of Chinese weapons were of US origin, 20 percent of Soviet origin, 15 percent of Japanese origin, 5 percent of Chinese origin, and 34 percent of unknown origin.[8]

It would be a logistic nightmare to keep a force thus armed supplied with ammunition. No wonder so many Chinese soldiers appeared on the battlefield with no individual weapon at all, except the four or five grenades they carried. They were told to find their weapons on the battlefield. They usually found American ones.

The US IX and X corps in March had the central front from the junction of the Pukhan River with the Han eastward to just beyond Pyongchang, where the ROK Army took over the rest of the line to the coast. The X Corps area now, having moved eastward, was in extremely mountainous country and faced North Korean troops rather than Chinese, which had confronted it up to now. The IX Corps had moved eastward also, so that it included the old 2nd Division sector around Hoengsong and Wonju, which the 1st Marine Division now took over for the IX Corps. The Chinese units had also extended their line eastward, so that their portion of the line extended to a point just east of Hoengsong. Thus, in March the IX Corps faced Chinese units, while X Corps now confronted reorganized and reequipped North Korean units, and eastward from it the ROK Army also had North Korean troops in front of it.

From west to east, beginning at the Pukhan River, the IX Corps had on line the US 24th Division, 1st Cavalry Division, British 27th Brigade, and 1st Marine Division; adjacent to and east of it the X Corps had the ROK 3rd Division, US 2nd Division and the attached French Battalion and Netherlands detachment, and the US 7th Division. Eastward to the coast, the ROK III Corps had the ROK 7th, 9th, and Capital divisions, with the latter division responsible for the coastal area.

Opposite the UN line and beginning also at the Pukhan River and extending eastward, the CCF 38th Army, with its 114th, 112th, and 113th divisions, was opposite the US 24th Division; the CCF 42nd Army, with its 126th, 124th, and 125th divisions, was opposite the 1st Cavalry Division and the British 27th Brigade; the CCF 40th Army held a narrow front with its three divisions echeloned behind one another north to south, with the 120th Division on line facing and opposite the ROK 6th Division, and the 119th and 118th behind it; the CCF 66th Army, with its 196th and 197th divisions on line and the 198th behind them, was opposite the US 1st Marine Division in the Hoengsong area.

From Hoengsong eastward to the coast North Korean units took over the line, with the NK 12th, 7th, 6th, 3rd, 15th, 1st, 2nd, 27th, 9th, and 31st divisions opposite the South Korean 3rd, the US 2nd Division and the French Battalion, the US 7th Division, and the ROK 7th and Capital divisions. The ROK 9th Division was deep in the mountains south of and between the ROK 7th and Capital divisions. For about 16 air miles eastward from the US 7th and ROK 7th divisions to the coast there were no UN troops. The ROK Capital Division was in place in the narrow coastal low ground around the town of Kangnung and the approaches to it. The North Korean 69th Brigade was north of it in the Yangyang area. A feature of the east coast here is that the highest mountains in Korea almost rim it, dropping from their crests precipitously to the Sea of Japan.[9]

The 25th Division's crossing of the Han River on 7 March at the Pukhan River's confluence with it brought a related action from the 24th Division, which was on line just east of it along the Pukhan River. The CCF 38th Army there on the north side of the Han and along the east side of the Pukhan, with its 114th and 113th divisions, faced the 24th Division. These enemy troops fought well in an organized withdrawal, defending key high-terrain features in company-sized units, often bitterly contesting every inch of ground. The terrain was the roughest the 24th Division had yet fought in. Hill 1157, six air miles northwest of Chipyong-ni and the same distance west of Piryong-ni, was the highest terrain feature to be attacked in the IX Corps zone of action. It was the key terrain immediately in front of the 24th Division. An estimated enemy regiment defended it with hand grenades. Another regiment was in front of the peak to the east in the 5th RCT sector. The 21st Infantry, commanded by Lt. Col. Gines Perez, was heading for Hill 1157, but it had hard fighting on lower hills before it got there.

The 19th Infantry Regiment was the left-flank unit of the 24th Division. It crossed the Han River on 5 March and assembled behind the 21st Infantry. That night the Chinese attacked the 5th RCT on its right; had they penetrated that regiment, they could have wrought havoc in the assembly area of the 19th Infantry. But the 5th RCT turned back the attack. When the 25th Division crossed the Han on 7 March, the 19th Infantry began moving forward and slanting left toward the Pukhan River, eventually crossing it in front of the 35th Infantry, 25th Division, and headed upstream on its western bank for the Hwachon Reservoir.[10]

In its sector east of the 24th Division, the 1st Battalion, 5th Cavalry Regiment, finally captured Hill 318 from the Chinese after four air strikes and concentrated artillery barrages. The hill had elaborately constructed defenses, and A and C companies occupied the crest only after close combat with bayonet and grenades. The next day the 7th Cavalry Regiment relieved the 5th Cavalry. That was a bad day for airdrop of supplies. There were no panels out, and three planes dropped in the wrong place, one drop landing in an uncleared minefield.[11]

The 9th and 23rd regiments of the 2nd Infantry Division fought hard battles in the first part of March in extremely rough terrain east and northeast of Wonju, the hill crests they had to attack being at least 1,000 meters high more often than not. A main objective was to gain control of the lateral highway running through the mountains east from Hoengsong to Saemal, Ungyo-ri, and Pangnim-ni. At Pangnim-ni this lateral road connected with the main north-south road from Chechon via Yongwol to Pyongchang and northward to Changpyong, where the road turned northeast to Kangnung and the east coast. The hills lining either side of both these major roads through the eastern mountains were rough and high. Here the enemy was stubbornly entrenched. Every hill was a major battle for the US 2nd and 7th divisions. Such were the battles for Hills 726 and 688 which the 9th Infantry, 2nd Division, took from the NK 5th Division after four days of fighting. Air strikes and artillery fire helped gain the victories.[12]

The 23rd Regiment had an easier time driving the North Koreans from

Hills 1145 and 778, but the French Battalion attached to it had a harder time in its attack on towering Hill 1037, north of the road, about halfway between Saemal and Pangnim-ni. Air strikes and artillery barrages seemed to have only limited effect on the dug-in enemy, although later, when the crest was gained, the deaths of 300 enemy there were credited to air strikes. The French Battalion finally had to make a costly frontal attack at 11 A.M. on 5 March to gain the hill. Elements of the ROK 5th Division relieved the French on the hill that night. The terrain was so cut-up and rough on Hill 1037 that evacuation of wounded was a difficult task.[13] That night the enemy in front of the 23rd Infantry withdrew; when the regiment resumed the attack on the sixth, they found only vacated positions. During the first part of the month, the 38th Infantry, 2nd Division, was in X Corps reserve.

The 7th Infantry Division was on X Corps's right flank attacking north with the objective of capturing Pyongchang on the north-south MSR. From the NK III Corps, the NK 1st Division was on its left front, and the NK 15th Division was on its right side and astride the MSR. The enemy fought well at times, but the NK 15th Division seemed more mercurial, sometimes abandoning a good position without a fight. The enemy seemed to be armed mostly with automatic weapons but had a problem in maintaining an ammunition resupply. In the 7th Division the 31st Infantry Regiment was in X Corps reserve, still reequipping and training replacements after the Chosin Reservoir campaign, and at first most of the combat in the eastern mountains fell to the 17th Regiment.

On 2 March the 1st and 3rd battalions, 17th Infantry, had a rather odd battle for Hill 980. The 3rd Battalion, attacking from a flank, got to within 200 yards of the crest undetected and at that distance had an extremely favorable enfilade fire position on the enemy, which apparently was giving its attention to the frontal approach of the 1st Battalion. The surprise deadly enfilade fire caused the North Koreans to break from their foxholes and run. This fire then caught them in the open. There were 202 dead enemy on the hill, and five prisoners taken from the 1st and 3rd regiments of the 15th NK Division. In contrast to this fight, three days later the 2nd Battalion, 17th Infantry, came up against strong opposition at Hill 982 and at 4 P.M. broke off the battle and returned to its original position. A heavy snow that night and the next day (5–6 March), which limited visibility to 50 yards, delayed further attack.[14]

East of the X Corps boundary the ROK III Corps was in bad shape. Only along the east coast, where the ROK Capital Division held its sector, was there any semblance of stable defense. The ROK 3rd Division was still in the line for X Corps just east of Hoengsong, but the ROK III Corps wanted it back. That could not be done at once, however, because the ROK 8th and 5th divisions were still combat ineffective from the mauling they received at Hoengsong on 11–12 February. In late February, North Korean units had penetrated the ROK 7th and 9th divisions of the ROK III Corps in the eastern mountains, creating a void between them. General Ridgway had at this point ordered the ROK Army to have the ROK Capital Division attack southwest from the Kangnung area along the Yangpyong-ni–Pangnim-ni road to restore some semblance of communication in the eastern part of the UN defense line. In this effort, the leading cavalry regiment of the ROK Capital Division was ambushed on 3 March at Soksa-ri, seven miles northeast of Changpyong-ni, and dispersed.[15]

Meanwhile the 1st Marine Division had to open the road north of Hoengsong that led to Hongchon. The 1st and 7th Marine regiments had the task of crossing flooded rivers just north of Hoengsong and then entering the infamous Massacre Valley, where the ROK 8th Division and supporting artillery and tanks, together with the 38th Infantry Regiment of the US 2nd Division, were cut to pieces by the CCF attack two weeks earlier. The Marines had hard fighting for Hills 536 and 333 on the road north of Massacre Valley but achieved their objectives by 4 March after heavy battles on 3 March, when the 1st Marine Division reported it had 14 killed and 104 wounded. The enemy withdrew during the night.[16]

At the same time, the 23rd Infantry of the 2nd Division, with the attached French Battalion, suffered casualties almost equally heavy east of the Marines. On 5 March the 23rd Infantry reported 2 killed and 93 wounded, while the French Battalion reported 10 killed and 40 wounded.[17]

More information was available on 6 March about the furious battle the French Battalion had fought the day before in capturing the highest ground at Hill 1037, which had overlooked both the 23rd Infantry Regiment of the 2nd Division and the ROK 3rd Division. The French Battalion now was revealed to have lost 17 killed and 61 wounded in that fight. All this action came at a time when the US 2nd Division was relieving the ROK 3rd Division in the line, and the ROK 3rd was returning to the ROK III Corps farther east. The 2nd Division completed this relief of the ROK 3rd Division on 6 March.[18]

This realignment in X Corps now placed the US 2nd Division on the lateral Hoengsong–Saemal–Pangnim-ni road in an attack north along the Chunchon-Inje axis, and the US 7th Division on the right or east from the Pyongchang–Pangnim-ni area north in attack toward Changpyong-ni and Soksa-ri. The hurried insertion of the ROK 5th Division between the two US divisions in the virtually roadless mountainous area between them, in a sense, was as a replacement for the ROK 3rd Division, which ROK officials demanded be returned from X Corps to the ROK III Corps, and it had to be supplied from either flank by the 2nd and 7th divisions. Enemy use of mines had markedly increased as the North Koreans withdrew slowly and stubbornly northward. The NK V Corps was now in front of the US 2nd Division and the ROK 5th Division, while the NK III Corps faced the US 7th Division farther east. Still farther east was the NK II Corps.

Mention was made earlier of the North Korean ambush of the Cavalry Regiment of the ROK Capital Division on 3 March near Soksa-ri. By 6 March more information on what had happened had come in from this isolated mountain area. The leading elements of the ROK Cavalry Regiment, advancing from the east, were within a mile of Soksa-ri when an estimated enemy regiment ambushed them from both north and south in company-sized forces. There were four such attacks in four hours. By that time the ROK Regiment had suffered 59 killed, 119 wounded, and 802 missing in action, and the regiment was dispersed. Two of the ROK battalions retreated on Kangnung, and the other assembled at Kusan-ni, four miles west of Kangnung.[19]

During this period of heavy fighting in IX and X corps, the new IX Corps commander arrived in Korea to replace the acting commander, Maj. Gen. Oliver P. Smith. Maj. Gen. William M. Hoge arrived from Trieste on 5 March, and his principal staff officers at IX Corps were Brig. Gen. William L. Mitchell, deputy corps commander; Brig. Gen. George B. Peploe, chief of staff; Col. John F. Greco, G-2; and Col. William B. Kunzig, G-3. Peploe had previously been the highly rated commander of the 38th Regiment of the 2nd Division.[20]

It appears that General Ridgway, on the death of IX Corps commander Bryant Moore, had submitted the names of three officers, with Hoge at the head of the list, from which he recommended that one be selected to command IX Corps. Hoge was chosen, so Ridgway got the man he wanted. General Hoge was 57 years old at the time, a native of Missouri and a member of the West Point class of 1916. He had been commissioned as an engineer officer. In France in World War I, Hoge commanded a battalion at St. Mihiel and in the Meuse-Argonne offensive. In the crossing of the Meuse River, he so distinguished himself that General Pershing personally presented him with the Distinguished Service Cross. He served with the Philippine Scouts in the Philippines, and in 1942 he built the Alcan Highway to Alaska, cutting the 1,023-mile road through the forests of Canada and Alaska. He was on Omaha Beach in the Normandy landings of World War II, and in 1944 he returned to his old command of Combat Command B, 9th Armored Division, and was with it at St. Vith, a critical action in the Battle of the Ardennes. General Ridgway, commanding the XVIII Airborne Corps, was his superior at this action. Ridgway had known Hoge when they were cadets at West Point and had always regarded him as calm, courageous, and imperturbable. In March 1945, when Hoge's lead elements of Combat Command B reached the Rhine, they found the Remagen railroad bridge still intact. It had been prepared for demolition, and the American forces did not expect to find it standing. Hoge decided quickly to take the great risk of trying to capture the bridge intact and cleared his decision with only his division commander, General Leonard of the 9th Armored Division. After the war, Hoge commanded the Engineer Center at Fort Belvoir, Virginia, and later, the US forces at Trieste, Italy.

When the author met General Hoge at his IX Corps headquarters in Korea in 1951, he found him entirely unpretentious, and in the conversations with him found him to be always quiet, genial, reminding one of a kindly, fatherly type. His face was rugged, but calm and thoughtful. His body, of medium stature, was solid and strong. He answered questions readily and intelligently.

On 7 March General Ridgway's Operation Ripper jumped off in an extended attack across the entire army front. It was really a continuation of the fighting already under way. It was more ambitious than any previous attack he had planned and ordered and, if successful, was expected to carry the UN forces back north to the 38th Parallel. The time for it seemed right because the first part of the Chinese 4th Offensive had just been turned back, and the Chinese and the North Koreans were in the process of a slow withdrawal. As a part of Ripper, the western front again became active with the 25th Division's crossing of the Han River east of Seoul. If the operation succeeded, Seoul would be outflanked on the east, and the enemy would have to withdraw from the Seoul area if they were to save their troops there.

As this large operation got under way on 7 March, the point of contact in IX Corps was about five miles north of Chipyong-ni for the 1st Cavalry Division and about four miles north of Hoengsong on the Massacre Valley road for the 1st Marine Division. In X Corps, the point of contact for the US 2nd Division and the French Battalion was the string of high hills north of the MSR between Hoengsong and Pangnim-ni. Everywhere the terrain was snow covered and forbidding. There were increasing reports and rumors that the Chinese were bringing new armies to the front. The six armies of the CCF Fourth Field Army that had fought the war in the west against Eighth Army from the end of October to the present were all but used up and had to be replaced. Rumors were also increasing that the commander of the CCF Fourth Field Army, incorrectly assumed to be Lin Piao, was leaving or had left Korea in a dispute with the top command of the Chinese People's Liberation Army.

The 19th Infantry of the 24th Division, on the division's left flank throughout most of March, faced the 337th and 339th regiments of the 113th Division, CCF 38th Army, and at the end of the month, the 349th Regiment of the 117th Division, 39th Army. Enemy resistance to it was heavy most of the month.[21]

On the first day of Ripper, 7 March, Sfc. Nelson V. Brittin, I Company, 19th Infantry, led his squad on one of the most heroic single-man attacks of the war. Enemy soldiers held their hill in strength with a massing of automatic weapons. Brittin's squad covered him as he raced for the nearest enemy automatic position and threw a grenade into it. In returning to his squad, he was hit by a grenade and knocked to the ground. He refused medical attention, resupplied himself with grenades, headed back into the enemy positions, grenaded another machine-gun position, and shot the crew when they fled. Then his rifle jammed as he attacked an enemy foxhole, but he leaped into the hole and killed the enemy soldier with bayonet and rifle butt strokes. He attacked another machine-gun position from the rear with a grenade and rushed to its front and killed the three crew members with his rifle. Another hundred yards up the hill his squad again was pinned down by an enemy with a camouflaged and sand-bagged automatic weapon. Brittin charged this position and ran directly into a blast of automatic-weapon fire that killed him instantly. Brittin was credited with killing 20 enemy soldiers and destroying four machine guns in the battle. I Company captured the hill later in the day—Brittin's heroics had been a dominant factor in its success. He was awarded the Medal of Honor, Posthumously.[22]

The 3rd Battalion, 19th Infantry, received three strong attacks during the night of 9–10 March in reinforced company strength but repulsed each. On the tenth the Chinese still resisted and used 82-mm and 120-mm mortar fire in defense. The next morning it was found that the enemy had withdrawn during the night.

In the attack across the army front beginning with Operation Ripper on 7 March, the I Corps sector on the west was supplied from the main Korean railhead at Suwon and from Yongdongpo; the IX Corps was situated eastward in a sector where there was no railhead, and it had to be supplied by truck from outside its sector from either the eastern X Corps or western I Corps railroad; the X Corps received its land transportation of supplies by truck from the Chechon railhead, and east of it transportation had to be mostly by air during the late winter and early spring. All sectors had a considerable quantity of air supply from landing fields or by airdrop in the more inaccessible parts of the line, often high in mountain areas devoid of cart trails.

During the night of 7 March, the 19th Infantry of the 24th Division moved up to the line and passed through the 5th RCT. The 19th and 21st regiments then were the attack regiments of the division on either side of the key town of Yangpyong on the east bank of the Han River. The central railroad from Wonju passed through it on the way to Seoul. The 21st Regiment attacked Hill 1157, Yongmun-san, the dominant terrain six air miles northeast of Yangpyong. Grenade-throwing Chinese held the peak, but A Company was nearly on top by 7:15 P.M. The next day the 1st Battalion cleared the hill. The 19th Infantry made less progress, and for the next two days, 9–11 March, the two regiments had hard fighting in mountainous terrain as they slowly pressed the Chinese north with their back to the Hwachon Reservoir on the Pukhan River. By 13 March enemy units

just south of the Hwachon Reservoir were in untenable positions and began to abandon them. On 16 March the 24th Division now was almost
to the Hwachon Reservoir, and the enemy deployments there forced it to
cross the Pukhan River to its west bank and attack through elements of
the 25th Division to the north and west. Resupply to it was almost entirely by airdrop and Korean carriers. Fifty fresh laborers had to be hired
every day to take the place of Korean carrier casualties and deserters.[23]

There can be no doubt that the reduction of Hill 1157, the highest terrain feature in the IX Corps sector, was a difficult and costly attack. Prisoners said they had been ordered to defend it to the last man, but aerial observers said they saw some leaving the hill at the end and withdrawing
north.

During the heavy action at the beginning of Operation Ripper, General
Ridgway had left the front momentarily to attend the graveside services
for Lt. Col. den Ouden, the Netherlands Battalion commander, who had
been killed at Hoengsong on 11 February. He was buried in the UN cemetery at Pusan on 8 March.

On the right of the 24th Division, the US 1st Cavalry Division was
driving through the mountains slowly north of Chipyong-ni toward Hoengsong with many heavy battles on the higher hills, the Chinese troops slowly
withdrawing only when forced to. The British 27th Brigade was in the
mountains east of the 1st Cavalry Division, and on 7 March, at the beginning of Operation Ripper, it had been attached to that division. It, too,
had slow and heavy fighting for the hills southwest of Hongchon. The British Brigade failed in three efforts to take Hill 532, just north of Hagal-li,
which the 370th and 376th regiments of the CCF 42nd Army held. On
13 March the 5th Cavalry Regiment relieved the British 27th Brigade in
the line.[24]

As an example of the type of fighting and withdrawal the CCF of the
42nd Army carried on in front of the 1st Cavalry Division and the British
27th Brigade in the mountains southwest of Chongchon, on 12 March the
Royal Australian Rifles 1st Battalion took Hill 703 without opposition, an
objective that it could not take the day before with heavy attack. In the
night the enemy had withdrawn.

The 5th Cavalry Regiment now had the same kind of fighting the British 27th Brigade had been having. Previous to relieving the British Brigade, I Company of the 5th Cavalry had sent out an officer-led squad on
patrol, 9 March. It ran into a minefield just after noon, and three men were
killed and four wounded by the mines. The patrol, however, was careless
in that it saw lines strung on the ground. At that point it should have halted,
considered the situation, and suspecting mines ahead, turned around. When
the first mine exploded, the patrol scattered and, in doing so, set off other
mines. As a result of this incident, Col. Marcel Crombez, the regimental

commander, ordered refresher courses on minefield procedures for all his regimental troops.

Another incident, this time an accident, afflicted the 5th Cavalry a week later. A muzzle burst of an 81-mm mortar in H Company killed five and wounded nine. On 14 March the 1st Battalion discovered a large cache of enemy-buried ammunition near its CP. This was the first such buried ammunition encountered. This same day, the regiment captured Hill 499, which the enemy seemed to have abandoned hurriedly. The hill had elaborate defensive works, including barbed wire, good bunkers, and deep foxholes, nearly all having ammunition of some kind. A large amount of equipment was left behind.[25]

On 17 March the Greek Battalion, attached to the 7th Cavalry Regiment, repulsed four enemy counterattacks against it on Hill 325 and then itself attacked again, this time with bayonet, and took the hill. The 7th Cavalry itself at the same time took related Hill 349 in a bayonet attack. The net was now closing on Hongchon with this steady but costly hill-to-hill fighting from the southwest. At the same time, the 1st Marine Division was approaching from the south.

On 25 February General Ridgway flew to Yoju for a conference with General Smith, in the course of which Ridgway asked about his views on the proper future use of the 1st Marine Division. Smith replied that he thought the division should continue its attack along the Hoengsong-Chongchon axis. Ridgway then changed the boundary of the 1st Marine Divison so that the 5th Marines on the right flank gave way to the ROK 3rd Division, and the Marine division had a narrower zone in Operation Ripper, which began on 7 March.

At the end of February the Marine Division had reached Hoengsong and the Som River, just north of the town. The Som was in flood, and several days were spent in improvising a bridge. In the attack north of Massacre Valley, just north of Hoengsong, in early March the 7th Marine Regiment had the hardest assignment. Hills 536 and 333, which were in the area where the 3rd Battalion, 36th Infantry, had established its perimeter on 10 February in support of the ROK 8th Divison, were the most formidable obstacles in its path. In the fighting for these hills the 1st and 3rd battalions, 7th Marines, on the afternoon of 3 March lost heavily. They lost 14 killed and 104 wounded that day, and at evening the Chinese 66th Division defenders still held the crest. The next morning when the Marines climbed the hills to resume their attack, the Chinese had withdrawn, leaving behind only a few outpost troops. The 7th Marine Regiment had control of its objectives north of Hoengsong on 4 March. The division's casualties in eight days of fighting were 395: 48 killed, 345 wounded, and 2 missing in action. In that period it counted 274 enemy dead and had taken 48 prisoners.[26]

During this period, the 1st Marine Division was not satisfied with the close air support the Fifth Air Force gave its ground troops. The 1st Marine Air Wing, which had previously supported the division, was now under the control of the Fifth Air Force Joint Operations Center for combat assignments where most needed. In a conference between Generals Shepherd and Harris of the US Marine Corps and General Partridge of the Fifth Air Force, a settlement of the issue was reached that committed more of the 1st Marine Air Wing to the 1st Marine Division for close support of its ground troops.

Hill 930, a 2,900-foot peak, lay ahead of the Marines between them and Hongchon. The Hongchon road curved around the west side of the peak. In a sharp fight there on 8 March, a high-explosive shell made a direct hit on a platoon led by 2nd Lt. Clayton O. Bush, killing two men, wounding three others, and mangling Bush's right arm. The rest of A Company continued the fight and had cleared enemy from the area by night. On the ninth, the Marines remained in place waiting for army troops on their right to come up abreast. When the Marines moved up on the eleventh, there was only slight resistance, and by 14 March the enemy in front of them was in general withdrawal.

After the 1st Marine Division had passed north over the Hoengsong-Hongchon road, General Ridgway on 12 March drove through Massacre Valley in a jeep and had a firsthand view of the places where the ROK 8th Division and the X Corps support forces from the 2nd Division artillery and the 38th Infantry Regiment had suffered such a catastrophe at the hands of the Chinese a month earlier. The next day, Ridgway went to Yongwol, where he conferred with General Farrell, commander of KMAG. Ridgway was dissatisfied with ROK performance in the east, and he wanted them to move their tactical CPs to forward areas. He also felt that the ROKs were not climbing hills and fighting for the peaks but were moving up the valleys instead and leaving enemy behind them. Farrell discussed the political problems he was having with the ROKs; he was especially concerned that General Kim, commanding the ROK I Corps on the east coast, had health and temperament problems that affected his efficiency. He wanted Kim replaced.[27]

During mid-March, when General Ridgway was trying to impress the ROK III Corps with his view that success against the enemy rested with its actions to a considerable extent, he disapproved its plan to attack from south to north, saying it was unsound. Instead, he wanted it to hold where it was and attack the base of the enemy salient in its sector from east to west, and destroy the enemy there.

West of the ROK III Corps sector, the 23rd Infantry of the 2nd Divison and the attached French Battalion had fought enemy forces in the vicinity of Ungyo-ri in the high mountains along the lateral MSR between Hoengsong and Pangnim-ni. The enemy fought bitterly to hold the high hills north of the road because it had a large assembly area in a number of small valleys on the north side of these mountains. On 10 March, finally, the enemy withdrew from in front of the 23rd Infantry during darkness. On 12–13 March the 38th Infantry relieved the 23rd Regiment, which had been in the line for 74 consecutive days. It went into X Corps reserve near Saemal.[28]

In Operation Ripper the US 7th Division was on the right flank of X Corps, the easternmost American division on the line, and in the high mountains through which the Pyongchang–Pangnim-ni–Changpyong-ni–Soksa-ri road twisted its way to the east coast at Kangnung. Many of the peaks in the 7th Division sector were more than 4,000 feet high. It had the worst terrain faced by any American division then fighting in Korea. Yet, on 7 March, the first day of the new offensive Ridgway had ordered, C Company, 32nd Infantry, of the division had good fortune in its attack on the 200 to 300 North Koreans holding Hill 1171. Under cover of an impressive array of artillery, tank, mortar, and antiaircraft fire, it reached a point within 100 yards of the crest. The company then fixed bayonets as the artillery fire lifted and assaulted the crest. The result was anticlimax. When the North Koreans saw the bayonets, they immediately abandoned their positions. C Company pursued the fleeing enemy over the crest and fired on them as they ran. There were more than 100 dead NK 1st Division soldiers scattered around the crest. Most of them had been casualties of the heavy preassault supporting fire.[29] This must have been satisfying to men of this unit, whose battalion had been all but annihilated on the east side of Chosin Reservoir three months earlier.

On the same day, the 3rd and 1st battalions, 17th Infantry, encircled North Koreans from the NK 1st Division on Hill 982, who had held out against previous attacks by the 2nd Battalion, and virtually annihilated that enemy force. They counted 105 enemy dead on the hill after they gained it, captured 7 prisoners, and estimated there were more than 150 wounded. The two attacking battalions had only 4 killed and 12 wounded in this action.[30]

The NK 1st Division now withdrew to Taemi-san Mountain (Hill 1232), 4,037 feet high. The 17th Regiment's attack on it proved to be the most difficult mission the regiment had undertaken thus far in Korea. The peak was the highest in an east-west ridge three air miles north of the MSR between Hoengsong and Pangnim-ni, six air miles southwest of Changpyong-ni, and west of the MSR south-north from Pyongchang. The 1st and 2nd battalions were the attack force. The 3rd Battalion at the same time was to attack west against Hill 1043 to protect the other battalions on their left flank. Time-on-Target (TOT) artillery barrages were delivered all night of 8–9 March against both hills. Early predawn of the ninth, an enemy force from Hill 1232 counterattacked the 2nd Battalion but was repulsed. When daylight came on 9 March, there was a low cloud ceiling hanging over the mountain, which precluded air support. During the day all three battalions suffered badly from their straight-up attacks. It was thought there were two North Korean regiments of the NK 1st Division on the peak, about 3,000 to 4,000 men. The third regiment of the enemy division held Hill 1043 on its western flank. During the day 4,374 rounds of artillery were fired in support of the 17th Regiment and the 35th ROK Regiment, which joined the 3rd Battalion against Hill 1043. The 17th Regiment lost 17 killed and 76 wounded during the day. Evacuation of wounded in this battle among the clouds required more than eight hours in some instances. At night all attacking units withdrew to reorganize – a tangle of men slipping and falling in a driving rain. In some places where the sun, when out, had not penetrated, the snow was waist deep. Under clearing skies the next day the attack resumed with 25 air strikes and continuing TOT artillery barrages.[31]

The costly fighting on 9 March earned the Medal of Honor for one man and a Distinguished Service Cross for another in the 17th Regiment. M. Sgt. James M. Wightman of E Company in action near Twigot (Twigol) was a platoon leader who led his men against enemy entrenchments on Hill 1232. When enemy automatic and small-arms fire pinned the platoon to the ground, Wightman located an enemy machine gun and single-handedly assaulted it. An enemy burst of automatic fire hit and killed him. But his leadership and courage stimulated his platoon to charge nearby emplacements and destroy them.

Likewise, Capt. Raymond L. Harvey, C Company commander, 17th Infantry, found enemy automatic fire on Hill 1232 so heavy that his company could not move against it. He made his way close to the nearest enemy machine gun and succeeded in killing its crew with hand grenades. He went on swiftly to another gun position and killed the crew with carbine fire. He then was able to get his 1st Platoon forward a short distance, but it was soon pinned down again by automatic fire. Harvey for the third time knocked out an enemy automatic-fire position. But he had to continue to lead the assault. He next went against an enemy pillbox of logs, well camouflaged. He got close enough to fire his carbine into the openings and throw grenades into the pillbox, finally killing all five occupants. By this time he had been painfully wounded, but he continued to command his company in the fight, refusing evacuation until C Company had accomplished its immediate mission.[32] It was a miracle that he escaped with his life.

The next day the 17th Infantry consolidated its position on the parts of Hill 1232 it had won and brought in 25 air strikes and delivered 26 artillery TOT barrages to help them hold. The following day, 11 March, plans were made to continue the infantry attack, and that night there were 80 flares dropped by planes over the defense positions. On 12 March the troops moved out to climb upward and make enemy contact. But there was no enemy. By 9:15 A.M. it was apparent that the North Korean 1st Division had withdrawn during the night. By 9:30 A.M. I Company had possession of Hill 1043. At 10 A.M. K Company had Hill 1197, and half an hour later both the 1st and 2nd battalions of the 17th Infantry were on top of forbidding Hill 1232. Not a shot was fired. On the eleventh and twelfth all available persons in the regiment—clerks, drivers, cooks, and others who could be spared from their normal duties—were organized into carrying parties, and with the 235 Korean carriers assigned to the regiment, were occupied in carrying supplies and ammunition to the front-line troops on Hill 1232. The next day elements of the ROK 5th Division relieved the 17th Regiment, 7th Division, on Hill 1232, and the regiment went into X Corps reserve.[33]

On 10 March an important document was captured on the eastern front. It was signed by the chief of staff, NK III Corps, ordering the NK 69th Brigade on the east coast above Kangnung to fight a holding action south of the 38th Parallel in the Yangyang area while the corps withdrew to Inje, 30 miles inland westward on a main road, 18 miles southeast of the Hwachon Reservoir, and a few miles north of the 38th Parallel.[34]

An increasing number of prisoners were being captured in the March fighting everywhere. Their interrogations showed that the Chinese and the Korean units both were losing heavy casualties and that their formations were far below strength. On 9 March, for instance, a CCF lieutenant from a mortar platoon, 196th Division, CCF 66th Army, on the extreme right (east) flank of the Chinese part of the enemy line, surrendered to the US 503rd Field Artillery Battalion. He gave his platoon strength as 20 men, his 5th Company as 40 men, the 2nd Battalion as 100 men, the 586th Regiment as 300 men. This was only a fourth or a fifth of what the units would have been at full strength. The lieutenant also said that at night some houses had as many as 30 CCF soldiers in them.[35] This situation may have been representative of most of the six CCF armies of the Fourth Field Army that had intervened in October 1950 and had fought the war in the west ever since then, with no addition of new infantry units, although with some individual replacements. They were, in effect, worn out and virtually combat ineffective. During the 4th Phase Offensive the Chinese high command saw the need to return the XIII Army Group to China and to bring in fresh formations.

On 12 March the 23rd Infantry of the US 2nd Division captured 42 NK soldiers of the NK 12th Division. They reported that the US 23rd Infantry and the heavy supporting artillery fire and air strikes had almost annihilated their division and that the NK 6th Division had replaced it in the line but had been just as roughly treated.[36]

From 12 March on through the month, and in some areas from 10 March onward, there was evidence of a general enemy withdrawal northward in the central and eastern front, as well as in the west above Seoul, although there was still extremely heavy fighting at places chosen by the enemy to make holding stands. During the period of 8–12 March two American prisoners escaped at night from the Chinese in the Chunchon-Hongchon area. During these days and nights, they observed very heavy enemy troop movements, estimated to total 25,000 soldiers, with vehicles and artillery in convoys, moving north from Hongchon toward Chunchon. The enemy movements usually began about midnight.[37]

Everywhere on the UN line there was trouble getting supplies to the front-line troops, usually high in the mountains where the troops could be reached only by mountain trails. The 24th Division, below the Hwachon Reservoir, sometimes had a round trip of 20 miles to hand carry supplies to the combat troops in their foxholes, and it had to send trucks on a round trip of 300 miles to Sangju to get the Korean laborers who would serve as carriers. Once they had been brought to the front, their loss was high due to bad feet, poor physical condition, some casualties, and much desertion. The Korean transportation companies were just being organized, and the situation later improved. March 1951, however, was a bad month in all respects relating to supplies for the soldiers fighting in the mountains.[38]

A month earlier, on 12 February, Chinese had captured two wounded American officers in the vicinity of Hoengsong. Later, on 23 February, at a collection point for American prisoners south of Hongchon, they had seen 152 US prisoners. The CCF released 29 enlisted men at that time, and they returned to their own lines. The rest were started for a POW camp they were told was 90 miles north. The two wounded officers were put in carts that also carried wounded CCF. The group arrived at Chunchon on 7 March. Six unarmed and wounded CCF continued on with the group as guards. The two officers saw their chance to escape and left the group the next day, and on the ninth they were back at Chunchon. There they persuaded a North Korean security policeman they had been released "up north," and he gave them a safe-conduct pass. They reached friendly lines on 12 March after passing through Hongchon. They saw no enemy in Hongchon, which seemed to be deserted.[39]

In the 1st Cavalry zone, north of Piryong-ni and Chipyong-ni, the 3rd Battalion, 7th Cavalry, was unable to take an enemy position defended from strong bunkers. At dusk an enemy column of about 700 soldiers, marching in a column of twos and extending more than a mile long, was observed moving south on a ridge toward the 2nd Battalion. The 1st Cavalry Division artillery placed TOT concentrations on the column and brought in air strikes. Three times the enemy column tried to organize for attack, but each time VT fuse artillery shells brought them under showers of exploding-shell steel fragments, as well as heavy mortar fire. The column was virtually destroyed, with an estimated 400 killed and 200 wounded. The survivors ran wildly back north. The 2nd Battalion, however, did not that day or night gain its objectives, as the enemy continued to defend its hill from many bunkers. On the morning of 14 March, though, the 2nd Battalion found the enemy position had been abandoned during the night.[40]

The 1st Cavalry Division on the left (west) and the 1st Marine Division on the right (east) were driving on Hongchon in the high mountains from the southwest and the south. The 1st Cavalry Division in general was proceeding up the Hongchon valley, but they were fighting in the mountains on either side of the valley—a narrow one where steep mountain sides slanted up sharply from the stream banks. The Hongchon River was a tributary of the Pukhan and ran southwest to empty into the latter at an arm of the Hwachon Reservoir. The Hongchon's source was in the high mountains eastward in the vicinity of Pungam-ni. The boundary between the 1st Cavalry Division and the 1st Marine Division as they converged on Hongchon was along the road that ran north-south for a few miles just south of the town. The Marines were on the right of the road, the 1st Cavalry on the left of it. The terrain in both divisions was difficult until they reached the Hongchon valley and the bulging bowl of level ground at Hongchon.

General Ridgway had planned to drop the 187th Airborne RCT on the north side of Hongchon and, with the 1st Marine Division arriving on the town's south side and the 1st Cavalry Division coming up from the southwest, to trap a sizable part of the CCF 66th Division in the Hongchon area. But the enemy escaped from Hongchon before the airborne troops could be dropped, and only ground troops were involved in the capture and occupation of the devastated town. When the 7th Marines arrived at Hongchon, it was deserted, and they entered it unopposed on the afternoon of 15 March. Maj. Webb D. Sawyer's patrol went through the deserted town without finding any Chinese soldiers. At noon the Marines had intercepted an enemy radio message, which said, "We cannot fight any longer. We must move back today. We will move back at 2 P.M. Enemy troops will enter our positions at 1 P.M. or 2 P.M. Enemy troops approaching fast."[41]

But if the Marines did not find any Chinese in Hongchon, the patrol found plenty of US-dropped butterfly four-pound bombs. They usually were in clusters on the ground and exploded on being disturbed. It took D Company, 1st Engineer Battalion, three days to clear them from Hongchon.

The 7th Cavalry Regiment at the same time was on the south and west sides of Hongchon, but in its zone it faced Hill 655 on the west side of the Hongchon River. This mountain mass and its subordinate Hills 325 and 320 controlled the Hongchon River valley and blocked any further advance northward west of the river. The 7th Cavalry had to find a way to reduce Hill 655. Although the enemy had abandoned Hongchon and the flat bowl in which it lay, they were in great strength on the surrounding critical, dominant hills. The terrain west of the Hongchon River at the town was such that the 7th Cavalry could not get their mortars and supporting weapons close enough to the base of Hill 655 to support an infantry attack. A combat patrol was sent out to find a crossing of the Hong-

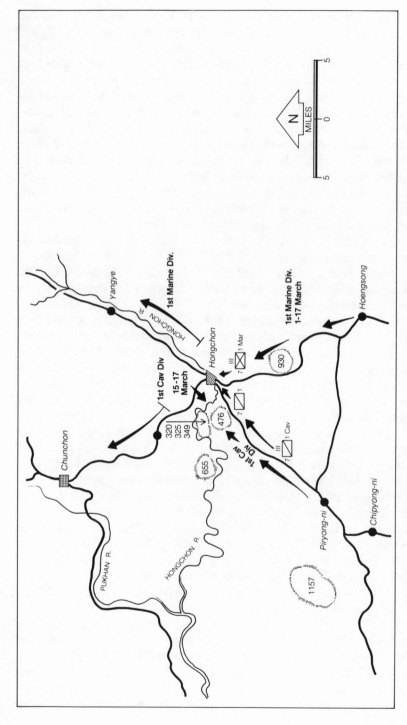

MAP 15. 1st Cavalry and 1st Marine divisions' capture of the Hongchon basin, 1–17 March 1951

A Marine tank and infantry patrol move along a war-torn street into Hong-chon, the first armored patrol to enter the town, 16 March 1951. *US Marine photograph, A 8613*

chon River farther north in terrain that would permit bringing up supporting weapons and allow an infantry approach to Hill 655 itself.

On 16 March the partrol found a feasible crossing site at the northwest edge of the town and, once across the river, a network of roads and trails that would permit an attack approach to Hills 320 and 325 on eastern spurs of Hill 655. After they had been taken, Hill 655 would be vulnerable to attack. But it promised to be a tough job. A patrol reported eight machine guns on Hill 320 alone, and it was only the first approach to the main objective. Artillery and air strikes were put on the enemy's positions on all three hills. Intelligence and reconnaissance, aerial and ground, arrived at an estimate of a regiment of Chinese holding the Hill 655 positions. The Chinese were well entrenched, with underground emplacements covered by several layers of tree logs and entrenchments that connected between emplacements. The order to seize Hill 655 was issued at 7 P.M., 15 March. The sixteenth was spent in reconnaissance.[42]

The 1st and 4th (Greek) battalions were the assault battalions; the 1st Battalion was to cross the river and seize Hills 320 and 349, and the 4th Battalion was to seize Hill 325 and be prepared to continue the attack to Hill 655. The 3rd Battalion, in regimental reserve, was to support the attacks with 81-mm mortar, recoilless-rifle, and heavy machine-gun fire on the southern slope of Hill 655. Artillery and mortar preparations on the objectives were fired during the night of 16–17 March. Air strikes were to start at 7:15 A.M. on 17 March. All supporting weapons would be used to the maximum.

At 8 A.M., 17 March, after the artillery preparation and an air strike, O Company of the Greek Battalion crossed the Hongchon River, the line of departure for Hill 325, which was directly east of Hill 655. The company was immediately brought under enemy fire. At 9:30 A.M. machine guns wounded the company commander. The executive officer took command, and the advance continued slowly and methodically. The Chinese were so well dug in and their defenses so well prepared that only grenades and bayonets would in the end get them out. Tanks took great chances in operating over very rough terrain, but some of them succeeded in reaching enemy emplacements and bunkers and caved them in by running over them. The Chinese continuously reinforced Hill 325 and stubbornly held it. After three hours of fighting and maneuvering and the help of all supporting weapons, the Greeks fixed bayonets and, with the cry of "Aera!" they assaulted and drove the Chinese from the hill. The Chinese immediately counterattacked with 100 men. The Greeks met them with bayonets and repulsed them. The Chinese at once made a second, and then a third, suicidal counterattack. But the Greeks, once in control of the crest, fought with equal ferocity and with bayonets drove off each counterattack. After the third encounter failed, the remaining Chinese withdrew.

The key hill and ridge were now secured. The Chinese Hongchon River line was broken. Preparations were made during the late afternoon and during the night to attack Hill 655 from Hill 325 the next day. But the next day when Greek Company N moved out, it found Hill 655 deserted. The Greeks counted 187 Chinese dead at Hill 325 and estimated another 300 had been wounded. The capture of Hill 325 at the western edge of Hongchon and the lower reaches of Hill 655 was one of the really great battles the Greek Battalion fought in the Korean War.[43]

Meanwhile, A Company, 1st Battalion, 7th Cavalry, crossed the line of departure on the morning of 17 March at the same time as the Greek Battalion and headed for Hill 320, a little closer to the river and east-northeast of Hill 325. Following closely behind supporting fire, A Company captured the first knob of the hill. But enemy fire from a second knob 100 yards west stopped further advance. At 2:30 P.M. the enemy was still further reinforced, and it then launched a counterattack. Still without a requested ammunition resupply, the company relied mostly on heavy artillery and mortar fire to interdict the Chinese counterattack. A Company was able to repulse it and immediately made one of its own, which was unusually successful, causing the Chinese to flee and scatter. A Company's attack carried it across Ridge-Hill 320. In continuing pursuit down a western finger spur of the ridge, a platoon of the company flushed nearly an equal number of enemy and, in the heat of their frenzied attack, killed 19 of them in a bayonet charge and took 12 prisoners. After they had secured Hill 320, the 1st Battalion counted 96 enemy dead, 14 prisoners, and estimated 200 Chinese wounded. The surviving Chinese fled to the north. Many weapons and much ammunition was captured on the hill. At 3 P.M. C Company, 7th Cavalry, received orders to pass through A Company and continue the attack against Hill 349, a short distance northwest of Hill 320. The company secured Hill 349 without opposition by 5 P.M. The battle for Hill 655 was over.[44]

Although Major Sawyer's 1st Battalion, 7th Marines, had gone through Hongchon on the afternoon of 15 March and found it deserted of enemy, the Marines did not have to go far from the town before they found plenty of enemy—on the hills outside. They held the hills north and northeast of Hongchon in great strength, where they occupied well-built bunkers. There the Marines had to dig them out in hand-to-hand fighting. Enemy on Hills 356, 246, and 428, east-southeast of Hongchon, fought the Marines to a standstill during the next two days, 16–17 March. The 2nd and 3rd battalions, 7th Marines, in that time lost 7 men killed and 86 wounded. There were 93 counted enemy dead. The Chinese abandoned Hill 428 during the night. On one hill east of Hongchon the Chinese resisted so stubbornly that Marines had to attack each bunker with grenades.[45]

The 7th Marines found three enemy ammunition dumps at and near Hongchon, which included more than 2,000 rifles and assorted automatic weapons and small arms, 11 heavy machine guns, 12 60-mm mortars, 9 US heavy machine guns, 12 57-mm recoilless rifles, 17 rocket launchers, 35 US Thompson submachine guns, bangalore torpedoes, grenades, and 44 cases of ammunition.

On 17 March General MacArthur visited the Marine front at Hongchon. Generals Ridgway and Oliver Smith accompanied him in a jeep from Wonju. MacArthur had asked to visit a Marine battalion in a combat area. He was driven to Major Sawyer's 1st Battalion area, where the troops were still mopping up on Hill 399, where the day before they had fought bunker to bunker with grenades. In crossing the Hongchon River, MacArthur's jeep stuck in a ford and had to be towed out. Marine engineers were still clearing mines from Hongchon.[46]

The 5th Marines now passed through the 7th Marines and continued the advance north; the 1st Marines were on their right, the 1st Cavalry Division across the boundary to the west. The 5th Marines had little opposition as they advanced to Hill 330. The enemy had generally withdrawn, and on 20 March, when they occupied Hill 330, not a single Marine had been killed or wounded in the three-day advance. The Hongchon valley road running northeast toward Hangye paralleled the 5th Marines' advance on the hills to the right of it, and B Company, 1st Marine Tank Battalion, was able to knock out many enemy bunkers from the road. On the twentieth, the 5th Marines continued on north from Hill 330 and captured Hill 381, again with tank help and without a casualty. After the heavy fighting in the hills immediately surrounding Hongchon, the enemy had withdrawn from contact, except for small outposts and screening units left behind, and they generally escaped before contact.[47]

On 13 March the 38th Infantry Regiment relieved the 23rd Regiment of the US 2nd Division in the high country east of the 1st Marine Division. It and the 9th Infantry, which fell in behind the 38th Regiment, carried the main fight for the next week for X Corps. The 2nd Division and X Corps aimed for Pungam-ni, a road junction for the minor roads and trails deep in the mountains, 16 air miles east of Hongchon. The best road or track to it from the south and southwest came from Hoengsong through Yudong-ni and Kuram-ni. It was steep mountains and gorges all the way.

On 14 March the 3rd Battalion, 38th Infantry, led the attack forward from just beyond Yudong-ni. The 2nd Battalion followed on the road, which was heavily mined. The 1st Battalion was behind the other two in the vicinity of Saemal. The 38th Infantry lost four tanks and one M16 quad-50 to mines during the day. On the fifteenth the 3rd Battalion, in the lead, had the mission of seizing the pass just south of Kuram-ni, and the 2nd Battalion was then to secure it. The two key hills at the pass were 570 and 719. But E and L companies failed to take Hill 570, and K Company made slow progress for the 3rd Battalion against Hill 719. In one stretch of 25 yards, elements of the 9th Infantry found more than 14 mines in the road.[48]

On 15 March the 2nd and 3rd battalions of the 38th Infantry captured 139 North Korean prisoners and counted 348 dead at Hill 570. The 38th Infantry itself had 12 men killed and 156 wounded, attesting to the severity of the fighting. The prisoners were from the NK 7th, 12th, and 6th divisions. The NK 6th and 12th divisions were the main delaying forces in front of the 38th Infantry, 2nd Division. One prisoner said that two enemy battalions defended Hill 570. In his company of 50 men, he said 30 were former South Korean soldiers who had been forced into service.[49]

Just after midnight the 38th Regiment ordered the 2nd and 3rd battalions to resume the attack at 7:30 the next morning, 16 March. The two battalions jumped off on schedule. By 8:15, E and L companies had taken Hill 570 against almost no resistance, and F Company took the remainder of Hill 719. The enemy had pulled out during the night. The 2nd Battalion left small holding forces on the two hills, pending their relief by the 9th Infantry Regiment. I and K companies of the 3rd Battalion captured Hill 650 and the ground to the left of the hill. During the night an enemy holding force had abandoned this hill as well as the others. The pass was now secure. K Company loaded on tanks and rumbled down the road to Pungam-ni, which they reached at 5:30 P.M. The 2nd and 3rd battalions joined and established a defense perimeter there. During the sixteenth the North Koreans avoided any contact with the 38th Infantry. On 17 March the 9th Infantry coming up behind the 38th Infantry had only to move north on the road, making a 12-mile advance in eight hours.[50] The 38th Infantry now consolidated the high ground positions northeast of Pungam-ni, its objective gained.

Farther east on the X Corps right (east) flank, the 3rd Battalion, 32nd Infantry, US 7th Division, had equally hard fighting in high mountains north and northwest of Soksa-ri, where the MSR turned east through Hajinbu-ri toward the east coast. Many North Koreans were dug in on Hills 1008 and 1286, according to civilian testimony. On 16 March I Company of the 3rd Battalion had orders to take Hill 1008 from the west, and L Company was to attack Hill 1286, while a platoon of the Reconnaissance Company screened and protected the 3rd Battalion's right flank. K Company was held in reserve. Both companies moved to the attack by daylight. When L Company received intense fire from the crest of Hill 1286, it called for artillery barrages, which 105-mm howitzers delivered. At the same time, two sections of antiaircraft weapons and two tanks fired direct support. Then came an air strike on the crest, employing napalm, rockets, and strafing. Two platoons of L Company then assaulted the crest, using more than 100 grenades. The L Company men pulled 32 enemy dead from their foxholes. Meanwhile, I Company moved up the rear slope of Hill 1008 and surprised dug-in enemy halfway down the forward slope. After a close-in fight among the foxholes, 15 North Koreans were dead, and others escaped. This was the first time the 7th Division had found enemy dug in halfway down the forward slope.[51] NK prisoners and an escaped ROK officer reported that, in the eastern sector, North Koreans were withdrawing to Inje and Yanggu behind screening forces.

K Company, 32nd Infantry, 7th Division, now attacked Kyebang-san, at 1577 meters the highest mountain in east-central Korea, 6 air miles north of Soksa-ri and 15 air miles east of Pungam-ni, but found no enemy on it. The 7th Division thus also attained its objectives on 16 March.[52]

Of all the NK guerrilla units that penetrated south in January 1951 along the east coast and through the central mountains to reach the rear area of X Corps and Eighth Army, none had a more memorable operational history than the NK 10th Division. It deserves a brief notice and some recognition of its amazing record. In early January 1951, when the entire eastern, mountainous part of central Korea was wide open to enemy infiltration just at the time the Chinese captured Seoul and crossed the Han River in the west, the NK 10th Division moved south from the vicinity of the 38th Parallel through the eastern mountains, brushing aside the feeble

ROK forces there, causing trouble all the way, and even more fear of what it might do later. It reached the outskirts of Andong in the south and the approaches of Taegu in the west, the headquarters of Eighth Army Main CP. Other rehabilitated NK divisions, all understrength, did the same thing as the NK 10th, but they were hunted down, destroyed, or dispersed. Not so with the NK 10th Division. It caused more trouble behind the UN lines—it killed or wounded more UN soldiers and South Korean police, destroyed more military property, and carried out successfully more sabotage actions—than any other guerrilla unit operating behind the lines. It fought innumerable engagements and skirmishes with ROK military units, South Korean police, and on occasion elements of the US 7th Infantry Division, and for a time the 1st Marine Division, which was given the special mission of destroying it.

Through all this time the NK 10th Division received no resupply of food, clothing, ammunition, or equipment from the north. It had no medical supplies. It lived on the land, capturing enemy weapons and ammunition when it could. It must have had superb leadership and discipline. After the 1st Marine Division was moved north into the IX Corps line in the middle of February, the ROK 2nd Division received full-time responsibility for hunting down the remaining elements of the NK 10th Division. But it did not succeed in its mission.

On or about 10 March, the NK 10th Division remnants began to move slowly back north. On 13 March elements of the division were encountered on the east coast about 18 miles south of Kangnung. There, four regiments of ROK troops, elements of the 28th, 29th, 30th, and 9th divisions, and a part of the ROK 26th Regiment, spent five days trying to destroy the NK 10th Division survivors. Most of them, however, escaped to enter the ROK 9th and 3rd Division sectors or the eastern mountains about 17 or 18 March. The ROK 9th Division had the most extensive contact and combat with the NK 10th Division. It later reported that, as a result of its operations in the period between 10 and 21 March, it killed 2,611 members of the NK 10th Division, captured 798 prisoners, and captured 874 rifles (including 180 M-1s), 224 submachine guns, and 16,645 rounds of small-arms ammunition.[53]

On 17 March the ROK 27th Regiment reported ambushing an enemy force, killing 485, and capturing much equipment. The North Koreans in this engagement were not identified. They may have been from the NK 10th Division. The day before, however, the Cavalry Regiment of the ROK Capital Division had tried to cut off the NK 10th Division 7 miles south of Kusan-ni, a few miles southwest of Kangnung, but had little success. On 18 March the 3rd Battalion, 28th Regiment, of the ROK 9th Division claimed to have engaged elements of the NK 10th Division in the Sokpyong-san mountain area 12 air miles south of Kangnung, where it said it killed 241 and captured 12. At this time about 300 soldiers of the NK 10th Division entered the 23rd Regiment, ROK 3rd Division, lines from the south, causing much confusion, and then escaped north, still maintaining unit integrity and under responsible command, after spending three months behind enemy lines. After slipping away from the ROK 3rd Division, the remnants of the enemy division joined other North Koreans in the Yangyang coastal area and presumably withdrew to the Inje area.[54]

The results of the IX and X corps operations in the middle part of March in the mountains of central Korea in the Chunchon, Pyongchang, Ungyori, Yudong-ni, Soksa-ri, and Pungam-ni areas, together with a large number of accumulated prisoner interrogation reports and agent reports, indicated clearly that the Chinese troops in the western border of the central zone and the North Koreans elsewhere eastward to the coast were engaged in a well-organized and successful withdrawal northward and westward toward the Chunchon and Inje areas. It seemed that the enemy was withdrawing to its old fortifications and defense line just above the 38th Parallel. There it was anticipated that the CCF would bring in massive new formations of troops, reorganize the North Koreans, and prepare to launch another major offensive. But for the present, the enemy was on the run in the central and eastern mountains.[55]

15

Eighth Army across the 38th Parallel

THE HARD FIGHTING in the mountains of central and east Korea during the third week of March had taken the US IX and X corps north of Hongchon and Soksa-ri, and from there the ROK III and I corps' jagged line slanted northeast to the coast some miles north of Kangnung. This UN line was now north of Seoul in the west. The clear evidence that developed in this mountain warfare indicates that, by the middle of March, the Chinese and North Koreans were carrying out an organized withdrawal, fighting hard where they needed to in screening that withdrawal, after the fall of Seoul in the west, from which the enemy also had withdrawn. Combat intelligence developed increasingly to indicate this withdrawal would carry the enemy forces as far north as the 38th Parallel, where the Chinese and North Koreans could rally and hold in the extensive field fortifications, trenches and bunkers, and chosen terrain features, where the North Koreans had built their border-line defenses between 1945 and 1950 and from which they had launched their invasions of the South on 25 June 1950. Behind this line, intelligence indicated the Chinese would reorganize their forces and bring in fresh formations to launch a new offensive.

In the west in the US I Corps sector, after crossing the Han River on 7 March and the fall of Seoul a week later, the UN advance virtually halted for some days until the occupation of Seoul could be consolidated, bridges built across the Han to carry men and supplies to the north side, and reconnaissance made of the enemy's screening forces to the north of the city. I Corps had the ROK 1st Division in Seoul and its environs to the west and north, the US 3rd Division on the east side of the city, and the US 25th Division farther east, as far as the Pukhan River.

On 27 March the American people heard Radio Peking broadcast to the United States that "the Chinese Peoples Volunteers and the Korean Peoples Army temporarily withdrew from Seoul on 14 March."[1]

In the 25th Division sector just west of the Pukhan River, stubborn enemy resistance developed on 22 March, and that night L Company, 27th

Infantry, received the first enemy night attacks since crossing the Han River two weeks earlier. These counterattacks were repulsed with the help of artillery fire from the 8th Artillery Battalion. At the end of the month the 25th Division had strong opposition and began to receive increasing numbers of casualties. E Company, 27th Infantry, for instance, had 25 battle casualties on 31 March. The main push north of Seoul would come from the US 3rd Division, which would advance along the main road north to Uijongbu, and the ROK 1st Division, which would be on its left (west) flank on the axis of the main road northwest to Munsan-ni and the Imjin River.

Before these two divisions could undertake any advance, the two floating vehicular bridges across the Han River would have to be completed. The "Seoul" bridge, from the east side of Yongdongpo in the ROK 1st Division sector, was finished on 17 March and was 732 feet long. The next day the "Al Jolson" bridge, 990 feet long, was completed in the 3rd Division sector on the east side of Seoul. Rail transportation from the port of Inchon to Yongdongpo started on 17 March, and by the twentieth, rail transportation on the main Korean rail line from Pusan reached Yongdongpo, and an army supply point was opened there.[2]

On 18 March the ROK 11th Regiment, ROK 1st Division, and the 65th Regiment, US 3rd Division, crossed to the north side of the Han. Crossing of other units of these two divisions continued daily. General Milburn, I Corps commander, in response to General Ridgway's inquiry, estimated that I Corps could attack north from the Seoul area on the morning of 22 March. Ridgway then ordered an attack for the three divisions of I Corps to jump off at 8 A.M. on that day.[3]

A patrol from C Company, 15th Infantry, 3rd Division, and C Company from the Belgian detachment, went north on 18 March to scout enemy defenses. It had a bad accident on the mission, detonating a mine estimated to contain 50 pounds of TNT. The explosion killed Capt. Harold Everitt, commander of C Company, and Lieutenant Beauprez, commander of the Belgian C Company contingent, and wounded three others.[4] This was only one of a large number of deadly encounters with enemy mines north of Seoul. The enemy had mined virtually every road and bridge bypass, as well as many stream beds and their banks, from Seoul to Uijongbu. The 3rd Division, especially, had a major problem with them, and they slowed its advance materially when the division moved out in attack on 22 March.

On 18 March a Chinese deserter, carrying a UN safe-conduct pass, surrendered to the I&R Platoon of the 24th Regiment, 25th Division. He was considered so important that he was flown immediately in a light plane to Taegu for interviewing by the Eighth Army Main CP interrogation team. His surrender was important because he was the first soldier captured from the CCF 26th Army, thus verifying that a new army had appeared on the west-central front, opposite the 25th Division, although there had been some intelligence indicating this army might be moving into the enemy line. According to Pvt. Lyu Kie Lyang's account, he was from the 3rd Company, 1st Battalion, 264th Regiment, 77th Division, 26th Army. [The CCF order of battle has the 264th Regiment in the 88th Division, 26th Army, and not in the 77th Division.] The 26th Army was one of three (others were the 20th and 27th) from the IX Army Group, Third Field Army, which had fought the Chosin Reservoir campaign in November and December 1950. After the X Corps evacuation from Hungnam, the exhausted and decimated Chinese divisions of the IX Army Group had remained in the Hungnam, Hamhung, and Wonsan areas taking in replacements and reorganizing. There had been countless speculations in the Far East Command and Eighth Army as to the location of these divisions and their probable movement to the Eighth Army front and reentry into combat. Now it had become a fact. On 24 and 30 March the 25th Division captured other prisoners from the 77th and 78th divisions of the 26th Army.[5]

It happened that an entire Chinese army, new to Korea, crossed the Yalu at this time and began a forced march toward the front. Two orders, one issued on 17 March by the CCF 60th Army, and the other issued on 18 March by its 180th Division, disclose all the details of a remarkable foot movement of three CCF divisions, the 179th, 180th, and 181st, from Antung, Manchuria, on the Yalu, to an assembly area at Ichon in Korea. The division made this march of 800 li, or approximately 286 miles in a period ranging from 16 to 19 days. The 60th Army Headquarters made the same movement on foot.

Antung is on the Manchurian side of the Yalu River opposite Sinuiju. Ichon is a major road junction in central Korea 25 air miles northwest of Chorwon at the southwest corner of the Iron Triangle and on the main invasion route to Seoul. Ichon would be an ideal assembly area for a new Chinese combat force intended for a planned new offensive against UN forces in Korea. The route of the 60th Army was from Antung across the Yalu to Sinuiju, and hence through Sonchon, Chongju, Anju, Sunchon, Chasan, Kangdong, Samdung, Suan, to Ichon.

The movement of the CCF 60th Army was not discovered between 22 March and 6 April, when it averaged 18 miles a day in night marches. The schedule given for one regiment, the 538th, shows that it covered 600 li, or 215 miles, in nine days, for an average of 24 miles a day. The Roman legions could do no better. A few excerpts from the division order will give an idea of the precision and discipline that made the march possible.

This division will depart at 1500 to 1800 hours on 22 March, with one hour intervals between regiments and division headquarters in the order given below:
    The 538th Regiment departs at 1500 hours; the 540th Regiment departs at 1600 hours; the Division Detachment departs at 1700 hours; and the 539th Regiment departs at 1800 hours.

All units of this division will reach the assembly area by 6 April. Routes of deployment and areas of assembly are shown on the attached sketches.

The distance of march from the present location of this Division to the assembly area is about 800 li. An average daily march of 60 li is required. . . . The march will start at 1900 hours each day and stop at 0300 hours the following morning. Defense measures against air attack must be completed before 0530. The bivouac parties will start at 0600 hours every day, proceed to the bivouac area ahead of the troops and make final arrangements as to the exact spot of bivouac, procurement of provision, defense measures against air attack, et cetera. . . .

Attention must be paid to air defense measures by all units during the march and after entering the bivouac area. Personnel, animals, and vehicles must be dispersed, concealed and thoroughly camouflaged. No smoke or reflecting object will be exposed during the day. At night fires and lights are strictly prohibited. . . .

Units will not begin or stop the day's march too long before or after the time scheduled. It is important that they start after dark and be protected against enemy air attack before dawn. . . .

Traffic regulations must be strictly observed. During the march, units will proceed along one or both sides of the road (on first and second class highways, proceed along both sides; on third class highways, along one side). Proper intervals must be maintained between regiments, battalions, and companies. When vehicles seek to pass along the roads, troops will make way for them. . . .

Collecting team: Each battalion will organize a collecting team to recover the sick and persons wounded by enemy air-craft and have sent to the Division hospital (patients must be in before 0400 hours). . . .

All units will carry with them the prescribed amount of rations, no more and no less, so they will neither starve nor be overburdened. . . .

All units must carry with them standard ammunition stocks which should be carefully maintained and camouflaged.

The 60th Army order indicated that it was to join the 12th and 15th armies, stated to be on the east of the Imjin River and northwest of Yonchon, to help stop the current UN offensive, and to launch a counteroffensive. If one may look ahead for a moment, all three of these Chinese armies were identified as being committed to action in the last part of April or the first part of May. The details revealed by the two captured orders of the CCF 60th Army and of the 180th Division indicate that a Chinese division, moving entirely by foot, could cross the Yalu from China into North Korea and be in the combat line near the 38th Parallel within a month. One may assume that most of the Chinese forces that took part in the massive offensives in April and May 1951 arrived at their combat destinations in much the same manner as the CCF 60th Army. In analyzing and commenting on the march of the 60th Army in March and in early April, the Far East Command stated:

In a final analysis it can only be concluded that this march was a major military accomplishment, that the troops concerned displayed superior stamina and courage, that despite a lack of transportation the CCF can move large bodies of troops over considerable distances in a comparatively short time. It also shows that they can meet military emergencies, that they are capable of planning and executing a well conceived march plan and that they are masters of improvisation as regards the maintenance and repair of roads, bridges and fords as well as the full utilization of every available means of transport to supply their units on the march.[6]

At the same time as new Chinese formations were marching from China across the Yalu and then south to assembly areas a short distance north of the 38th Parallel, the Chinese and North Koreans, with Soviet help in supplying weapons, ammunition, and logistic supplies, were running a maximum number of trains and trucks from the border south to the vicinity of the front. These were part of a massive buildup of war matériel that would be needed when they launched a planned new offensive. On the night of 19–20 March UN aircraft succeeded in placing three 500-pound bombs on a 35-car ammunition train. All cars exploded, one after the other, when the first one ignited, and smoke rose to 5,000 feet. The next night UN aircraft caught seven trains on the tracks just south of Sinuiju, near the Yalu, destroyed two of them, and damaged the other five. Aerial observation at this time along the important Chorwon-Wonsan rail line that connected with the Soviet rail system at the Siberian border found that trains ran on it nightly, and had been doing so since 13 February. The trains were usually short ones, from seven to nine cars long. The locomotives that pulled these trains were hidden in tunnels and other places along the track and appeared to pull the trains in relay fashion. Rail operations along this track extended usually from 10 P.M. to 4 A.M. nightly.[7]

Resistance of North Korean units that had been left behind in the Seoul area as screening and delaying forces when the CCF and North Koreans evacuated the city was now rapidly disappearing, and troops surrendered readily to UN forces after only token resistance. For instance, on 20 March, 25 enemy soldiers surrendered to elements of the ROK 1st Division after a firefight and said the rest of its force would surrender if safe-conduct passes were air-dropped to them. And at another point near Seoul, a North Korean major and 22 enlisted men surrendered that afternoon to a ROK 1st Division patrol. Farther east in the 25th Division sector of I Corps, the advancing troops found it was becoming harder to identify Chinese officers. Normally they had worn uniforms with red piping on them, but now their uniforms were generally plain. More of an effort had to be made in examining enemy dead and in interrogating prisoners to identify Chinese officers. An increase in enemy artillery fire was noticed in March, signifying that this aspect of enemy weaponry was changing. Earlier, enemy artillery fire was rarely encountered.[8]

In its advance northward near the Pukhan River, the 27th Infantry of the 25th Division discovered that, by 20 March, the 264th Regiment of the 26th Army, CCF Third Field Army, was in its front — a new formation. It appeared to be interested only in delaying actions. It was believed its mission was relieving the CCF 38th Army, a veteran organization of the CCF Fourth Field Army.[9]

On 21 March, Eighth Army had a new assistant chief of staff, G-3, for operations. Col. William C. Mudgett replaced Brig. Gen. John A. Dabney, who had held that post since 15 August 1950. On this date, General Ridgway ordered I and IX corps to continue their attacks to the general line of the Imjin River, and General MacArthur in a dispatch to the Joint Chiefs of Staff asked that no further military restrictions be imposed on the UN command in Korea.[10]

On 22 March the 1st ROK Division, the US 3rd Division, and the 25th Division of I Corps moved out northward from the Seoul area in attack. The main assault was by the ROK 1st Division toward Munsan-ni and the 3rd Division toward Uijongbu, 12 miles due north of Seoul. General Ridgway went to the ROK 1st Division CP at West Gate in Seoul to see that division, and then on to General Soule's 3rd Division lines northeast of Seoul.[11]

With the attack getting under way, I Corps closed its CP at Suwon and reopened it at Yongdongpo on 22 March. It expected to secure quickly the junction of the Imjin River with the Han on its left flank in the zone of the ROK 1st Division. The most important feature of the attack starting on the twenty-second in the I Corps sector, however, was the forming of Task Force Growden in Seoul to drive north to Munsan-ni, where it was to make junction with the 187th Airborne RCT, which was to make an airdrop there the next day. The 187th Airborne had had a hectic time during the past few days in its planning. First it was to drop at Chunchon in central Korea, but that plan was canceled on 19 March when an armored patrol of the 1st Cavalry Division entered Chonchon and found it a deserted and destroyed town; Marine patrols found the situation the same. The enemy had abandoned the town as indefensible but was dug in on the surrounding hills. General Ridgway then decided there was a chance for an airdrop of the regiment at Munsan-ni to cut off large numbers of North Korean troops between Seoul and the Imjin River. The drop was scheduled for 23 March. Eighth Army intelligence estimated that the NK I Corps, a force of about 20,000 men, composed of the 8th, 17th, and 47th divisions north and northwest of Seoul, had not yet crossed the Imjin River in its withdrawal and might be cut off and destroyed or dispersed.[12]

Task Force Growden was named for its commander, Lt. Col. John S. Growden, commander of the 6th Medium Tank Battalion. This ground task force that was to link up with the airdrop at Munsan-ni included the following units:

6th Medium Tank Battalion
2nd Battalion, 7th Infantry Regiment, US 3rd Division (mounted in
    M-39 personnel carriers from 3rd Division)

58th Armored Field Artillery Battalion (less one battery)
One battery, 999th Armored Field Artillery Battalion
A Company, 14th Engineer (C) Battalion
Two bridge-laying tanks of the British 29th Brigade (BIB)
Two TAC Parties

The task force was primarily an armored force. It was divided into four teams, each of which had a tank company and at least a platoon of infantry.

Plans for the task force were begun on the evening of 21 March. The units of the task force assembled in Seoul on the morning of 22 March. A planning meeting of unit commanders and staffs was held at I Corps Headquarters, and Corps Operation Directive 51 (Operation Tomahawk) was issued. The main route of advance was the Seoul–Munsan-ni MSR, with secondary routes to be used if the situation required it. At 2 P.M. the commanders and staffs of the task force assembled at the Seoul CP, and the attack order was issued verbally. At 6:30 P.M. the order was given to cross Line Cairo, the line of departure at 6:30 A.M. the next morning, 23 March.[13]

While preparations were going forward for the 187th Airborne RCT to jump at Munsan-ni, the 3rd US Division drove north along the Uijongbu road, the 65th Infantry on the west side of the MSR, and the 15th Infantry with the Belgian Battalion attached on the east side of the road. They reached Uijongbu, 12 miles north of Seoul, with little resistance, but once through the town they encountered stiff opposition from enemy dug in on the hills north of it. The heaviest resistance developed northeast of Uijongbu, where the MSR divided into a second important road branching off to the northeast toward Chorwon. Task Force Hawkins, comprising the 64th Heavy Tank Battalion and two platoons of the 15th Regimental Tank Company, entered and secured Uijongbu at 9:05 A.M. on 23 March. The next day there was hard fighting for the hills north of the town, the 15th Regiment of the 3rd Division counting 400 CCF dead there at the end of the day. Hills 337 and 368 were heavily defended by units of the CCF 26th Army. On 24 March the 1st Battalion, 15th Infantry, captured Hill 337 on the east side of the road, but the 3rd Battalion, 65th Infantry, failed to get Hill 368 on the west side.[14] The CCF 26th Army drew an east-west line just north of Uijongbu, where it meant to slow and delay the UN advance.

Brig. Gen. Frank S. Bowen, Jr., commander of the 187th Airborne RCT, had his men ready to load into 100 twin-tail C-119 Flying Boxcars at K-2 airstrip at Kimpo at dawn on 23 March. The 2nd and 14th Ranger companies joined them for the drop. Once in the air it took only a few minutes for the planes to be over Munsan-ni, 20 miles to the northwest. The planes dropped the parachute troops in three serials. The first serial left Kimpo at 7:30 A.M. with the 3rd Battalion, 187th RCT, and dropped its troops

Troops of the 15th Regiment, 3rd Division, move up a hill to attack dug-in enemy near Uijongbu, 25 March 1951. *US Army photograph, FEC 9333*

one-half mile north of Munsan-ni. General Ridgway was over Munsan-ni to see this drop. The second serial dropped the 1st Battalion, 187th RCT, 7 miles off target, 2 miles northwest of Munsan-ni instead of 5 miles to the southeast of it. The third serial accurately dropped the 2nd Battalion, 187th RCT, northeast of the town at 10 A.M. The two ranger companies apparently dropped with it, as they took positions northeast of the town.[15]

The 187th Airborne was too late at Munsan-ni. The enemy had already withdrawn north across the Imjin River, and only stragglers were encountered. By the end of 24 March, however, the RCT captured 146 prisoners, including two officers, one of them Chinese. The 187th had 16 men wounded. There had been some enemy mortar and artillery fire on the landing zone from enemy emplacements on the north side of the Imjin River. When George Lynch, Ridgway's pilot, tried to land on a dirt road in the drop zone he found it filled with parachute infantry. The plane made five passes over the road before the troops realized that someone wanted to land there. They then cleared the road, and Lynch came down. Ridgway stepped out and went over the roadside to look into a culvert. Five dead Chinese were in it, so recently shot that blood still oozed from their head wounds. A few minutes later an M-1 rifle shot rang out a little distance up a slight slope, and another dead Chinese rolled down and out of the bushes. While Ridgway conferred with General Bowen, he said he heard five mortar rounds and some enemy small-arms fire.[16]

From the jump itself there had been 80 casualties, only one of them a serious injury. When Bowen learned that ROK 1st Division troops had already reached Kumchon-ni, a village only five miles south of Munsan-ni, he asked that they be halted. He feared there might be a mix-up if they continued on into Munsan-ni, for some of his airborne soldiers might mistake the ROK troops for enemy.

One planeload of the second serial that had dropped seven miles off target and south of Munsan-ni reported it was surrounded by enemy troops. A Company was sent to their rescue.

Task Force Growden crossed its line of departure at 6:30 A.M., 23 March, leaving Seoul on the Munsan-ni road to link up as soon as possible, but within a limit of 24 hours, with the 187th RCT parachute drop at Munsan-ni. It had continuous air cover after daylight, which kept it informed on observed enemy, the condition of roads and bridges, and any minefields detected. Fifteen minutes after starting, while bypassing a blown bridge, a mine disabled one of the lead tanks. From this point on, the road and bypasses were so heavily mined and booby-trapped that it took the armored column four hours to reach a point only five and a half miles from its line of departure. There were hundreds of mines and buried mortar shells, and 90 percent of the former were booby-trapped. These had to be pulled out by grappling hooks attached to long ropes or cable, or destroyed in place by demolitions. Between Seoul and Munsan-ni four tanks, a jeep, and a British armored car were disabled by mines, despite a slow and careful effort to locate them before the column passed. Secondary roads were tried, and even a river bed for a distance, but these too were mined. The wheeled vehicles could not use the river bed, so it was decided the column would have to keep to the main road and sweep it for mines as carefully as possible.

The task force encountered no enemy until it was within a few miles of Munsan-ni at midafternoon, when some small-arms fire fell on it. This stopped quickly, and the column proceeded. At the edge of Munsan-ni some mortar and artillery fire hit the column as it was bypassing a blown bridge, direct hits disabling two tanks. Task Force Growden bypassed the two disabled tanks, and at 6:30 P.M. it linked up with the 187th Airborne RCT north of Munsan-ni. Twenty minutes later the entire task force had closed into its assembly area.[17]

The next morning three armored patrols left the perimeter: one went north to the Imjin River, without enemy contact; a second went several miles east, captured one 57-mm gun, and took up a blocking position; the third team went northeast several miles, generally paralleling the Imjin River, until the lead tank hit a mine and was disabled. Enemy mortar and small-arms fire also hit the patrol at this place. The patrol thus far had picked up 22 prisoners and destroyed one 57-mm gun. Air strikes were now called for, and the tanks returned fire. The damaged tank could not be repaired or towed, and after some parts had been removed, it was destroyed as darkness came on. The patrol returned to the task force assembly area.

There was nothing further the Airborne RCT or Task Force Growden could do at Munsan-ni – the enemy had departed northward or eastward. I Corps gave the 187th Airborne RCT and the task force a new mission for 24 March. Task Force Kobbe, named after its leader, Major Kobbe, and composed of C Company, 6th Medium Tank Battalion; C Battery, 58th Armored Field Artillery Battalion; 2nd Ranger Company; and a platoon of A Company, 14th Engineers, was formed to lead an attack east across-country toward the US 3rd Division MSR from Seoul through Uijongbu. Enemy had stopped the 3rd Division at well-defended positions in the hills north of Uijongbu. The attack by the 187th RCT and Task Force Growden was to come to the rear of the enemy positions north of Uijongbu and help the 3rd Division break the enemy's blocking positions. Kobbe's advance force left its point of departure east of Munsan-ni at 6 P.M. on the twenty-fourth, two miles ahead of the main attack force.

Task Force Kobbe came to a defile seven and a half miles east of its starting point when the road caved in behind the lead tank. The road ahead was too narrow to proceed. The wall of the defile was prepared for blasting to widen the road, and reconnaissance was made ahead to learn the condition of the trail they were following. Three tanks got through the bypass and crawled another three miles before the ground became too soft and marshy, and the tanks had to stop. They found a way to get around the marsh and advanced another mile, when the trail again caved in. No way could be found or devised to bypass this area. Engineer work at the first cave-in was completed by 2 A.M., 25 March, and the lead tank there withdrawn. Major Kobbe now radioed back that his task force was holding up the advance of the 187th RCT and that the road ahead was impassable for tanks. He recommended that his task force clear the route of advance and that the 187th Airborne RCT pass through him and continue its mission. General Bowen concurred and directed the 6th Medium Tank Battalion to withdraw and return to Seoul via Munsan-ni after the 187th RCT had passed through it. I Corps approved this decision at 10 A.M., 25 March, and at noon the 6th Medium Tank Battalion was on its way back. A little after 7 P.M. the battalion arrived at its Seoul assembly area on the palace grounds and was dissolved at 8 P.M. On the morning of 27 March the tank battalion left Seoul and by noon had rejoined the 24th Division, its parent organization.[18] Task Force Growden had accomplished

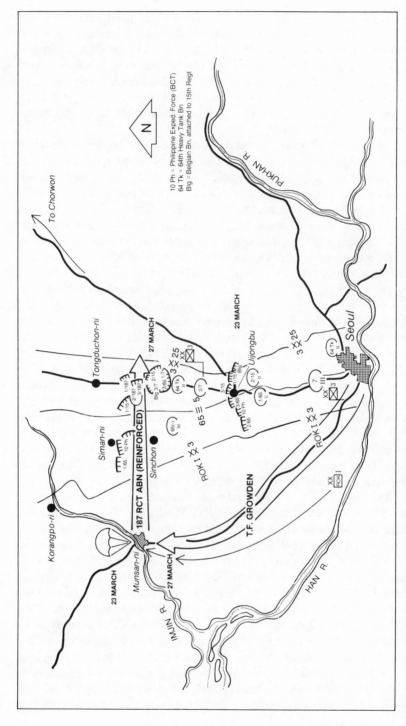

MAP 16. **Link-up of Task Force Growden and US 3rd Division, 27 March 1951**

its original mission, traversing the most extensively mined area yet encountered in Korea, losing one tank destroyed and three disabled. It had only 2 men killed, 1 when hit by a water can in an airdrop; 14 men were wounded.

Korean civilians in the Munsan-ni area informed the 187th Airborne RCT intelligence section that Chinese and North Korean units had passed through Munsan-ni and crossed to the north side of the Imjin River two or three days earlier. But there is specific information in a captured North Korean officer's diary that some units of the NK 8th Division had crossed the Imjin only in the predawn hours of 23 March, the day of the airdrop. Pertinent entries in the diary on this subject are the following:

23 Mar 51: River crossing of the 1st Regt commenced at 0100 hours and was completed at 0230 hours. River crossing of the 2nd Regt commenced at 0315 hours and was completed at 0430 hours. River crossing of Div Hqs commenced at 0440 hours and was completed at 0500 hours. Due to enemy air raid, at about 0340 hours, Korangpo bridge and Chahe-ri bridge were destroyed. River crossing of the 3rd Regt was completed at 2130 hours. . . .

24 March: The 8th Div is to defend north of the Imjin River. The 19th Div was dispersed.[19]

One aftermath of the 187th RCT parachute drop at Munsan-ni should be noted, as it illustrates lack of discipline in American troops and disregard for preservation of valuable matériel. The I Corps G-4 on 23 March sent a memorandum to the G-3 protesting that airdrop of matériel tonnage was two times as expensive as air landing of matériel, and that 10 to 30 percent of spoilage could be expected in an airdrop. The G-4 protested that airdrop of supplies should have been canceled when it became apparent during the day that land supply was feasible. Perhaps the most damaging information came during the next day from the ROK 1st Division that arrived at Munsan-ni almost as soon as the 187th Parachute drop on the twenty-third. The ROK Division reported to I Corps that the 187th Airborne troops had little regard for the value of their supplies and equipment, that they did not use the parachute bags for the packing of the chutes but cut up the chutes for souvenir scarves, that they cut up shroud lines for bundle ties, that they used chutes to line foxholes, that they allowed trucks to run over the chutes when some were being piled prior to evacuation, and that riggers displayed indifference to their duty of supervising the collection personnel. It was all too true. I Corps on 31 March ordered a report on the subject. Meanwhile, the corps ordered the ROK 1st Division on 26 March to assign not more than one battalion of its troops (the ROK 1st Battalion, 15th Regiment was assigned) to recover the equipment scattered about in the Munsan-ni drop area.[20]

Among the findings of the investigation were the inordinate demands of the 187th Airborne RCT for supplies for which there was no conceivable need, but known to be prepackaged in Japan, such as gasoline (no vehicles were available there for its use). The ROK battalion gathered up and recovered from the drop zone a vast quantity of matériel, including:

257 tons (approximately) of serviceable ammunition of all types (the ROK division retained 512,000 rounds of .30-caliber machine-gun ammunition for its own use; the US 3rd Division got 337,000 rounds more)

Demolished artillery: two 75-mm pack howitzers and one 105-mm howitzer

140 truckloads (approximately) of parachutes

Unstated amount of gasoline

97 tons of ammunition (recovered in the 3rd Division zone, to the east of the 187th RCT zone) and 3,000 rations; this matériel was turned over to the US 3rd Division.

On 30 March, when the 187th Airborne RCT was relieved in the line and moved south in reserve, its train stopped at an ASP, and the men dismounted in large numbers, built warming fires, and smoked in areas where signs prohibited it. They dumped trash and cans in the supply point, and some items were taken from the supply point. Among the many critics of the 187th RCT lack of discipline in this operation was Major Bowers, a KMAG advisor to the ROK 1st Division.

When the author asked General Ridgway if he knew at the time about the almost total lack of war-matériel supply discipline among the 187th RCT during the Munsan-ni operation, he said he did not. He added, however, that he did not consider the Munsan parachute drop a good one and said that, when he landed there in a light plane on 23 March, he learned that the 187th command group had landed at the wrong place.[22]

In his visits to his front-line troops north of Seoul in the latter part of March, in areas formerly held by CCF troops for several months, General Ridgway had noted that there appeared to have been little or no vandalism committed by them. He wanted none from his troops and instructed that there should be no destruction of private homes merely to get firewood.

The diary entry by Kim Dhong Hu on 23 March mentioned above told of UN aerial destruction of two bridges over the Imjin River near Korampo in predawn hours of 23 March, just at the time the UN troops would want to use them. General Ridgway noted the senseless destruction of bridges by aerial action and, in a memorandum at this time, said, "I think in general we distinctly over-do on bridges. Until and unless the Soviets enter this war, our enemies can make little use of vehicular bridges in the combat zone. We can."[23]

Another memorandum at this time reveals Ridgway's displeasure about what he considered poor intelligence reporting and complacent staff work. He wrote:

I wish you would please insure that every report to my headquarters contains the truth, the whole truth, and nothing but the truth, negative included, and that these reports be not unduly delayed because of these basic military requirements.

I find also too many cases of failure to attack at the time ordered, failure to report jump-offs until asked. I expect every commander to insist upon the launching of an attack when ordered, and the immediate initiation of reports back thru channels that the attack has been launched at the time directed.

I want to invite your attention to the high importance of the maintenance of direction of an attack. More attacks I expect, have failed from this one cause than all others combined.[24]

In spite of failures of some commanders and troops to carry out his directions as well as he would have liked, the overall performance of the Eighth Army had definitely improved in the past three months. On the very day the 187th Airborne RCT parachuted at Munsan-ni, Mrs. Margaret Visco wrote to General Ridgway: "I am writing you to tell you how much the morale of my son, Cpl. Visco, has improved since you have taken over command. He speaks of how much better the food and discipline has improved under your command, also how much better the news is. He looks up to you as some great God. You are a very great man. You have that greatness about you which is difficult to explain, but so easy to recognize in a person. He is so proud to be around you." Another letter, dated 30 March 1951, from Mrs. Violet Meyer to General Ridgway, told him about a visit to her from a Sergeant Jones, back in the United States. Her son, in the Marine Corps, had been under Sergeant Jones. Jones was looking through a scrapbook that Mrs. Meyer had kept about the war and noticed many items relating to the general. Mrs. Meyer wrote to Ridgway that Jones, as he looked at these clippings, "spoke so highly of you being such a wonderful man to the boys, regardless of what branch of the service they were serving."[25]

The morale factor worked both ways. Letters such as these could not but affect a commander's morale. From what the author saw and heard in Korea in 1951, he would judge these tributes to General Ridgway to be typical of what Eighth Army rank-and-file, and officers as well, felt about their commander.

On 24 March General MacArthur made another trip to Korea. He arrived in Seoul at 10:55 A.M., and after some conversation with General Ridgway, they went to the ROK 1st Division CP to see Gen. Paik Sun Yup, and then to see Maj. Gen. Robert H. Soule at his US 3rd Division CP. Afterward General MacArthur and his party went on up to several regimental CPs and to Uijongbu. The 3rd Division at this time was engaged in very heavy combat with the enemy on the hills just north of Uijongbu. Before he departed for the flight back to Tokyo, MacArthur gave Ridgway his views on Soviet intentions on intervention in Korea. He said

that the Soviet Union would decide to enter the war in Korea independently of events in Korea and elsewhere in Asia, that such a decision would
be taken by the Soviets based on a realistic, cold-blooded analysis of their
position in the world situation, but that a complete collapse of Red China
might bring Soviets directly into the war—that then they would be acting
on defensive considerations.[26]

Meanwhile, when the 187th Airborne RCT received a new mission to
attack east on 24 March toward the US 3rd Division north of Uijongbu,
the 11th Regiment of the ROK 1st Division secured the Munsan-ni area.
When the 187th Airborne RCT dropped at Munsan-ni, the US 3rd Division was engaged in heavy fighting with enemy forces only 16 air miles
southeast of it in the hills north and northeast of Uijongbu. The 1st Battalion, 15th Regiment, of the 3rd Division finally won Hill 337, east of
the Uijongbu MSR, that day after dark. The 3rd Battalion of the regiment
also had been in a heavy fight all day, and the Turkish Brigade likewise
had been heavily engaged. The 65th Regiment, west of the MSR north
of Uijongbu, was similarly held up by strong enemy defense. It was to help
break this enemy line north of Uijongbu that the 187th RCT now headed
almost directly east from Munsan-ni to the rear of the enemy line and the
MSR above Uijongbu. We have noted already that Task Force Kobbe on
25 March ran out of road just east of the village of Popwon-ni, about 7
miles from Munsan-ni. Five miles east of Popwon-ni the trail reached the
village of Sinchon, and there the trail forked, the southern branch going
to Yongju and the northern to Tokchong, both north of Uijongbu. The
187th RCT objective was the Tokchong vicinity, about 15 road miles north
of Uijongbu.[27]

On 25 March the 3rd Division made an effort to send armored tank
forces north and west to contact the 187th Airborne RCT, which was trying to reach its objective via the east-west road-trail that went from Munsan-ni
to Popwon-ni, Sinchon, Parun-ni, and Tokchong. The 3rd Division's 65th
Regiment, with the attached 10th BCT (Philippine Expeditionary Force),
was on the west side of the Uijongbu MSR and would be the unit expected
to make contact with the 187th RCT coming toward it from the west. In
an effort to make this contact between the two forces, Col. W. W. Harris,
commander of the regiment, formed Task Force Meyer, comprising the
65th Regiment's tank company of 17 tanks and a ten-man engineer squad.
Task Force Meyer started north on its mission on 24 March and soon lost
2 tanks to mines and found the road blocked. It took about an hour to get
the crews out of the damaged tanks, and at the same time the force came
under enemy mortar and small-arms fire. As dark was approaching, the
task force commander radioed to the regiment for permission to withdraw,
as he could not continue toward Sinchon, his objective to link up with
the 187th RCT. His request was denied, and he was ordered to continue.

Later, the task force was given permission to pull back, but in the dark and rain it could not find friendly lines and lost 4 more tanks to mines. Task Force Meyer ended up with one man killed and six wounded, and 4 tanks disabled and 1 stuck in the mud. During the twenty-fifth, another armored task force of 6 tanks was sent out to make contact with the 187th RCT, and it succeeded in doing so at 3 P.M. On 26 March the 3rd Division and the 187th Airborne RCT established effective contact with each other in the Parun-ni–Tokchong area.[28] The 187th RCT Command Report gives 1 P.M., 26 March, as the time of the link-up with the 65th Tank Company, 3rd Division. It appears that the 1st Battalion, 15th Infantry, 3rd Division, on the east side of the Uijongbu MSR, made the infantry link-up with the 187th RCT on the afternoon of the twenty-sixth.[29]

The 187th Airborne RCT had some hard fighting on 25 and 26 March in reaching its objective, a link-up with the US 3rd Division along the MSR about 15 road miles north of Uijongbu and east of Parun-ni at the high ground that flanked the MSR three to four miles due east of that village. Near Parun-ni on 25 March, M. Sgt. Erwin L. Muldoon of H Company, 187th Airborne, earned the Distinguished Service Cross, Posthumously. Muldoon commanded a machine-gun section attached to F Company to provide supporting fire in an attack on enemy positions. As the attack progressed, it developed that enemy opposition to F Company was slight but very strong against neighboring G Company, where an estimated enemy battalion was launching a fierce counterattack. Muldoon believed G Company would be quickly overrun if it did not get help. He made his own decision to move his machine-gun section across open rice paddies under fire to reach a point where he could support G Company. He was emplacing his guns in the new position when the enemy launched an assault to overrun his sector. They came from the front and both flanks. His machine guns repulsed the first assault, and then several successive ones, with heavy losses to the enemy. When one of his gunners was wounded, Muldoon took over as gunner, and a burst of enemy fire hit and killed him.[30]

Three days later, on 28 March, the 187th Airborne RCT had not made much advance, still being held up by strong and determined enemy forces on Hills 507 and 519 above Tokchong and near Parun-ni. There 1st Lt. Earl K. Wooley, G Company, distinguished himself in a grenade battle with enemy. Initially he led his platoon in a bayonet and grenade attack against enemy entrenchments on Hill 507. The enemy returned the grenade attack with grenade volleys of their own. Wooley picked up several of the enemy grenades that landed near him and threw them back before they exploded on him, killing several enemy with them. He was, however, wounded in a later enemy grenade shower. But he refused evacuation and led his platoon in a hand-to-hand fight with the entrenched enemy that won Hill 507. Then he took command of the company's Weapons Platoon as G Company moved on to assault Hill 519. He saw that the company's route of advance was under heavy enemy automatic fire. Thereupon he organized his 11 men into an assault team, and supported by machine-gun and mortar fire, he attacked the nearest enemy position. This attack silenced two enemy machine guns and killed 25 enemy. He had 4 men wounded. He put the remaining 7 men with himself in a tight perimeter on a knob and held it until relieved there by another unit at dusk.[31]

When the 187th Airborne RCT reached the MSR, it attacked across the front of the 15th Regiment, 3rd Division, on 27 March, while the latter held in place, until the 187th RCT gained its objective – the high ground east of the road – on 28 March. Elements of the 3rd Division completed relief of the 187th Airborne RCT at 1:30 P.M., 29 March, and the airborne regiment started south for reassembly at Taegu.[32]

General Ridgway went up to the 3rd Division's line north of Uijongbu on 26 March to see the progress there in the action looking to the junction of the 187th Airborne RCT with the 3rd Division. In a conference with General Soule the latter told Ridgway that some of his tanks had knocked out a Soviet-built T-34 tank that was trying to escape. This was the first enemy tank knocked out by ground action since Ridgway had taken command of Eighth Army in late December 1950. On this trip Ridgway witnessed an accident that might have ended in a tragedy for many Americans. Eight miles north of Uijongbu he saw the accidental release of a napalm container from an F-51 fighter plane. It landed only 100 yards from the MSR, which was crowded at the time with 3rd Battalion troops.[33]

As the 187th Airborne RCT neared the Uijongbu MSR on 26 March and an impending junction with the 3rd Division, the enemy broke contact with the 15th and 65th regiments. In the final actions of the 187th RCT, the 1st Battalion, 15th Infantry, blocked for and protected the left flank of the 187th RCT. The 3rd Division tanks helped the 187th RCT on the twenty-eighth take its final objective.[34]

On 29 March the 7th Infantry Regiment of the 3rd Division passed through the 15th Regiment, and the Belgian Battalion took over the position just released by the 187th Airborne RCT and faced east, where enemy still resisted. Although the 65th and 7th regiments met some scattered resistance on the twenty-ninth and on to the end of the month, the enemy in effect had withdrawn to and across the Imjin River to the 38th Parallel in the ROK 1st Division and the US 3rd Division sectors. Even so, Pvt. Knox Gilmore, K Company, 7th Infantry, at Hill 347 on 30 March, won the Distinguished Service Cross, Posthumously, when a grenade killed him as he was trying to throw it away from some comrades. The 7th Infantry met some enemy delaying forces 2,000 yards south of the 38th Parallel on 31 March. The 65th Infantry reached the south bank of the Imjin River that day and found some enemy on the north bank. Two battalions turned east along the south bank.

On 28 March the ROK 1st Division had reached the Imjin at Munsan-ni and sent a patrol across the river, where it engaged an estimated enemy company in a brief firefight and then withdrew to the south side. On 31 March the 3rd Platoon, 3rd Company, of the ROK 15th Regiment crossed the Imjin again and this time captured Hill 191, engaging an enemy company. The ROK company withdrew after dark back to the south side of the Imjin. The ROKs reported they had 4 killed and 4 wounded but estimated a larger number of enemy were killed or wounded, and it came back with 45 prisoners.

On 28 March the 8213th Ranger Company was deactivated. It had been the first of the ranger companies to be formed and committed to combat with Eighth Army—with Task Force Dolvin of the 25th Division at Ipsok, north of the Chongchon River late in November 1950.[35]

I Corps relieved 187th RCT and the 15th Infantry Regiment on 29 March, replacing them in the line with the British 29th Brigade (with the Belgian Battalion attached). This was a substitution of four battalions for six. On the same day, General Ridgway at 10:15 A.M. approved Operation Rugged, which was in reality a continuation of the action then in progress, for a short further advance to what was called "Line Kansas." In the I Corps area this would be to try to seize the roadnet in the Iron Triangle. Line Kansas followed the Imjin River from its junction with the Han River northwest of Seoul northeast to Majon-ni, then turned east past Yongpyong to the south side of the Hwachon Reservoir, through Yanggu, and on east to Yangyang on the coast at the Sea of Japan.[36]

East of the 3rd Division, on the eastern flank of I Corps, the US 25th Division and the attached Turkish Brigade had heavy fighting through 24 March, especially the Turks at Hills 639, 711, and 377. But on 26 March the Chinese troops of the newly committed CCF 26th Army abandoned their stubborn delaying tactics and fell back to prepared positions. At the end of the month, from 29 through 31 March, the 35th Infantry Regiment had hard fighting in the Changgo-ri area, astride the MSR up the Pakchon River on the road to Kumhwa at the southeast base of the Iron Triangle. A tank and two M16 AAA weapons vehicles were lost there. The 2nd Battalion failed to capture Hill 407 on the thirtieth, but the next day the 2nd and 3rd battalions gained it without much resistance.

The fighting in the Changgo-ri area at the end of the month provided an example of the tremendous value of M16 AAA to an infantry attack. On 29 March two platoons of infantry, four tanks, and four M16s of C Battery, 21st AAA AW Battalion, were to attack at Changgo-ri to help a hard-pressed unit of the 27th Regiment on their west. The main object was to overcome a force of Chinese that held a horseshoe-shaped ridge that overlooked the town from the north. Lt. Richard S. Craig commanded the M16s; the captain commanding the two platoons of 35th Infantry was the task-force commander. His plan was for the 1st Platoon with the four tanks to attack the lower loop of the horseshoe, while Lieutenant Craig and his four M16s and the 2nd Platoon supported the attack from within the town of Changgo-ri. The 1st Platoon's attack with the tanks took the lower loop of the ridge against enemy mortar, automatic, and small-arms fire. An artillery barrage hit the remaining part of the ridge. Two M16s moved out with the 2nd Platoon for the next assault, while the other two M16s gave covering fire on the higher portion of the ridge. The four tanks returned and joined in support of the assault. All tanks and M16s moved forward to get closer to the objective for the second phase of the attack. In this movement an enemy soldier in a foxhole pulled a cord that detonated a mine under one of the tanks and an adjacent M16, knocking both out of action. But the firepower and the approach of the 2nd Platoon in this attack caused the enemy to start leaving their bunkers and entrenchments, and the M16s cut them down almost to a man, as they huddled together in groups ranging from three or four to thirty men. The assistant division commander, Brig. Gen. John ("Mike") Michaelis, watched the attack. He remarked that this was as good a coordinated attack as he had ever seen. The 35th Infantry now had Changgo-ri and the ridge north of it, which had held up the regimental advance. Of the 250 enemy killed in this action, credit was given to the four M16s for 150 of them found dead in the dugouts, which had been shattered by the M16 .50-caliber fire, which expended a continuous stream of 50,000 rounds in the action.[37]

In the fighting west of Changgo-ri on 30 March, Sfc. Joseph P. Reeves, G Company, 27th Infantry, gave a remarkable combat performance. He took his rifle squad across open ground under fire to the base of Hill 764, which Chinese troops held. He led them up the slope under automatic-weapons and small-arms fire. After reaching a point where he formed his men to provide a base of covering fire, he crawled to within a few yards of an enemy machine gun. He killed the gun crew with a hand grenade and then killed four other enemy soldiers nearby with his carbine. Just after he returned to his squad, an enemy counterattack hit it. He and his squad repulsed the attack, but when it was over, he had only two unwounded men left. He called for reinforcements. Before they arrived, however, a second counterattack came in on him, which wounded his two men. Reeves, now alone in the fight, shot up all his remaining ammunition and that of his wounded men. At this point an enemy soldier armed with an automatic weapon rushed him in hand-to-hand fight. Reeves grappled with the enemy and wrested his weapon from his hands, killed him with it, and then turned the weapon on other Chinese coming at him, routing them.[38]

A bit of bad news came to General Ridgway and the UN command on 29 March with word that Maj. Gen. Kim Pak Il, commanding the ROK I Corps on the east coast, had disappeared the day before during a flight in an L-5 plane that left Hajinbu-ri at 3:30 P.M. headed for Kangnung. An intensive search had thus far provided no information of what had happened to him. General Ridgway flew to Kangnung the next day to check on the search for General Kim, but there was still no word.[39]

In the I Corps sector in March, in the western part of the Eighth Army line, Operation Ripper had not destroyed the enemy forces, but it had gained vital territory in a general advance of 30 miles, including the capture of Seoul, it had reached or neared the 38th Parallel, and it had inflicted very heavy casualties on both Chinese and North Korean forces.[40] I Corps casualties are shown in table 11.

At the end of the month there were about 30,000 South Korean laborers working in I Corps. Seoul was off-limits to all UN forces except those there on official business.[41]

A Chinese soldier named Choe San Sik kept a diary from 16 February to 6 May 1951, when it was found on his body in the 1st Cavalry Division sector. Choe's entry for 30 March shows an aspect of an enemy's thoughts not often seen: "30 March: Seeing the farmers busy on their farms, I could not help thinking of my family at home. They must be having a very hard time without me. All I want now is a peaceful settlement as soon as possible."[42]

We must now turn our attention to Operation Ripper in central and eastern Korea.

From the point where the US 25th Division crossed the Han River on 7 March at the right flank of I Corps, the IX Corps picked up the Eighth Army line, with the US 24th Division on its left flank and extended eastward with the US 1st Cavalry Division, a British brigade (sometimes the 29th and at other times the 27th), the ROK 6th Division, and the 1st Marine Division at its right flank. There the US 2nd Division held the left flank of X Corps and extended eastward with the ROK 5th Division; the US 7th Division was on the corps's right flank. There the ROK III Corps picked up the line with the ROK 7th and 3rd divisions carrying the line

TABLE 11. **I Corps Casualties, March 1951**

Unit	Battle Casualties	Nonbattle Casualties
25th Division	857	1,182
3rd Division	375	698
187th Airborne RCT	503	14
ROK 1st Division	188	271
British 29th Brigade	3	172
Turkish Brigade	24	14
Corps units	25	70
Total	1,975	2,421

Source: I Corps, Comd. Rpt., March 1951.

on eastward to the ROK I Corps sector, which extended eastward with the ROK 9th and Capital divisions to the coast. The ROK Capital Division held the coastal sector. During the latter part of March the ROK 6th Division exchanged places in the line with the 1st Cavalry Division. Otherwise, the Eighth Army alignment from west to east from the 24th Division at the left flank of IX Corps to the Sea of Japan remained the same.

We have already covered the advance of these units northward, often in heavy battles, to the end of the third week of March. From that time on, the action was less severe because the CCF and the NK forces there were in the midst of a general withdrawal to prepared positions and assembly areas just above the 38th Parallel, where Eighth Army intelligence believed new Chinese formations were moving into assembly areas preparatory to launching a 5th Phase Offensive. The original Chinese forces, most of them from Lin Piao's Fourth Field Army, had entered Korea in mid-October 1950 and had carried the war in the west since then, but they were by now so reduced by casualties and exhaustion that they were no longer combat effective, even though they had received some replacements. Intelligence reports speculated they were giving place to new, fresh CCF armies. But even as this withdrawal was under way, there was still stubborn holding action when the enemy saw fit to fight strong battles at chosen sites. General Ridgway expected his forces to reach Line Kansas, near or slightly above the 38th Parallel, in their current Ripper offensive by the end of March.

The 24th Division, adjacent on the east to the 25th Division, held a vital hinge area where the course of the Han River in the Yangpyong area turned sharply south. Directly north of the 25th Division was the Pukhan River and Kapyong, and beyond them the broken country that lay south of the Iron Triangle. On 18 March the 19th and 21st regiments of the 24th Division crossed to the west side of the southwest-running Pukhan River, below the Hwachon Reservoir. The 1st Cavalry Division's early capture of Chunchon eastward caused a realignment of the 25th and 24th divisions. The 5th RCT of the 24th Division on 21 March passed through the 35th Regiment of the 25th Division, thus pressing the 25th Division westward. The 5th RCT had hard fighting from 22 through 25 March. It captured key Hill 362 on 23 March in a bayonet attack, but it had only light opposition from 28 through 30 March.[43]

In its drive north toward the 38th Parallel in the latter part of the month, the 24th Division frequently had to use bridges and ferries on the Han and Pukhan rivers, which remained in control of the US 25th Division, I Corps, military police. Both divisions at various times used these river crossings. The 24th Division, of IX Corps, found the arrangement unsatisfactory and alleged that lack of cooperation (from its point of view) often led to delay in the crossing of supply vehicles for its units. It thought the control should have been in Eighth Army, or in a special coordinating unit.[44]

An important change in the Chinese order of battle was discovered on 19 March in the 24th Division sector. Three miles north of Chongpyong and below Kapyong, the 5th RCT captured 11 Chinese prisoners. They identified themselves as belonging to the 226th Regiment, 76th Division, of the Chinese 26th Army. This was one of the three armies of the IX Army Group of the Third Field Army, which had crossed the Yalu in mid-November 1950 and headed for the Chosin Reservoir. There it had engaged the 1st Marine Division at the end of November and in December 1950. The movement of these three armies from the Hamhung and Wonsan areas of northeast Korea to the central front had long been anticipated, and now it was confirmed. The CCF 26th Army in fact was relieving the CCF 38th and 50th armies of the Fourth Field Army.[45]

The new enemy formation apparently first appeared in front of the 5th RCT of the 24th Division. Eighth Army intelligence believed two unidentified CCF armies were in the Chorwon-Kumhwa area, and it expected all six CCF armies of the Third Field Army previously identified in Korea to be committed in the anticipated CCF 5th Phase Offensive. Dates often mentioned by Chinese prisoners for this offensive were 1 to 15 April. The CCF buildup obviously was centering on the Iron Triangle area as first priority.

When General Ridgway ordered Operation Rugged on 29 March, which was merely a cautious continuation of Ripper, he did so with the belief that it was safer to continue the advance while planning to meet the expected enemy attack.[46] On 31 March a tank-infantry patrol of the 2nd Battalion, 5th RCT, 24th Division, caught 25 enemy in the open near the 38th Parallel and killed them all. Later in the afternoon it came upon another group of 30 enemy and thought it killed them all; subsequently it fired on another group, with unknown results. The patrol then crossed the 38th Parallel for a short distance, but returned to its own lines at 4:30 P.M. This was one of the first American recrossings of the 38th Parallel in the current offensive.[47]

In the latter part of March the British 27th Brigade was in IX Corps reserve until 24 March. On the twenty-third, its commander, Brig. Basil A. Coad, left the brigade, relieved in command by Col. B. A. Burke, deputy commander of the British 29th Brigade. Coad had an excellent reputation as the brigade commander in the Korean War to date and had established good cooperative relations with the American forces of Eighth Army. Under Colonel Burke the 27th Brigade went back into the Eighth Army line, attached to the 24th Division, relieving the 19th Infantry on the division's right flank northwest of Kapyong. The ROK 6th Division was on its east, across the boundary from the 24th Division.[48]

Brigadier Coad called the country his brigade fought through during February and March "appallingly mountainous," and after five weeks of it he asked General Ridgway to put the brigade in reserve, as everyone was exhausted. Ridgway acceded to the request. Coad said all ranks then "had their second hot shower and took their boots off at night for a second time since they had been in Korea."[49] Coad's brigade had started off in the summer of 1950 in Korea with two battalions, the Argylls and the Middlesex, and a brigade headquarters. Now at the end of March 1951, when he gave up the command, he had added an Australian battalion, the Canadian Princess Pat Battalion, a New Zealand artillery regiment of 25-pounders, and an Indian field-ambulance unit.

In the last days of March the British 27th Brigade had followed the retreating enemy up the Chojong River, the Princess Pat Battalion crossing over five hills with Korean porters carrying supplies, and on 31 March it reached its objective, Hill 1036 on Line Benton, four miles south of the 38th Parallel. From there at the head of the Chojong valley, the brigade in April moved east over to the Kapyong River valley and continued its attack north toward the parallel and Line Kansas, three miles north of the 38th Parallel at this point.[50] At this time the British and Commonwealth governments opposed any military ground movement north of the 38th Parallel.

The 24th Division was one of three US divisions to receive a newly created Ranger company in March. The 3rd Ranger Company was assigned to the 3rd Division, the 8th to the 24th Division, and the 5th to the 25th Division, the latter a replacement for the earlier 8213th Ranger Company, which it had from late November 1950 but was deactivated on 28 March and its personnel assigned to the 25th Division. Altogether, there were six Ranger companies formed and assigned to the Far East Command by March 1951, one to each of the US divisions then in Korea. A few months later, however, high US military authorities decided that they were not needed in Korea and that regular US Army infantry units could do everything required.[51]

The ROK 6th Division on the east of the 24th Division and between it and the 1st Cavalry Division was in a virtually roadless, mountainous area between Yongpyong and Kapyong-Chunchon. Away from the main axes of north-south travel, it was in a sparsely inhabited wilderness, but an area nevertheless that had to be screened for enemy. On 19 March the 1st Battalion of the ROK 2nd Regiment of the 6th Division came upon an enemy bivouacked in a small valley without security outposts. The ROK battalion had almost surrounded the enemy force, being on three sides of it, before its presence was discovered. The surprised Chinese battalion was thrown into confusion and fled north, abandoning all its equipment, in an attempt to escape. The ROK soldiers shot down the Chinese as they fled. They counted 231 dead at the site and captured all the abandoned enemy equipment, which included 7 75-mm howitzers, 6 60-mm mortars, 14 heavy machine guns, 70 type-44 rifles, 5 US M-1 rifles, other small arms, 20 horses (killed), and 26 pack saddles.[52]

After the 1st Cavalry Division sent two tank forces into Chunchon in the afternoon of 21 March, both unopposed, General Palmer, the division commander, and Colonel Crombez, the 5th Cavalry Regimental commander, followed the tanks into the town. It had been so thoroughly destroyed by UN aerial attacks that no attempt was made to find any billeting there for troops. Tents were preferred to the rubble. The CCF had abandoned not only the town but the whole Chunchon basin. The 2nd Battalion, 5th Cavalry, made an interesting and very unusual discovery there of three embalmed and boxed Chinese bodies ready for shipment, presumably to China.

On 25 March the 3rd Battalion, 8th Cavalry Regiment, took over responsibility from the 7th Cavalry for the security of Chunchon. In the Chunchon prison, on a wall of Cell No. 6, 1st Cavalry troops found the names of 11 persons written in pencil, believed to be from Task Force Crombez, 5th Cavalry, that had cut its way through enemy forces to the relief of Chipyong-ni in February. These men had previously been carried as missing in action. The list of names was reported to the division headquarters at 6 P.M., 27 March.[53]

Interrogation of two US officers who had escaped from CCF capture and recorded observations of their imprisonment revealed certain things about the Chinese soldiers they saw. They said that, during the heavy B-29 raid on Chunchon, most of the enemy troops in the area were in caves on the ridgeline, and few casualties resulted. When trucks were moving on roads, there were usually troops in the same area; all cooking was done just after dark and just before daylight; and only an emergency would prompt any daylight activity. CCF troops stayed in Korean houses during the day and moved about outside only when necessary. CCF sentinels were on the top of every hill, and when one sighted an airplane, he would fire his weapons. All other sentinels who heard the shot would fire their weapons, and troops would take cover immediately.[54]

For several weeks there had been recurring reports of typhoid, typhus, smallpox, and whooping cough epidemics among Chinese and especially among North Korean forces and in the civilian population that had in several instances been so severe as to incapacitate some units. On 26 March agents obtained information from Umsong police on the epidemics in the area. The police reported there had been 88 deaths from the diseases in the past week, and listed 323 cases of typhoid, 305 of typhus, 431 of smallpox, and 3,316 of whooping cough. They reported a total of 1,456 deaths in the Umsong-gun population, which was estimated at 97,000.[55]

After the 1st Marine Division had successfully attacked the strongly held hills north and east of Hongchon, it prepared to jump off in a second phase of Operation Ripper from a line three miles north of Hongchon. On 20 March the 1st KMC (Korean Marine Corps) Regiment was attached to the Marine Division for this operation. It was placed on line between the 1st Marine Regiment on the right and the 5th Marines on the left. The ground allotted to the KMC regiment in the middle was "a roadless wilderness." Airdrop of supplies to the KMC was a necessity. Hill 975 lay in its path, and there the hardest fight of the 1st Marine Division during the rest of the month was fought – by the KMC. Its 2nd and 3rd battalions attacked the hill on 21 March, and for three days they made only slight gains, although they had heavy artillery support. On the morning of 24 March the 1st Battalion of the KMC maneuvered westward on the hill to threaten the Chinese right flank. This caused the enemy to order a withdrawal, and the KMC took the hill without further fighting.[56]

The 1st Marine Division and its attached 1st KMC moved up to their objectives, but on 29 March continued on under General Ridgway's order to attack to Line Kansas. In the meantime, X Corps prepared to relieve the 1st Marine Division on Line Kansas, with the exception of the 7th Marine Regiment, which was attached to the 1st Cavalry Division for the attack beyond Chunchon. But on 1 April there were changes in IX Corps orders. The Marines were not relieved but were ordered instead to relieve the 1st Cavalry Division north of Chunchon and to continue the attack northward with the 1st and 5th Marines and the KMC regiment. The Marine Division now had a front of nearly 20 miles.[57]

The US 2nd Infantry Division, on the right (east) flank of the 1st Marine Division in the last half of March, was in very mountainous country and had in front of it the NK V Corps, composed at the time of the NK 6th, 7th, and 12th divisions. The NK V Corps probably had no more than 10,000 men on March 1, and by the end of the month it had no more than half that number. It engaged chiefly in delaying actions, and before the month ended, its divisions were ineffective. They contained many captured ROK soldiers. These men were impressed into service usually as ammunition and litter bearers. Some would fight with the enemy as opportunists. Generally, these depleted NK units would avoid contact if possible and withdraw northward, but occasionally they would put up strenuous resistance. An example of the latter occurred on 22 March, when the 2nd Division crossed the Naechon River in the Pungam-ni area. In general, however, one may say that, between 23 and 31 March, enemy activity decreased and all but disappeared in front of the US 2nd Division. Its worst problem was in moving through the mountains over virtually impassable tracks. When it moved from its CP at Yudong-ni to Salbyon on 27 March, the 2nd Division had to use the 1st Marine Division MSR part of the way. The division had its own soldiers working in the hundreds on the roads to make them passable, and on the move to Salbyon it also had 400 Korean laborers on road work. They used stray oxen and cattle and A-frame carriers for transporting supplies. Fortunately, the North Koreans in this area had no main line of resistance but used only strongpoints along logical routes of movement. When these could be bypassed or flanked, they showed no inclination to withdraw but compelled the UN troops to stop to organize an attack, and then they withdrew. During this period Eighth Army made a study of whether it was best to use pack animals or Korean carriers with A frames to transport supplies in the mountains. The study favored use of human carriers with A frames. Out of this conclusion grew the decision to organize a Civil Transport Corps to assist in the logistic supply of troops in combat as described in chapter 13 above.[58]

During the drive north toward the 38th Parallel, the 2nd Division unfolded a poignant story relating to the Hoengsong catastrophe of a month earlier. On 17 March a tank-infantry patrol from G Company, 38th Infantry, came upon 16 American prisoners, captured by the Chinese at Hoengsong 11–12 February. They told the story of approximately 800 UN prisoners the Chinese brought together immediately following the Hoengsong action. They said the enemy broke down the total into groups of 200 and further divided these into groups of 20 and on 13 February started the entire body north, marching on foot. They continued north until 19 February, moving only at night and resting in villages during the day. On 19 February UN aircraft bombed the village they were in, and 25 of them were wounded in the air strike. Chinese guards left these wounded behind in the village when they continued on that night with the rest of the prisoners, telling them they would be returned to American lines. The wounded men remained in the village until 26 February, seven of them dying of wounds during that time. The Chinese had collected all money and valuables from their prisoners, calling it an involuntary contribution to the CCF cause. On 26 February, their Chinese guards placed the surviving Americans in a truck and drove south until they came under American artillery fire. At that point the truck turned around and took the men to the town of Changdae-dong, where they were kept until 17 March. On that day the G Company, 38th Infantry, patrol entered the town and found them. When the Americans were left in Changdae-dong, the Chinese gave them three letters, two addressed to North Koreans and Chinese units, and the third addressed to the commanding general of the US "invasion army." All NK units passing through the town left the group strictly alone after reading the letters. As it chanced, it was poetic justice that a patrol of the 38th Infantry found the men, since that regiment had suffered tremendous casualties at Hoengsong. Four of the recovered prisoners were in such bad condition that they were immediately evacuated by helicopter.[59]

In the last part of the month, the US 7th Division was virtually immobilized in the high mountains north of Changdong-ni and northeast of Pungam-ni in the Haeba-jae area. Kyebang-san, the 1,577-meter-high mountain, had now been passed and was to the southeast behind the division advance. The 31st Infantry had relieved the 32nd Regiment on 17 March and now led the advance, if it can be called that, since there was scarcely any movement because of the mud and the impassability of the mountain roads and tracks. The 2nd Battalion of the 31st Infantry patrolled to the north, while the rest of the regiment held defense positions on the Texas line. From 27 March on, heavy rains made the roads impassable. On 28 March 4,000 men could not keep the road passable and the regimental commander, Col. William J. McCaffrey, advised General Ferenbaugh that further operations northward were inadvisable until the road could be improved. Seven miles of road were under constant repair. Bad weather on 28–29 March prevented airdrop of supplies, but the regiment received 785 Korean laborers with A frames to carry in necessities. In addition, the 17th and 32nd regiments used all men not engaged in security duty (about 3,500) in working on the road. Those vehicles that could run had to make a 100-mile trip between the forward supply point to the division's forward element. The railhead was still at Chechon. On 30 March the weather improved enough to permit six planes to drop supplies for the 31st Infantry at Haebajae. From there hand carry took the supplies to the forward elements. Most of the supplies dropped were C rations, socks, and gasoline. The enemy in front of the 7th Division at this time was all North Koreans—their 1st, 15th, and 45th divisions.[60]

Beyond the 7th Division in the mountains eastward to the coast were the ROK III and I corps, with the 7th, 3rd, 9th, and Capital divisions. The Capital Division was the farthest north of any UN unit in Korea. Elements of both the ROK III and I corps had reached the 38th Parallel as early as 17 March, and by the end of the month they could cross the parallel at will. The Capital Division was north of the parallel at the coastal town of Yangyang and controlled the roads west and south of it. The two ROK corps in the east, however, had not performed satisfactorily, in General Ridgway's view, despite the fact that they were in command of the eastern coast up to the 38th Parallel. They were there primarily because there was no significant enemy force in front of them. The NK 29th Brigade had acted as a delaying force in front of the Capital Division, but near the end of the month it had withdrawn north of Kangnung. The ROK III Corps had its Advance Tactical CP at Hajinbu-ri, about 5 miles east of Soksa-ri on the MSR to Kangnung on the coast and 20 air miles southeast of Kangnung. There it was close to its boundary with the US 7th Division, but it had no contact with that division.[61]

On 26 March General Ridgway flew to the ROK Army's Forward CP at Hajinbu-ri and conferred with General Chung, the ROK Army chief of staff, and Major General Yu, commanding the ROK III Corps. General Ridgway told the two ROK commanders that the ROK I Corps on the coast lacked enveloping tactics and accordingly was not likely to punish the enemy much. He also directed that the ROK III Corps establish and maintain contact with the US 7th Division on its left (west).[62]

In view of the central importance of delivering airdrop supplies in the central and eastern mountainous fronts in the winter months of early 1951 to front-line troops, it seems justifiable to enter upon a slight digression to describe the main outline of how the airdrop system worked. It has been said that the 8081st Quartermaster Airborne Air Supply and Packaging Company is the most decorated quartermaster company in the US Army, and the only Army unit in Japan during the Korean War to earn combat credit. The work of this company was essential to the airdrop supply system in Korea. The 8081st was based at Ashiya Air Base on Kyushu, on the beach of the Sea of Japan. Capt. Cecil W. Hospelhorn had organized the company. The air-delivery platoons were responsible for loading planes and dropping the cargo. The 2nd Platoon repacked all parachutes. Japanese employees repacked cargo chutes, but only military members of the company ever repacked personnel chutes. In mid-February 1951 the company was loading and dropping from an average of 35 C-119 planes every day. The company's strength was then 4 officers and about 88 men. Several hundred Japanese civilians worked with the company.

Orders for a drop operation normally came to the company between 8 P.M. and midnight, through the Eighth Army G-4 to the 8247th Army Headquarters, Troop Movement Section, and then to the 8081st, giving the serial number of each plane, its capacity, the amount and type of cargo it would carry, and the on-station time, which was an hour before take-off. A manifest was made for each plane. There were a few rules about cargo. For instance, gasoline and rations were not loaded on the same plane, but gasoline and ammunition could be loaded together. The loading platoons checked tie-down bolts and put in the cargo rollers. The company had available 10 semitrailers and 90 2½-ton trucks to haul the cargoes to the planes. The drivers were Japanese, working on a 24-hour-a-day basis. The semitrailers were preferred for the loading because they carried more, their beds were higher, and the cargo would slide directly onto the rear floor of the C-119. It usually required four trucks to carry the cargo to a plane. Two American soldiers and four Japanese laborers loaded each plane. A platoon sergeant inspected the loading of each plane after it was completed. A loading platoon could load an average of five or six planes an hour. In-flight lunches were prepared at the consolidated Air Force–Army mess for the men who accompanied the planes. The normal flight time from Ashiya Air Base to a drop zone in Korea varied between two and three hours. Plane flight crews and quartermaster personnel who were assigned the flight were due at the plane an hour before take-off to draw their parachutes, pistols, in-flight lunches, and other equipment. The quartermaster crews inspected the cargo to make sure it was secured, obtained the white loading card, and notified the crew chief they were ready. While the plane was climbing after take-off, the dropmaster and his assistant checked the front cables, and later they checked the rear cables.

Twenty minutes before the plane was due over the drop zone, the quartermaster personnel went to the rear of the plane and removed the cables. Ties between bundles were removed, and the forward cable safeties were removed but remained tight against the bundles. The dropmaster and an assistant moved to the front of the cargo department and waited for the two-minute warning. They then removed the bomb-shackle-release safety and returned to the front to await the drop signal. The plane tried to come in over the drop zone at an altitude of 800 feet and at a speed of 110 miles an hour. This requirement carried some danger because that speed was close to stalling speed, and the plane that slow and at that altitude is a good target for automatic and small-arms fire when over an enemy front line. Planes following the leader were spaced about 1,000 feet apart. When the bell signal for drop sounded, the pilot pulled up the nose of the plane and jammed the throttle open. This tilt and lurch made the loads move on their rollers down toward the open tail-end of the plane. If any of the cargo failed to drop out of the plane, the pilot made another run over the drop zone. When the cargo was all out, the dropmaster had to reach out of the open end of the plane and pull back in the static lines. Then the plane headed for home.[63]

To speed up operations, the company normally kept all kinds of supplies prepackaged. Japanese workers did most of the packaging and were considered good at it. Large G-11 parachutes cost $1,300, G-1 chutes (24 feet) cost $43, and G-9 chutes (18 feet) cost $25. Each infantry division was supposed to gather up the chutes and return them to the nearest air base, and from there they were returned to Ashiya. The rate of recovery and return of chutes was estimated to be 40 percent. The drop-zone location was always provided to the Air Force, but the spot was also marked on the ground with a T panel. The Chinese soon learned of this practice, and sometimes, when they could do it, they put out a T panel at their position and on occasion got the drop. It became necessary to have an Air Force Mosquito plane meet the C-119s ten minutes short of the drop zone and guide them in to the correct one. There were occasions when enemy fire killed or wounded some of the drop crew, and some planes were well shot up. On one particular flight in May 1951, UN artillery fire hit and caused two C-119s to crash, killing two dropmasters.

One thing front-line infantrymen appreciated were the magazines for reading that the quartermaster crews tied into the drop bundles. One of the quartermaster company's officers said, "Helping the infantry out there made us feel more a part of it."[64]

By the end of March 1951, the overall logistic base for Eighth Army

in Korea had reached a level of 45 days' supply in Korea, 20 days of supply in the "pipeline," and 25 days' supply in Japan. This added up to a
90-day base of supply.[65]

March was a landmark month in several respects for Eighth Army in
Korea. Most important was the fact that it stood back at the 38th Parallel,
roughly where the two parts of Korea had their boundary in June 1950.
Also in March began the rotation of soldiers back to the United States.
The 1st Marine Division was the first major unit to rotate some of its men.
The Army system of rotation, which was announced at the end of March,
was to be based on release of men who had served in Korea for 6 months
or longer at division level or lower. Above division level and in service-type
duty, rotation would begin after 12 months of duty. The KMAG organization was unique in United States military operations, but rotation among
its personnel would be measured the same way as in the Eighth Army.
At the end of March 1951, there were approximately 70,000 persons in
Eighth Army eligible for rotation. Army rotation began in April 1951.[66]

Also, by the end of March 1951, the replacement problem began to
come under control with a sharp increase of trained replacements coming
to Korea from the United States. In March there were available 24,587 replacements (including those returning to duty after recovering from wounds),
with 18,900 going to the six US divisions and the 187th Airborne RCT
then serving in Korea. This number included 6,629 men who returned
to duty after convalescing from wounds or injuries.[67]

The Far East Command in Tokyo planned a rotation schedule of 25,000
a month in the future from Korea to Sasebo, Japan, and from there to the
United States. It did not reach that figure but was approximately 17,000
a month. Table 12 shows the number of replacements from the United

TABLE 12. **Replacement Troops from the United States**

Month	Number of Replacements
December 1950	16,756
January 1951	13,218
February	7,310
March	15,556
April	25,012
May	26,012
June	24,805
July	24,480
August	38,073
Total	191,222

Source: Far East, Comd. Rpt., August 1951.

States to the Far East Command for December 1950 to August 1951 and indicates the extent to which March was a turning point.

Gen. George C. Marshall, secretary of defense, in testimony before the Joint Congressional MacArthur Investigation panel on 13 May 1951, explained the replacement situation in Korea.

You see, up until March we couldn't even obtain enough men for the actual replacements of casualties, except by going into our units back here and taking them away from those units, and to that extent temporarily destroying, almost, the efficiency of those units.

Finally, in March we began to catch up in the production of trained men so that we reached a point toward the latter part of March where, for the first time, we could provide all the replacements from these trained men. . . .

As we get into this month, May, by the end of May, we ought to be approaching 20,000 for rotation, and be able to meet all of our replacements without touching any of our units in this country. . . .

Question: – You mean the divisions were something like 2,000 short and filled by South Koreans?

Answer: – Yes, sir.[68]

The authorized strength of a US infantry division in February 1951 was 18,855. To illustrate a typical American division's strength and makeup in February–March 1951, the 3rd Division, on 1 March 1951, had a strength of 15,735 US soldiers and 2,553 ROKs, or attached South Koreans, for a total strength of 18,288, or 97 percent of authorized strength.[69] In contrast to an Army infantry division, the strength of the 1st Marine Division in Korea was much greater. In February the 1st Marine Division strength was 25,000–26,000 men, and the strength of a Marine battalion was 800 to 1,000 men, all from the United States, and containing no ROKs or attached Koreans except for a few interpreters, in contrast to an Army infantry battalion strength of 600 to 700.[70] For the UN forces as a whole, at the end of March 1951 there were 16 different nations and independent commonwealths represented in Korea (see table 13).

In March 1951, these UN forces in Korea had suffered 23,859 total casualties (see table 14). UN forces had captured 143,952 prisoners of war: 103,625 North Koreans, 37,625 South Koreans that the North Korean Army had impressed into service, and 2,702 Chinese. This huge mass of prisoners was becoming an increasing problem to control, house, and feed. Up until this point they had been sent to the southern part of South Korea, but by March it had been decided that for security reasons they would have to be placed on islands in the Korean Strait. A larger prisoner-of-war compound was already under construction on the island of Koje-do, south of Chinhae and southeast of Pusan.[71]

In an interview on 31 March with Cpl. Dick Kemp, correspondent for the Army newspaper *Pacific Stars and Stripes,* General Ridgway said he

TABLE 13. **UN Forces in Korea, March 1951**

Contingent	Average Daily Supported Strength
US Eighth Army	185,229
Korean augmentation	13,475
US Marines	23,642
US Air Force	11,353[a]
US Navy	249
British and Australian forces	10,136
New Zealand detachment	816
Turkish detachment	4,383
Canadian detachment	858
Philippine detachment	1,277
Thailand detachment	1,050
French detachment	749
Greek detachment	777
Netherlands detachment	500
Belgian detachment	638
Danish Hospital Ship *Jutlandia*	186
60th Indian Ambulance Group	329
Swedish Evacuation Hospital Unit	156
Subtotal	255,803
ROK Army	249,815
Total	505,618[b]

Source: Eighth Army, Comd. Rpt., Mar 51, Plate 17; see Sec. 2, Book 5, Enclosures 1–31, Annexes (PIR Nos. 232–62), Box 1166.
[a]No figure was reported by USAF, G1, or G4 for 20 Mar 1951.
[b]Figures do not include personnel in hospitals or Clearing Stations.

TABLE 14. **UN Casualties, March 1951**

Contingent	KIA	WIA	MIA	Nonbattle	Total
United States	652	4,384	171	5,548	10,755
UN allies	76	265	2	628	971
Republic of Korea	1,068	3,557	1,053	6,455	12,133
Total	1,796	8,206	1,226	12,631	23,859

Source: Eighth Army, Comd. Rpt., G-1 Sec., G-1 Summ., Mar 51, Box 1166.

saw the American soldier at the end of March as being a "professional soldier." When Kemp asked what the greatest physical and idealistic attributes of the American soldier were, Ridgway replied, "He never does more physically than his spiritual strength permits. The spiritual is to the physical 3 to 1, or 1,000 to 1, you might say. There was a time when the men would walk in the valleys instead of on the ridges. Now they know they have to dominate the heights. It takes great physical endurance to do so, but the men have taken it in stride—they know it is a job they have to do, and they have done it."[72]

16

Across the 38th Parallel to Line Kansas

IN THE LAST WEEK of March the UN forces approached the 38th Parallel. Should the Army stop at the old line dividing North from South Korea, or should it continue its drive northward? A sharp debate had been in progress in the United Nations and in Washington, D.C., over the issue. Many of the UN allies, especially England, argued that the UN forces should not cross the parallel. The US State Department joined in favor of that position. The US Joint Chiefs of Staff and the Defense Department, however, argued that such a restriction would be a mistake, that the 38th Parallel was merely a line drawn on a map, that it followed no militarily defensible line, and that it had no terrain factors in its favor. As long as there were hostilities between the UN forces and the North Korean and Chinese forces, it would be foolhardy for the UN forces to stop there; they should have freedom for tactical reasons to cross the line if it was to their advantage for reasons of either defense or offense. The Joint Chiefs and the secretary of defense carried the day in their arguments with the Department of State before President Truman, who ruled that the question of whether to cross the 38th Parallel should be decided on tactical considerations. This decision made General Ridgway the arbiter in the matter. He decided at the beginning of April that the 38th Parallel would be no barrier to military operations.

Both ROK and American units had already crossed the parallel before the decision to do so had been given official sanction, but in most cases the crossings were by small units and for only short distances. But on the east coast, the ROK Capital Division had crossed on 24 March and attacked north. That same day General MacArthur officially authorized General Ridgway's Eighth Army to cross the parallel whenever tactical considerations made it advantageous or necessary to do so. The ROK Capital Division captured Yangyang on the coast some miles north of the parallel on 27 March. The same day, the ROK 1st Division on the western end of the line crossed the Imjin River, north of the parallel.

Ridgway's careful reconnaissance of the ground north of the 38th Parallel caused him to choose the first good defense line north of it as the objective of a renewed offensive in early April. He called this "Line Kansas." On the west, the line began at the mouth of the Imjin River, where it emptied into the Han, and followed its turns and twists northeast to the 38th Parallel, curved there slightly more to the northeast for a few miles, and then turned to run generally east to the coast at Yangyang.

Line Kansas was approximately 116 miles long, including at its western end about 14 miles of tidal water, and in its center the Hwachon Reservoir, a 16-mile-long east-west water barrier. From the reservoir on eastward to the coast, the terrain was rugged mountains virtually devoid of roads with a north-south axis. This was difficult terrain in which to engage in military operations; the logistic difficulties were enormous. The water barriers on both flanks and in the center shortened the army line that had to be held by troops in strength and made it easier for Eighth Army and the ROK Army to organize defenses in strength in other vital sectors. Throughout the remainder of the Korean War, Line Kansas was to be the centerpiece defense position of the UN forces in waging the war, either defensive or offensive, and finally it was to be a close approximation of the demilitarized zone when an armistice was negotiated. Kansas may be said to have been located on the dominating terrain, on average about 10 to 20 miles north of the 38th Parallel. Only at its western end did it dip below the parallel in following the course of the lower Imjin River. On 29 March General Ridgway published the order calling for the UN forces to advance and seize the terrain of this line.[1]

From the last week of October 1950 to the beginning of April 1951, five armies of the Chinese Fourth Field Army, one army from the North China Army Group, and three armies from the Third Field Army—nine armies altogether—had carried the battles for China in its 2nd, 3rd, and 4th Phase offensives. Now, suffering from heavy casualties in these campaigns, the divisions of the Chinese Third and Fourth field armies began to disappear from the front, replaced by fresh units from the Chinese First and Second field armies. This process continued through the first half of April as the Chinese prepared for what they called their 5th Phase Offensive, 1st Impulse. These preparations continued within or behind the original North Korean defense line along the 38th Parallel, as their screening forces fought delaying battles when UN forces approached the parallel. More will be said in a later section of this chapter about the Chinese forces brought into Korea at this time to replace those that originally came in as "volunteers."

General Ridgway named the general UN attack to seize Line Kansas "Operation Rugged" and scheduled it to begin on 5 April. It was not intended to be a defensive move primarily but included also the need to establish a base line from which offensive operations could be launched against the enemy-held Iron Triangle area. Within this triangle of land lay the most important concentration of rail and highway communications coming from the north, constituting a logistic center that was vital for enemy operations in central Korea. The UN command expected to make a major effort to capture this enemy military center at a later date.

The US I Corps was to make the major effort toward Line Kansas in the west, and for that reason the US 24th Division was shifted to it from the IX Corps on 2 April and the boundary between the two corps moved about five miles eastward. I Corps now had on line, from west to east, the ROK 1st Division and the US 3rd, 25th, and 24th divisions.

East of I Corps, the IX Corps had on line the British 27th Brigade, the ROK 6th Division, and the US 1st Cavalry Division, with the 1st Marine Division in reserve. East of IX Corps, in the central mountains and corridor, X Corps held the line with the US 2nd Division on its left flank, the US 7th Division in the center, and the ROK 5th Division on its right flank. Beyond X Corps eastward to the coast the ROK Army's III and I corps, with four divisions, held the line. The ROK III Corps had its 3rd Division up front, backed by the 7th Division; the ROK I Corps on the coast had its Capital Division up front, backed by the ROK 9th Division.[2]

The US I and IX corps were ready to begin Operation Rugged on 3 April. In the east the US X Corps and the ROK Army corps met the readiness date of 5 April. Since the US I and IX corps were ready on 3 April, General Ridgway gave them the order to begin operations in their sectors on that date. By 9 April the US I and IX corps in the west and the ROK I Corps on the east coast had reached their positions on Line Kansas. The US X Corps and ROK III Corps were not able to begin their advances until 5 April, and because of the greater difficulties in operating in almost trackless mountains and the greater enemy resistance against the US 7th Division and the ROK 3rd Division, the X Corps and the ROK III Corps were not on Line Kansas until 20 April.[3]

While the eastern units were struggling to reach Line Kansas, General Ridgway ordered I and IX corps in the west to continue on from Line Kansas in an attack on the Iron Triangle. He named this effort "Operation Dauntless," and the line to be reached, "Wyoming."

The deployment just described does not include the various UN contingents attached to the major division groupings. They should be noted. Most of these attachments remained constant during the month. In I Corps the 5th Battalion of the Korean Marine Corps was attached to the ROK 1st Division; the British 29th Brigade, the Belgian Battalion, and the 10th Philippine BCT were attached to the US 3rd Division; and the Turkish Brigade was attached to the US 25th Division.

In US IX Corps the British 27th Brigade was attached to the US 24th

Division. The Greek and Thailand battalions were attached to the 1st Cavalry Division, and the Korean Marine Corps 1st Regiment was attached to the US 1st Marine Division.

In the US X Corps, the French Battalion and the Netherlands Detachment were attached to the US 2nd Division. All these units shared the general combat conditions of the divisional units to which they were attached, the two British brigades and the Greek, Turkish, and French troops engaged in some of the hardest fighting of the month.[4]

While these forward movements were taking place in the first three weeks of April, General Ridgway also prepared for an expected general Chinese attack that might take place at any time. As a defense precaution against the expected enemy attack, the 1st Cavalry Division went into army reserve near Seoul for use in either the US I or IX Corps sector; the British 27th Brigade moved to Kapyong in IX Corps reserve; and the US 2nd Division, minus the 23rd Regiment (which stayed at Hongchon), became X Corps reserve. The ROK Army moved the ROK 9th Division to Yuchon-ni in reserve. The US 187th Airborne RCT remained at Taegu, where it was available for any emergency reinforcing mission. The above deployments were in effect for the first part of April as the UN forces advanced to, and took up positions on, Line Kansas.[5]

Within the above generally described UN deployments during the period 1 through 21 April, some incidents are worthy of mention. In a previous chapter it was noted that Maj. Gen. Kim Bak Il, the ROK commanding general of the ROK I Corps on the east coast, had disappeared on 29 March while on a reconnaissance flight in the mountainous area of his sector. Although a continuous search for his plane, presumed crashed, was made in the following days, its wreckage with his body was not found until 11 May, in the hills southwest of Kangnung.

Meanwhile the US 25th Division led the attack in the center of I Corps in the west toward Line Kansas. In front of it were elements of the Chinese 26th and 27th armies of the IX Army Group, Third Field Army. These units had engaged in the Chosin Reservoir campaign in Northeast Korea in late November and early December 1950. Their movement to another part of the front had long been predicted but had not materialized until they were identified in late March on the central front, now in front of I Corps.

With the ever-increasing evidence of large enemy troop movements from China and the northern part of Korea to the battle front, and large assembly areas 20 to 30 miles north of the front, the main lines of Chinese communications southward received mounting attacks from naval ships offshore. The rail lines were especially vulnerable to their gunfire attacks. At the same time, aerial attack continued day and night on enemy logistic centers and rail and truck movements southward.

Naval Task Force 77 on the east coast had long centered its bombardments on Wonsan and Songjin; the former had been under naval siege since 16 February. By 1 April all the important islands of Wonsan harbor were occupied by UN forces. In March mines were swept from Songjin harbor, 120 miles to the north, and it began to get the same treatment as Wonsan. The battleship *Missouri* took part in east-coast bombardments of military targets. By now enemy logistics in the north "depended on the two principal land transport nets, the western rail and road complex, in which the lines from the lower Yalu and from Manpojin joined in the north of Pyongyang, and the eastern route, in which the tracks south from Hoeryong and southeast from Hyesanjin met at Kilchu and continued down the east coast to join the transpeninsular line below Hungnam." In the west, the mission of interdiction had been assumed by the Bomber Command; the eastern rail and road lines became the responsibility of the Navy.[6]

Navy dive-bombers operating from carriers off the east coast could keep targets 400 miles from the nearest UN airstrip under attack, and coastal targets 300 miles behind the lines were subject to naval gunfire. The investment of Wonsan and the shelling of the city itself had been so heavy and destructive that Wonsan for some months was all but deserted. The enemy feared another Inchon-type landing of UN forces at Wonsan and kept several divisions of North Korean troops there in well-prepared fortifications. Similar but smaller fortifications and troop forces were stationed at Chinnampo on the west coast for the same reasons.

At the Far East Air Force's request, the Navy put the fast carriers of Task Force 95 on interdiction missions to interrupt land transport by knocking out rail and highway bridges along the east coast where the transport routes came close to the sea. They were frequently located there because the high mountains of the Northern Taebaek Range often came down precipitously to the sea, and the road and rail routes were virtually at the water's edge.

The demolition of concrete bridges required heavy hitting power, such as could be delivered by a battleship or a heavy cruiser, or by an AD plane (a heavy naval bomber). Experience showed that it required about 60 rounds of 16-inch battleship shells, or from 12 to 16 sorties of naval AD planes, to destroy two bridges a day. It was more difficult to keep a highway interdicted for a length of time than it was a rail line, because a truck can be more easily detoured than a train.

Perhaps the most important rail bridge on the east coast was the one across what became known as Carlson's Canyon, eight miles southwest of Kilju. There the railroad tunneled through hills, emerged briefly to cross a deep gully, and then disappeared in a tunnel again. Two sets of twin tunnels had been dug, and preparations had begun to double-track the railroad there, but only one track, 650 feet long and 60 feet high, had been completed. Commander Carlson led two AD strikes, which dropped one span and damaged a second. Four days later another aerial attack dropped the northernmost span.

Quickly a pile-up of supplies appeared at the northern end of the bridge, and at many places farther north where the rail line had been broken. Then came Corsair attacks from the carriers against these piles of supplies. The enemy did not falter, though, in amassing men and material to repair the bridge. Other air strikes resulted in destroying the repair work, and yet it continued. By 2 April only the concrete piers were left standing.

The enemy now dropped all effort to rebuild the bridge and instead started a four-mile serpentine to bypass both bridge and tunnels. This by-pass required eight new bridges, but they were low and short. The ease of repairing them made it unprofitable to try to keep them destroyed. In this intensive duel the Navy thus had to give up, and the enemy continued to run its trains south of Kilju. The episode shows the skill, determination, and industry the enemy put into keeping the east-coast railroad running. It eventually poured its military supplies into the Iron Triangle area and gave the sinews of war to the 5th Phase Offensive.[7]

On 4 April, after 38 days of continuous effort at interdicting enemy transport of supplies, Admiral Ostie turned over command of Task Force 95 and sailed in the *Princeton* to Yokosuka for overhaul and repair. His task force in that 38 days had rendered unusable 54 rail and 37 highway bridges and had damaged in varying degree 44 more; it had also broken the rail track in more than 200 places and destroyed or damaged large quantities of rail rolling stock. Task Force 77 also had an impressive record of interdiction destruction on the east coast.[8]

While US and UN naval forces on the east coast were making it hard in March and April for the enemy to get supplies from the Chinese and Soviet borders down to the fighting front for its armies, the Far East Air Force in Japan and southern Korea, and the US B-29 Bomber Command based on Okinawa, were pounding the enemy's transportation lines and airfields in central and western Korea. On 30 March, 38 B-29s flew from Okinawa to deliver the heaviest bombing strike of the war to date, against the twin bridges over the Yalu River at Sinuiju. During the 1950–51 CCF New Year's Offensive, the UN moved nearly all its tactical aircraft units from Korea to Japan, and most of them had remained there ever since, with a refueling base kept operational at Taegu. These fields were too distant for effective ground support as the front approached the 38th Parallel.[9]

But in March a new strip was opened at Hoengsong, the old ones at Pyongtaek in the west and at Kangnung on the east coast were made operational, and Mustang fighter planes began to reappear at Suwon and the Seoul municipal airfield. Engineers with rifles on their backs worked at Chunchon to open a short runway. But as the Chinese opened their 5th Phase Offensive in late April, jet fighter planes would still have to operate from Japan. The 27th Wing of Thunderjets flew from Itazuke. The 8th and 51st wings of Thunderjets were equipped with oversize fuel tanks that would carry them from Japan to the front lines in Korea, and from there they could get to Taegu for refueling. The 35th Group of Mustang fighters at Seoul gave invaluable close support for the front north of Seoul, but there was no comparable facility for the central Korean front.

By April the Eighth Army moved the US 24th Division from IX Corps to US I Corps, where it formed that corps's right flank, and the British 27th Brigade was attached to the IX Corps. That same day the 7th Company, 12th Regiment, ROK 1st Division, together with two platoons of the 11th Regiment, crossed the Imjin River northwest of Munsan-ni. The NK 8th Division on the north side of the Imjin apparently feared a major crossing was in the making and deployed battalion-sized units in a counter-attack against the ROKs, moving their battalions against them in the open. US artillery south of the river delivered observed fire on the enemy, and air strikes also caught these enemy troops in the open, causing an estimated 800 casualties. But even so, the North Koreans forced the ROK 1st Division units back across the Imjin.[10]

On this day the 1st Cavalry Division crossed the 38th Parallel. It headed toward the Hwachon Reservoir, which was one of the major objectives of the army advance. There was a certain amount of juggling of units in the first part of April between I, IX, and X corps to change boundaries, moving some units out of the line that had been long in it and needed a rest, sending them into reserve, and moving others back into the line. All this shifting was intended to keep the army moving forward cautiously at an average rate of two miles a day, and yet get the troops across the front in a good defensive posture with reserves stationed behind the front at critical points.

Among the changes that took place at this time was moving the British 29th Brigade to the Imjin River front, attached to the US 3rd Division, and forming its west, or left, flank. The ROK 1st Division was on line west of the British brigade. In front of the ROK 1st Division and the British 29th Brigade was the stretch of the Imjin that twice before in the Korean War had been one of the major enemy crossing points in major attacks. The 1st Battalion of the Gloucestershire Regiment was on the brigade's left flank.

Another troop movement in Eighth Army at this time involved the US 7th Division. It was to move from the X Corps sector to that of the IX Corps, relieving the 1st Marine Division there. This movement required traveling 100 miles on roads behind the lines to reach a point 30 miles west of its previous position. To make matters more difficult for the division, heavy rains had made the dirt roads all but impassable. The division's route led through Soksa-ri, Pungam-ni, Saemal, Hoengsong, Hongchon, and Yangye. The 17th Regiment with the 49th Artillery Battalion, and A Company, 13th Engineers, led the division movement. Its new zone was along the Hongchon-Yangye-Inje axis and north to the east end of the Hwachon Reservoir. From there eastward to the coast, the North Korean troops were responsible for the enemy front.

The Soyang (or Choyang) River was the largest barrier in the new 7th Division zone of action. North of the river the terrain rose abruptly to the east end of the Hwachon Reservoir, reaching heights of 2,700 feet (822 meters). South of the river the roads were barely adequate; north of it they were narrow and limited, and at some places there were no roads or trails. The division engineers had to build new roads or trails to supply some of the forthcoming combat operations. The 7th Division, at first in its new position, was in contact with the NK 15th Division, NK III Corps. In the latter part of April the NK II and V corps reinforced the III Corps.[11]

The 17th Regiment of the 7th Division reached its new MLR on 3 April and the next day relieved the Marines there at 6 P.M. The logistics for the division were difficult. It had to get its artillery supply at Chechon, a three-day round trip for 2½-ton trucks. The division was to go into attack on the morning of 5 April toward Line Kansas.

Still another major troop movement at the beginning of April was the movement westward of the US 2nd Division of X Corps to relieve the Marines in the eastern part of their zone. There the roads were even worse than in the new 7th Division sector, or altogether nonexistent on a north-south axis. The engineers improved stream beds as improvised roads for short distances and cut roads across rice paddies. Trucks in limited numbers could reach a point one and a half miles north of Sarang-chon, but from there supplies had to be hand-carried to the combat troops.

The first organized Korean labor companies for Eighth Army were assigned to the US 2nd Division, for use in carrying supplies over terrain impassable to motor vehicles. Their services were virtually indispensable. The army also attached 6 DUKWs to the division to ferry supplies across impassable streams. All ammunition for the division at this time had to come from the railhead at Chechon, 86 miles distant. CTC carriers had to supply one-third of the 2nd Division front in its roughest terrain. The supply problem was finally greatly relieved near the end of the month when a new railhead was opened at Wonju on 26 April—much closer to the front than Chechon.[12]

On the evening of 4 April the 23rd Infantry Regiment relieved the 5th Marine Regiment, with its 1st and 3rd battalions north of the Soyang River. The enemy defended strongly north of the Soyang, but the 23rd Infantry had seized Hill 578 by early afternoon of 6 April, and the French Battalion, also committed to attack, had reached the top of Hill 785. The next day, after a very strong concentration of all available supporting fire, the 23rd Infantry took Hill 1039, the strongest enemy position on the regiment's east flank. Little progress was made on 8 April, however, and all indications pointed to the enemy's intention to withdraw around the east end of the reservoir.[13]

The 38th Regiment of the 2nd Division spent the entire month of April in patrolling, training, resupplying, and rehabilitation. In April, for the first time since it landed in Korea as the lead element of the US 2nd Division, the 9th Infantry Regiment had no enemy contact for 30 consecutive days. It spent the entire month in either division or corps reserve, and in patrolling or in training. It received more replacements than ever before in Korea, and at the same time it lost more combat-hardened leaders through rotation than it had lost at Kunu-ri in late 1950. The 9th Regiment had its first group of rotatees leave on 13 April, when 9 officers and 50 enlisted men departed for the United States.

The rotation policy now going into effect required that an individual should have completed six months of service in Korea at division or lower level as of 31 March to be eligible for rotation home to the United States. Eligibility, however, gave no right to rotate. The combat effectiveness of the unit involved had to be given first consideration, and if that would be adversely affected in the face of impending battle, then rotation of experienced soldiers and officers could obviously be delayed. The middle of April 1951 generally marked the beginning of the rotation system. The 7th Infantry Division, for instance, had its first group of rotatees, 15 officers and 100 enlisted men, leave on 14 April. On the other hand, the 7th Division had 65 officers and 3,201 enlisted men report for duty in April as replacements. It then had a division strength of 16,924, against an authorized strength of 18,950.[14]

In its attempts to advance to Line Kansas in the first part of April, the 1st Cavalry Division encountered many enemy mines on roads and trails that damaged tanks and vehicles and caused many casualties. On 2 April the 8th Cavalry Regimental S-2 and adjutant walked on mines and both were seriously hurt and had to be evacuated by helicopter. The next day the enemy had evacuated their position, but a tank trap six feet deep and ten feet wide stopped B Company, 70th Tank Battalion, from advancing.

On 3 April General Ridgway ordered Operation "Dauntless," designed to destroy enemy and equipment, keep enemy units in front of I and IX corps off-balance, and advance those two corps toward Utah line, which, if attained, would create a salient of about 12 miles north of the 38th Parallel. Advance troops would then be within six miles of Chorwon and the edge of the Iron Triangle. X Corps and the ROK III and I corps farther east were to remain on Line Kansas when they reached it and to patrol from it.[15]

The same day, 3 April, General MacArthur made what was to be his last visit to Korea as commander in chief, Far East. He landed at Kangnung on the east coast and proceeded by jeep to the ROK I Corps and Capital Division's CP, hence north along the coastal road to Yangyang, and back to Kangnung. General Ridgway met MacArthur's party at Kangnung. MacArthur then returned to Japan without visiting the central and western parts of the front.[16]

On the same date, General Almond, X Corps commander, conferred with Colonel Martin, Far East Command assistant inspector general, regarding allegations appearing in *Fortnight* and *Time* magazines about the conduct of X Corps troops during the Chosin Reservoir campaign the preceding November and December. He also held planning conferences with Generals Ruffner and Ferenbaugh of the US 2nd and 7th divisions. He then designated Gen. Clark Ruffner to command X Corps temporarily while he was absent in Japan on R&R leave and temporary duty at the Far East Command. Almond returned to his command in Korea at 5 P.M., 9 April.[17]

An important logistic event occurred on 3 April in the US I Corps sector. A rail bridge over the Han River to Seoul was completed, and I Corps promptly established a railhead north of the river at Uijongbu. The next day petroleum products were delivered there by rail, and on 6 April rail transport delivered rations there.[18]

Lt. Col. William J. McCaffrey, now in command of the 31st Infantry Regiment, was putting his regiment in the 7th Division line along the Soyang River when, on 3 April, it was relieved by elements of the ROK 3rd Division. The NK 15th Division in front of them was engaged in a screening and delaying action as it withdrew slowly northward.[19]

Shifting of units and boundaries continued in Eighth Army as it moved toward establishing Line Kansas. On 4 April the boundary between IX and X corps was shifted 15 miles westward, and the 4th Ranger Company was attached to IX Corps. Eighth Army expected that the enemy attack, when it came, would hit hard at that corps. But two days later the IX Corps boundary was shifted back east three miles to give the corps responsibility for seizing the Hwachon Dam and the western part of the reservoir. The only land approach to the dam was in the IX Corps zone. Finally, on 5 April the US X Corps and the ROK III Corps jumped off in attack to reach Line Kansas in the east. But their advance was slow because of enemy resistance and a lack of roads.[20]

On 4 April the 7th Division completed its move westward, with the division establishing its CP in the Yangye area on the morning of the third. The next day the 17th and 32nd regiments relieved elements of the 1st Marine Division on line, and on 5 April attacked toward Line Kansas. The 31st Infantry Regiment was placed in reserve and was to be committed only on corps order. Enemy mines delayed the attack, but the division front had reached the 38th Parallel on 7 April, just south of the Soyang River. Two days later the 17th Infantry attacked across the Soyang River and gained a beachhead on the north side but was heavily engaged in the vicinity of Sinchon-ni.

In its crossing of the Soyang River on 9 April, the 1st Battalion, 17th

Regiment, of the 7th Division gave the lead to A Company. It began its crossing in the dark at 4:30 A.M. It had one and a half platoons across the river before the enemy knew the crossing was under way. This first group across at once came under heavy machine-gun cross fire and was unable to advance. The river ford, previously reconnoitered, had been blown, and the water was chest deep. The 7th Reconnaissance Company was able to get only five men across because of the water's depth, the swift current, and enemy opposition.

The unfavorable situation caused C Company to move downstream, and it crossed there under cover of an air strike. It then seized Hill 307. From there it helped cover B Company's crossing, and that company overran enemy on Hill 512. An enemy officer captured on Hill 512 said a battalion had held the hill, but the air strike had caused many of them to run off the hill into the valley, and afterward the American force had advanced so rapidly that they could not get back up in time to resist attack. It appears that C Company played the leading role in the capture of Hill 512, which dominated the crossing sites.[21]

The 2nd Battalion, with E Company leading, also crossed the river and was joined by the 7th Reconnaissance Company. They took Hill 322 in their attack. Thus, by evening of 9 April, the 17th Infantry, 7th Division, had secured a crossing of the Soyang River and held high ground at the crossing site.[22]

Farther west in the I Corps sector, the Belgian Battalion was attached to the British 29th Brigade, and the 10th Philippine BCT was taken from the 29th Brigade and attached to the 65th Infantry, US 3rd Division. The 1st Battalion, Gloucestershire Regiment, relieved the 10th Philippine BCT on line in this shift on 4 April. Meanwhile the 64th Heavy Tank Battalion, with F Company, 7th Infantry, US 3rd Division, attached, crossed the Hantan River and engaged enemy there. A Company of the tank battalion took up blocking positions on the road north of the river, and B and C tank companies swept the peninsula of land between the confluence of the Hantan and Imjin rivers. This action was accomplished by 9 April. The day before, I Corps changed the boundary between the ROK 1st Division and the British 29th Brigade, extending the ROK zone eastward. This change resulted in ROK troops' relieving the Northumberland Fusiliers Battalion, and the latter relieving the Royal Ulster Rifles Battalion, which went into brigade reserve.[23] This sector was to be a major point of enemy attack later.

A red-letter day came on 5 April for the 23rd RCT of the US 2nd Division, for on that date it was ordered into division reserve after 84 days in the lines, many of them in desperate combat, such as at Chipyong-ni. April was a less hectic month for nearly all of Eighth Army than the earlier months of 1951, and many units obtained some rest and time for rehabilitation.

The 7th Infantry Division, however, after a hard time in northeast Korea, was now back in the line with Eighth Army and had considerable hard going during the month. After the 17th Infantry crossed the Soyang River on 9 April, it met stubborn resistance in fighting its way toward Yanggu, at the eastern end of Hwachon Reservoir. It encountered numerous mines, 32 of them on one day, and there were many well-camouflaged and strongly built bunkers, probably dating from the fortification built prior to 1950 along the 38th Parallel demarcation line. But the NK 15th Division was forced from the high ground north of the Soyang River toward Yanggu, and the enemy shifted its strength toward Inje, some miles to the south-east of Yanggu and the reservoir.[24]

On 6 April the US I Corps moved its CP forward to Uijongbu, and the US X Corps also moved its CP much closer to the front lines, closing at Chungju, where it had remained so long, and opening at Hongchon. Both corps wanted to be closer to their forward units when the expected CCF offensive opened. It should not be thought that the expected forth-coming enemy attack, fully forecast by the heavy movement of fresh enemy forces to the front at this time, while Eighth Army advanced against re-duced enemy resistance, was taken lightly by any echelon of the UN forces in Korea or by the Joint Chiefs of Staff in the Pentagon. This is shown by a memo for the secretary of defense on 5 April 1951 from General Brad-ley for the Joint Chiefs of Staff, which said in part, "If the USSR precipi-tates a general war, UN forces should be withdrawn from Korea as rapidly as possible and deployed for service elsewhere. . . . The US should then mobilize in readiness for general war."[25]

Intelligence indicated that, by 6 April, the CCF high command had moved a fresh army group, the XIX, including the 63rd, 64th, and 65th armies, to within operating distances of the western front. This alignment reinforced the view that the Chinese would attack in the west. But as yet, of the ten CCF armies now accepted as being in Korea, only three were known to be in forward areas. But more were moving south daily, or rather, nightly. On 7 April aerial observers sighted 2,000 enemy vehicles, of which 1,400 were moving south. Similar reports had come in to Eighth Army for the past ten days. Among his busy days at this time, General Ridgway found time on 6 April to dedicate the UN cemetery at Pusan.[26]

The focal point of the massive movement of men and supplies south-ward at this time seemed to be the Chorwon-Kumhwa-Hwachon area of the Iron Triangle. An intelligence source reported that the CCF 27th Army left the Wonsan area on 7 March and was in the Chorwon area at the beginning of April. On the night of 7–8 April aerial night hecklers and radar planes reported observing 1,413 enemy vehicles moving south to forward areas, and huge supply dumps were being accumulated in the Samdung-Namchonjom areas. Patrols from Line Kansas reported stubborn resistance to their reconnaissance missions. At this time enemy-set brush fires began to burn and cover the areas near Line Kansas with heavy smoke clouds, making aerial observation in daytime more difficult, especially in the Hwachon Reservoir region.[27]

In its continuing effort to disrupt enemy rail and highway movement of supplies south to the battlefront along the east-coast transport network, the US Navy on 7 April made another strong attack on these facilities at Songjin. The heavy cruiser *St. Paul* and the three destroyers *Massey, Lind,* and *O'Brien* destroyed small coastal shipping vessels in the port and damaged rail and road junctions, and at Wonsan on the night of 5–6 April destroyers *Zellars* and *Hank* fired 297 rounds of 5-inch shells on vehicular traffic. On 8 April the British Royal Marine Commando landed under cover of naval gunfire against enemy small-arms fire and successfully blew up 110 feet of rail track to a depth of eight feet at a key rail bridge.[28]

On 7 April the British 27th Brigade left its reserve position and entered the line again in the IX Corps sector, with the US 24th Division on its left and the ROK 6th Division on its right, its attack objective Line Kansas. It crossed the 38th Parallel the next day and by 11 April had taken Hill 719. On the fourteenth the brigade changed its axis of attack to the northwest against Hill 826, which it captured on 16 April. The Australian Battalion on the left of the brigade met strong enemy resistance. The brigade had reached its sector of Line Kansas on 9 April, and at Hill 826 it was two miles north of Kansas. There it paused to consolidate its position.[29]

In I Corps on 7–8 April there was considerable skirmishing with enemy along the Imjin River. The 12th Regiment of the ROK 1st Division sent troops across the river and encountered enemy troops in company strength. These ROK troops were ordered to return to the south side of the Imjin at midafternoon. Farther east near the junction of the Hantan River with the Imjin, the US 3rd Division on 7–8 April sent F and L companies of the 7th Regiment across the Hantan with three companies of the 64th Tank Battalion to sweep the triangular-shaped area formed by the junction of the two rivers. They overran some enemy in their foxholes and inflicted an estimated 300 to 400 enemy casualties, taking 38 prisoners on the seventh. In this operation the 3rd Division lost three tanks to enemy mines and one to mechanical failure. The latter was left on the north side of the Hantan under guard.[30] The junction of the Hantan with the Imjin was considered a very sensitive area.

A disturbing factor to all of Eighth Army now appeared, apparently the result of the recently established Rest and Recreation program of sending groups of soldiers to Japan for relief from front-line duty in Korea. An epidemic of venereal disease broke out in the troops returning from R&R. General Soule told his troops in the US 3rd Division that any soldier showing up with venereal disease would automatically go to the bottom of the rotation list. All unit commanders were instructed to discuss the problem with their troops, and all battalion commanders in the US 25th Division were ordered to talk personally with any soldier who contracted the disease, stressing its effect on his future health and urging use of every protective measure possible to prevent contracting the disease, if one could not practice abstinence. In Korea venereal disease had not been a major problem thus far, no doubt owing to the limited opportunity to contract it.[31]

With Eighth Army's approach to the 38th Parallel and the launching of its attack to reach Line Kansas – the first high, defensible ground north of the parallel – increasing attention had to be given to the Hwachon Reservoir and Dam on the Pukhan River. The reservoir had been the principal source of water and electric power for the city of Seoul. It now lay under enemy control. Its southern shore, furthermore, was to constitute about 16 miles of Line Kansas. The reservoir also constituted a threat while under enemy control of being suddenly used for tactical purposes. If the enemy opened the 20 gates of the dam and released the reservoir's water when the reservoir was well filled, as it was now by spring snow melts and heavy rains in the upper Pukhan River drainage, it would result in flood conditions downstream and would destroy all or most of the low-level bridges the UN forces had recently installed over the Pukhan River, and in this way separate US IX Corps forces and divide their supply communications.

A IX Corps study issued on 4 April concluded the enemy could use the dam for tactical purposes and advantage. All the gates of the dam were closed at that time to raise the level of the reservoir to its maximum level. Engineers estimated that, if all the gates of the dam were opened at one time, the water level would rise 10 to 12 feet in the Pukhan River gorge area below the dam and up to 5 feet farther down in the Chunchon plain. This flooding would disrupt use of bridges and delivery of supplies to UN forces and would divide the corps's units.

On 7 April the 4th Ranger Company arrived at the 7th Cavalry Regiment CP at 9 P.M. and was sent at once to the 2nd Battalion, which was preparing to attack the Hwachon Reservoir. The battalion had received a message, confirming an earlier verbal order, that it should prepare to seize the Hwachon Dam, moving out against it at 7:30 A.M. the next morning, 8 April. The 4th Ranger Company was attached to the 2nd Battalion upon arrival at its CP. The attack force was to move through the 23rd Regiment and the French Battalion sectors of the US 2nd Division over Hill 621 and the river bed.[32]

On the morning of the eighth, G Company of the 7th Cavalry led off in the attack toward the reservoir, passing through the French sector at Hill 621, but there was little enemy contact. Patrols received some resistance and mortar fire, but nothing much happened.

The next morning at dawn, the enemy opened 8 of the dam's 20 gates,

Hwachon Dam under aerial attack by Navy AD Skyraiders using aerial torpedoes. *National Archives, 80-G 428678*

and by 7:20 A.M. a rise of one foot in the river below the dam washed out all the footbridges. The maximum rise during the day was about four feet. It broke one IX Corps floating bridge at one end. A detachment from the US 8th Engineer Battalion swung the loose end of the bridge against the opposite bank and anchored it there with bulldozers. The steel Treadway bridge farther downstream at Chunchon remained in place and could be used. The 19th Engineer Combat Battalion also went to the scene and secured the second floating bridge that was broken by the flooding Pukhan River. The water was running at 12 feet per second, a high velocity. The enemy made no attacks as a result of flooding the Pukhan River, but they gained about two days in delay of UN advances in the IX Corps area. It had to be counted an enemy tactical success.[33]

General Ridgway chanced to be at the IX Corps CP on 9 April, and he ordered General Hoge, the corps commander, to continue planning a raid on the dam to close the opened gates and to immobilize the dam machinery to prevent a reopening of some or all of the gates. Hoge, accordingly, organized Task Force Calloway, composed of the 2nd Battalion, 7th Cavalry Regiment; the 4th Ranger Company; and a platoon of engineers to continue the attack on the dam. The task force ran into strong resistance after it started its attack at 11:30 A.M. Air strikes tried to keep enemy forces away from the dam, and artillery fire was also registered on it. At the end of the day, the attack had reached to within about two and a half miles of the dam. F Company led the attack but had met small-arms and automatic fire from enemy dug in on higher ground covering the approach to the dam from the south. Captain Gray, F Company commander, was killed during the day, and six other men were wounded. Most of the enemy fire came from an area about two miles northwest of Yuchon. An estimated enemy company held the narrow neck of land between the Pukhan River and the Hwachon Reservoir. Task Force Calloway stayed in place overnight.[34]

The attempt to dislodge the enemy on the high ground south of the dam continued on 10 April. General Hoge visited the CP of the 1st Cavalry Division and discussed with the division commander the enemy resistance at Hwachon Dam. Hoge said he thought the resistance was not great and that the dam should be taken without delay.[35]

Task Force Calloway jumped off at 7:30 A.M. in a renewed effort to reach Hwachon Dam, this time using the 4th Ranger Company and the Engineer Platoon, but G Company of the 7th Cavalry led the attack. At 10:15 A.M. G Company received small-arms and automatic fire and 81-mm mortar shelling, although it did not report any casualties at that time. At midafternoon there was no change in the situation. At 3:30 P.M. it expected to be relieved at 6 P.M. But at 6:30 P.M., after breaking contact with the enemy an hour earlier, it learned it would not be relieved that night but was ordered again to take the dam. G Company at that time reported three men wounded in action. It would appear from such a limited number of casualties that the task force had really not made much of an effort during the day. A night attack on the dam was now under consideration, and ammunition and communication equipment was sent forward. During the day Task Force Calloway had advanced only 500 meters when it was stopped completely, and it then withdrew to its former position.[36]

The main difficulty in the attempted infantry attack on the Hwachon Dam on 9–10 April had been the limited avenues of approach by land to the dam site; there had been no room for maneuver. A short distance north of Yuchon-ni the road was squeezed into a narrow neck of land on a ridge between the Pukhan River on the west and a finger of the reservoir on the east. The dam ran in a straight east-west line across the Pukhan River at the beginning of a curve of the river where it made a U-bend back south.

The land approach to the dam along the narrow road on this ridge-neck of land was only half a mile wide between the western finger of the reservoir and the south-running Pukhan River just south of its U-bend. The enemy held this narrow neck of land. Air strikes on this area had not dislodged the enemy. A head-on assault on the dug-in enemy here probably would have resulted in heavy casualties, and it was not attempted. This was the situation at dark on 10 April, and no capture of this crucial neck of land seemed imminent. The tiny village of Kumanni-kogae marked the southern edge of this narrow neck of land south and southwest of the dam.[37]

After the complete failure on 10 April to make any progress toward capture of the Hwachon Dam, it was decided to try an amphibious night movement of the 4th Ranger Company across the west end of the reservoir to outflank the dug-in enemy defending the narrow neck of land southwest of the dam. The 4th Ranger Company and I Company of the 7th Cavalry would be the units used. The Rangers in small assault boats would lead the amphibious assault across the reservoir.

At 3:45 A.M., 11 April, the first group of Rangers crossed the west end of the reservoir and landed unopposed at 4 A.M. southeast of the dam. All the Rangers had crossed by 5:20 A.M. But at 6 A.M. enemy attacked from the west on the north side of the reservoir and halted the Rangers' advance toward the dam. Thereafter, the enemy force rapidly built up reinforcements by moving small groups across the top of the dam from west to east until they had about 500 troops in front of the rangers.

I Company of the 7th Cavalry crossed the reservoir in boats at 11:30 A.M. to reinforce the Rangers. The Rangers had obtained two of their initial objectives during the early morning, but an enemy counterattack at 1:30 P.M. by an estimated battalion drove both the Ranger and I companies back toward their landing point. At 6 P.M. they received orders to break contact and take up a defensive position; they returned to their landing site. There, at 6:30 P.M., the Ranger company embarked in the assault boats and returned to the south side of the reservoir. I Company followed at 9 P.M. The enemy interfered with neither company as it embarked to return to the south side. Both companies had closed in their assembly areas on the south side by 1:30 A.M., 12 April.

During the amphibious attack on 11 April, C Company, 70th Tank Battalion, tried to reach a point on the road from which it could support the attack, but road craters stopped its progress at 7 A.M. About noon, Lieutenant Gerrish, H Company, 7th Cavalry, was killed in action. The author could not determine the casualties incurred by the 2nd Battalion, the Ranger company, and attached units in the Hwachon Dam action, but they are believed not to have been great.

During 11 April the 1st Battalion, 7th Cavalry Regiment, made a diversionary movement from the west side of the Pukhan River toward the dam area. But at day's end it had not crossed the river, nor had it found a feasible crossing site. Its effort came to nothing. The only artillery support that could reach the enemy positions at and near the dam was from 155-mm howitzers, and they fired more than 2,400 rounds.

It was estimated that two enemy regiments defended the Hwachon Dam site, one battalion east of the dam against the 4th Ranger Company and I Company of the 7th Cavalry Regiment, and two battalions on the high ground south and west of the dam at the road on the narrow neck of land approach and astride the Pukhan River banks and the high ridge just west of the river at the dam site. Another regiment stood behind these forces to supply further reinforcements if needed.

The 7th Regiment was disengaged to go into reserve on the night of 11 April, and there is no way to determine whether the Hwachon attacks would have been successful if they had been continued on the twelfth. Boats were available on that morning to move 1,000 troops over the reservoir, and from there it was possible to outflank or overcome the enemy if the attacking forces had been reinforced. One wonders whether the 7th Cavalry troops on 11 April made their best effort, in view of the fact that they knew the entire division was to go into reserve that night.

The 7th Cavalry reported 126 prisoners taken, 537 enemy KIA counted, 1,729 estimated KIA, and 3,766 estimated wounded. Some enemy equipment and ammunition was recovered. The number of enemy reported killed and wounded seems excessive. If that number had been killed and wounded, the dam should have been taken.[38]

The US Marine Division relieved the 1st Cavalry Division in place on 12 April, and the latter went into army reserve. General Hoge, IX Corps commander, decided he should suspend efforts to capture the Hwachon Dam for the present and resume the attempt later when his corps had reached Line Wyoming. As events turned out, the Korean 1st Marine Corps Regiment, attached to the US 1st Marine Division, seized the dam on 18 April with no resistance—the enemy had withdrawn from it and the immediate front of the UN forces in their final preparations for the CCF 5th Phase Offensive.[39] The Hwachon Reservoir and Dam action never seemed to go right and did not reflect credit on the 7th Cavalry Regiment.

Other than the planned attack on the Hwachon Dam, the UN forces were engaged mostly in patrolling, building up the defenses north of Seoul, and in continuing their advance toward Line Kansas. This latter effort was especially difficult and involved some hard and hazardous fighting in the 7th and 2nd Division sectors in struggling through the roadless mountains south of the Hwachon Reservoir and eastward to Yanggu. On 8 April General Ridgway introduced a new procedure in his efforts to keep informed of the situation all along the line on a day-to-day basis. He requested that the several corps commanders give him, by electrical transmission at the end of each day's operations, a brief summary of significant actions in their zones and a personal estimate of enemy-projected attitudes and intentions whenever a substantial change had taken place from the preceding day's report, and to include the corps commander's operational plan for the next day. He ordered that these daily reports be "addressed to me personally at Army Advance Command Post." This meant they should be sent to him at Yoju. These reports started on the evening of 8 April.[40]

On the eighth another change was ordered in troop dispositions along the western part of Line Kansas, along the Imjin River. The boundary between the ROK 1st Division and the US 3rd Division was moved three miles eastward. Since the British 29th Brigade was on the western flank of the 3rd Division, to which it was attached, this change moved it farther east along the Imjin.

Aerial observation deep in the enemy's rear on this day reported that streets in Pyongyang, the North Korean capital, were being converted into runways. Homes and buildings were being razed for the new airstrips.[41]

The Engineer Section of Eighth Army was at this time fully occupied in establishing impressive defenses north of Seoul. On 8 April it requested 145,755 antitank mines and 35,950 antipersonnel mines for Lines Kansas, Delta, Golden, and Nevada. During April, 1,550 carloads of engineer supplies were sent from Pusan to Eighth Army forward areas. More and more attention was being given to Line Golden, originally called Line Lincoln, which was to be the ultimate defense line immediately around Seoul.[42]

On the east coast the naval bombardment of Wonsan continued and by 7 April had registered its 43rd consecutive day. Rear Adm. Allen E. Smith, in command of the naval task force off Wonsan, commented with perhaps some exaggeration, "In Wonsan, you cannot walk on the streets. You cannot sleep any time in the 24 hours unless it is the sleep of death." He said the only people in the city were "suicide groups" of soldiers living in caves and waiting to fight a possible UN landing.[43]

The tactical branch of Eighth Army, G-3 Section, under Colonel Tram, presented a plan on 9 April that it had been working on for an Eighth Army withdrawal from the Kansas line to one based directly on the Han River in the Seoul area, if expected enemy attacks in the near future made it desirable. General Ridgway approved the plan in general. For the present he ordered that the plan be issued only to the US I Corps and to the ROK Army Headquarters for planning purposes only. Ridgway ordered that written instructions be sent to the ROK Army Headquarters that it was not to publish the plan to lower units.

Since the beginning of the Korean War on 25 June 1950 Brig. Gen. Paik Sun Yup had commanded the ROK 1st Division. It was in the west of the ROK line and took heavy blows from the invading army with its Soviet-built T-34 tanks. General Paik had continued to command the ROK 1st Division from that beginning until 10 April 1951. He and his division became a part of US I Corps when that corps was organized in Korea and put into the line in the west in late summer of 1950. He quickly became well known throughout the UN forces as the most capable ROK division commander, and throughout the summer, fall, and winter he and his division were in some of the most desperate of the year's battles, always being stationed along an American division in the I Corps line. Generally, Paik's ROK 1st Division held its own alongside the American troops. Now, on 10 April 1951, General Paik was transferred to the east coast of Korea to command the ROK I Corps, replacing Major General Kim, who had been lost in an airplane crash in the eastern mountains. Upon his promotion and transfer, Lt. Gen. Frank Milburn, commander of the US I Corps, in a letter to General Paik, complimented him on his past services to I Corps. At the time of his assumption of command of the ROK I Corps, Paik passed to the direct command of the ROK Army Headquarters. His troops were already north of the 38th Parallel and Line Kansas and were astride the road junction in the east-coast town of Yangyang. General Ridgway could feel confident that the ROK I Corps was in good hands.[44]

Enemy resistance on 10 April was stiffening in front of the Turkish Brigade, and its troops had hard fighting in taking hills on the north side of the Hantan River. The 3rd Battalion crossed the Hantan during the day but apparently returned to the south side in the evening. It held observation positions there overlooking the Hantan and its north bank. The Turks were still attached to the US 25th Division, with whom they had established excellent rapport. The division knew by now that the Turks were excellent fighters.

In the central corridor, a railhead had just been established at Wonju. The main delay in getting rail transportation to and beyond Wonju on the east-central railroad from the south, to support that sector of the front, had been the rebuilding of the destroyed rail bridge at Wonju. US engineers had rebuilt the bridge on an emergency basis, working around the clock under night illumination of the site. Helping greatly in the logistics problems and supplying front-line troops in the central sector was the assignment of four Korean CTC companies to the US 7th Division, five to the US 2nd Division, and seven to several engineer groups there on 10 April. American troop units immediately gave them a favorable reception.[45]

On 10 April everything seemed to be moving forward favorably toward putting the UN forces on Line Kansas. In the west, I and IX corps already had occupied most of their positions on or beyond the line; in the central sector the US 7th and 2nd divisions were fighting hard in almost roadless, mountainous terrain to reach the line. On the east coast and inland for many miles, the ROK I Corps was on or beyond Line Kansas. On balance, affairs seemed to be going well. But General Ridgway and all major commanders knew that soon a big test would come; the CCF and North Koreans were massing just in front of them for their long-expected 5th Phase Offensive. Those who looked at their calendar could see that tomorrow was 11 April, a date to be remembered for major changes in UN command in Japan and Korea.

17

Changes in Command and an Enemy Buildup

ON 10 APRIL Secretary of the Army Frank Pace, Jr., arrived in Korea to hold conferences with General Ridgway and to make an inspection tour of the battlefront, with visits to major UN command units. The next day, 11 April, Ridgway started a tour of the front with Secretary Pace and members of his party from the United States, including Lieutenant General Hull, deputy chief of staff for administration, Department of the Army. The day was blustery and dreary, with hail and snow falling at some places. At one point in the inspection trip, a newspaper correspondent spoke to General Ridgway, congratulating him on something that had happened, but Ridgway did not know what he was talking about. Then, while the party was at the CP of the 5th RCT, US 24th Division, General Ridgway learned unofficially a little after 3 P.M. that he had been appointed commander in chief, Far East Command. Back at his Yoju Advance CP, it was confirmed to Ridgway at 10 P.M. that he was indeed taking General MacArthur's place. Later he wrote of that moment, "Late that night, back at my command post, an urgent message came for me, over the official radio. It told me that President Truman had relieved General MacArthur of command and I had been appointed in his place. For several hours, without my knowledge, I had been Supreme Commander in the Far East."[1]

This book presents a combat history of the Korean War, and it will not attempt to discuss the political, public-relations, and UN factors that led President Truman to remove General MacArthur from his Far East command and to appoint General Ridgway in his place. That action has already been discussed and debated in public, and in many books. Here, I include only those official orders that made the change and a brief statement on the chronology of discussions in Washington that led to President Truman's decision.

A letter from General MacArthur to Congressman Joseph Martin of Massachusetts, dated 20 March 1951, on MacArthur's views about the war in Korea came to President Truman's attention on 5 April. On the sixth the president called a meeting of his special assistant, Averell Harriman; Secretary of State Dean Acheson; Secretary of Defense George Marshall; and General Omar Bradley, chairman of the Joint Chiefs of Staff. There was a full discussion of the issue, and the president called for all the records that bore on the subject. The next day, Saturday, the president convened the same group at 8:30 A.M. for a further discussion of the matter. He then told the group individually to consider the issues over the weekend, and he directed Marshall to secure the views of the Chiefs of Staff from a purely military point of view. On Sunday, 8 April, the Chiefs of Staff met, and in the afternoon they stated their recommendations to Generals Marshall and Bradley. The next day, Monday, 9 April, General Bradley reported these recommendations to the president in a meeting that also included Secretary of Defense Marshall, Mr. Harriman, and Secretary of State Acheson. At that meeting, General Marshall later testified before a joint committee of the Congress, "With the unanimous concurrence of all those present, the President at that time took his decision to relieve Gen. MacA. On Tuesday, the 10th, at 3 P.M. there was another meeting of the President with the same group to pass on the form of the message from the President to Gen MacA, the form of the orders to Gen Ridgway notifying him of his succession to command, and the form of the release advising the public of the action taken and reasons therefore." The conferences in Washington that led to the dismissal of General MacArthur, therefore, lasted from 6 to 10 April. It may be well here to continue General Marshall's testimony as secretary of defense on how the decision was to be implemented.

Originally it was decided to transmit the notification to Gen. MacA at 8 P.M. Washington time on Wed April the 11th, that is 10 A.M. Tokyo time. Sec of the Army Frank Pace, then in Korea, was directed to make the delivery of the msgs to MacArthur at his residence, the Embassy, at the time indicated. However, late on Tuesday, April the 10th, there were indications that the action to be taken had become known publicly, and it was then decided by the President to accelerate the transmission of the official notification to Gen. MacA by approximately 20 hours. The exact timing of the public release was made so as to coincide with the arrival of this communication in Tokyo in midafternoon. Mr. Pace in Korea incidentally did not receive his instructions due to a breakdown in a power unit in Pusan.[2]

The Joint Chiefs of Staff, after meeting, went to Secretary of Defense Marshall's office, and General Bradley gave him their reasons for the opinion, from the military point of view, that General MacArthur should be relieved of his command.

1. That by his public statements and by his official communications to us, he had indicated that he was not in sympathy with the decision to try to limit the conflict to Korea. This would make it difficult for him to carry out Joint Chiefs of Staff directives. Since we had decided to try to confine the conflict to Korea and

avoid a third world war, it was nec to have a commander more responsive to control from Washington. The second reason advanced by the Chiefs was that Gen MacA had failed to comply with the Presidential directive to clear statements on policy before making such statements public. He had also taken independent action in proposing to negotiate directly with the en field commander for an armistice and had made that statement public despite the fact that he knew the President had such a proposal under consideration from a governmental level. The third reason advanced by the Chiefs was that they felt and feel now that the mil must be controlled by civilian authority in this country. They have always adhered to this principle and they felt that Gen. MacA's actions were continuing to jeopardize the civilian control over the mil authorities. These reasons were given by the Chiefs to Gen. Marshall on Sun afternoon. . . . We sat down afterward and wrote these down and agreed that these were the reasons they gave to Gen. Marshall on that Sunday afternoon. . . . I concurred.[3]

The message prepared by President Truman, relieving General Mac-Arthur of command, April 10, 1951, read as follows:

I deeply regret that it becomes my duty as President and Commander in Chief of the United States military forces to replace you as Supreme Commander, Allied Powers; Commander in Chief, United Nations Command; Commander in Chief, Far East; and Commanding General, U.S. Army Far East.

You will turn over your commands, effective at once, to Lt. Gen. Matthew B. Ridgway. You are authorized to have issued such orders as are necessary to complete desired travel to such place as you select.

My reasons for your replacement will be made public concurrently with the delivery to you of the foregoing order, and are contained in the next following message.[4]

General Ridgway was not certain in the instructions he received from the Joint Chiefs of Staff on the evening of 11 April what the extent of his authority was immediately in the command of Eighth Army while General Van Fleet was en route to Korea and of his employment thereafter, and he asked Secretary of the Army Frank Pace to obtain a clarification for him. Secretary Pace thereupon sent a message to Secretary of Defense Marshall for a clarification. This clarification came in a message on 12 April.

Message just received from Mr. Pace to Gen. Marshall reference to your uncertainty as to the extent of your authority in the matter of a Cmdr for 8th Army and employment of Van Fleet. We regret that time did not permit consulting you prior to announcement of appointment of Van Fleet. His appointment as your successor to command 8th Army was approved personally by the President. In Sec Def's message to you the last 7 words "for such duties as you may direct" were added to cover our thought that you would probably desire to designate Van Fleet as your Deputy Cmdr, retaining direct command in the field yourself, until such time as you thought it advisable to turn over top command of the 8th Army, presumably after the threatening hostile offensive. Aside, from the matter of Van Fleet's outstanding military qualifications, there is a special situation to be considered, which involves many reactions, both national and international, relating to Van Fleet's previous experience against Communist forces in Mountainous Greece and his relations there in dealing with the civil authorities. Already his name has been received with great favor especially in view of his services in Greece.[5]

This document makes clear that General Ridgway played no role in the selection of Gen. James Van Fleet to succeed him to command of Eighth Army in Korea. Ordinarily, an outgoing commander is asked for his views and recommendations in choosing his successor. The author believes in this case that Gen. J. Lawton Collins, the Army chief of staff, personally selected Van Fleet for command of Eighth Army and that Collins did not wish to ask Ridgway for his recommendation. The author also believes, from his examination of the Ridgway Papers, that, if asked, Ridgway probably would have recommended another officer, with, however, no reflection on General Van Fleet.

General MacArthur apparently received the first information of his dismissal from command about noon or shortly thereafter during a luncheon at his residence in the American Embassy in Tokyo. According to Maj. Gen. Courtney Whitney, an advisor and confidant on MacArthur's staff, General MacArthur was entertaining Sen. Warren Magnuson of Washington and William Stearns of Northwest Airlines at luncheon in his residence on Wednesday, 11 April. During the luncheon Mrs. MacArthur noticed that Col. Sidney Huff, MacArthur's aide-de-camp, was standing in the door of the dining room. She excused herself and went to him, knowing something important had happened. Colonel Huff told her that news of General MacArthur's dismissal had just reached him. She returned to the table and whispered it to General MacArthur.[6]

On the morning of 12 April, General Ridgway borrowed Secretary Pace's Constellation and flew from Korea to Japan for a conference with General MacArthur. Ridgway stopped at Pusan en route and at 4:30 P.M. arrived at Haneda Airport at the edge of Tokyo. Maj. Gen. Doyle Hickey, the Far East acting chief of staff, met Ridgway at Haneda and immediately drove him to the American Embassy for the meeting with MacArthur.[7]

In his book *Soldier,* Ridgway says of this conference:

I went directly to his office from Haneda airport, and he received me at once, with the greatest courtesy. I had a natural human curiosity to see how he had been affected by his peremptory removal from his high post. He was entirely himself—composed, quiet, temperate, friendly, and helpful to the man who was to succeed him. He made some allusions to the fact that he had been summarily relieved, but there was no trace of bitterness or anger in his tone. I thought it was a fine tribute to the resilience of this great man that he could accept so calmly, with no outward sign of shock, what must have been a devastating blow to a professional soldier standing at the peak of a great career. . . .

In the hours I spent with General MacArthur, we reviewed the whole scope and range of my responsibilities. I then started back from Tokyo to Korea, to wind up my affairs there and turn over my command. We flew by night, in Mr. Pace's Constellation, a far faster and more comfortable plane than my own old war-battered B-17.[8]

General Ridgway had told the crew to take him to the K-2 airfield at Taegu, but the pilot made a major mistake and landed instead at K-37, a small-plane strip that had just been lengthened to take twin-engined C-47s. He had never even seen K-2 and must have just barely missed slamming into a mountain alongside K-37. It was a close call for Ridgway.[9]

From Taegu on that day, 13 April, General Ridgway went on to his Advance CP at Yoju, and in a light plane from there he flew to the US 3rd Division CP for a conference with I Corps commander General Milburn and 3rd Division commander General Soule. From there he went to see Brigadier General Kang, the new commander of the ROK 1st Division, and General Chung, the ROK Army chief of staff. After this meeting with the ROK officers, he went to see Major General Palmer, commander of the 1st Cavalry Division, and then at 4:30 P.M. he flew back to the Eighth Army Tactical CP at Taegu. Half an hour later he met in a commanders' conference with the Army corps commanders, the ROK Army commanders, and the Fifth Air Force commander at Taegu. It had been a busy day and one in which General Ridgway had said many good-byes to friends and associates.[10]

Saturday, 14 April, was Ridgway's last day as Eighth Army commander of the UN forces in Korea. General Van Fleet arrived at Taegu, where Ridgway met him at the K-2 airport. In a simple ceremony there, Ridgway turned over command of the Eighth Army to Lt. Gen. James A. Van Fleet. In General Order 208, 14 April 1951, at Eighth Army Tactical Headquarters, General Van Fleet officially assumed command of Eighth Army.[11]

At 11:45 on 14 April General Ridgway received a good-bye call from ROK minister of defense Sihn. At 2 P.M. he held a press conference at Taegu, and at 6 P.M. he was airborne from K-2 airfield headed for Haneda Airport, Tokyo, where at 9:15 P.M. General Hickey and Ambassador Sebald met him. They drove him into the city, where Ridgway took temporary quarters at the Imperial Hotel, the famous hotel designed by American architect Frank Lloyd Wright.

Ridgway's last two weeks in Korea had been concerned primarily with troop deployments for the execution of Operations Rugged and Dauntless and preparations of defense positions in depth, planning for the possible withdrawal to these positions in the expected imminent CCF resumption of offensive operations, and in the rehabilitation of personnel and equipment of units placed in reserve.[12]

It remains to be said that General MacArthur left Japan on 16 April 1951. He had the letters "Scap" removed from his Constellation plane and the word "Bataan" placed on it instead. He and his family and party took off from Haneda Airport early in the morning, bound for the United States. He stopped overnight at Hawaii. He had arrived in Japan on 30 August 1945, almost five years and eight months earlier.[13]

General Van Fleet took over command of Eighth Army after General Ridgway had planned and ordered Operation Dauntless but before it was carried out. Operation Dauntless was to continue the advance through Phase Line Utah to Line Wyoming, in effect a drive toward Chorwon and the Iron Triangle, which, if successful, would create a bulge northward from Line Kansas.

It is appropriate at this point to let General Ridgway state in his own words what was very much on his mind – the relationship between himself and General Van Fleet and the corps commanders in Korea. He said he did not want to hold all the controls in his own hands, as MacArthur had done before. Ridgway wrote of his intention:

I was determined . . . to follow what I had seen habitually practiced in combat in Europe. That is, I would accord the Army Commander, General Van Fleet, the latitude his reputation and my high respect for his ability merited, while still retaining the right of approval or disapproval of his principal tactical plans. And in appraising these plans I intended on each occasion to consult personally and separately not only with the Army Commander himself, but with the Corps and Division Commanders of the Eighth Army, all of whom I knew intimately. I wanted in every instance to get for myself the feel of the situation as these officers responsible for execution of the plans might sense it. With this firsthand knowledge of their views added to all other relevant information, I would be in a position to make sound decisions – for which I as Theater Commander would accept full and sole responsibility.

In reaching my decisions I wanted to keep always in mind the clear policy decisions communicated to me by President Truman and the Joint Chiefs of Staff, the most immediate of which was to avoid any action that might result in an extension of hostilities and thus lead to a worldwide conflagration. General Van Fleet; Vice Admiral Joy, Commander Naval Forces, Far East; and General Stratemeyer, Commander Far East Air Forces, were all apprised of this basic guideline and each commander had expressed his full understanding and agreement. . . . I undertook to place reasonable restrictions on the advances of the Eighth and ROK Armies. Specifically I charged General Van Fleet to conduct no operations in force beyond the Wyoming Line without prior approval from GHQ. I wished to be informed ahead of time of whatever advances beyond the Utah Line the Eighth Army Commander felt were warranted. . . .

I had full confidence in General Van Fleet, a courageous and competent field commander. Moreover, I had always felt that the views of subordinate field commanders were entitled to the most thoughtful consideration. Even so, I had to walk that tightrope familiar to all top commanders in any profession, civilian as well as military: To maintain the proper balance between according sufficient latitude to the subordinate commander in carrying out broadly stated directives, and in exercising adequate supervision, as befitted the man who would bear the ultimate responsibility for the success or failure of the entire effort. I sought during all my time in Tokyo to maintain that balance.[14]

The day after General MacArthur left Japan, General Ridgway, on 17 April 1951, appointed Maj. Gen. Doyle O. Hickey his chief of staff for all the commands that Ridgway held in the Far East. Hickey had been acting chief of staff for General MacArthur since the latter had appointed Maj. Gen. Edward M. Almond his chief of staff, as commander of the US X Corps, organized for the Inchon operation in September 1950. General MacArthur apparently intended to return General Almond to his position as chief of staff after the X Corps had completed its operations in Mac-Arthur's plans to reunify all of Korea. When the X Corps evacuated northeast Korea in December 1950, General MacArthur, in a private discussion with General Almond, asked the latter if he wished to return to Tokyo as his chief of staff or to remain as X Corps commander in South Korea under Eighth Army control. Almond told MacArthur he wished to remain X Corps commander. But MacArthur retained Almond on paper as his chief of staff right up to the time of his dismissal on 11 April 1951.

Born in Coyesville, New Jersey, 19 March 1892, Lt. Gen. James Alward Van Fleet was 59 years old when he took command of Eighth Army in Korea on 14 April 1951. He was a member of the West Point class of 1915, which also included Dwight D. Eisenhower, Omar N. Bradley, and George E. Stratemeyer among its most distinguished members. Van Fleet entered the Army from Florida, which had become his adopted state. Upon graduating from the United States Military Academy, he was commissioned a second lieutenant of infantry. At West Point Van Fleet had been a halfback on the football team. "Big Jim" he was called, and rightly so, for his 6 foot, 1 inch frame was heavily covered with muscle; he was indeed a fine physical specimen. His background in football led him later to speak often of military matters and tactics in football vernacular.

In World War I, Van Fleet served as commander of a machine-gun battalion in France. After the war Van Fleet served in a number of posts as an instructor in military science, including ROTC at the University of Florida, where he also served as head football coach.

In World War II, Van Fleet commanded the 8th Infantry Regiment, 4th Division, which landed on Utah Beach on D day, and spearheaded the drive on Cherbourg, France. In that action he was wounded (he had also been wounded in the First World War), and he won the Distinguished Service Cross for superior leadership and personal bravery. Altogether, he collected two oak-leaf clusters to his DSC, and he had many other decorations as well in his military career, but the decoration he most liked to wear was the Combat Infantry's Badge. After Cherbourg, he commanded the 4th Division in the drive against the Siegfried line. Later, he commanded the 90th Division in the Battle of the Bulge, and in 1945–46, the US III Corps. Back in the United States after the war, he was deputy commander of the 1st Army at Governors Island, in New York Harbor, and was promoted to lieutenant general in 1948.

Then came his assignment as director of the Joint United States Military Advisory Group to Greece in 1948 to combat the Communist guerrillas, who seemed on the point of winning their battle for control of that strategic country. So successful was he in advising the Greek government and in providing for its army logistically that by 1950 the guerrillas in Greece were virtually nonexistent, and he was credited with saving that country for the West. He was known as a bitter foe of Communists. Back in the United States once again, he commanded the US 2nd Army in 1950–51 at Fort Meade, Maryland.

In early April 1951, General Van Fleet was on a ten-day vacation in his adopted state of Florida, when at 2 A.M., 11 April, he received a telephone call from Gen. J. Lawton Collins, the Army chief of staff. He was ordered to pack his bag and start for Korea at once. His departure from the United States was as precipitous as had been General Ridgway's four months earlier. Van Fleet later wrote of that event:

I had never been in the Orient before. All through the years I had listed China as my choice of station, but I had never been selected to go there. In my early career China and the Philippines were choice details, usually given to the deserving few who had had duty in Washington. I have never had duty in Washington.

It was 12 noon when I stepped off the plane in Taegu, then headquarters of our Eighth Army in Korea. General Matthew B. Ridgway, ordered to Tokyo to replace General Douglas MacArthur as Supreme Commander in the Far East, met me at the airport.

By 5 o'clock he had turned over the Eighth Army Command to me and was off to Tokyo. I was on my own. General Collins had said that I was to have a "free hand," that Matt Ridgway would give me a "free hand." What happened now on the Korea battlefront was my responsibility.[15] [In the author's view, the last sentence is at least a slight overstatement.]

Alva C. Carpenter, chief counsel and executive director of the Subcommittee of the Committee on the Judiciary, United States Senate, 83rd Congress, 2nd Session, did much of the questioning of General Van Fleet in 1954 in the hearings the subcommittee held. In one part of this questioning, on 29 September 1954, Mr. Carpenter brought out an interesting aspect of General Van Fleet's appointment to command of Eighth Army.

Mr. Carpenter. When were you first placed on a standby basis for Korea?
General Van Fleet. Early January 1951.
Mr. Carpenter. Who placed you on that standby basis?
General Van Fleet. The Chief of Staff, Gen. J. Lawton Collins, told me in the event of replacement for General Ridgway I would be next and that I must keep it quiet and only three other people would know about it.

Mr. Carpenter. When did he tell you this, on what occasion, General?
General Van Fleet. It was at the funeral of Gen. Walton H. Walker at Arlington.
Mr. Carpenter. Do you remember the exact date?
General Van Fleet. I think it was January 3.[16]

On the day General MacArthur was relieved of his command and General Ridgway was traveling with Secretary of the Army Pace around the I and IX Corps fronts in the west, 11 April, the US I Corps and the west flank of US IX Corps started a limited objective attack called "Operation Dauntless," which in the next seven days pushed a salient about 12 miles deep north of the 38th Parallel, the apex of which reached within 6 miles of Chorwon, at the southwest corner of the Iron Triangle. Any advance toward the Iron Triangle had been resisted for several days, and this attack was no exception. Indeed, the Chinese fought hard to halt the attack. The Turkish Brigade took three days, on occasion with hand-to-hand combat, to dislodge the enemy from dug-in positions, and elements of the US 24th Division, on the right of the Turks, used flamethrowers to dislodge the enemy. After 16 April, however, there was little opposition, the enemy seemingly having withdrawn from the fight. The perimeter formed as a result of this bulge in the line south of Chorwon was called the Utah line.[17]

West of the Utah bulge, the ROK 1st and the US 3rd divisions reached the Imjin River and sent patrols across it as far north as Kaesong. Enemy contacts there were light, but aerial reports indicated a heavy enemy buildup a little farther north. In the US IX Corps sector, the British 27th Brigade advanced toward Line Utah. Brigadier Coad had left the brigade, and Col. B. A. Burke, DSO, deputy commander of the British 29th Brigade, had taken over command. The 27th Brigade was attached to the US 24th Division. The brigade made slow but steady progress in the area north of Kapyong. The Argyll Battalion carried the advance for a time and lost two officers and several men in its last engagement. The Australian and Canadian battalions completed the drive to the Utah Line on 16 April. Three days later the ROK 19th Regiment of the ROK 6th Division relieved the British 27th Brigade on Line Utah, and it returned to Kapyong in IX Corps reserve.[18] All units were on Line Utah by 17 April, and until the twenty-first, only patrols went north of it.

Before daylight on 12 April, the Gloucestershire Battalion (the "Glosters") of the British 29th Brigade, attached to the US 3rd Division, moved out to seize the high ground north of Choksong. One company went farther and established a crossing of the Imjin River, without enemy contact, and patrolled farther north, still without enemy contact. It then returned to its assembly area south of the Imjin. On the west of the Glosters, patrols from the ROK 1st Division crossed the Imjin and went 8,000 yards beyond it. They returned with some prisoners and reported there was a CCF concentration north and northwest of Korangpo and the sharp eastward

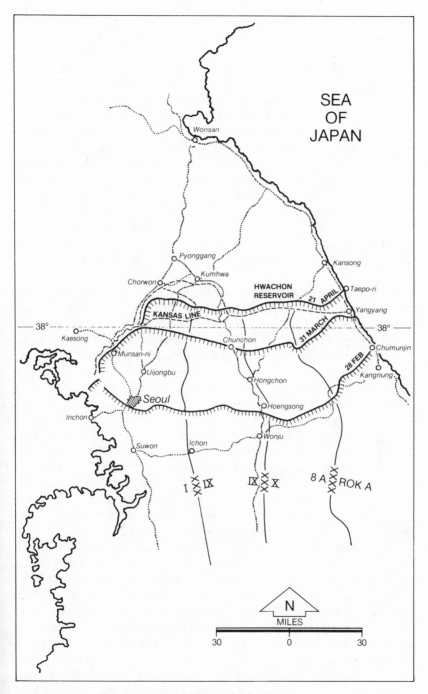

MAP 17. **UN offensive, 1 March–21 April 1951**

bend of the Imjin. The prisoners stated that the CCF 63rd Army had moved into the area.[19]

On this day, 12 April, Eighth Army completed its initial planning for a withdrawal of the army, if necessary, in the expected forthcoming enemy offensive. The plan was called "Audacious." It called for a withdrawal only on army orders to a series of phase lines south of Kansas. These successive phase lines were called Delta, Golden, and Nevada. These were designed to be for orderly, if not leisurely, withdrawals to throw the enemy out of close contact and bring the very large massed artillery and tank fire to play on pursuing enemy forces in daylight and cause heavy enemy casualties. Line Golden, which was to become the most important of the phase lines, was in reality a heavily fortified defense line around Seoul. The 1st Cavalry Division, just withdrawn from the line below the Hwachon Reservoir, was in army reserve at Kungong-ni, and the US 2nd Division was in reserve at Hongchon, both to be used as counterattack forces, as indeed also was the British 27th Brigade at Kapyong. General Ridgway had left nothing to chance.[20]

In reaching their sectors of Line Kansas, the US 7th and 2nd divisions had first to cross the Soyang River, which ran generally east-west in their sectors, and then try to find their way through the almost trackless high mountains between the river and the Hwachon Reservoir. The only lateral road in this area ran along the north bank of the Soyang River. There were no north-south roads here through the mountains, except poor tracks at either end of the reservoir. These led to the town of Hwachon a few miles west of the western end of the reservoir, and on the east a road led to Yanggu, a mile south of the eastern end of the reservoir. The two divisions began crossing the Soyang River on 11 April, and for the next week they fought their way, sometimes against strong resistance, toward the reservoir. The French Battalion was on the left flank, with the 23rd Regiment next to it for the 2nd Division. The 17th Regiment was east of the US 2nd Division and carried the advance for the US 7th Division.

Air strikes ahead of the 23rd Regiment had bombed Yanggu, at the eastern end of the Hwachon Reservoir, into a smoldering ruin on 13 April. A patrol of the 1st Battalion, 32nd Infantry, which entered Yanggu two days later found it deserted but came upon an enemy ammunition dump, which it destroyed. Between 11 and 15 April the 23rd Infantry scrambled slowly northward among the high, jagged peaks, the highest called Whitehead Mountain, 1198 meters (3930 feet) high. In places the enemy had prepared bunkers. The regiment used 900 Korean carriers during this time to bring supplies to it. Opposition was strongest in the eastern part of the 23rd Infantry sector.

The hardest fighting was probably on 12 April, when the 3rd Battalion, 23rd Infantry, strove by maneuver to break the enemy line. Artillery fired more than 2,000 rounds in support of the battalion that day. Holding the long, sharp-edged ridge running down from Hill 1198 were two regiments totaling about 5,000 enemy, many of them in bunkers. The battle of the twelfth must have been effective, for the next day there appeared to be no enemy in front of the 23rd Infantry south of the reservoir. They had apparently withdrawn northward around the east end of the reservoir. Three battalions of artillery, the 37th, 15th, and 503rd, had fired more than 29,000 rounds in support of the 23rd Regiment in the three days required to drive the enemy from the massive mountain. Two battalion volleys of TOT were used to a maximum extent.

Many enemy mines obstructed the regiment's advance, and 15 men were killed or wounded by them. A and B companies of the 2nd Engineer Battalion labored to clear mines and booby traps and to build new roads and tracks. These companies built a jeep trail through the mountains north from the Soyang River road and then used four Korean carrier companies of 240 men each to get food and ammunition to the men on the ridges and peaks. From high points overlooking the reservoir, units of the 23rd Infantry could see many enemy barges crossing the reservoir. An air strike on 11 April scuttled 15 boats and barges. West of the 23rd Infantry, the French Battalion was so far extended at the western end of the 2nd Division line that it took carrier parties from eight to ten hours to reach a supply point and the same length of time to return.

On 19 April A Company, 23rd Infantry, with a platoon of tanks, established contact with elements of the 17th Regiment of the US 7th Division on their right. Two days later the 1st Battalion, 23rd Infantry, received orders to proceed cautiously from Yanggu around the east end of the reservoir. B and C companies both sent out patrols; enemy fire hit the one from C Company.[21]

East of the 2nd Division, the 17th Infantry, 7th Division, had much the same kind of fighting that had characterized that of the French Battalion and the 23rd Infantry. The terrain north of the Soyang River near Inje is equally rough and mountainous. The 17th Regiment had almost constant contact with defending enemy from between 10 and 16 April. When it took one hill, there was another higher one ahead. Also, as the regiment approached the 38th Parallel, it found more and more enemy mines to contend with; on 12 April one mine explosion killed 8 American soldiers, wounded another 14, and wounded 2 ROKs. On the fourteenth, the 17th Regiment crossed the 38th Parallel into North Korea. The next day a K Company infantry-tank team secured Yanggu. The 32nd Regiment, which took over the continuation of the attack, encountered heavy resistance at the high ground northeast of Yanggu, where an estimated enemy force of 900 men defended with artillery and mortars. The regiment, however, secured its objective, Hill 700, on 17 April.[22]

Many miles farther west, one of the historic invasion routes to Seoul was near the junction of the Hantan with the Imjin River. The US 3rd

Division held this sector, with the British 29th Brigade attached and on its left flank in the vicinity of Choksong. The division boundary included the east side of the Imjin where it turned sharply north at its junction with the Hantan, which flowed into it from the east. The US 25th Division, with the Turkish Brigade attached, held the line east of the 3rd Division in a rough mountainous area with gorgelike stream channels, including that of the Hantan River. Hill 642 (or 643, on some maps), on the north side of the Hantan, dominated the river south of it where the Turks, on the division left, and the 24th Regiment had to construct crossing sites.

On 11 April C Company, 77th Engineer Battalion, converted a 3.7-mile trail to a two-lane road to the chosen bridge site, except for an 800-yard stretch that was within enemy small-arms fire. This stretch was soon thereafter finished to the bridge site, which had extremely high banks. The 27th Infantry S-2 report at the time says they were 40- to 60-feet-high sheer banks, the north side a wall of rock. Three engineer companies, aided by hundreds of Korean laborers, worked two days to complete the approaches to the crossing site, while B Company, 65th Engineers, worked on installing a 20-ton floating bridge. The work was completed by nightfall 11 April. The 1st and 3rd battalions of the 24th Infantry moved to the crossing site.

The 1st Battalion crossed at 4:30 A.M., 12 April, and caught an enemy force by surprise, asleep in their foxholes on the north bank. The assault company killed 34 in their foxholes. The 3rd Battalion, 24th Infantry, crossed the river to the west of the 1st Battalion, through the Turkish Brigade sector, and attacked Hill 463, where enemy in 20 bunkers defended the high point. They engaged in a grenade battle from the bunkers and drove the 3rd Battalion back down the slope. The battalion crossed back to the south side of the Hantan to reorganize.[23]

West of the 24th Regiment and the Turkish Brigade, on 14 April, the 65th Infantry, 3rd Division, sent patrols as far as a mile west and a mile north of Yonchon on the Chatan River, which flows south into the Hantan about three miles east of the latter's junction with the Imjin. These patrols saw enemy in Yonchon. Farther west, and along the Imjin in the Choksong area, patrols from the Gloster Battalion patrolled five miles north of its position without enemy contact, but an enemy patrol probed a Gloster outpost six and a half miles north of Choksong. After an hour-long firefight it was repulsed. That afternoon an aerial observer saw an estimated 1,500 enemy soldiers only two miles north of the ROK 6th Division positions.

Also on 14 April there was an apparent coordinated effort by the Chinese and North Koreans across the western part of the line to create a heavy smoke screen. The brush and woods on all the hills north of the front lines were set on fire, and the smoke was so dense that visibility during the day was obscured to the point that many aerial close-support missions had to be canceled. Of 70 air close-support missions scheduled, only 14 were completed that day because of smoke. The elevations at which missions had to be canceled varied from 1,000 feet over the 25th Division to 8,500 feet in the US 2nd Division sector eastward. Smoke covered the front to a depth of from six to ten miles. In this effort, the enemy used many smudge pots and burned villages as well as the ground cover. There was no wind, so the smoke hung overhead. The smoke screen lasted for about three days, from 14 through 16 April.[24]

The 25th Division held a vital part of the line between the 3rd Division on its left (west) and the ROK 6th Division on its right, along the Hantan River. The Chinese defended the crossings of the Hantan in this sector. South of the Hantan here the key terrain was Hill 456, which dominated the river on both sides and all the immediate surrounding terrain. On 15 April K Company, 27th Infantry, crossed the Hantan where it had clifflike banks, defended by the Chinese. But once K Company was across the river, enemy resistance lessened.

In F Company's zone of attack, 1st Lt. Derwood W. Sims, the company commander, assumed personal leadership of the assault platoon against an enemy-fortified position in mountainous terrain. He was soon seriously wounded by machine-gun fire but continued to lead the attack. In the latter phase of this assault Sims was mortally wounded by an enemy grenade burst. His example inspired his men to complete the attack and to occupy the enemy position.[25]

On 16 April the Belgian Battalion crossed the Imjin River and established a bridgehead about three miles northeast of Choksong. This battalion was now in front of part of the British 29th Brigade.

Farther east the long fight for control of the Hwachon Reservoir moved finally in favor of the UN forces. The 1st Korean Marine Regiment sent a patrol from its 2nd Battalion, which occupied a position on the dam. The next day the Korean Marine Regiment maintained its position there and improved its security.[26]

Enemy opposition was strongest against attempted UN advances in the 24th and 25th Division sectors. These divisions, especially the 25th, were drawing closer to the Chorwon corridor, and the Chinese did not want them to get closer to their own big supply and assembly areas in that vicinity. The 24th Regiment had hard fighting on 16 April in its attempt to capture Hill 616, where a dug-in enemy battalion resisted in a strong defense of this high ground. But the next day, the enemy abandoned this almost impregnable position to the 2nd Battalion, in an apparent ordered withdrawal. In its approach to Chorwon the 24th Regiment, together with B Company, 89th Tank Battalion, discovered or overran several large enemy ammunition dumps. From one of them the 25th Division removed 60 truckloads of ammunition, estimated at from 70 to 100 tons.[27]

From Korangpo on the Imjin westward during this time, there were no enemy smoke fires, but from there eastward over the I and IX corps sectors, they were continuous and heavy on 16 and 17 April. This seemed further proof that enemy ground forces were on the move there in daylight, concentrating in their assembly areas, preparing for attack. In this uncertain situation, D Company, 6th Tank Battalion, moved up the Uijongbu-Kumhwa road in the I Corps sector toward the Iron Triangle. But enemy fire stopped it at Chipo-ri. It engaged there and north of the town in a firefight with enemy forces, but in the afternoon it withdrew.

On 17 April Eighth Army headquarters rescinded Defense Plan 3, Lincoln, and issued Withdrawal Plan Golden 1. This plan called for Eighth Army's withdrawal to the Han River on army order only, to what it called Line Nevada. I Corps was to withdraw first to Line Delta, then to Golden. This withdrawal plan was given in great detail by phase lines, and it was to be coordinated with all units. It renamed Line Elgin as Delta, Lincoln as Golden, and Boston as Nevada. It ordered that no unit would attempt to *run* through fireblocks but that they were to be destroyed by aggressive attacks. When the plan was put into effect, the division commander of forces involved would move without delay all heavy equipment and nonessential equipment south of the Han River and to division rear areas. For the present the plan was to be known only at division level on a need-to-know basis. There was to be no scorched-earth action; a detailed plan indicated which bridges were to be demolished.[28]

The army had noted the heavy enemy concentrations in the Panam-ni area in front of the IX Corps area, which offered an excellent approach through rough terrain toward Kapyong. This terrain prevented tanks and artillery from approaching close enough to the enemy assembly areas here to disrupt their preparations. The IX Corps hastened the relief of the British 27th Brigade in this area by the ROK 6th Division and concentrated the brigade behind the ROK 6th Division at Kapyong on 17 April. The next day it attached A Company, 72nd Tank Battalion (less one platoon) to the British brigade for extensive reconnaissance along the Kapyong–Panam-ni route.[29]

By the middle of April in the east, there was no evidence of Chinese troops behind the North Korean units in the X Corps zone. North Korean resistance collapsed ahead of the ROK 5th Division, and by 16 April it seemed that North Koreans held the line from the high ground northeast of the Hwachon Reservoir on over the high ground north of Inje, and then in a jagged and broken manner on northeast to the coast. Their apparent tactic was to cut or control the road northeast from Inje to Kansong.[30] Evidently to further this aim, the NK V Corps reappeared on the X Corps east flank on 20 April.

On the western front, Eighth Army and I Corps were centering attention and work on getting Line Golden ready for the expected enemy offensive. The line was 24 miles long, arc shaped, or a semicircle around and north of Seoul. Its center was four miles north of the South Korean capitol building in Seoul. This line was built in April under American engineering supervision, largely by Korean labor. A total of 29 South Korean CTC companies were attached to I Corps in April for this work. I Corps and division engineers hauled 40,000 timber logs for use in defense works; sandbags, steel pickets, and barbed wire were used in huge quantities. Brigadier General Davidson coordinated the work, assisted by I Corps Engineer officers. Davidson had to be taken from this work on 8 April, and then the I Corps Engineers gave full time to it. In addition to building defenses and gun emplacements, they improved roads in the battle area and behind the lines, which later greatly aided the planned phase withdrawals during the enemy offensive. New, additional bridges were built, and new maps were issued that showed, in overlays, those places known to have had mines laid by the enemy and those freshly laid by UN forces.[31]

On 17 April intelligence learned that the CCF 19th Army Group had passed through the NK I Corps and was screening the enemy front between the ROK 1st Division and the US 3rd Division in I Corps in the west.[32] This action looked like a new enemy deployment preceding an attack.

The same day, the 3rd Division formed Task Force Hawkins for an attack north toward Chorwon. The task force included an artillery battery from the 58th Artillery, a battery from the 3rd AAA AW Battalion, the 3rd Ranger Company, two companies of the 7th Infantry, and the 64th Heavy Tank Battalion (less one company). The task force was to attack on 19 April and seize Chorwon. It was to link up there with a task force from the 25th Division, attacking toward it from the southeast. The operation was planned to last two days. General Milburn, I Corps commander, favored the operation, but the 25th Division did not. It agreed finally, however, to send an armored task force as far north as a small reservoir south of Chorwon, provided Task Force Hawkins would swing south from Chorwon to link up with it there. General Soule did not accept this proposal for the 3rd Division. The nearest that I Corps got to Chorwon was when a patrol came to within 500 yards of the town; there, on 18 April, enemy turned it back.[33]

It was clear to all by 18 April that, although the enemy might be withdrawing slowly almost everywhere along the line, it had no intention of allowing the UN forces to enter Chorwon and the Iron Triangle. The 3rd Division stated that enemy resistance would increase as any UN troops got close to the Chorwon–Sibyon-ni road. And the Eighth Army G-2, Colonel Tarkenton, estimated that the greatest enemy threat would come from the north and northwest sectors. He expected the Chinese 5th Phase Offensive would come in the period 20 April to 1 May. A deserter from the Chinese 27th Army said he was in an advance party sent out to reconnoiter the terrain held by the CCF 26th Army, which the 27th Army was to take over from it on or about 22 April, and then it was to attack. The Eighth Army accepted the CCF 27th Army as being in the Chorwon area.[34]

General Van Fleet at this time told General Soule that Eighth Army commanders were responsible for the combat efficiency of their commands and that they could not rotate any of their men until satisfactory replacements were found. He wanted the meaning of this order made clear to all the men.

By 18 April the enemy had pretty well withdrawn from the front to their rear assembly areas, where preparations were far advanced for their 5th Phase attack. It had always been a mark of a new CCF offensive in the works for them to withdraw from contact with the UN forces. They usually withdrew out of artillery range, and then when they were ready to reestablish contact, they could do so in one night's forced march.

On 18 April elements of the Korean 1st Marine Company entered Hwachon and returned with 11 prisoners without encountering enemy fire, and a platoon finally crossed the Hwachon Reservoir Dam and then held both ends of it.

In its effort to reach Chorwon during the period of 17 to 19 April, the 25th Division overran several huge enemy ammunition dumps, apparently intended for some of the new Chinese formations in assembly areas just a few miles north of the front. One of the large dumps was found by the 21st AAA AW Battalion. As much of this store of weapons and ammunition as possible was hauled to the rear; what could not be moved was destroyed. In one dump there were 600 cases of hand grenades alone, and the weapons ranged from rifles to machine guns, mortars, and 75-mm pack howitzers. There was also a considerable quantity of mines and TNT and other demolition explosives. Most of these enemy ammunition dumps were found by the 27th Infantry Regiment.[35]

On 19 April the 27th Regiment of the 25th Division was farther north than any other UN unit, with its forward position on high ground at the south edge of the Chorwon valley. On the twentieth it held this position while flank units came abreast. Chinese prisoners said 22 April was the date for their attack.

At the same time, the Gloster Battalion established a beachhead on the north side of the Imjin River above Choksong in preparation for patrols it intended to send northward from there on 20 April. The Belgian Battalion relieved the Royal Ulster Rifles Battalion. Eastward in the 24th Division sector the 19th Regiment received enemy counterattacks, and the 5th RCT relieved the 21st Regiment on the line.[36]

On 19 April the 25th Division had one of those tragic accidents that are all too frequent among trigger-happy and jumpy men on line. Before daylight a soldier in F Company, 27th Infantry, thought he "heard something." He threw a grenade, which killed two of his buddies. No enemy soldiers were in the vicinity.

On the twenty-first in the 25th Division sector, the attached Turkish Brigade had hard fighting, a precursor to the coming attack. The Turks advanced to Hills 541 and 638, and there the Chinese stopped them. Some of the fighting was hand-to-hand. The Turks had to withdraw to their original positions.

On 18 April the 35th Infantry of the 25th Division organized Task Force Lee, named after Lieutenant Colonel Lee of its 3rd Battalion, to cross the Hantan River and attack north. The task force included 300 men of the 3rd Battalion, 38 tanks, and two sections of AAA half-tracks and was supported by a battalion of field artillery and tactical aircraft on call. After crossing the Hantan, the need to sweep some sections of the road for mines slowed the advance. The task force saw only three enemy soldiers, who were killed by tank fire, but it came under very heavy and well-directed artillery fire, which the enemy had preregistered on a given section of the road five miles north of Task Force Lee's point of departure. This situation was reported to the 35th Regiment, and the task force was ordered to return to its assembly area.

At 6:30 A.M. the next day, the task force moved up the road again, but only three miles ahead it came to a bridge that the enemy had blown during the night. This stopped the armored vehicles, so on 19 April the task force did not get as far as it had the first day. Task Force Lee received orders to return to the 35th Infantry lines, having accomplished nothing except to establish the fact that strong enemy forces were only a few miles ahead of the 25th Division.[37]

An interesting intelligence report came from an agent who had established himself at Wonsan on the east-coast supply route. He reported on the convoy and supply routine the enemy had established to keep supplies moving south to the front. He said the organized route started at Chigyong, southwest of Hamhung, moved through Wonsan, and at Changdong-ni included a hideout and refueling stop for all trucks on a thickly forested hill west of the road, with 300 trucks finding sanctuary there at one time. There were no troops there, and the area appeared deserted. Drivers were under orders not to fire on aircraft. Traffic was heavy nightly over this road through Wonsan, and it disregarded naval gunfire. When a night intruder plane was sighted by the convoy leader, he had all lights turned off, and the trucks pulled off the road for cover and to evade flare illumination. This agent estimated that 500 trucks nightly passed through Wonsan.[38]

In the hectic preparation for the soon-expected enemy attack, an alarming item for the future was the capture, on 20 April in the US 25th Division sector, of a Chinese-made copy of the American Thompson submachine gun. Their manufacture in China in possibly large numbers could now be expected. Also on the twentieth, Col. John Throckmorton, commanding officer of the 5th RCT, 24th Infantry Division, left on rotation. His departure came at an awkward time, because this fine and highly praised regimental combat leader was the kind of officer who would be missed in the crisis that was at hand. The regiment also had two new commanders at the same time for its 1st and 3rd battalions.

All intelligence estimates on the I Corps front by 20 April had noted the capture of Chinese prisoners during the past week from new formations not previously encountered at the front—prisoners from the 61st, 64th, 63rd, and 27th Chinese armies, which represented the First, Second, and Third field armies. Up until now the Chinese divisions in the west had come from the Chinese XIII Army Group of the Fourth Field Army, except for one division. These prisoners all stated that a new offensive was to take place in the near future. That fresh troops would launch the new offensive was by now generally recognized in Eighth Army.[39]

On 21 April, I and IX corps of Eighth Army advanced toward Line Wyoming without resistance, except in the center of the 25th Division, where the front approached the Iron Triangle and Chorwon. Farther east, the 1st Marine Division, by use of the Korean 1st Marine Regiment, finally completed its control of the Hwachon Reservoir Dam area. It was unopposed there now, in contrast to the stubborn enemy resistance to any advance since 10 April. Generally, IX Corps had no resistance in its front. But by the end of day, 21 April, I Corps had noted a change taking place in the enemy situation to its front. Its report for the day said:

By evening enemy intentions began to show change. Previously large combat patrols of tank and infantry had been able to operate north and northwest in front of the ROK 1st and US 3rd Divisions to a considerable distance, meeting only scattered enemy groups. This evening such patrols met much stronger enemy positions along the line Kaesong to the northeast. Encounters began to look like general engagements of small forces. It seemed the enemy had established a screening force from Kaesong to the northeast. . . . The 25th Division also met increasing opposition. The enemy was also moving in daylight.[40]

In discussing the situation at the end of 21 April, General Soule of the 3rd Division said that the UN in the west apparently had reached an enemy MLR from just north of Kaesong to Chorwon, but he thought that any enemy attack would have to have a limited objective because of the unfordable Han River to the south.[41] While there was negligible enemy opposition in the IX Corps sector and gains were made across its front, they were made cautiously, as aerial observers reported large enemy concentrations just in front of them.[42]

18

The Chinese 5th Phase Offensive, 1st Impulse

THE CHINESE called their offensive against the UN Army that began on the night of 22 April 1951 their 5th Phase Offensive. The first part, lasting through 29 April, they called the 1st Impulse; there was a second phase, which they labeled the 2nd Impulse. It was their bid to overwhelm the UN forces in Korea and to end the war.

Before he succeeded to the Supreme Command in Tokyo on 11 April, General Ridgway had set the scene in Korea for the forthcoming battles. His plan had been put in place, with an intent to withdraw from the front line, where contact would be made, to succeeding lines of defense around Seoul, making the enemy forces deploy with each successive movement and keeping them off-balance. With each successive withdrawal massed artillery and air strikes would take a devastating toll of the enemy as it moved in the open in pursuit.

The Chinese and North Korean orders of battle for the 1st Impulse, 5th Phase Offensive, indicate there were four Chinese army groups, one each from the First, Second, Third, and Fourth field armies, the first three accounting for 9 divisions each, and the Fourth, for 6 divisions, for a total of 33 Chinese infantry divisions (see table 15). The three North Korean corps committed each had 3 divisions, for a total of 9 NK divisions. This gave a total of 42 enemy divisions. But the divisions were very unequal in numerical strength and also in arms.

Two new Chinese field armies, comprising six Chinese armies, were new, fresh troops, brought from the mainland of China into Korea during the first four months of 1951 at approximately full division strength of 8,000 troops each. Some had received new Soviet arms and equipment prior to entering Korea. These troops were from the First and Second field armies and had not previously fought in Korea.

In another category was the CCF IX Army Group from the Third Field Army, which had fought the Chosin Reservoir campaign in northeast Korea in late November and in December 1950. They had not fought against

TABLE 15. **Chinese Order of Battle, 22–29 April 1951,**
          5th Phase Offensive, 1st Impulse

Field Army	Army Group	Army	Division	Regiments
First[a]	XIX	63rd	187th	559th, 560th, 561st
			188th	562nd, 563rd, 564th
			189th	565th, 566th, 567th
		64th	190th	568th, 569th, 570th
			191st	571st, 572nd, 573rd
			192nd	574th, 575th, 576th
		65th	193rd	577th, 578th, 579th
			194th	580th, 581st, 582nd
			195th	583rd, 584th, 585th
Second	III	12th	31st	91st, 92nd, 93rd
			34th	100th, 101st, 106th
			35th	103rd, 104th, 105th
		15th	29th	85th, 86th, 87th
			44th	130th, 131st, 132nd
			45th	133rd, 134th, 135th
		60th	179th	535th, 536th, 537th
			180th	538th, 539th, 540th
			181st	541st, 542nd, 543rd
Third[b]	IX	20th[c]	58th	172nd, 173rd, 174th
			59th	175th, 176th, 177th
			60th	178th, 179th, 180th
		26th	76th	226th, 227th, 228th
			77th	229th, 230th, 231st
			78th	232nd, 233rd, 234th
		27th	79th	235th, 236th, 237th
			80th	238th, 239th, 240th
			81st	241st, 242nd, 243rd
Fourth[d]	XIII	39th	115th	343rd, 344th, 345th
			116th	346th, 347th, 348th
			117th	349th, 350th, 351st
		40th	118th	352nd, 353rd, 354th
			119th	355th, 356th, 357th
			120th	358th, 359th, 360th

Sources: Eighth Army Comd. Rpt., G-2 Sec., April 1951, map and chart of enemy strengths and locations, 22 April 51, Box 1181. Also, Organization Chart, Communist Field Forces (including units in Korea), FEC Intelligence Digest No. 28, 16–31 July 1952.

FEC Intelligence Digests: vol. 1, no. 3, 16–31 Jan 1953, History of Army Groups Active in Korea, pt. 2, Ninth Army Group, Box 225; vol. 5, 16–28 Feb 1953, Histories of CCF Army Groups Active in Korea, pt. 4, Nineteenth Army Group, pp. 27–32; No. 6, 16–31 August 51, Map No. A-5, Enemy Attack 5th Phase–1st Impulse, 22–30 April 51, Box 513. Also, FEC DIS No. 3207, 21 June 51, including translation of captured document, XIII Army Group Volunteer Headquarters, Box 473; and US Army Forces, Far East, G-2 Intelligence Digest, vol. 1, no. 1,

Eighth Army in the west, until a couple of divisions had moved to the central sector in March and helped briefly there in the Chinese 4th Phase campaign. This IX Army Group now was in position with all its nine divisions on line, although these divisions were not up to full strength.

The third category of Chinese divisions on line came from the XIII Army Group of the Fourth Field Army, Lin Piao's troops, which had fought the Chinese battles in the west ever since their initial crossings of the border in mid-October 1950—in the 1st, 2nd, 3rd, and 4th phases. Instead of its original six armies, only two—the 39th and 40th—were now left for front-line duty. Their task in the 5th Phase Offensive was a minor one, defense of the Chinese eastern flank. Their numerical strength was far below that of a full-strength division, perhaps each not much more than a full-strength regiment.

The fresh, new divisions from the First and Second field armies were placed on line in the west and were expected, with important help from the Third Field Army Group on their east, to carry the offensive down the ancient invasion route to Seoul. The Chinese timetable was to capture Seoul by 28 April. This offensive would take about one-third of the troops the Chinese then had in Korea. The Chinese high command expected the first attack groups to pause at Seoul and the Han River. It would then bring up the second third of their total forces in Korea to carry the attack from Seoul south, cross the Han, and penetrate deep into South Korea, possibly achieving final victory and the destruction of the UN troops. There would still be left the final third of their approximately 650,000 to 700,000 troops in Korea.

The 5th Phase Offensive had the enemy line up their formations just short of their projected line of departure, from west to east as follows: the NK I Corps on the extreme western coastal flank; then the Chinese armies took up the line in a solid chain from Munsan-ni on the Imjin River eastward to the western end of the Hwachon Reservoir in the following order: 64th and 63rd (with the 65th behind them) armies, of the XIX Army Group, First Field Army; the 15th, 60th, and 12th armies of the III Army Group, Second Field Army; the 27th, 26th, and 20th armies of

---

1–31 Dec 1952, Histories of CCF Army Groups Active in Korea, III CCF Army Group, pp. 31–37.

[a]The Chinese divisions of the First and Second field armies were new divisions introduced into Korea after 1950 and numbered about 8,000 men each.

[b]The Third Field Army divisions had fought in the northeast of Korea in the late fall and winter of 1950 in the Chosin Reservoir area. They took in many replacements in the Hamhung, Hungnam, and Wonsan areas before moving to the west-central front in March and April 1951. They may have averaged 6,000 to 7,000 in strength.

[c]Each division in this army is stated to have an artillery regiment.

[d]The two divisions of the Fourth Field Army had fought in all the major battles in Korea since October 1950. Their original strength had been much depleted, but they had from time to time taken in replacements. Their division strength probably averaged from 4,000 to 5,000 in late April 1951.

the IX Army Group, Third Field Army; and the 40th and 39th armies, XIII Army Group, Fourth Field Army. There at the Hwachon Reservoir area the North Korean Army III and V corps carried the line through high and almost roadless mountains eastward to the coast (see table 16). The NK II Corps was not on line but held a reserve position 25 air miles north and behind the other two corps. There were an estimated 180,000 Chinese and 35,000 North Koreans manning the battle stations. Behind them a few miles stood several hundred thousands more in assembly areas, but they were not intended for use in this first phase of their new offensive.

The Chinese and North Korean divisions were placed on line so that North Korean elements held both flanks; the NK I Corps was on the west flank, and the NK III and V corps were on the east flank. The Chinese divisions, constituting by far the greater military strength, held the west-central and central parts of the line, extending from the Imjin River on the west, northwest of Seoul, to the Hwachon Reservoir on the east. They confronted the US I and IX corps. It was in those sectors that the Chinese launched their 5th Phase Offensive, 1st Impulse, on the night of 22 April. The First and Second field armies made the main thrust in the US I Corps sector, using the XIX and III army groups respectively.[1]

The nine divisions of the XIX Army Group of the Chinese First Field Army and the nine divisions of the III Army Group, Second Field Army, entered Korea from February to April 1951. The 63rd Army of the First Field Army began crossing the Yalu from Antung into Sinuiju on 22 February and proceeded to assembly areas near Kunchon. The 64th Army had begun crossing the Yalu at the same place six days earlier, on 16 February, and it too assembled in the Kunchon area, closing there in early March. The 65th Army, the third of the XIX Army Group, which had been engaged in farming in Shensi Province in late 1950, moved by rail to Antung in early 1951 and was reequipped with new weapons. On 28 February 1951 it started crossing the Yalu into North Korea. The 64th and

TABLE 16. **North Korean Order of Battle, 22–29 April 1951, 5th Phase Offensive, 1st Impulse**

Corps	Divisions[a]
I	8th, 19th, 47th
III	1st, 15th, 45th
V	6th, 12th, 32nd

Sources: Eighth Army Comd. Rpt., G-2 Sec., April 1951, map and chart of enemy strengths and locations, 22 April 51, Box 1181; Organization Chart, Communist Field Forces (including units in Korea), FEC Intelligence Digest No. 28, 16–31 July 1951; FEC Intelligence Digest No. 6, 16–31 August 51, Map No. A-5, Enemy Attack 5th Phase—1st Impulse, 22–30 April 51, Box 513; FEC DIS No. 3207, 21 June 51, including translation of captured document, XIII Army Group Volunteer Headquarters, Box 473.

[a]The strength of the NK divisions in late April 1951 varied greatly but averaged about 3,000. The 19th, 45th, and 32nd divisions were strong, with about 8,000 men each.

63rd armies were set to attack abreast on a 12-mile front against the ROK 1st Division and the British 29th Brigade along the Imjin River, with the 65th Army behind them in reserve at first.[2]

The III Army Group of the Second Field Army had its headquarters in Chungking in 1949. In 1950, it moved to Manchuria for possible commitment in Korea. Its 12th Army started crossing into Korea on 21 March 1951, closing into its Koksan assembly areas by 9 April. The 15th Army left Luchow for Hankow via the Yangtze River in mid-January, and from Hankow it proceeded to North China, where it was equipped with Soviet weapons. It entrained by mid-March for Antung on the Yalu, closing there by late March. On the thirtieth of that month it began crossing the river into Sinuiju and from there marched south, closing into assembly areas near Singye on 20 April. The 15th Army on the west and the 12th Army on the east were lined up to attack south toward Yonchon against the US 3rd Division. The 60th Army came from South China to North China in 1950, where it was reequipped with Soviet weapons. It entrained for Antung on the Yalu and closed there in March 1951. It began crossing the river into Sinuiju on 17 February and made a record march south, closing into assembly areas near Ichon by 6 April. Its mission was to attack the Turkish Brigade and the US 25th Division, which were holding a vital sector of the UN front along the main road running from Seoul north through Uijongbu and Yonchon to Chorwon.[3]

The IX Army Group of the Third Field Army had entered northeast Korea in November 1950 and had fought the Chosin Reservoir campaign against the US X Corps. Its 20th Army had crossed the Yalu at Manpojin and had proceeded to Yudam-ni, where it relieved the Chinese 42nd Army, which then rejoined its parent organization, the XIII Army Group of the Chinese Fourth Field Army, facing Eighth Army in the west. The 26th and 27th armies of the IX Army Group followed the 20th Army into northeast Korea and fought the US 1st Marine Division and parts of the US 7th and 3rd divisions in the Chosin Reservoir campaign of November-December 1950. When the X Corps evacuated Hungnam at the end of December, the IX Army Group, decimated and exhausted by the Chosin campaign, remained in the Hungnam-Wonsan area for rehabilitation and reequipment. Not until 1 March did the 26th Army units start south to join units on the western front, relieving the 38th and 50th armies near the end of the Chinese 4th Phase campaign on 10 March. The 26th and 27th armies followed the 20th to the Kumhwa area. There, at the beginning of the 5th Phase Offensive, the 20th and 27th armies were in position to attack south along the Kumhwa-Uijongbu road toward Seoul. The 26th Army stayed behind to protect the Iron Triangle. The IX Army Group divisions would collide with the US 25th Division, positioned to defend the MSR.[4]

The 40th and 39th armies of the XIII Army Group, Fourth Field Army,

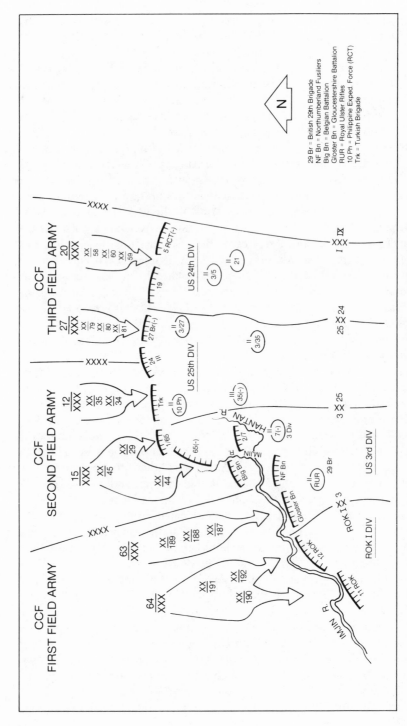

MAP 18. CCF and UN positions in I Corps sector, 22 April 1951, in the CCF 5th Phase Offensive

now much reduced in strength, were on the Chinese east flank in the Hwachon area to guard its flank against the 1st Marine Division. They were all that was left of the six armies that had carried the fight for the Chinese since their initial intervention in October 1950. The remnants of the other four were on their way to China, out of the war for good.

From the east end of the Hwachon Reservoir, the North Korean III and V corps carried the front line on to the east coast against the US X Corps and the ROK III and I corps.

Opposite and south of these enemy forces, and lined up generally along Line Kansas, with a bulge north of it toward the Iron Triangle area of Chorwon-Kumhwa, from west to east, were the ROK 1st Division along the Imjin River from Munsan-ni to the British 29th Brigade, which was attached to the US 3rd Division; and attached to the 29th Brigade in turn was the Belgian Battalion. The ROK 1st Division had its 11th Regiment on line in the Munsan-ni area and its 12th Regiment on line eastward to the boundary with the British 29th Brigade, with the ROK 15th Regiment in reserve.

The Gloster Battalion of the British brigade was on its western boundary, adjacent to the ROK 1st Division, with the Northumberland Fusiliers Battalion on its right, and the Royal Ulster Rifles Battalion behind the Fusiliers in reserve. The Belgian Battalion was north of the junction of the Imjin with the Hantan River, a critical point in the line, where the Imjin River made an abrupt turn northward. The 2nd Battalion of the 7th Regiment, 3rd Division, was north of the Hantan River near the junction. East of the British 29th Brigade, the US 3rd Division had responsibility for the MSR running north from Seoul through Uijongbu to Chorwon, with the 1st Battalion of the 65th Regiment on line above the Belgian Battalion northward on high ground west of the MSR. There the Turkish Brigade, attached to the US 25th Division, held a position on the east side of the MSR, and the line turned from a northerly direction to an eastern one. East of the Turkish Brigade, the 24th Regiment of the 25th Division extended the line to the 27th Regiment, which held the eastern flank of the 25th Division at its boundary with the US 24th Division. The 35th Regiment of the 25th Division was in reserve. The 24th Division formed the right flank of US I Corps, with its 19th Regiment on its left at the boundary with the 25th Division and the 5th RCT on its right flank at the IX Corps boundary. The 24th Division had responsibility for the main road from Kumhwa to Uijongbu, where it joined the MSR from Chorwon running south through the 3rd Division zone. The Kumhwa road slanted across the 19th Infantry sector for a short distance before the road crossed southwesterly into the 25th Division zone of responsibility.[5]

In the US IX Corps, the ROK 6th Division held the western flank sector, adjoining the US 5th RCT of the 24th Division, and beyond it eastward was the 1st Marine Division, with its attached 1st Korean Marine Regiment on the corps's eastern flank southeast of Hwachon at the western end of the Hwachon Reservoir. There it met the US X Corps boundary, where the French Battalion, attached to the US 2nd Division, held that corps's left (western) flank, with the 23rd Regiment on its right. The US 7th Division was next eastward in the Yanggu area, and the ROK 5th Division formed the X Corps's eastern flank. The ROK III Corps, with the 7th and 3rd ROK divisions, extended the line eastward to the ROK I Corps boundary, where the ROK Capital and 11th divisions carried the line to the east coast.

Eighth Army held the 1st Cavalry Division in reserve in the Seoul area, and the 187th Airborne RCT at Taegu. The British 27th Brigade was in IX Corps reserve below Kapyong near the lateral road from Seoul to Chunchon.[6]

It will be seen from this troop deployment that Eighth Army had the bulk of its strength in the western I Corps zone. There it covered the approaches to Seoul from the Munsan-ni MSR northwest of the city and the ancient invasion route from the north through Uijongbu and the adjacent approach from the Kumhwa area.

It happened that 22 April was the day General Ridgway in Tokyo issued his instructions to General Van Fleet in Korea on the guidelines that would control his conduct of Korean operations. He reminded Van Fleet that the Soviet Union might at any time elect to exercise its present capability of direct military intervention by its military forces — ground, sea, and air — against the UN forces in Korea, coordinated with the Chinese Communist and North Korean forces, timed to take maximum advantage of weather and its effect on terrain. Ridgway further advised him that his own forces would be brought to and maintained at approximate full strength but that he would receive no major reinforcements in combat organizations or service support. General Ridgway then continued, noting:

That the duration of your operations cannot now be predicted; that you may, at any time, be directed by competent authority to withdraw to a defensive position and there be directed to defend indefinitely; that you may at any time be directed by competent authority to initiate a retirement designed to culminate in an early evacuation of the Korean Peninsula.

Your mission is to repel aggression against so much of the territory (and the people thereof) of the Republic of Korea, as you now occupy and, in collaboration with the Government of the Republic of Korea, to establish and maintain order in said territory. In carrying out this mission you are authorized to conduct military operations, including amphibious and airborne landings, as well as ground operations in Korea north of the 38th parallel. . . .

B. In the execution of this mission you will be guided by the following prescriptions:

(1) Advance of major elements of your forces beyond the general line: Junction

of Imjin and Han Rivers–Chorwon–Hwachon Reservoir–Taepo-ri (DT 6625) will be on my order only.

(2) You will direct the efforts of your forces toward inflicting maximum losses on hostile forces in Korea, consistent with the maintenance intact of all your major units and safety of your troops. The continued piecemeal destruction of the offensive potential of the Chinese Communist and North Korean armies contributes materially to this objective, while concurrently destroying Communist China's military prestige.[7]

It is clear in these instructions that Ridgway meant to keep a close rein on Van Fleet's handling of Eighth Army in Korea; in effect it would be a continuation of his own policy during the past three and a half months.

On the morning of 22 April the US 25th Division continued its attempt to advance toward the Iron Triangle on the road running northeast from Uijongbu toward Kumhwa but met stubborn resistance. The 1st and 2nd battalions of the 24th Regiment tried to clear out the enemy bunkers on Hill 687, engaging in hand-grenade battles with the occupants, but the attack petered out during the day as signs multiplied of heavy enemy build-up across the front.[8]

Air sightings during the day included large enemy columns moving toward the front lines, indicating an impending attack. The enemy seemed suddenly to have abandoned all efforts at concealment, and the greatly increased troop movements were especially noticeable to the north and northwest of I Corps. The Eighth Army command was not sure at the end of the day whether the enemy troop movements meant a large counteroffensive or a coordinated effort to prevent the UN forces from seizing the Iron Triangle area. UN patrols were resisted all across the front. Air observers reported that all trails, gullies, and ravines running southwest out of Chorwon along the MSR and railroad were loaded with vehicles bumper to bumper for approximately three to four miles.[9]

But the most certain evidence as to the meaning of all the sudden enemy activity to the front of the I and IX corps came about 8 A.M. on the morning of 22 April, when Turkish soldiers noticed an enemy group moving through the position of the Turkish 2nd Battalion. The enemy party was intercepted by a Turk tank patrol, which captured six prisoners. Two of them were officers equipped with artillery aiming circles, range finders, slide rules, and other surveying equipment. They said they were from the 1st Battery, 28th Artillery Regiment, on a mission to set up an artillery observation post from which to locate UN positions and from which they could support the CCF offensive that was to begin that night. The officer avowed that the Chinese 12th Army of the Second Field Army was to attack that night, as part of a general offensive against the UN forces. This capture of the survey party and the information it disclosed was rapidly relayed to the 25th Division Headquarters, and thereafter throughout the army units on line. All units were warned to be prepared for an attack that night.[10]

Many tank sightings were recorded among enemy formations to the north, and it was expected they would make an appearance in the 5th Phase Offensive, but they did not. The ROK 1st Division had recently been strengthened by having the 73rd Heavy Tank Battalion give direct support to it. Equipped with new M-46 tanks, it was a powerful addition to the ROK division. The ROKs were proud of it and showed an aptitude for tank-infantry team warfare, and they took very good care of the 73rd tank helpers. Lt. Col. Duff Green, commanding officer of the 73rd, said he was entirely satisfied with the cooperation and care given to his tanks by the ROK 1st Division.[11]

The US 3rd Division took the prospect of an imminent enemy attack very seriously. At 2:15 P.M. on 22 April it ordered the 7th Regiment, its division reserve, to have counterattack plans and transportation ready to move on three hours' notice and to check its signal communication equipment to move the division CP to the rear if necessary. General Soule felt concern about the positions he held. He thought the CCF would hit in the vicinity of the confluence of the Hantan and Imjin rivers and imperil the 65th Infantry in its positions along the MSR. To strengthen the junction point, he placed the Belgian Battalion diagonally across the triangle formed by the junction of the two rivers. He placed the reserve 2nd Battalion of the 65th Infantry and the 64th Heavy Tank Battalion north of the Hantan River along the MSR, and the Ranger Company south of the MSR bridge across the Hantan River to keep it open as a withdrawal route. The British 29th Brigade held a series of disjointed high points along the south side of the Imjin River to the junction of the Hantan, where the Imjin turned north. All units outposted their lines two miles in front to prevent surprise. The Gloster Battalion was on the west of the brigade position, adjacent to the ROK 1st Division; the Northumberland Fusiliers was on its east, next to the 3rd Division; the Royal Ulster Rifles Battalion was behind the Northumberland Battalion in reserve.[12] On the twenty-second the Gloster patrols met those of the enemy much farther south than on previous days, and at 6 A.M. they were withdrawing from the enemy patrols.

The G-4 section of Eighth Army was well prepared for the enemy offensive. It closed all ammunition points north of the Han River on 22 April. An I Corps dump was established in Seoul with a two-day supply of ammunition, with several backup points south of the river. At Hongchon the dump was reduced to not more than two days' supply, with the backup at Wonju. Construction north of the Han River stopped, and machinery was moved south of the Han. One ammunition ship and one petroleum products ship were held in Inchon harbor.[13]

That night, with a full moon illuminating the landscape, between 10 P.M. and midnight, the Chinese 5th Phase Offensive struck all along the line in I Corps and part of IX Corps, and even had the coordinated action of

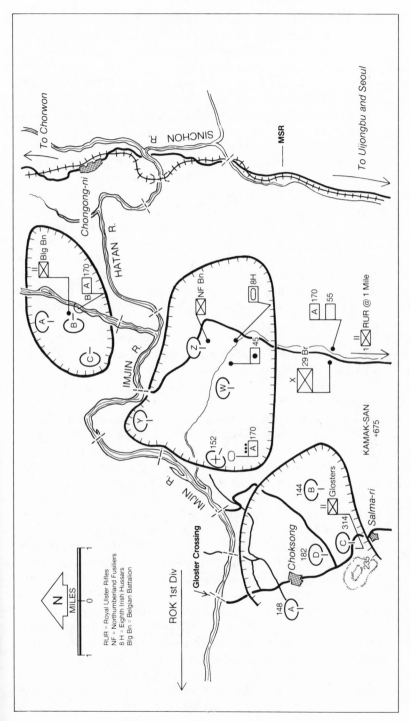

MAP 19. **British 29th Brigade (BIB) position, 22 April 1951**

North Korean troops in the eastern part of Korea. The fighting continued throughout the night into the morning of 23 April, with the enemy making devastating penetrations at a few places and setting into play withdrawals elsewhere. The first heavy attack hit the Turkish Brigade on the right flank of the US 3rd Division, on the east side of the MSR running almost due south from Chorwon to Uijongbu and Seoul.

At 8:30 P.M. the Turkish Brigade reported receiving a heavy volume of enemy artillery fire across the entire brigade front, which continued for a time. Half an hour before midnight the brigade reported heavy mortar and small-arms fire, which indicated an infantry assault would come next. It did. By 2 A.M., 23 April, the Chinese had penetrated the brigade at several points, disrupting communications with it and causing a withdrawal. The 3rd Division on the left flank of the Turks felt great concern when elements of the Turks' artillery displaced south through its right flank sector and Turk infantry stragglers began to assemble in their artillery positions. Inquiry disclosed that the Turks had been hit hard and that communication with the brigade was gone.[14] After withdrawing some distance, the Turkish Brigade rallied, reorganized its forces, resumed a position in the line, and then began to withdraw through blocking positions the 35th Infantry held.

On the right of the Turkish Brigade, the 24th Regiment of the 25th Division came under heavy attack at the same time; its 1st Battalion was soon penetrated, and Chinese pressure forced it back. The uncertain situation in the 24th Infantry led the division commander to inform Colonel Kelleher of the 35th Infantry that he might have to withdraw. At 10 A.M. on 23 April Kelleher ordered all units to send vehicles to the rear and to reconnoiter new positions south of the Yongpyong River.[15] At 5 P.M. on the twenty-third, all three battalions of the 35th Infantry were on Line Kansas on the west flank of the 25th Division sector, and the Turkish Brigade was closing behind the regiment. The 24th and 27th regiments were assembling on Line Kansas.

To the east of the 25th Division, the enemy struck simultaneously at the US 24th Division, the 19th Regiment on the division left being attacked at 9 P.M. This series of attacks forced the 19th Infantry to withdraw from its positions five miles south of Chigyong. By daylight enemy penetrations of the regiment had gained half a mile, and they were still advancing. At the same time artillery fire began to fall on the 5th RCT on the division right, and its outposts were driven in. At 10 P.M. an enemy infantry force attacked F Company with small-arms fire and hand grenades, causing the company to withdraw. Chinese pressure against the 5th RCT continued throughout the night, causing it to readjust its positions to south of Sinsul. Large enemy groups were observed moving toward and around the regiment. Concentrations of artillery fire did not stop them. After daylight, between 9 A.M. and 11 A.M., 23 April, numerous enemy troops were observed immediately in front of the entire division line. The division received orders to withdraw to Line Kansas. Tactical air strikes in the morning were hitting groups of enemy in the Sinsul area.

The greatest calamity suffered during the first night of the enemy offensive came in the sector of the ROK 6th Division, where it had its 9th and 2nd regiments on line at the western flank of the IX Corps sector. The initial attack hit the 2nd Regiment, which was followed almost simultaneously with a second blow at the 9th Regiment. Both regiments – the entire division line – began to withdraw. At this point a third enemy force drove a wedge between the two regiments, which created a panic and resulted in a complete rout of the ROK forces. The 7th Regiment, in reserve, moved north to buttress the 2nd Regiment and to block off the penetration between the two regiments. But it met a strong Chinese force and joined in the flight southward. This flight from the Chinese continued during the night into the next day, 23 April. By 6 P.M. the ROK 6th Division was trying to reorganize about 12 miles south of Line Kansas. The division had not suffered high combat casualties but was the victim of panic and disorganization. But its flight to the rear left open a huge gap in the UN line between the 24th Division of I Corps on the west and the 1st Marine Division on the east in the IX Corps. Into this gap moved elements of the CCF 20th and 40th armies. This was the third time the ROK 6th Division had faced the CCF 40th Army in the war, each time with disastrous results.

With the flight of the ROK 6th Division from the battle front, the British 27th Brigade, which had been held in IX Corps reserve below Kapyong, was rushed forward and by 6 P.M. had established defensive positions three to four miles north of Kapyong, just before the Chinese pursuit arrived there. Eighth Army also ordered the 5th Cavalry Regiment from its reserve to the Kapyong area. These two forces fought a hard battle with the onrushing Chinese and held them back. While this action was taking place, Eighth Army ordered all units not already on Line Kansas to coordinate their movements to that line.[16]

In the fight just north of Kapyong, the Princess Patricia's Canadian Light Infantry and the 3rd Royal Australian Regiment held positions on either side of the Kapyong valley, the Australians on the right of the road. The Australian-held hill rose to 1,600 feet. They had to fight both on the hill and along the road at its base near battalion headquarters. It was difficult for them to distinguish between the fleeing ROKs and the pursuing Chinese. A company of the Middlesex Battalion and A Company from the American 72nd Heavy Tank Battalion were sent to the aid of the Australians, who were then ordered to withdraw through the Middlesex and the covering fire of the tank company. The Chinese followed the Australians closely, and they had to fight for their escape. Artillery fire now came to the rescue and halted the pursuing Chinese. The 5th Cavalry Regiment arrived on the scene on the morning of 25 April and, under the command of the 27th Brigade, went into positions on either side of the road.

Before midnight of 24 April the Canadians were attacked on their side of the road and had two platoons overrun. Their commander called for close-in supporting fire from mortars and artillery, and this fire was effective. But the Patricias were surrounded, and the Chinese attacked them again. About noon of the twenty-fifth, an airdrop of supplies was made to the battalion. About 4 P.M. quiet descended on the area. The Chinese, despite their having routed the ROK 6th Division, had failed to cut the road from Seoul to Chunchon. The two British 27th Brigade battalions and A Company of the US 72nd Heavy Tank Battalion were given the Presidential Unit Citation for their extraordinary services at Kapyong.[17] Late on 24 April the 27th Brigade reported that the Chinese penetration to Kapyong had been contained, although heavy fighting was still in progress.

The 24th Division passed to control of IX Corps on 27 April, and the ROK 6th Division was attached to it. The 24th Division was instructed to place the ROK division south of the Pukhan River.

The British 28th Brigade replaced the 27th Brigade on 25 April and assumed control of all attachments except the Argyll and Sutherland Battalion, which departed for Inchon. The Kings Own Scottish Borderers replaced it in the 28th Brigade.

On the IX Corps right flank the 1st Marine Division was entirely exposed by the collapse of the ROK 6th Division on its left. The enemy's frontal attacks there were all repulsed, and withdrawals were made to effect a refused left flank to turn aside efforts to exploit the gap there by an enemy attack toward the southeast. But the enemy's main effort continued to be to the west of the 1st Marine Division in the I Corps sector. The enemy's plan of action centered on a headlong drive on Seoul and its capture.

On the western end of the UN line in the sector of the ROK 1st Division, the Chinese 64th Army pressed all the ROK patrols across the Imjin River by midnight of 22 April, and at 2:50 A.M. on the twenty-third the Reconnaissance Company of the ROK 12th Regiment was forced across to the east side of the Imjin. Enemy patrols crossed the Imjin at two points, three and a half and five miles northwest of Choksong. Estimated platoon-sized enemy groups crossed the river and established beachheads for the crossing of larger formations, which forded the river northwest of Choksong. Platoon-sized enemy groups had penetrated to a point seven miles southwest of Choksong by 11 A.M., 23 April. There appeared to be some confusion among the ranks of the Chinese after crossing the Imjin into the ROK 1st Division sector, as they scattered along the river valley floor, where one group of an estimated 2,000 were attacked by aircraft at 8:45 A.M., resulting in heavy casualties. Other formations were caught in the open, west and northwest of Choksong during the morning, and suffered heavily from air attacks. Meanwhile the ROK 12th Regiment directed tank and artillery fire at the enemy who had crossed the river, with good results, and held its position during the day. A ROK 12th Regimental task force swept the area north of the division's right flank and reported an estimated 1,500 enemy casualties in the area.[18] The eastern boundary of the ROK 1st Division passed just west of Choksong, where the British 29th Brigade, with the Gloster Battalion on its left flank next to the ROK 12th Regiment, continued the line along the Imjin River eastward.

On 22 April the brigade had three patrols north of the Imjin; the one from the Northumberland Fusiliers was the first to make contact with the Chinese, much farther south than in preceding days. The patrols observed numerous groups of Chinese all along the brigade front moving south. By dark all three patrols had returned south of the river.

The river was at a low stage, and it was easy to ford at numerous places. The main road in the area led from Choksong to the river a mile north and crossed it by a ford, known to the brigade as "Gloster Crossing." The valley of the Imjin here was relatively wide, with sharp rising hills dotting the valley floor. The Gloster Battalion had three of its four rifle companies on these hills: A Company on Castle Hill (148), just outside Choksong to the northwest; D Company on Hill 182, southeast of Choksong; B Company on Hill 144, east of Choksong. The fourth rifle company, C, was a few miles away, just above the battalion CP at the north end of Salma-ri. Salma-ri was at the northern end of a defile where a small stream emerged from the hills southward to flow into the Imjin valley floor and hence into the Imjin. A Company was closest to the Imjin River. Behind the Gloster position to the southeast rose towering Kamak-san, Hill 675, nearly 2,000 feet in elevation. Lt. Col. James P. Carne commanded the Gloster Battalion.

As darkness fell, Lieutenant Guy Temple and his 7th Platoon of C Company were posted at the Gloster Crossing to watch for an enemy crossing. After an hour's wait they heard splashes on the other side as groups of three and four Chinese stepped into the water. The line seemed continuous in the moonlight. Temple held his fire until the leading Chinese had almost reached the southern bank. Then the platoon's Bren guns opened up, and the riflemen fired at point-blank range. The Chinese tried to cross four times, and each time the result was the same slaughter in the Imjin. Then with ammunition running low, and more and more Chinese piling up on the opposite shore, Temple withdrew his platoon. He estimated it had killed more than a hundred enemy at the crossing site, without loss to itself.

Unknown to the Glosters, the Chinese had in the meantime found an underwater bridge or built-up ford about a mile below (west of) the Gloster Crossing, and hundreds crossed the river there and assaulted A Company at its Castle Hill site. Soon all three companies surrounding Choksong

View toward the southeast showing the Gloucestershire Battalion zone of responsibility south of the Imjin River (seen at lower left). Choksong is on the road about a mile south of the river, the crossing of which was known as the Gloster Crossing. Gloster Hill (Hill 235) is just beyond the right edge of the picture. *US Army photograph, unnumbered*

were under attack, and the battle spread eastward to X Company of the Fusiliers Battalion, holding an outpost position overlooking a ford that the Chinese were already crossing. At daybreak the village of Choksong was filled with Chinese. A and B companies of the Glosters suffered heavy casualties during the night and were ordered to withdraw under the covering fire of D Company. Maj. P. A. Angier commanded A Company, Maj. E. D. Harding commanded B Company, and Capt. Mike Harvey commanded D Company.

In its isolated position north of the Imjin at the junction of the Hantan, the Belgian Battalion was under attack, and the 1st Battalion, 65th Infantry, three miles west of Yonchon, came under attack at 3:40 A.M. of the twenty-third. The Chinese 63rd Army was attacking all along the front of the British 29th Brigade.[19]

View toward the south over the Gloster Battalion position. Gloster Hill (Hill 235) is the dark conical hill to the right of the road. Salma-ri, originally the Gloster Battalion's CP, was at the base of Hill 235, on the left side of the road. *US Army photograph, unnumbered*

At 9:30 A.M., 23 April, General Van Fleet ordered I and IX corps to make a coordinated withdrawal to Line Kansas. This step was made necessary because of the Chinese breakthrough in the ROK 6th Division and because of the withdrawals in the US 24th Division sector. During the day all forward elements carried out the withdrawals.[20]

The US 3rd Division and its attached units held the key to preventing a rapid enemy advance down the ancient invasion route from Chorwon through Uijongbu to Seoul. The division troops were largely on the eastern flank of its front, guarding the MSR. The attached units – the British 29th Brigade, the Belgian Battalion, and the 10th BCT (the Philippine Detachment) – were on the western flank along the south bank of the Imjin

View from above Gloster Hill (foreground). Kamak-san is the high mountain at upper right. Salma-ri can be seen at left, along the first bend of the road. *US Army photograph, unnumbered*

River and the area of the junction of the Hantan River with the Imjin.

The 187th Division of the 63rd Chinese Army struck the Gloster Battalion on the left flank and, during a night of vicious fighting, drove A and B companies from their hill positions near the village of Choksong. On the morning of the twenty-third, these companies, with D Company, withdrew to new positions south and east to points near the battalion CP, just north of Salma-ri and close to C Company, located just above the CP, which was located in the narrow valley at the base of Kamak-san. There they fought off enemy attacks during the night of 23–24 April until C Company was overrun by the Chinese before dawn. Lieutenant Colonel Carne then ordered all the companies to make for Hill 235 on the west side of the road at Salma-ri and moved his own headquarters there at once. The assault pioneer platoon had been the only unit on Hill 235 up to this point.

Before daylight all the battalion, except B Company, were on Hill 235. Major Harding and a remnant of B Company escaped to Hill 235 during the morning of the twenty-fourth. Hill 235 became known as Gloster Hill.

On 23 April the 3rd Division had a number of pressing problems: it had an open right flank, it had to get the Belgian Battalion out of its position north of the Imjin, and it had a gap between the Glosters and the Northumberland Fusiliers. By the end of the day the division had succeeded in extricating the Belgian Battalion and in moving its right-flank position south of the Hantan. But the gap of two miles between the Glosters and the Northumberland Fusiliers still existed. The division held its positions on Line Kansas during the night against continued enemy attack, but the enemy pressure against the British 29th Brigade had been intense.[21]

The Chinese had found the gap between the Glosters Battalion and the Northumberland Fusiliers and had poured through it during the night, and other enemy elements went south through the gap that now existed between the Glosters and the ROK 1st Division. By morning of 24 April the 187th and 188th divisions of the Chinese 63rd Army were five miles behind the Glosters' position.[22]

With the onset of the Chinese 5th Phase Offensive, UN artillery ammunition use had soared and resupply at once became a problem. Airlift from Japan to Kimpo and Suwon airbases was expedited, as was the unloading from an ammunition ship at Inchon. General Van Fleet encouraged use of artillery far beyond what had been customary. On 25 April a radio message to the Japan Logistical Command asked that a stock of 300,000 hand-fragmentation grenades be maintained in Korea to support the present rate of use in defensive action across the front. And on 27 April Van Fleet requested Japan to ship immediately 40 105-mm howitzers to Korea to replace recent battle losses.[23]

The North Korean units on the army's right flank in the X Corps area joined in the offensive. On 23 April the 1st Battalion, 23rd Infantry, captured Hill 384 near Yanggu from the NK 1st Division. A radio intercept revealed that the regimental commander of the 3rd Regiment was reprimanded and ordered to retake the hill. That afternoon 400 troops of the NK 1st Battalion assembled in a draw to make the effort. The 1st Battalion called for an artillery concentration to be placed on the assembly area, which was delivered, allegedly killing 300 of the enemy force. The next day the NK 45th Division relieved the NK 1st Division.[24]

On the same day, the 1st Regiment of the NK 45th Division attacked the 3rd Battalion, 32nd Infantry, 7th Division, on Hill 902, eastward of the 2nd Division. This was a very heavy battle during the night, with part of the battalion on Hills 610 and 680 also involved. All the companies were attacked by a regiment of the NK 45th Division. Second Lieutenant Boyle, a platoon leader of K Company, was killed, along with 9 enlisted men, and 45 enlisted men were wounded. In turn, K Company counted 200 enemy dead in and around its position; L Company counted 42 dead enemy; and M and I companies counted 130.[25]

A calamity occurred on 23 April during a shifting of two divisions, the ROK 5th and the ROK 7th, at the junction of the US X Corps and the ROK III Corps boundary. The ROK 5th Division was moving west, being relieved by the 3rd and 5th regiments of the ROK 7th Division. At this point, the NK III and V corps mounted an attack in the Inje area in which it surrounded and dispersed the ROK 5th Regiment, and in its retreat it became intermingled with the 36th Regiment of the ROK 5th Division. Both regiments became disorganized and withdrew south. The commanding general of the ROK 5th Division thereupon took command of all ROK troops in his former sector and got the 36th Regiment back on line. But the next day the ROKs withdrew to a defense position south of Inje and there finally halted the North Koreans.[26]

The ROK 5th Division then counterattacked the North Koreans on 25 April and recaptured Inje and the high ground north of the town. But on 28 April this ground was given up when the X Corps withdrew to adjust to the Eighth Army line in the west.[27]

In the meantime, the situation changed around Kapyong, where the British 27th Brigade and A Company of the US 72nd Tank Battalion had successfully checked the Chinese pursuit of the routed ROK 6th Division. The 5th Cavalry Regiment took over the front line there on 25 April from the British 28th Brigade (successor to the British 27th Brigade), to which it was attached, and attacked north with some success. It continued the attack on the twenty-sixth, reestablishing former 27th Brigade positions north of Kapyong, but at 3:30 P.M., General Hoge, the IX Corps commander, gave verbal orders to Colonel Crombez to withdraw the 5th Cavalry Regiment and to move to an assembly area northeast of Seoul. The regiment was to leave Kapyong at 6 A.M. on 27 April. The British 28th Brigade withdrew from the Kapyong area during the night. The 5th Cavalry departed Kapyong on the morning of the twenty-seventh, but en route to its assembly area north of Seoul it received new orders to move into a defensive position north of Seoul on Line Golden. Crombez selected the top of the high mountain ridge north of Seoul, instead of the position prepared by the engineers, as his MLR, and he attributed to this change his successful defense there against a Chinese penetration of the line of 29 April.[28] The withdrawal of the British 28th Brigade and the 5th Cavalry Regiment from the Kapyong area allowed the Chinese to press south and cut the Seoul-Chunchon east-west lateral road.

On 24 April the Chinese seemed to be on the point of breaking through the ROK 1st Division, for an enemy battalion drove a wedge between the ROK 11th and 12th regiments. But Task Force Able, composed of the 2nd

Battalion, ROK 15th Regiment, and A Company, 73rd Tank Battalion, counterattacked against this penetration and succeeded in tying in the separated flanks of the two regiments with the front line. The enemy, however, had pressed the ROK 12th Regiment back two kilometers. Naval air had joined in the battle on the ROK 1st Division's left flank in the lower Imjin area and reported having destroyed two enemy regiments during the day; another enemy force estimated at 6,000 was attacked by carrier air strikes with good results.[29]

The next day, 25 April, the Chinese massed their forces from four divisions of the 63rd and 64th armies in an assault designed to break through the ROK 1st Division. All the attacks were contained by the ROK 1st Division, which fought brilliantly, with heavy artillery support, but one or more enemy groups of company size were behind its lines moving in the direction of Uijongbu. Coordinating their action with that of the Chinese on their left, the NK 8th Division, on the left flank of the ROK 1st Division, tried to cross the Imjin River at the railroad bridge northwest of Munsan-ni, but the combined action of air strikes, artillery barrages, and ground action forced it back. General Milburn thought the ROK 1st Division performed as well during the CCF 5th Phase Offensive as any US division, and Col. Harold K. Johnson, his chief of staff, agreed with him. One reason for its sterling performance may have been the 11 battalions of artillery massed behind it at the end of April, including naval bombardments and carrier strikes from offshore.[30]

On the right side of I Corps, the US 25th and 24th divisions were pressed back all day long into one withdrawal after another in some of the bitterest fighting of the Korean War, the 24th Infantry of the 25th Division suffering many casualties.[31] On 25 April the 24th Division fell back to Line Delta through the blocking position of the 5th RCT. The apex of the Chinese penetrations on 25 April was at Kapyong in the IX Corps area, caused by the headlong flight of the ROK 6th Division, and in the British 29th Brigade area south and east of Choksong.

On 24 April General Ridgway had enplaned for Korea and was at Yoju by noon. General Van Fleet had already conferred with General Hoge of IX Corps at Hongchon. The two generals then went to the 3rd Division CP, where they conferred with General Soule, and subsequently they conferred with General Milburn at I Corps. As a result of these conferences, General Van Fleet decided to withdraw the army to the Delta line.[32]

In the next valley east of the Gloster Battalion, on Hill 235 at Salma-ri, the Northumberland Fusiliers Battalion and the Royal Ulster Rifles, three air miles away and separated from the Glosters by massive Kamak-san (Hill 675), were hard pressed by unceasing attack but escaped south with the help of the 65th Infantry. It was then planned that the 65th Infantry would move to relieve the Gloster Battalion and clear Hill 675 of enemy. The 10th Philippine BCT reverted to the 65th Infantry at this time. But by the morning of 25 April, the MSR from the British 29th Brigade's CP north to the Northumberland Fusiliers and the Royal Ulster Rifles was interdicted by enemy fire, and the 65th Infantry, the Belgian Battalion, the 10th Philippine BCT, and the 29th Brigade CP were all under mortar and small-arms fire. This situation made it mandatory that the 1st and 3rd battalions, 65th Infantry, be used to prevent the enemy from getting behind the troops withdrawing on the MSR.[33]

General Soule of the 3rd Division had expected to restore the line between the Glosters and the Northumberland Fusiliers, just south of the juncture of the Pukhan River with the Imjin, with the 1st Battalion, 7th Infantry, but the situation with the Fusiliers was so bad he had to strengthen them. The 3rd and 2nd battalions of the 7th Infantry were on line on the right of the division and fully engaged in holding off Chinese attacks. In a series of attacks before daylight on the morning of 25 April, the Chinese broke through between E and G companies and overran both of them. The 2nd Battalion was ordered to withdraw, as was the 1st Battalion. The 3rd Battalion, with the Heavy Tank Company attached, covered the withdrawal of the 1st and 2nd battalions, and then the entire regiment withdrew. It was estimated that two enemy divisions had attacked the 7th Regiment.[34] Two men, Capt. Hiroshi Miyamura of H Company, 7th Infantry, and Capt. Clair Goodblood of D Company, 7th Infantry, 3rd Division, won the Congressional Medal of Honor for their desperate sacrifices in the fighting of 24–25 April 1951.

With the large gap now existing between the rest of the 29th Brigade and the Gloster Battalion, enemy in very large numbers passed around the right flank of the latter on Hill 235 during the night of 24 April. Similarly, a large gap existed on the left flank of the Glosters, adjacent to the ROK 1st Division. By morning of 25 April the Gloster Battalion was completely isolated and surrounded. Enemy moved around both sides of the Glosters and behind them at will.

On the morning of 24 April, after the remnants of B Company reached Hill 235 from the lower slope of Hill 675 across the road north of Salma-ri, Lt. Col. James P. Carne's Gloster Battalion had been reduced from more than 700 to only about 400 effectives. The 188th Division of the 63rd Army had crossed the Imjin east of the Gloster Battalion and had overrun Kamak-san east of Salma-ri and the road from Choksong to Salma-ri, and hence south toward the 29th Brigade Headquarters. About 50 wounded were evacuated during the morning before the enemy cut this road south with a roadblock about noon. This act completed the isolation of the Gloster Battalion on Hill 235. The battalion was still supported by the fire from 25-pounders of the 45th Field Artillery, Royal Artillery, and the 4.2-inch mortars of C Troops of the 170th Mortar Battery, which was attached to the battalion. Brig. Thomas Brodie, the Scottish 29th Brigade commander, also had the huge Centurion tanks of the King's Royal Irish Hussars at his disposal in the rear.

Prior to the start of the Chinese 5th Phase Offensive, US Army engineers had improved the track that led to the Gloster Battalion to a two-way road in most places that would be capable of carrying traffic to get supplies to the Gloster position. This road from Salma-ri was the only exit available to the battalion. A second track on the east side of Kamak-san, in the valley where the Fusiliers and the Royal Ulster Rifles were concentrated and where the brigade headquarters was located some miles south of them, was now in the hands of the Chinese in its northern reaches, and they were attacking down it against the withdrawing brigade troops.

The Gloster Battalion positions from the start had not been good. The rifle companies were located on separate hills scattered around the village of Choksong and were not mutually supporting, thus lending themselves to enemy attack separately and to the danger of being overrun separately. That is what had happened after desperate battles at each one. The fiercest was at Castle Hill, held by A Company, and was the nearest of the Gloster positions to the river. The name "Castle Hill" came from a concrete observation bunker built by the US Army earlier on the forward slope of the hill. Lt. Philip Curtis, leader of the 1st Platoon of A Company, gave his life in the struggle there in a series of heroics that won him the Victoria Cross, and the company commander, Maj. P. A. Angier, was killed by machine-gun fire.

From daylight of 24 April on, it was clear that the Gloster Battalion had only a limited time to escape. An attempt was made on the twenty-fourth to rescue the Gloster Battalion. The 3rd Division G-3 Journal summary on the 29th BIB (British Independent Brigade) action 22–25 April states:

29th BIB instructed to move an infantry-tank force NW to relieve Gloster Psn. 29th BIB stated the relief unit was to move early on 24th (Annex 6, journal entry #52, 240625 April 51). The 10th [Philippine] BCT, with its own M-24 tanks (4), plus one-half "C" Squadron 8th Hussars (10 tks) embarked on this mission and encountered heavy resistance in pushing to a point 2000 yards (196005) from the Glouster position on Hill 235 (184010). The lead tank (M-24) hit a mine (or was hit by a mortar round) at this point and blocked the road. Brigadier Brodie considered it unwise to go farther that night and 10th BCT was withdrawn initially to positions Vic 2097 (then later to positions Vic 235965) and the 8th Hussars returned to Vic BIB CP. . . . Contrary to air observation reports, there was no link-up on this date.[35]

An entry in the 3rd Division G-3 Journal for 24 April, dated 4:00 P.M., Serial No. 109, from 29th BIB, states, "Elms 8th Hussars and 10th BCT lead Elms at 203983. Command decision is for this force to continue to GLOS and remain with them for night." Journal entry no. 129 at 6:45 P.M. from 29th BIB states: "GLOS still in Psn – fairly safe. Have had some equip

and weapons shot up. Don't believe their casualties to be heavy considering their situation. . . . Relief force of 10th BCT and Tks have been ordered back because leading Tk became immobilized in a ravine blocking
road completely about 2000 yds short of GLOS psns—further progress of
10th BCT was considered by Brigadier to be unwise. BCT being returned
to 2097, Tks go back to Brig."

Col. O. P. Newman, chief of staff of the US 3rd Division, made a statement of his conversations with Brigadier Brodie on 23–24 April, in which
he included the following:

About 1730, 24 April, Brig. Brodie called me asking for permission to withdraw
the Philippine Battalion, which had made an attempt to reach the Gloster Position
and to order the withdrawal of the Gloucester Battalion that night. During the
conversation the Division Commander [Gen. Soule] walked into my office and he
talked to Brig. Brodie on the subject. I heard him direct Brig. Brodie to leave the
Philippine and Gloucester Battalions in their present positions. He stated that he
was certain that the Gloucester would suffer severe losses if they attempted to break
out at night; that he was ordering an attack by two battalions of the 65th Infantry
the following morning to relieve the pressure on the Gloucesters. About 1900 I
received word that the Philippine Battalion had withdrawn about 5000 yards from
their most forward position. I do not know who directed this withdrawal.[36]

On this matter of the 10th Philippine BCT rescue attempt on 24 April,
Lt. Gen. Frank W. Milburn, commander of the US I Corps, made a report
to the commanding general, Eighth Army, on the Gloster Battalion operations. In it he said:

On the morning of 24 April, the 10th BCT with ½ squadron of the 8th Hussars
(10 tanks) was committed to the relief of the Glosters. The 10th BCT advanced
to within about 2000 yards of the Gloster position when the lead tank was immobilized due to enemy action, blocking the defile through which the column was
forced to pass. At this time the brigade commander felt that any further advance
was unwise due to the lateness of the hour (1735). Some confusion exists as to the
instructions issued to the 10th BCT. The division commander directed that they
hold their position for the night. The brigade commander's orders to the 10th BCT
are not clear, but the accompanying tanks were directed to withdraw and since the
10th BCT withdrew as well, it is presumed that they had orders from brigade to
do so. No journal entry exists covering this point in the brigade journal and staff
members queried have no recollection of the orders issued.[37]

At midafternoon on 24 April Brig. Gen. Armistead D. Mead, assistant
commander of the 3rd Division, stopped at Brigadier Brodie's CP to discuss
the situation on the brigade front and at that time asked him about the
progress of the 10th Philippine BCT toward the Glosters. Brodie replied
that the 10th BCT was still advancing. Mead reminded Brodie that the
division had plenty of artillery to reinforce his fire and advised him to call
for it. Brodie replied that he was doing so.

The next morning, 25 April, General Mead left the 3rd Division CP at 7:30 A.M. for the 29th BIB's CP. He went to the mess tent where Brodie, Col. W. W. Harris, commander of the 65th Regiment, and others were conferring. He learned that the group was discussing the composition of a task force to relieve the Glosters. A British tank commander was recommending that it should contain only a small number of tanks – that one platoon of the 65th Infantry Tank Company was being considered. Mead interrupted the discussion to express concern that tanks were not already en route and to emphasize the need for speed. Colonel Harris thereupon spoke up and stated that he understood the mission perfectly, that he and Brigadier Brodie were together on it, and that, if left alone, he could assure him they would handle it. Brigadier Brodie nodded in agreement. Mead wrote, "I repeated injunction as to necessity for speed in getting under way and stepped outside in order to allow them to finish."

Colonel Harris soon came out of the mess tent and told Mead that he and Brodie were in agreement, that it was a job for M-4 tanks rather than for M-46s and that a platoon was all that could be profitably employed. He said his instructions had been issued and that his platoon was about to move out. Mead asked if he was prepared to use greater strength if it should prove necessary, and Harris replied that he was.[38]

General Mead returned to the 3rd Division CP and reported on his conversation with Brodie and Harris. At 1 P.M. Mead returned to the 29th BIB, and Brodie told him he had no recent word about the Gloster Battalion and that CCF were attempting to block the pass over which the Northumberland Fusiliers and the Royal Ulster Rifles would have to withdraw but that he was attempting to keep the pass open and that the two battalions were instructed to withdraw as best they could and to assemble in the vicinity of Uijongbu. Brigadier Brodie was in the act of displacing his own CP at the time. I Corps had ordered Plan Golden effective at 8 A.M., and all units of the division were then heavily engaged and having difficulty in withdrawing for movement to Line Golden, just north of Seoul.

After the conference broke up early in the morning of 25 April in the 29th BIB mess tent, Colonel Harris gave orders to Capt. Claud Smith, commander of the 65th Tank Company, to send a platoon of his tanks up the road to the Gloster position, about five miles to the north. The road was one-way from the tank company's position. This order was given about 8:30 A.M. M. Sgt. James A. Branch commanded the platoon, and he set forth about midmorning. He and his platoon were back in about three hours and reported they had never come to within sight of the Glosters. They had got into a firefight on the way, perhaps three miles out, and had expended about all of their ammunition and had to fight their way out of the engagement.

About 2 P.M. Smith said he received orders from Colonel Harris to send another platoon up the road to reach the Glosters. Lt. Dale E. Broughton led this platoon, which included a TAC officer, Lt. William D. Mole. About a mile or so from the departure point, the platoon met a British major with some Centurion tanks, who said they could not get up to the Glosters. Lieutenant Broughton and Mole talked with the major for several minutes. They were convinced by his statements, and they turned around and returned to the tank company area. Thus ended the two feeble efforts on the morning and the afternoon of 25 April to reach the Glosters' position.[39]

It seems strange that these efforts were even made because Brigadier Brodie, already at 9:25 A.M. in his last radio communication with Lieutenant Colonel Carne, had authorized him to try to get out in any way he could, and the Gloster Battalion had in fact left Hill 235 before either of the two efforts could have reached him, had they been successful.

Lt. Col. Alvin L. Newberry, commanding officer of the 19th Field Artillery Battalion, supporting the 65th Infantry, attended the conference in the morning of 25 April in the 29th BIB mess tent when the relief of the Glosters was being discussed. He felt that Brigadier Brodie, representing a nation proud in all military matters, did not want to ask for help soon enough. In the conference Colonel Harris asked Brodie if British Centurion tanks should not participate with the light M-24 tanks from the 65th Tank Company. After a brief reflection, Brodie answered no. The tanks left on their mission before a forward observer from the artillery could come up, and consequently there was no communication with the tanks.[40]

In the meeting of Generals Ridgway and Van Fleet at the US 3rd Division airstrip on 24 April, the situation of the Glosters was discussed. At that time, General Soule said he thought Brigadier Brodie had enough strength to get them out. On the same day, General Milburn had talked with Brodie, who convinced him the Glosters were all right. Soule privately expressed the opinion that Brodie was not as aggressive as he had expected him to be. It seems clear that the higher command was misled about the real condition of the Gloster Battalion. General Soule said that the 3rd Division had no direct communication with the battalion, that everything went through the 29th BIB both ways. Soule also said that he was hesitant about stepping on another UN commander.[41]

The evidence seems to show that the effort of the 10th Philippine BCT on 24 April was the only one that came close to the Glosters and that it was the only one that might have succeeded in rescuing them. But that effort was aborted on the evening of the twenty-fourth, when Brigadier Brodie countermanded the order of General Soule, the 3rd Division commander, for the 10th BCT to remain in place overnight and resume its nearly successful effort to reach the Glosters the next morning. Brigadier Brodie ordered the 10th BCT and the Hussar tanks to withdraw from their position soon after his telephone conversation with General Soule, in which the latter had reiterated his order that they should hold in place overnight. This appears to have been a direct disobedience of orders. Whether the 10th BCT and the Hussar tanks would have been able to reach the Glosters the next morning and deliver them from their impending doom will never be known.

Little is known as to how much of an effort, if any, had been made to remove the light tank that had been disabled when the 10th BCT column approached the Gloster position at midafternoon on 24 April. Apparently no effort was made to push it aside. Maj. Henry Huth commanded C Squadron of the Hussar Centurion tanks, some of them included in the column. He told the author that six of the Centurions were moved from the eastern valley, where they were supporting the Northumberland Fusiliers and the Royal Ulster Rifles, to accompany the 10th Philippine BCT up the road to the Glosters position. Reconnaissance the day before by the second-in-command of C Squadron had resulted in him telling Huth that the Hussars could not go the full way because of the narrow defile in the road about a mile and a half short of Salma-ri. The Centurions are more than 11 feet wide and were not made for tank operations on Korean roads. His Centurions, moving from the eastern valley, caught up with the 10th BCT about midday.

They decided to push on another 1,500 yards, with the infantry on the right side of the road, which would bring them to what was called "the Pass," the defile just short of the Gloster position. One of the Centurions slid off a bridge just as the column started uphill to the Pass, and they had to guide it by hand signals. Huth told the Philippine Battalion to go through, and they did, taking the lead with their smaller tanks. The lead tank was knocked out as they entered the defile about 3 P.M. Chinese ran up to it, trying to stick something on the side, but they were knocked over, and they failed to attach any charges. Huth managed to get two Centurions past the small tanks on the side of the road about 100 yards back from the lead knocked-out tank, at a spot where they could pull off. Three Filipinos got off the knocked-out tank and came back to the others.

Huth radioed to Brigadier Brodie at this time and told him that they could not move forward without more infantry, that the three companies of the 10th BCT were not able to control the Chinese in the vicinity and were in a firefight with about a battalion of Chinese on two hills. Huth said Brodie accepted the fact the tanks could go no farther. Huth had told Brodie the 11-foot, 6-inch wide Centurions could not pass on the narrow road of the defile—it was only a jeep track. The Philippine light tanks could turn around where they had pulled off the road; the Centurions could not turn but had to go into reverse and back out. Huth said the Philippine commander thought he could not get his infantry forward. Huth agreed and then told him what Brigadier Brodie had authorized: to pull back the 10th Philippine BCT and to have the tanks follow, after covering their disengagement. The tanks and the infantry used a leapfrog method in do-

ing this, the Chinese trying to cut them off, without succeeding. They
got back to the 29th BIB CP about 7 P.M. This is the account Major Huth
gave the author of what happened at the site of the blown-out lead tank
within 2,000 yards of the Gloster position.[42] The next morning in the conference at the 29th BIB mess tent, Huth told Colonel Harris that tanks
were no good in that defile and that, unless a brigade of infantry went up,
they could not get through to the Glosters.

Capt. Anthony Farrar-Hockley, the adjutant of the Gloster Battalion,
has recorded that, on 24 April, he heard Lieutenant Colonel Carne's radio
conversation with Brigadier Brodie, in which Carne told Brodie his battalion was no longer an effective fighting force but would hold if ordered
to do so—that he had less than 400 effective men, and many wounded.
Hockley said he heard Brodie's voice reply "that the battalion had to stay
and hold, that tomorrow he planned to send armor and a regimental combat team for their relief."[43]

Lieutenant Colonel Carne decided to bring all parts of the battalion to
the crest of Hill 235 and form a tight perimeter for the night of the twenty-
fourth. They remained under enemy attack but survived the night. The
next morning the CCF captured a slight rise at the west end of the perimeter
and then pushed the Glosters off the summit. Captain Farrar-Hockley led
a counterattack that restored the position on the crest. A force of F-80 planes
came in with a napalm strike on the west side of the hill that was amazingly successful. They made seven runs in this strike. The napalm fell so
close to the Glosters that the bursts blew red dust on Farrar-Hockley and
his group. This strike gave some respite to the Glosters. The last communication with the Gloster Battalion was at 9:30 A.M. on the morning of 25 April,
when Brigadier Brodie talked on the radio with Carne.

Within a few minutes after the conclusion of his radio talk with Brodie,
Lieutenant Colonel Carne told all his company commanders that he had
just had a conversation with Brigadier Brodie and that the latter had told
him that artillery support from the 45th Royal Artillery would end, that
they were under enemy attack themselves and could no longer fire support.
Brodie told Carne that every man would have to try to get out on his own.
Carne told his men that they would make their breakout at 10 A.M. The
medical officer, Capt. R. P. Hickey, and the chaplain, Capt. S. J. Davies,
and their helpers would stay behind with the wounded.

The remnants of A, B, and C companies and Headquarters Company
formed into three parties, one of them under the command of Capt. Farrar-
Hockley. They all went south from the crest of Hill 235. All were stopped
during the day by enemy forces that held the ground south of the hill in
force, and they surrendered to the Chinese. Lieutenant Colonel Carne with
a few companions left by themselves, and he succeeded in escaping capture for two days.

The last to leave Hill 235 was Capt. Mike Harvey with the remnants of D Company and a small group of others. He chose to go off the hill to the north, apparently into the heart of enemy forces. According to Harvey's own comments to the author on Hill 235 itself a few months later, he had 81 members of D Company and 10 to 12 members of the medium machine-gun crew in his force when he started off Hill 235. Harvey told the group before they started that they would have to travel fast and that any who could not keep up or who got hit would be on their own, as the rest would not wait, including himself. He waited about three minutes after the others had started down the south side of the hill before he started off in the opposite direction, to the north, toward Choksong. Once off the hill without meeting any Chinese, Harvey led the group about a mile north and then turned west. They ran into two Chinese soldiers as they rounded a little spur of ground and immediately killed them. They went west about two miles, south of the road that runs east-west in the flat land, crossed a low saddle of ground, and then turned south into a narrow valley from which a small stream emerged from high hills to the south. After about a mile this little valley narrowed as the hills closed in, and the party found itself in a sort of defile, with Hill 211 on their left (east). They had been guided to take this route from the valley by a small plane that appeared overhead and sought to guide them to safety. In the area where the hills closed in on the small stream, the party came under fire from the high ground on the sides of the defile, mostly from the west side, which extended about a mile. Here Harvey said he lost about 60 men to Chinese fire. Most of the men sought shelter in the small stream bed. In places it was knee-deep in water, and they soon were wet and covered with mud.

Rounding a curve in the winding stream, the party came in sight of a group of tanks about half a mile ahead. They were firing on the Chinese on the hillsides. They soon saw Harvey's party and at first thought they were Chinese and fired on them, hitting six, who had jumped to their feet and run ahead of Harvey, who had stopped to look back. One definitely was killed. Harvey, still in the ditch, put his beret on a stick and waved it aloft to attract the attention of the tank drivers. (Harvey had his men earlier put their blue berets inside their tunic so that they would not attract attention.) A bullet soon hit his stick and knocked it and his beret out of his hand. The tank drivers quickly realized their mistake, though, and lifted their fire.

At this Harvey and the survivors rose to their feet and raced toward the tanks as fast as they could run. They had encountered a group of five tanks of the 73rd Heavy Tank Battalion, which was in support of the ROK 1st Division. The tanks were at an opening in the hills through which the little stream made its way, about half a mile north of the little village of Taechon. Harvey and his surviving group reached the tanks and rode out a short distance on them, with six of the group in a jeep. Then all were loaded on one tank, which was detailed to carry them out. From the tank he was able to establish radio communication with Brigadier Brodie, who told him to make his way back to Yongdongpo. That evening they reached Yongdongpo, on the south bank of the Han River, opposite Seoul. Early the next day, Brodie came to see Harvey.

Harvey's group got to the tanks about noon. The tankers gave the group American-made coffee, the first drink Harvey said he had had in three days. Harvey was the only one to come out with a weapon, an American .45 Colt pistol. This was in fact the only weapon to get out of the Gloster battles on the Imjin. The rest of the men had been ordered to drop everything and run for the tanks when they made their break. Most of the men who got out with Harvey were reservists and in their 30s. Harvey was the youngest at 28. He had volunteered for Korea in August 1950. He had studied judo since he was 12 years old and held the black belt in it at the time of the Imjin River battles. Harvey said 41 in his group made it to the tanks and escaped – he and three other officers and 37 enlisted men.[44]

Capt. Farrar-Hockley and his party were captured and taken to Choksong. There he saw several prisoners who were captured on top of Hill 235 after he and the others left. He learned from them that, about 20 minutes after his party had left the hill, a group of Chinese came cautiously over the hilltop and, finding the ridge deserted, then rushed forward. Bob Hickey, the battalion medical officer, came forward carrying a Red Cross flag. The leading Chinese opened fire on him but missed. An officer or a senior noncommissioned officer ran forward and stopped the shooting, except for one Chinese who continued firing his burp gun. The Chinese officer shot him. They did not harm the wounded, numbering about 50, but they would not allow the medical officer to organize their evacuation.[45]

At the Imjin River, Farrar-Hockley said there was great confusion, with a throng of personages, mule drivers, and bearers carrying ammunition on both ends of a bamboo pole. There was no traffic control, but two streams of people, one going north, the other south, the latter three times as big as the former. In passing through Choksong, they met hundreds of CCF reserves moving up, each carrying a pine branch to be used for camouflage when airplanes were in view. Choksong was full of piles of their dead. Once a group of soldiers passed the prisoners on English-made Hercules bicycles, baseball caps on the riders' heads. Ironically enough, that night the prisoners crossed the Imjin to the north side by the Gloster Crossing.[46]

On 8 May 1951, the G-1 of the 3rd Division reported that the Gloucestershire Battalion had 5 officers and 15 enlisted men killed, 35 enlisted men wounded, and 21 officers and 554 enlisted men missing in action, for a total of 630 casualties. The same report gave the losses for the 29th BIB as 1,160 men.[47]

On the evening of 10 September 1951, the author had an interview with Brigadier Brodie in his van at the 29th BIB CP. The talk centered on why the British 29th Brigade had not been able to get the Gloster Battalion out. Brodie refused to answer some of my questions, especially the one about whether or not he had countermanded General Soule's order to him that the 10th Philippine BCT be left in position on the night of 24 April, when it was within 2,000 yards of the Glosters on Hill 235. But he answered some questions and made a few comments on the situation then.

Brodie said he thought it made little difference what the 10th BCT did on the afternoon of 24 April. He thought that the tanks could not be left sitting at the road defile overnight but had to be pulled back. In retrospect, he said he thought 24 April was the latest time the Gloster Battalion could have been rescued (the author agrees with this judgment). He said the American help he had received in the Gloster situation "was quite phenomenal"—the Americans gave all that was needed. And he added that he would take 50 percent of the responsibility for failing to make clear to General Soule how serious the situation was. There was an obvious difference between American and British statements on the critical issue of the seriousness of a military situation—the British tended to understate the case, while the Americans sought a realistic understanding.[48]

At 12:35 P.M. on 25 April, the 29th Brigade Headquarters arrived at Uijongbu, about 12 miles north of Seoul, and continued its withdrawal toward the Han River. By the twenty-seventh, the brigade had reached Yongdongpo, where it went into I Corps reserve. On 8 May General Van Fleet presented the Presidential Unit Citation to the Gloucestershire Battalion. Lt. Col. D. B. Grist became the new commander of the battalion, which took in replacements and was reequipped.

On 25 April the entire I Corps line was withdrawing, hard pressed nearly everywhere by closely pursuing Chinese. The 25th and 24th divisions had trouble in their withdrawals in the crucial area of the MSR running north from Uijongbu toward Chorwon. At daylight on the twenty-fifth, the 5th RCT, on the 24th Division's right flank, was blocking for the withdrawal of the 21st and 19th regiments. These units cleared the blocking point, and at 11 A.M. the 5th RCT began to clear its own area under enemy pressure. The 3rd Battalion cleared first, followed by the 1st Battalion, while the 2nd Battalion and the 5th Tank Company covered their movements from the valley below. The 5th RCT hurriedly reorganized and prepared to move farther south.

As the 1st Battalion was passing through a long mountain defile near Pisi-gol, an enemy ambush brought it under fire. At the same time, C Battery, 555th Field Artillery Battalion, which supported the 5th RCT, was fired on. This was the beginning of an afternoon spent in desperately trying to escape from a large enemy force that had moved east of the 5th RCT down its open right flank in the gap left by the fleeing ROK 6th Division on 22–23 April. The enemy force had cut west behind the 5th RCT and

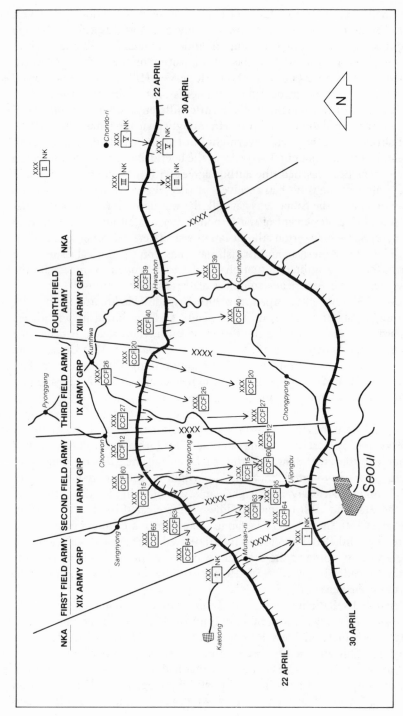

MAP 20. CCF 5th Phase Offensive, 22–30 April 1951

had it trapped at a mountain pass just south of a crossroads on its line of retreat. All batteries of the 555th Artillery, the entire 2nd Battalion, the 5th Tank Company, elements of the 6th Medium Tank Battalion, and most of the 1st Battalion were caught north of the pass.[49]

The artillery caught in the pass area unlimbered and started firing, but the narrow road allowed little maneuvering, and the scene became one of destruction of artillery pieces and vehicles. Many men were wounded and killed. When Lt. Edward P. Crockett's tanks from the 5th Tank Company reached the artillery, the situation was critical. Included among the wounded there were Lieutenant Fay, the TACP leader, Captain West of A Company, Captain Lamb of F Company, and Major Wells, who died of his wounds during the action. The artillery was about out of ammunition, and so were the quad-50s that had been in the midst of the fight. Crockett's tanks tried to push through the vehicles that were on fire. A radio SOS reached the 21st Infantry south of the pass, and it sent Capt. Herman Stein with a tank force and an infantry company riding the tanks to try to force the pass open from the south, but this attempt failed. The Chinese knocked out two of these tanks and killed the infantry riding on them, forcing back this relief column.

Lt. Col. Clarence E. Stuart, commander of the 555th Field Artillery Battalion, saw that the road south of the intersection, where the ambush had taken place, could not be used, as it was completely blocked. He undertook a reconnaissance of the road running west at the intersection and found it clear of enemy. B and A and HQ batteries had moved into the defile; C Battery was south of the crossroads. Infantry cleared the enemy from the high ground to the west, and six quad-50s kept up a heavy defensive fire. Stuart said eight or nine tanks were left at the roadblock, as they could not get through. He could not turn the 105-mm howitzers around on the narrow road, and he lost 11 of them. But he got 7 howitzers out, 4 from C Battery, and 3 from A Battery. The 555th Artillery lost about 100 killed, wounded, and missing in the ambush fight.[50]

Maj. Joe B. Lamb said he flew over the area of the 5th RCT ambush and counted seven burned-out tanks, with many vehicles south of the tanks. A sergeant told Major Lamb that he had burned the tanks because he could not get them out past the enemy roadblock.

When Stuart reported to Lieutenant Colonel Wilson, the 5th RCT commander, that the road west from the intersection, a mere track, could be used by all the equipment and men north of the crossroads to escape, Wilson ordered the withdrawal of that part of the force over it. This part of the column escaped into the lines of the 19th Infantry after dark.[51]

In a memorandum for record on 26 April, the 24th Division reported that the 555th Field Artillery Battalion had lost 11 of its 105-mm howitzers the day before (25 April) in the ambush and had brought out 7, with 2 of them unserviceable. On 27 April I Corps reported that the 5th RCT had lost 12 tanks in the ambush on the twenty-fifth; the 6th Tank Company lost 9 tanks, and the 5th Tank Company lost 3. Furthermore, the British 8th Hussars reported the loss of 6 Centurions when they were aiding the withdrawal of the Northumberland Fusiliers and the Royal Ulster Rifles in the valley to the east of the Glosters on the twenty-fifth. These forces barely made it out to Uijongbu.[52]

The US I Corps was in general retreat on 25 April all along its front. At 6:30 A.M. the corps ordered all units to begin moving all heavy equipment and vehicles south of the Han River. And at 10:30 A.M. I Corps closed its CP at Uijongbu and opened its new CP at Yongdongpo, south of the Han River.[53] On the right in the 3rd Division sector, its 7th Regiment was engaged in a bitter withdrawal battle. Two men during the day, Cpl. John Essebagger, Jr., of A Company and Cpl. Charles L. Gilliland of I Company, earned the Congressional Medal of Honor in fighting defensive battles during withdrawals.

The British 29th Brigade withdrew from the Imjin River front during the day in some distress, and the US 3rd Division felt it necessary to replace the brigade in the front lines. It accordingly requested I Corps to release the 15th Infantry Regiment to it from corps reserve so it could go into Line Delta instead of the British 29th Brigade. The 15th Infantry was released to the 3rd Division at 7:15 P.M. and relieved the disorganized Northumberland Fusiliers and the Royal Ulster Rifles, whose tactical unity had been impaired after three days of heavy engagement with the enemy, on Line Delta at 11:30 P.M. The British 29th Brigade, with the Belgian Battalion attached, went into I Corps control.[54]

On the main Uijongbu road the 35th Infantry of the 25th Division withdrew through an almost constant series of enemy roadblocks. At 1:30 in the morning there were enemy soldiers 2,000 yards south of the regimental CP, firing small arms and automatic weapons and throwing grenades into gun positions of A Battery, 64th Field Artillery Battalion. At 2:05 P.M. the regiment received orders to move out and for about three miles encountered a series of enemy roadblocks. They got through these roadblocks largely because of the effective hail of fire delivered on the Chinese by tanks and AAA quad-50 gun carriages. All the time the surrounding hills echoed with Chinese bugle calls urging on the attack. The regimental executive officer's Daily Journal states that the roadblocks extended for five miles, with enemy on both sides of the road, and that burning vehicles on the road had to be pushed out of the way by tanks.[55]

The ROK 1st Division was under attack all day by enemy company- and battalion-sized groups but held its positions. It was greatly aided by close air support, which killed hundreds of enemy caught in the open. During 25 April the Air Force flew 1,075 sorties, 408 of them in close support, 279 in I Corps sector. That day the Air Force must have accounted for several thousand enemy killed or wounded.[56] The main Chinese effort continued to be down the Yonchon-Uijongbu corridor. The 1st Cavalry Division, less the 5th Regiment, was attached to I Corps from army reserve and assembled in the vicinity of Seoul, and the 187th Airborne RCT closed at Yongdongpo.

Hectic work had been in progress during the preceding days in preparing defenses on Line Golden, just north of Seoul. By 25 April the 25th Division sector of the line had 786 crew-served weapons installations completed and 74,000 yards of double-apron tactical wire fence built, using 510,000 sandbags, 122,800 pickets, 5,400 rolls of barbed wire, 25,000 logs, and 30,000 demolitions prepared.[57]

On 26 April General Van Fleet visited the X Corps CP and conferred with Generals Almond and Hoge. Because of the situation in I Corps he told them he thought the X and IX corps should withdraw south to the area known as No Name line. The last three days of the month were spent in making this withdrawal.[58]

Differing from an earlier opinion, General Van Fleet on 26 April believed Seoul worthy of defense and said he meant to hold it. He drew a defense arc north of the city east to the center of IX Corps, and from there northeast to Yangyang on the east coast, and directed I, IX, and X corps to defend that line.[59]

During the day the 24th and 25th divisions fell back under enemy pressure. Sfc. Ray E. Duke of C Company, 21st Infantry, 24th Division, won the Congressional Medal of Honor during the day's fighting. In the 3rd Division sector, the 2nd Battalion, 65th Infantry, and elements of the 10th Philippine BCT were surrounded at 4 A.M. The 15th Regimental Tank Company attacked north to get them out and succeeded. The 7th Cavalry Regiment, with the Greek Battalion attached, went into blocking positions behind the center of the 3rd Division. The ROK 6th Division was reorganized and put on Line Delta. There was a perceptible decrease in enemy movement south in the central and western sectors of the front. Enemy prisoners reported that the five-day supply of food carried by them at the beginning of the offensive was now in its last day.

Enemy attacks in the west on 26 April centered on the ROK 1st Division. Elements of five enemy divisions pressed attacks during the night of 25–26 April and the following day. During a night attack two enemy regiments pressed back the ROK 11th Regiment, but at daylight a counterattack restored its position. Air and artillery support imposed many enemy casualties. An enemy division infiltrated between the US 3rd Division and the ROK 1st Division during the night, but air attacks on this division during the day caused many casualties.[60]

On the twenty-sixth there was a change in the enemy's behavior. For the first time since the offensive began, there was a noticeable increase in the use of cover and concealment during the day – during the previous four days they had moved in the open. And during the day, Eighth Army moved

Troops of the 35th Regiment, 25th Division, riding on M4 tanks of D Company, 89th Tank Battalion as they withdraw on the west central front, 25 April 1951. *US Army photograph, FEC 14442*

the boundary between IX and I corps 15 kilometers west, giving IX Corps control of the 24th Division and releasing the 5th Cavalry Regiment to I Corps. The X Corps and ROK Army in the east coordinated their withdrawals there to meet the situation in the west.[61]

On 26 April the US 3rd Division withdrew generally to a line 3,000 meters north of Uijongbu. The enemy continued to press hard in this area. At noon the 7th Cavalry Regiment was committed on the division's left flank, where the 65th Cavalry Regiment was in trouble, and the 3rd Reconnaissance Company was ordered there also to maintain contact with the ROK 1st Division. The 65th Infantry then reverted to 3rd Division reserve.[62] Two enemy battalions penetrated to within 3,000 yards of the 3rd Division CP and dug in there.

At noon on the twenty-sixth the British 29th Brigade relieved the ROK

The 204th FA Battalion fires its 155-mm guns on enemy positions, 26 April 1951. Their accuracy caused heavy enemy casualties. *US Army photograph, FEC 13489*

1st Division of responsibility for the Kimpo peninsula. At this time the NK 47th Division was attacking the ROK division from the Munsan-ni area and forcing it back. Air support came to help the ROKs and inflicted heavy casualties on the North Koreans.[63]

At the end of the day, 26 April, General Milburn reported to General Van Fleet that the enemy had built up its penetration through the gap between the ROK 1st Division and the 3rd Division and had also built up strength on the left side of the 3rd Division. At 11 A.M. Milburn had ordered the corps to withdraw generally 6,000 to 9,000 yards south of Line Delta, but there had been difficulty in extricating units in the middle of the division zone.[64]

In the morning of the twenty-sixth, Eighth Army had ordered all front-line divisions and the 29th BIB to button up for the night—there were to be no night withdrawals except in most unusual circumstances. Anything that moved at night would be considered enemy, and they were to hold each position. At first daylight they were to take aggressive action to restore any lost positions.[65]

Meanwhile, an investigation of the actions of the ROK 6th Division on the night of 22–23 April in fleeing to the rear at the outset of the Chinese attack was under way. On 24 April General Ridgway radioed General Van Fleet for information on troop leadership in the ROK division. That day Van Fleet ordered General Hoge, commander of IX Corps, to make a full investigation of the ROK debacle. Hoge in turn ordered General Mitchell, deputy corps commander, to make the investigation. Mitchell, already on 23 April, had gone to the ROK 6th Division to find out what had happened.[66]

On 25 April Lt. Gen. John B. Coulter, deputy Eighth Army commander, reported on a conference he and Ambassador Muccio had held with President Syngman Rhee that afternoon on the failure of the ROK 6th Division to remain on line during the Chinese attack and the consequences of its flight to the rear. In the course of Coulter's comments to President Rhee Coulter said, "We are fighting for our existence and your army is fighting for its homeland, and every soldier must die in place, if he is not ordered to withdraw. Such failure not only threatens his own unit but every U.N. force fighting in Korea."

President Rhee asked, "What can I do?"

In reply, Coulter said, "Appoint a board of inquiry at once, establish the facts, fix the responsibility, try and severely punish the guilty. This not only maintains discipline and obedience of orders but sets an example for all others in the army."

President Rhee said he would do that. He then sent for "the Vice Minister of Defense and directed that he send a message to the Defense Minister and General Chung to appoint a board of inquiry composed of qualified senior officers to establish the facts concerning the actions of the 6th ROK Division and submit them to him."[67]

On 28 April General Hoge wrote to Brig. Gen. Chang Do Young, commander of the ROK 6th Division, expressing his disappointment on the conduct of the division. At the time of the action, Lt. Col. Willard Pearson was KMAG senior advisor to the ROK 6th Division. On 2 May 1951 he wrote to the chief of KMAG on General Chang's behalf, saying in part:

During the two days in which the Division was disorganized the Division Commander General Chang Do Young, did everything possible to bring order out of chaos. He went 48 hours with practically no sleep; missed most his meals during this period; personally returned one regimental commander to the front lines in his, the general's jeep; collected stragglers, made speeches to them and returned them to the lines; and kept the Division CP near the front until it was attacked by the enemy. I do not recommend his relief as I believe he is far more capable than the average Korean general.[68]

General Chang was left in command of the ROK 6th Division.

Lt. Gen. Chung Il Kwon, chief of staff, ROK Army, on 4 May 1951 wrote to the commanding general, Eighth Army, on the investigation of officers in the ROK 6th Division, stating that Col. Kim Pong Chuh, 2nd Regimental commander, was to be tried by court-martial and that the battalion commander of the 1st Battalion, 2nd Regiment, was in confinement awaiting court-martial.[69]

On 25 April Maj. P. B. Ford, KMAG advisor to the ROK 6th Division, reported to the G-4, IX Corps, that the ROK 6th Division G-4 had informed him that equipment and ordnance loss by the division between 22 and 24 April included the following:[70]

M-1 rifle	3,373
Carbine	1,633
BAR	167
Submachine gun	84
Light machine gun	57
Heavy machine gun	71
3.5-inch rocket launcher	105
60-mm mortar	59
81-mm mortar	23
105-mm howitzer	9
Jeep	22
2½-ton truck	17

A memo of 28 April from Ford to IX Corps showed a lesser figure for some of the items on that date, some having been recovered in the interval. The above losses were reported to Van Fleet and by him to the commander in chief, Far East.[71]

ROK equipment losses from 25 June 1950 to 28 April 1951, inclusive, were put at the following staggering total (a partial list):[72]

M-1 rifle	68,295
Carbine	37,560
BAR	3,659
Submachine gun	1,815
Light machine gun	1,815
Heavy machine gun	1,363
.50-caliber machine gun	1,081
Rocket launcher	3,079
Mortar	1,575

Howitzer	229
Jeep	1,751
2½-ton truck	1,263

On 27 April in the east, the X Corps ordered its troops to withdraw south of the Soyang River. The 17th Infantry of the US 7th Division protected the bridge site north of Umyang-ni for the crossing of troops. An enemy breakthrough in the corps center caused a further withdrawal in the 7th Division west of the 2nd Division and the ROK 5th Division. All troops were across to the south side of the Soyang River by the close of 29 April and occupied No Name line.[73]

In the central part of the line, the US 24th Division continued further withdrawals on 27 April without incident and established new positions with the 19th and 21st regiments and the British 28th Brigade west of the Pukhan River, and the ROK 6th Division east of the river. The 5th RCT was in reserve.[74] The 1st KMC Regiment and the 1st Marine Regiment in the Hwachon area broke contact and withdrew to the Chunchon area.

But in the western sector of the line, the battle still continued with unabated fury down the MSR from Yonchon toward Uijongbu and Seoul. On 27 April the 1st Battalion, 5th Cavalry Regiment, was ordered from the Kapyong area to a position just north of Seoul. It hurried to reach its new assigned position. As the battalion approached its assigned high ground from the south, enemy approached it from the north. The 1st Battalion reached its position only minutes before the enemy and was able to hold it against the enemy attack. This position was repeatedly attacked during the day, but with artillery and air support the 5th RCT turned back all enemy efforts to seize the position, with heavy enemy casualties.[75]

It was noticed that the enemy had ceased to use its own artillery after the first few days. The reason apparently was the inability to move the artillery forward to new positions after UN withdrawals began. They simply did not have the capability of moving the artillery forward fast enough to support their advancing infantry. They were limited to use of pack animals or human carry.

On 27 April the 3rd Division lines stabilized. Its withdrawal, however, continued. Its 65th Regiment cleared through Uijongbu at 1 P.M., and the 10th Philippine BCT withdrew from its blocking position and closed with the regiment at 8 P.M. K and B companies were under heavy attack and became cut off from the rest of the regiment. The two companies combined forces and made a bayonet assault to escape and rejoin the regiment.[76]

At 1 P.M. the 7th Cavalry Regiment engaged an estimated enemy regiment three miles southwest of Uijongbu. This battle continued for an hour. The 7th Cavalry Regiment then withdrew four and a half to five miles south to southwest of Uijongbu to prearranged positions. The Chinese took control of the devastated town.

The 7th Infantry was surprised at 7 A.M. on the morning of 27 April to see a battalion of the NK 47th Division coming down the road from Munsan-ni in march formation. The CCF had informed them that there no longer were any UN troops north of the Han River. This misinformation caused heavy casualties in the battalion, and also many prisoners were taken.[77]

The ROK 1st Division was under heavy enemy pressure all day. Both the 11th and 15th regiments had been forced to withdraw 3,000 yards by dawn. The ROK 15th Regiment then contained the attack and counterattacked and restored its lost position. But several enemy groups were behind the UN lines. Also, the Tank Destroyer Battalion of the ROK 1st Division was penetrated by 7:15 A.M. and became disorganized and withdrew. It was then absorbed by the 1st Battalion, 11th ROK Regiment, and the joint group counterattacked. At noon the 2nd Battalion, 11th Regiment, was forced to withdraw 1,500 yards. The 1st Battalion, on the left of the 2nd, contained this attack. At 1 P.M. all units of the ROK 11th Regiment counterattacked and pushed the enemy back 3,000 yards. The enemy broke contact at 4 P.M. The 11th Regiment then withdrew, and the 15th Regiment also withdrew without contact at 3:50 P.M.[78]

Action in the 3rd Division sector was uneventful during the night of 27–28 April, and early on the morning of 28 April the division began its final withdrawal to assembly areas behind Line Golden. These withdrawals were made under certain pressure but did not result in any grave incident. On passage through Line Golden, the 65th Infantry was attached to the 25th Division, and the 3rd Division, minus, passed to I Corps reserve. The 65th Regiment was subsequently released by the 25th Division, and the entire 3rd Division closed into assembly areas within the Seoul region and immediately began rehabilitating personnel and equipment. At the close of April the 3rd Division CP was in Yongdongpo in the vicinity of the I Corps CP.[79]

The Eighth Army withdrawals had been faster than the enemy follow-up, and as a result, by 28 April contact along the western front was relatively light. But the enemy was prepared for a continuation of the offensive. In the area north of Seoul and in the bridgehead area north of Tokso-ri, UN defensive positions were well entrenched and surrounded by wire entanglements and minefields. These had been prepared during the preceding six weeks. Elsewhere, occupying forces were prepared to defend on the best possible terrain. General Van Fleet ordered that this final defensive line be maintained and that further withdrawals, if they seemed necessary, would be made only on his order. In the changes that were made in the units along this final defensive line, the 1st Cavalry Division relieved the British 29th Brigade and the US 3rd Division. And the ROK Army ordered the ROK 2nd Division to assemble at Chechon, where it was attached to the IX Corps.[80]

On 28 April the Gloucestershire Battalion reported as present for duty 43 men, missing in action 740 men. This is the final report on the battalion. The other two battalions of the 29th BIB also suffered heavy casualties in the period 22–25 April: the Royal Ulster Rifles Battalion had 204 killed, wounded in action, or missing; the Northumberland Fusiliers had 134 killed, wounded, or missing.[81]

All units of I Corps would start for Line Golden at 9 A.M. on 28 April. Four hours later, General Milburn announced to General Van Fleet, "In compliance with your personal msg to me, it is my intention to hold firmly on Line Golden as design in my Opn Dir. 54. Withdrawals of this line [will] be initiated only under extreme pressure imperilling our pos. and will be made only at my personal direction upon orders of the Army commander." The I Corps situation map of 28–29 April showed Line Golden as an arc surrounding Seoul on the north side of the Han River, with both ends anchored on the river, and the apex of that arc about five miles north of Seoul. Three divisions formed the line: on the west was the ROK 1st Division, in the center was the 1st Cavalry Division, and on the east was the 25th Division. The line was about 34 miles long. Line Golden had been built between 3 and 23 April while the UN general advance had been under way. It was a massive effort and included preparing covered weapons emplacements, wire obstacles, and minefields. It had been begun by the 25th Division and employed 2,000 Korean laborers.[82]

On 28 April the Turkish Brigade was ordered to assume responsibility for securing the Al Jolson bridge, near the 25th Division's right flank anchor on the Han River.[83] On the same day, IX Corps left the deserted town of Chunchon and withdrew south. The next day the IX Corps CP closed at Chunchon and opened at Yoju, south of the Han River. The Chinese 5th Phase Offensive was spent on 27 April, but this fact did not become apparent until 30 April. Its active phase had lasted six days.

During the night of 27 April elements of the 24th and 65th infantry regiments lost some positions to enemy attack. The regimental reserves were committed and restored the positions. Both regiments continued mopping up remnants in the rear of the MLR until the 27th and 35th infantry regiments of the 25th Division relieved them on position on Line Golden. The 65th Infantry then reverted to control of the 3rd Division at 5 P.M. on the twenty-ninth.[84]

Activity continued against the ROK 1st Division on the west flank. During the night, outposts of the ROK 11th Regiment were driven in by the NK 8th Division and a Chinese regiment. UN artillery was then directed on those positions. After daylight a tank-infantry force composed of a company of tanks and a battalion of infantry counterattacked and, by 10:30 A.M., restored the outpost line. They found 900 enemy dead—400 in the barbed-wired-enclosed position, 400 more along the rail line, and 100 nearby. Tank and artillery fire accounted for most of the casualties. Two companies of the ROK 15th Regiment were surrounded during the night, but after daylight on 29 April, a tank-infantry force got to them, and the enemy retired northward.[85] The weather, which had been bad during the past two days, began to clear at 9 A.M. on the twenty-ninth, and air support resumed.

In the afternoon of 29 April General Bradley, commander of the 25th Division, informed Col. Harold K. Johnson, I Corps chief of staff, that all three regiments were on Line Golden, the 24th Infantry on a narrow front with all three battalions on line. He still did not feel confident about that regiment. He had no doubts about the 27th and 35th regiments. An Engineer battalion and a tank company guarded the Al Jolson bridge.[86] General Milburn left the I Corps CP at 8:45 A.M. to inspect the corps front-line units.

In the east, the 1st Marine RCT withdrew from security positions at Chunchon and Inje. The 5th RCT of the 24th Division moved south along the west bank of the Pukhan River and the next day closed into the division-reserve area, northeast of the junction of the Han and Pukhan rivers. The 5th RCT left many dead and wounded in its battleground of 22–25 April because recovery teams had not been able to enter that area.[87]

A POW, Assistant Company Commander Chun Su Hwan, captured on 29 April, said that the 1st Battalion, 537th Regiment, 179th Division, 60th Army, was nearly wiped out the night of 28 April, that only eight men were left in the 1st Company. And another prisoner from the same division said the 179th Division had used enveloping tactics three times since 26 April, only to find each time that they were enveloping a vacuum. This resulted from the Eighth Army withdrawal policy.[88]

General Van Fleet made a statement to the press at 5 P.M. on 29 April saying that he believed 600,000 enemy were available from five different CCF army groups and the I, III, and V NK corps to continue their attacks, that about half of them had been used in the current offensive. Air and ground reports estimated that at least 70,000 enemy casualties had been inflicted in the offensive, now in its seventh day, and that the present lull resulted from the enemy's need to resupply, reorganize, and to bring up reinforcements.[89]

On 30 April the 27th Infantry, 25th Division, organized a combat patrol, composed of an infantry platoon and a tank platoon, to patrol north to locate the enemy. The next day the patrol set out north toward Uijongbu. They saw several groups of enemy dead, many of them burned by napalm. In one group 70 percent seemed to have been killed in an assembly area by artillery. Many abandoned weapons were found and destroyed. At one point, in screening the high ground on both sides of the road, the patrol found 150 dead and wounded. At a village the patrol found a platoon of enemy, and a brief firefight flared. There the patrol found 200 dead, estimating that 75 percent of them were killed by air strikes and 25 percent by artillery. In certain sections the road was covered by dead. During the patrol it estimated that it had seen 1,000 enemy dead, an estimated 65 percent of them killed by air strikes and 35 percent by artillery. Several groups of enemy were seen and engaged during the patrol.[90]

During the night the enemy drove in the ROK 1st Division outpost line at one point, but after daylight on 30 April an infantry battalion and a tank company task force restored the line, meeting no enemy. The 29th BIB on the Kimpo peninsula destroyed boats along the Han River and prepared bridges for demolition. I Corps patrolled up to 5000 yards north of Line Golden and, only in the 1st Cavalry sector, had one minor contact. All along the line the enemy seemed to have pulled back. Some of the patrols went 10,000 yards from the line, encountering only light enemy resistance from small enemy groups.[91]

Within the Golden defense line it was found that the water-cooled machine gun was best for maintaining a sustained rate of fire. They were emplaced in pairs. The gun crews thus could fire one while the other was being cooled or repaired. It was found, however, that the Chinese had one superior weapon, the 120-mm mortar. It had long range and could be sited well back from the front and in defilade. Its burst was almost equal to that of US medium artillery, and it got results, causing many US casualties and also damage to tanks.

During the 5th Phase Offensive the rotation of officers and noncommissioned officers almost stopped, since they were needed in the current action and could not be spared from front-line duty. As an example of this situation, the 1st Cavalry Division stopped rotation, even though 79 percent of its lieutenant colonels and 73 percent of its majors were eligible for rotation.[92] Infantry noncommissioned officers were especially not available for rotation in any of the US divisions.

After the Chinese 5th Phase Offensive started, the civilian population of Seoul began to leave the city, and by the end of April its population was down to 100,000. About 200,000 refugees accumulated at Inchon, waiting in vain for water transportation out of the area.

Transportation was strained to the utmost during the 5th Phase Offensive. Yongdongpo was the main supply point for I Corps, Hongchon for the IX and X corps. Wonju was the railhead for the Hongchon Supply Point, and it took nine truck companies to keep it operating, hauling from Wonju.

Enemy prisoners indicated that there was a general withdrawal of enemy forces from in front of Line Golden on the night of 29–30 April, involving elements of the 12th, 15th, 20th, 27th, and 60th CCF armies. The 63rd Army conducted only defensive operations north and northeast of Seoul. Whether the Chinese high command ordered a general withdrawal from the front on 30 April is unknown, but conditions there seemed to indicate that they did.[93]

On the night of 29–30 April air sightings of enemy vehicles numbered 3,240, with 2,825 of them moving south. This movement indicated a major enemy effort at resupply of its front-line troops.

On 30 April Eighth Army issued Plan Stubborn, which was for the army withdrawal to Line Waco, on the south bank of the Han River in I Corps sector. The plan was never implemented, but it was nevertheless an elaborate one, contemplating a daylight withdrawal over the Han River pontoon and Shoo-fly bridges.[94]

The depth of the enemy general advance south in the 5th Phase Offensive measured along the Seoul-Chorwon MSR was 26 miles – from Line Golden to Line Kansas. The latter was well above the 38th Parallel; Golden was well south of it. Most of the withdrawals of this period used battalion combat teams with tanks, heavy mortars, and AAA dual-40 and quad-50 platoons, all of which gave heavy firepower, the vehicles transporting the infantry, with battalions leapfrogging and blocking for the withdrawals.

The Eighth Army line that was marked for defense on 30 April was No Name line, as mentioned earlier. It ran generally along Line Golden in I Corps area (but in some instances was slightly north of it), from Haengju, on the north bank of the Han west of Seoul, in an arc 6 miles north of Seoul. East of the Uijongbu MSR it bent down to the Han east of Seoul at Tokso-ri, a distance of about 30 miles. From there it ran east for 21 miles, and then slanted northeast to the coast. Only the western part had prepared defense positions; the eastern half was in rough terrain with few roads.[95]

In the western I Corps sector it was a three-division line, with the ROK 1st Division's 11th and 15th regiments on line west to east, the 5th and 8th cavalry regiments on line in the center, and the 25th Division's 35th, 27th, and 24th regiments on line down to Tokso-ri. The Philippine Battalion was behind the 24th Regiment at the end of the line, and the Turkish Brigade was in reserve.

The Eighth Army casualties for April, most of them in the 5th Phase Offensive, were tabulated as shown in table 17. Eighth Army had 24,492 replacements during the month. Perhaps the most prominent one was Maj. Gen. Gerald C. Thomas for Maj. Gen. Oliver P. Smith, commanding general of the 1st Marine Division, on 26 April. Smith had commanded the

TABLE 17. **UN Casualties, April 1951**

Contingent	KIA	WIA	MIA	Nonbattle	Total
United States	607	4,324	891	6,487	12,309
UN allies	217	611	924	530	2,282
Republic of Korea	518	1,979	7,465	5,505	15,467
Total	1,342	6,914	9,280	12,522	53,917

Source: Eighth Army, Comd. Rpt., April 1951, G-1 Sec., Box 1180.

Marine division throughout its time in Korea up to then and was considered by all an outstanding commander.

The supported strength in April in Korea is shown in table 18. Casualties for I Corps during April are listed in table 19.

At 2 P.M. on the afternoon of 30 April, General Van Fleet called a conference of the three US corps commanders at Eighth Army Headquarters at Yoju. It was attended by Lt. Gen. E. M. Almond, X Corps; Maj. Gen. W. M. Hoge, IX Corps; and Brig. Gen. Rinaldo Van Brunt, representing I Corps; selected staff officers from each corps, including the G-3s; Col. G. C. Mudgett, Eighth Army G-3; Maj. Gen. Henry I. Hodes, deputy chief of staff, Eighth Army; and Maj. J. E. Pizzi, Eighth Army G-2 Section. In reviewing the Chinese offensive just finished, Major Pizzi esti-

TABLE 18. **UN Forces in Korea, April 1951**

Contingent	Average Daily Supported Strength
US Eighth Army	201,797
Korean augmentation	14,495
1st Marine Division	26,032
US Air Force	13,073
British and Australian Army	11,259
ROK Army	251,917
Other units	165,360
Total	683,933

Source: Eighth Army, Comd. Rpt., Plate 17, 30 Apr 51, Box 1190.

TABLE 19. **I Corps Casualties, April 1951**

Unit	Battle Casualties	Nonbattle Casualties	Administrative Loss	Total
25th Division	1,118	1,159	1,700	3,977
3rd Division	823	682	936	2,441
24th Division	1,706	780	1,731	4,217
1st Cavalry Division	208	94	353	655
ROK 1st Division	1,274	411	655	2,340
British 29th Brigade	1,182	99	29	1,310
Turkish Brigade	250	8	0	258
Belgian Battalion	42	22	0	64
Philippine 10th BCT	81	140	37	258
Other corps units	98	118	356	572
Total	6,782	3,513	5,797	16,092[a]

Source: I Corps, Comd. Rpt., G-1 Sec., Apr 51, Box 1523.
[a]Replacements for the month were 18,475, yielding a net gain for I Corps of 2,383.

mated that the enemy had suffered 70,000 casualties out of a probable 350,000 troops committed.

General Van Fleet then commented about the battles just completed.[96]

> The main battle has been on the left—so far it has been an I Corps fight. The weight of three of our five US Divisions were located in the wrong place—the eastern half of the peninsula. We have a threat just east of the I Corps zone—generally in the Pukhan corridor. To offset this threat and to be better prepared to counter the enemy main forces I have ordered the 187th Abn RCT to IX Corps immediately—its primary use is to be in the Pukhan corridor. Also the 7th US Division is to move early 1 May to IX Corps. The 1st Marine Division will pass to the control of X Corps—also the 7th ROK Division. The boundary between IX and X Corps is moved east to a general line thru present east flank of 5th Marine Regiment. Summarizing, assignment of major elements will be:
>
> I Corps—no major change
> IX Corps—24th Inf Div
> 6th ROK Div
> 2nd ROK Div
> 7th US Div
> 187th Abn RCT
> X Corps—1st Marine Div
> 5th ROK Div
> 2nd US Div
> 7th ROK Div

Col. Mudgett exhibited the operations map and new boundary between IX Corps and X Corps. After a slight modification, the two corps commanders agreed to it.

General Van Fleet then commented about his concept of operations.

> We have successfully defended against about one-half of the enemy offensive strength, so far. He had in addition to the other half of his force, salvaged probably 50% of his original attack force. He has used so far no armor, no air, and little artillery.
>
> May is the month in which to defeat him. We can do it better in this area than in any other. If he is not given a bad set-back here, he can infiltrate forever. To stop him then in that type of operation we would have to meet the enemy man for man which we can't do. If we don't beat him now we will have more and more unfavorable weather for some months—less air—less mobility; the enemy will have better concealment. *Now is the time to destroy him. I would like to make this our maximum effort and do it north of the Han.*
>
> The following are briefly the Corps missions:
> I Corps—destroy the enemy generally north of Seoul.
> IX Corps—protect the east flank of I Corps; prevent an envelopment of I Corps right flank. Hold the general line extending northeast thru present positions of the 24th Division. Meet an enemy buildup north of the Han by inflicting maximum destruction to his forces.
> X Corps—meet an enemy push along the Hwachon-Chunchon-Hongchon axis as primary mission; along the Inje-Hongchon axis as secondary mission.

General Van Fleet added that he wanted no needless sacrificing of units. "Don't want to lose a company," he said, "certainly not a Bn. Keep units intact. Small units must be kept within supporting distance, I want to emphasize again, don't let units get 'cut off'. An example is the Gloucestershire Bn. Don't use *any* UN forces that way." Van Fleet concluded his remarks:

Button up at night. In general, there should be no night withdrawal. Beginning at first light vigorous action must be taken to mop-up and wipe out forces that have gotten in the rear. Give every consideration to the use of armor and infantry teams for limited objective counter-thrusts. For greater distances, have ready and use when appropriate, regiments of infantry supported by artillery and tanks. I Corps will have one of these regimental teams prepared to counter across the front of the western part of the IX Corps zone. Similarly the IX Corps will have one prepared for use across the eastern part of the I Corps zone. X Corps have one prepared to operate in the vicinity of the Chunchon axis.

Van Fleet's comments on operation tactics were the same as those enunciated earlier by General Ridgway. His estimation that the enemy would renew the attack in the west where it had left off in the 1st Impulse of the 5th Phase Offensive proved to be wrong.

The new lineup along the Eighth Army front the next day, 1 May, following the changes Van Fleet had just announced was as follows. In the US I Corps, from west to east: the ROK 1st Division, the 1st Cavalry Division, and the 25th Division on line, with the 3rd Division in reserve in the vicinity of Seoul and the British 29th Brigade on the Kimpo peninsula. In the IX Corps, from west to east: the British 28th Brigade, the 24th Division, with the 187th RCT behind it in reserve, the ROK 6th Division, and the US 7th Division. The X Corps would have on line from west to east: the 1st Marine Division, the US 2nd Division, the ROK 5th Division, and the ROK 7th Division.

The ROK Army sector would have, in the ROK III Corps zone, the 9th and 3rd divisions; in the ROK I Corps it would have the Capital and the ROK 11th divisions. Thus matters stood on 1 May 1951.

19

Interlude

THE CCF 5th Phase Offensive, 1st Impulse, had spent itself by 29 April, and on 1 May the enemy troops were withdrawing almost everywhere from contact with Eighth Army. But General Van Fleet looked upon this as only a temporary reprieve and fully expected the enemy to renew attacks as soon as resupply and reinforcements could be accomplished. His view was that the renewed attacks would occur in the west, and possibly in the Pukhan River corridor to the east of Seoul. For that reason he shifted some troops at the beginning of May to put more strength there. The I Corps at the western end of the line was on Line Golden and No Name line, with the ROK 1st Division on the western flank, the 1st Cavalry Division in the center just north of Seoul, and the US 25th Division on the northeast and east of Seoul. The US 3rd Division and the British 29th Brigade were behind this line. Eastward from the 25th Division, the IX Corps had been built up so that it had the British 28th Brigade, the US 24th Division, the ROK 2nd Division, the ROK 6th Division, and the US 7th Division on line. Behind them the 187th Airborne RCT and two ROK divisions were in reserve. The army's right flank was weaker. There the X Corps had the 1st Marine Division, the US 2nd Division, and the ROK 5th and 7th divisions on line. Beyond them eastward were the ROK III Corps and the ROK 9th and 3rd divisions; and in the mountainous east coastal area the ROK I Corps had the ROK 11th and Capital divisions on the extreme eastern flank.

Patrolling in front of the defense line was begun to reestablish contact with the enemy. Patrols went as far as ten miles into enemy territory with little contact, except in the western end in the ROK 1st Division sector. On 3 May the 64th Tank Battalion, 3rd Division, entered Uijongbu but encountered some enemy small-arms and automatic fire. Also on 3 May General Van Fleet ordered the US I, IX, and X corps to establish regimental patrol bases 12,000 yards in front of No Name line, and from them to send out armored patrols to search out the enemy. On 8 May, 7th Cavalry armored patrols reached high ground 6,000 yards north of Uijongbu, where they estimated an enemy regiment was entrenched.[1] In IX Corps there was no change in the expectation that the enemy would attack south again along the Pukhan River axis following the Kapyong-Seoul axis.

The big question for Eighth Army in the first part of May was, Where is the enemy and what is he doing? But the strong patrols that went deep to the north made only negligible contact. This was typical of CCF tactics when they broke contact after an attack; they withdrew far enough to be out of range of UN artillery so that they could reorganize and resupply with a minimum of hindrance, usually a five- or six-hour march from the front.

A high priority for the UN command at this time was to establish a main supply route for the ROK Army in the east so that its troops there could be supplied from the coast at Kansong. In the past, resupply had relied largely on airdrop and hand carry. On 7 May the ROK divisions there launched an attack to try to establish such a lateral supply route in that area of few roads.[2]

At this time, General Ridgway in Tokyo found it necessary to answer a request from the Department of the Army in Washington that President Syngman Rhee had been pressing on it for some time. He had made the same requests of General Ridgway in the past when he had commanded Eighth Army, which Ridgway had always refused to consider. President Rhee wanted the United States to provide arms for an additional ten ROK divisions, saying that he had the manpower to form the divisions but that they would need arms. Ridgway's view had always been that no additional ROK Army divisions should be provided with US equipment until present ROK divisions demonstrated that they could perform suitably on the battlefield. On 1 May Ridgway replied to the Department of the Army's inquiry by forwarding a message from Van Fleet of 28 April to him on the subject, in which he concurred.

The basic problems with ROKA are leadership and training; not manpower or equip. Lack of leadership extends throughout except in rare instances. If excess trained officers and non-commissioned officers are available they are needed in units presently constituted. Until such time as above deficiencies are corrected it would be a waste of vitally needed equip and supplies to permit organization and supply of additional units. It is estimated that since the beginning of the Korean campaign equip losses in ROKA have exceeded that necessary to equip 10 divisions; this without inflicting commensurate losses on the enemy and in some cases without the semblance of a battle. During this week the equip of approx 3 arty bns (2 ROKA and 1 US) in addition to other equip has been lost due primarily to lack of proper ROKA leadership and the will to fight.[3]

Following up on this message to the Department of the Army, General Ridgway on 3 May went to Korea, where he had an hour's conference with

President Syngman Rhee on the subject. General Van Fleet and Ambassador Muccio were present at the meeting. Ridgway prepared a memorandum of the meeting for his diary. In it he said the purpose was "to tell the President very frankly we wanted better performance of the ROKA in battle than we had so far gotten. No words were minced. In summation I told him that we must have better leadership in his officer corps; that the responsibility for getting that leadership rested with the civil authorities." He said that both he and Van Fleet had confidence in General Chung, but the latter must have the support of civil superiors, and no interference with his exercise of command. The cooperation of the ROK Army "had been very satisfactory. The performance in battle had not."

Rhee responded that he had to get rid of all three ministers, although the Eighth Army had great confidence in Sihn. Ridgway told Rhee he was expressing his criticism to Rhee's ears alone and that he was careful to keep it from the public.[4]

In a meeting at Taegu with only Generals Van Fleet and Allen present, Ridgway asked Van Fleet if he knew the feeling in the 1st Marine Division of coming again under X Corps command. Van Fleet said he did, and that with the new Marine division commander, General Thomas, everything would be satisfactory. Ridgway also verified with Van Fleet at this meeting that now was the time to withdraw General Coulter as deputy commander of Eighth Army and to give that duty to Gen. Leven Allen. On 4 May Ridgway visited the ROK 1st Division and complimented it on its recent battle performance and made a round of visits to corps and division CPs. During this series of visits, General Almond of X Corps praised the 7th Infantry Division.[5]

The strongest resistance to UN patrols deep into enemy territory continued to be in front of the ROK 1st Division on the western flank of Eighth Army and in the high ground just north of Uijongbu, where the 1st Cavalry Division patrols were resisted 4,000 to 6,000 yards north of the ruined town. The roads had been mined by the enemy in the withdrawal, and tank support for patrols was hampered. Booby traps had also been set. In the IX Corps area one exploded on 8 May that killed 4 and wounded 17 men in the ROK 17th Regiment. Two days later another fragmentation bomb was set off in the ROK 6th Division that wounded 17 men.[6]

On 6 May another UN force, the Ethiopian Expeditionary Force, an infantry battalion of more than 1,150 men, arrived at Pusan.

Patrols nearly everywhere found little opposition on 7 May to deep penetrations. One of the 7th Marine Regiment patrols entered Chunchon in the center of the line without enemy contact, and again a 1st Cavalry Division patrol reached a point 5 miles north and northwest of Uijongbu. The ROK divisions in the eastern part of the front made slow but steady progress northward, and on 9 May a tank destroyer battalion of the ROK 11th Division occupied Kansong on the coast. POW reports indicated the

CCF in the west and central sectors were regrouping and resupplying about 12 miles back of the front, each army leaving a division as a screening force in front of it.[7]

On 4 May a patrol from the ROK 15th Regiment picked up 15 enlisted men, K Company, 5th Cavalry Regiment, who had been listed missing in action on 29 April. Chinese had captured them, held them a week, and then released them.

The X Corps G-2 report for 9 May reported that the presence of CCF in the eastern portion of the Eighth Army front was often reported but, on close checking, had never been confirmed. The feasibility of committing CCF in the eastern zone must be examined in the light of logistic difficulties, the report said, and pointed out that the only reasonable route to the east from the Iron Triangle area was a secondary and difficult road north of the Hwachon Reservoir and down its east side to Yanggu and Inje. Supply from the north to the east had not proven satisfactory, as evidenced by the difficulty of North Korean forces in opposing the ROK V Corps on the UN right flank.[8]

The UN command kept a close watch on the amount of enemy motor traffic coming to assembly areas near the front at this time, using night observation by aircraft on the main routes of travel from the border to the front. For the ten-day period of the nights from 29 April through 8 May, 24,000 vehicles, an average of 2,400 nightly, were observed by reconnaissance aircraft. Of this total an estimated 15,500 vehicles, an average of 1,550 nightly, were reported as moving south. During this period 2,100 of these vehicles, 210 nightly, were reported as being damaged or destroyed. Assuming that each vehicle southbound was overloaded with four tons, these figures could mean that a potential of 5,360 tons of supplies could have been arriving at enemy forward depots nightly. Deducting from this amount the assumed destruction of 210 vehicles, all moving south, nightly would still leave enough to furnish supplies adequate for 60 enemy divisions. In the quiet then prevailing, much of this could be stockpiled against future operations – the 50 tons daily needed for a division would not have been used. Wherever possible, motor hauls were shortened by use of rail facilities. A truck would need an estimated ten days for round trips between Manchuria and the front. It was estimated that the enemy had 5,000–6,000 trucks in use. By 10 May the UN command estimated that the enemy resupply of its forces at the front had been substantially accomplished, and the resumption of attack could be expected shortly.[9]

In a letter to Van Fleet on 9 May, Ridgway warned of a possible eastward shifting of CCF formations in Korea and of an enemy attack there. He suggested the possible shifting of some US forces eastward to meet that possibility, indicating that the placing of reserves may be "the decisive element." Ridgway, apparently, did not fully share Van Fleet's conviction that the expected enemy attack would be in the west or west-central sectors of the line. In the same letter Ridgway said he wanted to discuss another matter, relating "to the sacrifice of any unit, particularly of another nationality. The case of the Glouc. Bn is, of course, uppermost in my mind." He continued:

I cannot but feel a certain disquiet that down through the channel of command, the full responsibility for realizing the danger to which this unit was exposed, then for extricating it when that danger became grave, was not recognized nor implemented. There are times, as I am sure your experience in battle will bear out, when it is not sufficient to accept the judgment of a subordinate commander that a threatened unit can care for itself, or that a threatened situation can be handled locally. The responsibility in each case goes straight up the command chain, through regiment, Div., Corps to Army. Each commander should search his soul and by personal verification, satisfy himself that adequate action has been taken. It may be that such was the case of the Gloucesters. I have the feeling that it was not; that neither the Div, or the Corps Commander was fully aware by direct personal presence, as near the critical spot as he could have gotten, of what the actual situation was. Had he known it, I feel sure that instant vigorous action would have been taken to extricate the unit.

I feel in conscience bound to state these views at this time, lest some other avoidable tragedy occur.

I fully realize that the loss of these gallant men weighs as heavily in your heart as in mine or any others.[10]

It is obvious from this letter that Ridgway felt that there had been negligence in the matter, from the Eighth Army commander on down the chain of command. It is the author's opinion that the British 29th Brigade commander, the immediate superior in command of the Gloucestershire Battalion, was most remiss of all. The 3rd Division commander, who had no direct communication with the Glosters, since all communications both ways between it and the battalion went through the 29th Brigade, was obviously concerned about its plight while there was still time to rescue it. General Ridgway had always been very sensitive to the American command of Eighth Army and the UN forces and to the possibility of allowing any UN force to be cut off and destroyed. If that had to happen to any force, he wanted the risk taken by an American unit.

On the night of 6–7 May tactical air had sighted 3,700 vehicles behind enemy lines after dark, 2,300 of them moving south – an all-time high. But the enemy's intentions remained clouded. On 9 May Eighth Army ordered the US I Corps to release the US 3rd Division to army reserve and to assemble it in regiments in the Seoul-Ichon area for support or counterattack in either the Seoul, Pukhan, or Chunchon-Hongchon axes. General Almond had reported a buildup on the left front of his X Corps. This was the first definite move made to have the 3rd Division ready for use at different points of the front.[11] The three RCTs were to be ready to move on six hours' notice. Many in Eighth Army believed the enemy would attack

Left to right: Gen. William M. Hoge, IX Corps; Gen. Blackshear M. Bryan, 24th Division; Gen. James Van Fleet, Eighth Army; and Gen. Matthew B. Ridgway, FEC. *National Archives photograph, 111-SC 367550*

the west-central area, possibly at the junction of the Han and Pukhan rivers near the boundaries of the IX and X corps.

On 9 May Eighth Army issued a plan called "Detonate," which ambitiously called for an attack toward Line Kansas to be implemented on 12 May to spoil the enemy's preparation for resuming its own attack. But this plan was canceled on 11 May on receipt of intelligence of enemy massing west of the Pukhan River for an assault within 72 hours. Instead of attacking, Eighth Army now concentrated on defense to meet an attack south.[12] But even that was a bad guess.

On 11 May Lieutenant General Ridgway was promoted to the rank of four-star general.

The enemy on 10 May began a secret move of five armies from the west and central fronts eastward to reach the front of the X Corps and the ROK III Corps in the east. The first information on this surprise tactic came

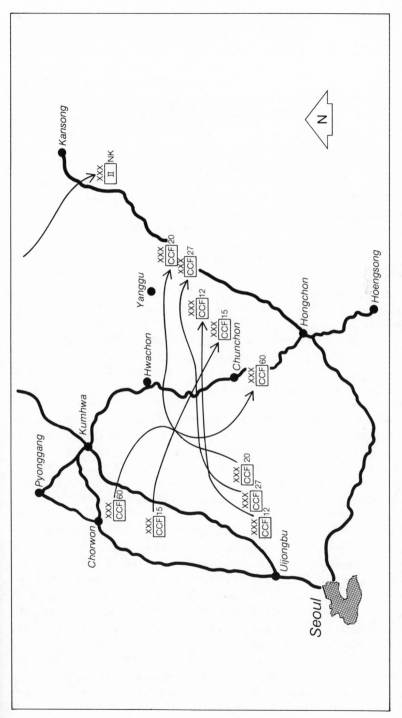

MAP 21. **CCF Redeployment for 5th Phase Offensive, 2nd Impulse, 1–15 May 1951**

from a prisoner the US 3rd Division captured from the 12th CCF Army. He said that the 12th Army and two others were to start southeast that night and march four nights to an undisclosed destination but that they would attack the US 2nd Division and adjacent ROK divisions. The offensive was to be concluded in 16 days, and the troops were issued 16 days' rations.[13] There is no evidence that this report was taken seriously.

On this same day General Van Fleet conferred with General Hoge of IX Corps and General Almond of X Corps, repeating to them General Ridgway's strictures to him about not allowing any UN unit to be cut off and sacrificed. In these conversations Van Fleet urged that artillery be used to the maximum. He was also dissatisfied with the use of protective wire and mines in front of the lines — he wanted three times as much used. He told General Hoge the IX Corps positions fell way short of his desires, and he wanted the work speeded up. On the twelfth, he reiterated he wanted massed artillery used lavishly in any forthcoming CCF offensive. Commanders should remember that "artillery is the greatest close-in weapon available."[14]

Enemy North Korean pressure had suddenly picked up on the east coast. On 10 May 1,000 enemy attacked the ROK 11th Division's Tank Destroyer Battalion that had just occupied Kansong, and the next day drove it out of the town and to a point five miles south. On 12 May the North Koreans attacked the 22nd Regiment of the ROK 3rd Division in the ROK III Corps area and drove it south, and on the same day they broke the ROK 20th Regiment, 11th Division. The ROK 26th Regiment, Capital Division, blocked the North Korean penetration. But General Van Fleet's attention was centered on the US 24th Division sector of IX Corps, which he thought the most sensitive of the entire line — there was little room there to fall back, without allowing the enemy to cross the Han.[15]

On 14–15 May there were very heavy rains in Korea. This weather drastically reduced aerial observation of enemy movements, and it made some bridges unusable and some of the MSRs dangerous in the mountainous parts of the front.

A captured document relating the experiences of the CCF 42nd Army with a mobile defense was translated and published in Eighth Army on 14 May. It realistically recounts the difficulties the CCF Armies were experiencing at this time, stating that the army had a 50-mile sector to defend and that it suffered heavy losses; the UN attacked day and night with artillery, tanks, and aircraft. They could do nothing in defensive positions. They received neither food nor ammunition and were slowly worn down. Without ammunition they could only wait for the UN forces to close, and then depend on a few hand grenades. They were killed when their positions were overrun. They also had difficulty in communications under bombardment and were unable to receive commands from higher authority. The document stated, "The offensive of a modern army brought us critical losses. Against such an enemy it is believed that it is better to practice a mobile defense than to hold one position to the death. We must master the defense, 'front light, rear heavy.'"[16]

On 14 May General Van Fleet held a conference at the IX Corps CP, accompanied by his G-3, the army ordnance officer, and his senior aide. There he met General Hoge, the corps commander, and General Soule, commander of the 3rd Division. They discussed the planned use of the army reserve (the 3rd Division) and of the IX Corps reserve (the 187th Airborne RCT). General Hoge stated that he planned on using the 187th RCT in the 19th Infantry, 24th Division, sector only in case of a deep penetration and that, because of terrain, it would be committed head-on, north along the west side of the Pukhan River.

Van Fleet expressed dissatisfaction with the limited use of wire in front of the IX Corps positions, stating that it was no more than a third of what he wanted. He then stressed placing the weight of artillery fire on the left flank and was assured that a withdrawal to the banks of the Han would not force the displacement of artillery on the south bank. Van Fleet stressed that he wanted the amount of artillery used in the next offensive to be twice what it had been in the offensive just ended. He also ordered that the 65th Infantry Regiment of the 3rd Division be moved to the threatened area on the left of IX Corps. He then ended his discussion with the following statement: "I want to stress again that my idea of obstacles and fire power is vast. We must expend steel and fire, not men. I want to stop the Chinaman here and hurt him. I welcome his attack and want to be strong enough in position and fire power to defeat him. I want so many artillery holes that a man can step from one to another. This is not an overstatement; I mean it!"[17] It seems clear that General Van Fleet expected the enemy's next offensive to strike the IX Corps, and especially its left flank.

This conclusion is reinforced by Van Fleet's meeting at his headquarters on 16 May. He directed that planning for ammunition resupply be based on the premise that Eighth Army would fire five days' worth of fire in one day during massed attacks. He discussed with his staff the question of whether the boundary between I Corps and IX Corps should be shifted east or west to gain unity of command in the area formed by the loop of the Han River directly east of Seoul. The present boundary bisected the loop. Van Fleet decided to give the entire loop area to I Corps on the basis that an attack in this area would threaten primarily I Corps's rear area and therefore should be an I Corps responsibility. As a result of this decision it followed that the 65th Infantry of the 3rd Division would have to come under I Corps control, since the 65th Infantry was occupying a critical part of the loop.[18]

There was no discussion or attention given to the massing of enemy in front of the US 2nd Division in the X Corps sector and the imminence of a major attack there. He expected the enemy attack in the IX Corps area, directed again at Seoul. The Eighth Army G-2 estimate of the situation at the close of 15 May supported this view. It said:

Considering the present enemy attack capability, recent PsW tend to reaffirm previously indicated troop dispositions, suggesting a shift of weight since the last attack phase so as to indicate a main attack in the west and west-central sectors and a strong secondary attack in the central sector along the Chunchon-Hongchon axis, in conjunction with a general attack along the front. . . .

The main effort of any renewed enemy effort continues to be indicated east of Seoul, in the west-central sector probably towards the lower Han River corridor.[19]

The army G-2 report for 15 May correctly listed the enemy units to be employed in the expected renewed offensive, but it put them in the wrong places and with the wrong objectives. We must now turn our attention to what was happening in the X Corps sector in the east-central and the ROK III Corps sector in east Korea between 10 and 16 May.

In the X Corps area No Name line ran southwest to northeast and was located on high ground five and a half miles south of the Soyang River. The 9th Infantry Regiment of the US 2nd Division held Hill 705 as the left anchor of the division line; the 38th Infantry Regiment held Hill 1051, the most dominant height on the line. Task Force Zebra was also initially on the line east of the 38th Infantry. A modified No Name line ran 3,000 to 6,000 yards south of Yangye.[20]

Late in the evening of 9 May, enemy soldiers were observed repairing a footbridge across the Soyang River. The next morning aerial observation discovered 150 enemy dug-in along a ridge between Hill 568 and Hill 545. Artillery fire and air strikes were immediately called in on the enemy position. A Company, 9th Infantry, attacked the hill, which overlooked the Chunchon valley, but was unable to dislodge the enemy force. Another enemy force of 300 was discovered in bunkers. G Company, 9th Infantry, attacked it, but was unable to dislodge it. By 11 May an enemy battalion was anchored on Hill 568, and aerial observation reported large numbers of enemy troops moving south on the road from Yuchon-ni, and this movement continued on the twelfth. The enemy appeared to be moving into an assembly area two and a half miles south of Yanggu.[21]

This appeared to be the beginning of an enemy movement that continued day after day thereafter. On 12 May observers saw large enemy forces moving laterally and strung out on the road from Hwachon to Yuchon-ni, and hence to the Soyang River and north to the Yanggu basin. Composition of the forces observed was not known definitely but was believed to be CCF. It indicated a threat to the X Corps east flank and a widening of the CCF area of operations eastward.[22]

On the same day, enemy continued to resist patrols in the Naepyong-ni area on the Soyang River. Earlier, the Soyang River crossing area at Naepyong-ni had become the center of enemy activity, as 2nd Division patrols kept finding enemy groups in the vicinity three to five miles south of the river. On the eleventh, air observers saw an enemy column on the road as far as he could see moving south into Hwachon, 200 moving out of the town, and another force of 300 moving southeast from nine and a half miles northwest to six miles north of Naepyong-ni. Other pilots saw enemy on the road two to five miles west and southwest of Naepyong-ni. One aircraft was damaged by enemy antiaircraft fire from northeast of the town.[23]

An enemy force meanwhile had seized Hill 699 and held tenaciously to it. General Ruffner, the 2nd Division commander, believed the enemy was engaged in a buildup and hiding its forces in draws and valleys until ready for jump-off. Ruffner had artillery fire placed on all suspected areas and called for air strikes against known enemy positions. On 14 May the translation of an intercepted CCF radio message said, "275 killed today on Hill 699 by air and arty." Shortly before dark on 14 May air observers reported masses of enemy marching down a trail between Naepyong-ni and Sapkyo-ri. Ruffner directed artillery fire and air strikes on the place. Parts of three artillery battalions fired on it. The 2nd Division had a concentration of artillery that could be brought to fire on its front; 94 pieces under the command of support artillery made a total of 300 artillery pieces at the division's disposal. It had also placed tanks for indirect fire missions.[24]

The division patrols continued to meet strong enemy units south of the Soyang River in the vicinity of Naepyong-ni. On the fourteenth, an air observer saw three company-sized groups cross the river one and a half miles southeast of the town. Critical Hill 1051 held by the 38th Infantry lay to the southeast.

On 15 May enemy activity increased south of the Soyang River in the Naepyong-ni and Umyang areas. Enemy tried to penetrate UN outposts and resisted all patrols. The weather was bad on this day, which curtailed aerial observation. But observers did see several groups entrenched south of the town and river and observed 100 to 150 enemy carrying supplies across the Soyang River.[25] The majority of the enemy movements seemed to be south of the Soyang River in a drainage leading into the high ground toward Kari-san, Hill 1051.

Unknown to the X Corps and the Eighth Army, the CCF had been engaged in a massive redeployment of two army groups laterally across the front from west to east: the IX Army Group, consisting of the 20th and 27th armies, to positions in front of the ROK III Corps, and the III Army Group, from the Uijongbu corridor to Seoul to positions in front of the 1st Marine Division and the US 2nd Division of X Corps. The III Army Group consisted of the 12th, 15th, and 60th armies. Thus these two CCF army groups, moving mostly by night, beginning on the night of 10 May and continuing to the night of 16 May, had moved a force of about 137,000 troops a distance of up to 40 miles to new battle positions. Also, the North Korean II Corps had moved from a rear position along the east coast to a battle position in front of the ROK I Corps near the coast. The NK II and V corps on the east end of the line added a force of about 38,000 to the 137,000 CCF committed, for a total strike force of approximately 175,000 men. The purpose of the 2nd Impulse of the 5th Phase Offensive was to destroy the ROK forces in the east and to destroy the US 2nd Division.

Four CCF divisions, the three from the 20th Army and one from the 12th Army, were given the mission of deep penetration together with the 6 North Korean divisions from the NK II and V corps, a force of 10 divisions in the east, to destroy the ROK Army there. The other 11 CCF divisions of the III and IX army groups would attack the X Corps, with the special mission of destroying the US 2nd Division.[26]

On 13 May the 7th Marine Regiment had the first new unit identification on the X Corps front, when a prisoner from the Engineer Battalion, 80th Division, CCF 27th Army, was captured. He said his unit's mission was to construct a bridge over the Pukhan River. He located the three divisions of the 27th Army as of 11 May. The bridgehead south of the Soyang River had been expanding south and east, and enemy company-sized groups were encountered in the defensive sectors of the ROK 5th and 7th divisions at the eastern part of the X Corps zone. A further identification of enemy forces in front of X Corps was made on 15 May when the 7th Marine Regiment picked up a CCF deserter from the 12th CCF Army. He located the three divisions of the 12th Army and said they were moving into the Chunchon area to make a frontal attack. On the night of 15–16 May there were two strong probing attacks against the right of the US 2nd Division line and two against the ROK 7th Division, which drove in the outposts. It was apparent by now that the rough terrain between the Hwachon Reservoir and the Soyang River had been taken over by enemy forces, and an attack against the X Corps and the ROK forces in the east was imminent. The few prisoners captured along the front of No Name line gave an inkling of the composition of the attack forces.

20

The Chinese 5th Phase Offensive, 2nd Impulse

ON THE NIGHT OF 16–17 MAY an enemy force of 137,000 CCF and 38,000 NK soldiers started the 2nd Impulse of their 5th Phase Offensive. This offensive was designed to destroy the six ROK Army divisions along the eastern flank of Eighth Army as well as the US 2nd Infantry Division.

The X Corps knew there was an ominous buildup of enemy units to its front, but it did not know the identity of this force. In the period 10 to 15 May its patrols and aerial sightings had established the fact that large numbers of enemy troops had moved into the Soyang River area south of Chunchon from the west and northwest and had crossed the Soyang River to the south side in an impressive bridgehead in the vicinity of Naepyong-ni. The center of the 2nd Division line on the high ridgeline south of the river, culminating in the dominating height known as Kari-san, or Hill 1051, lay only six air miles to the southeast. Only with the opening of the big offensive on 16 May did the UN forces identify the enemy order of battle and learn the size and composition of the enemy force attacking it. That day a patrol from the Netherlands Detachment (attached to the 38th Infantry Regiment of the US 2nd Division) captured a Chinese soldier who identified the 35th Division of the CCF 12th Army. Previous reports on that army had placed it 40 miles to the west. Then the next day, 17 May, with the attack generally all along the X Corps line, prisoners were taken from the 31st Division of the 12th Army and from the 44th Division of the 15th Army. These identifications were immediately reported to higher headquarters and pointed to the probable presence of the entire CCF III Army Group in front of the 2nd Division. One more day was needed to reveal the complete enemy order of battle in front of the 2nd Division when prisoners from the 44th and 45th divisions of the CCF 15th Army and from the 181st Division of the CCF 60th Army were taken. The 181st Division was attached to and participated in the attack by the CCF 12th Army. On the third day a prisoner identified the CCF 34th Division of the 12th Army.[1]

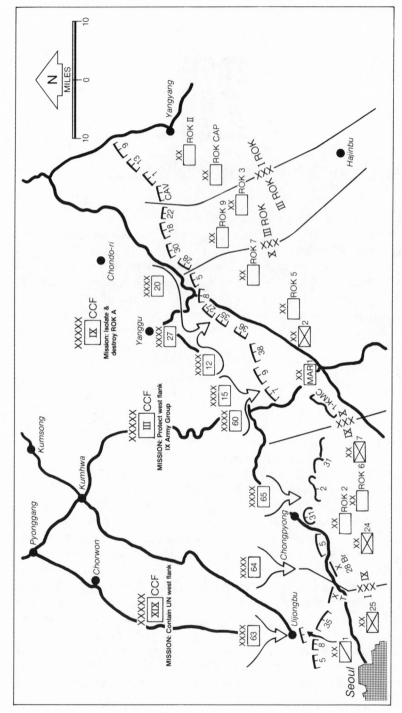

MAP 22. Positions at outset of CCF 5th Phase Offensive, 2nd Impulse, 16 May 1951

Hill 1051, No Name line, where Chinese ruptured the 2nd Division line in the middle of its sector, during the Chinese 5th Phase Offensive, 2nd Impulse, May 1951. *National Archives photograph, unnumbered*

By 6:30 P.M. on 16 May enemy probing attacks had started, and an hour later strong attacks were being made in the center and on the east side of the X Corps sector. It was immediately evident that the ROK divisions on the right of the US 2nd Division were becoming disorganized and being forced back.

The US 2nd Division occupied No Name line with four infantry battalions. The 9th Infantry (less 1st Battalion) occupied a regimental patrol base at Hill 899; the 2nd Battalion, 38th Infantry, occupied a battalion patrol base in front of the regimental line. The remainder of the 38th Regiment, with the Netherlands Battalion attached in regimental reserve, occupied defense positions on No Name line. The 3rd Battalion was on Hill 800 about three air miles southwest of Kari-san, where the 1st Battalion held the highest point of the ridgeline. The two battalions had adjacent boundaries. On the right of the 38th Infantry, Task Force Zebra of the

2nd Division held the division right. This task force consisted of the 72nd Tank Battalion (less one company); the 2nd Battalion, 23rd Infantry; the 2nd Reconnaissance Company; and the 1st Ranger Company. The 3rd Battalion, 36th ROK Regiment, was attached to the US 2nd Division and occupied a position to the front of Task Force Zebra. The 23rd Infantry Regiment of the 2nd Division was in X Corps reserve, less the 2nd Battalion.

During the afternoon of 16 May enemy probing attacks hit the right side of the 2nd Division, and by 6:30 P.M. enemy had closed with elements of the 3rd Battalion, 36th ROK Regiment, in the Task Force Zebra sector. To the west, the 38th Regiment had its 2nd Battalion in a patrol base 3,000 yards in front of its 3rd Battalion on Hill 800. The Netherlands Battalion occupied Hills 710 and 975 in rear of the 1st Battalion on Hill 1051. The Regimental Tank Company was south of the Netherlands Battalion, securing the regiment's right flank with indirect fire.

At 1:50 P.M. on the sixteenth, a probing attack hit C Company on the right of the 1st Battalion, and from that time on for 72 hours, enemy pressure on the 38th Regiment was almost continuous. Forward observers were continuously busy adjusting artillery fire during the afternoon and all night. During the night the 2nd Battalion, on the patrol base, and the 1st Battalion, on Hill 1051, were subject to heavy attack, with enemy making penetrations, but the battalions restored them by counterattacks. At 8:55 P.M. the 1st Battalion reported the ridge north of C Company's right flank was in enemy hands. By 2:20 A.M., 17 May, the situation in the 2nd Battalion patrol base position had become critical, and the battalion was ordered to withdraw to the rear of the MLR. The forward observer with F Company covered the battalion's withdrawal with artillery fire, placed with telling effect.

Enemy pressure against the 1st Battalion did not let up, and at 3:15 A.M. the enemy made a penetration on the east side of Hill 1051 in the saddle between it and Hill 914 farther to the east. Heavy artillery concentrations were placed on the area of this penetration, which was destined to be greatly exploited by enemy formations. A Company of the Netherlands Battalion was ordered to close this gap, but by 5:15 A.M. Hill 1051 was reported lost. The Dutch Battalion was ordered to go to Hill 710, where it was to join A Company and to make a coordinated attack to restore the regiment's positions on Hill 1051. It failed to attack, however.

The other regimental position, that of the 3rd Battalion, was still intact. It had received heavy attacks at the same time as the 1st Battalion, but they were not as intense, and although driven from its position on Hill 800 at one time, it restored the position by counterattack and then held it.[2]

Meanwhile, enemy were streaming through the gap between Hills 1051 and 914 unopposed, except for the artillery barrage laid down there. An intercept of an enemy radio message revealed that an enemy order said, "Send all troops east of Hill 1051." Targets were everywhere for artillery and air, and only the most promising were selected. At 11:55 A.M. 17 May the Netherlands Battalion was again ordered to retake Hill 1051, and maximum artillery support was planned. The attack was set for 1 P.M. Again the Netherlands Battalion did not attack.

The 44th Division of the CCF 15th Army made the main effort against the 2nd Division in the Hill 1051 area. The Chinese 45th Division suffered very heavy casualties in the effort to exploit the penetrations the 44th Division had made. The leading elements of this division were cut to pieces, and those who followed ran into murderous UN artillery fire and suffered thousands of casualties without ever engaging UN forces. But these two enemy divisions created havoc in the Hill 1051 area on 17 and 18 May.[3]

The failure to get the Netherlands Detachment to attack in the Hill 1051 sector where the enemy penetrations had been made, although repeatedly ordered, needs some explanation. The affair is glossed over in nearly all the official reports, but the matter is made clear in the journal of the Chief of Staff for the 2nd Infantry Division, 17 May. That journal for 17 May fills 21 legal-size single-space pages with entries that resemble stenographic reports in their detail of what was said over field telephone or radio between 2nd Division and X Corps personnel, especially between General Ruffner, commander of the 2nd Division, and General Almond, X Corps commander. To describe the situation on Hill 1051 on 17 May during the Chinese breakthrough, the following excerpts from the Chief of Staff Journal, 2nd Infantry Division, are presented.

0205 CG [Ruffner] to C/O 38 [Col. John G. Coughlin]: How about this 2nd Bn of yours? Have they been able to readjust? You have a FO [Forward Observer]? 38 C/O: – He's hurt, radio damaged by direct hit, no communications, so they started falling back. FO with G Co. is handling arty now.   Serial 8, 0205

0228 C/O 38 – We are shooting the place we vacated.   Serial 9, 0228

0230 CG to Index 6 [CO, 9th Inf.]: 38th forward 2nd Bn getting clobbered. Hold until cleared to pullback.   Serial 10, 0230

0721 G-3 to ADC [Assistant Division Commander Stewart] 1051 still in Impel Red [1st Bn., 38th Inf.] hands – about 40 CCF thru.   Serial [NA], 0721

0815 ADC to G-3: C/O of F Co says enemy still coming thru gap, about 500. G-3: – C/O 38 does not verify that French in trucks ready to go to gap. G-2 says L planes spotted en coming down valley, French going up. ADC: – 4 tanks up valley and in contact with them, shooting at them. CG: Up where E and F Cos are on line is thin, breakthrough be bad. Engineers activating minefields and closing road.   Serial 22, 0815

0825 G-3 to C/O 38th Inf: Is gap still there? Yes – Putting air on N slope of Hill 1051. No Pws. G-3 wants Pws – have every one look in front of pos. for WIA enemy. G-3 – Hope you can gather some Pws. 38 CO: – there are a lot of them dying in minefields. . . . Chinks came thru mines like they weren't there.   Serial 24, 0825

0840 ADC to CG: Chinese on 1051 and coming down slope. Air strike and mortars, wants arty, but can't get it because in 38th zone and won't clear.

Serial 25, 0840

0845 G-3 to Maj Jenson, Inspire White [2nd Bn., 23rd Inf.]: about CCF on 1051. Jenson said he could see about 500 in gap coming toward him. Wants artillery on them—told to call Coughlin, CO 38. Serial 26, 0845

0850 G-3 to CO 38: told him about above item. CO 38 said air strike on them and would follow with arty. Serial 27, 0850

0908 CG to CO 38: Asks for clear information on Hill 1051. 38 uncertain, long conversation on location of units. CG wants gap closed and info on 1051. At end of conv CO 38 says just got rpt now that 1051 is in en hands and they are swarming all over it. CG:—Now we can really lay the Arty on it. Serial 30, 0908

0925 CO Div Arty to CG: Just got word from 38th that 1st Bn gave up Hill 1051, and we are clobbering them. FOs been watching them for last half hour. French contact. Serial 33, 0925

0933 CG to CG X Corps: My 2nd Bn, 38th out on R line got knocked off there. . . . I have plenty troubles at 1051. 1st Bn of 38th. I am c-att with Dutch. I am fighting those that got thru with French, Tks, and flak. . . . Zebra line is very thin. Almond said he was on way up to 2nd Div. Serial 34, 0933

0950 G-3 to Maj. Spann: CG wants French less one Co join Co already sent up and help Dutch close gap at Hill 1051. We have intercept that CCF have said send all troops E of 1051 thru gap. Want you to reinf Fr Co before they get there.

Serial 35, 0950

1030 ADC to CG: French in contact. Other 2 Cos not here yet—Can see fight 1½ mi up valley. Getting Dutch ready to charge place. Serial 38, 1030

1045 C/S 2nd Div to Exec 38 Inf: Be sure to instruct Dutch to have panels and display as soon as they get on 1051. 38th: Don't know about that, sir. Have you heard thousands that are coming thru gap? The Dutch rpt them pouring over that saddle and Fr also rpt it. Are pouring arty in there. A Co on other side of 1051, C on shoulder. They kicked plat of C off 914. Firing arty on 1051 for 2 hours. Rpt of Red [1st Bn. 38th] is that thousands of CCF pouring thru saddle bet 1051 and 914. Serial 40, 1045

1122 CG to 23rd CO: My plane will be at your strip in 10–15 min. Get your whole outfit, less 1 Bn, pack up your Bn and move it up to where Stewart is to meet you. Will move Blue [3rd] Bn into that place. Get your staff cranked up and take command. We have that gap on high ridge. You can att from E and get that. We have got to close gap before tonight. Serial 43, 1122

1202 CG to ADC: Found Coughlin looking halfway over shoulder. Told him not to—take that place to get gap. Told him he could use Dutch. ADC: 2nd Bn, 23rd says he had killed thousands—shooting them with tanks, SA, and everything. CG: Be sure to understand I have assumed resp of taking care of guys that broke thru. Got 2 Cos coming in and think before p.m. will have sit under control. Have you got main breakthrough force in front of you? ADC: Yes. Serial 48, 1202

1250 CG to DG X Corps: Dutch going to jump off 1310 to take gap. Expect to tell you at 1500 line is intact.   Serial at 1250

1633 CG to CG X Corps: Dutch failed to get on Line Departure until 1310, latest rpt on Hill 910 on way to Hill 1051 – not there yet. On E side gap not being filled bec forces so involved to their front and 1000 coming down valley. Fr and tanks c-att.   Serial 75, 1633

1710 CO 38 to C/S 2nd Div: Are you getting en pix way they are pouring through. Just got rept 3000 bet 2 hills again east of 1051. Got it from arty. Air says 20 pack animals up to pass and 500 yds west of it. That means Dutch will never get there.
                                                        Serial 78, 1710

1827 C/S to X Corps C/S: Chinks beginning to come out. Req maximum air bet now and dark.   Serial 83, 1827

1828 CG to Index 6 [CO 9th Inf.]: I can't temporize. 38th is getting clobbered and I don't mean maybe. I feel I should take your 3rd Bn and move it over in re-serve behind 38th. Almond said tomorrow you will be pinched out and revert to me. We have got to have troops. We are taking on about 10 CCF Divs right in front of 38th. Believe should move your 3rd Bn at once – over new rd behind 38th. Index 6: OK will do, and I'll bring my 2nd back before dark.   Serial 84, 1828

2100 X Corps CG to CG: Just got rpt that 3000 + a Bn thru gap and going SW (Then talk about Dutch Bn.). Plan a curtain of fire in gap and valley all night.
                                                        Serial 91, 2100

2130 CO 23 Inf to CG: CCF coming around Fr left flank. Terrific gap bet them and Dutch, 3,000 meter gap. Expect some CCF at MSR by daylight.
                                                        Serial 92, 2130

2230 CG to CG X Corps: Discuss sit. Both decide to put night bombers on app routes and try to break up attack cols until late in night – disrupt their schedule.
                                                        Serial 93, 2230

1930 Impel 6 [CO, 38th Inf., Col. John Coughlin] to CG: Really bad news here now Dutch are refusing to occupy their pos. They have seen so many Chinamen and firing today. They think if our air and arty can't stop them then there's not much they can do. The officers are willing but the men are not and they can't do anything with them. They have come down off their pos. They let 2 Chinese Bns come down the ridge. CG: Best thing to do is tell Eckhout to assemble his unit as close as he can, rpt pos. to you, and not mention or say anything to any-one about this. Use what you can to fill up the gap. Treat the thing as highly secret. All my forces are committed.   Serial 89, 1930[4]

   The Netherlands Detachment's own journal for the day, attached to the 38th Infantry Command Report, states that, at 1 P.M. on the seventeenth, their A and B companies were ordered to attack at 2 P.M. behind a barrage on ridge leading to Hill 1051. But they were in the wrong position to do this. At 2:40 P.M. the companies started for the correct line of departure. At that time Maj. van der Meyde left to go to the companies' commanding officers to make sure the orders were understood – that the attack would be along the ridge east of Hill 1051. At 3:15 P.M. their journal stated that hundreds of CCF were moving through the saddle in a southerly direction. Half an hour later their journal stated, "Att impossible as en is ext from Hill 1051 SE along trail." At 4 P.M. the two companies were reported as being on Hill 975, from which they estimated there were from 3,000 to 4,000 enemy moving west and southeast toward the valley. A and B companies established a defense line between Hills 975 and 790, which came under enemy sniper and mortar fire. The Dutch withdrew from this position at 6:30 P.M. The commanding officer of the Netherland Detachment was at the CP of 1st Battalion, 38th Infantry, at 8 P.M. and decided there that he would take the Dutch Battalion to the rear to get some rest. He started with it at 8:30 and closed in an assembly area in the rear at 10:30 P.M.[5]

The plain fact is that the enlisted men of the Netherlands Detachment refused to attack the gap at Hill 1051 as ordered and actually approached mutiny. This fact was never publicly admitted or discussed in the 2nd Infantry Division command.

During the fighting in the 38th Infantry's sector in the Hill 1051 area on 17 May, the X Corps released to 2nd Division control the part of the 23rd Infantry Regiment that was not in Task Force Zebra, and the 2nd Division at 2:30 P.M. on the seventeenth directed the 23rd Regiment to assume control of all forces assigned to the task force, which Lt. Col. Elbridge L. Brubacker had commanded. The 3rd Battalion moved from its reserve position near Hongchon to the battle area and took its place on the line to the right of the 2nd Battalion, which had been the principal infantry force in Task Force Zebra. The 23rd Regiment closed in the battle area just prior to darkness. The French Battalion, attached to the regiment, had occupied blocking positions south of Chaun-ni and had been fighting enemy infiltrator groups the entire day. The 1st Battalion of the 23rd Infantry occupied reserve blocking positions north and northwest of Yangye.[6]

During the night enemy pressure continued, and the ROK 3rd Battalion, 35th Regiment, on the 2nd Division's right flank withdrew, and an enemy attack after dark against the French Battalion caused it to withdraw more than a mile into a perimeter defense with engineer and tank elements. At 1 A.M., 17 May, General Ruffner of the 2nd Division informed General Almond of X Corps that both ROK divisions, the 5th and the 7th, on the right side of X Corps had broken and were heading south.[7]

The chief of staff, ROK Army, had ordered the ROK III Corps to withdraw from its advanced positions to the No Name line, but it did not initiate that withdrawal until late on the 17th. Because the ROK 5th and 7th divisions had already pulled back on the west side of the ROK III boundary, there was created a 3,000-meter gap along the III Corps left (west) flank. An enemy division poured through this gap to establish a roadblock near Samgam-ni. This development placed a strong enemy force behind the army defense line and also blocked the ROK III Corps's only MSR.

This condition compelled a continued withdrawal in the eastern sector. In the meantime, the ROK 5th and 7th divisions had been under heavy attack, and they began a full retreat southward. This movement resulted in the complete exposure of the right flank of the US 2nd Division and the left flank of the ROK III Corps and put both in danger of enemy envelopment by the fast-moving Chinese division.[8]

During the first 24 hours of the enemy offensive in the 2nd Division sector, the division's artillery battalions fired 30,149 rounds of ammunition into the enemy formations—24,952 rounds from 105-mm howitzers and 5,197 from 155-mm howitzers. It was estimated that this artillery fire alone caused 5,000 enemy casualties.[9]

The situation in the 38th Infantry sector on the night of 16–17 May caused General Ruffner to order the 3rd Battalion, 9th Infantry, from the west flank of the 2nd Division to the center. It marched all night across country behind the line to reach the right flank of the 38th Regiment, where it filled the gap between the 38th and the 23rd regiments west of Yangye. The 2nd Battalion, 9th Infantry, also moved from the west flank to the center, where it secured the high ground due west of Yangye and contacted the 23rd Infantry. The 1st Battalion of the regiment joined the other two battalions in the Yangye area as soon as it was relieved in its position by the 1st Battalion, 1st Marine Regiment. The 9th Infantry, under Col. Edwin Messinger, was now concentrated in the center between the 38th and 23rd regiments. General Van Fleet had ordered a boundary change that moved the 1st Marine Division one regimental space eastward, which in turn moved the 2nd Division the same distance, effective at noon on the eighteenth.[10]

During the night of 17–18 May, the 23rd Regiment's 2nd and 3rd battalions had assembled near Chaun-ni on the 2nd Division's right, north of Yangye. There the 2nd Battalion came under heavy enemy attack. The MSR from Yangye to Chaun-ni was patrolled by tanks until 5 A.M. of the eighteenth, when they hit the first enemy roadblock and mines. Although not known at the time, during the night a division of the CCF 12th Army had moved across the 23rd Regimental sector. And the 181st CCF Division from the CCF 60th Army, moving from west to east, attached to the 12th Army, had reached the west side of the MSR south of Chaun-ni by daylight and was between the 23rd Regiment and the French Battalion farther south near Yangye. At 7:55 A.M. General Ruffner suggested to General Almond that the No Name line be modified on the right (east) to allow the 23rd Infantry to deny the right flank to the enemy who had penetrated the ROK sector. General Almond approved the suggestion and ordered its immediate execution. Colonel Chiles was ordered to move the 23rd Regiment down to Yangye, where he was to establish a perimeter as close as possible to the 2nd Division's right boundary. At 9:30 A.M. the division directed the 23rd Regiment to withdraw to a new defensive position generally east of Yangye. In the meantime its 2nd and 3rd battalions had been under enemy attack from the southwest, west, north, and northeast.[11]

In its withdrawal to Yangye, due south of Chaun-ni about six miles, the MSR followed the west bank of the Hongchon River. In beginning the withdrawal, a platoon of K Company, supported by a platoon of tanks, B Company, 72nd Tank Battalion, led off down the MSR to clear enemy from the road. This team knocked out two enemy machine guns on the east side of the road and inflicted an estimated 300 enemy casualties on the eastern slope. Intense enemy small-arms and automatic fire stopped the advance team.

Behind it came the two-battalion attack south down the MSR. The 2nd Battalion was to clear the high ground on the west side of the road; the 3rd Battalion was to do the same on the east side of the road. On the road between them K Company, with six platoons of tanks and the wheeled vehicles of the two battalions, moved in the protective sleeve as the two battalions cleared the high ground on either side. Movement was slow. On the west the 2nd Battalion led off in the attack with G Company in the lead. It got on the western ridge but came under small-arms and automatic-weapons fire from west and south. Enemy got between G and E companies and the rest of the battalion and penetrated F Company. The 2nd Battalion then ordered E and F companies, followed by G Company, to return to the 2nd Battalion CP, to withdraw through the 3rd Battalion, and to move out on the east side of the MSR. The accurate machine-gun fire and the 76-mm fire from the tanks of C Company, 72nd Medium Tank Battalion, attached to the two battalions, made this withdrawal possible. A platoon of tanks from B Company, 72nd Tank Battalion, near the 3rd Battalion CP, aided the 2nd Battalion movement by firing northwest into the former 2nd Battalion position, where the enemy was trying to cut off the 2nd Battalion from the 3rd Battalion.

The 3rd Battalion began to withdraw, with I and L companies under small-arms and mortar fire, to a defensive position southeast of K Company and its platoon of tanks. The 3rd Battalion headquarters personnel remained in the 3rd Battalion CP area to cover the withdrawal of the 2nd Battalion. This CP area had all the vehicles. The 2nd Battalion made no progress in its efforts to attack south.

It was then decided the road column would try to run the roadblock with the tank escort. One driver was allocated to each vehicle, and all heavy weapons were loaded on the vehicles, but each unit took its light machine guns and 60-mm mortars and what ammunition could be hand-carried. The vehicular column moved off down the road and passed through K Company. It was halted when the two lead tanks struck mines, blocking the road. Also they had broken through a bridge just before hitting the mines. The tanks had prevented enemy at the rear from getting up on the eastern slope and attacking the 2nd and 3rd battalions from there. They kept the slope free of enemy as far as their fire would reach.

Some vehicles tried to bypass the caved-in bridge and the knocked-out tanks, but they were destroyed by enemy fire. The drivers left the wheeled vehicles on the road, and ultimately only one vehicle got out. The tanks fared better, as 32 of 35 of them got out by going into the riverbed to bypass the roadblock.

The men of the two battalions took off across country on the east side of the road, headed south. Those carrying heavy equipment such as mortars, light machine guns, and radios soon became exhausted from their weight, and most abandoned them. The men tried to send wounded on to the front by CTC litter bearers, but enemy fire dispersed the bearers, and they abandoned the wounded.

The enemy roadblock and the two knocked-out tanks that stopped the road column were near the village of Yongnae-ri, about halfway between Chaun-ni and Yangye. From there, those who escaped walked out, and some of the tanks got through. Led by the 2nd Battalion, the units made a wide sweep to the east of the enemy block, the 2nd Battalion reaching Yangye shortly after 10 P.M. The 3rd Battalion followed, and came in there about half an hour later. Each had about 150 casualties.

The first figure on the number of men missing in action for the RCT was 886. But many stragglers came back through enemy lines or were rescued by attacking forces in following days, so that eventually the number of missing in action was reduced to 264. The loss of vehicles was almost total, and the loss of crew-served weapons that were loaded on the abandoned and destroyed vehicles was also very heavy.

The fire of the French Battalion in its position just northwest of Yangye greatly aided the men of the two battalions in reaching Yangye. When the 2nd Battalion men reached Yangye, they were assembled, reorganized, entrucked, and moved to the 23rd RCT CP, closing there at 1:30 A.M., 19 May. The main body of the 3rd Battalion men arrived at the 1st Battalion position at 10:30 P.M. and were reorganized and put in a defensive position.[12] The 23rd RCT logistics section calculated that the 2nd and 3rd battalions lost 102 vehicles in the debacle on the eighteenth, north of Yangye — 72 ¼-ton trucks, 16 ¾-ton trucks, and 14 2½-ton trucks, each having its organic load of kitchen equipment, heavy weapons, communication equipment, or battalion ammunition supplies. Losses included two full platoons of 4.2-inch heavy mortars.[13]

By 5 P.M. the French Battalion was endangered with encirclement north of Yangye, and it withdrew. On 19 May and afterward, the army defense line was south and southeast of Yangye.

In the 23rd RCT's 2nd and 3rd battalions' dilemma between Chaun-ni and Yangye, I Company of the 3rd Battalion held Hill 389 east of the MSR, which enabled most of the men to escape. The 3rd Battalion fought the rear-guard action all the way.[14]

By this time enough enemy prisoners had been taken to permit a construction of the enemy order of battle engaged in the 2nd Impulse attack against the X Corps and the ROK III Corps. The 20th and 27th armies of the CCF IX Army Group had shifted east and were in front of the ROK III Corps on the eastern end of the line, except for the North Korean V and II corps, which were on the extreme east flank. One Chinese division, the 31st, from the CCF 12th Army, was to help these forces effect a deep penetration in the east and destroy the ROK divisions. The III Army Group, comprising the 12th, 15th, and 60th armies, shifted east about 40 miles from the western front to positions in front of the west and central part of X Corps. This force, minus the 31st Division of the 12th Army, had the mission of destroying the US 2nd Division. From west to east the III CCF Army Group was deployed in the order 60th Army, 15th Army, and 12th Army. The 44th and 45th divisions of the 15th Army attacked the 38th Infantry of the 2nd Division ferociously at Hill 1051 on No Name line. The CCF 12th Army attacked the ROK 5th and 7th divisions on the eastern flank of the 2nd Division, where the 31st CCF Division made such great initial gains and demolished those divisions as fighting forces, quickly penetrating deeply to the southeast in the ROK III Corps area. It was this development that caused General Van Fleet, on 17 May, to order the 15th RCT of the US 3rd Division to make a rapid night march in a truck column from the vicinity of Seoul to that sector to confront the victorious 31st Division in the Soksa-ri area, north of Hoengsong. The Chinese had committed five armies of 15 divisions to the 2nd Impulse Offensive, aided by 2 North Korean corps, the V and II, having 6 divisions— a total of 21 divisions. Of this force, 11 divisions attacked the US X Corps.

The rapid retreat and demoralization of the 5th and 7th ROK divisions in the east side of the X Corps, and the immediate exploitation of this breakthrough by Chinese units, caused General Van Fleet to order the US 3rd Division to move quickly to the threatened area in X Corps. The 15th Regiment of the division moved first. At 10:15 P.M. it crossed the initial point at Ichon, south of Seoul, for the dash across the peninsula. It closed near Hoengsong at daybreak the next morning. The 2nd Battalion moved into a blocking position during the day, with orders to attack at dawn on the nineteenth.[15]

On 18 May X Corps commandeered 98 empty 2½-ton trucks at Hoengsong to move the 15th RCT from there to Pungam-ni. The rest of the US 3rd Division started from I Corps to make forced truck movement to an assembly area at Hoengsong on the eighteenth. Trucks were gathered for the movement from every conceivable source. Each corps had to provide 40 trucks, and the 52nd Transportation Truck Battalion was given six hours to provide 200 trucks to move the 3rd Division. Clearance was given at

8 A.M., 18 May, for the movement of 60 tanks and 280 other vehicles to leave Ichon for Wonju; the movement continued through 6 P.M. When the units of the 3rd Division arrived at Wonju, the highway regulating officer, Capt. Jasper N. Erskine, had to notify each unit of its destination and route.[16]

East of the ROK 5th and 7th divisions of the X Corps, the ROK divisions of the ROK III Corps rapidly disintegrated, the ROK 9th Division becoming mixed with the ROK 3rd Division the night of 17 May, with panic resulting. It was reported that Maj. Harold Duke Slater and 13 other KMAG advisors were lost in the debacle of the ROK III Corps. The X Corps reported that more than 300 vehicles and artillery pieces were lost at Hyon-ni.[17] No locations of the ROK III Corps units were known in Eighth Army on 17 May.

Farther east, the North Korean II Corps tried to move south on the coastal road in the ROK I Corps area, but the terrain and US naval gunfire all but stopped it, and it veered west into rugged terrain, following the North Korean V Corps and elements of the CCF 27th Army. In the vicinity of Hajinbu-ri the North Koreans met elements of the US 3rd Division. On 18 May large amounts of ammunition and demolitions were flown to Hoengsong for use of the US 3rd Division.[18]

The remaining elements of the 3rd Division, led by the 64th Tank Battalion, started from Ichon at 4 A.M., 18 May, on the 70-mile run for the X Corps and headed for an assembly area near Hoengsong. The 64th Tank Battalion, however, did not go beyond Wonju, where it refueled, because of the poor condition of the road to Hoengsong. It would not support heavy tank traffic. B Company of the tank battalion was later attached to the 187th Airborne RCT, but the rest of the tank battalion went to Chechon and was not used in X Corps because of the poor roadnet.[19]

Meanwhile on the eighteenth, the ROK III Corps withdrew farther south along the Hyon-ni–Pungam-ni road, with the ROK 9th Division in the lead, followed by the ROK 3rd Division. This withdrawal was orderly until the ROK 9th Division fled south into the hills, abandoning 327 vehicles and their artillery. Stragglers were collected, but on 21–22 May both ROK divisions' CPs were overrun.[20]

At 9 A.M. on 18 May General Almond had a conference with General Soule, 3rd Division commander, on use of the 15th RCT on the X Corps right flank in the Pungam-ni area. A few minutes later General Ruffner called Almond and told him ROK 5th Division men were coming onto his MSR. Almond ordered Ruffner to send them back southeast toward Pungam-ni, as previously ordered, and to assemble for the protection of a critical pass north of the town. He also passed this word on to Colonel Ladue, deputy commander of X Corps, who was trying to round up the disorganized ROK divisions in the east.[21]

On 18 May the North Korean penetration in the east reached the

Kangnung–Soksa-ri lateral road. That day the 15th RCT of the US 3rd Division arrived to go into position on the right of the US 2nd Division where the ROK 5th Division had retreated south from its position. With so much happening on its right flank, the 1st Marine Division held the line firm on the west flank after it took the place of the 9th Infantry, which moved east to help the 38th Infantry. On the eighteenth, the 2nd Division used 122 planes in strikes across its front, many on enemy roadblocks. The ROK 7th Division was still disorganized on the 2nd Division's eastern flank, and 700 of them had fled as far as Chechon, where they were being gathered together and regrouped. Some of the division was reported to be in the ROK III Corps area northwest of Soksa-ri.[22]

Meanwhile in the 2nd Division sector, remnants of the 38th Infantry still held a line along the lower slope of Hill 1051, but they were hard pressed indeed. In the morning of 18 May the regiment reported to the 2nd Division G-3, "We picked up 3 truckloads of stragglers, mostly Dutch and sending them up to join a platoon of tanks to break RB [roadblock] behind the 2nd Battalion, 38th Infantry. 1 man set emergency brake on lead truck and 2 truck loads piled off, 1 truck continued. These people are streaming back again."[23] The rebellious attitude and lack of effort on the part of the Netherlands Battalion seemingly was still in force. The same journal contained a 7:40 entry, which said of the ROK 7th Division, "We don't know where any of our units are. Nothing on your right."

The chief of staff, 2nd Division, told Colonel Coughlin at 1:30 P.M. that both General Ruffner and General Almond wanted him to clear the 38th Infantry out of its present positions and to clear the road before dark. An hour before midnight on 18 May, Colonel Coughlin gave to the 2nd Division G-3 the status of the 1st Battalion, 38th Infantry, that had come off Hill 1051:

A Co.	37 EM	1 Off
B Co.	74 EM	No Off
C Co.	39 EM	No Off
D Co.	68 EM	1 Off
HQ, 1st Bn.	58 EM	5 Off[24]

Before leaving the hill, a machine gunner stayed at his gun firing to his front at attacking Chinese until the gun was tipped over by an enemy from the rear.[25]

The Chief of Staff's Journal, 2nd Division, for 18 May included a message from the division G-3 to Colonel Coughlin at 9:15 A.M. saying that the "white [2nd] Bn is back in the rear and pretty well shot to pieces. Very few officers." The chief of staff also reported to General Almond at X Corps that he had just received an air report that the ROK III Corps had abandoned 327 trucks and artillery pieces and had taken off south. Vehicles backed up on the road. "With your permission would like to put air on them." Almond replied, "That's not in our Corps. You give that to Army. I am not going to destroy them."[26]

At 9:05 A.M., 18 May, General Almond gave General Ruffner orders over the telephone to readjust the 2nd Division line from the position held by Lt. Col. Wallace M. Hanes, 3rd Battalion, 38th Infantry, "due east along the high ground south of the road which crosses road at Yangye. I am sending that combat team [the 15th from 3rd Div.] to Pungam-ni. I want to block this threat around the flank. That will keep the lateral to our rear. I'll have Ladue push the ROKs out on that road."[27]

That day the G-2 of the X Corps summed up his estimation of the Chinese ability to keep their offensive moving. He thought it needed a north-south roadnet to carry resupply forward. Two of them ran through Hong-chon, which they did not possess. The third ran from Inje to Haeba-jae, which he deemed insufficient to carry the quantity needed. Accordingly, he doubted that the enemy could support logistically the resupply needed to hold a deep penetration.[28]

After the 2nd Battalion, 38th Infantry, was able to withdraw to the rear on 18 May, it was learned that its commanding officer, the battalion executive officer, most of the staff, and two company commanders had been killed, wounded, or evacuated.

Beginning at 6 P.M. the 1st Battalion, 38th Infantry, finally withdrew, under cover of fire from elements of seven artillery battalions. The massed artillery fire and fighter-plane cover that was planned would provide a box to cover the 1st Battalion. But a thunderstorm at 6:20 drove all planes back to their bases. The storm lasted all night, but the artillery fire was delivered. Communication with the 1st Battalion was lost, and the battalion filtered back in small groups during the night and in the morning of the nineteenth. On 20 May the 38th Regiment was placed in corps reserve.[29] During its withdrawal during the night of the eighteenth, a violent attack hit I and K companies at 9:20 P.M., with bugles blowing and whistles sounding. Within four minutes 600 rounds of artillery, some of it falling on the battalion position, hit this enemy attack. Such firepower effectively broke up the attack, which lasted less than an hour.

Throughout the day, General Van Fleet had kept in close touch with the situation on the X Corps front. At 8 A.M. he talked with General Almond about it, who was most concerned about the enemy penetration through the ROK 5th and 7th divisions on his right flank. Van Fleet at his 9 A.M. Eighth Army staff briefing emphasized that he wanted the Eighth Army line to hold and fight where it then was. He said,

Roll with the punch concept is out and I have made this point clear to Corps commanders. We move back only to prevent the loss of a major unit, i.e., a battalion. Units will withdraw only on orders from higher HQ. Regiment, division, and corps commanders must be alert to critical situation on battalion level and be quick to take needed action. Only an outpost line may be withdrawn at discretion of its unit commander. We must fight on this line and put a terrific toll on the enemy; here is our opportunity.

He said X Corps wanted the 7th and 65th RCTs of the 3rd Division, but he wanted to know more about the situation on the left before he gave them to it.[30]

Van Fleet visited the X Corps CP in the afternoon and promised to decide that night whether to release the 7th and 65th RCTs of the 3rd Division. Back at his headquarters, Van Fleet held a special briefing at 8:30 P.M. At that time he directed that the US 7th RCT was to move at first light to join the 3rd Division in X Corps and that the Canadian 25th Brigade, then in I Corps, should begin relief of the 65th RCT by noon, 19 May, and that the 65th should start for X Corps as soon as the relief was completed.[31] The Eighth Army collected 170 trucks from I and IX corps and several truck companies and transportation battalions on 19 May to transport the 65th Infantry from Yongdongpo to the X Corps front.[32]

On 19 May General Ridgway flew to Korea and spent two days making the rounds of virtually every corps and division CP. At the 2nd Division that afternoon, he asked for a report on the full details of the Chinese attack on the 23rd Infantry the previous day at Chaun-ni and on the MSR south toward Yangye. At Kangnung on the twentieth he met General Chung, the ROK Army chief of staff; General Coulter; Gen. Paik Sun Yup, the new commander of the ROK I Corps on the east coast; and General Farrell, chief of KMAG. He discussed with them the poor condition of the ROK forces in the east.[33]

The same day, the 15th RCT, US 3rd Division, was in position on the eastern front to attack through the ROK 3rd Regiment, ROK 5th Division, to secure Pungam-ni and the critical hill mass to the north of it. The 1st and 3rd battalions passed through the ROKs at 11 A.M. in attack, attached to the 2nd Division at noon. By 4:45 P.M. the 1st Battalion had the high ground north of Pungam-ni. A few minutes later the 3rd Battalion reported it had seized its objective and was continuing its attack to the northwest. The 2nd Battalion advanced against heavy opposition west of the town but took the high ground there.[34]

Meanwhile, the 7th Infantry RCT departed Seoul at 6 A.M. en route to the X Corps zone and closed at Amidong at 8 P.M. The 1st Battalion took up a blocking area, and the other two battalions went to an assembly area. The next morning the regiment was to attack Soksa-ri. The CCF 31st Division there was completely surprised to find these US troops confronting it, when it had expected nothing more than the past feeble resistance of ROK troops. In the fighting around Soksa-ri on 20 and 21 May, elements of the 65th RCT entered the fight piecemeal as they arrived.[35]

In its action against the enemy in the Soksa-ri area, the 7th Infantry engaged elements of the 93rd Regiment, 31st Division, CCF 12th Army; the 242nd and 243rd regiments of the 81st Division, CCF 27th Army; the NK 12th Division, NK V Corps; and the 14th Regiment, 27th Division, NK II Corps.

On 19 May the ROK III Corps had no control over its units – it did not even know where they were. Later it was learned that the 22nd and 23rd regiments of the ROK 3rd Division were in the ROK 9th Division's sector. The ROK 9th Division strength was reported during the day to be minimal, with the 28th Regiment having 370 men, the 29th Regiment 421, and the 30th Regiment 500. Only the ROK I Corps, Gen. Paik Sun Yup commanding, on the east coast carried out an orderly withdrawal and held the east end of the line with little or no enemy contact.[36]

In its own sector, the 2nd Division continued to have heavy fighting, reporting 38 killed, 165 wounded, and 343 missing in action for the day. During the nineteenth, the 2nd Division was busy withdrawing elements to a new defense line south of Yangye. The 5th Marine Regiment on the left flank of the 2nd Division enabled the 9th Infantry and the 38th Infantry to withdraw through it. The 38th Infantry withdrew to Hoengsong in corps reserve; the 9th Infantry assumed the central position in the division line. But an enemy battalion hit K Company of the 38th Infantry prior to its withdrawal, and only a maximum concentration of artillery support – firing 2,000 rounds in eight minutes – stopped this enemy attack. The enemy attacks decreased at midday and allowed the 23rd Regiment, the French Battalion, and the Netherlands Battalion to withdraw and adjust in the new defense line. The 23rd Infantry line was two miles south of Yangye, protecting a key pass on the Hongchon road.[37]

On 19 May General Van Fleet ordered I and IX corps in the west to make a full-scale advance as a diversion to the enemy in the east. Pressure was to be applied first in the Hwachon Reservoir area, and second in the Iron Triangle area. He shifted the IX-X Corps boundary east to give the western third of the reservoir to IX Corps and for it to capture the roadnet west of the reservoir. He also gave the 7th Infantry Division a separate MSR from that of the 1st Marine Division. On the east of the army line, Van Fleet on 21 May directed General Paik of the ROK I Corps to secure the Kangnung–Soksa-ri lateral road, to hold positions north of the road if at all possible, and at all costs to hold a defense perimeter around Kangnung.

The Chinese 31st Division's penetration between the X Corps and the ROK III Corps boundary on 19 May carried its spearhead to within 20 air miles of Wonju in the Umyang-Noyang area, where the 7th Infantry RCT confronted it on 20 May at Soksa-ri. The critical element in the situation was control of the north-south road where it entered a pass a few miles northwest of Soksa-ri, topping a 5,000-foot range of mountains. This north-south road intersection at Soksa-ri, the only lateral road from the Wonju-Hoengsong area to Yangyang on the east coast, was critical to military operations in the region. Control of the area around the road juncture was vital to any military force operating east or south of it. The mission of the US 3rd Division was to halt the penetration at this point, which is what it accomplished in action there from 21 to 23 May. The 7th Infantry, and less so the 65th RCT when it arrived on the twenty-first, fought a series of battles to wrest control of the pass from the CCF 31st Division and to occupy Soksa-ri. Elements of the NK 12th and 6th divisions moved south to relieve the CCF 31st Division, which shifted over to a withdrawal back north, with the two North Korean divisions acting as its rear guard and a screening force. There was considerable confusion during this process, and both the 31st Division and the North Koreans suffered heavy casualties.[38] The arrival of the US 3rd Division in the X Corps zone, after a 130-mile truck trip behind the front, and its operations in the Soksa-ri area ended the enemy penetration and started the Chinese retreat.

On 19 May the X Corps announced that a large warehouse in Hwachon containing the entire food supply of the CCF 15th Army had been destroyed by air attack and that the army thereby had a reduced ration supply and could not be resupplied. This incident may have affected the length of time the 15th Army could maintain its momentum against the 2nd Division.[39]

Lt. Col. Frederick Weyand, G-3 of the US 3rd Division (previously, commander of the 1st Battalion, 7th Infantry), described a typical battalion attack at the time as being made in a column of companies, a column of platoons within a company, and a column of squads within the lead platoon, so that only a squad was engaged initially at first. He said one was "damn lucky in this terrain if two platoons were in contact with the enemy 2 hours after the 1st squad had made initial contact."[40]

In the 3rd Battalion, 7th Infantry, action at Soksa-ri, the terrain was so rough that wounded had to be evacuated by litter teams led by an American or ROK soldier, using four Korean bearers and requiring a one-and-a-half-hour trip. One problem was the main channel of the Soksa-ri River, between the road and the mountain where the fighting was going on. The stream was waist deep and fast flowing and had large boulders in its bed. Litter jeeps were brought to a point only 50 yards from the base of the mountain. Seriously wounded were loaded two to a jeep; lightly wounded often were loaded seven to a jeep—one in the front seat, four in back, and two on the hood. The jeeps bypassed the battalion aid station and took the wounded to the Advanced Clearing Station. The battalion surgeon, Capt. Gilbert S. Campbell, had given first-aid treatment to the wounded right at the front line, he and his assistants working directly from their first-aid kits.[41]

On 20 May an incident occurred in front of the 1st Battalion, 9th Infantry, which had just completed its movement to the 2nd Division center in an overnight march. Air observers reported 1,500 to 2,000 enemy massing in a valley to its front, apparently unaware that the battalion was present. This concentration was taking place in full view of the 1st Battalion ground observers and within small-arms range. The enemy force proved to be the 100th and 101st regiments of the CCF 34th Division, 12th Army. The 1st Battalion, 9th Infantry, immediately called for fire on the massed enemy by the 15th Field Artillery Battalion, fire by all battalion weapons, and air strikes, in which 76 aircraft ultimately took part. This unexpected action almost completely destroyed this enemy force. There were 800 enemy dead counted in the valley, and 12 mortars and 24 machine guns were recovered.[42]

On this day the 2nd Division held its line near Yangye, with the 3rd and 1st battalions of the 23rd Regiment on its left with the French Battalion, all three battalions of the 9th Infantry on line in the center, and with all three battalions of the 15th RCT (3rd Division) attached on the division right. It had three battalions of artillery behind the 9th Infantry and three battalions behind the 23rd Infantry, and the 503rd Artillery Battalion was expected to add its firepower during the night. The artillery kept firing along the entire front with the increased rate of fire that Van Fleet was urging. That night a US escapee said a CCF battalion assembled 400 yards north of A Company, 9th Infantry, was just commencing to move out in attack formation when night bombers happened to drop their bombs on it, killing hundreds of them; the remaining men turned north in panic flight.[43]

On 20 May X Corps had support from 165 close-support air sorties, the fourth day the number had passed 150, which caused heavy enemy casualties. The 1st Marine Division, on the left of the 2nd Division, caught an enemy regiment and decimated it with 46 sorties. The next day the weather was bad, and the 2nd Division had only 16 sorties, but 21 B-29 bombers at night dropped 200 tons of bombs on massed troops on a road northeast of the 1st Marine Division. There were two US prisoners in the CCF battalion caught in this bomb drop, and a patrol of the 9th Infantry that rescued one of them found 200 to 300 fully armed dead CCF in the area.[44]

General Almond was on his way to the X Corps airstrip to meet Generals Van Fleet and Ridgway when he met them on the road. In the following conference, Almond asked Van Fleet for the 187th Airborne RCT, and the latter ordered Colonel Mudgett, his G-3, to order the 187th RCT to depart immediately for the vicinity of Hoengsong.[45] The 187th RCT went into an assembly area three miles north of Hoengsong the next day, and on the morning of the twenty-second, Almond ordered Brigadier General Bowen to attack north on the Hongchon-Inje road with the RCT to seize the high ground in the vicinity of the Soyang River.

On 21 May the 7th Infantry Regiment of the 3rd Division engaged at least two battalions of the CCF 31st Division at Soksa-ri and seized the town, but the enemy held the vital pass northwest of it. Aerial observers reported large numbers of enemy withdrawing north toward the pass. And elements of the 3rd Division engaged units of the NK II Corps at Hajinbu-ri during the day. By 22 May the NK II Corps was withdrawing north-ward, covering elements of the CCF 27th Army. On the twenty-fourth, the NK II Corps passed through Hyon-ni, leaving its 13th Division be-hind to delay pursuit. It appeared that the CCF offensive peaked on the twentieth and thereafter declined, with an increasing enemy withdrawal northward.[46]

On 20 May General Van Fleet ordered a general army counterattack against the Chinese and North Koreans. Advances were made in I and IX corps in the west, but elsewhere the enemy offensive still was maintained and gains against it were small. There had been a certain amount of action in IX Corps during the CCF offensive in the east. As early as 4 May Task Force Lindy had been formed to give artillery support to the ROK 2nd and 6th divisions of IX Corps, Lt. Col. Leon F. Lavoie commanding it. The task force consisted of the 92nd HQ Battery; its A Battery (155-mm howitzers, self-propelled); two batteries of 105-mm howitzers; the 2nd Bat-talion, 21st Infantry Regiment, 24th Division, for security; A and B com-panies, 194th Engineer Combat Battalion; and A Company, 74th Engi-neer Combat Battalion. On 17 May CCF forces began advancing against the ROK 31st Regiment of the ROK 2nd Division, with the objective of advancing down the Pukhan River. The artillery fire of Task Force Lindy eventually checked the enemy attack, and by 20 May the IX Corps was counterattacking in this sector. In fighting during this period, at least one platoon of the ROK 31st Regiment distinguished itself. The 2nd Platoon, A Company, 31st Regiment, 2nd ROK Division, was cited for extraordi-nary heroism on 16 and 17 May near Chongpyong in hand-to-hand fight-ing and received the Presidential Distinguished Unit Citation.[47]

On 21 May General Van Fleet gave to Lt. Col. Paul Smith, liaison of-ficer from General Ridgway with Eighth Army, for transmission to Ridg-way, his views of the current situation. They included his belief that "the enemy's initial punch on the East and Central East front appears to be shot." He was displeased over the slow progress of I and IX corps in ad-vancing, particularly the slow advances of the US 24th and 7th divisions. He requested the Air Force to concentrate to cut the enemy MSR in the Hwachon Reservoir area and wanted the corps commanders to press to achieve army objectives in the Hwachon area. Also he planned to have X Corps make the main effort on its left, with the 1st Marine Division using the Hongchon-Inje axis, and wanted the IX Corps to make its main ef-fort on its right, with the US 7th Division on the Hongchon-Chunchon-Hwachon axis. "In general, I still believe we should press on all fronts and not give the enemy any chance to regroup. This maximum weight should be directed towards the enemy MSR in Hwachon Reservoir area primarily, and later in the Kumhwa-Chorwon and Pyonggang areas."[48]

General Ruffner talked with the S-3 of the Netherlands Battalion on 20 May and reminded him that two days earlier the battalion had reported 127 men missing in action and the past two days there had been no change in the report. Ruffner said he wanted to know the facts. The Netherlands Battalion S-3 then said, "Some have returned." Later, the battalion S-3 gave to the 2nd Division chief of staff the numbers: on 18 May, 1 killed, 8 wounded, 121 missing in action; on the nineteenth, none killed or wounded, 6 missing in action. The 2nd Division chief of staff then commented to the Dutch S-3, "Then all the MIA have returned except the 6. Is that right?" The response was, "That is right."[49]

The above relates to the rebellious attitude of the enlisted men of the Netherlands Detachment on 18 May. After the chief of staff got the figures from the Netherlands Battalion S-3, General Ruffner called General Almond at X Corps and gave them to him and said, "Time Magazine asked me, 'Is there any truth to the rumor that the Dutch refused to fight?' I told them, not that I know of." Almond asked Ruffner, "Why didn't you tell them a flat 'No' and say nothing more?" The latter responded, "I had to give them some sort of answer."[50]

On the night of 21–22 May the Chinese put the heaviest possible pressure on the 2nd Infantry Division line, beginning about 2 A.M. of the twenty-second and lasting until after daybreak, but they were unable to break through the maze of barbed wire and the minefields in front of it, and the fire of the division weapons, aided by flares that illuminated the front, mowed them down. Four battalions of 105-mm artillery, one battalion of 155-mm artillery, and two battalions of heavy artillery, seven in all, delivered concentrated fire on the attackers and virtually annihilated the enemy forces. After daylight patrols went out more than half a mile in front of the lines and found no enemy. Only a patrol from the 9th Infantry encountered any enemy, and that was on a trail.[51]

On the twenty-second, the 187th Airborne RCT, attached to the 2nd Division at noon, entered the fight in starting up the Hongchon-Inje road, passing through the 23rd Infantry. It captured the high ground on the east and west sides of Yangye. The day before, the 2nd Battalion, 23rd Infantry, had attacked the high ground overlooking the Naechon River following an intense artillery barrage. The enemy stayed in their position despite the barrage, and G Company finally drove out the remaining troops with fixed bayonets. Very few enemy soldiers were seen to leave their positions, and it was estimated that 300 died there.[52] L Company of the 15th RCT was also successful in its attack on Hill 492, killing 140 and capturing 17.

On 21 May three wounded US soldiers came into the 2nd Division lines carrying safe-conduct passes from the enemy. They had just come down the Yangye-Hongchon road. They said the road was lined with "hordes of CCF, all on the sides of the road, each CCF with a shrub or bush." They believed they would advance to the attack that night and suggested that night bombers hit the road that night for a distance of four to five miles.[53]

In the east, all battalions of the 7th Regiment, US 3rd Division, were committed on 21 May in the Soksa-ri area. The 1st Battalion attacked north toward the pass at 7 A.M., and the 3rd Battalion followed it. The 2nd Battalion attacked the village of Soksa-ri and had secured it by 2:20 P.M., as well as high ground north of it. The 7th Infantry, however, did not secure the high pass northwest of Soksa-ri, Hill 1015, until the next day. There was heavy resistance to this attack on the east flank, where the 3rd Battalion carried the fight. The 7th Infantry consolidated its possession of the pass on the twenty-third. On that day the 2nd Battalion, 65th Infantry, relieved the 2nd Battalion, 7th Infantry, at Soksa-ri. On 25 May the 1st and 3rd battalions sent patrols north without enemy contact. On the twenty-sixth, F Company secured Hill 856 after a heavy artillery and mortar preparation. With its mission of turning back the enemy attack in the east at Soksa-ri accomplished, and the enemy everywhere in full retreat, the Eighth Army on 27 May ordered the US 3rd Division to return back west to I Corps. On the twenty-eighth it started for an assigned assembly area near Uijongbu.[54]

While the US 3rd Division was turning back the enemy spearhead in the ROK III zone in the east and then forcing the withdrawal of the Chinese 31st Division and the NK II Corps in that area, the ROK III Corps continued to display ineptness and complete ineffectiveness. On 21 May enemy forces overran both its 9th and 3rd divisions. The ROK III Corps had no control over them.

The senior KMAG advisor to the ROK 9th Division reported through the US 3rd Division that the ROK 9th Division was attacked by an unknown number of enemy at 8 P.M. on 21 May, dispersing the entire division. Its CP at Hajinbu-ri was also attacked by an estimated 300 enemy, and its commanding general, the chief of staff, the G-1, and the G-3 were as a result missing in action. The ROK 3rd Division CP was also overrun, with the commanding general believed killed or a prisoner. Its 18th and 19th regiments were believed to be surrounded. This information came in a roundabout way to Eighth Army through the ROK 3rd Division KMAG senior advisor through the Capital Division and hence through the ROK I Corps. On 23 May Eighth Army reported the ROK 3rd Division had 3,910 missing in action and the ROK 9th Division had 7,121 missing in action.[55] On the twenty-second, General Van Fleet ordered the chief of staff, ROK Army, to inactivate the ROK III Corps and attach its 9th Division to the X Corps and to give the 3rd Division to the ROK I Corps

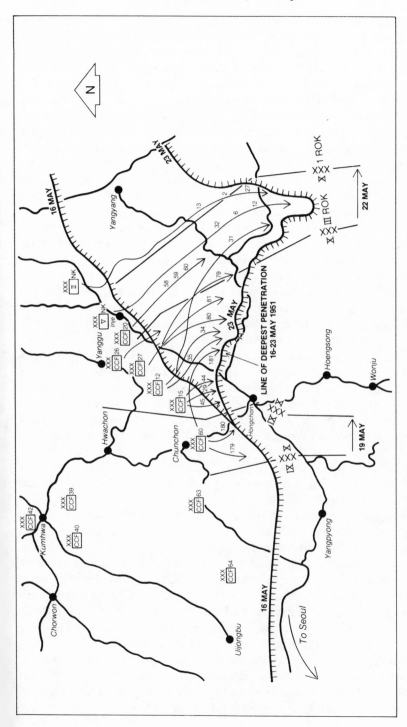

MAP 23. **CCF 5th Phase Offensive, 2nd Impulse, 16–23 May 1951 (boundary for X Corps moved twice)**

on the coast. This order gave most of the former ROK III Corps zone of responsibility to General Almond's X Corps.[56]

CCF prisoners told much about food shortages in the CCF forces and about the prevalence of dysentery. One prisoner said that 50 percent of his unit had it. After 22 April the combat ration had changed from a combination of baked cakes and rice to a less nutritious diet of ground meal. It and its container were sensitive to moisture, and the meal fermented or became moldy if exposed to moisture—rain, dew, humidity, or perspiration. Many men were sick from eating it. To compensate for vitamin deficiency, many soldiers ate grass, which contributed to dysentery and other intestinal disorders.[57] By 21 May the soldiers in the 2nd Impulse of the offensive had consumed the rations they had been given on or about 10 May to last for the duration of the offensive.

As late as 6 P.M., 21 May, aerial observers noticed large numbers of enemy troops moving south from Hwachon. The next day the UN counterattack began to make progress, and for the first time aerial observers saw several large groups of enemy moving north. But the enemy still made several local attacks on the twenty-second, and there was close contact along most of the front. The 2nd Division's determined defense of its position on 20 May had stopped the CCF 12th and 15th armies in their tracks. This result, followed by limited local counterattacks by the US 2nd and 3rd divisions the next day and the violent attack by the 187th Airborne RCT astride the Hongchon-Inje road, undoubtedly contributed to the CCF decision to call an end to their offensive and to withdraw. On 23 May there was a noticeable northward trend in the enemy's movements in rear areas, and withdrawal seemed to be in effect clear across the front.

In the counterattack already under way in the IX and I corps areas in the west, Pfc. Joseph C. Rodriguez of F Company, 17th Infantry, 7th Division, IX Corps, engaged on 21 May in heroic action that won him the Medal of Honor.[58]

Much has been said and written about the "Van Fleet rate of artillery fire" during the 2nd Impulse of the Chinese 5th Phase Offensive. Generally it meant that he wanted five times as much artillery fire as was considered normal in Korean combat up to that time. Prior to his leading Eighth Army, a normal daily rate was 50 rounds for 105-mm howitzers, 35 rounds for 155-mm howitzers, 25 rounds for 155-mm guns, and 30 rounds for 8-inch howitzers. When the Chinese 5th Phase Offensive started, Eighth Army had in forward ASPs a ten-day supply. But in terms of the Van Fleet rate of fire, that was equivalent to only a two-day supply.

On 17 May General Van Fleet authorized artillery ammunition expenditure at the daily rate shown in table 20, henceforth known as the Van Fleet rate of fire. Between 18 and 22 May the artillery battalions were trying to fire the Van Fleet rate of fire, each gun 250 rounds per day. The

TABLE 20. **The Van Fleet Rate of Fire**

Weapon	Daily Rate of Fire	Total Daily for Eighth Army
105-mm howitzer	250	43,750
155-mm howitzer	175	15,575
155-mm gun	250	3,000
8-inch gun	250	2,000

Source: Eighth Army, Comd. Rpt., G-4 Sec., May 51, Box 1198; X Corps, Comd. Rpt., 17 May 51, Box 2012.

peak was reached in X Corps on 19 May, at 49,785 rounds, and on 22 May, at 49,986 rounds.[59]

ASP 50 at Hongchon could not handle the tremendous demand, which required trucks to go to the railhead at Wonju, a day's trip, to get their loads. Heavy ammunition and hand grenades were flown into the K-46 airstrip south of Hoengsong, reducing the round trip for trucks by six hours. During the entire offensive the 2nd Magazine Platoon, 69th Ordnance Ammunition Company, remained in position at Hongchon ASP 50, even though most service units moved farther south. At one time enemy were only eight miles away, and an infantry company was assigned to guard it. ASP 50 supplied all the ammunition for the artillery battalions supporting the 2nd Division. During the seven days of the heaviest fighting, 16–22 May, the platoon loaded out 2,896 rounds of 8-inch howitzer, 4,396 rounds of 155-mm gun, 47,008 rounds of 155-mm howitzer, and 150,240 rounds of 105-mm howitzer—a total of 8,139.92 tons of ammunition. On or about 20 May, the platoon, with the help of 125 Korean laborers, loaded or unloaded 540 trucks in an eight-hour period between 8 P.M. and 4 A.M. the next morning. Each truck carried a load of approximately four tons.[60]

The Van Fleet rate of fire was never achieved during the 5th Phase Offensive for all guns at any one time, but some batteries burned up their gun barrels in trying. But the volume of fire was several times what it had ever been before in the Korean War. The curtain of steel laid down at some designated targets in front of the US 2nd Division was more than human flesh could bear. Many Chinese prisoners bore testimony to the great destruction it wrought in their ranks, in some cases canceling out entirely enemy attacks ready to jump off. The round-the-clock use of all 2½-ton trucks that could be found to deliver the ammunition from the ASPs or the railhead to the firing batteries soon took its toll of the number that continued operable. And there was a shortage of drivers, many of whom worked 18-hour shifts.

Expenditures of artillery ammunition in the seven days 17 May to 23 May by 21 artillery battalions supporting the X Corps, including four Marine and two ROK batteries, was stated to be 309,958 rounds, or more than

8,730 tons. This amount could be compared to the 94,230 rounds that 35 battalions fired in support of the Third Army's attack toward Bastogne of 22–31 December 1944, or to the 10,000 tons fired in ten days by the XX Corps in the assault on Metz in 1944.[61]

In the summer of 1951, the author was discussing the Van Fleet rate of fire with Col. Robert Halleck, commanding officer of the 24th Division Artillery. Halleck was a salty, outspoken officer. He recounted a story about a recent visit from General Van Fleet in which the latter asked him how much artillery had been fired. Halleck responded that he thought it was a lot. Van Fleet answered, "Chicken feed – shoot more."

By 22 May the Chinese offensive on a 20-mile front north of Yangye in the US 2nd Division sector had pushed the UN line south about 12 miles. In the severe fighting there during this period, combat elements equivalent to three enemy divisions were destroyed, and the remaining elements of the enemy there were then counterattacked and forced back 18 miles to the 38th Parallel. By 28 May, trapped enemy units were attempting to escape past the west end of the Hwachon Reservoir.

East of the vortex of the enemy offensive that swirled around the US 2nd Division, three enemy divisions attacked ROK forces on a 12-mile front from Inje to near the coast. Here the enemy scored repeated deep penetrations of the UN line, in a forward thrust that carried them 30 miles southward. But by 22 May the situation was stablized there in the vicinity of Changdong and Hajinbu-ri. The failure of the enemy offensive against the US 2nd Division just to the west of this deep penetration made this successful salient vulnerable. The appearance of the US 3rd Division there at this critical moment turned the enemy spearheads around and in the following counterattack drove them back to the 38th Parallel. Before the enemy was able to stop this counterattack, the UN line had been reestablished to run from west to east from Musan on the Imjin River to Chongdong, hence just south of Chorwon and the Iron Triangle, through Hwachon to Inje, southeast to Sori, and hence northeast to Yongchon.

Some of the more pertinent actions of this counterattack should be noted briefly. The counterattack north from Yangye to the Soyang River bridgehead site, and hence northeast to Inje, is perhaps the most important. The idea of a major counterattack in this area seems to have originated with Lt. Gen. Edward M. Almond, commander of X Corps. After the CCF and NK had penetrated far south in the eastern zone and the situation there was considered critical, both General Ridgway and General Van Fleet in a conference with General Almond asked the latter his views of what should be done. Almond asked for the US 3rd Division to be moved from the west and added to his corps, for the 187th Airborne RCT also to be attached to X Corps, and for him to be allowed to attack northeast in the direction of Inje to sever the enemy line of communication to the salient they had established. He said the idea for this maneuver came from General Foch's attack from Soissons across country and across the German line of communication in their effort to cross the Rhine and capture Paris in World War I. The Germans had pushed a large salient to the front of their line. This resulted in the Second Battle of the Marne, in which the German salient was cut off. Almond's recommendations were adopted, and when the 187th RCT was in place, he used it as a special task force to make the strike, to be followed by the 2nd Division.[62]

On 22 May the 187th Airborne RCT relieved the 23rd Infantry Regiment near Yangye and moved into attack against the Chinese there, taking its objectives during that and the next day. On the twenty-fourth, Almond ordered a special task force formed for a fast movement north toward the Soyang River, passing through enemy territory.

Also on 22 May the ROK Army announced the outcome of its investigation of the unwarranted withdrawal of the ROK 6th Division on the night of 16–17 May at the outset of the CCF 5th Phase Offensive. Six officers of the division, including a regimental commander, were court-martialed and sentenced to from 2 to 15 years of hard labor, and the other two regimental commanders were reprimanded and forfeited pay for two months.[63]

On the twenty-second the attacking 32nd Regiment, ROK 2nd Division, IX Corps, reached the Hwachon Dam, but elements that went to the north side were forced back to the south side for the night. At the same time, the 32nd Infantry of the US 7th Division sent a strong tank-infantry patrol into Chunchon. That day also the 38th Regiment returned to the front line after only a day or two out of it, taking position on the 2nd Division's right flank in relief of the 15th RCT of the 3rd Division.

The 2nd Division moved out in attack on 23 May, immediately after six days of enemy offensive. This was the first time in the Korean War that the UN forces had been able to resume the offensive so quickly after a major enemy attack. The 1st Battalion, 9th Infantry, led off in the center of the line; the other regiments followed. They received fire from the Chinese after crossing the lateral east-west road from Yangye to Tappang-ni. The 2nd Battalion, 9th Infantry, tied in on its left with the 187th Airborne RCT.[64]

In the east, the 1st Battalion, 7th Infantry, US 3rd Division, drove the Chinese from the vital pass northwest of Soksa-ri. It had to be supplied by airdrop during the day, since it was completely isolated.[65]

During the day, General Van Fleet visited the ROK I Corps headquarters and met the ROK Army chief of staff there. He told him that the ROK I Corps henceforth would be directly under command of Eighth Army and no longer under him. Van Fleet expressed confidence in Maj. Gen. Paik Sun Yup and told him to gain contact with the X Corps and that he must hold his own, as the UN command could not spare a US division to help him if his front collapsed.[66]

A Marine unit on its way to the central front marches along a dusty road, 28 May 1951. *US Marine photograph, A 8756*

In a conversation with General Soule of the US 3rd Division at the latter's CP in the afternoon, Van Fleet said he was considering using the 1st Cavalry Division on his right flank if the situation became desperate. This remark shows that General Van Fleet was by no means sure on the afternoon of 23 May that the tide had turned.[67]

At 9 A.M. on 24 May General Almond ordered the 2nd Infantry Division to form a task force to drive from the vicinity of Yangye to the Soyang River to seize the bridgehead there. The 1st Marine Division was to follow and exploit the area to the north and northwest of the task force's route (the main road north from Yangye to Chaun-ni and hence to Umyang-ni on the Soyang River and from there east to Inje), and the 23rd Infantry Regiment was to follow and exploit the area toward Inje. Col. William Gerhardt, executive officer of the 187th Airborne RCT, commanded this task force and gave it his name. The 2nd Division commander had named

Brigadier General Bowen as its commander, but he had delegated command to Colonel Gerhardt. The task force was formed at 1 P.M. at Yangye and consisted of the following units:

> 2nd Battalion, 187th Airborne RCT
> Reconnaissance Platoon, 187th Airborne RCT
> B Company, 72nd Tank Battalion (−)
> B Company, 64th Tank Battalion
> Four sections, 82nd AAA Bn
> A Company, 127th Engineer Battalion
> C Battery, 674th Airborne Field Artillery Battalion

Lt. Col. Elbridge Brubacker, commanding officer, 72nd Tank Battalion, commanded the tank contingent.[68]

There was a lack of initiative in the 187th Airborne RCT in organizing the task force, and there was confusion and delay in getting it completed and started on its mission. The 3rd Platoon, B Company, 72nd Tank Battalion, the task force's point, did not pass through the Marine outpost position until 2 P.M. and then halted while engineers probed the road for mines. A helicopter landed, and out stepped General Almond, who wanted to know what caused the slowdown. Maj. Charles A. Newman, executive officer of the 72nd Tank Battalion, said minesweepers were out and they were trying to establish communication between the tanks and the I&R Platoon. Almond blew up. He said, "I don't give a G—— damn about communications. Get those tanks on the road and keep going until you hit a mine. I want you to keep going at 20 miles an hour." Newman ordered the tanks to move and hit fifth gear (22 miles an hour). Almond then asked Maj. James H. Spann, S-3, 72nd Tank Battalion, who commanded the tanks. Spann said Brubacker did. Brubacker was not present. Almond told Spann to tell him to "get that G——d tank column moving whether they had infantry support or no." The road was full of other vehicles, and it was difficult to clear it for the movement of the tanks.

After passing Chaun-ni, the tank column began to run into enemy groups. Small groups it ignored, but other, larger groups it fired at and killed many of the surprised and confused enemy retreating groups. At one point a liaison plane dropped a message saying that a mile north there were 4,000 enemy and that jet aircraft were on their way to deliver a napalm strike. Lieutenant Gardner said to Major Newman, "What are we going to do now?" Newman replied, "We're going to attack the Chinese; we'll run into General Almond if we turn back." The jets arrived at 4 P.M. and dropped their napalm loads and then began to strafe the front of the enemy column. The Chinese scattered and fled to the northwest. The tanks reached the Soyang River about 6 P.M., and the rest of the task force soon arrived.[69]

General Almond came up to Task Force Gerhardt soon after it reached the Soyang River bridgehead. The tanks were just sitting there when they were supposed to be driving up the road toward Inje. Almond was upset about this, and Lieutenant Colonel Brubacker, the tank commander, again was not present. Almond summarily removed him from his command. Almond found Calvin S. Hannum, 72nd Tank Battalion, whose B Company was in the tank group. He put him in charge of the tank contingent and told him to get going toward Inje. Hannum took charge of the tank column, with infantry from the 2nd Battalion, 187th Airborne, riding on the tanks. After crossing the river, the road ran along the northern bank eastward toward Inje. Just beyond Inje pass the column ran into enemy in prepared positions. These had been built between 1945 and 1950 by North Koreans as defense positions along the 38th Parallel. Enemy rocket launchers knocked out three or four of the tanks, and enemy fire inflicted about 100 casualties on the infantry riding the tanks in a very short time. The column turned back.[70]

Meanwhile, to the west the 7th Infantry Division had the 32nd Regiment organize Task Force Hazel to force an entry into Chunchon. The task force comprised the 7th Reconnaissance Company, a platoon of the 32nd Tank Company, and a squad of the 13th Engineer Battalion. It met fleeing enemy groups all along the way and had several encounters with enemy small-arms fire, which was not able to stop it. It arrived at Chunchon at 5:05 P.M. and found 75 to 100 Chinese in the town. It rescued 19 Americans who had been held captive since the previous December, all but one of them Marines captured at Koto-ri near the Chosin Reservoir. A press account said there were 18 Marines and 1 Army man. When tanks of the task force surprised the Chinese at Chunchon, they ran off and left the POWs behind.[71]

Aerial observers over Chunchon and Task Force Hazel reported enemy groups in many places near the town. Many groups were fleeing in confusion. At 8 P.M. Task Force Hazel was ordered to return, and on a part of its return it had to run a gauntlet of heavy enemy fire.[72]

General Ferenbaugh of the 7th Division had a close call on 24 May. He passed through the 1st Battalion, 32nd Infantry, on his way to Chunchon. His party of two jeeps was ambushed, and two MPs in the front jeep were killed and another wounded. General Ferenbaugh and his aide, Captain Chandler, escaped from their jeep and hid in some dense foliage. Sgt. Lawrence O'Brien, in an M-20 armored car and on his way to join Task Force Hazel, discovered the two abandoned jeeps and notified the 1st Battalion. The battalion commander sent Lieutenant Stanaway with a tank platoon from the 32nd Tank Company to rescue the ambushed party. Stanaway had to go through intense small-arms fire to reach them, arriving at the scene at 9 P.M. Tank fire subdued enemy small-arms fire sufficiently to enable the tank platoon to rescue General Ferenbaugh and his aide, and also to pick up the wounded MP and Sergeant O'Brien and then return to the 1st Battalion without further incident.[73]

The X Corps lost an outstanding officer, Col. L. K. Ladue, deputy commander of X Corps, on the twenty-fourth. During the Chinese 5th Phase Offensive he had been tireless in trying to help hold the ROK forces together in the east, where the enemy penetrations had been deepest. He died in his sleep in his van of a heart attack the night of 23–24 May.

On the twenty-fourth Task Force Able took over the mission of Task Force Yoke, which had been the capture of Haeba-jae, to the east of the 2nd Division. Haeba-jae was an important road center on the main lateral road to the east coast, which had fallen to the enemy. Lt. Col. T. R. Yancey commanded the task force, which consisted of the 15th Infantry, minus; C Company, 72nd Tank Battalion; C Battery, 300th Field Artillery Battalion; and the 1st Battalion, 23rd Infantry. It had a four-hour foot march to reach its line of departure. The task force succeeded in entering Haeba-jae at 6 P.M., but the town was not secured until the following morning.[74]

On 24 May Eighth Army gave X Corps another mission, after it had seized Inje. It was to continue the advance attack northeast across the front of the ROK I Corps to Kansong on the east coast in an effort to trap and destroy elements of the NK II, III, and V corps, as well as elements of the CCF 12th, 20th, and 27th armies, all south of the Hongchon-Kansong road. The X Corps boundary was changed accordingly to run northeast to the east coast four miles north of Chosan-ni, and X Corps was to coordinate its actions with the ROK I Corps. This new and ambitious mission led to the formation of Task Force Baker the next day to carry it out.[75]

Task Force Baker was formed on the morning of 25 May in the vicinity of Umyang-ni, near the bridgehead site across the Soyang River. Brigadier General Bowen, of the 187th Airborne RCT, commanded it. In addition to the 187th Airborne RCT, it consisted of an attached tank battalion, a company of combat engineers, a battalion of armored field artillery, a naval gunfire team, two transportation truck companies, and a signal detachment– a powerful task force, under the command of X Corps.

Before following the action of Task Force Baker to Inje from the Soyang River bridgehead at Umyang-ni on the south bank and Kwandae-ri on the north bank, it will be necessary to get the 187th Airborne RCT to the river from Yangye. Only Task Force Gerhardt had reached the river on the twenty-fourth. That night 20 of its vehicles, with an officer and 22 enlisted men, returning to Yangye, were ambushed and destroyed. Two men got through to the 187th Airborne RCT and reported the situation and the fact that Task Force Gerhardt was running low on ammunition.

It was decided that it would be necessary to clear the high ground along the road before the 187th Airborne RCT would link up with Task Force Gerhardt. The 23rd Infantry, with all three battalions abreast, attacked the roadblock on 25 May, reinforced by the French Battalion and a company of tanks. But the 106th Regiment, CCF 34th Division, 12th Army, had been placed across the road to deny it to UN forces while cutoff elements to the south and east escaped across it. The assignment was a suicidal one, but it was well executed. The enemy 106th Regiment denied the road to the 23rd Infantry and the Marine Division for 24 hours while Chinese streamed across it north of the roadblock and escaped toward Hwachon. The enemy regiment succeeded in fighting off all three battalions of the 23rd Infantry all day. Only a platoon of tanks broke through in the afternoon and reached the Soyang River. The 7th Marine Regiment on the left of the 23rd Infantry was also held to only slight gains. Joining in the attack on the enemy roadblock during the day were 85 Marine aircraft.[76]

The next day, 26 May, enemy resistance disappeared in the morning, and the 23rd Infantry had cleared the road and the hills alongside it by noon. The 187th Airborne RCT command group started for the Soyang River at 12:45 P.M. and arrived there at 3 P.M. Upon arriving there, it learned that its 2nd Battalion with Task Force Gerhardt had probed four miles ahead and was in contact with an estimated 3,000 enemy dug in on high ground on the north side of the Soyang.

It was 27 May before Task Force Baker really got started on its way to Inje from the Soyang River bridgehead. The 187th Airborne RCT crossed the river, and its 3rd Battalion screened the hills on the left and the 2nd Battalion those on the right. At 10 A.M. resistance was so great that the 1st Battalion joined the 3rd Battalion. Its A Company attacked and secured Hill 490. C Company passed through K Company and attacked Hill 592. B Company crossed the river flats in front of Inje and secured the town, then went on to the high ground on the approaches to Inje from the north. C Company took its objective in a bayonet attack, after which it was ordered back to Inje. One platoon stayed on Hill 592 until it was relieved by elements of the 23rd Infantry at 10 P.M.[77]

On 26 May and thereafter no organized CCF units were encountered by X Corps units as they advanced toward Yanggu and Inje. Only stragglers and wounded CCF were captured. The North Korean II and V corps had taken over responsibility for the zone and were covering the retreating CCF organizations. The latter withdrew north through the Inje area, passing to the east and then north of the Hwachon Reservoir to rejoin parent organizations by a long and circuitous route. The NK V Corps had managed to slip through Inje prior to the arrival of the 187th Airborne RCT and formed a delaying line with two divisions abreast, opposing the 1st Marine Division when it tried to advance toward Yanggu. The NK II Corps made persistent attempts to recapture Inje on 30 and 31 May and opposed Task Force Baker in its attempt to drive east from Inje toward the coast.

On 27 May, the same day that the 187th Airborne of Task Force Baker seized Inje, the 17th Infantry Regiment of the 7th Division captured Hwachon, five miles from the western end of the reservoir, and cut the escape route around the west end of the reservoir toward the Iron Triangle area.

On that day and the next UN forces captured more than 6,000 Chinese in this area.[78]

After its capture of Inje and the high ground to the north of the town on the twenty-seventh, Task Force Baker attempted a rapid advance eastward the next day along the Inje-Kansong road. Kansong and the east coast was 52 miles away. But the way was blocked by elements of the NK II Corps, who fought bitterly for every foot of ground. On 28 May the task force had 18 men killed, 104 wounded, for a total of 122 casualties. The next day it had 10 killed and 69 wounded. The reason for a rapid advance to Kansong to cut off the enemy caught south of the Inje-Kansong road no longer existed, as they had escaped the trap and now were north of the road and in full retreat, covered by the NK V and II corps. So Task Force Baker never accomplished its purpose.[79] The ROK I Corps on the east coast was given the mission of holding the high ground north of the road.

The 3rd Battalion of the 23rd Infantry, in the regimental attack north from Yangye, had with it the Treadway bridge units for bridging the Soyang River. The 23rd Infantry and the French Battalion reached the bridge site at 10:30 A.M. 26 May, and the Treadway bridge across the Soyang, the longest in Korea, was completed at 5 P.M. It was named the Ladue Bridge, in honor of Colonel Ladue.[80]

Task Force Hazel, 7th Infantry Division, returned to Chunchon on 25 May, after its initial entry on the twenty-fourth. It found many enemy soldiers trying to escape from the valley to the northwest, ambushed them in the low ground, and overran their positions on higher ground. Some tank crew members fired through escape hatches to kill enemy in trenches underneath tanks. On the twenty-sixth, the 32nd Infantry secured Chunchon, capturing five ammunition dumps and ten 57-mm recoilless rifles. Meanwhile, on Hills 565 and 453 the 1st and 3rd battalions, 17th Infantry, attacked enemy dug-in positions. Two platoons of tanks went north on the Hwachon road and reached positions from which they could fire on the reverse slopes of Hill 565, and this fire caused the enemy to flee in confusion. Captured POWs indicated these enemy troops were from the 2nd and 3rd battalions, 537th Regiment, 179th Division, CCF 60th Army. POW reports stated that elements of the 12th and 15th CCF armies had been trying to move toward Hwachon by all trails and routes for the past three days and nights. The 17th RCT continued the attack north from Chunchon, crossed the 38th Parallel for the third time, and took the high ground overlooking the Chunchon-Hwachon road.[81]

On 25 May more than 10,000 enemy tried to move north in the Chunchon-Hwachon area. Mostly they used the main road, but all east-west trails emptying into this road were also used. Air strikes and artillery fire were directed on them. There was a frantic move of enemy from the X Corps area west into the IX Corps area. Air observers from the 7th Division reported enemy on every trail and road leading north—5,000 to 10,000 men, 500 horses, 25 artillery pieces, 50 trucks on the main road between Chunchon and Hwachon. Destroyed vehicles on the road hindered the enemy retreat. Similar conditions were reported in the vicinity of Naepyong-ni. The main enemy withdrawal route was via the road south of the Hwachon Reservoir. There were poor roads and bad terrain east and north of the reservoir. Since the three NK corps had to use these roads, the CCF turned to the northwest.[82]

At noon 25 May the enemy abandoned the practice of night movement only, and 10,000 to 12,000 enemy soldiers with vehicles appeared on roads and trails south of the Hwachon Reservoir moving northwest toward the town of Hwachon. Entire fighter groups turned their efforts on these targets and kept after them until dark. They estimated 2,000 men and 100 vehicles were destroyed. The next day the mass movement continued, and many enemy escaped via Hwachon before the ROK 6th Division could move to the right of the 7th Division to block off the route between the reservoir dam and the town. By the twenty-eighth this route was blocked. As the 7th Division approached Hwachon, Chinese counterattacked. The enemy continued to oppose the 7th Division at Hwachon the rest of the month, and the latter made only limited gains there.[83]

West of the 7th Division in IX Corps, the US 24th Division virtually destroyed the CCF 180th Division, 60th CCF Army, at this time. This division was trapped between the 24th Division and the 7th Division and acted in a very confused manner. In the period 25–31 May the 24th Division captured 3,305 Chinese prisoners, 3,098 of them from the 180th Division. Another reference in the division records places the number of prisoners from the 180th Division at 3,295. The 19th Regiment, which captured half of them, noted a marked tendency of bypassed enemy to surrender.[84]

The counterattack in the west was beginning to have an effect in moving the relatively quiescent enemy units there back north. On 25 May the 1st Cavalry Division moved to positions eight miles north of Uijongbu, and on the thirtieth the division CP had moved all the way north to the vicinity of Tongduchon-ni. On 26–28 May the enemy had retreated across the Imjin River. But at these points the enemy again resisted further advances.[85]

Reports began to multiply as I Corps moved back north that the minefields placed along Line Golden were very dangerous affairs. Most of them had been laid by careless crews with little training, and they had kept scanty and confusing records about their locations. They were now killing UN troops, who did not know where they were.[86]

On 26 May the enemy retreat continued in full swing from the east to the west and northwest. General Ruffner, 2nd Division commander, radioed a message to de Shazo, 2nd Division Artillery commander, while flying over the Hyon-ni to Inje road, "I just saw a million Chinamen on the road to Inje. They were on the road thicker than flies. Your arty is registered

Men of the 2nd Battalion, 7th Regiment, 3rd Division, crossing a burned bridge after driving the enemy from their positions on the east central front, 28 May 1951. *US Army photograph, FEC 17360*

and firing on them now. . . . Your spotter had them firing right on the button."[87] A large enemy column was reported on the road north of Inje with lots of equipment and vehicles, and two groups of planes were reported as being on their way to deliver strikes on it.

X Corps issued the order for Operation Chopper on 26 May. It was a bold plan to have the 1st Marine Division seize Yanggu, the US 2nd Division secure the Hyon-ni–Inje road, and Task Force Baker strike northeast from Inje to the coast to intercept and destroy enemy trying to escape to the north. This plan was slow in execution, apparently because some commanding officers were hesitant about entering boldly into the exploitation and pursuit phase of the counterattack.[88]

General Almond was disappointed in the execution of his plan for pursuit and exploitation of the counterattack. He met General Bowen of the 187th Airborne RCT and General Thomas, commander of the 1st Marine Division, at the Soyang River bridgehead at 10:50 A.M. on the twenty-sixth. He instructed Bowen to move immediately on Inje and to plan on using it as a future base of operations to drive to the coast as soon as the 23rd RCT, 2nd Division, had secured the high ground north of Inje. General Thomas wanted to move the 5th and 7th Marines from the high ground west of the bridgehead as soon as the enemy cleared from it and then send the 1st Marines to Yanggu. Almond ordered him to start the 5th and 7th Marines immediately for Yanggu and not to wait further on the high ground west of the bridgehead.[89]

On 27 May the 38th Infantry Regiment, with the Netherlands Battalion attached, continued its drive on Hyon-ni. The 1st Battalion took Hill 558, west of the town, and the Dutch Battalion took the hill east of the town. Tanks went into the town at the same time and surprised a large force of enemy there, which was trying to flee from it. As they passed along the road at the foot of Hill 558, A Company of the 38th fired on them from the slopes of the hill, killing hundreds and wounding an estimated 300 more. The 38th Regiment took 156 prisoners during the day. At 5:50 P.M. the 38th Infantry informed the G-3, 2nd Division that it had taken Hyon-ni and the high ground east and west of it.[90] The next day the 38th Infantry reached Inje.

During the day an agent captured on 23 May at Kumhwa, who later escaped, traveled the road from there to Hwachon, where he regained UN lines on the twenty-seventh. He reported seeing 20,000 enemy on the high ground around Kumhwa and in valleys and villages. On the road to Hwachon he said he passed 30,000 CCF moving northwest, and he overheard two lieutenants talking about plans to defend Kumhwa with 50,000 troops if the UN succeeded in reaching the town.[91]

The 5th RCT, 24th Division, working with the ROK 19th Regiment, 6th Division, surrounded an enemy regiment on 27 May and captured 2,000 prisoners, with an unknown number killed or wounded. Similarly, an enemy regiment was surrounded during the day northwest of Chunchon and most of its members taken prisoner.

On 25 May the 23rd RCT captured a prisoner from the Headquarters, CCF 35th Division, 12th Army, who said the 12th Army had withdrawn north on 23 May, leaving behind the 106th Regiment, 34th Division, to cover its withdrawal (the regiment that blocked the Yangye–Umhung-ni road to the Soyang River on 25 May). The prisoner said the 105th Regiment of the 35th Division had lost all but 100 men, the 103rd Regiment had 33 percent casualties, and the 104th Regiment had 50 percent casualties. The 106th Regiment that covered the withdrawal had been virtually annihilated, and the other two regiments of the 34th Division had been so crippled as to be not combat effective.[92]

Enemy reaction was strong in opposing the 7th Division attack on Hwachon on 27 May. Tanks entered Hwachon at 1 P.M. and 2 P.M., and infantry of the 17th Regiment flanked the town and engaged enemy a mile and a half west of it. The 2nd and 3rd battalions, 17th Infantry, took Hills 389 and 348 after hard fights. On the twenty-eighth, enemy counterattacked at Hwachon in an effort to keep the route open, and 100 enemy soldiers actually reentered the town from the northwest. An enemy battalion regained Hill 313 only half a mile north of Hwachon, and air strikes and artillery barrages were needed to regain the hill about dusk.[93] There was no easy advance beyond Hwachon, ten miles north of the parallel, from the twenty-seventh on through the remainder of the month. General Hoge of the IX Corps reported to General Van Fleet on 27 May that elements of the 7th Division entered Hwachon at 2 P.M. but that the enemy was resisting there and along the withdrawal route skirting the south and west edges of the reservoir.[94]

On 28 May the 31st and 32nd regiments arrived at Hwachon, and the 7th Division consolidated its positions there. The G-4 had to ask all units to help bury the enemy dead and animals that littered the road in the vicinity.[95]

Blocked at the Hwachon passage around the reservoir, some enemy units were pushed farther west in their efforts to escape. This put them in the sector of the US 24th Division, and there they got trapped behind UN lines. The 180th Division, CCF 60th Army, was virtually destroyed there on 27–28 May, large numbers of them surrendering. The G-2 section of the 24th Division reported 4,411 CCF prisoners for the day. The 2nd Battalion, 5th Infantry, alone reported 1,141 prisoners. At some places the enemy division made desperate efforts to break free and lost many killed and wounded. Survivors fled east.[96]

On 27 May General Van Fleet issued Operational Order Piledriver, directing Eighth Army to attack toward three objectives: I Corps to drive to the areas bounded by Chorwon and Kumhwa, IX Corps to seize the area from Hwachon north to Samyang-ni, and X Corps to attack north from the east side of the reservoir and, with the ROK I Corps, seize the area to Kojin-ni on the east coast.[97] The enemy held so stubbornly on the approaches to Chorwon and Kumhwa and north of Inje that accomplishing the objectives seemed doubtful.

On 28 May General Van Fleet made plans for the 1st Marine Division to make an amphibious landing on 6 June on the east coast at Tongchon, where a major road ran southwest to Kumhwa. At the same time, the IX Corps would drive northeast on the Kumhwa road to meet the 1st Marine Division. But the plan was canceled the next day when Ridgway visited Korea. He disapproved of the idea.[98]

On the twenty-eighth, the enemy attitude changed across the front. Now it became one of obstinate resistance to further UN advance. The exploitation phase of the UN counterattack was over. Again it became a situation of hard fighting for any gains and of repulsing enemy counterattacks. This situation predominated in the vicinity of Inje, where the 23rd and 38th regiments of the US 2nd Division were concentrating to relieve the 187th Airborne RCT so that it could take up its scheduled drive to the east coast, and it also was very much the order of the day at Hwachon, where the US 7th Division was poised to continue its advance northwest to Kumhwa.

North of Inje there was a snafu when the 23rd Infantry moved up to relieve the 187th Airborne RCT on the hills north of the town. Enemy got on the hills vacated by the 187th RCT before the 23rd Infantry arrived, and the latter had to fight to retake them. North Koreans fought the battles around Inje and were very tenacious indeed. The NK II and V corps had taken over the defense of the area, as the CCF sought to escape to the northwest around the east side of the Hwachon Reservoir. On the MSR from Hyon-ni to Inje, a force of North Koreans tried to cut the road behind the 38th Infantry, and it took a battalion all afternoon to prevent it. On the next day, 29 May, the 38th Infantry closed into Inje. But the 2nd Battalion trains ran into a fireblock on the road, which was not cleared until the thirtieth, when all but three vehicles were recovered.[99]

On both 28 and 29 May the weather was good and favored the massive use of air strikes. On the twenty-eighth there were 192 sorties in the X Corps zone, and Navy planes from the east coast flew cover over the 187th RCT with great success. On the twenty-ninth there were 141 close-support sorties below Yanggu and in the vicinity of Inje, 90 of them controlled by the 187th RCT.[100]

The 2nd Battalion, 9th Infantry, 2nd Division, arrived at Umyang-ni at the Soyang River bridgehead on 28 May and had the task of patrolling the MSR to Inje. The rest of Col. Edwin J. Messinger's regiment arrived the next day and secured the bridgehead and the airstrip in X Corps reserve.[101]

The mission of the US 3rd Division in the east accomplished, the division received orders on 27 May to return to I Corps. The next day, with the ROK 9th Division attached, it began the long 190-mile road march back to the Seoul area.[102]

By the end of 28 May, the enemy had cleared out of the area south of the Hwachon Reservoir, and an estimated division held the high ground east of the town and north of it along the road to Kumhwa, 20 miles to the northwest. Aerial observers reported enemy moving new units into the Hwachon area to defend north, east, and west of the town. Prisoners taken during the day said the 58th Division of the 20th Army, Third Field Army, had moved into the area. More prisoners the next day confirmed this. And on the thirtieth, prisoners said the 174th Regiment of the 58th Division was withdrawing after having suffered heavy casualties in the past three days of combat with the US 17th Regiment. But air observers at the same

Men of the 3rd Division Reconnaissance Company carry the body of one of their buddies killed in a firefight with Chinese, May 1951. *US Army photograph, FEC 16468*

time reported more large numbers of enemy moving south toward Hwachon. It was clear by the end of the month that the Chinese had established a definite line north of Hwachon to defend the Kumhwa road.[103]

The 1st Cavalry Division of I Corps advanced north and crossed the 38th Parallel for the third time on 28 May, and on the same day I Corps issued its Operational Order 7 instructing the ROK 1st Division and the 29th and 28th British brigades to defend Line Kansas, while the 1st Cavalry, the 3rd and the 25th divisions, moved to seize the Chorwon-Kumhwa area at the base of the Iron Triangle, 1 June.[104]

On 28 May General Van Fleet ordered the Eighth Army staff to plan on moving the army tactical headquarters to Seoul in the near future, and then he went to Pyongtaek to meet General Ridgway and Mr. Sebald, chief of the Diplomatic Section, Tokyo. In his meeting with General Ridgway, General Van Fleet discussed with him the use of the 1st Marine Division in an amphibious operation on the east coast. Ridgway opposed this proposal for many reasons: the extreme dispersion of the front lines, the continued capability of the enemy for offensive action, the danger of removing a division from the army line, the small reward to be gained if successful, the need to request the Joint Chiefs of Staff for approval, the impossibility of clearing enemy forces from Korea, and the necessity of choosing positions Eighth Army could hold.[105]

On the twenty-ninth Ridgway visited the major command posts of Eighth Army across the front, returning to Eighth Army Main CP at Taegu in the evening. He returned to Tokyo on the morning of the thirtieth.

In the US 24th Division sector on 29–30 May, the 19th and 21st regiments were busy gathering up the enemy who were still trapped behind its lines. The two regiments captured a total of 730 more POWs in those two days, most of them surrendering without a fight. The 19th Infantry captured 516 POWs on the twenty-ninth.[106]

The ROK 2nd Division in IX Corps had success in helping to destroy or capture enemy caught in the withdrawal west of Hwachon. On 29 and 30 May it killed about 1,000 and captured 229 prisoners and 13 truckloads of matériel. The ROK 6th Division shared in a successful day on the thirtieth when its 21st Regiment secured the Hwachon Dam at noon.[107]

According to POWs, the 12th, 15th, and 60th CCF armies of the Second Field Army were assembling in the Iron Triangle area. They also said the 39th, 40th, and 42nd CCF armies had left Korea and had returned to China.[108]

On 30 May Task Force Baker could not overcome strong enemy resistance at a roadblock just a few miles northeast of Inje, and its advance toward Kansong was halted. General Van Fleet now ordered X Corps to halt the operation. Meanwhile, the ROK I Corps had successfully carried out its part of the operation and had turned west from Kansong to meet Task Force Baker. It now was ordered to halt its advance and hold the high ground north of the Kansong-Inje road.[109]

Meanwhile, large groups of North Koreans were in evidence all around Inje, and gains there were virtually halted. The North Koreans established a defense line about five miles north of the town. The 38th Infantry Regiment of the US 2nd Division continued to hold Inje.

Enemy action around Hwachon continued to be severe; the enemy was indeed intent on stopping the 7th Division from making further gains. On 30 May a strong enemy force attacked the 31st Infantry a mile and a half north of Hwachon and forced it into three successive withdrawals to the edge of the town before artillery fire halted the enemy attack.[110]

On 30 May a patrol from the 1st Battalion, 21st Infantry, 24th Division, came upon a gruesome sight – seven bodies from A Company, 19th Infantry, shot in the forehead and in the temples. They were from an eight-man patrol. The eighth man was still living, but his throat had been cut. He was evacuated by helicopter. Bodies of five Marines were also found by the 21st Infantry patrol.[111]

In his conference with the 2nd Division staff and its regimental commanders at the 23rd Infantry CP at Inje on 31 May, General Almond modified the 38th Regiment's plan to replace the 23rd Infantry there by ordering it to occupy additional high ground that the 23rd Infantry held. And General Almond ordered General Bowen to suspend for 24 hours his attack from Inje toward Kansong on the coast. This was in effect the end of Task Force Baker, because its advance never resumed. On this last day of its attack, Cpl. Rodolfo P. Hernandez, G Company, 187th Airborne RCT, won the Medal of Honor for his valor in holding a position.[112]

On 31 May General Van Fleet assigned Brig. Gen. Garrison H. Davidson to the ROK Headquarters at Taegu as Eighth Army's temporary KMAG advisor. By that day the 38th Infantry had completed relief of the 23rd Infantry north of Inje, and the 3rd Battalion had relieved elements of the 9th Infantry in that area. And on the same day a tank-infantry team from the 7th Marine Regiment entered Yanggu under intense small-arms, automatic, and mortar fire but was then withdrawn from the town. West of Yanggu, the 1st Korean Marine Corps Regiment reached the south bank of the Hwachon Reservoir.[113]

Other advances occurred on 31 May when the ROK 6th Division seized high ground two miles north of the Hwachon Reservoir that had to be gained before further advances could be made in that area. And on the same day, IX Corps moved its CP to Chunchon from Yoju.[114]

Heavy rains fell on 30 May and hampered all troop movements. Most rivers in the zone of operations flooded, washing out bridges. Han River bridges were affected by high water. The bridge at Yoju was being pulled out because of a big rise in the river; the bridge at Tanyang was out; the Chechon bridge was closed to traffic; and the bridge at Chungju could not be reached because of high water. Roads everywhere were made almost impassable. Numerous bypasses around bridges previously blown by UN forces in their retreat in January were not fordable. The indiscriminate destruction of bridges in that retrograde movement created a greater handicap to UN forces afterward in moving back north than it had ever been a hindrance to the enemy. This was also true of the railroad track destroyed.

The 2nd Infantry Division suffered greater casualties during the last two weeks of May during the enemy offensive than any other US division, having 2,744 battle casualties. Its personnel losses were offset, however, by receiving 5,341 replacements and having 1,163 returnees from hospitals. The US Eighth Army losses during May were 745 killed, 4,218 wounded, and 572 missing in action. Only the ROK Army suffered greater casualties, having 1,221 killed, 4,659 wounded, and 9,714 missing in action. All the

UN allies together totaled only 71 killed, 312 wounded, and 46 missing in action.[115]

The rotation of officers constituted a serious problem. A scheduled rate of 15,000 replacements a month was in effect. But it was difficult to rotate experienced officers and men in the midst of heavy battle when their experience and leadership were so much needed. At the end of May 1951, 4,553 officers in Eighth Army were eligible for replacement, but in the period 15 April to 31 May only 932 officers in field and company grade had been assigned to Eighth Army. And of this number only 637 proved to be qualified for assignment to combat units. There was no way to keep a combat-effective army without delaying the replacement of many officers who had been in service in Korea for as long as 11 months in continuous and severe combat. Field commanders were reluctant to release proven combat officers for rotation. And the same was true for experienced and proven noncommissioned officers and riflemen.[116]

For the period of the 2nd Impulse, 5th Phase Offensive, Eighth Army claimed the Chinese and North Korean forces had suffered a total of 105,000 casualties, 17,000 of them being counted dead, and 10,000 of them prisoners.[117] It is impossible to know the number of enemy casualties, but it certainly was very large, rendering several enemy divisions completely combat ineffective. In the case of the 180th Division, it was almost certainly destroyed. In no other of its offensives since it had entered the war had the Chinese forces suffered to the same extent as in the 2nd Impulse of the 5th Phase Offensive. And in no other had the number of prisoners taken even approached the number taken in this last offensive.

General Ridgway, supreme commander in Tokyo, sent a dispatch on 30 May 1951 to the Joint Chiefs of Staff in Washington giving his estimate of the situation in Korea at the end of the CCF 5th Phase Offensive. The greater part of it deserves to be incorporated here.

1. Have discussed Eighth Army tactical situation in details on the ground with Van Fleet and all 3 US Corps comdrs. Following is my estimate covering the period beginning 22 April, Van Fleet concurring.

2. a. The enemy has suffered a severe major defeat. Estimates of enemy killed in action submitted by field comdrs come to a total so high that I cannot accept it. Nevertheless, there has been inflicted a major personnel loss far exceeding in my opinion the loss suffered by the enemy in the Apr 22 offensive. The ratio of wounded to killed is undetermined but is probably not less than 3 to 1. POWs captured total 8,492 of which vast majority are Chinese and the total is increasing daily. In assessing the effect of these losses, I believe consideration should be given to 2 factors. First, fewer of his wounded will be returned to duty than would be the case with ours. Second, a majority of his casualties have been in his infantry so that the loss in combat effectiveness of his major tactical units is much greater than the mere reduction in numbers of effectives would indicate.

b. Within the past few days there has been a rapidly increasing deterioration of the Chinese forces opposing our IX and X Corps. There has been a marked increase in the number of Chinese surrendering. At least 1 unit of company size has surrendered as a unit with its officers. Prisoners are being taken in the zones of all 3 US Corps from CCF Armies across our entire front. Enemy ammo dumps are being overrun in quantities far exceeding anything previously captured. There has been a very great increase in the number of hostile mortars, machine guns, automatic hand weapons and rifles captured. There has been a marked increase in PW complaints of inadequate food. In many cases Chinese POWs have reported that their units have had to eat grass and roots because of the exhaustion of their rations. All 3 US Corps comdrs have reported a noticeable deterioration in the fighting spirit of CCF forces. A plainly evident disorganization now exists among both CCF and NKPA forces. . . .

3. a. Eighth Army at near full strength with morale excellent and confidence high and with logistic capabilities little affected to date by deteriorating weather, is now regrouping with its principal weight in the US First Corps zone, and is attacking toward the general line: Chorwon-Kumhwa-Hwachon Reservoir thence to the East Coast, for the purpose of inflicting maximum casualties on a defeated and retiring enemy and destroying or capturing maximum enemy equipment and supplies. . . .

5. I therefore, believe that for the next 60 days the United States govt. should be able to count with reasonable assurance upon a military situation in Korea offering optimum advantages in support of its diplomatic negotiations.[118]

An analysis by the Far East Command Intelligence Section estimated that the total CCF and NKPA strength at the beginning of the 2nd Impulse, 5th Phase Offensive, on 16 May was 383,000. On 1 June, at the end of the offensive and the UN counterattack, the strength of the same enemy formations was 286,000, for a loss of 25 percent of its strength.[119]

The same intelligence analysis presents an opinion on probable future enemy intentions and actions that is on the mark and stands up as a knowledgeable and realistic projection of enemy future actions:

There is nothing in the current picture to suggest that the enemy intends to relinquish his hold on any major portion of North Korea; on the contrary, both current indications and past performance are indicative of an intention to eventually mount further efforts to expel UN forces from the Peninsula. Naturally, he desires the line of departure the least distance north of the 38th Parallel that he can secure, and the area between the 38th and the narrow waist of Korea confers special advantages for the extensive regroupment and refitting which his forces must undergo before he can again mount an offensive effort powerful enough to offer hope of any decisive success. Even if he be willing or desirous to accept a stalemate, it would be necessary to his purpose that the situation be stabilized as far south as possible. The present line of contact offers the advantages he desires, and if he would insure their retention, would be about as far north as he could go.

The Kumhwa-Chorwon-Pyonggang triangle has lost none of its importance to the enemy. Retention of this area, sprawling across the heart of North Korea between the 38th and the "waist," confers advantages which he cannot afford to relinquish, whether his purpose be to regroup and attack or merely hold such gains as he still retains. Numerous past studies have emphasized that within this complex lies the vortex of one of the most important roadnets north of the 38th Parallel, whose retention or loss vitally influences the measure of flexibility and control enjoyed by the enemy. Within this area lie numerous important supply installations. As long as he retains this roadnet he has excellent lateral and vertical communications with his front lines, and he can expeditiously dispatch supplies and/ or dispose reserve formations from this advantageous assembly area to east or west. Loss of this complex would particularly aggravate his already difficult logistical problems with respect to the eastern front. He cannot afford to relinquish this net if he intends to hold south of the "waist."

There is little doubt that the UN reaction to his May offensive caught the enemy off balance and ill-disposed to meet a strong retaliatory effort; that many of his units were scattered and badly disorganized in the resultant hasty withdrawal. His losses in personnel and materiel were terrific. On some portions of the front, retrograde movement has still not entirely ceased. On the other hand, denial of the vital Kumhwa-Chorwon-Pyonggang complex to advancing UN forces was mandatory. That the enemy has been able to go a long way toward meeting this requirement is evidenced by the notable recent increase in both the quality and quantity of resistance as the advancing UN forces have closed in on the near approaches to the triangle. Within the past few days opposition has offered less and less suggestion of a general delaying action, and taken on the aspects of that conducted by an outpost. New, semi-permanent fortifications are being encountered in an increasing number of zones of action. Key terrain features are bitterly defended. Local counter-attacks are delivered with increasing frequency and violence. Daily the action provides fresh indications that the forward edge of a battle position covering the south edge of the triangle is being developed.[120]

Believing that the above analysis presents the true situation of enemy intentions and options at the end of the 5th Phase Offensive at the end of May, the author also believes that the views of Generals Van Fleet and Almond on the weakened condition of the enemy forces and the relative ease with which a continuation of the UN attack north could destroy the enemy forces, possibly employing an amphibious operation on the east coast in the Wonsan area, were unrealistic and euphoric. As subsequent events were to show, the UN could not even seize the Iron Triangle area and hold it. General Ridgway's more cautious views were in order.

21

End of the War of Maneuver

THE END of the pursuit phase of the UN counterattack to the enemy's 2nd Impulse, 5th Phase Offensive, came on 1 June, when Task Force Baker was officially dissolved and the drive of the 187th Airborne RCT to the east coast from the Inje area was abandoned. By this date the enemy forces across the Korean front had stiffened their resistance, and in key areas had stopped the UN advance. In a press statement on 2 June, General Van Fleet said, "The 8th Army pursuit phase has now ended with the clearing, again, of the enemy units from South Korea,—less those in the former border areas west of the Imjin River."[1] The Eighth Army stood north of the 38th Parallel almost everywhere across the breadth of Korea. It had substantially regained its Line Kansas, the first good defensive line north of the 38th Parallel.

It had become clear in the pursuit phase that there was a difference between the CCF and the NKA in how they fought: the CCF withdrew great distances when the situation dictated it and would not fight just to hold land; the NKA fought bitterly for every foot of ground—it was their country, and they did not readily withdraw from an area unless forced to do so, and then they formed a defense line as soon as possible. This difference was shown best perhaps by the NKA in the vicinity of Inje and northward from it, while the CCF withdrew as rapidly as possible from the area south of the Hwachon Reservoir. The CCF would still fight a war of maneuver; the NKA would not.

At the beginning of June 1951, the enemy forces were lined up from west to east across Korea, with NK I Corps located along the northwest bank of the Imjin River, then the CCF 65th, 63rd, 15th, and 60th armies eastward to the Hwachon Reservoir. There were no CCF elements east of the reservoir. From the eastern end of the Hwachon Reservoir to the coast, the NK II and V corps held the line, and there the fighting became bitter.

Since the Eighth Army did not have the strength to undertake a war of maneuver against the combined enemy forces, the question on 1 June became one of where it should take its stand in a basically defensive posture. There were three possible lines, combining shortness with terrain features, that could be considered: (1) the Kansas line, the first good defense line north of the 38th Parallel, essentially where UN forces currently stood; (2) a line about 40 to 45 miles farther north, which ran from the Yesong River on the west to Wonsan on the east coast, a line that was vulnerable on its east end; or (3) a line that ran across the waist of Korea, the narrowest line across the peninsula, from the west coastal area north of Pyongyang in the vicinity of Sukchon east to Wonsan. The farther north the defense line, the shorter was the line of supply and communication for the enemy and the longer for Eighth Army. Because UN air and naval forces had systematically destroyed the bridges, railroads, highways, and communication centers north of Seoul, Eighth Army would have a monumental task of rebuilding these facilities for its use if it tried to establish a defense line north of the Kansas line, on either the second or third option. These considerations caused Eighth Army to choose to regain the Kansas line as its basic defense line and to fortify it systematically to such an extent that it would be likely to withstand any offensive the enemy could launch against it with its forces then in Korea.

With this in mind, General Van Fleet on 1 June issued "a letter of Instruction," the only formal tactical plan Eighth Army issued during June. All operations during the month were for the accomplishment of the missions outlined in this letter. It ordered Eighth Army to construct strong fortifications on the Kansas line and to continue its attack in the west to seize the enemy's vital Chorwon-Kumhwa area. To do the latter, Line Wyoming was delineated to encompass the area wanted, and hasty field fortifications were to be set up once it was obtained.

Line Wyoming was a bulge extending on the Kansas line 18 to 20 miles north of it. It started at a point on the Kansas line at the town of Yugong-ni on the Imjin River and ran northeast to Hill 487, then eastward north of Chorwon to Hill 577, where it turned southeast and skirted the southern edge of Kumhwa, and thence ran east to Pungam-ni on the road from Hwachon, then southeast to a point on the Hwachon Reservoir near Tongchon-ni. The boundary between IX and X corps was extended north across the Hwachon Reservoir to follow the Pukhan River northward to Oun-ni.

Patrol bases were to be established just beyond Line Wyoming. Limited-objective attacks and patrols were to be made on the judgment of corps commanders. Each corps commander was to organize Line Kansas in depth, employing civilians under military supervision when practicable. These fortifications were to include tactical and protective wire, prepared fields of fire, minefields and trip flares, foxholes with overhead cover for combat personnel and crew-served weapons, and obstacles and roadblocks.

To provide added security to the defensive line, General Van Fleet or-

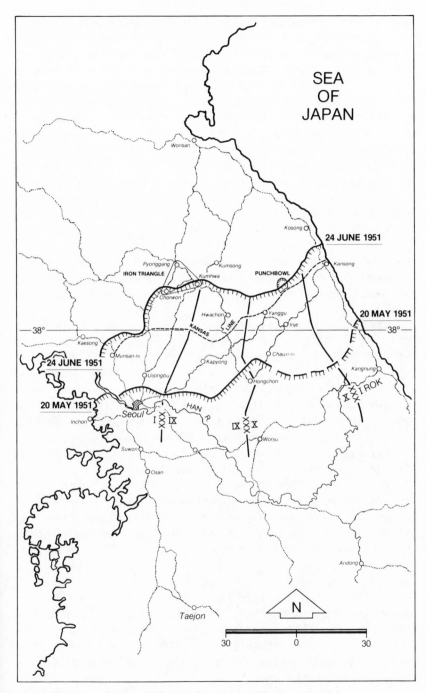

MAP 24. **UN offensive, 20 May–24 June 1951**

dered all corps commanders to clear the general battle area of all civilians except those employed on military projects. All civilians who had entered this area were to be considered hostile and treated accordingly.[2]

As reserve forces concentrated just north of the Iron Triangle area, the enemy had the CCF 12th, 20th, 40th, and 26th armies. The CCF 27th Army was situated north of the eastern end of the Hwachon Reservoir, the NK VI Corps was on the west coast behind the line, and the NK III Corps was in a similar position on the east coast.[3]

On 3 June Operation Piledriver became operational at 6 A.M. There had been a buildup on the east flank of I Corps in front of the 25th Division. In moving forward, the 1st Cavalry Division hit three lines of enemy defenses in the Yonchon area. The enemy fought from the first two lines and held firm at the third line, where there were log bunkers. On the hills southeast of Yonchon two enemy regiments of the 195th Division, CCF 65th Army, held off the 7th Cavalry Regiment. At the same time, the US 3rd Division attacked north toward Chorwon, with the 7th Regiment on its left and the 65th Regiment on its right. The 64th Heavy Tank Battalion lost seven tanks at Chipo-ri, five to 57-mm antitank-gun fire and two to mines.[4]

In its drive toward Chorwon during the first ten days of June, the US 3rd Division was opposed by four enemy regiments, the 565th and 566th of the 189th Division and the 562nd and 563rd of the 188th Division of the 63rd Army. The ROK 9th Division, attached to the 3rd Division and participating in the action, faced the 564th Regiment of the 188th Division.[5]

Farther east in the vital Hwachon area, the 172nd, 173rd, and 174th regiments of the 58th Division, CCF 20th Army, stood in front of the US 7th Division. The 58th division was in good condition, as it had not been in action since the Chosin Reservoir campaign of November–December 1950, and it was well supplied with automatic weapons, mortars, and artillery. The rugged terrain around Hwachon had been fortified prior to the 1950 invasion with mutually supporting bunkers, made of logs 14 inches thick and covered with two to three feet of earth, some with concrete. They were almost impervious to artillery and aircraft attack – they had to be taken by assault. In them the 58th Division defended stubbornly by day, and at night counterattacked.

The 17th Regiment consolidated its position and mopped up in the vicinity of Hwachon. The 31st and 32nd regiments of the 7th Division were employed southwest of the town. They had to advance and come abreast of the 17th before there could be a general advance, which they did by 4 June. The battle line then ran generally about two miles north of Hwachon.[6] The objective of the division was then to seize the high ground astride the Hwachon-Kumhwa road.

Kumsong, northeast of Kumhwa, was reported to be a straggler collection point and an assembly area. An agent reported that an estimated 30,000

enemy had moved from Kumsong northeast from 31 May to 2 June and
that on 5 June 700 CCF had moved there from Kumhwa. A POW from
the 243rd Regiment, 81st Division, CCF 27th Army, reported that the 27th
Army's mission was the defense of the Kumsong area. Air sightings of enemy groups indicated that the area north of Kumsong was an enemy assembly area.[7]

On 2 June the 3rd Battalion, 9th Infantry, US 2nd Division, relieved
the 2nd Battalion, 187th Airborne RCT, at 4 P.M. on Hill 579, the extreme
right flank of the 2nd Division at Inje. The NKs beat off the subsequent
attack, and the battalion had to withdraw. Air strikes and artillery then
hit the hill. During this action about 250 rounds of enemy mortar struck
the 3rd Battalion.

The 23rd Regiment encountered less resistance and by night had taken
the high ground between Inje and Yanggu. The 1st Battalion, 38th Infantry, relieved the French Battalion east of Inje, and the 2nd Battalion, 38th
Infantry, and the Netherlands Detachment held off two enemy attacks where
they protected the MSR between Inje and the Soyang River bridgehead.[8]

The US 25th Division had hard fighting in its zone of advance toward
the Iron Triangle. On 2 June Sgt. Cornelius H. Charlton, C Company,
24th Regiment of the division, won the Medal of Honor there in repeated
daring exploits after he took over the leadership of his platoon when the
platoon leader was wounded and evacuated. Repeatedly wounded, Charlton stayed on his feet until the last enemy position on the hill had been
silenced. He personally eliminated two enemy positions and killed six enemy with rifle and grenades. He died of his wounds.[9]

On 2 June the 1st Marine Division, together with the attached South
Korean Marine Regiment, attacked north through Yanggu to the eastern
tip of the Hwachon Reservoir and Line Kansas. Two platoons of the CCF
60th Army surrendered voluntarily during the day when a ROK force surrounded them.

General Van Fleet moved the Eighth Army Advance Headquarters to
Seoul on 4 June, with strong representation of the G-2 and G-3 sections
and token representation from the other General Staff and Special Staff
sections.[10]

One more old-timer in Korea, Brig. Gen. George B. Barth, commander
of the 25th Division Artillery, left Korea on 3 June for the United States.
He had been with the 25th Division since it had landed there, the second
division to enter the battle.

The 15th Regiment was the last of the US 3rd Division to return to
I Corps, on 3 June, from the X Corps zone of action. On the night of the
fifth it received orders to pass through the 65th Infantry and resume the
attack on the seventh toward Line Wyoming. It went over to the attack
at daylight on 7 May and slowly forged ahead against enemy opposition
until it reached Line Wyoming on 11 June, where it started digging in. It

sent patrols out into the Iron Triangle, where they met small enemy groups in the vicinity of Hills 717 and 682.[11]

On the third an unusual accident happened. Two C-119 cargo planes were knocked out of the sky by VT fused artillery shells in the 38th Infantry sector near Inje. The planes were on their way to air-drop supplies to the ROK 5th Division. The 2nd Infantry Division CP alleged that the Combat Cargo Command had not notified the X Corps or the 2nd Division the flight was to take place, and they had not lifted artillery fire at that time.[12]

During the day, air observers reported the enemy was reinforcing the Chipo-ri area, where the 3rd Division was engaged in a hard fight. The 65th Infantry fought off a two-battalion attack, but the 64th Tank Battalion on the Uijongbu-Kumhwa road near Chailli came under attack from 12 enemy guns, and one platoon lost three tanks to the fire of Soviet-made 57-mm antitank weapons in ten minutes. Half an hour later two more tanks were hit. UN air and artillery destroyed four of the enemy guns. The 27th and 35th regiments of the 25th Division were involved in a heavy fight in an adjacent area. The enemy was resisting bitterly all efforts to approach the Iron Triangle.[13]

Enemy resistance in the west continued to be strong during 4 June on the approaches to the Iron Triangle, and in the Hwachon area it was more bitter than elsewhere. There the battle centered three miles north of the town in the 7th Division sector. The 31st Regiment had to drive the enemy out of their bunkers. In the afternoon the CCF counterattacked the 31st Infantry there and drove them back nearly a mile. On the other side of the road, the 32nd Infantry fought an enemy regiment and made slight gains. On the east side of the reservoir, just north of Yanggu, the 1st Marine Division had heavy resistance.[14]

In the three successive days 5–7 June, enemy resistance diminished in front of the Iron Triangle in the I Corps area. When the 1st Battalion, 65th Infantry, of the 3rd Division took Hill 466 on 5 June after a two-day battle, it found 200 dead CCF on it. During the day the ROK 9th Division, attached to the US 3rd Division, arrived from the X Corps zone and was assigned a sector of the line, relieving the 1st Battalion, 7th Infantry.[15] There was indication at this time that the CCF 64th Army had moved back west and had replaced the NK I Corps on the western end of the line along the Imjin River.

Operation Piledriver was initiated by the 7th Infantry Division in the Hwachon area on 5 June. The 31st Regiment took the east side of the Hwachon-Kumhwa road; the 32nd Regiment took the west side of it. The third regiment, the 17th, blocked in the vicinity of Hwachon as division reserve. The enemy defended against this attack almost to the last man. Progress was slow, even though ten battalions of artillery and a battalion of 4.2-inch mortars supported the two regiments. Between 4 and

22 June artillery expended 89,547 rounds in support of the 7th Division. On 10 June the 17th Infantry passed through the 31st Infantry and continued the attack north. On 17 June the 17th and the 32nd regiments reached the Kansas line. There they consolidated their positions and prepared hasty defenses. The US 24th Division relieved the 7th Infantry Division on Line Wyoming on 23 June, whereupon the 7th Division went into IX Corps reserve. It needed a rest after three weeks of heavy battle with a determined enemy. One of its members, 1st Lt. Benjamin F. Wilson, I Company, 31st Infantry Regiment, received the Medal of Honor for his outstanding heroic action on 5 June near Hwachon. Another member of the 31st Infantry, Pfc. Jack G. Hanson, of F Company, earned the Medal of Honor, Posthumously, on 7 June.[16]

On 6 June the CCF 60th and 63rd armies withdrew through the CCF 20th Army, and thereafter that army, with the 58th, 59th, and 60th divisions, having a total strength of approximately 27,000 was the only unit identified in front of IX Corps. In the east, where the NK 12th and 32nd divisions of the NK V corps opposed the 1st Marine and the 2nd Infantry divisions and the ROK 7th and 5th divisions, prisoners said they were under orders to defend to the last man, and they did exact a high rate of casualties from the UN units attacking them in the high mountains in that sector.[17]

The 1st Marine Division and the ROK 7th Division had gained part of their objectives on Line Kansas on 7 June in heavy fighting in which the North Koreans had used artillery and mortar concentrations against them. At the same time, the ROK 5th Division gained the high ground just east of Kumi. The slowest advance was on the right flank, where the 5th Marines and the ROK 5th Division had to fight over sharp edged ridges. The Kansas line was not secured there until 12 June.[18]

Secretary of Defense George C. Marshall and a party that included General McAuliffe, the Army G-1, and General Ridgway arrived at the Seoul airport in the early afternoon of 8 June. They were met by General Van Fleet and deputy chief of staff, Eighth Army, General Henry I. Hodes. The party visited the Eighth Army Advance CP and then journeyed to the command posts of I Corps, the 1st Cavalry Division, the IX and X Corps, and the Eighth Army Main CP at Taegu, where General Marshall met the ROK Army chief of staff and Brigadier General Davidson, Eighth Army chief of KMAG. At the 1st Cavalry Division CP all the UN commanders in I Corps were present. After a press conference the secretary of defense and his party left Taegu and returned to Japan. General Marshall seemed pleased with his reception and what he saw on his quick trip.[19]

On 8 June General Van Fleet requested of General Ridgway ten additional artillery battalions for Eighth Army: five 155-mm howitzer battalions, four 8-inch howitzer battalions, and one 155-mm gun battalion.

In June the 2nd Division G-4 and the Quartermaster Graves Registration unit, with the help of several hundred Korean laborers, began the collection of UN bodies left on the battlefield in May. They recovered 78 bodies and buried hundreds of enemy dead. Also, 593 truckloads of matériel were salvaged.[20]

On 9 June enemy resistance was light as UN forces approached the base of the Iron Triangle, and Eighth Army's position across Korea was almost the same as on 22 April, when the CCF mounted their 5th Phase Offensive. The lessening of the crisis in Korea was marked by Eighth Army's alerting the 187th Airborne RCT for movement to Japan. This was the first time in the Korean War that a major unit had been taken out of the line for any length of time. In the western section of the front, the 7th Cavalry Regiment and the attached Greek Battalion secured their objectives on Wyoming line, the Greek Battalion securing its objective by the bayonet.[21]

When the troops crossed the 38th Parallel once again, they left a lot of equipment on the battlefield. There was so much of it that a salvage operation was organized in I Corps, and in a three-and-a-half-day cleanup 90 railcar loads were picked up, sorted, and outloaded. Eighth Army assigned to I Corps a platoon of the 58th Quartermaster Salvage Company for further salvage work.[22]

On 11 June, just before noon, a patrol of B Company, 1st Battalion, 7th Infantry, 3rd Division, entered Chorwon, capturing 5 prisoners in the process. In 11 days of hard fighting the 7th Regiment had counted 692 enemy dead, had captured 134 prisoners, and had captured Chorwon, at the southwest corner of the Iron Triangle. On the same day, a Turkish patrol on the right flank of the US 25th Division entered the southeast edge of Kumhwa but saw no enemy, although they were in view on high ground southwest of the town.[23] Civilians in Chorwon informed UN patrols who entered the town on 12 June that on 9 June 10,000 CCF had withdrawn north through Chorwon, and the last of them had left the town early on the eleventh.[24]

From 10 June to the end of the month, the enemy CCF 64th and 65th armies held the line on the northwest bank of the Imjin River and as far east as Chorwon; the CCF 26th Army defended the area between Chorwon and Kumhwa; and the CCF 20th Army was on line east of the 26th Army and north of the Hwachon Reservoir. To the east of it the North Korean V and II corps defended to the coast.[25]

The North Korean units had come back to life with a vengeance after having been all but destroyed in the fall of 1950. By ruthless methods and with Soviet aid, remnants of the original North Korean Army had taken in replacements and trained with Soviet equipment along the Manchurian border. In June 1951, the North Korean Army was organized into eight corps of 24 divisions. Four of the corps had seen much action in April and May; the I, II, and V corps had been heavily engaged and were thoroughly seasoned units. Although they had suffered heavy losses, they had recuperated fast and, after a short interval, had been able to make further strenuous efforts. The II and V corps in the east became noted for their fierce defense, and it was commonly said by their opponents, the 1st Marine Division, the 2nd Infantry Division, and some ROK units, that they were more to be feared than CCF formations.[26]

Approaching Kumhwa from the southeast on 11 June, the 1st Battalion, 17th Infantry, 7th Division, was held up by enemy resistance on Hill 566 and was forced to withdraw from it. The next day the battalion resumed its assault on this key hill on the approach to Kumhwa, and A and C companies, coordinating their attacks from different directions, secured the hill.[27] In its approach to Kumhwa on 11 June, the 1st Battalion, 32nd Infantry, 7th Division, received a mortar hit in its command group that was costly; the explosion wounded the battalion commander, the S-2 and S-3, the artillery liaison officer, and 15 enlisted men.[28]

While the enemy seemed to pull their forces back west of the Hwachon Reservoir at this time, the North Korean resistance was stiffer than ever on the east side of the reservoir, where the 1st Marine Division was trying to reach the Kansas line in the midst of sharp-edged, high mountains. Cpl. Charles G. Abrell, E Company, 1st Marine Regiment, on 10 June earned the Medal of Honor in assaulting an enemy bunker that had pinned down the assault squad by accurate and heavy automatic weapons fire. Although wounded for the third time in the engagement, Abrell stormed the bunker and hurled himself bodily into it with a grenade in his hand. The grenade explosion fatally wounded Abrell, but it also killed the entire enemy gun crew inside the bunker. His platoon then gained its objective.[29]

After the UN counterattack in the Chinese 2nd Impulse, 5th Phase Offensive, had ended, the 2nd Division ordered Maj. Jack Young and his 2nd Division Security Force to make a thorough reconnaissance of the area between Naepyong-ni and Yangye, the area of intense battle, to get data on enemy dead and the cause of their casualties. Young was to count only complete bodies; single graves, but not mass graves, were to be counted, and where decomposition had taken place, the remains were not tallied. The number counted was 2,916; of that number 22 percent of the deaths were caused by artillery, 14 percent by air-dropped napalm, and 30 percent by combined artillery and air action. This tabulation showed the great destructive effect of artillery and air, with artillery getting credit for almost 50 percent of the casualties.[30]

On 12 June both the US 3rd and the US 25th divisions were on Line Wyoming, at the base of the Iron Triangle – the US 3rd Division on the west at Chorwon, the US 25th Division on the east at Kumhwa. The 25th Division formed Task Force Hamilton on the eleventh, consisting of A and B companies of the 27th Regiment and two companies of the 89th Tank Battalion. Task Force Hamilton patrolled to a point four kilometers north of Kumhwa on the twelfth, meeting only scattered resistance. At the same time, a Turkish task force comprising a platoon of infantry and two platoons of tanks went three kilometers north of Kumhwa, against some small-arms and automatic-weapons fire. No troops went into Kumhwa itself. The 25th Division wanted to envelop Kumhwa completely before entering it to avoid being trapped in the town.[31]

On 12 June both the US 3rd and the US 25th divisions ordered a tank-infantry patrol to go to Pyonggang the next day and return before dark. Task Force Hamilton would go for the 25th Division; Task Force Hawkins would go for the US 3rd Division. They would meet at Pyonggang, one traveling the eastern road, the other the western road, across the two sides of the Iron Triangle from Kumhwa and Chorwon respectively. Task Force Hawkins from the US 3rd Division consisted of the 64th Tank Battalion; I Company, 7th Infantry Regiment; A Battery, 58th AFA Battalion; two platoons of the 65th Tank Company; a 10th Engineer Battalion detachment; and a CIC detachment. A TACP from the 9th Field Artillery Battalion would provide fire support. A battalion of the ROK 9th Division would block to the west and northwest; the 15th Infantry would make an effort on the Chorwon-Kumhwa road; and there would be continuous air cover and artillery support throughout the reconnaissance in force.[32]

Task Force Hamilton from Kumhwa crossed its line of departure at 8:15 A.M., 13 June. At one point on the way north it engaged an estimated 120 enemy, killing 21 of them and taking 21 POWs. It also encountered a roadblock at a low pass before descending to the low plain in which Pyonggang was situated. The task force counted 32 enemy bodies along the road. At Pyonggang Task Force Hamilton met Task Force Hawkins from Chorwon. The former returned to Kumhwa at 4:40 and was dissolved.[33]

Task Force Hawkins left Chorwon about the same time that Task Force Hamilton left Kumhwa and started up the somewhat longer but flatter western road to Pyonggang. The 2nd Platoon of the 65th Infantry Tank Company patrolled and kept open the road behind it. The task force entered Pyonggang and searched the surrounding country but encountered no opposition of consequence. In Pyonggang it met one platoon of Task Force Hamilton. Most of that task force had been unable to get through because of mines, roadblocks, and resistance en route. The enemy were on the high ground that surrounded the Iron Triangle, but for the moment they had almost vacated the triangular-shaped bowl itself. General Soule of the 3rd Division was in Chorwon following the progress of Task Force Hawkins. It returned there before dark without incident.[34]

The next day, 14 June, Tactical Air observers reported every peak on Hill 1062, four miles north of Kumhwa, occupied by enemy. Estimated to number 500, they were dug in with piles of supplies evident on another hill two miles southeast of the town, and another 150 enemy were dug-in on a ridge three and a half miles north of Kumhwa. Hill 1062 was east across the valley road, eight air miles from Hill 717 in the Sobang Hills in the southeastern part of the Iron Triangle.

The Sobang Hills were about eight miles northwest of Kumhwa on the west side of the road running northwest from Kumhwa and about six miles south of Pyonggang. They lay just within the boundary of the 3rd Division sector. They were really the end of the chain of hills that extended northwest from below Kumhwa and were the only high ground of consequence in the Iron Triangle. Hill 717 was the highest point in the Sobang Hills, but Hill 682, a mile southwest of Hill 717, was also important, and together they constituted a formidable position that had visual control of the entire triangle. On 13 June Task Force Hamilton from Kumhwa had an encounter near them and found roadblocks at the low pass where the road crossed their northern tip at Yongmi and Chiam-ni to enter the flat area stretching northwest to Pyonggang. After the thirteenth, the enemy occupied both hills in some strength. Two battalions, the 2nd from each of the 233rd and 234th regiments of the CCF 78th Division, occupied and deployed in depth the north slope of the two hills. It looked as if the enemy meant to hold this terrain to prevent observation of its forward areas.[35]

On 13 June the US IX Corps received orders to get possession of the area north of the Hwachon-Pyonggang road to a depth of four to six kilometers north of Line Wyoming. The ROK 2nd Division and the 32nd Regiment of the 7th Division got the assignment to take this terrain. The 32nd Infantry had hand-to-hand fighting on Hill 1073, where resistance centered in its zone, before it captured the hill. The Turkish Brigade drew an equally hard assignment in attacking Hill 507, which was commanding terrain just north of Kumhwa. The Turks took the hill on the fourteenth, but lost it that night to the CCF.[36] Not until 16 June was the Turkish Brigade finally able to capture and occupy this key and bitterly contested hill. UN forces could now occupy the southeast corner of the Triangle.[37]

Notice should be taken of the Triple-Single Bailey, M-2 Panel Bridge — 772 feet in length, comprising seven spans, having a total weight of 340 tons, and containing 40 piles and 552 panels — that was completed across the Soyang River on 13 June. It was started on 15 April by the 185th Engineer Combat Battalion, but when the CCF 5th Phase Offensive got under way on 22 April, all work on the bridge halted, and 36 truckloads of Bailey parts were hauled away. Work was resumed on the bridge at the end of May. Completed on 13 June, it had taken 14 days to build. The work involved 4,051 military man-days and 4,278 civilian man-days of labor. At the time of its completion the bridge was the longest bridge Army engineers had built north of the 38th Parallel and was the longest Bailey bridge in Korea.[38] It was a main feature in the supply of X Corps troops henceforth.

On 14 June another UN contingent, a battalion from Colombia, arrived at Pusan. It numbered 1,010 enlisted men, half regular army and half volunteers.

The 65th Infantry of the US 3rd Division took unopposed the remaining high ground south of Chorwon on 16 June. It was then estimated that Chorwon held about 30,000 refugees, and because of that fact the division stopped just south of the city. The next day the 3rd Division established a patrol base consisting of the 3rd Reconnaissance Company, the 3rd Ranger Company, one infantry company, and an artillery battery 4,000 yards north of the Wyoming line and sent out patrols from it to within 6,000 yards of Pyonggang. Heavy enemy automatic fire forced the patrols to turn back at that point. One patrol of the 15th Infantry engaged an enemy company 7,000 yards southeast of Pyonggang on 17 June. Aerial observers saw several hundred enemy west of Pyonggang and others dug in on a ridge northeast of Kumhwa.[39]

While action in June centered in the west on the Iron Triangle area, in the east it centered in the X Corps area on a feature called the "Punchbowl." This was an extinct volcano that had a semilevel area on top in a crater, surrounded by a sharp-edged rim, located in the high mountains north of Inje. The Punchbowl lay in the path of the 1st Marine Division and was fiercely defended by North Korean troops. It was hard fighting for the Marines and the attached South Korean Marine Corps regiment. On 18 June, in a day of very hard fighting, the ROK 1st Marine Regiment seized Hill 1100, at the southwest corner of the Punchbowl. The 5th Marine Regiment at the same time had light resistance in the southeast part of the Punchbowl. The next day the 1st Marine Division continued its attacks in the area. Enemy on Hill 873 held commanding terrain there in spite of four attempts by the 7th Marine Regiment to get it. In the last ten days the 1st Battalion, 5th Marines, had taken 69 killed and 364 men wounded. (About this time, General Almond complained to Colonel Hayward, the Marine regimental commander, about the number of flies in the area as a result of unburied dead. The situation, however, had precluded burying them.) Finally on 21 June, the 5th Marines sent patrols into the Punchbowl and to Hill 792 without enemy contact.[40]

At the Iron Triangle the 15th Regiment of the 3rd Division sent patrols daily to the Sobang hills, especially to Hills 682 and 717, beginning on 18 June. In each case they encountered enemy automatic fire, and they called in artillery and air strikes on the two hills, each of which they estimated contained an enemy company. On 21 June the 1st Battalion patrols tried to determine the location of the enemy positions for an attack planned to be launched against the hills on 23 June. One tank hit a mine on that occasion, and patrols from the 2nd and 3rd battalions were driven back. An enemy plane that night dropped flares, napalm or gasoline, and rockets on the Wyoming line. On the twenty-second, the 1st Battalion, 7th Infan-

Stretcher bearers with troops on Hill 1179 at the southwest edge of the Punch-bowl, 1951. *National Archives photograph, 111-SC 376719*

try, relieved the 1st Battalion, 15th Infantry, on the Wyoming line, as the latter prepared to attack the Sobang hills.

On 23 June the 1st Battalion, 15th Infantry, Lt. Col. Julius W. Levy, commanding, turned out in battle formation at 2 A.M. with C Company on the left, B Company on the right, and A Company in reserve with the support tank company. The battalion strength was 916 officers and men, including 44 ROKs. A novelty was the presence of two dogs and their handlers to each rifle company to warn of enemy hiding along the approach march—in this case, a seven-and-a-half-mile walk in the dark. This first use of dogs in an operation was a dismal failure. The dogs got tired before the approach march ended, and some of them even had to be carried by their handlers. The battalion arrived at the foot of Hill 717 about 9 A.M., three hours late, tired out, and in no condition to make an attack on the heavily forested hill.

An artillery preparation was fired at 8:50 A.M., and at 9:03 A.M. C and B companies began their attack. It went slowly, and at one point several men were lost to a deadly accurate enemy sniper who hit his target with every shot. At 3:35 in the afternoon, after hours of heavy fighting, B and C companies took Hill 717 – after a fashion. It developed that the 2nd Battalion, 233rd Regiment, 78th Division, of the 26th Army had defended Hill 717 but had suffered so many casualties that the 2nd Battalion, 234th Regiment, was sent from Hill 472 to relieve it and to continue the battle. This new battalion arrived on Hill 717 soon after midnight with about 500 men, with 120 men and 6 officers in each of four companies. They counterattacked beginning about 2 A.M. on 24 June, and communication with the hill was lost half an hour later. They penetrated the 1st Battalion's perimeter. Lieutenant Dinkle, commanding C Company, was killed in this action, and 1st Lt. John Bessmer, commanding B Company, was badly wounded. Lieutenant Brinson was now left in command of both companies, although he did not know the two company commanders were out of action. The CCF had bayonets fixed (using bayonet points shaped like a trident) and used a lot of flares to light up the area, and there were many bugles and whistles sounding as control signals.

There was no contact between B and C companies now. Many American soldiers broke in panic, and suddenly everyone "took off." The Chinese did not pursue very far. A Company at the time was on its way to Hill 717 and met stragglers from the other companies as it reached the hill. It took up a blocking position through which B and C companies passed. There is no clear statement of the 1st Battalion's casualties in this engagement. One source says 6 enlisted men were killed, 52 wounded, and 7 missing. Lieutenant Dinkle's body was left behind, and three other officers were wounded. This was not a high casualty rate under the circumstances.[41]

In the battle on Hill 717 during the night, Pfc. Emory L. Bennett, B Company, a BAR man, stayed behind to cover the withdrawal of his unit in the enemy counterattack about 2 A.M. of the twenty-fourth and died in the effort to hold off the enemy assault long enough to allow his unit to escape. For his self-sacrificing action he received the Medal of Honor, Posthumously.[42] The 1st Battalion withdrew from the scene entirely, returning to regimental lines at noon.

Regimental patrols got a deserter from the 3rd Battalion, 234th Regiment, 78th Division, 26th CCF Army, a fresh unit on the Sobang hills that now held Hill 717. His regiment had been in the process of relieving the 2nd Battalion, 233rd Regiment of the division, which had many casualties in the battle, during the night of 23–24 June.[43] At 6:15 A.M. on the twenty-fourth, 200 men were unaccounted for in the 1st Battalion, US 15th Infantry, but by 10:45 A.M. this number had been reduced to 22 men.[44]

In the days that followed, patrols from the 15th Infantry reconnoitered the Sobang hills area, and the enemy always reacted, coming out of their positions on Hills 682 and 717 to harass the patrols. By 20 June the CCF had outposted almost every bit of high ground in the Pyonggang plain.

On 20 June an unusual incident occurred along the Wyoming line. An enemy aircraft made a rare bombing and strafing run on the position of the 3rd Battalion, 24th Infantry, 25th Division, killing 7, wounding 10, and damaging 14 vehicles, only 4 of which could be salvaged. Five small fragmentation bombs did most of the damage in an area of 40 yards; other bombs landed in soft ground in two clusters of five each and were less effective.[45]

Prisoner reports in June frequently spoke of a 6th Phase Offensive that the enemy had in preparation, to be launched not later than mid-July. The cultural officer of the CCF 29th Division, 15th Army, captured on 12 June, said that this 6th Phase Offensive was to be fought by new armies from China, including the 10th Army and 50,000 recruits from China, and that the war was to be ended by late September in time to celebrate the Chinese fall festival. Aerial sightings throughout June of enemy forces moving from the north to enemy rear areas back of the front led the Far East Command Intelligence Section to accept the projection that the enemy was indeed preparing for a new offensive.[46]

In the IX Corps area, the US 7th Division had a grim struggle in advancing 23 miles from Hwachon toward Kumhwa in the three weeks from 1 to 23 June, when it was relieved by the 24th Division. In that time the 32nd Regiment alone had encountered elements of the 58th, 59th, and 60th divisions of the CCF 20th Army and had suffered losses of 46 killed and 330 wounded. In this time it had inflicted on the enemy a counted 787 dead, another 178 estimated to have been killed, and an estimated 537 wounded and had taken 192 prisoners.[47]

At the western end of the Eighth Army line, the ROK 1st Division mounted a reconnaissance in force on 21 June that entered Kaesong without opposition, but it encountered some enemy near Korangpo-ri. By the twenty-third the enemy in this area had stiffened its opposition, and an enemy regiment turned back elements of the ROK 11th and 12th regiments near Korangpo-ri and caused them to withdraw back south of the Han River. And in the Iron Triangle, an enemy company attacked the 15th Infantry Regiment's patrol base near Hill 717. In the Punchbowl area in east Korea, a North Korean attack regained Hill 872 from the ROK 1st Marine Regiment and then lost it again to a counterattack in which UN artillery drove the North Korean force northward.[48]

On 22 June General Ridgway, at the Far East Command Headquarters in Tokyo, informed the Joint Chiefs of Staff that he had requested Eighth

Army in Korea to submit a plan not later than 10 July for a general advance beyond the Kansas-Wyoming line.[49]

The UN advance to the Wyoming line had given Eighth Army control of the lateral east-west roadnet, centering at the base of the Triangle between Chorwon and Kumhwa, and thereby disrupted the ease with which the CCF had hitherto been able to shift troops from west to east on the battlefront, but it had not given control of the Iron Triangle area otherwise to UN forces. The setback in the Sobang hills on 23–24 June had made this fact clear, and plans were already under way to mount a new attack on Hills 682 and 717 to regain possession of them. By the middle of June intelligence had established that, while the enemy at first seemingly had vacated the Iron Triangle plateau bowl, it really had not done so. The enemy had five armies deployed on the high ground on either side of the Triangle and to the north of Pyonggang, and two more armies were in the immediate rear. And in the latter part of the month it had undertaken to outpost most of the higher spots in the Triangle itself.[50]

When the ROK 9th Division, attached to the US 3rd Division, had first taken position on the right flank of the 3rd Division on Line Wyoming, it developed that it had not taken the most favorable positions for defense of its sector. Hills 603 and 861 in front of it were the dominating features, and enemy forces had now occupied these points. The ROK 9th Division, accordingly, was ordered to attack on 24 June to seize the enemy-held dominant terrain. At 5 A.M. the ROK 29th Regiment attacked Hill 603. After a day of seesaw battle in which both sides at different times held the hill, the ROK regiment withdrew from the hill at 5 P.M., and air strikes and artillery barrages were placed on it. The ROK regiment then attacked it again and took the hill at 10 P.M. After midnight the enemy counterattacked and won the hill back. At dawn the ROK 29th Regiment, aided by the 1st Battalion, 28th Regiment, renewed its attack on the hill and, after fighting throughout the day, succeeded in gaining control of Hill 603 and surrounding hill masses. But again, during the night of 25–26 June, enemy counterattacked and drove elements of the ROK 9th Division from the hill, completely disorganized. At this point the 3rd Division ordered the 3rd Battalion, 7th Infantry, into blocking positions to prevent the enemy from exploiting its success in the ROK 9th Division sector and to secure the division's right flank.

During 26 June the ROK division was reorganized, and the 28th and 29th regiments attacked and secured Hill 603 at 4 P.M. Preparations were immediately made to wire in the defense positions and coordinate artillery fires to prevent the loss of the hill again. On 27 June the ROK 9th Division was not engaged by enemy and spent its time in improving its defensive positions on the hard-won new sector.[51]

The 1st Cavalry Division in I Corps, just west of the Iron Triangle, encountered strong enemy resistance day after day as it tried to advance to the Wyoming line. On 24 June Task Force Croft was formed to attack west along the road running from Chorwon to Sibyon-ni. This was the main lateral road running west from the Iron Triangle, and it was bitterly defended by the enemy. The task force included the 1st Battalion, 7th Cavalry (−); the 4th Ranger Company; C Company, 70th Tank Battalion; two batteries of the 77th Field Artillery Battalion; one battery of the 82nd Field Artillery; a bomb-disposal squad; and a platoon of engineers. After advancing 12 kilometers, the task force ran into a roadblock at Changpo-ri defended by enemy artillery fire. This stopped the task force, but it engaged in a five-hour fight before it broke contact and returned to 1st Cavalry Division lines, where it was dissolved.[52]

The next day, the 8th Cavalry committed all three of its battalions in an effort to take some high ground in this area, some of the fighting hand-to-hand, but failed in its effort. And on 26 June the 1st Battalion, 5th Cavalry, attacked an enemy-held ridge but was unable to dislodge the enemy, although they sustained artillery and mortar fire all day. In an action with a 7th Cavalry Regimental patrol on the twenty-ninth, an enemy platoon still fought effectively after 500 rounds of artillery had been fired on its position. At the end of the month it was still touch and go with the 1st Cavalry Division in the area west of the Iron Triangle.[53]

On 24 June General Van Fleet ordered all ROK divisions, except the 1st ROK Division, to turn in to Eighth Army Ordnance all but ten 3.5-inch rocket launchers and to substitute 2.36-inch rocket launchers for them within authorized allowances. This order came as a result of heavy ROK losses of the 3.5-inch rocket launchers to the enemy, who then used them against American units.[54]

According to air reports, Kumsong in the central sector, about 15 miles northeast of Kumhwa on the main road to the east coast, had the densest supply and troop movement activity of the entire front in the latter part of June. There were no gains in that direction.

On 25 June the UN forces were generally about ten miles north of the 38th Parallel, except in the extreme western part of the line, west of the mouth of the Imjin River. The first year of the war ended with no major change in positions of the two contending forces, although the UN forces were somewhat more favorably situated. The ROK 1st Division was ordered to withdraw all forces, except one infantry battalion south and east of the Imjin River, as there appeared to be a buildup of enemy forces to the west, and it was decided not to risk losing the floating bridge over the Imjin. The 1st Battalion of the ROK 15th Regiment remained on the west side in a patrol base. The rest of the regiment withdrew into a reserve assembly area south of Munsan-ni. The floating bridge was then removed.[55]

The Civilian Transport Corps companies, organized in March to carry military supplies from division rear boundaries to front lines, had been a great success. Initially planned for 82 companies of 240 men each, or a total of 19,680 carriers, it had reached a total of 84 companies by 19 May, with 20,160 carriers. On 25 June the responsibility for the CTC was transferred to Eighth Army G-4. Each company had four platoons, with a sergeant for platoon leader, a corporal, and 54 carriers. By the end of June 1951, there were a total of 25,825 CTC carriers in the army.[56]

On 23 June Jacob A. Malik, the Soviet Union's delegate to the United Nations, made a surprise radio announcement that a cease-fire was possible in Korea—but there was no change in activity on the front.[57]

On 26 June President Syngman Rhee of the Republic of Korea made a statement referring to the cease-fire proposals made by Soviet Deputy Foreign Minister Malik. President Rhee said Malik's statement had been considered by his cabinet, which had reached a unanimous conclusion that South Korea could not and should not recognize the Soviet Union's cease-fire proposal. His statement served notice that "any so-called peace plan which involves the division of this nation along any artificial border is entirely unacceptable to the people of Korea, north and south." General Ridgway flew from Japan to Korea for a quick conference with President Rhee at his residence in Pusan. It was a short meeting, lasting only from 4:30 to 5 P.M. No statement was released on the nature of the conference, but it was generally assumed that Ridgway gave Rhee a warning about any further statements he might make on the Malik proposal.[58]

The 7th Infantry Regiment relieved the 15th Infantry on Line Wyoming on 27 June, and the next day it was alerted to attack Hills 682 and 717 in the Sobang hills. On 29 and 30 June the 7th Regiment sent patrols to the vicinity of the hills and prepared to attack them. Intelligence indicated an enemy battalion was on each hill. Patrols went to within three miles of Pyonggang before they met resistance.[59]

It became increasingly apparent on 28 June that the enemy was sensitive to any UN effort to penetrate the area north of Kumhwa and the approaches to Kumsong. Company- and battalion-sized attacks were made against any UN advances attempted north and east of Kumhwa.[60]

While General Van Fleet was at the 24th Division CP on 28 June, IX Corps and the 24th Division proposed to him that the division be allowed to displace forward of the Wyoming line to more favorable terrain. Van Fleet vetoed the idea, saying, "We are as far as I want to go"—it would be bad from the Army point of view, although advantageous to the 24th Division. I Corps also complained to General Van Fleet about the changed Air Force operations, which relied now on L-19 Mosquito planes instead of AT-6 planes, which were free to look for targets and make direct strikes on them.[61]

On 29 June the 19th and 5th RCTs of the US 24th Division advanced into enemy-vacated territory and destroyed a large number of enemy fortifications. The 19th Infantry reported it had destroyed 519 enemy bunkers and 82 trenches, found vacant but formerly occupied, and collected many abandoned weapons; the 5th RCT reported it had destroyed 112 enemy bunkers and obtained many weapons and much ammunition.[62]

The last week of June saw a large increase in the number of enemy vehicle sightings moving south, 14,199 from 23 to 29 June, a daily average of 2,028. This number was almost as large as it was during the first week of June in the enemy's large buildup then. The direction of flow was toward the Kumhwa-Kumchon area. The traffic along the Wonsan-Singosan-Kumhwa road greatly increased over previous periods as contrasted with that over the Sinanju-Pyongyang-Sariwon-Kaesong traffic, which had previously carried the bulk of the enemy's traffic; the eastern routes were now being favored.[63]

The most important development of 29 June was a message from the Joint Chiefs of Staff for the commander in chief, United Nations Command in Tokyo. It read:

The Pres has directed that at 0800 Saturday Tokyo Daylight Saving Time you send following message by radio in clear addressed to Comdr in Chief Communist Forces in Korea and simultaneously release to press:

"As Commander in Chief of the United Nations Command I have been instructed to communicate to you the following:

"I am informed that you may wish a meeting to discuss an armistice providing for the cessation of hostilities and all acts of armed force in Korea, with adequate guarantees for the maintenance of such armistice.

"Upon the receipt of word from you that such a meeting is desired I shall be prepared to name my representative. I would also at that time suggest a date at which he could meet with your representative. I propose that such a meeting could take place aboard a Danish hospital ship in Wonsan Harbor.

"(Signed MB Ridgway, Gen, USA, C-in-C UN Command)"[64]

The Ridgway offer was broadcast at 15-minute intervals in English, Chinese, and Korean by Army, Japanese, and South Korean radio stations and by the Voice of America in 45 languages. At 11 P.M., July 1, a broadcast in Chinese over the Peking radio gave an answer to Ridgway's announcement. A translation of the Mandarin version stated the following:

Your statement of June 30 this year concerning peace talks has been received. We are authorized to inform you that we agree to meet your representative for conducting talks concerning cessation of military action and establishment of peace. We propose that the place of meeting be in the area of Kaesong on the 38th parallel; if you agree, our representatives are prepared to meet your representatives between July 10 and 15, 1951.[65]

The message was signed jointly by Premier Kim Il Sung, as "Supreme Commander of the Korean People's Army," and by Gen. Peng Dehuai, as "Commander of the Chinese Volunteers." Kaesong was barely south of the 38th Parallel, but at the time was in North Korean possession in a kind of no-man's-land. For several centuries, dating from 913, it had been the first capital of a united Korea. It had had a population of about 88,000 when the Korean War started in June 1950.

In the meantime the war went on. For the month of June the 1st Marine Division had 2,265 casualties, by far the largest number of casualties of any American division.[66] Up to this point in the war, however, the US 2nd Division had suffered more casualties than any other American division, totaling more than 16,000, or 300 more than it had suffered in World War II. But no other division had inflicted more casualties on the enemy in the Korean War than had the 2nd Division.

In May, Seoul's population had dropped to about 80,000. At the end of June it had risen to 300,000 with the changing fortunes of war. But 3,245,000 of South Korea's population were refugees. During the last half of June, the US 3rd Division reported that 40,000 refugees were trucked from the Chorwon-Kumhwa area to places south of the Han River.

In June the US Army in Korea had promoted 89 men to second lieutenant, 6 of them from warrant officers and 83 from enlisted-man status, and Major General Hoge had been promoted to lieutenant general. During June the Far East Command had accepted the Department of the Army's plan for integration of white and black men into Army units. This proposal included the deactivation of the all-black 24th Infantry Regiment and the activation of a new regiment, the 37th, in which black soldiers would be integrated in the proportion of 12 percent. This same proportion was to be maintained in future integration of combat units.[67]

In the last half of June there was a noticeable change in the number of agents that were able to penetrate enemy lines. Of 27 agents sent out since 13 June, only 15 returned, and 10 were overdue. And of the 15 that returned, only 7 had been able to penetrate enemy lines a satisfactory distance. It was held by some American G-2 officers that the enemy had better battlefield intelligence than the UN did, that the enemy patrols were more aggressive and better trained and that American captives talked freely and gave intelligence to the enemy.[68]

Operation Doughnut, in the US 3rd Division, was a major operation in the first days of July. It started on the evening of 30 June, when attack forces moved toward their line of departure for attack on 1 July. The main objective was to seize Hill 717 and its subordinate high ground in the Sobang hills, northwest of Kumhwa. The 1st and the 3rd battalions, 7th Infantry; the 3rd Battalion, 65th Infantry (less I Company); K Company, 15th Infantry; and the 64th Tank Battalion, with several detachments attached, including TAC parties and part of the 10th Engineers, the 3rd Platoon, Medical Company; and Forward Observer parties from B Battery, 39th Field Artillery Battalion, constituted the attack force. Four battalions of field artillery supported the attack on Hills 717 and 682. The 3rd Battalion, 7th Infantry, was to attack Hill 717; the 1st Battalion, 7th Infantry, was to attack Hill 682; and the 3rd Battalion, 65th Infantry, was to attack Hill 581 and link up with the 3rd Battalion, 7th Infantry, on Hill 717.

On 1 July the 7th Infantry attack got only part of the south slope of Hill 717, which was defended by an estimated two enemy battalions. Two columns tried to envelop the hill but failed to dislodge the enemy. The attack was supported by 23 flights of 90 fighter planes. The 3rd Battalion, 7th Infantry, went into a perimeter defense for the night on the south peak. On 2 July the 7th Infantry continued the attack but gained little, as most of the enemy bunkers had to be taken in close-up infantry attack. It withdrew for the night to its perimeter of the night before on the south slope. During the day the 3rd Battalion, 65th Infantry, moved from Chorwon along the Pyonggang road in preparation for an attack on 3 July against the north slope of Hill 717.

On 3 July the 7th Infantry, with the help of the 10th Philippine BCT, seized Hills 717 and 682 against a reinforced enemy and dug in on a perimeter defense for the night. There they repulsed all counterattacks during the night. During the day the 3rd Battalion, 65th Infantry, had taken Hill 608.

In the predawn hours of early 4 July, the 7th Infantry repulsed several counterattacks. In one of them Sgt. LeRoy A. Mendonca of B Company, 7th Infantry, won the Medal of Honor, Posthumously, when he sacrificed himself by single-handedly holding off an attack on his platoon while it withdrew. He fought with rifle and grenades, and after expending his ammunition, he continued to fight with clubbed rifle and bayonet until he was mortally wounded. After his platoon regained the lost position, an inspection of the area around Mendonca's body indicated that he had been responsible for 37 enemy casualties.[69]

After daylight on 4 July all attacking units gained their objectives without enemy opposition. Under cover of their last counterattacks the CCF had withdrawn from Hills 717 and 682 and vicinity to the northeast of Pyonggang. The 7th Infantry had the 3rd Ranger Company put platoon-sized listening posts on Hills 717 and 682, and it then withdrew back to Line Wyoming. The 3rd Ranger Company was to warn the main positions whenever the enemy tried to reoccupy the recently won hills, and registered artillery fire would then be brought down on them. The Ranger company stayed on the hills until 14 July. The 7th Infantry Regiment then took over outposting them. There were frequent contacts with enemy patrols, but the CCF made no effort to retake the hills. The 3rd Division used them as a patrol base. The four-day fight for Hills 717 and 682 cost the UN forces 26 men killed and 170 wounded for a total of 196 casualties. In turn the CCF lost 575 counted dead, an additional estimated 802 killed and 791 wounded, plus 39 POWs, for an estimated total of 2,207 casualties.[70]

As the negotiations proceeded apace in the first part of July for the be-

Troops of the 7th Regiment, 3rd Division, attack Hill 717 in the Iron Triangle, south of Pyonggang, 3 July 1951. *National Archives photograph, 111-SC 373296*

ginnings of truce talks, General Ridgway in Tokyo became alarmed at the emphasis in the press and radio of talk of "Let's get the boys back home." On 4 July he sent a message to the Joint Chiefs of Staff on the need to limit such talk and to avoid the debacle in that respect that accompanied the end of World War II. He said in part:

I wish with great earnestness to point out the importance I attach to the retention by UN forces of so much of Korea as will permit occupation and defense of the Kansas Line with a suitable outpost zone for its protection.

This line follows the strongest defensive terrain in that general area. It is the most advanced strong defensive terrain which the tactical situation under your directives permits me to reach, and there logistically to support my forces.

Into the organization of this line has gone a tremendous amoung of effort.

Any position taken by our govt which would compel me to abandon the Kansas Line or deny me a reasonable outpost zone for its protection would vitally prejudice our entire military position in Korea. Request that copy of this message be furnished to Secy of Defense, personally.[71]

The heavy action in the Punchbowl area of east Korea continued. On 8 July the 2nd Battalion, ROK 1st Marine Regiment, assaulted Hill 1100 at the Punchbowl, going up the spur ridge southeast on Hill 1001. It was stopped by intense small-arms and automatic-weapons fire from the front and both flanks and by extensive fields of mines and booby traps. On the ninth, in continuing fighting for Hill 1100, the North Koreans forced the ROK 1st Marine Regiment to withdraw south of the hill, the ROK Marines losing 10 killed and 100 wounded to mines and booby traps alone.[72]

Meanwhile, negotiations proceeded for initiating the meetings of the truce proposal. On 3 July General Ridgway proposed that the liaison officers of both sides meet on 5 July to ensure satisfactory arrangements for the first meeting of the accredited representatives. Peking radio responded the next day that his proposal was accepted, except it proposed 8 July for the date of the meeting. After some exchange of messages, 8 July was accepted as the date of the meeting of the liaison officials at Kaesong, at which time discussions were held on arranging for the first meeting of the delegations, to be held on 10 July.

At Kaesong on 10 July the first meeting of the two delegations was held. The UN command delegation consisted of Vice Adm. C. Turner Joy, Maj. Gen. L. C. Craigie, Maj. Gen. Henry I. Hodes, Rear Adm. Arleigh A. Burke, and Maj. Gen. Paik Sun Yup. The Communist delegation consisted of Gen. Nam Il, Maj. Gen. Lee Sang Jo, Maj. Gen. Chang Pyong-San, Lt. Gen. Tung Hua, and Maj. Gen. Fang Hsieh. The first meeting considered an agenda, after each side made opening remarks. The opening remarks of Vice Admiral Joy included an important principle that guided what followed during all the dreary months that the armistice talks lasted. He said: "It is understood, of course, that hostilities will continue in all areas except in those neutral zones agreed upon, until such time as there is an agreement on the terms governing the armistice, and until such time as an approved armistice commission is prepared to function."[73]

Immediately an argument arose over the UN proposal that 20 journalists be included as part of its delegation, but not to be admitted to the conference room. At the first meeting Communist armed guards were constantly in evidence and tried to restrict the movement of the UN delegates to and about the conference site. On 12 July the Communist armed guards denied the journalists access to the conference area. General Ridgway instructed the UN delegation to recess until there could be established "a neutral zone around Kaesong free of armed personnel and the exclusion of armed personnel from routes to the zone." The Communist leaders agreed to this proposal on 14 July, and the talks resumed, in a meeting lasting from two to four o'clock, on the afternoon of 15 July.[74]

Concurrent with these initial meetings of the truce talks, military operations continued. Neither side, however, undertook large-scale operations, but there were numerous small-unit contacts as UN reconnaissance patrols sought to gain intelligence of enemy dispositions. The report to the United Nations on this aspect of the situation surrounding the opening of armistice talks had the following to say:

On the western part of the front, from Changdan to Kumwha [sic], United Nations patrols advanced up to six miles before eliciting counteraction. Bitter opposition was consistently encountered in the Otan-Amhyon area, astride the Imjin River where every United Nations approach drew violent reaction from hostile groups of substantial strength, well supported by artillery and mortars. On the fifty mile front from Kumwha eastward to Changjong, the enemy screening forces remained within one or two miles of the United Nations front, and promptly disputed advance by United Nations patrols. Action was virtually continuous to the north and east of Kumwha where the enemy undertook persistent probing attacks at rates of two to four per night, usually executed by platoons or companies, relatively well supported by artillery and mortar fire. Farther east, numerous local thrusts and counterthrusts occurred south of Chuktong and Hoegok. In the Pia area, there was evidence of increased artillery strength, and to the south of Changjong, small enemy units made several light probing attacks. Front lines remained stable throughout the period, except for a slight southward adjustment on the extreme east flank. The front extended from Munsan northeast to Kumwha, eastward to Wolsan, and northeast to the vicinity of Pohang.

The most significant military development during the period was continuance of hostile activities which heretofore have presaged a new major offensive. The enemy continued to augment his supply installations, particularly near the central and eastern fronts, and markedly increased the artillery and mortar support to practically all his forward elements as far east as Pia. Vehicle sightings have reached proportions similar to those which preceded earlier major offensives, and once more there are indications through prisoners of war that fresh forces are being readied for action. On the other hand, the extensive system of anti-tank defenses previously noted opposite the western front has been extended more than forty miles eastward to the vicinity of Pia, and now covers all trafficable north-south routes except those along the east coast.[75]

On 10 July the Joint Chiefs of Staff sent to General Ridgway the instructions that would guide him in the military operations in Korea during the armistice talks at Kaesong.

1. Fol instructions which are a compilation and condensation with minor modifications, of existing directives, constitute your authority as CINCUNC for conduct of mil operations in Korea. All previous directives or portions of directives in conflict herewith are rescinded. . . .

5. As CINCUNC you will, consistent with the security of forces under your command, inflict the maximum personnel and materiel losses on the forces of North Korea and Communist China operating within the geographical boundaries of Korea and waters thereto. The policy objective of your mil mission is to create condi-

tions favorable to a settlement of the Korea conflict which would, as a minimum:

(a) Terminate hostilities under appropriate armistice arrangements;

(b) Establish the authority of ROK over all Korea south of a northern boundary so located as to facilitate, to the maximum extent possible, both administration and military defense, and in no case south of the 38th parallel;

(c) Provide for the withdrawal by appropriate stages of non-Korean armed forces from Korea;

(d) Permit the building of sufficient ROK mil power to deter or repel a renewed North Korean aggression.

6. In pursuit of your mission in Korea, you authd to conduct air and naval operations within geographic boundaries of Korea and waters adjacent thereto as deemed by you to be necessary or advantageous to successful attainment of your mission. This specifically does not include authority to conduct air and naval action against Manchuria or other Chinese territory, against USSR territory, or against hydroelectric installations on Yalu River, except with approval of JCS, and as a matter of policy no air operations or naval surface operations will be conducted within 12 miles of USSR territory on the Asiatic Mainland.

7. With regard to ground operations you are authorized to conduct such tactical operations as may be necessary or desirable to support your mission, to insure the safety of your command, and to continue to harass the enemy. This includes authority to conduct guerrilla operations and limited amphibious and airborne operations in enemy rear areas. . . .

17. It is agreed in principle that, in event of Soviet attack against the FECOM, United States and other UN forces will be withdrawn from Korea and you should plan accordingly. Situation may require some immediate movement of your forces both in Korea and in Japan, you will initiate major withdrawal from Korea only upon instructions furnished you after receipt of info from you as to conditions obtaining. Pending further instructions, you should not count on the use of any UN forces other than those of US, in defense of FECOM outside Korea.[76]

Kaesong, for five centures capital of Korea until replaced by Seoul about 1450, was 42 road miles northwest of Seoul. The meetings of the delegates to the armistice talks were held in a small teahouse on the edge of Kaesong. The UN delegates arrived each day from Munsan-ni, a small village of mud-thatch huts on the south bank of the Imjin River, 30 miles south of Kaesong. At Munsan-ni the UN command had built a base camp of canvas squad tents scattered around an apple orchard. Here the UN armistice delegation had its headquarters. The delegates made a daily helicopter flight from this base camp to the Kaesong teahouse for their meetings, and at their termination each day the delegates flew back to the camp at Munsan-ni to spend the night. Each day a procession of 16 vehicles, including mess trucks bearing the equipment and mess detail for the noontime meal, and other trucks and jeeps bore liaison officers, stenographers, interpreters, and the 20 allotted reporters. This cavalcade of vehicles carried about 130 officers and men.

A train with steam up stood at the little railroad station at Munsan-ni,

Jeep drivers waiting outside the Kaesong teahouse as armistice negotiations get under way inside, 10 July 1951. *National Archives photograph, 111-SC 372280*

ready to move quickly south if there was a threatening incident from across the river. The train served mostly as a briefing structure when Brig. Gen. William P. Nuchols came from the conference teahouse in Kaesong to give a report on the day's proceedings. This was the source for the hundreds of press dispatches that were disseminated to the world through the news bureaus in Seoul and Tokyo. The usual story of the day was "no progress."

On 15 July Lt. Gen. Edward M. Almond, who had been in Korea ever since the Inchon landing, left the peninsula forever, rotated back to the United States to take up his next assignment, as commandant, the Army War College, at Carlisle Barracks, Pennsylvania. Farewell honors were accorded him by the X Corps Honor Guard and the assembled officers and men of the X Corps Headquarters at 1:35 P.M. By radio the "parting shot" was fired simultaneously by all of X Corps artillery batteries—274 guns and 12 tanks. At 1:45 Almond left the X Corps CP in an L-19 plane for Chunchon. There he transferred to a Constellation, which General Ridgway had sent from Japan, for the flight to Seoul. In Seoul he drove from the airport to Eighth Army's Advance CP to say good-bye to General Van Fleet, the army commander. At 3:35 he left the army's Advance CP for K-16 airfield at Taegu and at 4 P.M. departed for Haneda airfield, Tokyo, arriving there at 7:28 P.M.[77]

This aggressive, patriotic soldier left an indelible mark upon the war in Korea. Sometimes controversial, he was a man of action and impatient of delay and incompetence. After his X Corps joined Eighth Army in South Korea following the evacuation of the X Corps from northeast Korea at Hungnam in December 1950, the X Corps went into the line in east-central Korea and remained there throughout 1951 and Almond's tenure of command. When he left it, the X Corps had just wrought the defeat of the Chinese and North Korean 2nd Impulse of the CCF 5th Phase Offensive and had won back in a massive counterattack all the ground that had been lost in the earlier fighting in that sector. It was the greatest defeat of the Chinese in the war to date. General Ridgway evaluated General Almond as his "best corps commander."[78]

The talks begun at Kaesong on 10 July 1951 to effect a truce in the Korean War went on for more than two years, with many interruptions, and it was not until 27 July 1953 that the truce documents were signed at Panmunjom, which had become the site of the truce talks, beginning on 25 October 1951. A demarcation line between the two Koreas was agreed upon the same day, establishing a demilitarized zone 151 miles long, and two kilometers wide, extending from the north side of the Imjin River opposite Munsan-ni and ending on the east coast just south of the town of Kosong.

In those two years many bitter and deadly engagements were fought over hills and points of advantage to one side or the other in or close to what became the Demilitarized Zone, and the territory held by both sides changed from time to time. But all these battles were localized engagements, and there were no operational maneuvers on a major scale. The war of maneuver came to an end in June 1951. The events of the two years between 1 July 1951 and 27 July 1953 are covered very well in Walter G. Hermes, *Truce Tent and Fighting Front: United States Army in the Korean War* (Washington, D.C.: Office of the Chief of Military History, US Army, Superintendent of Documents, GPO, 1966).

I cannot end this volume without including my appraisal of General Matthew B. Ridgway. He took command of a defeated and demoralized army on 26 December 1950 in Korea. His hope that it would fight the enemy and hold Seoul in January 1951 was doomed to sharp disappointment. The army and its officers, with few exceptions, were intent on going south—and quitting Korea. It required a patient but persistent effort on Ridgway's part to change the direction of Eighth Army from south to north.

It was for the most part a solo performance—he had no help from the army staff and its men. One man, a leader with high resolve, made the difference. In the end his cautious turnaround gained momentum when the officers and men saw that the enemy was vulnerable and overextended and that victories could be won.

If there was one turning point in the war that was critical to eventual success and disheartened the enemy and invigorated Eighth Army with a heightened morale, it was the battle of Chipyong-ni in mid-February in central Korea. All subordinate commanders involved wanted to withdraw from the place when it was threatened with being surrounded by superior forces. But Ridgway had determined that the 23rd Infantry Regiment and its attached units would remain there and fight a battle against seemingly overwhelming odds from within a tight perimeter, and he promised to provide the support needed to win. It turned out to be a crucial battle. In my opinion Ridgway was its principal architect. Without him it would not have been fought.

Ridgway succeeded in establishing a line across the breadth of Korea, and each month that passed saw it forged more firmly. He insisted on unit contact with adjacent units and an end to gaps between units, a policy that required them to be mutually supporting. He dealt harshly with commanders who ignored this principle. His conduct of the turnaround operations was not spectacular but was based on what was possible at the moment. As morale in the army increased with each small success, what became possible with Eighth Army mounted steadily, until by April 1951, it was able to face and defeat the Chinese 5th Phase Offensive. By the end of May 1951, Eighth Army had won another major battle and had counterattacked successfully, with the enemy demoralized and suffering very heavy casualties in personnel and matériel. The Eighth Army had regained virtually all of Korea south of the 38th Parallel and had gone north of the parallel on a line north of Seoul along the Imjin River to Chorwon at the southwest corner of the Iron Triangle and hence generally northeast to the Sea of Japan.

Ridgway was at one and the same time an inspiring leader of men and a pragmatic commander. He believed the point of balance between the two sides had been reached, and he withheld risking the loss of what had been gained and spending an unrewarding amount of American blood for possible additions that would not materially change the military situation in Korea. His judgment was sound. Ridgway redeemed the military honor of the United States in the eyes of the world.

Appendix: Lament of Suwon

WHILE AT THE I CORPS CP in 1951 I came upon a quaint, interesting document entitled "Lament of Suwon," which presumably reflects the general impression then held of the men mentioned in its text. I was never able to establish the identity of its author, although the information at I Corps was that a lieutenant colonel had written it when the corps CP was at Suwon in February 1951. Whoever its author was, he must have been familiar with some of the medieval writers and perhaps Froissart's chronicles, which record the medieval wars of England and France. In the medieval tradition that styled Richard "the Lion Heart" and William "the Conqueror," the author of "Lament of Suwon" added descriptive phrases to the first names of prominent men. The names of many officers of the I Corps staff appear: Matthew the Good (Gen. Matthew B. Ridgway), Ned the Anointed (Gen. Edward M. Almond), John the Nervous (Gen. John Coulter, IX Corps), William Cross at Remagen (Gen. William Hoge, IX Corps), Frank the Little (Maj. Gen. Frank Milburn, CG, I Corps), Rinaldo the Chief Shepherd (Brig. Gen. Rinaldo Van Brunt, CS, I Corps), Carl the Redfaced (Maj. Carl Armail, CO, HQ Co., I Corps), John of the Many Ciphers (probably Lt. Col. John MacIndoe, G-3 Sec., I Corps, who usually gave the morning briefings of operations).

And it came to pass that the tents of the Legion of Frank the Little were assembled in the city called Suwon in the land of the Koreanites. And there came one day a herald bringing tidings and great news of the arrival in this camp of him who was called Matthew the Good. Much preparation was evoked and Rinaldo the Chief Shepherd among the disciples of Frank the Little called unto him all his chief disciples, among them being Master of the Household. Carl the Redfaced; James the Freezer of Mare's Milk; Ray Keeper of the Peace; Charles the Dour, Guardian of Pastures; and many others and spake unto them; Lo, I say unto ye, there comes among us he who is known as Matthew the Good. I command ye make haste and prepare for him the welcome befitting his greatness. Let all multitude be forewarned. Prepare for him a feast of kimches and native wine. For great should be our honor that he hath selected this camp to come unto. Then the Chief Shepherd turned to Charles the Dour and questioned him saying, wherefore shall we find a caravan for his use befitting his position? And Charles the Dour spake saying, be thou not concerned, O Chief, for this great one may have all that is called mine. Which came to pass.

The Chief Shepherd then called unto him certain other of the disciples. To him who is known as Thomas the Undoubting he spake saying, Know thou the quantity of bread loaves and the number of fishes and grain which repose in thy storehouses? Harken unto my word that thou shalt expand each and every last small morsel of information.

Then he called unto him the lesser disciple known as John of the Many Ciphers and spake unto him saying, Verily I say unto thee if thou delivereth thy sermon unto Matthew the Good and bringeth not the wrath of him down upon us thou shalt be rewarded with wine and thou shalt be sent unto that land surrounded by water over which the Great White Father reigneth. But shouldst thou fail and cause wrath and scorn of the Good Matthew to become rife amoung us thou shalt be cast into the dungeon of despair and thy wine casks shall be broken.

And it came to pass on the appointed day that early in the morn were assembled in great numbers the cohorts of Frank the Little.

Rinaldo the Chief Shepherd gathered about him his master shepherds of the smaller flocks and bade them to be not afraid against the coming of him who was known as Matthew the Good, Chief Inquisitor of Joseph — he of the lightning and of many fierce weapons unknown to mortal man. He spake thus giving encouragement, for all the assembled knew that this Matthew was Chief over many Chief Shepherds and asked many questions and accepted few answers.

Then came Matthew the Good bearing pomegranates upon his chest into the habitation of the vassals and smiled. The cohorts rose and greeted their Chief of Chiefs. Then did all sit except him who was known as John of the Many Ciphers who took his wand in hand and saith unto his Chief without any further preparation, for had he not already repeated the same words over to Rinaldo the Chief Shepherd.

Lo there were many enemies of our Lord on many sides.

And Matthew the Good spake, saying:

How knowest thou that there were many and not a mere many?

And John of the Many Ciphers was sore troubled within though he showed it not and resumed, saying:

Lo and there were a mere many. Our flocks were sore set upon by bands of wolves.

Say not more, spake Matthew the Good. What color were the wolves?

John of the Many Ciphers had prepared himself for such a question, and spake thus:

They were of grey hue, my lord, and numbered seven of the large dog and three of the old and nine of the young bitches.

Matthew the Good nodded and spake no more. Rinaldo the Chief Shepherd nodded gravely and uttered a silent sigh of great relief though he was duly proud, for were not these his very own words? Frank the Little also spake not a word.

Then did Thomas the Undoubting rise to his feet and say, Thou shalt keep thy basic load intact, thy ass in fine fettle that it may bear its burdens in seemly fashion. We lack, my lord, many of the promised goods.

Then did Matthew the Good say, How much of the substance do you lack?

And Thomas the Undoubting, trumpeting, answered in parables of the Widow's Mite and many things.

Matthew the Good faltered not and said, Lo you have the shekels unto the fifth day of consumption as promised.

And all were silent for none wished to gainsay the Lord in their midst.

Then rose James [the] Freezer of Mare's Milk and counter of the cohorts and said, Many sheep have been lost to the total of ninety and three. The first of these had blue eyes and golden hair. He reclineth in a special tent near the sheep and returneth to the flock.

Thus did James the Freezer of Mare's Milk tell of all that had befallen the flocks unto the last or least thereof. And Rinaldo the Chief Shepherd rested in ease, for were these not the very words just as rehearsed?

And so lived Matthew the Good amongst the Legions of Frank the Little for many days and nights. But troubles midst the flocks of Ned the Anointed and the flocks late of John the Nervous brought much new worry unto the mind of Good Matthew. Sorely taxed and in tribulation he had need depart his vast camp and go forth to calm the troubled waters in the lands of Ned the Anointed and in the lands lately of John the Nervous but now of William Cross at Remagen.

Tents folded in the night and sorrow thus came to the disciples of Frank the Little and especially to Rinaldo the Chief Shepherd. Good spirit and cheers accompanied Matthew the Good as he sped away in his winged chariot. Such was the good cheer that later a great feast was prepared with much wine and all partook in the merrymaking.

Notes

ALL OPERATIONS REPORTS and documents from the Korean War as well as the intelligence data obtained in the operations, are preserved in the National Archives in Record Group 407, where they are grouped in numbered boxes. It can be assumed that, unless otherwise indicated, any citation of an item that lists merely a box number is in Record Group 407. In addition to abbreviations used in the text and listed after the preface, the following acronyms appear in the notes: ACG, assistant commanding general; CIC, Counter Intelligence Corps; CS, chief of staff; DIS, Daily Intelligence Summary; WD, War Diary.

CHAPTER 1

1. Telecon NR Z 30793, CincFe to DeptAR, Wash, 23 Dec 50, Personal for Gen. J. L. Collins, signed MacArthur; Telecon MC IN 71151, CincFe to DeptAR, Personal for Ridgway, signed MacArthur, 23 Dec 50, Box 16, Ridgway Papers, US Army Military History Research Collection, Carlisle Barracks, Pa. In his book *MacArthur, His Rendezvous with History* (New York: Knopf, 1956), p. 432, Maj. Gen. Courtney Whitney says that, when Gen. Collins received MacArthur's message, he at first demurred. On MacArthur's insistence, however, he consented to Ridgway's appointment to Eighth Army command. Whitney also says that MacArthur asked Gen. Collins to have Gen. James Van Fleet in readiness to send to the Far East to replace Ridgway or himself if either should become casualties. Whitney was a member of MacArthur's small circle of top advisors in Tokyo and a strong partisan. Also, Ridgway, review comments on "Ridgway Duels for Korea" (hereafter cited as Ridgway, Comments), and letter to author, 8 Mar 1980.

2. Matthew B. Ridgway, *The Korean War* (New York: Doubleday, 1967), pp. 79–80. This volume is Ridgway's personal story of his role in the Korean War and as commander in chief, United Nations forces, in Korea. Ridgway had previously published a work entitled *Soldier: The Memoirs of Matthew B. Ridgway*, as told to Harold Martin (New York: Harper and Brothers, 1956), in which chapters 22–27 concern his role in the Korean War. The first four chapters of *The Korean War* were probably written by Robert Smith as a quick survey of the war up to the time Gen. Ridgway assumed command in Korea. These chapters contain numerous

errors of fact and should be considered less than fully reliable as to detail. I believe Gen. Ridgway's own contributions begin with chapter 5. Thereafter the book may be considered reliable and valuable in connection with his role in the Korean War.

3. *Washington Post,* 3 Oct 1954, Dr. Gordon Prang in a review of Maj. Gen. Charles A. Willoughby and John Chamberlain, *MacArthur: 1941–1951.* Prang was close to Gen. Willoughby at the time as a member of his G-2 staff in the FEC. Ridgway, interview with author, 21 Oct 1975, Ridgway's home, Pittsburgh, Pa.

4. Historical Record Folder, Box 16, Ridgway Papers.

5. Ridgway, interview with author, 21 Oct 1975; Ridgway, interview with Col. John M. Blair, 6 Jan 1972, vol. 2, p. 84, Box 51, Ridgway Papers.

6. Personal Correspondence, Box 16, Ridgway Papers.

7. Eighth Army Correspondence, Dec 50–Apr 51, Box 17, Ridgway Papers.

8. Ridgway, *Soldier,* pp. 195–201; Ridgway, *The Korean War,* pp. 79–81.

9. Memorandum of Record of Conference with MacArthur, 26 Dec 50, Tokyo, in Unclassified Binder, Box 17, Ridgway Papers. The conversation with MacArthur is also covered in Ridgway, *The Korean War,* pp. 82–83.

10. Ridgway, *The Korean War,* p. 83. In my interview with Gen. Ridgway, 21 Oct 1975, I asked if he thought Lin Piao had commanded the CCF forces opposed to him in Korea. He answered, "Yes, I was told in the Far East Command that Lin Piao was my opposite number in Korea." He apparently thought that this was the case right up to 1975, when I talked with him about it.

11. HQ, EUSAK, Gen. Ord. No. 215, 26 Dec 50, copy in Folder M–R, Box 17, Ridgway Papers; Eighth Army, Comd. Rpt., Summ., Dec 50, Box 1134; Ridgway, *The Korean War,* App. 2, p. 262, reproduces text of Ridgway's order, sent initially as Personal for Allen, Eighth Army chief of staff. Ridgway, Comments, and letter to author, 8 Mar 1980.

12. Maj. Gen. Leven C. Allen, Eighth Army chief of staff (1950–51), interview with author, 15 Dec 1953. For Allen's conversation with Ridgway, see Ridgway, *Soldier,* p. 203. In connection with Eighth Army demolition policy then in effect, Gen. Allen told me that FEC GHQ had ordered it, and he confirmed that Col. Pascal Strong, Eighth Army engineer, had opposed it.

13. Allen, interview with author, 15 Dec 1953.

14. Ridgway, Comments, and letter to author, 8 Mar 1980.

15. Cpl. Randle M. Hurst, 502nd Recon. Plat., MS, Binder 1, Addendum 2, p. 96 (in author's possession); Ridgway, *Soldier,* p. 93.

16. Cpl. Randle M. Hurst, letter to his parents, Mr. and Mrs. Irvin Hurst, 1 Jan 1951.

17. Ridgway, *Soldier,* p. 204.

18. Lt. Col. Paul Smith (who had accompanied Gen. Ridgway from Eighth Army CP at Taegu as a temporary aide, pending the arrival from Washington of Lt. Col. Walter Winton, who would be Ridgway's regular aide-de-camp), interview with author, 1951; Memorandum to Ridgway from Lt. Col. Smith (Scotch 303), 27 Dec 50, "Highlights of Conferences and Command Visits, 27 Dec 50," Special File, Box 20, Ridgway Papers.

19. Memorandum to Ridgway from Lt. Col. Smith, 27 Dec 50; Ridgway, *The Korean War,* pp. 84–85.

20. Memorandum to Ridgway from Lt. Col. Smith, 27 Dec 50; Smith, inter-

view with author, 1951; Eighth Army, Comd. Rpt., Summ., Dec 50, Box 1134; Ridgway, Comments, and letter to author, 8 Mar 1980.

21. Lt. Gen. Edward M. Almond, Diary, 27 Dec 50; Almond, interview with author, 23 Nov 1954.

22. Almond, Diary, 27 Dec 50. The passage quoted was in Almond's handwriting in black ink at the bottom of the typed page, date not indicated. Entries in Almond's diary were made at the end of each day by one of his two aides and approved by Almond. They were usually made a part of the X Corps monthly command report. In this diary Almond did not usually include personal or sensitive information, although it was complete and precise as to his movements and meetings with others. In his personal copy of the diary, however, Almond would at times add observations in his own hand that were not found in the diary included in the X Corps command report. The observation quoted in the narrative for the 27 Dec 1950 diary entry is one of several found only in Almond's personal copy. I have in my possession, with Gen. Almond's approval, a copy of his personal copy of the diary.

23. Eighth Army, Comd. Rpt., Summ., Dec 50, Box 1134.

24. Ridgway, *Soldier*, pp. 204-205.

25. Ridgway, *The Korean War*, pp. 88-89.

26. Ridgway, interview with Col. John M. Blair, 24 Nov 1971, vol. 1, pp. 1-10, Folder K-M, Box 18, Ridgway Papers; Ridgway, interview with Virgil Pinkley, 12 Apr 1951; War Dept. listing of M. B. Ridgway promotions, service, and decorations up to 1 Aug 1947 (copy in author's possession); Ridgway, interview with author, 21 Oct 1975.

27. War Dept. list of Ridgway personnel actions; Ridgway, *Soldier*, pp. 30-50. In *Soldier* Ridgway gives many details about his various assignments between 1917 and 1942. Those years gave him varied experience in the Army schools, in command and staff assignments, and in military diplomacy under the tutelage of Gen. Frank McCoy, whom he never ceased to admire.

28. Ridgway, *Soldier*, pp. 55-56.

29. War Dept. listing of Ridgway decorations; Ridgway, *Soldier*, pp. 51-151; Ridgway, Comments, and letter to author, 8 Mar 1980.

30. The quotations are from my record of two interviews with Gen. Ridgway in his office in the Dai-Ichi Building (FEC Headquarters), Tokyo, 8 and 9 Oct 1951.

31. Ridgway, *Soldier*, pp. 97-98.

32. Ridgway, interview with author, 21 Oct 1975.

33. Ridgway, interview with Col. John M. Blair, 24 Mar 1972, Box 51, Ridgway Papers.

34. Lt. Gen. William J. McCaffrey, USA, Ret., letter to author, 5 June 1979.

35. Brig. Gen. Brittingham, interview with author, 29 July 1951.

36. Col. David M. Butler, DSO, Australian Military Forces, letter to author, 5 Sept 1972.

37. Lt. Gen. William J. McCaffrey, USA, Ret., letter to author, 5 Dec 1975. I have discussed this and other incidents of the Korean War with Gen. McCaffrey. He emphasized that all commanders in Korea during Ridgway's command knew he would deal harshly with them if they did not follow his orders and carelessly

lost men to enemy action. He had great respect for Ridgway and said that, after Ridgway assumed command, a new army evolved.

38. Ridgway, interview with Caulfield and Elton, 29 Aug 1969, Box 51, Ridgway Papers.

39. Theodore A. Dodge, *Great Captains* (New York and Boston: Houghton Mifflin, 1889), pp. 74, 302–303.

40. Ibid., p. 211. (An abbreviated version of Dodge's views appears in a volume originally given as a series of lectures. References are to the full published work cited here.)

41. Ridgway, Comments, and letter to author, 8 Mar 1980.

42. Antoine Henri Jomini, *Summary of the Art of War*, a condensed version, edited by Lt. Col. J. D. Hittle, USMC (Harrisburg, Pa.: Military Service Publishing, 1947), is a convenient and easily used edition of Jomini's greatest work. To this day Jomini is considered one of the most brilliant military thinkers in the history of war. It is evident that the Chinese leaders of the Korean War had studied Jomini, as their tactics often seem taken directly from him.

43. Ridgway, letter to author, 24 Mar 1978. In this letter in a passage that preceded the part quoted, Gen. Ridgway mentioned "the details which follow, and which I have never before released. You are welcome to use them."

44. Ridgway, *Soldier*, pp. 82–83.

CHAPTER 2

1. 2nd Log. Command., Comd. Rpt. (C), Dec 1950, p. 4.

2. Eighth Army, Comd. Rpt., Summ., 27–29 Dec 50, Box 1134; 38th Inf., 2nd Div., Comd. Rpt., Narr., 27–29 Dec 50, Box 2474.

3. Eighth Army, Comd. Rpt., Summ., 30 Dec 50, Box 1134.

4. I Corps, Comd. Rpt., Narr., 27 Dec 50, Box 1502; 24th Inf., 25th Div., Comd. Rpt., Narr., 27 Dec 50, Box 3766.

5. Eighth Army, Comd. Rpt., Summ., 27 Dec 50, Boxes 1137 and 1134. (The Eighth Army Comd. Rpt. for 1–16 Dec 50 is in Box 1136, and for 17–31 Dec 50, in Box 1137.)

6. 2nd Div., Comd. Rpt., G-2 Staff Sec., 27 Dec 50, Box 2436; 9th Inf., Comd. Rpt., Narr., 27 Dec 50, Box 2471; Eighth Army, Comd. Rpt., G-3 Sec. and G-3 Jnl., 27 Dec 50, Box 1137.

7. 2nd Div., Comd. Rpt., Summ., Dec 50, p. 12, Box 2436; 23rd Inf., 2nd Div., Comd. Rpt., Narr., 28 Dec 50, Box 2473; 9th Inf., Comd. Rpt., Narr., 28 Dec 50, Box 2471.

8. I Corps, Comd. Rpt., Narr., 28 Dec 50, Box 1502.

9. 25th Div., Comd. Rpt., Narr., Dec 50, Box 3766.

10. 2nd Div., Comd. Rpt., Narr., p. 13, and G-3 Jnl., 29 Dec 50, Box 2436; FEC DIS No. 3035, 31 Dec 50, Box 99.

11. Eighth Army, Comd. Rpt., G-3 Sec. and G-3 Jnl., 29 Dec 50, Box 1137.

12. 25th Div., Comd. Rpt., 29 Dec 50, Box 3766; Eighth Army, Comd. Rpt., Summ., 29 Dec 50, Box 1134; FEC DIS No. 3035, 31 Dec 50, Box 99.

13. 2nd Div., Comd. Rpt., Dec 50, 30 Dec, Summ., p. 14; Eighth Army, Comd. Rpt., Narr., 30 Dec 50, Box 1134; Eighth Army, Comd. Rpt., G-3 Sec. and G-3 Jnl., 30 Dec 50, Boxes 1136–37; FEC DIS No. 3034, 30 Dec 50, Box 99.

14. 2nd Div., Comd. Rpt., G-3 Staff Sec. and Narr. Summ., Dec 50, pp. 13–14; 23rd Inf., 2nd Div., Comd. Rpt., 30–31 Dec 50, Box 2473; 9th Inf., Comd. Rpt., 30–31 Dec 50, Box 2471.

15. Eighth Army, Comd. Rpt., G-3 Jnl., 30 Dec 50, Box 1137.

16. Ibid., G-2 Sec., and Encl. 2, PIR No. 171, 30 Dec 50, Box 1135. The army's PIR No. 172, 31 Dec 50, confirmed the first interrogation of the thirtieth and adds more to it.

17. Eighth Army, Comd. Rpt., Summ., 30 Dec 50, Box 1134; FEC DIS No. 3036, 1 Jan 51, Box 386.

18. 3rd Div., Comd. Rpt., 30–31 Dec 50, Box 2881.

19. 2nd Log. Command, Comd. Rpt. (C), Dec 1950, pp. 3, 7.

20. Ibid., p. 16.

21. "Logistical Problems and Their Solutions, 25 Aug 50 to 31 Aug 51," Hist. Sec., Japan Logistical Command (JLC), 15 Feb 52, pp. 16–17; 25th Div., Comd. Rpt., Summ., Dec 50, p. 19. By the end of August 1951, 82,000 American troops, 5,100 British troops, and 3,500 other UN soldiers had enjoyed R&R trips to Japan.

22. 2nd Log. Command, Comd. Rpt. (C), Dec 50, pp. 5, 9; ORO-T-6 (FEC), "An Evaluation of Service Supply in the Korean Campaign," 1 Mar 51, pp. 50–53.

23. Eighth Army, Comd. Rpt., G-3 Jnl., 31 Dec 50, Box 1137; FEC DIS No. 3036, 1 Jan 51, Box 386; 23rd Inf., 2nd Div., Comd. Rpt., 31 Dec 50, Box 2473; 2nd Div., Comd. Rpt., Narr., 31 Dec 50, Box 2436; 38th Inf., Comd. Rpt., Narr., 31 Dec 50, Box 2474.

24. Eighth Army, Comd. Rpt., Logistics Sec. and Narr., Dec 50, Box 1134.

25. Ibid., Narr. and G-4 Sec., Dec 50, Boxes 1134 and 1138.

26. Ridgway, interview with Caulfield and Elton, 29 Aug 1969, pp. 5–27, Ridgway Papers; Ridgway, *The Korean War*, p. 87.

27. Copy in Ridgway Papers; see also Ridgway message, personal for Bolling and his personal delivery to Gen. Collins, TSW 233, 25 Apr 51, on this subject, correcting Courtney Whitney's statement for the press on 24 Apr 51, copy in Ridgway Papers; Ridgway, interview with author, 21 Oct 1975. Gen. Ridgway told me in this interview that only after he had reached Korea and estimated the situation there, on the basis of his conversations with numerous officers of Eighth Army, I Corps and IX Corps, and ROK officers, and had seen the situation with respect to the enlisted men as he toured the front between 27 and 29 December 1950, did he decide to send the message to Gen. Collins recommending the use of Chiang Kai-shek's Nationalist Chinese troops in an invasion of South China's mainland opposite Formosa.

28. Ridgway, *Soldier*, p. 209.

29. Ridgway, personal letter to Collins, CS, 8 Jan 1951, Folder A–C, Box 17, Ridgway Papers. Only the first page of this letter was in the file.

CHAPTER 3

1. Two copies are in my possession. The copies differ slightly in translation from each other, but the substance is the same throughout. The document is a booklet mimeographed in Chinese, entitled "A Collection of Combat Experiences Issued by HQ XIX CCF Army Group, 29 March 51." One copy is marked "belonging to Chin, Chief of Staff, 4th Ta-tui." It covers all the important battles from the Chinese entrance into the war in October 1950 through the battle of Chipyong-

ni, in the middle of February 1951. The section entitled "Penetration of the Imjin River" extends from p. 142 through p. 151 of the translation. In the second copy there is a sketch map showing initial crossing and penetration of the UN line. The document obviously had been prepared by elements of the XIII Army Group that were involved in the events.

2. A study of a 1:50,000-scale map, 1¼ inch to the mile, will show this area clearly.

3. "Collection of Combat Experiences."

4. I Corps, Comd. Rpt., G-3 Sec., 1 Jan 51, Box 1507; Eighth Army, Comd. Rpt., Summ., 1 Jan 51, Box 1134; ibid., G-2, PIR No. 173, 1 Jan 51, Box 1144; I Corps, Comd. Rpt., 1 Jan 51, Box 1505.

5. Author's interviews with Maj. Lamb, Lts. James T. Jones and Snell; Maj. Daly, KMAG advisor to ROK 1st Div.; and Capt. Harley F. Mooney, US 3rd Div.

6. Mooney, interview with author, Sept 1951.

7. IX Corps, Comd. Rpt., G-3 Sec., 1 Jan 51, Box 1779; I Corps, Comd. Rpt., G-2 Sec., Box 1506; Eighth Army, Comd. Rpt., Summ., Box 1134.

8. ATIS, Enemy Doc., Issue 44, p. 79, Combat Rpt. of unspecified CCF regt., undated. The document mentions that "our regt" began to penetrate at 1830 hours on 31 Dec 50.

9. 24th Div., Comd. Rpt., 1 Jan 51, Box 3545; 25th Div., Comd. Rpt., 1 Jan 51, Box 3545; 19th Inf., Comd. Rpt., Narr. and combined G-2 and G-3 Rpt., Box 3523.

10. Col. Robert Halleck, CO, 24th Div. Arty., interview with author, Aug 1951; FEC DIS No. 3037, 2 Jan 51; I Corps, Comd. Rpt., G-3 Sec., 1 Jan 51, Box 1134.

11. Ridgway, Soldier, p. 210.

12. Ridgway, The Korean War, p. 94.

13. Ridgway, Soldier, pp. 210–11.

14. Eighth Army, Comd. Rpt., 1 Jan 51, Box 1143.

15. Brig. T. Brodie, Order of the Day, 1 Jan 51, Hist. Rec., Dec 50–Oct 51, Box 22, Ridgway Papers; Eighth Army, Comd. Rpt., G-3 Jnl., 1 Jan 51.

16. I Corps, Comd. Rpt., 1 Jan 51, Box 1505; Eighth Army, Comd. Rpt., G-3 Jnl., 1 Jan 51.

17. Eighth Army, Comd. Rpt., G-3 Jnl., 1 Jan 51, Box 1146; Norman Bartlett, With the Australians in Korea (Canberra: Australian War Memorial, 1954), p. 59.

18. US 25th Div., Comd. Rpt., G-3 Sec., 1 Jan 51, Boxes 3773–74; 25th Div., Comd. Rpt., 1 Jan 51, Box 3773; 2nd Bn., 27th Inf., 25th Div., Comd. Rpt., 1 Jan 51, Box 3850 (Lt. Col. Gordon Murch, a great battalion commander, CO of the 2nd Bn., was ordered to protect the left flank of the British 29th Brigade); Eighth Army, G-3 Jnl., 1 Jan 51 (according to a journal entry at 1655 hours, I Corps issued its operational order to the 25th Division at that time to take its position on the left of the British 29th Brigade and to protect its flank and to block on the Kaesong road); 27th Inf., 25th Div., Comd. Rpt., 1 Jan 51, Box 3850.

19. 1st Bn., 27th Inf., 25th Div., Jan 51, and 27th Inf., Comd. Rpt., Jan 51, Box 3850.

20. FEC DIS No. 3038, 3 Jan 51, Box 386; I Corps, Comd. Rpt., 1 Jan 51, Box 1503.

21. Eighth Army HQ, Gen. Ord. No. 155, 20 Mar 51, awarding the Distinguished Service Cross to Maj. Harold H. Meisner for action near Kapyong.

22. 2nd Bn., 27th Inf., Hist. Rpt., 2 Jan 51, Box 3850; 25th Div., Comd. Rpt., 2 Jan 51, Box 3773.

23. 25th Div., Comd. Rpt., G-3 Sec. Jnl. File, copy of Instr. No. 39, Box 3774.

24. Eighth Army, Comd. Rpt., G-3 Sec., 2 Jan 51, Box 1146; ibid., G-2 Sec., PIR No. 174, Box 1144; I Corps, Comd. Rpt., 2 Jan 51, Box 1505, and G-3 Sec., Box 1507.

25. IX Corps, Comd. Rpt., G-3 Sec. Jnl., Serial 221; Eighth Army, Comd. Rpt., G-3 Jnl., messages at 1720 and 2152 hours.

26. Lt. Col. Clarence E. Stuart, CO, 555th FA Bn., interview with author, 9 Aug 1951; 24th Div., Comd. Rpt., 2 Jan 51, Box 3545; 5th RCT, 24th Div., Comd. Rpt., 2 Jan 51, Box 5237; Eighth Army, Comd. Rpt., G-3 Sec., 2 Jan 51, Box 1146; FEC DIS No. 3038, 3 Jan 51, Box 386.

27. FEC DIS No. 3038, 3 Jan 51 (reporting events of 2 Jan), Box 386; Eighth Army, Comd. Rpt., 2 Jan 51; G-3 Jnl. messages, 2 Jan 51, at 1830, 1600, 1800, and briefing for CG, 3 Jan 51.

28. Ridgway, *Soldier*, p. 211; Gen. Frank Milburn (I Corps commander), interview with author, Dec 1951.

29. Ridgway, *The Korean War*, p. 95.

CHAPTER 4

1. "Demolition Policy in South Korea," 2 Jan 51, to CG, I Corps, IX and X corps, ROK Army, 5th Air Force, Special File, Dec 1950–Mar 1951, Box 20, Ridgway Papers.

2. Daily Hist. Rpt., 3 Jan 51, Hist. Rec., Dec 50–Oct 51, Box 22, Ridgway Papers; Ridgway, *The Korean War*, pp. 95–96; Eighth Army, Comd. Rpt., Narr. Summ., CG Activities, 3 Jan 51, Box 1143.

3. Eighth Army, Comd. Rpt., 3 Jan 51, Box 1143, and Eighth Army, G-3 Sec., Box 1146.

4. Eighth Army, Comd. Rpt., G-2, PIR No. 175, Encl. 2, 3 Jan 51, Box 1144.

5. IX Corps, Comd. Rpt., G-3 Sec., 3 Jan 51, Box 1779.

6. Eighth Army, Comd. Rpt., G-3 Jnl., 3 Jan 51, Box 1146.

7. Ibid., 3 Jan 51, Box 1134; ibid., G-2, PIR No. 175, 3 Jan 51, Box 1144; FEC DIS, 5 Jan 51, Situation Map, scale 1:125,000, to accompany DIS No. 3040, Box 386.

8. 21st Inf., 24th Div., Comd. Rpt., and 21st Inf., S-2 Jnl., Serial 3447, Box 3664.

9. 24th Div., Comd. Rpt., 3 Jan 51, Box 3545.

10. Eighth Army HQ, Gen. Ord. No. 136, 12 Mar 51, awarding the Distinguished Service Cross to Cpl. Billy Mosier, Med. Co., 21st Inf., 24th Div., for heroic action 3 Jan 51, near Uijongbu.

11. FEC DIS No. 3039, 4 Jan 51, Box 386; 24th Div., Comd. Rpt., 3 Jan 51, Box 3545, and 24th Div., G-2 and G-3 Consolidated Rpt., 3 Jan 51; IX Corps, Comd. Rpt., 3 Jan 51, Box 1779.

12. Capt. Martin Blumenson, "Chinese New Year's Offensive," 29 Aug 51, based on interviews with Lts. Fahy and Shea in Korea, mimeographed copy, B-51, in Office Chief of Military History, DA, Washington, D.C.

13. Maj. Gen. B. A. Coad, "My Land Campaign in Korea," *Journal of the Royal United Service Institution* 97, no. 585 (Feb 1952): 10.

14. Ibid.
15. Bartlett, *With the Australians in Korea*, pp. 59–60.
16. 25th Div., Comd. Rpt., 1–5 Jan 51, Boxes 3773–74.
17. Maj. Apgar, asst. G-1, 25th Div., interview with author, 4 Sept 1951.
18. 25th Div., Comd. Rpt., 3 Jan 51, Box 3773; 27th Inf., 25th Div., Comd. Rpt., 3 Jan 51, Box 3850; 35th Inf., 25th Div., Comd. Rpt., 3 Jan 51, Box 3859.
19. 25th Div., Comd. Rpt., G-2 Sec. and G-2 Jnl., Serial 3654, 3 Jan 51, Box 3774.
20. 25th Div., Comd. Rpt., G-3 Sec Jnl. File, 0300-1100, 3 Jan 51, Box 3774.
21. 25th Div., Comd. Rpt., 3 Jan 51, Box 3773; 27th Inf., 25th Div., Comd. Rpt., 3 Jan 51, Box 3850; 1st Bn., 27th Inf., 25th Div., Comd. Rpt., 3 Jan 51, Box 3850.
22. Map of Korea, AMS 1, L552, scale 1:250,000, area from Suwon north to Imjin River, including Seoul; Brig. C. N. Barclay, *The First Commonwealth Division* (Aldershot: Gale and Polden, 1954), pp. 41–45; Bartlett, *With the Australians in Korea*, pp. 60–63; Eric Linklater, *Our Men in Korea* (London: Her Majesty's Stationery Office, 1952), pp. 40–43; 25th Div., Comd. Rpt., 3–4 Jan 51, Box 3774; I Corps, Comd. Rpt., 3 Jan 51, Box 1505.
23. ATIS, Enemy Docs., Issues 42, 11, notes in Chinese on combat news and enemy situation (source, date, and place of capture unknown), 14 Feb 51.
24. I Corps, Comd. Rpt., G-3 Sec., 3 Jan 51, Boxes 1507 and 1505; Barclay, *First Commonwealth Division*, p. 42.
25. I Corps, Comd. Rpt., 3 Jan 51, Box 1505; I Corps, Comd. Rpt., G-3 Sec., 3 Jan 51, Box 1507; Linklater, *Our Men in Korea*, pp. 41–42.
26. Folder M-R, Box 17, Ridgway Papers.
27. Map of Korea, 1950 AMS 1, scale 1:250,000. It is necessary to use a contemporary map, one similar to that used by the troops themselves, as later editions of this map do not always carry the same place-names. The locations, accordingly, are frequently difficult to locate on later maps.
28. 2nd Bn., 27th Inf., 25th Div., Comd. Rpt., 3–4 Jan 51, Box 3850. This battalion report has the most significant information from American sources of the sequence of events and of what happened to the British rear guard. Lt. Col. Murch was perhaps as good a battalion commander as could have been assigned this dangerous and crucial mission. He had proved himself many times. In late November 1950 in the Chinese 2nd Phase Offensive, he and his battalion had saved Task Force Dolvin north of Ipsok from almost certain destruction.
29. Bartlett, *With the Australians in Korea*, p. 60, citing Rene Cutforth, *Korean Reporter* (London: Allan and Wingate, 1952), p. 103.
30. Bartlett, *With the Australians in Korea*, p. 60.
31. 25th Div. HQ, reproduced as Annex 1 to Periodic Report No. 176, 11 Jan 51, the Annex No. 1 to I Corps PIR No. 11. The account of Phillips's experiences was made the subject of a news dispatch to the Eighth Army public information officer on 8 Jan 51.
32. ATIS, Enemy Docs., Issue 42, 111, notes in Chinese, captured 14 Feb 51.
33. Linklater, *Our Men in Korea*, pp. 42–43; Barclay, *First Commonwealth Division*, p. 43; I Corps, Comd. Rpt., 3–4 Jan 51, p. 31; 25th Div., Comd. Rpt., G-2 Sec., 3 Jan 51, Box 3774.
34. 2nd Bn., 27th Inf., 25th Div., Comd. Rpt., 3–4 Jan 51, Box 3850.

35. Ibid.

36. I Corps, Comd. Rpt., G-3 Sec., 4 Jan 51, Box 1507.

37. Folder M–R, Box 17, Ridgway Papers.

38. Memo, I Corps HQ to Ridgway, 4 Jan 51, in ibid.

39. Eighth Army, Comd. Rpt., Daily Hist. Rpt., 4 Jan 51, Box 1143.

40. 25th Div., Comd. Rpt., 4 Jan 51, G-3 Jnl. File, Box 3774. The I Corps Comd. Rpt. for 4 Jan, Box 1505, had reported that at 3:30 A.M. the 29th Brigade, less 11 tanks and 40 men of B Co., Royal Ulster Rifles Bn., had reached safety.

41. Memorandum from Maj. James W. DeLoach, liaison officer with I Corps, deputy chief of staff, I Corps, 8 Jan 51, reporting on traffic control, 2–4 Jan 51, in Seoul, I Corps, Comd. Rpt., G-3 Sec., 4 Jan 51, G-4 Logistics Sec., Box 1507 (enclosed as an affidavit with I Corps, G-3 Rpt., 4 Jan 51).

42. 3rd Bn., 27th Inf., 25th Div., Comd. Rpt., 4 Jan 51, Box 3850.

43. DeLoach's memorandum covers some of the meeting and efforts being planned to rescue the cut-off members of the British 29th Brigade. DeLoach apparently was present at some of these meetings.

44. 27th Inf., 25th Div., Comd. Rpt., 4 Jan 51, Box 3850.

45. Ridgway, interview with author, 21 Oct 1975.

46. Eighth Army, Comd. Rpt., G-3 Jnl. File, message at 1300, 4 Jan 51, location CS 1775.

47. The description of the bridges across the Han is based on Capt. B. C. Mossman, "Dismantling and Destruction of the Han River Bridges at Seoul, 1–4 Jan 1951," typescript MS in Office Chief of Military History, based on interviews with Capt. D. J. Haden, Lt. Rodman M. Davis, Lt. Jack R. Wheatley, C Co., and Capt. Donald E. Roush, S-4 14th Eng. Comb. Bn., in Korea 1951. Other sources used in connection with the bridges in the evacuation of Seoul are indicated in the citations.

48. I Corps, Comd. Rpt., 2 Jan 51, Box 1505.

49. Eighth Army, Comd. Rpt., G-3 Jnl., briefing for CG, Eighth Army, 4 Jan 51, Box 1146.

50. 1st Cav. Div., Comd. Rpt., 3–4 Jan 51, Box 4434.

51. 21st Inf., 24th Div., Comd. Rpt., 4 Jan 51, p. 6, and S-3 and S-2 Jnl. entries, Box 3664. For the report of the investigation, see S-3 Jnl. entries at 1245, Serial 3467 at 1330, and Serial 3468 at 1500; IX Corps, Comd. Rpt., 3–4 Jan 51, Box 1779.

52. Mossman, "Dismantling and Destruction of Bridges."

53. Ibid.; I Corps, Comd. Rpt., G-4 Logistics Sec., 4 Jan 51, Box 1505; and Comd. Rpt., Narr., 4 Jan 51. Army Signal photographs taken on 4 Jan 51 show both the Shoo-fly and the M4-M4A2 bridges before and at the time of destruction. See John Miller, Jr., Owen J. Carroll, and Margaret E. Tackley, *Korea, 1951–1953* (Washington, D.C.: Office Chief of Military History, DA, published apparently in the mid-1950s).

54. I Corps, Comd. Rpt., 4 Jan 51, Box 1505; Box 22, Ridgway Papers.

55. 1st Bn., 27th Inf., 25th Div., Comd. Rpt., 4 Jan 51, Box 3850; FEC DIS No. 3040, 5 Jan 51 (covering events of 4 Jan), Box 386.

56. I Corps, Comd. Rpt., 4 Jan 51, Box 1505; 25th Div., Comd. Rpt., G-2 Sec. Jnl., Serial 3948, at 7:30 P.M., discusses a Joint Operations Center report that

the enemy flag raising was at 1300; IX Corps, G-3 Sec. Jnl., Serial 385, 4 Jan 51, Box 1779.

57. 25th Div., Comd. Rpt., Operations, p. 25, 4 Jan 51.

58. Cpl. Randle M. Hurst, "The History of the 502nd Reconnaissance Platoon in Korea, December 1950 to October 1951," Binder 2, pp. 41–45, original in author's possession.

59. Bartlett, *With the Australians in Korea*, pp. 61–62, quoting Monson.

60. Ibid., pp. 62–63, quoting from Cutforth, *Korean Reporter*, pp. 115–16.

61. Capt. Pierce W. Briscoe and Capt. Billy B. C. Mossman, "Rehabilitation of Tidal Locks, Inchon Korea, 50th Engineer Port Construction Company, Jan–Feb 1951," BA 23, copy in Office Chief of Military History.

62. Ibid.

63. The information in this paragraph and the next is from *Kunlun*, July–Aug 1984. The translation is by Ellis L. Melvin, of Tamaroa, Ill., and a copy was given to me. Melvin, who has read Chinese sources on the Korean War published since the war, concludes that they show that Mao Zedong and Peng Dehuai, commander of the Chinese People's Volunteers, decided to stop around the 38th Parallel (Melvin, letter to author, with attachments, 19 Dec 1987). The quotation from Section VI of Peng's biography was translated also by Ellis L. Melvin and provided as an enclosure to his letter of 10 Oct 1988.

64. Eighth Army, Comd. Rpt., 4–5 Jan 51, Box 1143; Maj. Gen. Garrison H. Davidson, interview with author, 24 Jan 54; Memo Conf. Record, 5 Jan 51, EUSAK HQ, Unclassified Binder, Ridgway Papers.

65. Maj. Caleb A. Cole, "The Operations of the 2nd Bn., 15th Inf., 3rd Div. in Offensive Action," Student Monograph, Adv. Inf. Course, Cl. 1, 1952–53; Combined G-2/G-3 Situation Map, FEC DIS No. 3043, Map A-1, 9 Jan 51, Box 386.

66. Eighth Army, Comd. Rpt., 5 Jan 51, Box 1143.

67. IX Corps, Comd. Rpt., 5 Jan 51, Box 1779.

68. Eighth Army, Comd. Rpt., G-3 Jnl., 5 Jan 51, and G-2, PIR No. 177, 5 Jan 51, Boxes 1146 and 1144; I Corps, Comd. Rpt., 5 Jan 51, Box 1505; 25th Div., Comd. Rpt., G-2 Sec., 5 Jan 51, Box 3774; FEC DIS No. 3041, 5 Jan 51, Box 386.

69. Copies of Muccio Telex to Secy. of State, Nos. 651 and 648, 6 Jan 51, Folder D-L, Box 17, Ridgway Papers.

70. Ridgway, interview with Col. John M. Blair, USA, 6 Jan 72, third of four interviews, vol. 2, Box 51, Ridgway Papers.

71. I Corps, Comd. Rpt., 6 Jan 51, Box 1505; ibid., G-2 Sec., PIR No. 6, 6 Jan 51, Box 1506; FEC DIS No. 3042, 6 Jan 51, Box 386; 25th Div., Comd. Rpt., G-2 Sec., 6 Jan 51, Box 3774.

72. 25th Div., Comd. Rpt., G-3 Sec., 6 Jan 51, Box 3850; 2nd Bn., 27th Inf., 25th Div., Comd. Rpt., 6 Jan 51, Box 3850.

73. Lt. Sam D. Starobin, S-2, 65th Eng. Comb. Bn., "Causeway at Osan," Item 3 in Capt. John G. Westover, *Combat Support in Korea* (Washington, D.C.: Combat Forces Press, 1955), pp. 13–15.

74. I Corps, Comd. Rpt., G-4 Rpt., 6 Jan 51, Box 1508.

75. Eighth Army, Comd. Rpt., G-3 Sec., 7 Jan 51, Box 1146; 25th Div., 27th Inf., Comd. Rpt., 6–7 Jan 51, Box 3850.

76. Ridgway, *The Korean War,* p. 98.

77. I Corps, Comd. Rpt., 7 Jan 51, Box 1505; ibid., G-2 Sec., 7 Jan 51, Box 1506; FEC DIS No. 3043, 8 Jan 51, Box 386.

78. IX Corps, Comd. Rpt., G-2 Sec., Jan 51, Box 1779; FEC DIS No. 3041, 6 Jan 51, Box 386.

79. Eighth Army, Comd. Rpt., 7 Jan 51, Box 1143 (also see sec. 3, bk. 4, incl. p. 7, G-3 Rpt.); I Corps, Comd. Rpt., Jan 51, pp. 51–52.

80. Ridgway, letter to Gen. J. Lawton Collins, CS, 8 Jan 1951, Folder A–C, Box 17, Ridgway Papers.

81. MacArthur, letter to Ridgway, 7 Jan 1951, Unclassified Binder, Ridgway Papers; James F. Schnabel, *Policy and Direction: The First Year* (Washington, D.C.: DA, GPO, 1972), pp. 312–13.

82. "To CINCUNC TOKYO FROM JCS NR: JCS 80254 4 Jan 51," in *Pertinent Papers on Korean Situation,* II, 390–91.

83. "From CINCFE TOKYO TO DEPTAR For JCS, NR: C 52879 6 Jan 51," in *Pertinent Papers on Korean Situation,* II, 393–94.

84. Memo, Eighth Army G-2 to Chief of Staff, NK and CCF Weapons, 6 Jan 51, Folder S–Z, Box 17, Ridgway Papers.

CHAPTER 5

1. 2nd Div., Comd. Rpt., Jan 51, Box 2476; X Corps, Comd. Rpt., Jan 51, Intelligence Sec., pp. 18–22.

2. X Corps, Comd. Rpt., Jan 51, Intelligence Sec., pp. 18–22.

3. Almond, Diary, 31 Dec 50.

4. Lt. Gen. William J. McCaffrey, USA (Ret.), interview with author, 4 Feb 1976; McCaffrey, letter to author, 6 Mar 1980.

5. Robert F. Futrell, *The United States Air Force in Korea, 1950–1953* (New York: Duell, Sloan, and Pearce, 1961), pp. 259–60.

6. Almond, Diary, 3 Jan 51.

7. X Corps, Comd. Rpt., Jan 51, POR No. 97, 1 Jan, and POR No. 98, 2 Jan 51, Box 1991; Maj. Gen. David G. Barr, notes, 1 Jan 51 (in author's possession).

8. Eighth Army, Comd. Rpt., G-3 Jnl., message at 1620, 1 Jan 51, Box 1146.

9. 2nd Div., Comd. Rpt., 1–3 Jan 51, Box 2476.

10. Dept. of Army, Gen. Ord. No. 13, 1 Feb 1952, Congressional Medal of Honor, Posthumously, to Sfc. Junior B. Edwards, E Co., 23rd Inf., for action near Changbong-ni, 2 Jan 51; X Corps, Comd. Rpt., Annexes, POR No. 98, 2 Jan 51, Box 1991.

11. 2nd Div., Comd. Rpt., G-1 Rpt., and POR No. 99, 2 Jan 51, Box 2476; Maj. Dick Leonard, I Corps, interview with author, 26 July 1951.

12. Ridgway, letter to Almond, 2 Jan 1951, Box 17, Ridgway Papers.

13. X Corps, Comd. Rpt., G-2 Sec., PIR No. 106, 10 Jan 51; FEC DIS No. 3052, OB 2–3, 17 Jan 51, Box 387.

14. Eighth Army, Comd. Rpt., G-3 Jnl., 3 Jan 51, Box 1146.

15. 2nd Div., Comd. Rpt., 4 Jan 51, Box 2476.

16. Eighth Army, Comd. Rpt., G-3 Jnl., 4 Jan. 51, Box 1146.

17. 1st Lt. Jerrell F. Wilson, exec. off., G Co., 23rd Inf., 1951, interview with 1st Lt. Martin Blumenson, "Action at Wonju, 5–20 Jan 51," MS, BA 31, Office Chief of Military History.

18. 2nd Div., Comd. Rpt., 5 Jan 51, Box 2476; FEC DIS No. 3042, p. 5, 7 Jan 51, Box 386.

19. 2nd Div., Comd. Rpt., 5 Jan 51, and G-3 Sec., Box 2476.

20. Capt. Edward C. Williamson, 1st Lt. John Mewha, and 1st Lt. Martin Blumenson, "Action at Wonju and Vicinity, 5–20 January 1951," mimeographed MS, BA 31, Office Chief of Military History, based on interviews with members of the 2nd Div., in the summer of 1951 in Korea (hereafter cited as "Action at Wonju and Vicinity"). The MS has several sketch maps of Wonju and vicinity prepared by participants of the action there.

21. Ibid.

22. Brig. Gen. George B. Peploe, CS, IX Corps, interview with author, 12 Aug 51.

23. "Action at Wonju and Vicinity."

24. Ibid.

25. Ibid.

26. "Destruction of Wonju," sec. 6 in Westover, Combat Support in Korea, pp. 18–23, based on 1st Lt. John Mewha, "Withdrawal from Wonju, 6–7 Jan 51," MS, Office Chief of Military History. I have examined Mewha's MS, which is based on his interviews with 1st Lt. William Champion, 2nd Eng. Comb. Bn., and M. Sgt. Julius R. Grupe, and have used it as the primary source on the demolition work at Wonju.

27. Mewha, "Withdrawal from Wonju," and Westover, Combat Support in Korea.

28. Mewha, "Withdrawal from Wonju."

29. Almond, Diary, 7 Jan 51; X Corps, Comd. Rpt., Jan 1951, p. 6, Boxes 1990–91 (Annexes to Comd. Rpt.). The X Corps POR No. 103 and PIR No. 103 for 7 Jan 51 state that 114 prisoners were captured at Wonju on 7 Jan 51.

30. X Corps, Comd. Rpt., Annexes, PIR No. 103, 7 Jan 51, Box 1991.

31. "Action at Wonju and Vicinity"; Mewha, "Withdrawal from Wonju."

32. ATIS, Interrogation Reports (Enemy Forces), Issue 25, No. 2881, p. 106, on Chang Sok Chang, 2nd Bn., 15th Regt., NK 6th Div., 16 Jan 51; and ibid., No. 2872, p. 66, Pyon Sun Bong, 2nd Bn., 15th Regt., NK 6th Div., 16 Jan 51.

33. Eighth Army, G-2 Sec., PIR No. 180, 8 Jan 51, covering action of 7 Jan, Box 1144; 2nd Div., Comd. Rpt., G-2 Sec., 7 Jan 51, Box 2476.

34. 2nd Div., Comd. Rpt., G-3 Sec., 7 Jan 51, Box 2476; 7th Div., Comd. Rpt., 7, 10, 11 Jan 51, Box 3186; Eighth Army, Comd. Rpt., G-3 Jnl., 7 Jan 51, Box 1146.

35. A copy of Hartell's long letter was given to me during the war by Mr. Bruce Jacobs, who told me that Lt. Hartell's father had the original handwritten letter. Unable to trace the current owner of the letter, I have not quoted it directly. I also paraphrase it below relative to later actions.

36. Col. Gerald G. Epley, interview with author, 12 Dec 1951.

37. Capt. Marvin L. Nance, E Co., 2nd Bn., 23rd Inf., interview with author, Aug 1951; Maj. Sam Radow, CO, 1st Bn., 23rd Inf., interview with author, 16 Aug 1951.

38. Maj. Will G. Atwood, Jr., and Capt. Daniel E. Sullivan, X Corps Hist. Sec., interview with author, 23 Aug 1951; Maj. Gen. Clark L. Ruffner, CG, 2nd Div., interview with author, 27 Aug 1951.

39. Ridgway, letter to author, 12 June 1984.

40. Futrell, *US Air Force in Korea,* p. 260.

CHAPTER 6

1. Maj. Gen. Clark L. Ruffner, interview with author, 15 Aug 1951.

2. X Corps, Comd. Rpt., G-3 Annex, 8 Jan 51, Box 1991; Almond, Diary, 8 Jan 51; Almond, interview with author, 28 Apr 1977.

3. Almond, Diary, 8 Jan 51.

4. X Corps, Comd. Rpt., Annexes, POR, 8 Jan 51, Box 1991.

5. "Action at Wonju and Vicinity."

6. Ibid., citing interviews with 1st Lt. Frank J. Barnes, F Co., 38th Inf., and Lt. Heath, G Co., 23rd Inf.; Col. Paul L. Freeman, CO, 23rd Regt., "Wonju through Chipyong-ni: An Epic of Regimental Combat Team Action in Korea," p. 3, typescript, undated but apparently written shortly after the battle of Chipyong-ni in the period Feb-Apr 1951, copy in author's possession. It bears a stamp from Office of Public Information, Department of Defense, 16 May 1951. See also 2nd Div., Comd. Rpt., 9 Jan 51, Box 2476.

7. Almond, Diary, 9 Jan 51; X Corps, Comd. Rpt., Annexes, Box 1992; 2nd Div., Comd. Rpt., 9 Jan 51, Box 2476.

8. X Corps, Comd. Rpt., Annexes, POR No. 105, 9 Jan 51; FEC DIS No. 3043, Map No. A-3, 8 Jan 51, Box 386; 7th Inf., Comd. Rpt., 1-10 Jan 51, Box 3186.

9. 7th Div., Comd. Rpt., 1-13 Jan 51, Box 3186.

10. Eighth Army, Comd. Rpt., G-2 Sec., PIR No. 180, 8 Jan 51, Box 1144.

11. Eighth Army, Comd. Rpt., 8 Jan 51, Box 1143; 1st Cav. Div., Comd. Rpt., 8 Jan 51, Box 4434.

12. Hist. Rec., Dec 50-Oct 51, Box 22, Ridgway Papers; Eighth Army, Comd. Rpt., Daily Hist. Rpt., 9 Jan 51, Box 1143.

13. 9th Inf., 2nd Div., Comd. Rpt., 10 Jan 51.

14. Memo to Ridgway, 13 Jan 51, information from Lt. Col. Monclar and Col. Freeman to Lt. Col. John H. Chiles, G-3, X Corps, Box 17, Ridgway Papers.

15. "Action at Wonju and Vicinity"; 2nd Div., Comd. Rpt., 10 Jan 51, Box 2476; ibid., Annexes, POR No. 105, PIR Nos. 106-107; FEC DIS No. 4046, 11 Jan 51 (covers 10 Jan), Box 387.

16. Hist. Rec., 30 Dec 50-Oct 51 (for 15 Jan 51), Box 22, Ridgway Papers.

17. X Corps, Comd. Rpt., POR No. 108, 12 Jan 51, Box 1992; Eighth Army, Comd. Rpt., G-3 Jnl., 12 Jan 51, Box 1146; 1st Lt. Lee R. Hartell, 15th FA Bn., 2nd Div., letter to his brother, 20 Mar 51; Freeman, "Wonju through Chipyong-ni," pp. 3-4.

18. Harold Martin, "Who Says the French Won't Fight?" *Saturday Evening Post,* 5 May 1951, p. 19; also Ridgway, *The Korean War,* p. 107 and note.

19. 25th Div., Comd. Rpt., Summ., Dec 50, p. 23; Maj. Gen. Basil A. Coad, "The Land Campaign in Korea," *Journal of the Royal United Service Institution* 97, no. 585 (Feb 1952). The official records contain innumerable references to the shoepac and to difficulties of keeping vehicles and weapons operational in sub-zero weather at night.

20. Maj. Wayne L. Hauselman, 38th FA Bn., interview, 1951, in "Action at Wonju and Vicinity."

21. Lt. Col. Charles E. Henry, 21st AAA AW Bn (SP), "In Support of the Infantry," *Antiaircraft Journal* 94, no. 1 (Jan-Feb 1951).

22. Ridgway, interview with Col. Blair, 6 Jan 1972, vol. 2, Box 51, Ridgway Papers.

23. Paraphrased from Hartell, letter to brother, 20 Mar 1951.

24. Almond, Diary, 13 Jan 51, one of the longest daily entries in the entire diary. Also, see X Corps, Comd. Rpt., Jan 51, pp. 8-9.

25. Almond, Diary, 13 Jan 51, his personal copy. This handwritten note is not on copies of the official X Corps Comd. Rpt. for Jan 1951.

26. Spec. File, Dec 50-Mar 51, Box 20, Ridgway Papers.

27. X Corps, Comd. Rpt., Jan 51, p. 9.

28. Lt. Gen. Edward M. Almond, USA, Ret., letter to author, 29 Oct 1975.

29. Almond, letter to Brig. Gen. Hal C. Pattison, chief of Military History, DA, 7 Mar 1969, and enclosure of Almond's "Review of Policy and Direction: The First Year (Korean War)," 20 Feb 1969. This enclosure is a 23-page single-spaced typed review of a MS the Office Chief of Military History was preparing for publication on the Korean War. The above quoted comments of Almond on McClure's relief are on p. 16 of that review.

30. 9th Inf., 2nd Div., Comd. Rpt., 13 Jan 51.

31. 7th Div., Comd. Rpt., 13, 15 Jan 51, Box 3186; X Corps, Comd. Rpt., Jan 51, p. 9.

32. 187th Abn. RCT, Comd. Rpt., 13-19 Jan 51, and S-2 Sec., Box 3432.

33. Eighth Army, Comd. Rpt. 7-12 Jan 51, Box 1146; 24th Div., Comd. Rpt., G-4 Sec., Jan 51, Box 3547; 5th Cav. Regt., 1st Cav. Div., Comd. Rpt., 13-15 Jan 51, Box 4434.

34. Futrell, *US Air Force in Korea*, p. 260.

35. FEC DIS No. 3052, 17 Jan 51, Box 387.

36. Eighth Army, Comd. Rpt., G-3 Sec., 15 Jan 51, Box 1146; 2nd Div., Comd. Rpt., 14 Jan 51, Box 2476.

37. X Corps, Comd. Rpt., Enclosures, 15 Jan 51 (this document was misfiled and found in the Feb 51 Comd. Rpt.), Box 1995; Freeman, "Wonju through Chipyong-ni," pp. 4-5, 51.

38. X Corps, Comd. Rpt., Annexes, PIR Nos. 110-11, 14-15 Jan 51, Box 1992.

39. 7th Div., Comd. Rpt., 13-15 Jan 51, Box 3186.

40. Eighth Army, Comd. Rpt., 15 Jan 51, Box 1143.

41. 2nd Div., Comd. Rpt., 17 Jan 51, Box 2476; X Corps, Comd. Rpt., 17 Jan 51, and Annexes, PIR No. 113, 17 Jan 51, Boxes 1992-93 and 1995; "Action at Wonju and Vicinity," 17 Jan 51.

42. 1st Lt. Philip Mallory, asst. S-4, 2nd Bn., 9th Inf., interview with Capt. Edward C. Williamson, 19-20 Jan 51, in "Action at Wonju and Vicinity."

43. 9th Inf., 2nd Div., Comd. Rpt., Jan 1951.

44. Eighth Army, Comd. Rpt., G-3 Sec., 16 Jan 51, Box 1146.

45. 187th Abn. RCT, Comd. Rpt., 16-31 Jan 51, Box 3432.

46. 1st Lt. Walter Hurtt, interview with Capt. Edward C. Williamson, in "Action at Wonju and Vicinity."

47. M. Sgt. Olen MacGregor, F Co., 38th Inf., interview with 1st Lt. John Mewha, in "Action at Wonju and Vicinity."

48. X Corps, Comd. Rpt., 20–21 Jan 51, Annexes and Enclosures, Box 1993 and 1995. The enclosures for the 21 Jan annexes were misfiled in Feb 1951 documents.

49. X Corps, Comd. Rpt., 20–21 Jan 51, Summ. of Operations and POR No. 116, 20 Jan 51; ibid., Comd. Rpt., Annexes, 22–24 Jan 51, including POR Nos. 119–20, Box 1993; 2nd Div., Comd. Rpt., 19–23 Jan 51, Box 2476.

50. 2nd Div., Comd. Rpt., 24 Jan 51, Box 2476; X Corps, Comd. Rpt., 24 Jan 51, Annexes, POR Nos. 119–20, Box 1993.

51. X Corps, Comd. Rpt., A, Command Sec., Jan 51, p. 10, and X Corps HQ Combat Notes No. 7, "Infantry Battalion Tactical Air Parties," with map, 1 Feb 51.

CHAPTER 7

1. James A. Field, Jr., *History of United States Naval Operations, Korea* (Washington, D.C.: GPO, 1962), pp. 313–14.

2. Eighth Army, Comd. Rpt., Jan 51, Box 1134; 25th Div., Comd. Rpt., G-3 Sec., 7–13 Jan 51, Box 3774; 2nd Bn., 27th Inf., 25th Div., Comd. Rpt., 9 Jan 51; FEC DIS No. 4046, 11 Jan 51.

3. Lt. Col. Norwood G. Read, G-2 Sec., I Corps, interview with author, 28 July 1951.

4. Ridgway, interview with Maj. Matthew P. Caulfield, USMC, and Lt. Col. Robert M. Elton, Inf., USA, 29 Aug 1969, Box 51, Ridgway Papers.

5. M. B. Ridgway, Lt. Gen., US Army, Commanding, letter to Gen. Chung Il Kwon, chief of staff, Republic of Korea Army, 11 Jan 51, printed in full in Ridgway, *The Korean War*, p. 263.

6. Cyril Falls, "Theory and Practice in Korea," pt. 2, *Illustrated London News*, 27 Jan 1951.

7. Ridgway, personal letter to Gen. Wade H. Haislip, 11 Jan 51, Folder D–L, Box 17, Ridgway Papers.

8. MacArthur to DA, Washington, D.C., personal for JCS, 10 Jan 51, Unclassified Binder, Ridgway Papers.

9. Personal from JCS to MacArthur, No. JCS 80680, 9 Jan 51, Unclassified Binder, Ridgway Papers; Defense Secretary George C. Marshall, testimony before MacArthur hearings, 7 May 1951.

10. Defense Secretary George C. Marshall, testimony before the Joint Senate Armed Services and Foreign Relations Committees in the MacArthur hearings, 7 May 1951, pp. 322ff.

11. Marshall testimony in MacArthur hearings, 7 May 51, pp. 325ff.; Schnabel, *Policy and Direction*, discusses the Far East Command and the JCS messages on this subject.

12. See *New York Times*, 8 May 1951, p. 16, for a long article discussing the Korean situation in mid-January 1951, as disclosed in the MacArthur hearings, 7 May 1951.

13. Karl von Clausewitz, *Principles of War* (Harrisburg, Pa.: Stackpole, 1960), p. 62. This edition is a much-compressed compilation of Clausewitz's views. A longer treatise is his *On War*, trans. Col. J. J. Graham (London: Kegan Paul, Trench, Trubner, 1918).

14. Clausewitz, *Principles of War*, p. 14.

15. Quoted in Dodge, *Great Captains*, p. 205.

16. An extract found in Folder D–L, Box 17, Ridgway Papers.

17. Lt. Charles Hoyt, 2nd Bn., 35th Inf., 25th Div., interview with author, 4 Sept 1951.

18. IX Corps, Comd. Rpt., Eng. Sec., 11 Jan 51, Operation Order 2, Box 1779; I Corps, Comd. Rpt., 11 Jan 51, Box 1505.

19. Eighth Army, Comd. Rpt., G-3 Jnl., 11 Jan 51, and G-3 Daily Summ., Box 1146; 25th Div., Comd. Rpt., 11 Jan 51, CIC Detach. Rpt., Daily Summ., 18 Mar 51, has details.

20. I Corps, Comd. Rpt., Logistics Sec., 12 Jan 51, pp. 197–98, Box 1505, and I Corps, G-4 Rpt., Comd. Rpt., 13 Jan 51, Box 1508; Eighth Army, Comd. Rpt., G-3 Jnl., 12 Jan 51, Box 1146. Another I Corps document, the G-2 Intelligence Summ. No. 37, 13 Jan 51, Box 1506, says the ambushed train was southbound. Apparently this is in error.

21. Eighth Army, Comd. Rpt., 12 Jan 51, p. 31, Box 1143.

22. Author's interviews with Maj. Gen. Leven C. Allen, 15 Dec 1953, and with Ridgway, 21 Oct 1975, also confirmed by Ridgway in MS review comments to author, 21 May 1984; Col. Richard W. Stephens, CO, 21st Inf., 24th Div., interview with author, 8 Oct 1951.

23. Col. Robert Halleck, interview with author, Korea, Aug 1951.

24. Ridgway, The Korean War, pp. 104–105.

25. 25th Div., Comd. Rpt., G-2 Sec., Daily Summ. and G-2 Jnl. Serial No. 4630.

26. Eighth Army, Comd. Rpt., 14 Jan 51, Box 1143.

27. I Corps, Comd. Rpt., 14 and 15 Jan 51, Box 1505.

28. Eighth Army, Comd. Rpt., 15 Jan 51, Box 1143; 27th Inf., 25th Div., Comd. Rpt., 15 Jan 51, Box 3850; 21st Inf., 24th Div., Comd. Rpt., 15 Jan 51, Box 3664; I Corps, Comd. Rpt., G-3 Sec., 15 Jan 51, Box 1508.

29. Eighth Army, Comd. Rpt., 15 Jan 51, Box 1143; 27th Inf., 25th Div., Comd. Rpt., 15 Jan 51, Box 3850; 3rd Bn., 27th Inf., Comd. Rpt., 15 Jan 51, Box 3850; I Corps, Comd. Rpt., G-3 Sec., 15 Jan 51, Box 1508.

30. The account of Operation Wolfhound, which reached the edge of Suwon on the afternoon of 16 January, is based on 2nd Bn., 27th Inf., 25th Div., Comd. Rpt., 16 Jan 51, and 27th Inf., Comd. Rpt., 15–16 Jan 51, Box 3850; I Corps, Comd. Rpt., G-3 Sec., 15–16 Jan 51, Box 1508; Eighth Army, Comd. Rpt., 15–16 Jan 51, Box 1505.

31. Milburn Rpt. to Ridgway, 18 Jan 51, on Operation Wolfhound, Folder S–Z, Box 17, Ridgway Papers.

32. Eighth Army, Comd. Rpt., 16 Jan 51, Box 1505. Milburn's report to Ridgway differs from the Eighth Army Comd. Rpt. in naming one POW from the CCF 56th Div. instead of from the 55th.

33. Eighth Army, Comd. Rpt., 16 Jan 51, Box 1143; 21st Inf., 24th Div., Comd. Rpt., Box 3664.

34. I Corps, Comd. Rpt., 16 Jan 51, Box 1505.

35. Bartlett, With the Australians in Korea, pp. 64–68.

36. Eighth Army, Comd. Rpt., Daily Hist. Rpt., 17 Jan 51, Box 1143.

37. ATIS Enemy Documents, Issue 44, p. 62, notes in Chinese, Oct 50 to 17 Jan 51, owner unknown, presumably a company CO, 50th Army (place and date of capture unknown), recd. ATIS 12 Mar 51.

38. *Pertinent Papers on Korean Situation,* II, 296–98, including JCS Memo for Secretary of Defense, 17 Jan 51.

39. I Corps, Comd. Rpt., G-3 Sec., 17–18 Jan, Box 1508; Armor Combat Lesson Bulletin, 28 Feb 51, 5 pp. mimeographed, on Ambush of [US 3rd Div.] Reconnaissance Co., 18 Jan 51, HQ I US Corps. ATIS Enemy Documents, Issue 37, p. 37, a Chinese circular, issued by the 1st subunit, 50th Unit, CCF, identifies the enemy force that ambushed the 3rd Recon. Co. at Kumyangjang-ni as the "2nd Co." It claimed killing 50 men, capturing 1, and capturing weapons and 7 jeeps.

40. 25th Div., Comd. Rpt., G-2 Sec., 19 Jan 51, Box 3774; 27th Inf., Comd. Rpt., 19–20 Jan 51, Box 3850; Eighth Army, Comd. Rpt., 19 Jan 51, Box 1143.

41. I Corps, Comd. Rpt., 20 Jan 51, Box 1505; IX Corps, Comd. Rpt., 20 Jan 51, Box 1779; Eighth Army, Comd. Rpt., 20 Jan 51, Box 1143.

42. Eighth Army, Comd. Rpt., Daily Hist. Rpt., 20 Jan 51, Box 1143.

43. 5th RCT, 24th Div., Comd. Rpt., 21 Jan 51, Box 5237; 24th Div., Comd. Rpt., 21 Jan 51, Box 3545.

44. Eighth Army, Comd. Rpt., G-2 Sec., 21 Jan 51, Box 1143.

45. Ridgway, *The Korean War,* App. 4, pp. 264–65. The text is not dated, nor is any other copy of the statement I have seen. The Eighth Army Comd. Rpt., Daily Hist. Rpt., 21 Jan 51, Box 1143, however, states that Eighth Army issued the statement on that date. In answer to my question concerning the date Ridgway dictated the statement, the general answered, "I think 21 Jan" (Ridgway, letter to author, with enclosure, 15 May 1984). It appears, therefore, that the statement was dictated on 21 Jan 51, and Eighth Army reproduced and circulated it to all units of its command the same date. On 23 Jan Ridgway recorded the "Why We Are Here" statement for the Defense Department radio program (Box 22, Ridgway Papers).

46. Ridgway, letter to Capt. William J. Whitener, 13 June 1957, Box 21, Ridgway Papers.

47. IX Corps, Comd. Rpt., 22 Jan 51, pp. 21–22, Box 1779; Eighth Army, Comd. Rpt., 22 Jan 51, p. 8, Box 1143, and G-3 Jnl. File and G-3 Daily Summ., 22 Jan 51, Box 1146, and G-2, PIR No. 194, 22 Jan 51, Box 1144.

48. Eighth Army, Comd. Rpt., 23 Jan 51, Box 1143.

49. Conference Notes EUSAK HQ, 23 Jan 51, on planned attack north, Unclassified Binder, Ridgway Papers.

50. Hist. Rec., 23 Jan 51, Box 22, Ridgway Papers.

51. Chung Il Kwon, letter to Ridgway, 23 Jan 51, Box 17, Ridgway Papers.

52. 25th Div., Comd. Rpt., G-2 Sec., 23 Jan 51, Box 3774.

53. Eighth Army, Comd. Rpt., Daily Hist. Rpt., 24 Jan 51, Box 1143.

54. Ridgway, *Soldier,* p. 216. Ridgway mentions this reconnaissance flight also in *The Korean War,* p. 105.

55. Hist. Rec., 25 Jan 51, Box 22, Ridgway Papers; Eighth Army Comd. Rpt., 25 Jan 51.

56. Henry, "In Support of the Infantry."

57. Eighth Army, Comd. Rpt., G-2 Sec., PIR No. 197, 25 Jan 51, Box 1144; and Eighth Army, Daily Hist. Rpt., 25 Jan 51, Box 1143; 27th Inf., Comd. Rpt., 25 Jan 51, Box 3850; I Corps, Comd. Rpt., 25 Jan 51, Box 1505.

58. 1st Cav. Div., Comd. Rpt., 25 Jan 51, Box 4434; IX Corps, Comd. Rpt., 25 Jan 51, Box 1779.

59. 25th Div., Comd. Rpt., G-3 Sec., 26 Jan 51, Box 3774; I Corps, Comd. Rpt., G-3 Sec., 26 Jan 51, Box 1508; Eighth Army, Comd. Rpt., 26 Jan 51, Box 1134.

60. Eighth Army Comd. Rpt., G-3 Jnl. and Daily Summ., 26 Jan 51, Box 1146; I Corps, Comd. Rpt., 26 Jan 51, p. 154, Box 1505; Eighth Army, Comd. Rpt., G-2 Sec., PIR No. 198, 26 Jan 51, Box 1144.

61. Bartlett, *With the Australians in Korea*, pp. 210–14; US Presidential Unit Citation, DA, General Orders No. 49, 11 July 1951 (listing Battery A, 25th AAA AW Bn. among those included in the citation is apparently a mistake; it should instead be the 21st AAA AW [SP] Bn.); I Corps, Comd. Rpt., G-3 Sec., 26 Jan 51, Box 1508; Lt. Col. John W. MacIndoe, I Corps G-3 Staff, interview with author, July 1951.

62. Henry, "In Support of the Infantry." Each track carried 12,000 rounds in the bed and on the guns. The infantry regiment held 100,000 rounds for the battery at the regimental CP.

63. 1st Cav. Div., Comd. Rpt., 26 Jan 51, Box 4434; Eighth Army, Comd. Rpt., G-2 Sec., PIR No. 198, 26 Jan 51; Garry Owen, "The Seventh Cavalry Regiment," 7 pp. (n.d.), mimeographed sketch of the regiment, apparently issued during the Korean War, copy in author's possession.

64. Hist. Rec., 26 Jan 51, Box 22, Ridgway Papers; Eighth Army, Comd. Rpt., G-1 Sec., 26 Jan 51, Box 1143.

65. Ridgway, letter and attachments to author, 15 May 1984.

66. 25th Div., Comd. Rpt., G-3 Sec., 27 Jan 51, Box 3774.

67. 1st Cav. Div., Comd. Rpt., 26–27 Jan 51, Box 4434.

68. ATIS Bulletin, Enemy Doc. No. 9, p. 11, combat order issued 27 Jan 51 by Paek Hak Kim, CO, 1st Inf. Regt., NKA.

69. There is some discussion of this subject in Eighth Army, Comd. Rpt., 27 Jan 51, Box 1146, and in Eighth Army, G-2 PIR No. 199, 27 Jan 51, Box 1144.

70. Eighth Army, Comd. Rpt., 27 Jan 51, Box 1143.

71. 1st Cav. Div., Comd. Rpt., 28–29 Jan 51, Box 4434.

72. Ibid., 30 Jan 51, Box 4434; Bartlett, *With the Australians in Korea*, p. 69.

73. 1st Cav. Div., Comd. Rpt., 29–30 Jan 51, and enclosure no. 9, Box 4434.

74. Ibid., 29 Jan 51.

75. Ibid., 30 Jan 51, Box 4434; 1st Lt. Martin Blumenson, after-action interview report, "Hill 312, 1st Bn., 5th Cav. Regt., 28–30 Jan 51," mimeographed copy, Office Chief of Military History, BA 32; Congressional Medal of Honor, Posthumously, awarded to 1st Lt. Robert M. McGovern, DA, Gen. Ord. No. 2, 8 Jan 1952, but awarded 7 Nov 51; Distinguished Unit Citation, A and B companies, 1st Bn., 5th Cav. Regt., 1st Cav. Div., for action near Kumyangjang-ni, 30 Jan 51, DA, Gen. Ord. No. 36, 4 June 1951.

76. Blumenson, "Hill 312."

77. Ibid.

78. I Corps, Comd. Rpt., 30–31 Jan 50, Box 1505; 27th Inf., Comd. Rpt., 30–31 Jan 51, Box 3850; 25th Div., Comd. Rpt., G-3 Sec., 30–31 Jan 51, Box 3774.

79. Eighth Army, Comd. Rpt., 31 Jan 51, Box 1143.

80. Cole, "Operations of the 2nd Bn."

81. I Corps, Comd. Rpt., 29–30 Jan 51, Box 1505.

82. EUSAK HQ, Gen. Ord. No. 310, 15 May 1951, awarding Distinguished Service Cross to Cpl. Gerald L. Dilley, B Co., 19th Inf., 24th Div., for heroism near Hyonbang-ni, 30 Jan 1951.

83. DA, Gen. Ord. No. 37, 4 June 59, awarding the Congressional Medal of Honor to 1st Lt. (promoted from 2nd Lt.) Carl H. Dodd, E Co., 5th RCT, 24th Div., for action near Subuk, 30–31 Jan 51; 5th RCT, 24th Div., Comd. Rpt., 29–31 Jan 51, Box 5237.

84. Eighth Army, Comd. Rpt., G-3 Jnl. and G-3 Daily Summ., 29–31 Jan 51, Box 1146.

85. Eighth Army, Comd. Rpt., 30 Jan 51, Box 1134.

CHAPTER 8

1. Almond, letter to Ridgway, 2 May 51, Folder A, Box 18, Ridgway Papers.

2. Ridgway, letter to Coulter, 31 Jan 51, Folder A–C, Box 17, Ridgway Papers.

3. Hist. Rec., 1 Feb. 51, Box 22, Ridgway Papers.

4. Ridgway, interview with Col. Blair, Sec. 4, 24 Mar 1972, Box 51, Ridgway Papers.

5. Map to accompany EUSAK, G-2 PIR No. 203, 31 Jan 51 (2400); map to accompany 3rd Div., Comd. Rpt., 1 Feb 51, Illustration No. 1, Box 2891.

6. 3rd Div., Comd. Rpt., 1 Feb 51, Box 2891; 25th Div., Comd. Rpt., 1 Feb 51, Box 3776, and 24th Inf., Comd. Rpt., 1 Feb 51, Box 3841; I Corps, Comd. Rpt., Box 1511; FEC DIS No. 3068, 2 Feb 51, Box 400.

7. 21st Inf., 24th Div., Comd. Rpt., 1–4 Feb 51, Box 3665.

8. Ridgway, letter to MacArthur, 3 Feb 51 (delivered personally to MacArthur 041100 Feb 51), Unclassified Binder, Ridgway Papers.

9. Ibid.

10. MacArthur letter to Ridgway, Unclassified Binder, Ridgway Papers.

11. I Corps, Comd. Rpt., 3 Feb 51, Box 1511.

12. Ibid.; FEC DIS No. 3070, 4 Feb 51, Box 400.

13. 65th Inf., 3rd Div., Comd. Rpt., 2–3 Feb 51, Box 2961.

14. Field, *Naval Operations Korea*, pp. 322–24.

15. 1st Cav. Div., Comd. Rpt., 3 Feb 51, Box 4428.

16. 19th Inf., 24th Div., Comd. Rpt., 1–3 Feb 51, Box 3655, and 24th Div., Comd. Rpt., 1–3 Feb 51, Box 3550.

17. 19th Inf., 24th Div., Comd. Rpt., 1–17 Feb 51, Box 3655.

18. DA, Gen. Ord., 2 Aug 1951, awarding Congressional Medal of Honor to M. Sgt. Stanley T. Adams for action near Sesim-ni, 4 Feb 51. Adams actually received the Medal of Honor before the official order announcing it was published; the Washington *Evening Star* announced the award in an article on 2 July 1951.

19. Eighth Army HQ, Gen. Ord. No. 365, 28 May 1951, awarding the Distinguished Service Cross to Cpl. Bobby G. Stuart, A Co., 19th Inf., 24th Div., for heroic action against the enemy near Sesim-ni, 4 Feb 1951.

20. Hist. Rec., 4 Feb 51, Box 22, Ridgway Papers; Eighth Army, Comd. Rpt., Command Summ., 4 Feb 51, Box 1154.

21. 24th Div., Comd. Rpt., G-3 Sec., 4–5 Feb 1951, Box 3550.

22. 1st Cav. Div., Comd. Rpt., 4 Feb 51, Box 4438.

23. IX Corps, Comd. Rpt., G-2 Sec., PIR No. 131, Annex 1, 4 Feb 51.

24. 1st Cav. Div., Comd. Rpt., 5 Feb 51, Box 4438; Hist. Rec., 5 Feb 51, Box 22, Ridgway Papers.

25. 27th Inf., Comd. Rpt., 4 Feb 51, Box 3850; Hist. Rec., 5 Feb 51, Box 22, Ridgway Papers.

26. FEC DIS No. 3072, 6 Feb 51; Capt. John Popovics, "Baker Battery Supports the 'Wolfhounds,'" *Antiaircraft Journal* 94, no. 1 (Jan–Feb 1951): 12.

27. 27th Inf., Comd. Rpt., 4 Feb 51, Box 3850. (The 25th Div. records seem to have renamed the 21st AAA AW Bn. as the 25th AAA AW Bn., after the division to which it was now attached); I Corps HQ, Armor Combat Lesson Bulletin No. 11, "Notes on Task Force Bartlett" (reproduced from Memo, 64th Hvy. Tank Bn., dated 27 Feb 51), 13 Mar 51.

28. 25th Div., Comd. Rpt., G-3 Sec., 5 Feb 51, Box 3777.

29. 3rd Div., Comd. Rpt., 5–6 Feb 51, Box 2891.

30. I Corps, Comd. Rpt., Eng. Sec., 1–5 Feb 51, Box 1515.

31. 27th Inf., Comd. Rpt., 6 Feb 51, Box 3850; Eighth Army, Gen. Ord. No. 312, 15 May 51, awarding the Distinguished Service Cross to Pfc. Paul L. Strickler, G. Co., 27th Inf., for action 6 Feb 51.

32. I Corps, Comd. Rpt., G-3 Sec., 6 Feb 51, Box 1512.

33. 1st Cav. Div., Comd. Rpt., 6 Feb 51, Box 4438.

34. Ibid.

35. 21st Inf., Comd. Rpt., 6–8 Feb 51, Box 3665.

36. Eighth Army, Gen. Ord. No. 194, 7 Apr 51, awarding the Distinguished Service Cross to Capt. Anthony Dannucci, Jr., CO, G Co., 19th Inf., 24th Div., for heroic action near Sangho-ri, 6 Feb 51.

37. 25th Div., Comd. Rpt., 7 Feb 51, Box 3776; I Corps, Comd. Rpt., 7 Feb 51, Box 1511; FEC DIS No. 3074, 8 Feb 51, Box 400; Lt. Col. MacIndoe, G-3 Sec., I Corps, interview with author, July 1951. MacIndoe said the high ground around Anyang constituted the last important enemy defense positions short of the Han River south of Yongdongpo. Hill 429 seemed to be the key to the complex of enemy positions.

38. I Corps, Comd. Rpt., 7–8 Feb 51, pp. 64–71, Box 1511.

39. 2nd Bn., 27th Inf., 25th Div., Comd. Rpt., 7 Feb 51, Box 3850.

40. DA, Gen. Ord. No. 69, 2 Aug 1951, awarding the Congressional Medal of Honor to Capt. Lewis L. Millett for action on 7 Feb 1951, near Soam-ni.

41. S. L. A. Marshall, "Bayonet Charge," *Combat Forces Journal,* June 1951, pp. 22–32. On 11 Feb 51, Marshall interviewed members of E Co. on the events of 7 Feb. His article cited here includes great detail and is based on accounts given by several participants. The article is highly dramatic. Marshall says it was "the most complete bayonet charge since Cold Harbor" (a battle in the US Civil War during Grant's advance on Petersburg, Va.). The 2nd Bn., 27th Inf., report says that "the number of enemy killed in the engagement with the bayonet exceeds that of any engagement in U.S. military history." I make no attempt to evaluate these statements, as I know of no way to arrive at reliable figures on the subject.

42. 3rd Div., Comd. Rpt., G-2 Sec., 7 Feb 51, Box 2891.

43. 1st Cav. Div., Comd. Rpt., 7 Feb 51, Box 4438; FEC DIS No. 3074, 8 Feb 51, Box 400.

44. IX Corps, Comd. Rpt., G-2 Sec., PIR No. 135, Encl. to Annex 2, 8 Feb 51, Box 1786.

45. Ibid., PIR No. 134 Annex 1, 7 Feb 51, Box 1786.

46. I Corps, Comd. Rpt., 8 Feb 51, Box 1511.

47. Ridgway, letter to Almond, 8 Feb 51, Box 17, Ridgway Papers.

48. I Corps, Armor Combat Lesson Bulletin No. 4, 3 Mar 51, "Observations Made with TF Dolvin, 8 Feb 51."

49. 1st Cav. Div., Comd. Rpt., 8 Feb 51, Box 4438.

50. FEC DIS No. 3089, 23 Feb 51 (discussing events of 6–8 Feb 51), OB-3, Box 402.

51. I Corps, Comd. Rpt., 9 Feb 51; 24th Inf., 25th Div., Comd. Rpt., 9 Feb 51, Box 3841.

52. I Corps, Comd. Rpt., 9 Feb 51, p. 83.

53. 27th Inf., Comd. Rpt., 9 Feb 51, Box 3850.

54. 65th Inf., Comd. Rpt., Box 2961; FEC DIS No. 3076, 9 Feb 51, Box 400; Newsweek, 19 Feb 1951, pp. 27–28.

55. 21st Inf., 24th Div., Comd. Rpt., 9 Feb 51, and 2nd Bn., Jnl. File, message 7, 1615, Encls. 1, 9, Annex A, and Encl. 7, Box 3665; IX Corps, Comd. Rpt., 9 Feb 51, Box 1784.

56. Ridgway, letter to MacArthur, 9 Feb 51, Unclassified Binder, Ridgway Papers.

57. Lt. Col. Herbert Fairlee Wood, Strange Battleground: Official History of the Canadian Army in Korea (Ottawa: Ministry of National Defense, Roger Duhamel, Queen's Printer, 1966), pp. 60–61.

58. Hist. Rec., 10 Feb 51, Box 22, Ridgway Papers; Eighth Army, Comd. Rpt., Summ., 10 Feb 51, Box 1154.

59. FEC DIS No. 3078, 12 Feb 51, Box 401.

60. 27th Inf., 25th Div., Comd. Rpt., Box 3850; map overlay to the 27th Inf. Comd. Rpt., covering Task Forces Dolvin and Bartlett, 1–14 Feb 51, scale 1:50,000, shows the routes of both task forces. For a critique of Task Force Allen, see I Corps, Armor Combat Lesson Bulletin No. 5, 4 Mar 51, "Task Force Allen, Operation Pacemaker, 10–11 Feb 51."

61. 35th Inf., 25th Div., Comd. Rpt., 10 Feb 51, Box 3860.

62. 24th Inf., 25th Div., Comd. Rpt., 10 Feb 51, Box 3841.

63. 25th Div., Comd. Rpt., 10 Feb 51, Box 3776; I Corps, Comd. Rpt., 10–11 Feb 51, Box 1511; Newsweek, 19 Feb 51, pp. 27–28.

64. I Corps, Comd. Rpt., 10 Feb 51, Box 1511; 25th Div., Comd. Rpt., 11–12 Feb 51, Box 3776.

65. Newsweek, 19 Feb 51, p. 28.

66. Capt. H. D. McCallum, "The M19 as an Offensive Weapon," Antiaircraft Journal 94, no. 3 (May–June 1951): 20; 15th Inf., 3rd Div., Comd. Rpt., 10 Feb 51, Box 2955.

67. FEC DIS No. 3084, 18 Feb 51, OB-2, Box 401.

68. Briscoe and Mossman, "Rehabilitation of Tidal Locks."

69. 3rd Div., Comd. Rpt., Feb 1951, 13–14 Feb.

70. I conducted interviews and had conversations with many members of the I Corps staff while I was with the I Corps CP in July 1951.

CHAPTER 9

1. 2nd Div., Comd. Rpt., G-2 Jnl., Serial 1898, 28 Jan 51, Box 2480; X Corps, Comd. Rpt., 28 Jan 51, Box 1995.

2. Freeman, "Wonju through Chipyong-ni," pp. 6–7.

3. 21st Inf., 24th Div., Comd. Rpt., 28–29 Jan 51, pp. 21–23, and 21st Inf., S-2 Jnl., Serial 4077, oral report, 30 Jan 51, Box 3664; Freeman, "Wonju through Chipyong-ni"; Capt. Russell A. Gugeler, "Twin Tunnels Patrol Ambush," chap. 8 in *Combat Actions in Korea* (Washington, D.C.: The Association of the US Army, 1954), pp. 88–107, is a detailed study of this patrol, based on interviews with members of Mitchell's group; correspondence with Lt. Mueller of the 21st Inf., and official records of the 23rd Inf. and the 2nd Div. I question whether the action should be called an ambush. It seems to me that the fighting resulted from a chance engagement when the patrol encountered a large enemy force moving into and occupying the Twin Tunnels area. Had it been an ambush, enemy units would have been emplaced at the beginning of the fight, and the Chinese would have been able to destroy the patrol completely.

4. There are various references to the total strength of the patrol in the official records. The 21st Inf. Comd. Rpt. gives 2 officers and 25 men from the 23rd Inf., which, together with its own contingent of 15 men, adds up to a total of 3 officers and 39 enlisted men—42 men in the patrol. X Corps, G-3 Sec., "Combat Notes," n.d., p. 4, gives Mitchell's contingent as numbering 2 officers and 34 enlisted men. Both these figures are obviously incorrect. I accept Gugeler's figures of 44 men from the 1st Bn., 23rd Inf., plus Capt. Stai and 15 men from the 21st Inf., for a total of 60 men in the joint patrol after it left Iho-ri and when it reached the Twin Tunnels area.

5. Terrain sketch map, scale 1:50,000, in X Corps Combat Notes, Twin Tunnel Fight, n.d., following p. 6, copy in author's possession, and sketch map in Gugeler, *Combat Actions in Korea*, p. 92.

6. Gugeler, *Combat Actions in Korea*, pp. 92–93.

7. Ibid., p. 93.

8. 21st Inf. Jnl., 291700 Jan 51 to 301700 Jan 51, entry no. 4077, Action of info to CO, Exec. Off., G-2 by Liaison Off., 24th Div., Comd. Rpt., 29–30 Jan, Box 3664.

9. Gugeler, *Combat Actions in Korea*, pp. 95–97.

10. Ibid., pp. 98–99; X Corps, G-3 Sec., Combat Notes on the Twin Tunnels Patrol Action, n.d, pp. 4–5; 21st Inf., 24th Div., Comd. Rpt., 28–29 Jan 51, Box 3664.

11. Gugeler, *Combat Actions in Korea*, p. 99; 21st Inf., Comd. Rpt., 28–29 Jan 51, pp. 21–23, Box 3664; Maj. Sam Radow, S-3, 1st Bn., 23rd Inf., interview with author, 16 Aug 1951.

12. The number of casualties in Mueller's contingent from the 21st Inf. seems firm. The number from Mitchell's 23rd Inf. is subject to some uncertainty, but the number given is believed to be at least approximately correct. The casualty figure is culled from various statements in Gugeler, *Combat Actions in Korea;* X Corps, Comd. Rpt., Annexes, including POR No. 126, 30 Jan 51, Box 1993; 21st Inf., 24th Div., Comd. Rpt., S-2 Jnl., two-page, single-spaced typed entry based

on oral testimony, item 4077, 29–30 Jan 51, Box 3664; X Corps, G-3 Sec., Combat Notes on Twin Tunnels fight, pp. 4–6, including three excellent sketch maps of the scene of action, copy in author's possession. This combat report, with detail on Tyrrell's relief mission, gives the total casualties as 4 killed, 30 wounded, and 5 missing in action. Also see 2nd Div., Comd. Rpt., G-2 Jnl., 29 Jan 51, Box 2480; 23rd RCT, After Action Rpt. to CG, 2nd Div., 13 Mar 51.

13. Freeman, "Wonju through Chipyong-ni," p. 10.

14. Ibid., pp. 10–11; X Corps, Comd. Rpt. and enclosures, 30–31 Jan 51, Box 1995 (I found the X Corps documents misfiled among the Feb 1951 documents at the National Archives).

15. X Corps, Comd. Rpt. and enclosures, 31 Jan 51, Box 1995; X Corps, Combat Notes on Twin Tunnels Battle, 31 Jan–1 Feb 51, copy in author's possession; Freeman, "Wonju through Chipyong-ni," pp. 11–14. Both the X Corps Combat Notes and Freeman's MS contain sketch maps of the area and perimeter defense locations.

16. Freeman, "Wonju through Chipyong-ni," pp. 14–15.

17. X Corps, Comd. Rpt., and enclosures, 31 Jan 51, Box 1995; X Corps, Combat Notes on Twin Tunnels Battle, 31 Jan 51, p. 3; Freeman, "Wonju through Chipyong-ni," pp. 17–18; HQ, Eighth Army, Gen. Ord. No. 366, 28 May 51, awarding the Distinguished Service Cross to Lt. Craig for action at the Twin Tunnels.

18. Freeman, "Wonju through Chipyong-ni," p. 19.

19. Ibid., pp. 19–21; X Corps, Combat Notes, The Action at the Twin Tunnels, 1 Feb 51, pp. 3–4; Memo to CG Eighth Army, from Patterson for Dabney (Eighth Army G-3), 3 Feb 51, Folder D–L, Box 17, Ridgway Papers.

20. 23rd RCT, After Action Rpt., 29 Jan–15 Feb 51, to CG, 2nd Div., 13 Mar 51; Memo from Patterson for Dabney, 3 Feb 51, Ridgway Papers; Freeman, "Wonju through Chipyong-ni," p. 22; Eighth Army, Comd. Rpt., G-3, 3 Feb 51, Box 1157; Presidential Unit Citation; 3rd Bn., 23rd Inf., 2nd Div., for action 30 Jan–2 Feb 51, DA, Gen. Ord. No. 36, 4 June 51; Presidential Unit Citation, the French Bn., UN Forces in Korea, for action 30 Jan–2 Feb 51, DA, Gen. Ord. No. 16, 20 Mar 51; 2nd Div., Comd. Rpt., 1 Feb 51, Box 2495. Freeman gives his casualties as 225 and remarks that the Twin Tunnels fight was the end of the Chinese 125th Division. The latter is an overstatement. Those of the division that escaped fought another day, as the 23rd RCT learned within a week.

21. Freeman, " Wonju through Chipyong-ni," pp. 22–23; 23rd RCT, After Action Rpt. to CG, 2nd Div., 29 Jan 51–15 Feb 51, 13 Mar 51, copy in author's possession.

CHAPTER 10

1. FEC DIS No. 3088, OB-1, 22 Feb 1951, Box 402. Address given by Gen. Peng Te-huai (Dehuai), CG, Joint NKA-CCF HQ, 4 Feb 51, in enemy document captured 14 Feb 51.

2. X Corps, Almond Diary, 1 Feb 51; X Corps, Comd. Rpt., Feb 1951, Operations Sec., p. 3.

3. Almond, Diary, 1, 8 Feb 51; X Corps, Comd. Rpt., Feb 51, Operations, pp. 24–25; X Corps, G-3 Sec., Combat Notes No. 9, n.d., but apparently issued in Mar 1951, with three map annexes.

4. Eighth Army, Comd. Rpt., 5–7 Feb 51, Box 1154; FEC DIS Nos. 3073-74, 7–8 Feb 51, Box 400.

5. Eighth Army, Comd. Rpt., G-3 Sec., 5–9 Feb 51, Box 1157; Eighth Army, Comd. Rpt., Narr., 5–8 Feb 51, Box 1154; 17th Inf., 7th Div., Rpt., 8 Feb 51, Box 3222.

6. 9th Inf., Comd. Rpt., 3–8 Feb 51, Box 2689; HQ, Eighth Army, Gen. Ord. No. 159, 21 Mar 51, awarding Distinguished Service Cross to Capt. Frank W. Lucas, KMAG advisor to 2nd Bn., ROK 26th Regt., for action 6 Feb 51 near Kangnung.

7. X Corps, Comd. Rpt., Annexes, PIR No., 135, 8 Feb 51, Box 1997.

8. 9th Inf., 2nd Div., Comd. Rpt., 9 Feb 51, Box 2689; X Corps, Comd. Rpt., 9 Feb 51, PIR No. 136, Box 1997; 17th Inf., 7th Div., Comd. Rpt., 8 Feb 51, Box 3222; 187th Abn. RCT, Comd. Rpt., 9 Feb 51, Box 3434.

9. X Corps, Comd. Rpt., Daily Summ., 10 Feb 51, Box 1997; 187th Abn. RCT, Comd. Rpt., S-2 Sec., 10 Feb 51, Box 3434.

10. X Corps, Comd. Rpt., Encl. 4, 11 Feb 51, Box 1995; and Oper. Narr., p. 25; 38th INf., 2nd Div., Comd. Rpt., 11 Feb 51, Box 2705.

11. FEC DIS No. 3077, 11 Feb 51, Box 401; X Corps, Comd. Rpt., Annexes, PIR No. 137, 10 Feb 51, Box 1997; 38th Inf., 2nd Div., Comd. Rpt., 10 Feb 51, Box 2705; Eighth Army, G-3 Sec. Jnl., 10 Feb 51, Box 1156.

12. X Corps, Plan Roundup, Annex C, 1 Feb 51; Eighth Army, Comd. Rpt., G-3 Sec., 11 Feb 51, Box 1157; X Corps, Comd. Rpt., Annexes, POR No. 138, 11 Feb 51, Box 1997.

13. Almond, Diary, 11 Feb 51; X Corps, Comd. Rpt., Annexes, Box 1997.

14. Eighth Army, Comd. Rpt., Sec. 5, After Action Interviews, Feb 1951, 1st Lt. George W. Gardner, CO, A Co., 1st Bn., 38th Inf., Summary of Combat Action of Company A, 11–12 Feb 51, to CO, 1st Bn., 16 Feb 51 (hereafter cited as Gardner, Summary).

15. Lt. Col. William P. Kelleher, CO, 1st Bn., 38th Inf., to CO, 38th Inf., 14 Feb 51, "Summation of Action of the 1st Bn., 38th Inf. during the Period 1–12 Feb 51," in Eighth Army Comd. Rpt., Sec. 5, After Action Interviews, Feb 1951 (hereafter cited as Kelleher, Summation).

16. Combat Notes No. 9, X Corps, G-3 Sec., n.d., p. 10, signed by Almond.

17. Eighth Army, Comd. Rpt., 11 Feb 51, Box 1154. The Eighth Army Comd. Rpt. said it was the CCF 117th Division (or possibly the 116th Division) that cut the road behind the ROK and American troops north of Hoengsong.

18. Mimeographed booklet, in Chinese, titled "A Collection of Combat Experiences," issued by HQ, 19th Army Group, CCF, 29 Mar 51, belonging to Chin, Chief of Staff, 4th Ta-tui, 58 pp., p. 151 of ATIS publication captured by 25th Div., date unknown, but received by ATIS 25 June 51.

19. Ibid., p. 154.

20. A document captured by 1st Cav. Div. Arty., 17 Feb 51, Eighth Army, Comd. Rpt., G-2 Sec., Encl. 2 to G-2 PIR No. 234, 3 Mar 51, Box 1167.

21. Capt. William E. Manning, S-3, 3rd Bn., 38th Inf., using his diary, interview with author, 20 Aug 1951, and in report on the action north of Hoengsong in 2nd Div. Comd. Rpt., Annexes of subordinate units, Feb 51, report by Capts. Manning and Valentine, CSHIS-5 (R-1).

22. Eighth Army, Comd. Rpt., 11 Feb 51, Box 1154.

23. Gardner, Summary. The chain of command to Support Force 21 is a confused issue. It seems that at first its orders came from the 2nd Div. Arty. The 2nd Div. Comd. Rpt., G-3 Sec. Jnl. file, has an entry at 2:50 A.M., 12 Feb, from the Div. Arty. to the Div. G-3, stating that it ordered Support Force 21 at 2:45 A.M. to withdraw, Serials 13 and 14, Box 2503.

24. Gardner, Summary.

25. Lt. Col. Walter Killilae, CO, 82nd AAA AW (SP) Bn., *Antiaircraft Journal* 94, no. 3 (May–June 1951): 4.

26. Lt. Col. Kelleher, "Supplemental to Summation of the 1st Bn. 38th Inf. during the Period 11–12 Feb 51," to CO, 38th Inf., 15 Feb 51. There were six howitzers to each of the three batteries of the 15th FA, and six also to A Btry., 503rd FA Bn. The one 155-mm howitzer and its tractor prime mover that got on the road were abandoned or destroyed there.

27. Gardner, Summary.

28. Kelleher, Summation. The Gardner and Kelleher reports give location point with six-digit map coordinates. The author has checked these coordinates on a 1:50,000-scale map and translated them into mileages from located village or other identifiable features. Maps of Korea, 1:50,000 scale, covering the area from Hongchon south to Hoengsong have been used in this work.

29. Ibid.

30. 38th Inf., 2nd Div., Special Rpt. on Hoengsong, Feb 1951, p. 3, Box 2707.

31. DA, Gen. Ord. No. 18, 1 Feb 1952 (awarded 7 Nov 51), granting the Medal of Honor, Posthumously, to Sgt. Charles R. Long, M Co., 38th Inf., 2nd Div., for action 12 Feb 51, near Hoengsong.

32. 38th Inf., 2nd Div., Special Rpt. on Hoengsong, Feb 1951, Box 2707.

33. 38th Tank Co., Comd. Rpt., 11–13 Feb 51; 2nd Div., Comd. Rpt., Feb 51, quoted in 1st Lt. John Mewha, "Changbong-ni to Hoengsong, 11–13 Feb 51," BA 83 MS, in Office Chief of Military History, Washington, D.C.

34. Cpl. James J. Lee, of the Security Platoon, and an eyewitness to all that happened, gave his account of it to Capt. Valentine in an interview, 4 Apr 1951, Special Rpt., 38th Inf., Comd. Rpt., in 2nd Div., Comd. Rpt., Feb 51, Box 2707; Mewha, "Changbong-ni to Hoengsong"; 38th Inf., 2nd Div., Spec. Rpt., "Hoengsong," n.d., pp. 7–9, Box 2707.

35. 38th Inf., 2nd Div., Spec. Rpt., "Hoengsong," pp. 9–10; Kelleher, Summation, p. 2.

36. Gardner, Summary; Kelleher, Summation.

37. Kelleher, Summation; 38th Inf., 2nd Div., Spec. Rpt., "Hoengsong," pp. 11–12.

38. 38th Tank Co., Comd. Rpt., 11–13 Feb 51, cited in Mewha, "Changbong-ni to Hoengsong"; Brig. Gen. Stewart and 2nd Div. Insp. Gen. Lt. Col. Duvall, Rpt. on Hoengsong action, 16 Feb 51 (brought to me at Maj. Gen. Ruffner's instructions in Korea; hereafter cited as Stewart and Duvall, Report); Col. Coughlin, interview with author, 13 Dec 51; Lt. Col. Earl M. Williamson, X Corps G-3, interview with author, 26 and 28 Aug 1951.

39. Gardner, Summary.

40. Lt. Col. Walter Killilae, "Crew Protection on M16s," *Antiaircraft Journal* 94, no. 4 (July–Aug 1951): 28.

41. 38th Inf., 2nd Div., Spec. Rpt., "Hoengsong," pp. 13–14.

42. Testimony of Lt. Meyer (17 Feb 51) and Sgt. Perrone, in Stewart and Duvall, Report.

43. Paraphrased from 1st Lt. Lee Ross Hartell, 15th FA Bn., letter to his brother "Chic," 20 Mar 1951.

44. Remarks of Gardner to Mewha, made while walking through the stretch of road just north of the bridge, at Hoengsong, Feb 1951, in EUSAK, Comd. Rpt., Feb 1951, Sec. 5.

45. 2nd Div., Comd. Rpt., Summ., 12 Mar 51, p. 8.

46. A summary of three typed pages, single spaced, prepared by the S-2 and S-3 of the Netherlands Battalion, on the CP attack at Hoengsong, is among the papers of the 2nd Div. in the National Archives and is the basis of the account given here. At the time I found this summary, the archives officials would not permit me to make copies of it or to prepare extensive notes. I studied the document carefully, and that night while the information was still fresh in my mind, I wrote out the details I wanted. Other sources are IX Corps, Comd. Rpt., 12 Feb 51, G-2 Jnl., PIR No. 153, Annex 2, 26 Feb 51, Box 1786; Presidential Distinguished Unit Citation, the Netherlands Detachment, United Nations Forces in Korea, DA, Gen. Ord. No. 36, 4 June 1951; 2nd Div., Comd. Rpt., 12 Feb 51, G-2 Summ., Box 2495.

47. 17th Inf., 7th Div., Comd. Rpt., 12–13 Feb 51, Box 3222; Eighth Army, Comd. Rpt., G-3 Sec., 12 Feb 51; FEC DIS No. 3079, Box 401; X Corps, Comd. Rpt., Encl. 4, 12 Feb 51, including "Action of 11th ROK FA Bn.," Box 1995.

48. Eighth Army, Comd. Rpt., 12–13 Feb 51, and G-3 Sec., 12 Feb 51, Box 1154; X Corps, Comd. Rpt., 12 Feb 51, Box 1995.

49. X Corps, Comd. Rpt., 7, 12 Feb 51, Box 1995, and ibid., Annexes, POR No. 139, Box 1997; Eighth Army, Comd. Rpt., G-3 Sec., 12 Feb 51, Box 1157.

50. 2nd Div., Comd. Rpt., G-3 Jnl., Serial 83, 1445, 12 Feb 51, in X Corps, Comd. Rpt. file, G-3 Sec., 12 Feb 51, Box 2503; X Corps, Comd. Rpt., 12 Feb 51, Box 2495.

51. 2nd Div., Comd. Rpt., 12 Feb 51, Box 2495.

52. Memo for Record–R., 13 Feb 51, Special File, Dec 50–Mar 51, Box 20, Ridgway Papers.

53. GC EUSAK to MacArthur, 9 Mar 51, [re] Hoengsong, 11–13 Feb 51, Folder M–R, Box 17, Ridgway Papers.

54. Ridgway to Almond, note, 13 Feb 51, Box 17, Ridgway Papers.

55. Almond to CG, 2nd Div., 13 Feb 51, Box 17, Ridgway Papers.

56. Capt. Guy P. McMurray, C Btry., exec. off., 49th FA Bn., 7th Div., 8 Feb 52, Training Publications and Aids, Debriefing Rpt. No. 70, Artillery School, Fort Sill, Okla.

57. Testimony of Coughlin, in Stewart and Duvall, Report.

58. Ibid.

59. Radio Message, X Corps to 2nd Div., personal from Almond to Ruffner and Ridgway, 122341 Feb 51, requesting investigation of Hoengsong; Investigation of Heavy Losses of Material and Personnel in 2nd Div. Task Force Operating in Support of 8th ROK Div., 23 Feb 51, in Stewart and Duvall, Report.

60. Maj. Gen. Clark L. Ruffner, interview with author at 2nd Div. CP, Korea, 27 Aug 51; X Corps, Plan Roundup, Annex C, Artillery, 1 Feb 51, p. 3a, seems

to place artillery units of Support Force 21 and Team Baker under control of the 2nd Div. Arty. commander. But actually, in the action, Gen. Chae of the ROK 8th Div. seems to have controlled it, and only the X Corps Arty. commander exercised any higher control.

61. Col. William P. Ennis, X Corps Arty. commander, testimony before Stewart-Duvall panel.

62. 2nd Div., G-3 Jnl., messages at 10:30, and 11:20 A.M. and at 12:00 P.M., 12 Feb 51, from G-3 to Advance CP, and from 2nd Div. Advance CP to G-3, 2nd Div.

63. Lt. Col. James T. Quirck, Eighth Army Information Officer, Memos 6 and 17, Mar 1951, to Ridgway, 17 Mar 51, Folder M-R, Box 17, Ridgway Papers.

CHAPTER 11

1. Freeman, "Wonju through Chipyong-ni," pp. 23-26; Freeman, interview with author, 17 Apr 1952.

2. Freeman, "Wonju through Chipyong-ni," pp. 26-27.

3. Ibid., p. 20. See Chinese booklet, "Collection of Combat Experiences." Sec. 6 of it is entitled "A Critique of Tactics Employed in the First Encounter with the Enemy at Chop Pyong ni." This document is valuable for enemy unit identification and movements at Chipyong-ni.

4. Almond, Diary, 12 Feb 51. The conference was held between 12:15 and 1:15 P.M.

5. IX Corps, Comd. Rpt., 14-17 Feb 51, Box 1784; Eighth Army, Comd. Rpt., G-3 Sec., 13 Feb 51, Box 1157.

6. X Corps, Comd. Rpt., G-3 Sec., and 2nd Div. G-3 Jnl., Serial 89, 1610, 12 Feb 51, Box 2503.

7. 2nd Div., Comd. Rpt., G-3 Sec. Jnl., Serial 79, 1422, 13 Feb 51.

8. Ibid., G-3 Jnl., Serial 80, 1428. Also see earlier Jnl. Serial 56, 1056, 13 Feb 51.

9. Gen. Ridgway, interviews with author, Dai-Ichi Building, Tokyo, 8-9 Oct 51; Lt. Gen. Edward M. Almond, letters to author, 29 Oct and 13 Nov 1975; Maj. Gen. Clark L. Ruffner, CG, 2nd Div., interview with author, 15 Aug 51; and Lt. Col. Earl M. Williamson, G-3, X Corps, interview with author, 26 Aug 51. All agreed that Gen. Ridgway insisted on holding at Chipyong-ni after all subordinate commanders had recommended withdrawing the UN forces from the place.

10. I walked around the perimeter with a good map in hand and could literally follow the perimeter line most of the way by following the field-telephone line that lay on the ground. Capt. Henry L. Poole, 37th FA Bn. liaison officer with the 2nd Bn., 23rd Inf., interview with author, 21 Aug 51.

11. Freeman, "Wonju through Chipyong-ni," and sketch map of battle positions, 12-16 Feb 51; X Corps, Comd. Rpt., Encl. 1, Map A, sketch of 23rd RCT in Perimeter Defense at Chipyong-ni, Feb 1951, Box 1995.

12. Freeman, "Wonju through Chipyong-ni"; X Corps, Comd. Rpt., Encl. 1, Map A, Feb 1951; Map of Korea, Ipo-ri sheet, scale 1:50,000.

13. Freeman, "Wonju through Chipyong-ni," pp. 29-30; X Corps, G-3 Sec., Combat Notes, Defense of Chipyong-ni, n.d., p. 2-3.

14. Col. Paul L. Freeman, interview with author, 17 Apr 1952; Lt. Gen. William J. McCaffrey, USA, Ret., letter to author, 16 Feb 1980; Lt. Col. James W.

Edwards, CO, 2nd Bn., 23rd Inf., Memo to Col. Freeman, n.d. (but in 1951); Gen. Almond, in his diary entry on 14 Feb 51, says that Maj. Gen. Ruffner, in conference with him at 2:15 P.M., asked that Chiles be sent to Chipyong-ni to replace Freeman, and he ordered Chiles to leave at once. Ruffner, in an interview with the author, said that Almond himself decided to send Chiles to Chipyong-ni and that Ruffner had nothing to do with making the assignment. There is some evidence that Gen. Almond had previously planned to replace Freeman. The same mortar shell that hit the 23rd RCT CP and wounded Freeman also wounded the regimental S-2 and S-3 and killed one man.

15. Maj. John B. Dumaine, S-3, 23rd RCT, Report, "Operations at Chipyong-ni," n.d., but bearing an official stamp 8 June 1951 (hereafter cited as Dumaine, Report); X Corps, Comd. Rpt., Encl. 1, Battle of Chipyong-ni, pp. 6–7, Combat Notes, Defense at Chipyong-ni, with maps, n.d. (but within a month or two after the battle), Box 1995; 1st Lt. Donald O. Miller, HQ Co., 2nd Bn., 23rd Inf., to unnamed person but addressed "Dear Sir" (apparently in response to a request from either Lt. Col. Edwards, CO, 2nd Bn., at Chipyong-ni or Col. Freeman, CO, 23rd Inf., at time of battle), 11 Sept 51, Korea, copy in author's possession; Gugeler, *Combat Actions in Korea*, pp. 113–14, and map sketch of G Co.'s position, p. 110. Gugeler has a detailed account of G Co. in the battle of Chipyong-ni up to about 8 A.M. on 15 Feb, when B Co. relieved it. His account also covers most of the action involving B Btry., 503rd FA Bn., which emplaced its six 155-mm howitzers in a bowl-shaped area just behind (north of) G Co. Gugeler's account of the infantry action is based largely on Maj. Edward C. Williamson's typescript MS "Chipyong-ni: Defense of South Sector of 23rd Regimental Combat Team Perimeter by Company G, 13-15 February 1951." Williamson interviewed members of the 2nd Bn. in Korea, copy in Office Chief of Military History. Gugeler's information on B Btry., 503rd FA Bn., is based on his own interviews with members of B Btry. and several interviews with Capt. John A. Elledge, 37th FA Bn. liaison officer with B Btry., 503rd FA Bn.

16. Chinese booklet, "Collection of Combat Experiences," pp. 157–58.

17. Dumaine, Report, p. 5.

18. Lt. Col. Walter Killilae and Capt. Clyde T. Hathaway, "Accompli at Chipyong-ni," *Antiaircraft Journal* 94, no. 4 (July–Aug 1951): 11–12; Dumaine, Report, pp. 4–5.

19. Killilae and Hathaway, "Accompli," p. 12; Gugeler, *Combat Actions in Korea;* Freeman, "Wonju through Chipyong-ni," p. 32.

20. Freeman, "Wonju through Chipyong-ni," p. 32.

21. 23rd RCT, Comd. Rpt., Feb 51, Annex 7, Role of the Regimental Clearing Station and Battalion Aid Stations in the Perimeter Defense of Chipyong-ni, 13–15 Feb 51.

22. X Corps, Comd. Rpt., Feb 51, Annex 1, Battle of Chipyong-ni, p. 8, copy in author's possession.

23. Freeman, "Wonju through Chipyong-ni," pp. 35–36; Dumaine, Report; X Corps, Comd. Rpt., Feb 51, Encl. 1, Battle of Chipyong-ni, pp. 8–9, 6–7; Gugeler, *Combat Actions in Korea*, pp. 111–26, gives a grim account of this battle on G Co.'s hill.

24. Gugeler, *Combat Actions in Korea*, pp. 129–31.

25. Ibid., pp. 124–29.

26. Chinese booklet, "Collection of Combat Experiences," p. 158, copy in author's possession.

27. Freeman, "Wonju through Chipyong-ni," p. 36; Capt. Henry L. Poole, 37th FA Bn., liaison officer with the 2nd Bn., 23rd Inf., interview with author, 21 Aug 51; X Corps, Combat Notes, Defense of Chipyong-ni, n.d., pp. 5–6; Gugeler, *Combat Actions in Korea,* pp. 129–31.

28. Freeman, "Wonju through Chipyong-ni," p. 37; X Corps, Comd. Rpt., Feb 51, Encl. 1, Battle of Chipyong-ni, p. 9; X Corps, Combat Notes, Defense of Chipyong-ni, pp. 5–6; Chinese booklet, "Collection of Combat Experiences."

29. Lt. Col. James W. Edwards, CO, 2nd Bn., 23rd Inf., letter to Col. Paul L. Freeman, 7 May 1951, copy in author's possession. Col. Freeman had written to Edwards and asked him to send an account of what happened at Chipyong-ni after Freeman left by helicopter just before noon on 15 Feb. Edwards's letter is a somewhat detailed account of his personal effort to regain the G Co. position. The fight there continued during 15 Feb until late in the afternoon, when the battle ended with the arrival of Task Force Crombez, 5th Cav. Regt.

30. X Corps, Comd. Rpt., Encl. 1, Map A, Sketch of 23rd RCT in Perimeter Defense at Chipyong-ni, Feb 1951, Box 1995. Gugeler, *Combat Actions in Korea,* p. 110, has a sketch of the immediate G Co. troop positions. The scale 1:50,000 map of Korea, Ipo-ri sheet, is needed to understand the relationship of the various hills and terrain surrounding Chipyong-ni to the Chinese attacks.

31. Edwards, letter to Freeman, 7 May 1951; the Chinese booklet, "Collection of Combat Experiences," speaks of "the 3rd Battalion of the 344th Regiment occupying three hilltops situated on the southeast of the railroad station" (p. 159).

32. 1st Lt. Donald O. Miller, letter to unnamed person in response to a request for his information on F Co.'s action during the battle, copy in author's possession. Probably, the letter was to Lt. Col. Edwards, CO, 2nd Bn., 23rd Inf., but it may have been to Col. Freeman. During the battle Miller was probably exec. off. of F Co., but at the time he wrote the letter, 11 Sept 51, he was in HQ Co., 2nd Bn., 23rd Inf. In this letter he said he wrote the official F Co. after-action report.

33. Edwards, letter to Freeman.

34. Ibid.; X Corps, Comd. Rpt., Feb 51, Encl. 1, The Battle of Chipyong-ni, p. 10, Box 1995.

35. Chinese booklet, "Collection of Combat Experiences," p. 159.

36. 21st Inf., 24th Div., Comd. Rpt., 12–14 Feb 51, Box 3665.

37. Bartlett, *With the Australians in Korea,* pp. 70–71.

38. 1st Lt. Martin Blumenson, "Task Force Crombez, 5th Cavalry Regiment," typed MS of a series of interviews he had in Korea in Apr 1951 with members of Task Force Crombez and others in IX Corps, copy in Office Chief of Military History (now US Military History Center), catalogued as OCMH BA 29 (hereafter cited as Blumenson, MS). Blumenson, interview with Lt. Col. George B. Pickett, 1 Apr 51, and interview with Col. Crombez.

39. Brig. Gen. Frank A. Allen, interview with author, 28 Jan 54; Blumenson, MS. Capt. Russell A. Gugeler has an excellent account of Task Force Crombez, based on Blumenson interviews, as Item 10 in his *Combat Actions in Korea,* pp. 134–44. Ridgway's comment about Col. Crombez's courage in leading the task force was in a review comment on the draft for this chapter, 10 Jan 1985. Ridgway further commented in that letter, "The Chipyong-ni action was a key factor in my

primary objective of restoring confidence of the troops in their leadership and their own self-respect."

40. Blumenson, MS; his interview with Capt. Barrett was on 21 Apr 51. Gugeler, *Combat Actions in Korea,* pp. 136–37.

41. Written statement by Col. Marcel G. Crombez, "Task Force Crombez," 5th Cav. Regt. RCT, 1st Cav. Div., Comd. Rpt. Feb 51, pp. 60–61, Box 4438.

42. Col. Marcel G. Crombez, interview with author, 12 Jan 1956.

43. Maj. Robert A. Humphrey, S-2, 5th Cav. Regt., interview with Blumenson, 27 Mar 51.

44. Capt. Joe W. Finley, CO, F Co., 5th Cav. Regt.; M. Sgt. Lloyd L. Jones, plat. sgt., 3rd Plat., L Co.; and Sfc. George W. Miller, 3rd Plat., L Co., interviews with Blumenson, 28 Mar 51.

45. M. Sgt. Joe Kirland, D Co., 6th Tank Bn., interview with Blumenson; Unit Hist., D Co., 6th Tank Bn., 15–16 Feb 51.

46. Cpl. Paul Campbell, 2nd Plat., Cpl. Wayne O. Kemp, 1st Plat., and CWO Clarence L. Umberger, all of L Co., 5th Cav. Regt., interviews with Blumenson.

47. Crombez, "Task Force Crombez."

48. 1st Lt. William R. Bierworth, plat. leader, 3rd Plat., D Co., 6th Tank Bn. (Bierworth succeeded Hiers to command of the tank company), interview with Blumenson; 5th Cav., Comd. Rpt., S-3 Sec., Feb 51. D Co., 6th Tank Bn., had two tanks damaged at the Pass, and altogether in the advance of Chipyong-ni, one officer killed, two enlisted men killed, one officer wounded, and four enlisted men wounded. Lt. Col. George Pickett, CO, Armor, IX Corps, interview with Blumenson, 1 Apr 51, for Growden's evidence.

49. Col. Crombez, interview with Blumenson.

50. Sfc. James Maxwell, D Co., 6th Tank Bn., statement in Blumenson interviews.

51. Capt. John C. Barrett, CO, L Co., 5th Cav. Regt., interview with Blumenson, 26 Apr 51.

52. Ibid.

53. HQ I Corps, Armor Combat Lesson Bulletin No. 7, 7 Mar 51, Observations on Task Force Crombez, 15 Feb 51.

54. Barrett, CO, L Co., 5th Cav. Regt., interview with Blumenson.

55. Chinese booklet, "Collection of Combat Experiences" (italics mine in para. B.1).

56. Col. Crombez, interview with Blumenson; FEC DIS No. 3083, 17 Feb 51, Box 401.

57. Dumaine, Report.

58. Barclay, *First Commonwealth Division,* p. 51; Almond to Ridgway, correspondence, 7 Mar 51, Box 17, Ridgway Papers.

59. Folder M–R, Box 17, Ridgway Papers.

60. Lt. Col. Ray W. Horton, Insp. Gen. Div., memo to Ridgway, 13 May 1951, Folder S–Z, Box 17, Ridgway Papers.

CHAPTER 12

1. X Corps, Comd. Rpt., Annexes, G-4 Daily Summ., 11 Feb 51; Eighth Army, Comd. Rpt., G-4 Sec., 11–19 Feb 51, pp. 92–94.

2. Hist. Rec., 14 Feb 51, Box 22, Ridgway Papers.

3. Eighth Army, Comd. Rpt., G-3 Sec. and G-3 Jnl. File, 14 Feb 51, Box 1157.

4. Map of Korea, Yangdongwon-ni Sheet, 1950, 1:50,000 scale, shows this situation clearly.

5. Paraphrased from Hartell, letter to his brother "Chic," 20 Mar 1951.

6. *Medal of Honor Recipients—1863–1963*, 88th Cong., 2nd sess. (Washington, D.C.: GPO, 1964), p. 255, Medal of Honor award to 1st Lt. Lee R. Hartell, USA, A Btry., 15th FA, 2nd Div., for action 27 Aug 1951, near Kobangsan-ni.

7. Eighth Army, Comd. Rpt., G-2 Sec., PIR No. 217, 14 Feb 51, Box 1155; X Corps, Comd. Rpt., 14 Feb 51, Box 2495; *Newsweek*, 26 Feb 1951, pp. 26–27; FEC DIS No. 3081, 15 Feb 51, Box 401.

8. 2nd Div., Comd. Rpt., G-3 Jnl. Serials 109 and 119, 14 Feb 51, Box 2504; X Corps, Comd. Rpt., POR No. 141, 14 Feb 51, Box 1998.

9. X Corps, Comd. Rpt., Annexes, G-2 Sec., PIR No. 142, 15 Feb 51, Box 1998.

10. 2nd Div., Comd. Rpt., G-3 Sec., 14 Feb 51, Box 2504.

11. Ibid., G-3 Sec. Jnl. File, Serial 124, 14 1822, Feb 51.

12. Eighth Army, Gen. Ord. No. 359, 27 May 1951, awarding the Distinguished Service Cross to Capt. John H. Nelson, CO, F Co., 38th Inf., 2nd Div., for service at Hill 325, 14 Feb 51; 38th Inf., Comd. Rpt., 14 Feb 51, Box 2705; 187th Abn. RCT, Comd. Rpt., 14–15 Feb 51, Box 3434, and S-2 Sec. Jnl. File. The 674th FA Bn. fired 3,250 rounds during the day in support of the 187th Abn. Bn.

13. X Corps, Comd. Rpt., Feb 51, Encl. 3 with panoramic sketch, "Assault on Hill 255 by 1st Platoon, E Company, 187th Abn. RCT 141430 Feb 51," Box 1995.

14. Ibid.; DA, Gen. Ord. No. 41, 6 June 1951, awarding the Presidential Unit Citation to E Co., 187th Abn. Inf. Regt., for action in vicinity of Wonju, 14 Feb 51; Eighth Army, Gen. Ord. No. 174, 28 Mar 51, awarding Distinguished Service Cross to 1st Lt. James H. Nix, 3rd Plat. leader, E Co., 187th Abn. Inf. Regt., for action 14 Feb 1951, near Wonju; Eighth Army, Gen. Ord. No. 151, 20 Mar 51, awarding the Distinguished Service Cross to 1st Lt. William J. Dolan, 1st Plat. leader, E Co., 187th Abn. Inf. Regt., for action near Wonju, 14 Feb 1951. The frontal assault by E Co., 187th Abn. RCT, on 14 Feb 51 was considered a classic example of a well-led and courageously executed infantry company attack against a numerically superior dug-in enemy force. Eighth Army reproduced the special report of the 1st Plat. on 14 Mar 51, as Combat Information Bulletin No. 15, "Platoon in the Assault," but omitted names of persons and units.

15. Eighth Army, Comd. Rpt., 14–16 Feb 51, Box 1154.

16. Eighth Army, Gen. Ord. No. 318, 17 May 1951, awarding the Distinguished Service Cross to 1st Lt. David N. White, plat. leader, G Co., 187th Abn. Inf. Regt., for action 15 Feb 51 in vicinity of Wonju; 187th Abn. RCT, Comd. Rpt., S-2 Sec., 15 Feb 51.

17. Eighth Army, Comd. Rpt., 15 Feb 51, Box 1154, and Eighth Army, Comd. Rpt., G-3 Sec., 15 Feb 51, Box 1157.

18. Eighth Army, Comd. Rpt., 15 Feb 51, Box 1154.

19. Ridgway, private conversation with Col. Guthrie, CS, X Corps, 16 Feb 51, Unclassified Binder, Ridgway Papers.

20. Eighth Army, Comd. Rpt., 16 Feb 51, and Eighth Army CG, Daily Summ.,

Box 1154. A summary of these meetings is also in the Hist. Rec., 16 Feb 1951, Box 22, Ridgway Papers.

21. *All Hands: The Bureau of Naval Information Bulletin,* Nov 1951, pp. 22ff.

22. 187th Abn. RCT, Comd. Rpt., S-2 Sec. and Jnl. File, 16–17 Feb 51, Box 3434. In the recent heavy fighting around Wonju, Eighth Army intelligence believed the 119th and 120th divisions of the 40th Army and the 197th and 198th divisions of the 66th Army had been committed. East and northeast of Wonju the NK II, III, and V corps had been committed toward the Chechon objective.

23. 2nd Div., Comd. Rpt., G-3 Jnl. File, 16 Dec 51.

24. 38th Inf., 2nd Div., Comd. Rpt., 16 Feb 51, Box 2705. The official records of the 5th Cav. Regt., 1st Cav. Div., and the 187th Abn. RCT for the period Nov–Dec 1950 and Jan–June 1951 frequently cannot be found in the National Archives, Federal Records Center, in Record Group 407, where they should be. There are not even index cards for them in the files, which would indicate they were never received.

25. Eighth Army, Comd. Rpt., G-3 Sec. and Jnl. File, 16–17 Feb 51; X Corps, Comd. Rpt., Annexes, PIR No. 143, 16 Feb, and POR No. 143, 16 Feb 51, 1998.

26. 7th Div., Comd. Rpt., 16 Feb 51, Box 3188.

27. 187th Abn. RCT, Comd. Rpt., 16–17 Feb 51, Box 3434; 1st Cav. Div., Comd. Rpt., 17 Feb 51, Box 4438; IX Corps, Comd. Rpt., G-2 Sec., PIR No. 144, 17 Feb 51, Box 1786; FEC DIS No. 3084, 17 Feb 51, Box 401; X Corps, Comd. Rpt., Feb 51, pp. 8–9.

28. 1st Cav. Div., Comd. Rpt., 18 Feb 51, Box 4438.

29. Eighth Army, Comd. Rpt., Summ., 18 Feb 51, Box 1154, and G-3 Sec., 18 Feb 51, Box 1157.

30. X Corps, Comd. Rpt., Feb 1951, Evaluation of Operations Sec., p. 9; Operation Ord. No. 14, 19 Feb 51, and X Corps, Comd. Rpt., Feb 51, p. 54.

31. Barclay, *First Commonwealth Division,* p. 53.

32. Almond, Diary, 19 Feb 51.

33. Eighth Army, Comd. Rpt., Summ., 18 and 20 Feb 51; X Corps, Comd. Rpt., Annexes, Almond's Diary, 18 Feb 51, and G-2 PIR No. 147, Box 1154, and PIR No. 149, 22 Feb 51, Box 1999.

34. X Corps, Comd. Rpt., Feb 51, pp. 22–23, Boxes 1995 and 1157.

35. 187th Abn. RCT, Comd. Rpt., S-2 Sec., Box 3434.

36. Ibid., 26–28 Feb 51, Box 3434.

37. Bartlett, *With the Australians in Korea,* pp. 72–73.

38. X Corps, Comd. Rpt., 24 Feb 51, Annexes, G-2 Sec., PIR No. 151, Box 1999.

39. 1st Cav. Div., Comd. Rpt., 25–28 Feb 51, Box 4438.

40. DA, Gen. Ord. 68, 2 Aug 1951, awarding the Medal of Honor to Sgt. Einar H. Ingman, Jr. (promoted from Cpl.), E Co., 17th Inf., 7th Div., for action near Maltari, 26 Feb 1951.

41. Folder M–R, Box 17, Ridgway Papers; Register of Graduates, USMI, 1975, item 5845, p. 340; *Newsweek,* 5 Mar 1951, p. 32.

42. Ridgway, letter to Gen. Wade Haislip, vice chief of staff, 24 Feb 1951, Special File, Box 20, Ridgway Papers.

43. R. Memo for Record, 24 Feb 51, Special File, Box 20, Ridgway Papers; Gen. Ridgway discusses this episode in some detail in *The Korean War,* pp. 108–10.

44. Handwritten statement by Tarkenton to Ridgway, Disposition Form, 24 Feb 51, Folder S-Z, Box 17, Ridgway Papers.

45. 1st Cav. Div., Comd. Rpt., 23 Feb 51, and Daily Summ., 24 Feb 51, Box 4438.

46. *Richmond* (Va.) *Times-Dispatch,* 28 Feb 1951, p. 12, UP dispatch from Hoengsong, with the US Marines, 27 Feb 1951.

47. Eighth Army, Comd. Rpt., G-2 Sec., Encl. 2, PIR No. 236, 5 Mar 51, Box 1167.

48. X Corps, Comd. Rpt., Annexes, 28 Feb 51, G-2 Sec., PIR No. 155, 28 Feb 51.

CHAPTER 13

1. Field, *Naval Operations, Korea,* p. 324. This work is a dependable survey of naval operations in the Korean War.

2. Ibid., pp. 326-27.

3. Ibid., pp. 328-29.

4. Futrell, *US Air Force in Korea,* pp. 267-70.

5. Ibid., p. 320.

6. Eighth Army, Comd. Rpt., 14 Feb 51, Box 1154, and Eighth Army, G-2 Sec., PIR No. 217, 14 Feb 51.

7. Eighth Army, Gen. Ord. No. 318, 17 May 51, awarding the Distinguished Service Cross to Cpl. Albert V. Erickson for action near Chungung-ni, 14 Feb 51.

8. 3rd Div., Comd. Rpt., 14-15 Feb 51, Box 2891.

9. FEC DIS No. 3081, 15 Feb 51, Box 401.

10. Ibid., No. 3087, 21 Feb 51, C/M-3, Box 402.

11. IX Corps, Comd. Rpt., 15 Feb 51, Box 1784.

12. 25th Div., Comd. Rpt., 15 Feb 51, Box 3776.

13. Eighth Army, Comd. Rpt., G-4 Sec., 10-16 Feb 51, Box 1154; 25th Div., Comd. Rpt., 15 Feb 51, Box 3776.

14. FEC DIS No. 3084, 18 Feb 51, Box 401; IX Corps, Comd. Rpt., G-2 PIR No. 144, 17 Feb 51.

15. *Richmond* (Va.) *Times-Dispatch,* 18 Feb 1951, p. 7.

16. I Corps, Comd. Rpt., 17-18 Feb 51, Box 1511; 21st Inf., Comd. Rpt., 18-20 Feb 51, Box 3665.

17. Eighth Army, Comd. Rpt., Summ., 18 Feb 51, Boxes 1154 and 1158; 5th RCT, 24th Div., Comd. Rpt., 17-20 Feb 51, Box 5237.

18. 35th Inf., 25th Div., Comd. Rpt., 19 Feb 51, Box 3860.

19. Eighth Army, Comd. Rpt., G-2 Sec., PIR No. 223, 20 Feb 51, Box 1155; I Corps, Comd. Rpt., 17-21 Feb 51, pp. 175-98, Box 1511; 15th RCT, 3rd Div., Comd. Rpt., 20 Feb 51, Box 2955; FEC DIS No. 3088, 22 Feb 51, Box 402.

20. FEC DIS No. 3088, OB-1, 22 Feb 51, Box 402.

21. Eighth Army, Comd. Rpt., G-3 Jnl., 20-21 Feb 51, Box 1158.

22. IX Corps, Comd. Rpt., 22 Feb 51, Box 1784.

23. Eighth Army, Comd. Rpt., G-3 Sec., 21-23 Feb 51, Box 1158; IX Corps, Comd. Rpt., 21-24 Feb 51, Box 1784; X Corps, Comd. Rpt., Logistics Sec., 21-28 Feb 51, Box 1995; 1st Cav. Div., Comd. Rpt., 21-22 Feb 51, Box 4438.

24. 19th Inf., 24th Div., Comd. Rpt., S-4 Sec., Feb 51, Box 3655.

25. Report of officer from Korea, Training Bulletin No. 2, Office Chief Army

Ground Field Forces, Ft. Monroe, Va., 9 Nov 1950, p. 14; ORO-T-8 (EUSAK), NK Logistics and Methods of Accomplishments, p. 7, 13 Feb 51.

26. Mossman and Middleton, "Logistical Problems and Their Solutions" (EUSAK) June 1952, pp. 89–90, MS copy in Office Chief of Military History.

27. IX Corps, Comd. Rpt., G-3 Sec., Daily Summ., 22 Feb 51, Box 1784.

28. Eighth Army, Comd. Rpt., G-2 Sec., Annex, PIR No. 225, 22 Feb 51, Box 1155.

29. Ibid., PIR Nos. 226 and 227, 23–24 Feb 51.

30. Futrell, US Air Force in Korea, pp. 319–20.

31. Eighth Army, Comd. Rpt., G-2 Sec., Annex A to Enclosure 2, PIR No. 224, 21 Feb 51, translation of enemy document, 112th Div. HQ (CCF 38th Army), Box 1155.

32. 1st Cav. Div., Comd. Rpt., 24 Feb 51, Box 4438.

33. 25th Div., Comd. Rpt., 25 Feb 51, pp. 11–12, Box 3776; I Corps, Comd. Rpt., G-3 Sec. and Eng. Sec., 25 Feb 51, Box 1512.

34. Eighth Army, Comd. Rpt., G-2 Sec., PIR No. 230, 27 Feb 51, Box 1155; and Eighth Army, Comd. Rpt., 28 Feb 51, p. 27, Box 1154; I Corps, Comd. Rpt., 28 Feb 51, Box 1511.

35. IX Corps, Comd. Rpt., G-2 Sec., PIR No. 155, 28 Feb 51, Box 1786.

36. CG, Eighth Army, teletype to subordinate commands, 28 Feb 51, Folder A-C, Box 17, Ridgway Papers.

37. 24th Div., Comd. Rpt., G-4 Sec., Feb 51, Box 3554.

38. Memo for the Secretary of Defense, 27 Feb 1951, Subject: Action to be taken by UN Forces with respect to the 38th Parallel; signed by Gen. Omar N. Bradley for JCS, in Pertinent Papers on Korean Situation, III, 407–11.

39. Ridgway, The Korean War, pp. 108–109.

40. Ibid., p. 108.

41. I Corps, Comd. Rpt., Mar 51, pp. 37–39, Box 1517.

42. 25th Div., Comd. Rpt., Summ., Mar 51, Box 3779; Map of Korea, 1950, 1:250,000 scale.

43. Eighth Army, Comd. Rpt., G-3 Sec., Mar 51, Box 1170; 3rd Div., Comd. Rpt., Mar 51, Box 2814.

44. Eighth Army, Comd. Rpt., Mar 51, Box 1166.

45. 25th Div., Comd. Rpt., G-3 Sec., 2–7 Mar 51, Box 3780; Eighth Army, Comd. Rpt., 2–3 Mar 51, Box 1166.

46. Capt. Pierce W. Briscoe and Capt. B. C. Mossman, MS Rpt., "Rehabilitation of Tidal Locks, Inchon, Korea, 50th Engineer Port construction company, Jan–Feb 51," copy in Office Chief of Military History.

47. Eighth Army, Comd. Rpt., Mar 51, pp. 19–20, Box 1166.

48. Ibid., ACG Actions, 4 Mar 51, Box 1164.

49. 27th Inf., 25th Div., Comd. Rpt., 4–6 Mar 51, Box 3851; Eighth Army, Comd. Rpt., ACG Activities, 5–6 Mar 51, Box 1164.

50. I Corps, Comd. Rpt., Mar 51, p. 50, Box 1517.

51. 25th Div., Comd. Rpt., Summ., 1–7 Mar 51, Box 3779.

52. 25th Div., Comd. Rpt., 7 Mar 51, pp. 64–66, Box 3779; 3rd Bn., 27th Inf., 25th Div., Comd. Rpt., 7 Mar 51, Box 3851; 25th Div., Comd. Rpt., Mar 51, Sketch A, Tactical Positions, 7–15 Mar 51, Box 3779.

53. 27th Inf., 25th Div., Comd. Rpt., S-2 Sec., 7 Mar 51, Box 3851.

NOTES TO PAGES 338-346

54. 3rd Bn., 27th Inf., Comd. Rpt., S-3 Jnl., 7 Mar 51.

55. 25th Div., Comd. Rpt., 7 Mar 51, Box 3851; and ibid., 25 Mar 51, Box 2779; I Corps, Comd. Rpt., 7 Mar 51, pp. 54-55, Box 1517; Maj. Gen. William F. Marquat, "Antiaircraft Artillery in Korea," *Antiaircraft Journal* 94, no. 4 (July-Aug 1951): 7.

56. 35th Inf., 25th Div., Comd. Rpt., 7 Mar 51, Box 3861.

57. Ibid., I Corps, Comd. Rpt., 7 Mar 51, Box 1517.

58. Gugeler, *Combat Actions in Korea,* pp. 145-51, has an excellent detailed account of this tank crossing.

59. 35th Inf., 25th Div., Comd. Rpt., 7 Mar 51, Box 3861; I Corps, Comd. Rpt., Mar 51, pp. 54-55, Box 1517; 25th Div., Comd. Rpt., Mar 51, Sketch A, Tactical Positions, 7-15 Mar 51, Box 3779.

60. 25th Div., Comd. Rpt., G-3 Jnl. 1125, 7 Mar 51, Box 3780; 35th Inf., Comd. Rpt., 7 Mar 51, Box 3861.

61. I Corps, Comd. Rpt., 7 Mar 51, Box 1517; 25th Div., Comd. Rpt., Summ., Box 3779; HQ, I Corps, Armor Combat Lesson Bulletin No. 10, 12 Mar 51, Armor Support of 24th Inf. Regt. Crossing of Han River," with attached sketch map; also I Corps, Armor Combat Lesson Bulletin No. 9, 11 Mar 51, "Tanks in an Indirect Fire Role"; 25th Div., Comd. Rpt., Mar 51, Sketch A, Tactical Positions, 7-15 Mar 51, Box 3779.

62. 25th Div., Comd. Rpt., Summ., 7 Mar 51, Box 3779.

63. 25th Div., Comd. Rpt., 7 Mar 51, pp. 57-58, Box 1517; ibid., G-4 Daily Summ., 8 Mar 51, Box 3780; Westover, *Combat Support in Korea,* pp. 219-20.

64. 24th Inf., 25th Div., Comd. Rpt., 8 Mar 51, pp. 5-6; 25th Div., Comd. Rpt., G-3 Sec. Jnl., 8 Mar 51, Box 3780.

65. 27th Inf., 25th Div., Comd. Rpt., 8-9 Mar 51, Box 3851.

66. Eighth Army, Comd. Rpt., G-2 Sec., Encl. 5, PIR No. 271, 9 Apr 51, Notebook belonging to Wang Ying Shun, 230th Regt., 77th Div., 26th Army, IX Army Group, Third Field Army.

67. R–Memo for Records, 8 Mar 51, Unclassified Binder, Ridgway Papers.

68. Hist. Rec., 7 Mar 51, Box 22, Ridgway Papers; Eighth Army, Comd. Rpt., 10 Mar 51, Box 1166. Ridgway believes 7 Mar 51 is the correct date for the opening of his CP at Yoju (Ridgway, letter to author, 13 Mar 1985).

69. 25th Div., Comd. Rpt., 9 Mar 51, Box 3779.

70. 35th Inf., 25th Div., Comd. Rpt., 9-10 Mar 51, Box 3861.

71. 27th Inf., 25th Div., Comd. Rpt., 13 Mar 51, Box 3851; 25th Div., Comd. Rpt., 10-13 Mar 51, p. 12, Sketch A, Tactical Positions, 7-15 Mar 51, Box 3779.

72. 27th Inf., 25th Div., Comd. Rpt., 1-16 Mar 51, Box 3851; 25th Div., Comd. Rpt., Mar 51, and Sketch A, Tactical Positions, 7-15 Mar 51, Box 3779.

73. US 3rd Div., Comd. Rpt., 12-15 Mar 51, pp. 9-10, Box 2814.

74. I Corps, Comd. Rpt., 13-15 Mar 51, Box 1517; Eighth Army, Comd. Rpt., 14 Mar 51, Box 1166.

75. 3rd Div., Comd. Rpt., 15 Mar 51, pp. 2-4, Box 2814; Eighth Army, Comd. Rpt., 15 Mar 51, p. 71, Box 1166; I Corps, Comd. Rpt., 15 Mar 51, pp. 81-85, Box 1517.

76. 21st Inf., 24th Div., Comd. Rpt., 15 Mar 51, Box 3666; 24th Div., Comd. Rpt., 15-16 Mar 51, Box 3556.

77. Eighth Army, Comd. Rpt., 16 Mar 51, Box 1166; and ibid., G-3 Sec.,

16 Mar 51, Box 1170; Eighth Army, Comd. Rpt., ACG Activities, 16 Mar 51, Box 1164; Hist Rec., 16 Mar 51, Box 22, Ridgway Papers; I Corps, Comd. Rpt., 16 Mar 51, pp. 88–89, Box 1517; 65th Inf., 3rd Div., Comd. Rpt., 16–18 Mar 51, Box 2962; 15th Inf., 3rd Div., Comd. Rpt., 16 Mar 51, Box 2955.
78. FEC DIS No. 3111, 17 Mar 51, Box 415.
79. 25th Div., Comd. Rpt., Mar 51, pp. 72–73, Box 3779.
80. Ridgway, letter to Col. R. P. Eaton, 16 Mar 51, Folder D–L, Box 17, Ridgway Papers.
81. Dwight D. Eisenhower, *Mandate for Change, 1953–1956* (New York: Doubleday, 1963), p. 178.

CHAPTER 14

1. Ridgway, letter to Gen. George C. Marshall, 12 Mar 51, Folder M–R, Box 17, Ridgway, Papers.
2. Ridgway, *The Korean War*, p. 102.
3. Maj. Warren J. Rosengren, "KMAG–Its Mission in Korea," p. 11, Student Monograph, Adv. Inf. Officers Course, Cl. 1, 1952–1953, Fort Benning, Ga. By 1952 there were 13 ROK divisions.
4. Westover, *Combat Support in Korea*, pp. 23–24.
5. 25th Div., Comd. Rpt., Mar 1951, p. 72.
6. Brig. Gen. Paul F. Yount, interview with author, 21 July 1951, Pusan. Engineering materials in Korea were limited to sand and rock. Native timber of usable size was all but nonexistent.
7. Training Memo No. 3, 13 Mar 51, Office Chief of Army Field Forces, Fort Monroe, Va.
8. Eighth Army, Comd. Rpt., G-2 Sec., Encl. 3, PIR No. 242, 11 Mar 51.
9. Eighth Army, Comd. Rpt., G-2 Sec., Mar 1951, Box 1167; Combined G-2/G-3 Map, for Eighth Army Intelligence Summ. No. 3099, 5 Mar 51, FEC DIS, 5 Mar 51, Box 413.
10. 19th Inf., Comd. Rpt., S-3 Sec. and G-4 Sec., 5–15 Mar 51, Box 3656; IX Corps, Comd. Rpt., Mar 51, pp. 15–18, Box 1790; 24th Div., Comd. Rpt., 1–6 Mar 51, Box 3554.
11. 5th Cav. Regt., Comd. Rpt., 1–2 Mar 51, Box 4499; 1st Cav. Div., Comd. Rpt., 1–2 Mar 51, Box 4499.
12. 9th Inf., 2nd Div., Comd. Rpt., 1–4 Mar 51, Box 2690.
13. 23rd Inf., Comd. Rpt., 1–5 Mar 51, Box 2696.
14. 17th Inf., 7th Div., Comd. Rpt., 1–6 Mar 51, Box 3223; 7th Div., Comd. Rpt., 1–15 Mar 51, Box 3190; 31st Inf., 7th Div., Comd. Rpt., 1–16 Mar 51, Box 3242.
15. Eighth Army, Comd. Rpt., G-3 Sec., 3 Mar 51, Box 1170.
16. Lynn Montross, Maj. Hubbard D. Kuokka, and Maj. Norman W. Hicks, *The East-Central Front*, vol. 4 of *U.S. Marine Operations in Korea, 1950–1953* (Washington, D.C.: US Marine Corps, 1962), pp. 74–76; FEC DIS No. 3097, Box 413.
17. Eighth Army, Comd. Rpt., 5 Mar 51, Box 1166.
18. X Corps, Comd. Rpt., 5–6 Mar 51, Box 2001; 2nd Div., Comd. Rpt., Summ., Mar 51, p. 8; Eighth Army, Comd. Rpt., G-3 Daily Summ., 6 Mar 51, Box 1170.
19. Eighth Army, Comd. Rpt., G-3 Sec., Daily Summ., 6 Mar 51, Box 1170.

20. IX Corps, Comd. Rpt., Mar 51, Box 1790.

21. 19th Inf., 24th Div., Comd. Rpt., Mar 1951, and S-2 Sec. Rpt.

22. DA, Gen. Ord. No. 12, 1 Feb 52, for action 7 Mar 1951, near Yonggong-ni, awarded the Congressional Medal of Honor to Sfc. Nelson V. Brittin, I Co., 19th Inf., 24th Div.

23. 21st Inf., 24th Div., Comd. Rpt., 7–10 Mar 51, Box 3666; 24th Div., Comd. Rpt., 6–16 Mar 51, Box 3554; ibid., G-3 Sec., 6–13 Mar 51, Box 3556; and ibid., 7–8 Mar 51, Box 3555.

24. 1st Cav. Div., Comd. Rpt., 6–8 Mar 51; 8th Cav. Regt., 1st Cav. Div., Comd. Rpt., 8–14 Mar 51, Box 4517; Wood, *Strange Battleground,* map, Operations 27th British Commonwealth Infantry Brigade, 19 Feb–11 Mar 1951, opp. p. 66.

25. 5th Cav. Regt., 1st Cav. Div., Comd. Rpt., 9–16 Mar 51, Box 4499.

26. Montross, Kuokka, and Hicks, *The East-Central Front,* pp. 72–76.

27. Eighth Army, Comd. Rpt., CG Activities, 12–13 Mar 51, Box 1164.

28. 23rd Inf., 2nd Div., Comd. Rpt., 3–13 Mar 51, Box 2696; 9th Inf., 2nd Div., Comd. Rpt., 7–15 Mar 51, Box 2690, Eighth Army, Comd. Rpt., 7–12 Mar 51, Box 1166; 38th Inf., 2nd Div., Comd. Rpt., 13 Mar 51, Box 2708; 2nd Div., Comd. Rpt., G-3 Sec., 13 Mar 51, Box 2511.

29. 32nd Inf., 7th Div., Comd. Rpt., 7 Mar 51, Box 3253; 7th Div., Comd. Rpt., 7 Mar 51, Box 3190.

30. 17th Inf., 7th Div., Comd. Rpt., 7 Mar 51, Box 3223.

31. Ibid., 8–10 Mar 51, Box 3223.

32. DA, Gen. Ord. No. 67, 2 Aug 1951, awarding Congressional Medal of Honor to Capt. Raymond L. Harvey, CO, C Co., 17th Inf., 7th Div., for action 9 Mar 1951 in vicinity of Taemi-dong.

33. 17th Inf., 7th Div., Comd. Rpt., 10–14 Mar 51, and Regt. S-3 Rpt. for same period, Box 3223.

34. Eighth Army, Comd. Rpt., 10 Mar 51, p. 75, Box 1166.

35. IX Corps, Comd. Rpt., G-2 Sec., Spot Rpt., 10 Mar 51, Box 1795.

36. 2nd Div., Comd. Rpt., 12 Mar 51, Box 2511.

37. Eighth Army, Comd. Rpt., G-2 Sec., Encl. 2, PIR No. 244, 13 Mar 51.

38. 24th Div., Comd. Rpt., Mar 51, p. 14, Box 3554.

39. IX Corps, Comd. Rpt., G-2 Sec., Annex 1, PIR No. 168, 13 Mar 51. An extensive report on the debriefing of these two officers is given in the PIR. It supplied a wealth of information on conditions behind the enemy's lines in the Hongchon and Chunchon areas and about the massive withdrawal of Chinese from the Hongchon area.

40. 7th Cav. Regt., 1st Cav. Div., Comd. Rpt., 13–14 Mar 51, Box 4508.

41. Montross, Kuokka, and Hicks, *The East-Central Front,* p. 88 and nn. 16–17.

42. 7th Cav. Regt., Comd. Rpt., Mar 51, Annex 1, "Summary of the Attack on Hill 655 by 1st Bn and 4th Bn (GEF) 7th Cavalry Regiment," 15–17 Mar 51, by Maj. James B. Webel, S-3 deputy for operations, together with an operations overlay illustrating the objectives and troop movements. "GEF" stands for the Greek Expeditionary Force, which was frequently referred to as the 7th Inf., 4th Bn. This terminology is confusing unless the situation is understood. The Greek battalion had been attached to the 7th Inf. Regt., which gave it lettered companies, such as "N" and "O."

43. Ibid.

44. Ibid., Eighth Army, Comd. Rpt., Mar 51, pp. 75–78, Box 1166; IX Corps, Comd. Rpt., G-2 Sec., Spot Rpts., 14–15 Mar 51, Box 1795.

45. Eighth Army, Comd. Rpt., 15–16 Mar 51, Box 1166; ibid., G-3 Sec., Daily Summ., 15 Mar 51, Box 1170; Montross, Kuokka, and Hicks, *The East-Central Front*, pp. 90–91 and Map No. 9, p. 87.

46. Montross, Kuokka, and Hicks, *The East-Central Front*, pp. 91–92.

47. Ibid.

48. 2nd Div., Comd. Rpt., 13–15 Mar 51, and G-3 Sec., 13 Mar 51, Box 2511; 38th Inf., 2nd Div., Comd. Rpt., 13–15 Mar 51, Box 2708; 9th Inf., Comd. Rpt., 15–16 Mar 51, Box 2690.

49. 38th Inf., Comd. Rpt., S-2 Sec. and Jnl., 15 Mar 51, Box 2708; Eighth Army, Comd. Rpt. and G-3 Sec., Daily Summ., Boxes 1166 and 1170.

50. 38th Inf., Comd. Rpt. and S-2 Sec. and Jnl., 16–17 Mar 51, Box 2708; 9th Inf., Comd. Rpt., 15–17 Mar 51, Box 2690; X Corps, Comd. Rpt., 16–21 Mar 51, Box 2001.

51. 7th Div., Comd. Rpt., Summ., 16 Mar 51, pp. 17–18, Box 3190; Eighth Army, Comd. Rpt., 16 Mar 51, Box 1166.

52. 7th Div., Comd. Rpt., Daily Summ., 16 Mar 51, Box 3190.

53. Eighth Army, Comd. Rpt., G-3 Sec., Daily Summ., 22 Mar 51, Box 1171.

54. Eighth Army, Comd. Rpt., Mar 51, pp. 70–71, Box 1166; ibid., G-3 Sec., Daily Summ., 16–20 Mar 51, Box 1170.

55. FEC DIS No. 3117, 23 Mar 51, Box 417.

CHAPTER 15

1. FEC DIS No. 3121, 27 Mar 51, C/M = 3, Box 418.

2. I Corps, Comd. Rpt., 17–18 Mar 51, Box 1517.

3. Ibid., 20–23 Mar 51, Box 1517.

4. 15th Regt., 3rd Div., Comd. Rpt., 18 Mar 51, Box 2955.

5. 25th Div., Comd. Rpt., G-2 Sec., 18 Mar 51, pp. 3–4, and ibid., CIC Det. Daily Summ., 21 Mar 51, Box 3779; ibid., G-2 Daily Summ., 24, 30 Mar 51, Box 3799.

6. FEC Intelligence Digest No. 16, 16–31 Jan 1952, "March of a CCF Army," pp. 33–40, including four sketch maps and one chart. I have used a 1:1,000,000-scale map of Korea to correlate the distances to Inchon to other places mentioned, such as Chorwon, the Iron Triangle, and Seoul.

7. FEC DIS No. 3116, 22 Mar 51, p. 9, and OB-2, Box 417.

8. 25th Div., Comd. Rpt., Mar 51, pp. 12–13, and p. 20, 24 Mar 51, G-2 Daily Summ., Box 3779.

9. 27th Inf., 25th Div., Comd. Rpt., S-2 Sec., 20 Mar 51, Box 3851.

10. NR: C58203, 21 Mar 51, *Pertinent Papers on Korean Situation*, III, 415.

11. 3rd Div., Comd. Rpt., 22 Mar 51, Box 2962; 15th Regt., 3rd Div., Comd. Rpt., 22 Mar 51, Box 2955; Eighth Army, Comd. Rpt., CG Activities, 22 Mar 51, Box 1164.

12. 187th Abn. RCT, Comd. Rpt., 19–22 Mar 51, Box 3435; I Corps, Comd. Rpt., 22 Mar 51, pp. 115–17, Box 1517.

13. Armor Combat Lesson Bull. No. 18, "Task Force Growden: Ground Link-up with an Air Drop (Operations of the 6th Medium Tank Battalion, 21–27 March 51)," HQ, I Corps, Armor Sec., 20 Apr 51.

14. 3rd Div., Comd. Rpt., 24 Mar 51, Box 2814; 15th Regt., 3rd Div., Comd. Rpt., 22–24 Mar 51, Box 2955; I Corps, Comd. Rpt., 23 Mar 51, Box 1517.

15. 187th Abn. RCT, Comd. Rpt., 23–24 Mar 51, Box 3435; Eighth Army, Comd. Rpt., 23 Mar 51, Box 1166.

16. Ridgway, *Soldier*, pp. 217–18; Hist. Rec., 23 Mar 51, Box 22, Ridgway Papers.

17. Armor Combat Lesson Bull. No. 18, "Task Force Growden," pp. 1–2.

18. Ibid., p. 2, and sketches of Task Force Growden's movements, p. 4; I Corps, Comd. Rpt., 25 Mar 51, Box 1517.

19. 187th Abn. RCT, Comd. Rpt., 24 Mar 51, Box 3435, for Korean civilian information. ATIS Bulletin, Enemy Docs. No. 2, p. 5, Document 202884, Diary, 10 Mar to 22 Apr 51, owned by Kim Chong Hu, CO, Eng. Bn., 8th Div., NKA, captured 28 Apr 51. Korangpo identifies the river as the Imjin.

20. I Corps, Comd. Rpt., G-4 Sec., Apr 51, Box 1528. Brig. Gen. Rinaldo Van Brunt, asst. corps commander, ordered the I Corps G-1, G-2, G-3, G-4, and the signal officer on 31 Mar to investigate the ROK 1st Div. charges as to the situation at the Munsan-ni parachute drop area. The report was included in the April command report. It supported the charges. Col. T. F. Taylor, assistant chief of staff, G-4, I Corps, signed the report.

21. Ibid.

22. Ridgway, interview with author, 21 Oct 1975.

23. Special File, Dec 50–Mar 51, Box 20, Ridgway Papers. This memo is only partial and is undated but appears to have been written after the parachute drop of the 187th RCT at Munsan-ni.

24. Undated, partial memo written in Mar 51, in Special File, Dec 50–Mar 51, Box 20, Ridgway Papers.

25. Mrs. Margaret Visco, letter to Ridgway, 23 May 51, and Mrs. Violet Meyer, letter to Ridgway, 30 Mar 51, Next of Kin items, Box 21, Ridgway Papers.

26. Eighth Army, Comd. Rpt., CG Activities, 24 Mar 51, Box 1164; Gen. MacArthur, private conversation with Ridgway in Korea, Classified Memo for Record (declassified 14 Nov 1973), 24 Mar 51, Ridgway Papers.

27. Eighth Army, Comd. Rpt., 24 Mar 51, Box 1166; I Corps, Comd. Rpt., 24 Mar 51, Box 1517; FEC DIS No. 3118, 24 Mar 51, and No. 3120, 26 Mar 51; Map of Korea, 1950, 1:250,000 scale.

28. 65th Inf., 3rd Div., Comd. Rpt., 23–25 Mar 51, Box 2962; 3rd Div., Comd. Rpt., 25–26 Mar 51, Box 2814; I Corps, Comd. Rpt., 25–26 Mar 51, Box 1517; 187th Abn. RCT, Comd. Rpt., 26 Mar 51, Box 3435; 1st Lt. Dushkin, exec. off., 65th Tank Co., 3rd Div., interview with author, 8 Sept 1951; Map of Korea, 1950, 1:250,000 scale, for road and place-name information.

29. 15th Regt., 3rd Div., Comd. Rpt., 26 Mar 51, Box 2955.

30. Eighth Army, Gen. Ord. No. 349, 26 May 1951, awarding the Distinguished Service Cross, Posthumously, M. Sgt. Erwin L. Muldoon, H. Co., 187th Abn. Inf. Regt., for valorous action 25 Mar 51, near Parun-ni.

31. Eighth Army, Gen. Ord. No. 820, 23 Oct 51, awarding the Distinguished Service Cross to 1st Lt. Earl K. Wooley, platoon leader, G Co., 187th Abn. Inf. Regt., for action on 28 Mar 51 in the vicinity of Parun-ni.

32. 15th Inf., 3rd Div., Comd. Rpt., 27–28 Mar 51, Box 2955, 187th Abn. RCT, Comd. Rpt., 26–29 Mar 51; 3rd Div., Comd. Rpt., Illustration No. 5, Mar 51, Box 2814.

33. Eighth Army, Comd. Rpt., CG Activities, 26 Mar 51, Box 1164; Hist. Rec., 26 Mar 51, Box 22, Ridgway Papers.

34. 3rd Div., Comd. Rpt., 26–28 Mar 51, Box 2814.

35. 65th Regt., 3rd Div., Comd. Rpt., 27–31 Mar 51, Box 2962; 7th Regt., 3rd Div., 27–31 Mar 51, Box 2950; 3rd Div., Comd. Rpt., 29–30 Mar 51, Box 2814; I Corps, Comd. Rpt., 28–31 Mar 51, pp. 136–58; Eighth Army, Comd. Rpt., 27–29 Mar 51.

36. Hist. Rec., 29 Mar 51, Box 22, Ridgway Papers; Eighth Army, Comd. Rpt., 27–29 Mar 51, Box 1166.

37. 35th Inf., 25th Div., Comd. Rpt., 29 Mar 51, Box 3861; Lt. Richard S. Craig, Arty., "M16s in the Attack on Changgo-ri," *Antiaircraft Journal* 94, no. 4 (July–Aug 1951): 23–24.

38. HQ, Eighth Army, Gen. Ord. No. 347, 26 May 51, awarding Distinguished Service Cross to Sfc. Joseph P. Reeves, G Co., 27th Inf., 25th Div., for heroism, 30 Mar 51, near Yongju. Why he was not awarded the Medal of Honor is unclear.

39. Eighth Army, Comd. Rpt., CG Activities, 29 Mar 51, Box 1164; Hist. Rec., 30 Mar 51, Box 22, Ridgway Papers.

40. 25th Div., Comd. Rpt., 23–30 Mar 51, Box 3779; Map of 35th Inf. positions, 28–31 Mar 51, Box 3861; 35th Inf., Comd. Rpt., Mar 51, Box 3861.

41. I Corps, Comd. Rpt., Mar 51, pp. 11ff., Box 1517.

42. ATIS Bulletin, Enemy Doc. No. 19, p. 17, diary entries from 16 Feb to 6 May 51 captured 6 May belonging to Choe San Sik, rank and unit unknown.

43. 24th Div., Comd. Rpt., 17–25 Mar 51, Box 3556; 5th RCT, 24th Div., Comd. Rpt., 22–30 Mar 51, Box 5238.

44. 24th Div., Comd. Rpt., Mar 51, p. 12, Box 3554.

45. FEC DIS No. 3115, 21 Mar 51, Box 416; IX Corps, Comd. Rpt., G-2 Sec., PIR Nos. 174 and 176, 19 and 21 Mar 51, Box 1792; 24th Div., Comd. Rpt., G-2 Sec., 24 Mar 51; Eighth Army, Comd. Rpt. G-2 Sec., PIR No. 258, 27 Mar 51, Box 1167.

46. Eighth Army, Comd. Rpt., G-3 Sec., 29 Mar 51, pp. 10–11, Box 1170.

47. IX Corps, Comd. Rpt., G-2 Spot Rpts., 31 Mar 51, Box 1795.

48. Barclay, *First Commonwealth Division,* p. 55, and sketch map, p. 54.

49. Coad, "Land Campaign in Korea," p. 11.

50. Wood, *Strangle Battleground,* pp. 70–71, and Map 3, Operations 27th British Commonwealth Infantry Brigade, 29 Mar–16 Apr 51, opp. p. 70.

51. Eighth Army, Comd. Rpt., G-3 Sec., 24–27 Mar 51, Box 1171; Maj. Gen. W. B. Bradford, "Sec. 1, Requirements for Ranger-Type Units," Report of Conference of Commandants of Army Service Schools, vol. 1, conducted at Command and Gen. Staff College, Fort Leavenworth, Kans., 13–16 Nov 51, p. 71.

52. IX Corps, Comd. Rpt., G-2 Spot Rpts., 19 Mar 51, Box 1795; IX Corps, Comd. Rpt., 19 Mar 51, p. 39, Box 1700; Eighth Army, Comd. Rpt., 20 Mar 51, p. 79, Box 1166.

53. IX Corps, Comd. Rpt., 17 Mar 51, Box 1790; ibid., G-2 Spot Rpts., 27 Mar 51, Box 1795; 1st Cav. Div., Comd. Rpt., 21 Mar 51; 5th Cav. Regt., 1st Cav. Div., Comd. Rpt., 21–25 Mar 51, Box 4499; ibid., Daily Narr., 21 Mar 51, Box 4499; 7th Cav. Regt., 1st Cav. Div., Comd. Rpt., 22–25 Mar 51, Box 4508.

54. FEC, G-2 Rpt., Mar 51, p. 41, citing X Corps, PIR No. 171, DIS No. 3119, 25 Mar 51.

55. IX Corps, Comd. Rpt., G-2 Spot Rpts., 26 Mar 51, Box 1795.

56. Montross, Kuokka, and Hicks, *The East-Central Front*, pp. 93-94.

57. Ibid., p. 94.

58. 38th Inf., 2nd Div., Comd. Rpt., S-2 Jnl. and S-2 Summ., 20-21 Mar 51, Box 2708; 2nd Div., Comd. Rpt., 17-31 Mar 51, and G-2 Sec., pp. 1, 7, Box 2511; IX Corps Comd. Rpt., Apr 51, p. 3, Box 1797; X Corps, Comd. Rpt., 16-31 Mar 51, Box 2001; Eighth Army, Comd. Rpt., 29 Mar 51, pp. 20-21, Box 1166.

59. 38th Inf., 2nd Div., Comd. Rpt., Narr., 18 Mar 51, Box 2708; 2nd Div., Comd. Rpt., G-2 Sec., pp. 12-13, PIR No. 146, 18 Mar 51, App. C-2.

60. 31st Inf., 7th Div., Comd. Rpt., 17-30 Mar 51, Box 3242; 7th Div., Comd. Rpt., 28-31 Mar 51, pp. 20-22, Box 3190.

61. Eighth Army, Comd. Rpt., Apr 51, Box 1179; ibid., G-2 Sec., 20 Mar 51, Boxes 1166-67.

62. Eighth Army, Comd. Rpt., CG Activities, 26 Mar 51, Box 1164; Hist. Rec., 26 Mar 51, Box 22, Ridgway Papers.

63. The comments about the airdrop system are based on Capt. William J. Dawson, Jr., 8081st Quartermaster Abn. Air Supply and Packaging Co., "Deliver by Air," in Westover, *Combat Support in Korea*, pp. 153-59.

64. Maj. Gen. George L. Eberle, G-4, FEC, interview with author, July 1951.

65. Eighth Army, Comd. Rpt., Mar 51, pp. 27-28, Box 1166.

66. Ibid., pp. 25-26. There is some discrepancy in the figures on replacements in Mar 1951, since in the same report, G-1 Sec., the number of replacements in Eighth Army is given as 17,691.

67. "Logistical Problems and Their Solution, 25 Aug 1950 to 31 Aug 51," prepared by Hist. Sec. HQ, Japan Logistical Command, 15 Feb 52, p. 10, reproduced by Office Chief of Military History (a copy is available there).

68. *New York Times*, 14 May 1951, p. 12, col. 6-7, reporting on Gen. Marshall's testimony of 13 May 1951. There are discrepancies in Marshall's figures on replacements with the figures given in reports I have used, but I make no effort here to reconcile them.

69. US 3rd Div., Comd. Rpt., 1 Mar 51, Box 2814.

70. Eighth Army, Comd. Rpt., G-1 Sec., Chart, Enclosures 36-37, Box 1154.

71. Eighth Army, Comd. Rpt., Mar 51, pp. 32-33, Box 1166.

72. Kemp article on interviews with Gen. Ridgway in *Pacific Stars and Stripes*, printed in many newspapers in the US, including the *Richmond Times-Dispatch*, 1 Apr 1951.

CHAPTER 16

1. Eighth Army, Comd. Rpt., G-3 Sec., Apr 1951, Book 2, Annex J, 1 Apr 51, Box 1179.

2. Ibid., Book 2, Annex C, 2-4 Apr, and Annex J, 4 Apr 51, Box 1179.

3. Eighth Army, Comd. Rpt., G-3 Sec., Apr 51, p. 3, Box 1179.

4. Ibid., Apr 51, p. 4, Box 1179.

5. Ibid., G-3 Sec., Book 3, Annex J, Book 4, Annex J, Book 2, Annex D, Apr 51.

6. Field, *Naval Operations, Korea*, p. 332.

7. Ibid., pp. 333-36; FEC DIS No. 3150, 25 Apr 51, Box 437, says that there were seven small bridge crossings in this bypass in a canyon at its lowest level and that the tremendous effort in constructing it took only 20 days (p. 10).

8. Field, *Naval Operations, Korea,* pp. 337–38. Field has an excellent detailed account of the US Navy in the Korean War. It contributed more to the ground action than is generally known.

9. Ibid.; for details concerning these technical developments, see pp. 328–34.

10. I Corps, Comd. Rpt., 3 Apr 51, Box 1523; Eighth Army, Comd. Rpt., 3 Apr 51, Box 1179.

11. 7th Div., Comd. Rpt., Narr., Apr 51, Box 3192; 17th Inf., 7th Div., Comd. Rpt., 1–3 Apr 51, Box 3224.

12. 2nd Div., Comd. Rpt., G-4 Sec., Apr 51, Box 2526.

13. Ibid., Narr., 4–9 Apr 51, Box 2526; 23rd Inf., 2nd Div., Comd. Rpt., 3–10 Apr 51, Box 2696.

14. 7th Div., Comd. Rpt., Narr., Apr 51, Box 3192.

15. Eighth Army, Comd. Rpt., G-3 Sec. and G-3 Jnl., Summ., 3 Apr 51, Box 1181.

16. Eighth Army, Comd. Rpt., 3 Apr 51, Box 1179.

17. Almond, Diary, 3, 9 Apr 51; X Corps, Comd. Rpt., 3 Apr 51. Col. Boram (X Corps inspector gen.) began an investigation on 13 Apr of the 31st Inf. Regt. and found the charges against it at variance with the facts.

18. Eighth Army, Comd. Rpt., 3–6 Apr 51, Box 1179.

19. 31st Inf., 7th Div., Comd. Rpt., 3–6 Apr 51, Box 3243.

20. Eighth Army, Comd. Rpt., 5 Apr 51, and ibid., G-3 Sec., Apr 51, Box 1181.

21. 17th Inf., 7th Div. (Commander's Notes, 1st Bn., 17th Inf.), 9 Apr 51, Box 3224.

22. 7th Div., Comd. Rpt., Narr., 4–9 Apr 51, Box 3192.

23. 3rd Div., Comd., 4–9 Apr 51, Box 2898.

24. 17th Inf., 7th Div., Comd. Rpt., Intelligence Summ., 5–21 Apr 51, Box 3224; X Corps, Comd. Rpt., 6–21 Apr 51, Box 2006.

25. *Pertinent Papers on Korean Situation,* III, 423–24.

26. Eighth Army, Comd. Rpt., 6–7 Apr 51, Box 1179; WD, Office of CG, Eighth Army, in Eighth Army, Comd. Rpt., 6 Apr 51, Box 1180.

27. FEC DIS Nos. 3131, 3133–34, 6, 8–9 Apr 51, Box 433.

28. Eighth Army, Comd. Rpt., G-3 Sec., 7–8 Apr 51, and Briefing for CG, 9 Apr 51, Box 1181.

29. Wood, *Strange Battleground,* operations map of British 27th Brigade, 7–19 Apr 51, opp. p. 70; see also Fairlee chap. in ibid., pp. 70–71.

30. 7th Inf., 3rd Div., Comd. Rpt., 7–8 Apr 51, Box 2950; I Corps, Comd. Rpt., G-3 Sec. and POR No. 613, 7 Apr 51, Box 1526.

31. 3rd Div., Comd. Rpt., Apr 51; 25th Div., Comd. Rpt., 7, 9 Apr 51, Box 3862.

32. 7th Cav. Regt., Comd. Rpt., S-2 Jnl., Summ., 7 Apr 51, and 2nd Bn., 7th Cav. Regt., Comd. Rpt., S-3 Jnl., message Serial 29, 2350, 7 Apr 51, Box 4508.

33. IX Corps, Eng. Sec., Comd. Rpt., 9 Apr 51, Box 1798; ibid., G-3 Sec., 9 Apr 51, Box 1797; IX Corps, Comd. Rpt., 4, 9 Apr 51, Box 1797; Eighth Army, Comd. Rpt., 9 Apr 51, Box 1179.

34. IX Corps, Comd. Rpt., G-3 Sec. and Jnl. File, see Serial 606, 091410, and Hist. Summ., 10 Apr 51, S. W. Holderness, G-3; 2nd Bn., 7th Cav. Regt., Comd. Rpt., 9 Apr 51, S-3 Jnl. File, Serial 16, 1800, and Summ., Box 4508; Eighth Army,

Comd. Rpt., 9 Apr 51, Box 1179; FEC DIS No. 3135, 10 Apr 51, Box 433.

35. IX Corps, Comd. Rpt., CS Daily Jnl. Summ., 10 Apr 51, Box 1797.

36. 2nd Bn., 7th Cav. Regt., Comd. Rpt., 10 Apr 51, Box 4508; Eighth Army, Comd. Rpt., G-3 Sec., POR, 10 Apr 51; FEC DIS No. 3136, 11 Apr 51, p. 2, Box 433.

37. Map study of Hwachon Reservoir, the dam site, and the only road approach to the dam from the south. Scale 1:50,000 Yanggu Sheet is essential for an understanding of the terrain situation.

38. 1st Cav. Div., Comd. Rpt., Apr 51, pp. 9, 11, Box 4445; 7th Cav. Regt., Comd. Rpt., 11 Apr 51, Box 4508; ibid., S-3 Jnl., with time given for movements and attack action, 11 Apr 51, Box 4508; 1st Cav. Div., Comd. Rpt., G-2 Sec., 11 Apr 51, Box 1797; FEC DIS No. 3136, 11 Apr 51, Box 433; Eighth Army, Comd. Rpt., G-3 Sec. and G-3 Jnl., Summ., 11 Apr 51, Box 1183. In the cross-reservoir assault by the 4th Ranger Co. and I Co., 7th Cav. Regt., on 11 Apr 51, Korean carrying parties, working from the engineer companies, transported 35 assault boats, 20 outboard motors, 245 paddles, and 160 life preservers to the launching site at the south side of the reservoir.

39. IX Corps, CS Daily Jnl. Summ., Comd. Rpt., 12 Apr 51, Box 1797; IX Corps, Comd. Rpt., G-3 Sec., 18-19 Apr 51, Box 1797.

40. I Corps, Comd. Rpt., G-3 Sec., 8 Apr 51, Box 1526.

41. Eighth Army, Comd. Rpt., 8 Apr 51, Box 1179.

42. Ibid., Eng. Sec., 8 Apr 51, pp. 24-27, Box 1187.

43. *Time,* 9 Apr 1951, p. 35.

44. Eighth Army, Comd. Rpt., 10 Apr 51, Box 1179; I Corps, Comd. Rpt., G-3 Sec., 10 Apr 51, Box 1526.

45. X Corps, Comd. Rpt., 10 Apr 51, pp. 21-22, Box 2006.

CHAPTER 17

1. 3rd Div., Comd. Rpt. (CG Jnl.), 11 Apr 51, Box 2898; Eighth Army, Comd. Rpt., 11 Apr 51; WD, Office of CG, Eighth Army, 11 Apr 51, Box 1180; Ridgway, *Soldier,* p. 220.

2. *Military Situation in the Far East,* Hearings before the Committee on Armed Services and the Committee on Foreign Relations, United States Senate, 82nd Cong., 1st sess., to Conduct an Inquiry into the Military Situation in the Far East and the Facts Surrounding the Relief of General MacArthur from His Assignments in That Area, pt. 1 (Washington, D.C.: GPO, 1951). These hearings were printed in five parts, or volumes, in 3,691 pages, including an index, covering a period of hearings from 3 May to 17 Aug 1951. The quotations are from Secretary of Defense Marshall's testimony before the Joint Committees, 7 May 1951, pt. 1, pp. 344-45.

3. Testimony of General of the Army Omar N. Bradley, 21 May 1951, in ibid., pt. 2, pp. 878-79.

4. Ibid., pt. 5, p. 3,546.

5. "To CINCFE Tokyo, Japan, From JCS Personal for Gen. Ridgway, NR JCS 88374, 12 Apr 51," in *Pertinent Papers on Korean Situation,* III, 426.

6. Maj. Gen. Courtney Whitney, *MacArthur: His Rendezvous with History* (New York: Knopf, 1956), p. 471.

7. Eighth Army, Comd. Rpt., WD of CG, Eighth Army, 12 Apr 51, Box 1180.

8. Ridgway, *Soldier*, p. 223.

9. Ibid., p. 224.

10. Eighth Army, Comd. Rpt., WD of CG, Eighth Army, 13 Apr 51, Box 1180.

11. Ibid., 14 Apr 51, Box 1180, and Eighth Army, Comd. Rpt., 14 Apr 51, Box 1179.

12. Eighth Army, Comd. Rpt., WD of CG, Eighth Army, 14 Apr 51, and statement of Lt. Col. W. F. Winton, Jr., aide-de-camp to Gen. Ridgway, Box 1180.

13. Whitney, *MacArthur*, p. 480.

14. Ridgway, *The Korean War*, pp. 162–68. In this work Gen. Ridgway gives the orders he issued to Gen. Van Fleet and to the air and naval commanders and the range of his new duties in some detail, many of them not directly applicable to the war in Korea.

15. James A. Van Fleet, "The Truth about Korea: From a Man Now Free to Speak," pt. 1, *Life*, 11 May 1953, p. 127. Information about Van Fleet's previous Army career is based on *1975 Register of Graduates, US Military Academy*, p. 332, Item 5405; *Hearings before the Subcommittee to Investigate the Administration of the Internal Security Act and Other Internal Security Laws of the Committee on the Judiciary, United States Senate, 83rd Congress, 2nd Session*, Testimony of Gen. James A. Van Fleet, 29 Sept 1954, pt. 24 (Washington, D.C.: GPO, 1954).

16. *Hearings before the Subcommittee . . . on the Judiciary*, p. 2,026.

17. Eighth Army, Comd. Rpt., G-3 Sec., Apr 1951, p. 4.

18. Ibid.; IX Corps, Comd. Rpt., Apr 51, p. 35; Barclay, *First Commonwealth Division*, p. 55.

19. I Corps, Comd. Rpt., G-3 Sec., 12 Apr 51, Box 1526.

20. Eighth Army, Comd. Rpt., 12 Apr 51, Box 1179, and ibid., G-3 Sec. and G-3 Jnl. Summ., 12 Apr 51, Box 1183.

21. The narrative concerning the 2nd and 7th divisions' capture of Yanggu and the area between the Soyang River and the Hwachon Reservoir is based on the following sources: 23rd Inf., 2nd Div., Comd. Rpt., and Operations Sec., 11–12 Apr 51, Box 2696; 2nd Div., Comd. Rpt., Narr., 11–15 Apr 51, Box 2526.

22. 17th Inf., 7th Div., Comd. Rpt., 1–16 Apr 51, Box 3224; 32nd Regt., 7th Div., Comd. Rpt., 11–16 Apr 51, Box 3254; 7th Div., Comd. Rpt., 14–17 Apr 51, Box 3192.

23. 24th Inf., 25th Div., Comd. Rpt., 11–15 Apr 51, Box 3843.

24. FEC DIS No. 3140, 15–16 Apr 51, Box 435; Eighth Army, Comd. Rpt., G-3 Sec., 12–16 Apr 51, Box 1183.

25. 27th Inf., 25th Div., Comd. Rpt., 15 Apr 51, Box 3852; 3rd Bn., 27th Inf., 25th Div., Comd. Rpt., 15 Apr 51, Box 3852; Eighth Army, Gen. Ord. No. 331, 23 May 1951, awarding the Distinguished Service Cross, Posthumously, to 1st Lt. Derwood W. Sims, CO, F Co., 27th Inf., for heroism in action, 15 Apr 51, near Chitkan.

26. Eighth Army, Comd. Rpt., G-3 Sec., 16–17 Apr 51, Box 1183.

27. 24th Inf. 25th Div., Comd. Rpt., 17 Apr 51, Box 3843.

28. I Corps, Comd. Rpt., G-3 Jnl. Sec. and G-3 Daily Summ., 17 Apr 51, Boxes 1525–26.

29. IX Corps, Comd. Rpt., 16–18 Apr 51, Box 1797.

30. X Corps, Comd. Rpt., 16 Apr 51, Box 2006.

31. I Corps, Comd. Rpt., G-4 Sec., Apr 51, pp. 179–90, Box 1523.

32. I Corps, Comd. Rpt., G-2 Sec., 17 Apr 51, Box 1524.

33. 3rd Div., Comd. Rpt., 17–19 Apr 51, Box 2898; Eighth Army, Comd. Rpt., G-2 Sec., PIR No. 280, 18 Apr 51, Box 1181.

34. 3rd Div., Comd. Rpt., Staff Briefing Minutes, 18 Apr 51; Eighth Army, Comd. Rpt., G-2 Sec., 18 Apr 51, PIR No. 380, Enclosures, PW Rpts., 18 Apr 51.

35. 27th Inf., 25th Div., Comd. Rpt., 17–19 Apr 51, Box 3852; ibid., G-2 Sec., Enclosure 5, 18–19 Apr 51; 25th Div., Comd. Rpt., G-4 Sec., Box 3785; 25th Div., Comd. Rpt., 19–20 Apr 51, Box 3783.

36. Eighth Army, Comd. Rpt., G-3 Sec., 19–20 Apr 51, Box 1184.

37. 35th Inf., 25th Div., Comd. Rpt., 18–19 Apr 51, pp. 7–8; and ibid., G-3 Sec., 19 Apr 51, Boxes 3862 and 3784.

38. FEC DIS No. 3145, 20 Apr 51, OB-5, Box 436.

39. Eighth Army, Comd. Rpt., G-2 Sec., 20 Apr 51, Box 1181; 3rd Div., Comd. Rpt., G-2 Sec., 19–20 Apr 51, Box 2899.

40. I Corps, Comd. Rpt., 21 Apr 51, Box 1523.

41. 3rd Div., Comd. Rpt., Staff Briefing Minutes, 21 Apr 51, Box 2898. I have found that the US 3rd Div. documents, including its Command Reports, are of a superior nature, perhaps the best of any US division in the Korean War.

42. IX Corps, Comd. Rpt., G-3 Sec., 21–22 Apr 51, Box 1797.

CHAPTER 18

1. Eighth Army, Comd. Rpt., G-2 Sec., Apr 1951, map and chart of enemy strengths and locations, 22 Apr 51, Box 1181; Organization Chart, Communist Field Forces (including units in Korea), FEC Intelligence Digest No. 28, 16–31 July 1952; FEC Intelligence Digest No. 6, 16–31 Aug 51, Map No. A-5, FECID No. 6, Enemy Attack 5th Phase – 1st Impulse, 22–30 Apr 51, Box 513; FEC DIS No. 3207, 21 June 51, including translation of captured document, XIII Army Group Volunteer Headquarters, Box 473.

2. FEC Intelligence Digest, vol. 5, 16–28 Feb 1953, Histories of CCF Army Groups Active in Korea, pt. 4, Nineteenth Army Group, pp. 27–32.

3. US Army Forces, Far East, G-2, Intelligence Digest, vol. 1, no. 1, 1–31 Dec 1952, Histories of CCF Army Groups Active in Korea, III CCF Army Group, pp. 31–37.

4. FEC Intelligence Digest, vol. 1, no. 3, 16–31 Jan 1953, History of CCF Army Groups Active in Korea, pt. 2, Ninth Army Group, Box 225.

5. I Corps, Comd. Rpt., Apr 51, Plate 2, Troop Disposition prior to Chinese Offensive 22–23 Apr 51, Box 1523.

6. Gen. HQ, Combine G-2/G-3 Map No. 3, for FEC DIS No. 3149, 240200 Apr 51, Box 437.

7. "From CINCFE Tokyo Japan Sgd Ridgway, to: JCS Wash DC, NR: C 60965, DA IN 5595 (25 Apr 51)," in *Pertinent Papers on Korean Situation*, III, 438–40.

8. 25th Div., Comd. Rpt., 22 Apr 51, Box 3783.

9. IX Corps, CS Daily Jnl. Summ., 22 Apr 51, Box 1797; Eighth Army, Comd. Rpt., 22 Apr 51, Box 1179; ibid., G-2 Sec., 22 Apr 51, Box 1181.

10. 25th Div., Comd. Rpt., G-2 Sec. Jnl., Serials 1147, 1189, 1200, 22 Apr 51, Box 2898; I Corps, Comd. Rpt., G-2 Sec., 22 Apr 51, Box 1525.

11. I Corps, Comd. Rpt., Armor Sec., Narr. Summ., Apr 51, Box 1528.

12. 3rd Div., Comd. Rpt., 22 Apr 51, Box 2898.

13. Eighth Army, Comd. Rpt., G-4 Sec., 22 Apr 51, Box 1185.

14. 3rd Div., Comd. Rpt., G-3 Sec., Narr. of Operations, Apr 51, Box 2900; FEC DIS No. 3149, 24 Apr 51, Box 437.

15. 35th Inf., 25th Div., Comd. Rpt., Apr 51, Box 3862.

16. Eighth Army, Comd. Rpt., G-3 Sec., Apr 51, Book 5, Annex C, 22–25 Apr 51, Box 1183; IX Corps, Comd. Rpt., Apr 51, 23 Apr, p. 36, Box 1797.

17. Linklater, *Our Men in Korea*, pp. 61–63; IX Corps, Comd. Rpt., 23–25 Apr 51, pp. 37–38, Box 1797.

18. FEC DIS No. 3149, 24 Apr 51, p. 7, Box 437; I Corps, Comd. Rpt., 23 Apr 51, Box 1523; Eighth Army, Comd. Rpt., G-2 Sec., 23 Apr 51, Box 1181.

19. I Corps, Comd. Rpt., 23 Apr 51, Box 1513; FEC DIS No. 3149, 24 Apr 51, p. 7, Box 437; Eighth Army, Comd. Rpt., G-3 Sec., 23 Apr 51, Box 1184.

20. Eighth Army, Comd. Rpt., 23 Apr 51, Box 1179.

21. 3rd Div., Comd. Rpt., Apr 51, G-3 Sec., Narr. Account of Operations, Box 2900; David Scott Daniell, *Cap of Honour: The Story of the Gloucestershire Regiment*, with chapters covering the period from 1945 to 1975 by Maj. Gen. A. H. Farrar-Hockley and Maj. E. L. T. Capel (London: White Lion, 1975), pp. 342–52.

22. 3rd Div., Comd. Rpt., 23 Apr 51, Box 2898.

23. Eighth Army, Comd. Rpt., Ordnance Sec., Apr 51, Box 1189.

24. 23rd Inf., 2nd Div., Comd. Rpt., 23 Apr 51, Box 2696.

25. 32nd Inf., 7th Div., Comd. Rpt., 23 Apr 51, and S-1 Unit Rpt., Box 3254; DA, Gen. Ord. No. 81, 14 Sept 51, Distinguished Unit Citation, 3rd Bn., 32nd Inf., 7th Div.

26. Eighth Army, Comd. Rpt., 23–24 Apr 51, Box 1179; ibid., G-3 Sec., p. 8, Box 1183.

27. X Corps, Comd. Rpt., 25–28 Apr 51, Box 2006.

28. 5th Cav. Regt., Comd. Rpt., 25–29 Apr 51, Box 4499.

29. Eighth Army, Comd. Rpt., 24 Apr 51, Box 1179; ibid., G-2 Sec., 24 Apr 51, Box 1181.

30. I Corps, Comd. Rpt., 25 Apr 51, Box 1523; Gen. Milburn and Col. Johnson, interview with author, 6 Nov 51; Brig. Gen. James F. Brittingham, I Corps Arty. Off., interview with author, 25 July 51.

31. 25th Div., Comd. Rpt., G-3 Jnl. 24 Apr 51, Box 3784; 24th Inf., Comd. Rpt., 25 Apr 51, Box 3843.

32. Eighth Army, Comd. Rpt., 24 Apr 51, Box 1179.

33. 3rd Div., Comd. Rpt., 24–25 Apr 51, Box 2898.

34. 7th Inf., 3rd Div., Comd. Rpt., 24–25 Apr 51, Box 5950.

35. G-3 Summ. on 29th BIB Action, 22–25 Apr 51, inclusive, HQ, 3rd Div., G-3 Sec., 3rd Div. Comd. Rpt., Apr 51, Box 2898.

36. HQ, 3rd Div., Comd. Rpt., Operations of 29th BIB 22–25 Apr 51, to CG, US I Corps, 14 May 51, Annex 13, Apr 51, Box 2898.

37. HQ, I Corps, Report to CG, Eighth Army, on Gloucestershire Battalion, 15 May 51, in Supplementary Documents, Eighth Army, Comd. Rpt., Apr 51, Box 1184.

38. Brig. Gen. A. D. Mead to CG, 3rd Div., 7 May 51, on his conversations with Brig. Brodie on 24–25 Apr 51 regarding relief of the Gloucestershire Bn., Annex 14, HQ, 3rd Div., Operations of 29th BIB, 22–25 Apr 51, 3rd Div., Comd. Rpt., Apr 51, Box 2898.

39. Author's interviews with Capt. Claude Smith, CO; 1st Lt. Dushkin, exec. off.; and Sgt. Young Gladen, all in 65th Tank Co., Sept 1951.

40. Lt. Col. Alvin L. Newberry, CO, 10th FA Bn., interview with author, Sept 1951.

41. Maj. Gen. Robert H. Soule, interview with author, Korea, 8 Sept 1951.

42. Maj. Henry Huth, CO, C Squadron, 8th Hussars, interview with author, Korea, Sept 1951.

43. Capt. Anthony Farrar-Hockley, *The Edge of the Sword* (London: Frederick Muller, 1954), pp. 50–51.

44. Capt. Mike Harvey, interview with author on Hill 235, Imjin River, Korea, 10 Sept 1951. As we talked, Harvey marked on a 1:50,000-scale map of the area I was holding the route he took on leaving Hill 235 and in reaching the tanks on 25 April. The Glosters had come back to the area at the last of May and were holding the same area in September that they had occupied on 25 April.

45. Farrar-Hockley, *Edge of the Sword*, pp. 75–76.

46. Ibid., p. 77.

47. Lt. Col. James W. Friend, G-1, 3rd Div., Memo to CG, 3rd Div.

48. Brig. Brodie, interview with author, Korea, 10 Sept 1951.

49. 5th RCT, 24th Div., Comd. Rpt., G-3 Sec., Apr 51, Box 5239.

50. Lt. Col. Stuart, interview with author, 9 Aug 1951.

51. Ibid.; 5th RCT, 24th Div., Comd. Rpt., 25 Apr 51, Box 5239.

52. I Corps, Comd. Rpt., Armor Sec., 27 Apr 51, Box 1528; Armor Sec. Jnl., Serial 3, 1020, 27 Apr 51.

53. I Corps, Comd. Rpt., G-3 Sec., 25 Apr 51, Box 1527.

54. 3rd Div., Comd. Rpt., 25 Apr 51, Box 2898.

55. 35th Inf., 25th Div., Comd. Rpt., Apr 51, Box 3862.

56. Eighth Army, Comd. Rpt., G-3 Sec. and G-2 Sec., 25 Apr 51, Boxes 1184 and 1181, respectively.

57. 25th Div., Comd. Rpt., Apr 51, p. 66, Box 3783.

58. X Corps, Comd. Rpt., 26 Apr 51, Box 2006.

59. Eighth Army, Comd. Rpt., 26 Apr 51, Box 1179.

60. Ibid., G-2 Sec., 26 Apr 51, Box 1181.

61. Ibid.

62. 3rd Div., Comd. Rpt., 26 Apr 51, Boxes 2898–99.

63. I Corps, Comd. Rpt., 26 Apr, Boxes 1523 and 1525; I Corps, PIR No. 116, G-2 Sec., 26 Apr 51.

64. I Corps, Comd. Rpt., G-3 Daily Summ., 26 Apr 51, Box 1527.

65. Ibid., Enclosure with G-3 Jnl.

66. IX Corps, CS Daily Jnl. Summ., 24 Apr 51, in IX Corps, Comd. Rpt., 24 Apr 51, Box 1797.

67. Lt. Gen. John B. Coulter, Memorandum for CG, EUSAK, Subj. Conf. with Pres. Rhee, 25 Apr 51, in Eighth Army Comd. Rpt., Office of CG, Apr 51, Box 1180.

68. Lt. Col. Willard Pearson, senior advisor, ROK 6th Div., letter to Chief KMAG, 2 May 51.

69. Enclosure with Eighth Army CS Jnl., Eighth Army Comd. Rpt., May 51, Box 1193.

70. IX Corps, Comd. Rpt., G-4 Sec., 25 Apr 51, Box 1797.

71. Eighth Army, Comd. Rpt., Ordnance Sec., Apr 51, p. 136, Box 1179.

72. FEC and UNC, Comd. Rpt., No. 6, 1–30 Apr 51, p. 77.

73. X Corps, Comd. Rpt., 27–28 Apr 51, Box 2006; 7th Div., Comd. Rpt., Narr., 28 Apr 51, Box 3192.

74. 24th Div., Comd. Rpt., 27 Apr 51, p. 13, Box 3561.

75. 1st Bn., 5th Cav. Regt., Comd. Rpt., 27 Apr 51, Box 4499.

76. 65th Inf., 3rd Div., Comd. Rpt., 27 Apr 51, Box 2963; Eighth Army, Comd. Rpt., 27 Apr 51, Box 1184.

77. 3rd Div., Comd. Rpt., G-2 Sec., 27 Apr 51, Box 2899.

78. Eighth Army, Comd. Rpt., G-2 Sec., 27 Apr 51, Box 1181; I Corps, Comd. Rpt., G-2 Sec., PIR No. 117, 27 Apr 51, Box 1525; I Corps, Comd. Rpt., 27 Apr 51, Box 1523.

79. 3rd Div., Comd. Rpt., G-3 Sec., Rpt. Narr. of Operations, Apr 51, Box 2900.

80. Eighth Army, Comd. Rpt., G-3 Sec., 26–30 Apr 51, Box 1183.

81. Ibid., Jnl. Summ., 28 Apr 51, Box 1184.

82. 25th Div., Comd. Rpt., 28–30 Apr 51, Box 3783; I Corps, Comd. Rpt., 28 Apr 51, Box 1523; and I Corps, G-2 Sec., Situation Map, 28–29 Apr 51, Box 1525; FEC DIS No. 3155, 28 Apr 51, Box 438.

83. 25th Div., Comd. Rpt., 28 Apr 51, Box 3783.

84. Ibid., G-3 Sec., 29 Apr 51, Box 3784.

85. I Corps, Comd. Rpt., G-3 Sec., 29 Apr 51, Box 1527; Eighth Army, Comd. Rpt., G-3 Sec., 29 Apr 51, Box 1184.

86. I Corps, Comd. Rpt., 29 Apr 51, Box 1523.

87. 5th RCT, 24th Div., Comd. Rpt., 29 Apr 51, Box 5239.

88. 25th Div., Comd. Rpt., G-2 Sec., 29 Apr 51, Box 3783.

89. Eighth Army, Comd. Rpt., Office CS, 29 Apr 51, Box 1180.

90. 2nd Bn., 27th Inf., 25th Div., Comd. Rpt., 30 Apr 51, Box 3852.

91. I Corps, Comd. Rpt., G-3, 30 Apr 51, Box 1527; 25th Div., Comd. Rpt., 30 Apr 51, Box 3783.

92. 1st Cav. Div., Comd. Rpt., Narr., Apr 51, Box 4445.

93. FEC DIS Nos. 3160–61, 5–6 May 51, Box 450.

94. I Corps, Comd. Rpt., Narr., 30 Apr 51, Box 1531.

95. Eighth Army, Comd. Rpt., 30 Apr 51, Box 1192, and Plate 3, Troop Dispositions 30 Apr 51, in I Corps, Comd. Rpt., Apr 51, Box 1523.

96. Eighth Army, Comd. Rpt., Office of CG, Memorandum for Record, Conf. held by Army Commander with the three US Corps Commanders at Yoju 301400 Apr 1951, Box 1180. Quotations below are from the same conference.

CHAPTER 19

1. Eighth Army, Comd. Rpt., 1–7 May 51, Box 1192; I Corps, Comd. Rpt., Narr., 1–8 May 51, Box 1531.

2. Eighth Army, Comd. Rpt., G-3 Sec., 7 May 51, Box 1196.

3. Personal for Collins, 1 May 51, in *Pertinent Papers on Korean Situation,* III, 452.

4. Ridgway Memo for Diary, 4 May 51, Spec. File, Apr–Dec 51, Box 20, Ridgway Papers.

5. Ibid.

6. IX Corps, Comd. Rpt., 8–10 May 51, Box 1803; I Corps, Comd. Rpt., G-2 Sec., 2–9 May 51, Box 1532.

7. Eighth Army, Comd. Rpt., 4–9 May 51, Box 1192; 5th Cav. Regt., Comd. Rpt., 10 May 51, Box 1532.

8. X Corps, Comd. Rpt., G-2 Sec., PIR No. 225, 9 May 51, Box 2013.

9. FEC DIS No. 3165, 10 May 51, Box 451.

10. Ridgway, letter to Van Fleet, 9 May 51, Folder T–Z, Box 19, Ridgway Papers.

11. Eighth Army, Comd. Rpt., 9 May 51, Box 1192.

12. Ibid., G-3 Sec., Narr., 9–11 May 51.

13. FEC DIS No. 3188, M-1, 2 June 51.

14. Eighth Army, Comd. Rpt., 12 May 51, Box 1192.

15. Ibid.

16. Ibid., G-2 Sec., Enclosure 6 to PIR No. 306, 14 May 51, Box 1194.

17. Ibid., CG Jnl., 14 May 51, Box 1193.

18. Ibid., 16 May 51, Box 1193.

19. Ibid., G-2 Sec., PIR No. 307, 15 May 51, Box 1194.

20. 2nd Div., Comd. Rpt., G-3 Sec., May 51, Box 2543.

21. Ibid., 9–12 May 51, Box 2543.

22. X Corps, Comd. Rpt., G-2 Sec., 12 May 51, Box 2013.

23. FEC DIS No. 3168, 13 May 51, pp. 4, 7, Box 452.

24. 2nd Div., Comd. Rpt., 13–14 May 51, Box 2543, cites CS Jnl., 14 May 51, for the CCF radio intercept regarding CCF losses on Hill 699.

25. FEC DIS No. 3170, 15 May 51, pp. 3, 5, Box 452.

26. FEC Intelligence Digest No. 6, 2 Sept 51, "Redisposition of CCF in Preparation of 2nd Impulse, 5th Phase Offensive, 1–15 May (Map A-6)," pp. A-14–A-16 and Map 6; X Corps, Comd. Rpt., May 51, Box 2012.

CHAPTER 20

1. 2nd Div., Comd. Rpt., May 51, Narr., Staff Sec., Rpt. of G-2, pp. 15–16, Box 2543.

2. X Corps, Comd. Rpt., May 51, Operations of the 38th Inf. RCT, 16 May–2 June 51, 16–17 May, pp. 3–4, Box 2012. A detailed account of the 3rd Bn.'s action on Hill 800 appears in Gugeler, *Combat Actions in Korea*, pp. 174–90.

3. X Corps, Comd. Rpt., May 51, Operations of 38th Inf., pp. 4–5, Box 2012; 2nd Div., Comd. Rpt., Staff Sec., Rpt. of G-2, May 51, pp. 2–3, Box 2543.

4. 2nd Div., Comd. Rpt., CS Jnl., 17 May 51, Box 2543.

5. Netherlands Detachment Jnl., 17 May 51, attached to 38th Inf. Comd. Rpt. for May 51, Box 2714.

6. 23rd Inf. Operations, p. 6, in 2nd Div., Comd. Rpt., May 51, Box 2012.

7. 2nd Div., Comd. Rpt., 17 May 51, CS Jnl. 17 May, Serial 2, 0100, Box 2543.

8. Eighth Army, Comd. Rpt., May 51, pp. 16–17, Box 1192.

9. 2nd Div., Comd. Rpt., Staff Sec., Rpt. of G-2, May 51, p. 19, Box 2543.

10. Eighth Army, Comd. Rpt., 18 May 51, p. 17, Box 1192; 2nd Div., Comd. Rpt., May 51, p. 23, Box 2543; 9th Inf., Operations Rpt. for May 51, pp. 2–3, Box 2012.

11. 23rd Inf., Operations Rpt., 18 May, in 2nd Div., Comd. Rpt., May 51,

Box 2012; 2nd Div., Comd. Rpt., G-3 Sec., POR No. 613, 18 May 51, Box 2557; ibid., G-2 Sec., Staff Rpt., May 51, pp. 23–24, Box 2543.

12. 23rd Inf., Comd. Rpt., in 2nd Div., Comd. Rpt., Narr., May 51, pp. 11–16, Box 4697; 2nd Div., Comd. Rpt., G-3 Sec., POR No. 613, 18 May 51, Box 2557.

13. 23rd Inf., 2nd Div., Comd. Rpt., Logistics Sec., May 51, p. 37, Box 4691.

14. 2nd Div., Comd. Rpt., G-3 Sec., Jnl. entries on 18 May, Box 2553.

15. 3rd Div. Papers, Box 4, Ridgway Papers; Capt. Edward F. Frick, Jr., Student Monograph, Adv. Inf. Off. Course Cl.1, 1952–53, pp. 4–5.

16. 1st Lt. John Mewha, "Supply Battle of the Soyang River, 10 May–7 June, 1951," MS, BA 62, in Office Chief of Military History; IX Corps, Comd. Rpt., Trans. Sec., 18 May 51, Box 1805.

17. Lt. Col. Emmerich, KMAG advisor with ROK 3rd Div., interview with author, 1951; X Corps, Comd. Rpt., 17 May 51, Box 2012.

18. X Corps, Comd. Rpt., 18 May 51, Box 2012.

19. 3rd Div., Comd. Rpt., 18–19 May 51, Box 2902.

20. Eighth Army, Comd. Rpt., G-3 Sec., May 51, pp. 5–6, Box 1196.

21. X Corps, Comd. Rpt., 18 May 51, Box 2012.

22. Eighth Army, Comd. Rpt., G-3 Sec., 18 May 51, Box 1196; X Corps, Comd. Rpt., G-3 Sec. and POR No. 234, 18 May 51, Box 2014.

23. 2nd Div., Comd. Rpt., G-3 Jnl., Serial 27, 0545, 18 May 51, Box 2553.

24. Ibid., CS Jnl., 18 May 51, Box 2543.

25. Ibid., G-3 Sec., POR No. 613, 18 May 51, Box 2557.

26. Ibid., CS Jnl., Serial 18, 1100, 18 May 51, Box 2543.

27. Ibid., Serial 10, 0905, 18 May 51, Box 2543.

28. X Corps, Comd. Rpt., G-2 Sec., PIR No. 234, 18 May 51, Box 2013.

29. 38th Inf., Comd. Rpt., 18–20 May 51, Boxes 2012 and 2712.

30. Eighth Army, Comd. Rpt., CG Jnl., 18 May 51, Box 1193.

31. Ibid., Narr., May 51, p. 102, Box 1192.

32. Eighth Army, Comd. Rpt., G-4 Sec., 19 May 51, Box 1198.

33. Hist. Rec., 19–20 May 51, Box 22, Ridgway Papers; X Corps, Comd. Rpt., Command Sec., 19 May 51, Box 2012.

34. 15th RCT, 3rd Div., Comd. Rpt., 19 May 51, Box 2956.

35. 7th Inf. RCT, 3rd Div., Comd. Rpt., 19–20 May 51; 3rd Div., Comd. Rpt., G-2 Sec., PIRs, 19–20 May 51, Box 2902.

36. Ibid., 19 May 51, p. 105, Box 1192.

37. 23rd Inf., 2nd Div., Comd. Rpt., Narr., 19–20 May 51, Box 4697.

38. 3rd Div., Comd. Rpt., G-2 Sec., 18–23 May 51, Box 2902; FEC DIS Nos. 3175–76, 19–20 May 51.

39. X Corps, Comd. Rpt., G-2 Sec., PIR No. 224, 8 May 51, Annex 4, Summ. PW Interrog., Box 2013.

40. Col. Frederick Weyand, interview with author, Aug 1951.

41. Westover, *Combat Support in Korea*, pp. 110–11.

42. 9th Inf., 2nd Div., Comd. Rpt., Narr., 20 May 51, p. 14, Boxes 2691 and 2012.

43. 2nd Div., Comd. Rpt., CS Jnl., 20 May 51, Box 2543; ibid., G-3 Jnl., 20 May 51, Box 2554.

44. X Corps, Comd. Rpt., G-3 Sec., POR Nos. 236–37, 20–21 May 51, Box 2014.

45. Almond, Diary, 20 May 51.

46. 3rd Div., Comd. Rpt., G-2 Sec., PIR Nos. 128–29, 20–21 May 51, Box 2902; X Corps, Comd. Rpt., 20–24 May 51, Box 2012; Eighth Army, Comd. Rpt., G-2 Sec., 20–31 May 51, Box 1194.

47. DA, Gen. Ord. No. 35, 8 Apr 52, awarding the Distinguished Service Unit to the 2nd Plat., A Co., 31st Regt., ROK 2nd Div.; 1st Lt. Martin Blumenson, "Task Force Lindy, May 1951," MS, BA 36, Office Chief of Military History.

48. Eighth Army, Comd. Rpt., CG Jnl., 21 May 51, Box 1193.

49. 2nd Div., Comd. Rpt., CS Jnl., 20 May 51, Serial 27, 2050, and Serial 33, 2140, Box 2543.

50. Ibid., Serial 34, 2158, Box 2543.

51. 2nd Div., Comd. Rpt., Narr., 21–22 May 51, pp. 32–33, Box 2543.

52. Ibid., 21 May 51, Box 2543.

53. 2nd Div., Comd. Rpt., G-3 Jnl., Serial 50, 2000, 23rd Inf. to Div. G-3, 21 May 51, Box 2554.

54. 7th Inf., 3rd Div., Comd. Rpt., 21–28 May 51, Box 2951.

55. Eighth Army, Comd. Rpt., G-3 Sec., Jnl., Serials 1735, 1325, 1755, and 1545, 22 May 51, and G-3 POR for 23 May 51, Box 1197.

56. Eighth Army, Comd. Rpt., 21–22 May 51, Box 1192.

57. FEC DIS No. 3188, 2 June 51, M-2, Box 468.

58. DA, Gen. Ord. No. 22, 5 Feb 53, awarding the Medal of Honor to Sgt. Joseph C. Rodriguez (then Pfc.), for action on 21 May 51 near Munye-ri.

59. X Corps, Comd. Rpt., 19 May 51, Box 2012; 1st Lt. John Mewha, "Battle of the Soyang River, Logistical Support, Artillery," MS, Office Chief of Military History, 1951, p. 1.

60. Mewha, "Battle of Soyang River," p. 3.

61. Maj. James A. Huston, "Time and Space," MS, Office Chief of Military History, p. 161.

62. Lt. Gen. Edward M. Almond, letter to author, 29 Oct 1975, and subsequent conversations.

63. Eighth Army, Comd. Rpt., CS Jnl., 22 May 51, Box 1193.

64. Ibid., Narr., 23 May 51, p. 36.

65. 3rd Div., Comd. Rpt., Narr., May 1951, p. 12, Box 2902.

66. Eighth Army, Comd. Rpt., Narr., 23 May 51, p. 118, Box 1192.

67. X Corps, Comd. Rpt., Command Sec., 23 May 51, Box 2012.

68. 1st Lt. John Mewha, "Task Force Gerhardt," based on field interviews in Korea, Aug 1951, MS BA 54, Office Chief of Military History; 2nd Div., Comd. Rpt., Narr., 24 May 51, Box 2543. Mewha uses the name William Gerhardt as the leader of Task Force Gerhardt. Russell A. Gugeler uses the same name, but since his sec. 15, pp. 191–200, in *Combat Actions in Korea* is based largely on Mewha's MS, he may merely have followed Mewha. I am unsure of the name William, since the first name George appears in the 2nd Div. Comd. Rpt. narrative for 24 May 51, which gives an account of the task force. Although unable to resolve the issue, I decided to follow Mewha in the name usage.

69. Mewha, "Task Force Gerhardt"; see also 2nd Div., Comd. Rpt., CS Jnl., 24 May 51, Box 2543, and 2nd Div., G-3, POR No. 619, 24 May 51, Box 2557, for more on the task force.

70. Col. Calvin S. Hannum, interview with author, 21 July 1953.

71. 7th Div., Comd. Rpt., Narr., 24 May 51, and G-3 Sec., POR No. 232, 24 May 51; *New York Times*, 26 May 51.

72. IX Corps, Comd. Rpt., Narr., 24 May 51, p. 136, Box 1803; and ibid., G-2 Sec., Spot Rpts., 24 May 51, Box 1809.

73. 32nd Inf., 7th Div., Comd. Rpt., 24 May 51, Box 3225.

74. 15th Inf., 3rd Div., Comd. Rpt., 24-25 May 51, Box 2956.

75. Eighth Army, Comd. Rpt., 24 May 51, p. 120, Box 1192.

76. 2nd Div., Comd. Rpt., G-3 Sec., POR No. 620, 25 May 51, Box 2557; 187th Abn. RCT, Comd. Rpt., 25 May 51, Box 3439; ibid., G-2 Jnl., 25 May 51, Box 3439.

77. 187th Abn. RCT, Comd. Rpt., 27 May 51, Box 3439.

78. Eighth Army, Comd. Rpt., 27-28 May 51, Box 1192.

79. X Corps, Comd. Rpt., Combat Notes No. 12, G-3 Sec., undated but prepared in summer of 1951, 8 pp. with maps, copy in author's possession.

80. X Corps, Comd. Rpt., G-3 Sec., POR No. 242, 26 May 51, Box 2014; 23rd Inf., 2nd Div., Comd. Rpt., 26 May 51, Box 2012.

81. 32nd Inf., 7th Div., Comd. Rpt., 25-26 May 51, Box 3225; 17th Inf., 7th Div., Comd. Rpt., 25-26 May 51, Box 3225; 7th Div., Comd. Rpt., G-3 Sec., POR No. 233, 25 May 51, Box 3194.

82. Eighth Army, Comd. Rpt., 25 May 51, Box 1192; IX Corps, Comd. Rpt., G-2 Hist. Rpt., 24-25 May 51, Box 1803; FEC DIS No. 3180, 25 May 51, Box 455.

83. IX Corps, Comd. Rpt., Narr., 24-28 May 51, pp. 36-39, Box 1803.

84. 24th Div., Comd. Rpt. and G-2 Sec., 25-31 May 51, Box 3567; 19th Inf., 24th Div., Comd. Rpt., 25 May 51, and S-3 Jnl., 25 May 51, Box 3658.

85. 1st Cav. Div., Comd. Rpt., G-2 Sec., Narr., and Signal Sec., 25-30 May 51, Boxes 4452 and 4449.

86. I Corps, Comd. Rpt., G-4 Sec., 25 May 51, Box 1532.

87. 2nd Div., Comd. Rpt., CS Jnl., entry 14 1825, 26 May 51, Box 2543.

88. X Corps, Comd. Rpt., 26 May 51, Box 2012.

89. Almond, Diary, 26 May 51, in X Corps Comd. Rpt., Command Sec., Box 2012.

90. 2nd Div., G-3 Jnl., 27 May 51, Box 2555, and ibid., Comd. Rpt., Narr., 27 May 51, Box 2543.

91. IX Corps, Comd. Rpt., G-2 Spot Rpts., 27 May 51, Box 1809.

92. Eighth Army, Comd. Rpt., G-2 Sec., Encl. 2, PIR No. 319, 27 May 51, Box 1194.

93. 17th Inf., 7th Div., Comd. Rpt., 27 May 51, Box 3225; 7th Div., Comd. Rpt., G-3 Sec., POR Nos. 238-39, 30-31 May 51, Box 3194; 7th Div., Comd. Rpt., Narr., 27-28 May 51, Box 3194.

94. IX Corps, Comd. Rpt., CS Jnl., 27 May 51, Box 1803.

95. 7th Div., Comd. Rpt., Narr., 28 May 51, Box 3194.

96. 24th Div., Comd. Rpt., G-2 and G-3 Secs., 27 May 51, Boxes 3567 and 3668, and ibid., Narr., 27 May 51, pp. 13-14, Box 3567; Eighth Army, Gen. Ord. No. 557, 18 July 1951, Unit Citation, HQ and HQ Co., and Medical Co., 21st Inf., 24th Div., for performance in action 27 May 51; Unit Citation, HQ and HQ Btry., and A Btry., 213th Armored FA Bn. (supporting 21st Inf., 24th Div.), 27 May 51, DA, Gen. Ord. No. 35, 8 Apr 1952.

97. Eighth Army, Comd. Rpt., G-3 Sec., Narr., 27 May 51, pp. 8–9.

98. Ibid., G-3 Sec., 28 May 51, Box 1197.

99. 38th Inf., 2nd Div., Comd. Rpt., 28–29 May 51, Box 2012; 2nd Div., Comd. Rpt., 28–29 May 51, Box 2543.

100. X Corps, Comd. Rpt., G-3 Sec., POR Nos. 244–46, 28–30 May 51, Box 2014.

101. 9th Inf., 2nd Div., Comd. Rpt., G-2 Sec., 28–29 May 51, Box 2691.

102. 2nd Div., Comd. Rpt., G-3 Narr., 27–28 May 51, Box 2903.

103. 17th Inf., 7th Div., Comd. Rpt., S-2 Sec., 28–30 May 51, Box 3225; IX Corps, Comd. Rpt., G-2 Hist. Sec., 28–31 May 51, Box 1803.

104. 1st Cav. Div., Comd. Rpt., Narr., 26–29 May 51, p. 23, Box 4449; I Corps, Comd. Rpt., G-3 Sec., 28 May 51, Box 1534.

105. Memo for Record, 31 May 51, conference between Ridgway and Van Fleet, EUSAK (Tac), 28 May 2100, 1951, Ridgway Papers.

106. 19th Inf., 24th Div., Comd. Rpt., 29–30 May 51, Box 3658; 24th Div., Comd. Rpt., Narr., 29–30 May 51, p. 14, Box 3567; Eighth Army, Comd. Rpt., G-3 Sec., 29 May 51, Box 1197.

107. Eighth Army, Comd. Rpt., 29–30 May 51, Box 1192.

108. FEC DIS No. 3189, 3 June 51, Box 468.

109. Eighth Army, Comd. Rpt. and G-3 Sec., 30 May 51, Boxes 1192 and 1197.

110. FEC DIS Nos. 3185–86, 30–31 May 51, Box 456.

111. 21st Inf., 24th Div., Comd. Rpt., S-2 Jnl., Serial 41, 2235, 30 May 51.

112. Almond, Diary, 31 May 51, and X Corps, Comd. Rpt., Command Sec., Box 2012; DA, Gen. Ord. No. 40, 21 Apr 1952, granting Medal of Honor to Hernandez.

113. X Corps, Comd. Rpt., G-3 Sec., POR Nos. 245–47, 29–31 May 51.

114. IX Corps, Comd. Rpt., G-3 Jnl., 31 May 51, Box 1803.

115. Eighth Army, Comd. Rpt., G-1 Sec., May 51, Box 1193.

116. Ibid., June 51, p. 21, Box 1206.

117. Ibid., G-3 Sec., Narr., May 1951, p. 9, Box 1196.

118. "From CINCFE Tokyo Japan, Sgd. Ridgway To: DEPTAR Wash DC for JCS, NR C 63744, May 51, DA in 18477, 30 May 1951," in *Pertinent Papers on Korean Situation*, III, 477–80.

119. FEC DIS No. 3197, 11 June 51, p. 8, Box 470.

120. Ibid., p. 9, Box 470.

CHAPTER 21

1. Eighth Army, Comd. Rpt., Narr., 2 June 51, pp. 57–58.

2. Ibid., 1 June 51, pp. 8–10, Plate 4, illustration of Letter of Instruction, 1 June 51, Box 1206.

3. Ibid., p. 16, and G-2 Sec., 1 June 51, Box 1208.

4. I Corps, Comd. Rpt., Narr., 3 June 51, Box 1538.

5. 3rd Div., Comd. Rpt., G-2 Sec., 1–10 June 51, Box 2907.

6. 7th Div., Comd. Rpt., Narr., 1–4 June 51, Box 3196.

7. IX Corps, Comd. Rpt., G-2 Sec., 1–27 June 51, Box 1810.

8. 2nd Div., Comd. Rpt., Narr., 3 June 51, Box 2561.

9. DA, Gen. Ord. No. 30, 19 Mar 52, awarding the Medal of Honor, Post-

humously, to Sgt. Cornelius H. Charlton, C Co., 24th Inf., 25th Div., for heroic action 2 June 51, near Chipo-ri.

10. Eighth Army, Comd. Rpt., Staff Sec., Office of CG, Monthly Narr. Summ. for June 1951, Box 1207.

11. 15th Inf., 3rd Div., Comd. Rpt., 3–16 June 51, Box 2956.

12. 2nd Div., Comd. Rpt., Narr., 3 June 51, Box 2561.

13. Eighth Army, Comd. Rpt., Narr., 3 June 51, pp. 57–61, Box 1206; 3rd Div., Comd. Rpt., Narr., 3 June 51, Box 2906.

14. Eighth Army, Comd. Rpt., Narr., 4 June 51, p. 63, Box 1206.

15. 3rd Div., Comd. Rpt., Narr., 5 June 51, Box 2906; I Corps, Comd. Rpt., Narr., 4–8 June 51, Box 1538.

16. 7th Div., Comd. Rpt., Narr., 5–23 June 51, Box 3196; 31st Inf., 7th Div., Comd. Rpt., Narr., 5–6 June 51, Box 3245; DA, Gen. Ord. No. 69, 23 Sept 1954, awarding the Medal of Honor to 1st Lt. Benjamin F. Wilson, I Co., 31st Inf., 7th Div., for action near Hwachon, 5 June 1951; and DA, Gen. Ord. No. 15, 1 Feb 1952, awarding the Medal of Honor to Pfc. Jack G. Hanson, 1st Plat., F Co., 31st Inf., 7th Div., for action 5 June 51, near Hwachon.

17. X Corps, Comd. Rpt., G-2 Sec., PIR No. 254, 7 June 51, Box 2019.

18. Ibid., Operation Narr., 6–12 June 51, Box 2018.

19. Eighth Army, Comd. Rpt., Narr., 8 June 51, p. 69, Box 1206.

20. 2nd Div., Comd. Rpt., G-3 Operations and G-4 Sec., June 51, Box 2561.

21. Eighth Army, Comd. Rpt., Narr., 9 June 51, Box 1206; 1st Cav. Div., Comd. Rpt., Narr., 9 June 51, 4453.

22. I Corps, Comd. Rpt., G-3 and G-4 Secs., 10 June 51, Box 1541.

23. 7th Inf., 3rd Div., Comd. Rpt., S-3 Sec., 11 June 51, Box 2951; 25th Div., Comd. Rpt., 10–11 June 51, Box 3791; Eighth Army, Comd. Rpt., 10–11 June 51, Box 1206.

24. 3rd Div., Comd. Rpt., Narr., 12 June 51, Box 2906.

25. Eighth Army, Comd. Rpt., G-2 Sec., 10–30 June 51, Box 1208.

26. FEC DIS No. 3197, 11 June 51, Box 470.

27. 17th Inf., 7th Div., Comd. Rpt., Narr., 11–12 June 51, Box 3227.

28. 32nd Inf., 7th Div., Comd. Rpt., Narr., 11 June 51, Box 3257.

29. *Medal of Honor Recipients, 1863-1963*, p. 229, giving text of citation to Cpl. Charles G. Abrell for action 10 June 51.

30. 2nd Div., Comd. Rpt., "Ivanhoe Security Force Operation Ghoul, 11 June 51," May 51, Box 2560.

31. 27th Inf., 25th Div., Comd. Rpt., 11 June 51, Box 3854; Eighth Army, Comd. Rpt., Narr., 12 June 51, p. 77, Box 1206.

32. 3rd Div., Comd. Rpt., Narr., 13 June 51, pp. 13–14, Box 2906.

33. 25th Div., Comd. Rpt., and G-3 Jnl. 13 June 51, Box 3791.

34. 3rd Div., Comd. Rpt., Narr., 13 June 51, pp. 13–14, Box 2906.

35. 15th Inf., 3rd Div., Comd. Rpt., June 51, Box 2956.

36. Eighth Army, Comd. Rpt., Narr., 13–14 June 51, pp. 80–81, Box 1206; I Corps, Comd. Rpt., G-2 Sec., 13–16 June 51, Box 1539.

37. 25th Div., Comd. Rpt., G-3 Sec. and Jnl., 14–16 June 51, Box 3792.

38. 1st Lt. Civil Engineer James P. Godsey, "The Soyang River Bailey Bridge," *Military Engineer* 43, no. 29 (Nov–Dec 1951): 395ff.; X Corps, Comd. Rpt., CG Daily Jnl., 14 June 51, Box 2018.

39. I Corps, Comd. Rpt., Narr., 15–17 June 51, pp. 45–49, Box 1538.

40. Eighth Army, Comd. Rpt., Narr., 18–21 June 51, pp. 89–91, Box 1206; X Corps, Comd. Rpt., CG Daily Jnl., 20–21 June 51, Box 2018.

41. Capt. William J. Fox, "Hills 717 and 682 in the Iron Triangle Area," 15th Inf., 3rd Div., 23–24 June 51, MS BA 2, Office Chief of Military History.

42. DA, Gen. Ord. No. 11, 1 Feb 1952, awarding Medal of Honor, Posthumously, to Pfc. Emory L. Bennett, B Co., 15th Inf., 3rd Div., for gallantry in action, 24 June 51, near Sogangsan.

43. 15th Inf., 3rd Div., Comd. Rpt., 22–24 June 51, Box 2956.

44. Ibid., S-3 Jnl., Serial 115 entry.

45. 24th Inf., 25th Div., Comd. Rpt., 20 June 51, Box 3845.

46. I Corps, Comd. Rpt., G-2 Sec., 21 June 51, PIR No. 172, Box 1540; FEC DIS No. 3207, 21 June 51, Box 473.

47. 32nd Inf., 7th Div., Comd. Rpt., Narr., 1–21 June 51, Box 3257; Eighth Army, Comd. Rpt., Narr., 23 June 51, Box 1206.

48. Eighth Army, Comd. Rpt., Narr., 21–23 June 51, Box 1206.

49. "From Cincfe Tokyo Japan to JCS Wash., DC; NR C 65529, 22 Jun 51, DA IN 6910, 22 Jun 1951," in Pertinent Papers on Korean Situation, III, 484.

50. FEC DIS No. 3208, 22 June 51, Box 473.

51. 3rd Div., Comd. Rpt., June 51, pp. 20–21, Box 2906.

52. 1st Cav. Div., Comd. Rpt., Narr., 24 June 51, Box 4453; Eighth Army, Comd. Rpt., Narr., 24 June 51, p. 94, Box 1206.

53. 1st Cav. Div., Comd. Rpt., Narr., 24–29 June 51, pp. 17–18, Box 4453.

54. Eighth Army, Comd. Rpt., Narr., Logistics Sec., 24 June 51, p. 123, Box 1206.

55. Ibid., G-4 Sec., 25 June 51, Box 2510; I Corps, Comd. Rpt., Narr., 25 June 51, pp. 63–64.

56. Eighth Army, Comd. Rpt., G-4 Sec., June 1951, Box 1210.

57. Eighth Army, Comd. Rpt., 23 June 51, Box 1206.

58. New York Times, 27 June 1951, special dispatch by George Barrett, from Korea, 26 June 51.

59. 7th Inf., 3rd Div., Comd. Rpt., S-3 Sec., 27–30 June 51, Box 2951; I Corps, Comd. Rpt., G-2 Sec., 27 June 51, Box 1539.

60. I Corps, Comd. Rpt., Narr., 28 June 51, Box 1538; FEC DIS No. 3215, 29 June 51, Box 475.

61. Eighth Army, Comd. Rpt., Narr., 28 June 51, Box 1206; and ibid., CG Jnl., 28 June 51, Box 1207.

62. Eighth Army, Comd. Rpt., Narr., 29 June 51, Box 1206.

63. FEC DIS No. 3212, 2 July 51, Box 488.

64. "To CINCFE Tokyo Japan, From JCS for CINCUNC eyes only, Personal for Ridgway. NR: JCS 95258, 29 June 51," in Pertinent Papers on Korean Situation, III, 491.

65. "To CINCFE Tokyo Japan, From JCS for CINCUNC eyes only, Personal for Ridgway, NR JCS 95438, 2 July 51," in Pertinent Papers on Korean Situation, III, 502–503.

66. Eighth Army, Comd. Rpt., G-1 Sec., June 1951, Encl. 34, G-1 Rpt., Box 1207.

67. Ibid., Narr., June 51, p. 49, Box 1206.

68. 1st Cav. Div., Comd. Rpt., Narr., June 51, p. 607; Lt. Col. Read, I Corps, interview with author, July 1951.

69. DA, Gen. Ord. No. 83, 3 Sept 1952, awarding Medal of Honor, Posthumously, to Sgt. LeRoy A. Mendonca for action 4 July 51, near Chichon.

70. 3rd Div., Comd. Rpt., Narr., 1–14 July 51, Box 2911; I Corps, Comd. Rpt., Narr., 1–4 July 51, Box 1545; Eighth Army, Comd. Rpt., Narr., 1–4 July 51, Box 1219; DA, Gen. Ord. No. 33, 31 Mar 1952, Distinguished Unit Citation, the 3rd Bn., 7th Inf., 3rd Div., and attached units for action near Segok, 30 June–4 July 1951.

71. "From CINCFE Tokyo Japan, sgd Ridgway, to Dept AR for JCS Wash., D.C., 4 July 1951," in *Pertinent Papers on Korean Situation*, III, 505–506.

72. Eighth Army, Comd. Rpt., Narr., 8–9 July 51, Box 1219; FEC DIS No. 3226, 10 July 51, Box 490.

73. Report of the UN Command Operations in Korea for the period 1–15 July 1951 (Report No. 25), pp. 289–90.

74. Ibid., pp. 291–92.

75. Ibid., pp. 292–93.

76. "To CINCFE Tokyo Japan, From JCS for CINCUNC Pearl Harbor TH, NR JCS 95977, 10 Jul 51," in *Pertinent Papers on Korea Situation*, III, 514–19.

77. X Corps, Comd. Rpt., CG Diary, 15 July 51.

78. Gen. Ridgway has expressed his evaluation of Almond to the author several times.

Bibliographical Note

OFFICIAL RECORDS AND MANUSCRIPT COLLECTIONS

The most important sources for the operational history of the UN forces covered in this volume are the war diaries (through November 1950) and the command reports (after November 1950). All of these documents are in the National Archives, Record Group 407, which is located in Building No. 1 of the Federal Records Center at 4205 Suitland Road in Suitland, Maryland. The diaries and command reports are monthly summaries, with their supporting documents, prepared by all levels of command from the Far East Command down through army, corps, division, regiment, and battalion levels, with battalion reports sometimes attaching company-level reports, although the latter were not mandated.

The most important manuscript collections are the Matthew B. Ridgway Papers and the Gen. Edward M. Almond Papers, both in the US Army Military History Research Collections, Carlisle Barracks, Pennsylvania.

OFFICIAL HISTORIES

Army. Roy E. Appleman, *South to the Naktong, North to the Yalu,* 1961 (reprinted 1975, 1987); James F. Schnabel, *Policy and Direction: The First Year,* 1972 (reprinted 1978); Walter G. Hermes, *Truce Tent and Fighting Front,* 1966.

Navy. Malcolm W. Cagle and Frank A. Manson, *The Sea War in Korea,* 1957. Another volume may be considered as semiofficial: James A. Field, Jr., *History of United States Naval Operations in Korea,* 1962.

Air Force. Robert Frank Futrell, *The United States Air Force in Korea, 1950–1953,* 1961.

Marine Corps. Lynn Montross and Nicolas Canzona, *The U.S. Marine Operations in Korea, 1950–1953,* 4 vols. (vol. 4 is most pertinent to this work), 1957.

Except for Futrell's book, which was published by Duell, Sloan, and Pearce in New York, all the official histories were published by the Superintendent of Documents, Government Printing Office, Washington, D.C.

OTHER PUBLISHED WORKS

The works listed here include only those books actually used in the writing of this book. They do not include the many books on the Korean War that consist of generalizations or are heavily derivative of previously published works or that deal mainly with the political aspects of the war.

Appleman, Roy E. *East of Chosin: Entrapment and Breakout in Korea, 1950*. College Station: Texas A&M University Press, 1987.

Barclay, Brigadier C. N., CBE, DSO. *The First Commonwealth Division: The Story of British Commonwealth Land Forces in Korea, 1950–1953*, with a foreword by Field-Marshal Alexander of Tunis. Aldershot: Gale and Polden, 1954.

Bartlett, Norman. *With the Australians in Korea*. Canberra: Australian War Memorial, 1954.

Carew, Tim. *The Glorious Glosters*. London: Leo Cooper, 1970.

Daniell, David Scott. *Cap of Honour: The Story of the Gloucestershire Regiment (the 28th/61st Foot, 1694–1975)*, with chapters covering the period 1945–1975 by Maj. Gen. A. H. Farrar-Hockley, DSO, MBE, MC, and Maj. E. L. Capel, ERD. London: White Lion, 1975. Farrar-Hockley contributed the chapters on the Gloucestershire Battalion in the Battle of the Imjin River in April 1951.

Farrar-Hockley, Capt. Anthony, DSO, MC. *The Edge of the Sword*. Foreword by Maj. Gen. Thomas Brodie. London: Frederick Muller, 1954. Farrar-Hockley was the adjutant of the Gloucestershire Battalion at the Battle of the Imjin River and was captured there and held captive until the armistice in July 1953.

Holles, Robert O. *Now Thrive the Armourers*. London: George G. Harrap, 1952. This story relates action with the Gloucestershire Battalion in April 1951.

Kahn, E. J., Jr. *The Peculiar War: Impressions of a Reporter in Korea*. New York: Random House, 1951.

Karnow, Stanley. *Mao and China: From Revolution to Revolution*. New York: Viking Press, 1972.

Khrushchev Remembers: The Last Testament. 2nd ed. Boston: Little, Brown, 1974.

Linklater, Eric. *Our Men in Korea*. London: Her Majesty's Stationery Office, 1952.

Malcolm, Lt. Col. G. I. *The Argylls in Korea*. London: Thomas Nelson and Sons, 1952.

Ridgway, Gen. Matthew B. *The Korean War*. Garden City, N.Y.: Doubleday, 1967.

———. *Soldier: The Memoirs of Matthew B. Ridgway*, as told to Harold H. Martin. New York: Harper and Brothers, 1956.

Thompson, Reginald William. *Cry Korea*. London: MacDonald, 1951.

Whitney, Courtney. *MacArthur: His Rendezvous with History*. New York: Knopf, 1956.

Wood, Lt. Col. Herbert Fairlee. *Strange Battleground: The Operations in Korea and Their Effects on the Defense Policy of Canada* (official history of the Canadian army). Published by the authority of the Minister of National Defense, Roger Duhamel, FRSC. Ottawa: Queen's Printer and Controller of Stationery, 1966.

Extensive interviews and correspondence with survivors of the Eighth Army and X Corps actions, who often provided key information not available in the official records or any other source, are detailed in the notes. General Ridgway gave each chapter of the manuscript a careful reading and clarified important information.

Index

(Italicized page numbers refer to photographs. Chinese military units are listed under CCF. North Korean military units are listed under NK. South Korean military units are listed under ROK.)

Index prepared by Renee G. Loeffler, System Analytics of Virginia.

Hill 700, 441
Hill 703, 360
Hill 717, 563, 564, 566, 567, 570, 572, 573, *574*
Hill 719, 372, 421
Hill 800, 511, 512
Hill 873, 564
Hill 899, 511
Hill 902, 467–68
Hill 930, 222, *224*, 225, 226, 362
Hill 975, 400, 512
Hill 980, 355
Hill 982, 355, 363
Hill 1008, 373
Hill 1037, 355, 356
Hill 1039, 416
Hill 1043, 364, 365
Hill 1051 (Kari-san), 507, 509, *511*, 512–16, 522, 530
Hill 1062, 562–63
Hill 1073, 563
Hill 1100, 564, 575
Hill 1157, 354, 359, 360
Hill 1171, 363
Hill 1198, 440–41
Hill 1232 (Taemi-san), 363, 364–65
Hill 1286, 373
Hinton, Capt. Reginald J., 240
Hodes, Maj. Gen. Henry I., 119, 494, 559, 575
Hoengsong, 103, 135, 137, 219, 220, 221, 414, 521; disaster at, 226, 235–46, 248–53; US prisoners from battle at, 401
Hoengsong-Hongchon road, 229
Hoengsong–Pangnim-ni road, 354, 355, 362–63
Hoengsong-Wonju-Chungju MSR, 103, 104
Hoeryong-to-Wonsan railroad, 316–17
Hogan, Capt. Harold F., 242–43
Hoge, Maj. Gen. William M., 312, 357–58, *502*, 505, 572, 581; and attack on Hwachon Dam, 424, 426; in 5th Phase Offensive, 468, 469, 483, 486, 494
Hongchon, 29, 30, 221, 360, 361, 367, *369*, 371, 420, 492
Hongchon-Inje road, 527, 529
Hongchon River valley, 367, 369–71, 372
Hongchon-Wonju-Chechon corridor, 9, 26

Hongchon-Yongpyong road, 219
horses: as pack animals, 102, 326
Horton, Lt. Col. Roy W., 291
Hospelhorn, Capt. Cecil W., 403
Howden, Lt. James, 235, 237
Hsueh Fu-li, 228
Hugg, Col. Sidney, 433
Hull, Lt. Gen., 430
Humphrey, Maj. Robert A., 280
Hurst, Cpl. Randle M., 8, 80
Hurtt, 1st Lt. Walter, 136
Huth, Maj. Henry, 475–76
Hwachon, 540, 542, 545, 546, 548, 556, 558–59
Hwachon-Kumhwa road, 558
Hwachon Reservoir and Dam, 336, 359, 360, 421, *423*; Eighth Army attacks on, 415, 422–26, 440, 441, 443, 446
Hyon-ni, 544

Ichon, 172–73
Illustrated London News, 142
Imjin River, 34, *464*, 569; in 5th Phase Offensive, 458, 462, 463–64, 478; in 3rd Phase Offensive, 38, 40, 42–44, 46–49, 57; UN forces advance to, cross, 381, 388, 392–93, 415, 421, 441–42, 438
Inchon, 192, 195, 377; naval bombardment of, 180–81, 316; restoration of port facilities at, 196, 320, 335
Ingman, Cpl. Einar H., Jr., 311, 615n50
Inje, 468, 540, 546, 548, 557
Inje-Kansong road, 541
intelligence, enemy: US prisoners as source of, 572
intelligence, US: enemy prisoners as source of, 26, 30, 31, 130, 131, 133, 170, 183, 186, 189–90, 191–92, 195–96, 297–98, 365, 297–98, 365, 377–78, 438–40, 446, 448, 457, 483, 491, 503–504, 566, 567; estimate of enemy intentions, May 1951, 551–52; low quality of, 29, 177, 312, 352, 503–504, 506, 572; released prisoners as source of, 194, 399
Iron Triangle, 31, 393, 551–52; enemy buildup in, 414, 420, 548; UN offensive against, 411, 554, 557, 558–59, 560–63, 564–67, 568, 569, 570, 572–

Ridgway Duels for Korea was composed into type on a Compugraphic digital phototypesetter in ten and one-half point Plantin with one and one-half points of spacing between the lines. Permanent Headline was selected for display. The book was designed by Jim Billingsley, typeset by Metricomp, Inc., printed offset by Thomson-Shore, Inc., and bound by John H. Dekker & Sons, Inc. The paper on which this book is printed carries acid-free characteristics for an effective life of at least three hundred years.

TEXAS A&M UNIVERSITY PRESS : COLLEGE STATION